MW01224920

Human, Social, and Organizational Aspects of Health Information Systems

Andre W. Kushniruk
University of Victoria, Canada

Elizabeth M. Borycki
University of Victoria, Canada

MEDICAL INFORMATION SCIENCE REFERENCE

Hershey · New York

Acquisitions Editor: Kristin Klinger
Development Editor: Kristin Roth
Senior Managing Editor: Jennifer Neidig
Managing Editor: Jamie Snavely
Assistant Managing Editor: Carole Coulson
Copy Editor: Katie Smalley
Typesetter: Jeff Ash
Cover Design: Lisa Tosheff
Printed at: Yurchak Printing Inc.

Published in the United States of America by
    Information Science Reference (an imprint of IGI Global)
    701 E. Chocolate Avenue, Suite 200
    Hershey PA 17033
    Tel: 717-533-8845
    Fax: 717-533-8661
    E-mail: cust@igi-global.com
    Web site: http://www.igi-global.com

and in the United Kingdom by
    Information Science Reference (an imprint of IGI Global)
    3 Henrietta Street
    Covent Garden
    London WC2E 8LU
    Tel: 44 20 7240 0856
    Fax: 44 20 7379 0609
    Web site: http://www.eurospanbookstore.com

Copyright © 2008 by IGI Global. All rights reserved. No part of this publication may be reproduced, stored or distributed in any form or by any means, electronic or mechanical, including photocopying, without written permission from the publisher.

Product or company names used in this set are for identification purposes only. Inclusion of the names of the products or companies does not indicate a claim of ownership by IGI Global of the trademark or registered trademark.

Library of Congress Cataloging-in-Publication Data

Human, social, and organizational aspects of health information systems / A.W. Kushniruk and E.M. Borycki, editors.

    p. ; cm.

  Includes bibliographical references.

  Summary: "This book offers an evidence-based management approach to issues associated with the human and social aspects of designing, developing, implementing, and maintaining health information systems across a healthcare organization--specific to an individual, team, organizational, system, and international perspective. Integrating knowledge from multiple levels, will benefit scholars and practitioners from the medical information, health service management, information technology arenas"--Provided by publisher.

  ISBN 978-1-59904-792-8 (hardcover)

  1. Information storage and retrieval systems--Health services administration. 2. Health services administration--Data processing. 3. Management information systems--Human factors. 4. Management information systems--Social aspects. 5. Management information systems--Management. I. Kushniruk, A. W. (Andre W.) II. Borycki, Elizabeth, 1968-

  [DNLM: 1. Medical Informatics Applications. 2. Health Services Administration. WA 26.5 H918 2008]

RA971.6.H86 2008

362.10285--dc22

                        2007045014

British Cataloguing in Publication Data
A Cataloguing in Publication record for this book is available from the British Library.

All work contributed to this book set is original material. The views expressed in this book are those of the authors, but not necessarily of the publisher.

If a library purchased a print copy of this publication, please go to http://www.igi-global.com/reference/assets/IGR-eAccess-agreement.
pdf for information on activating the library's complimentary electronic access to this publication.

Table of Contents

Section I
Usability and Human-Computer Interaction in Healthcare

Andre W. Kushniruk, University of Victoria, Canada
Elizabeth M. Borycki, University of Victoria, Canada
Shige Kuwata, University of Victoria, Canada
Francis Ho, Tottori University Hospital, Japan

Morgan Price, University of Victoria, Canada and University of British Columbia, Canada

Section II
Supporting Healthcare Work Practices

Craig E. Kuziemsky, University of Ottawa, Canada

Christian Nohr, Aalborg University, Denmark
Niels Boye, Aalborg University, Denmark

Section IV
Strategic Approaches to Improving the Healthcare System

Section V
Legal, Ethical, and Professional Issues

Section VI
Knowledge Translation in Healthcare

Detailed Table of Contents

Section I
Usability and Human-Computer Interaction in Healthcare

Andre W. Kushniruk, University of Victoria, Canada
Elizabeth M. Borycki, University of Victoria, Canada
Shige Kuwata, University of Victoria, Canada
Francis Ho, Tottori University Hospital, Japan

It is essential that health information systems are easy to use, meet user information needs, and are shown to be safe. However, there is currently a wide range of issues and problems with health information systems related to human-computer interaction. Indeed, lack of ease of use of health information systems has been a major impediment to the adoption of such systems. To address these issues, the authors have applied methods emerging from the field of usability engineering in order to improve the adoption of a wide range of health information systems in collaboration with hospitals and other healthcare organizations throughout the world. In this chapter, we describe our work in conducting usability analyses that can be used to rapidly evaluate the usability and safety of healthcare information systems, both in artificial laboratory and real clinical settings. We then discuss how this work has evolved towards the development of software systems ("virtual usability laboratories") capable of remotely collecting, integrating and supporting analysis of a range of usability data.

Morgan Price, University of Victoria, Canada and University of British Columbia, Canada

The purpose of this chapter is to provide the reader with an overview of several models and theories from the general HCI literature, highlighting models at three levels of focus: biomechanical interactions, individual-cognitive interactions, and social interactions. This chapter will also explore how these models have been or could be applied to the design and evaluation of clinical information systems, such as electronic medical records and hospital information systems. Finally, it will conclude with how an understanding at each level compliments the other two in order to create a more complete understanding of the interactions of information systems in healthcare.

Section II
Supporting Healthcare Work Practices

Chapter III

The design and implementation of healthcare information systems (HIS) is problematic as many HIS projects do not achieve the desired outcomes. There exist a number of theories to enhance our ability to successfully develop HIS. Examples of such theories include 'fit' and the sociotechnical approach. However, there are few empirical studies that illustrate how to understand and operationalize such theories at the empirical level needed for HIS design. This chapter introduces a practice support framework that bridges the gap between the theoretical and empirical aspects of HIS design by identifying specific process and information practice supports that need to be considered to actively produce fit of an HIS within a healthcare setting. The chapter also provides an empirical case study of how practice support was used to develop a computer based tool in the domain area of palliative care severe pain management.

Chapter IV

The introduction of electronic health records (EHR) to the clinical setting has led healthcare professionals, policy makers, and administrators to believe that health information systems will improve the functioning of the health care system. In general such expectations of health information system functionality, impact, and ability to disseminate have not been met. In this chapter, we present the findings of three empirical studies: (1) the structured monitoring of EHR implementation processes in Denmark from 1999-2006 by the Danish EHR observatory, (2) a usability study based on human factors engineering concepts with clinicians in artificial but realistic circumstances—a "state of the art (2005)" for Danish CPOE (computerized physician order entry system) and (3) user reactions to a conceptual "high level model" of healthcare activities—the Danish G-EPJ model in order to better understand the reasons for health information system failures and to suggest methods of improving adoption. The authors suggest that knowledge handling as a science seems immature and is not in line with the nature of clinical work. The prerequisites for mature knowledge handling are discussed in the second part of this chapter. More specifically, the authors describe one way of improving knowledge handling: the development of a more true digital representation of the object of interest or the virtual patient/citizen that interacts with computer based health care services on behalf of and for the benefit of the citizen's health.

Chapter V

Pervasive healthcare is a vision for the future of health care stating that some healthcare provisions can be delivered in high quality at low cost and with higher patient-experienced quality and satisfaction as a service on top of a pervasive computing infrastructure, which can be built by integrating communicating computer-power into industrial products and fixed structures in urban and rural spaces. For pervasive healthcare integration with on body networks sensors, and actuators may also be needed. The chapter discusses the prerequisites of this vision from a point of a healthcare professional. A number of parallel advances in concepts have to take place before pervasive healthcare (PH) is matured into a general method for delivering health care provisions. The contemporary most widespread model of healthcare provisions as industrial products with consumer-goods characteristics has to mature into the concepts of welfare economics and new market models have to be developed for PH to pervade society and add value to the health aspects of an individual's life. Ethical and legal aspects must also be further matured. Maturation of technology is also needed. This includes all the components of the "pervasive loop" from sensors to the central intelligence back to the actuators. The "virtual patient/healthy human" as an operational digital representation of the "object/subject of care" also has to be developed.

Section III
Organizational Aspects: Change Management, Best Practices, and Evaluation

In this chapter, we describe the transition phase (capability crisis) of the change process linked to health IT projects, indicate how it can be identified and outline the ways in which we can use change management to intervene and assist people in their journey of change. Despite IT projects being considered a failure more often than not, we continue to implement IT innovations encapsulated in health information systems in healthcare services. These projects bring about considerable organizational change. Good project management includes the use of critical success factors such as change management in our attempts at ensuring success. The purpose of this chapter is to examine the ways in which we can identify (diagnose) the capability crisis and intervene (with change management) by means of learning, leadership, communication and workload management.

Chapter VII

This chapter introduces a multi-level, multi-dimensional meta-framework for successful implementations of EHR in health care organizations. Existing implementation frameworks do not explain many features experienced and reported by implementers and have not helped to make health information technology implementation any more successful. To close this gap, we developed an EHR implementation framework that integrates multiple conceptual frameworks in an overarching, yet pragmatic meta-framework to explain factors which lead to successful EHR implementation, in order to provide more quantitative insight into EHR implementations. Our meta-framework captures the dynamic nature of an EHR implementation through their function, interactivity with other factors and phases, and iterative nature.

This chapter introduces a framework to analyze the pre-requisites to move from an evolutionary stage to a revolutionary one when using ICT in healthcare. It argues that the degree of transformation should be determined by the role ICT has in the organization when initiating the redesigning process, but also by the aims technology is supposed to achieve. The suggested framework can be used to identify preconditions and areas affected from the implementation and use of ICT providing a structure to evaluate how changes will affect key actors and the organization. The classification suggested to identify different steps of transformation should indicate stakeholders, healthcare personnel and managers how to refocus their priorities to be able to built organizations that can be adapted to the revolutionary stage to obtain the same benefits that the industry has previously identified from the implementation of use of ICT.

Health information technology has the potential to greatly improve health care delivery. Indeed in recent years many have argued that introduction of information technology will be essential in order to decrease medical error and increase health care safety. In this chapter we review some of the evidence that has accumulated indicating the positive benefits of health information technology for improving safety in health care. However, a number of recent studies have indicated that if systems are not designed and implemented properly health information technology may actual inadvertently result in new types of medical errors—technology-induced errors. In this chapter, we discuss where such error may arise and propose a model for conceptualizing and diagnosing technology-induced error so that the benefits of technology can be achieved while the likelihood of the occurrence of technology-induced medical error is reduced.

Chapter X

Data-sharing systems—where healthcare providers jointly implement a common reporting system to promote voluntary reporting, information sharing, and learning—are emerging as an important regional, state-level, and national strategy for improving patient safety. The objective of this chapter is to review the evidence regarding the effectiveness of these data-sharing systems and to report on the results of an analysis of data from the Pittsburgh Regional Healthcare Initiative (PRHI). PRHI consists of 42 hospitals, purchasers and insurers in southwestern Pennsylvania that implemented Medmarx, an on-line medication error reporting systems. Analysis of data from the PRHI hospitals indicated that the number of errors and corrective actions reported initially varied widely with organizational characteristics such as hospital size, JCAHO accreditation score and teaching status. But the subsequent trends in reporting errors and reporting actions were different. Whereas the number of reported errors increased significantly, and at similar rates, across the participating hospitals, the number of corrective actions reported per error remained mostly unchanged over the 12-month period. A computer simulation model was developed to explore organizational changes designed to improve patient safety. Four interventions were simulated involving the implementation of computerized physician order entry, decision support systems and a clinical pharmacist on hospital rounds. The results of this study carry implications for the design and assessment of data-sharing systems. Improvements in patient safety require more than voluntary reporting and clinical initiatives. Organizational changes are essential in order to significantly reduce medical errors and adverse events.

Chapter XI

Section IV
Strategic Approaches to Improving the Healthcare System

This chapter discusses the extent to which factors known to influence the success and failure of health information systems may be evaluated. More specifically, this is concerned with evaluation of such factors—for screening, diagnostic or preventive purposes—by means of existing evaluation methods designed for users. The author identifies that it is feasible to identify evaluation methods for most success factor and failure criteria. However, there is a need for situational methods engineering as the methods are not dedicated to answering the precise information needs of the project management. Therefore, demands are being placed on the evaluators' methical and methodological skills, when evaluating health information systems. The author concludes the paper by pointing at research needs and opportunities.

Chapter XII

Healthcare is one of the world's most information intensive industries. Every day volumes of data are produced which, properly used, can improve clinical practice and outcomes, guide planning and resource allocation, and enhance accountability. Electronic health information is fundamental to better health care.

There will be no significant increase forward in health care quality and efficiency without high quality, user-friendly health information compiled and delivered electronically. The growing use of information and communication technology (ICT) in the healthcare sector has introduced numerous opportunities and benefits to patients, providers and governments alike. Patients are being provided with tools to help them manage and monitor their health care, providers are able to seamlessly access up-to-date patient information and governments are showing transparency to the public by reporting health data and information on their Web sites. There is mounting evidence that national, regional and organizational e-health strategies are being developed and implemented worldwide. This chapter provides an overview of three different national e-health strategies, and identifies the lessons learned from the e-health strategies of Canada, England, and Denmark.

Healthcare IT (HIT) has failed to live up to its promise in the United States. HIT solutions and decisions need to be evidence based and standardized. Interventional Informatics is ideally positioned to provide evidence based and standardized solutions in the enterprise (aka, the medical center) which includes all or some combination of hospital(s), hospital based-practices, enterprise owned offsite medical practices, faculty practice and a medical school. For purposes of this chapter, interventional informatics is defined as applied medical or clinical informatics with an emphasis on an active interventional role in the enterprise. A department of interventional informatics, which integrates the science of Informatics into daily operations, should become a standard part of any 21st century medical center in the United States.

Chapter XIV

This chapter describes a framework for conducting economic analyses of health information technologies (HIT). It explains the basic principles of healthcare economic analyses and the relationships between the costs and effectiveness of a health intervention, and then uses these principles to explain the types of data that need to be gathered in order to conduct a health information technology economic evaluation study. A current health information technology study is then used to illustrate the incorporation of the framework's economic analysis methods into an ongoing research project. Economic research in the field of health information technology is not yet well developed. This chapter is meant to educate researchers about the need for HIT economic analyses as well as provide a structured framework to assist them in conducting these analyses.

Section V
Legal, Ethical, and Professional Issues

Chapter XV

This chapter discusses key legal issues raised by the contemporary trend to managing and sharing patient information via electronic health records (EHR). Concepts of privacy, confidentiality, consent and security are defined and considered in the context of EHR initiatives in Canada, the United Kingdom and Australia. This chapter explores whether patients have the right to withhold consent to the collection and sharing of their personal information via EHRs. It discusses opt-in and opt-out models for participation in EHRs and concludes that presumed consent for EHR participation will ensure more rapid and complete implementation, but at the cost of some personal choice for patients. The reduction in patient control over personal information ought to be augmented with strong security protections to minimize risks of unauthorized access to EHRs and fulfill legal and ethical obligations to safeguard patient information.

Chapter XVI

Existing literature often addresses the ethical problems posed by health informatics. Instead of this problem-based approach, this chapter explores the ethical benefits of health information systems in an attempt to answer the question "can health information systems make organizations more accountable, beneficent, and more responsive to a patient's right to self determination?" It does so by unpacking the accountability for reasonableness framework in ethical decision making and the concepts of beneficence and self-determination. The framework and the concepts are discussed in light of four commonly used health information systems, namely: Web-based publicly accessible inventories of services; Web-based patient education; telemedicine; and the electronic medical record. The objective of this chapter is to discuss the ethical principles that health information systems actually help to achieve, with a view to enabling researchers, clinicians, and managers make the case for the development and maintenance of these systems in a client-centered fashion.

Chapter XVII

The development of electronic health records marked a fundamental change in the ethical and legal status of health records and in the relationship between the subjects of the records, the records themselves and health information and health care professionals—changes that are not fully captured by traditional privacy- and confidentiality considerations. The chapter begins with a sketch of the nature of this evolution and places it into the epistemic framework of health care decision-making. It then outlines why EHRs are special, what the implications of this special status are both ethically and juridically, and what this means for professionals and institutions. An attempt is made to link these considerations to the development of secure e-health, which requires not only the interoperability of technical standards but also the harmonization of professional education, institutional protocols and of laws and regulations.

Section VI
Knowledge Translation in Healthcare

Because of the rapid growth of health evidence and knowledge generated through research, and as the health system is becoming increasingly complex, clinical care gaps increasingly widen where best practices based on latest evidence are not routinely integrated into everyday health service delivery. Therefore, there is a strong need to inculcate knowledge translation strategies into our health system so as to promote seamless incorporation of new knowledge into routine service delivery and education to promote positive change in individuals and the health system towards eliminating the clinical care gaps. E-health, the use of information and communication technologies (ICT) in health which encompasses telehealth, health informatics, and e-learning, can play a prominently supportive role. This chapter examines the opportunities and challenges of technology enabled knowledge translation (TEKT) —using ICT to accelerate knowledge translation—in today's health system with two case studies for illustration. Future TEKT research and evaluation directions are also articulated.

Chapter XIX

With advances in electronic health record systems and mobile computing technologies it is possible to re-conceptualize how health professionals access information and design appropriate decision-support systems to support quality patient care. This chapter uses the context of nursing sensitive patient outcomes data collection to explore how technology can be used to increase nurses' and other health professionals' access to patient outcomes information in real time to continually improve patient care. The chapter draws upon literature related to: (1) case-based reasoning, (2) feedback, (3) and evidence-based nursing practice to provide the theoretical foundation for an electronic knowledge translation intervention that was developed and tested for usability. Directions for future research include the need to understand how nurses experience uncertainty in their practice, how this influences information seeking behavior, and how information resources can be designed to support real-time clinical decision making.

This chapter presents a discussion and findings of health literacy and its relevance to health informatics. We argue that the Internet represents an increasingly important vehicle for knowledge translation to consumers of health information. However, much of the Internet-based information available to consumers is difficult to understand by those who need it the most. A critical factor to improve the comprehensibility, and therefore the quality, of health information is literacy. We summarize studies of various aspects of health literacy, such as readability and comprehensibility of risk information. We also point out ways in which the study of health literacy, including prose and numeric literacy, should inform researchers, health practitioners, and Web designers of specific ways in which consumer health information can be improved.

Foreword

It is safe to say that the deployment of what is commonly referred to as "Health Information Systems" in the "real world" has a history that exceeds a span of four decades. I would suggest that research in this field predates deployment by at least another decade, if not more. Traditional barriers to deployment were a combination of factors including: lack of funding, unwillingness of healthcare leaders to trust the concept of "computerization," lack of adequate technologies to support automation, and "political will" on the part of governing authorities.

The application of information technologies over that period of time, by and large, centered on the automation of processing data rather than the use of information inherent in the science of health informatics and bioinformatics. The systems that succeeded were isolated in the sense that they were designed and deployed to serve the needs of specific organizations rather than altruistically the patient or the caregivers and clinicians. That is not to say that these conflict. However, it suggests that the acceptance of these systems was based largely on senior management decisions rather than necessarily by consensus.

Over the past decade we have witnessed a number of systemic if not endemic global changes, likely prompted by the Internet and popularized by automated teller machines (ATMs) and online banking – with the consequence of creating a population which has faith in information and communication technology and which is rapidly integrating it in their day to day lives. This factor, together with research in bioinformatics and genomics, rapidly evolving useable technologies, media popularity, and political will (with associated funding) has created the need to transform the field of "Health" in its entirety.

The keystone to the transformation is the electronic health record (EHR) within a national or regional context – its definition is somewhat elusive, ranging from being a repository of an individual's contact and insurance information, chronic disease and drug allergies to being inclusive of encounter information, medication profiles, and diagnostic history. Several countries, notably the UK, Canada, and Australia have invested significant sums of public funds in these broad national strategies.

Another primary area is that of the electronic medical record (EMR) broadly and generally defined as a womb – to- tomb record of interactions of a specific individual with the health delivery system inclusive of reports, physician notes, images, diagnostic results, and basic information included in the aforementioned EHR. The EMR is normally seen as being held in the custody of the individual's general practitioner or family physician.

Inherent in the transformation are clinical information systems which are designed specifically to provide informatics support to clinicians in the delivery of clinical interventions to the patient inclusive of clinical decision support, best practices and outcomes.

Health surveillance systems are on the immediate horizon of needs as evidenced by the SARS pandemic and the Asian bird flux that is currently a significant issue.

On a global basis various components of the transformational changes have been implemented with varying degrees of success. The consultative processes that accompanied implementation or lessons learned after top-down implementation attempts have precipitated some broad challenges or opportunities:

- The need for thinking within a global context and adoption of internationally accepted standards specifically as they relate to interoperability, nomenclature and other standards.
- The need for preparing organizations for change through a facilitative collaboration process as opposed to "damage control' after the fact.
- The need to identify the client of applications and ensure that they are involved in the development and implementation process.
- The need for formal education for Health Informaticians, certification, codes of practice, i.e. the basic elements of a career choice.
- The need for consistent review of privacy, security and confidentiality legislation, policies & procedures and the penalties for breaching them.
- The need to be able to measure information – based health delivery systems or components thereof from both a patient outcome and return on investment perspective.

A recent (November 19, 2007) public opinion poll (funded by Health Canada, Canada Health Infoway, and the office of the Privacy Commissioner for Canada) indicated that 88% of Canadians supported the development of EHR's; of those who had personal experience with an EHR, 89% said that, in terms of overall effectiveness for the health care system, the electronic system was better.

The time is now.

The vision of Healthcare Transformation has positioned the human, social and organizational sciences specific to health information systems in the forefront of research and application in the real-word setting. This book brilliantly clarifies the enormous complexity and multiple dynamics of health care and the informatics sciences that support it.

Steven A. Huesing, CMA
Executive Director,
International Medical Informatics Association (IMIA)

Preface

Healthcare and healthcare delivery are currently undergoing major changes worldwide as they are increasingly being transformed through the application of technology. Over the past several decades a wide variety of information technologies have been deployed within an ever increasing variety of healthcare settings (ranging from clinical to hospital, community and home settings) in an effort to streamline and modernize healthcare delivery. Much of this effort has been in response to the limitations of ways that healthcare information has traditionally been collected, retrieved and communicated. For example, the limitations of handwritten paper-based medical records, which have been the predominant form of recording patient and medical information for over a century, have been well documented (Shortliffe & Cimino, 2006). This includes difficulty in obtaining information stored in paper-based records, illegibility of handwritten notes and lack of ability to connect information in the paper-based record with other relevant data being stored in growing clinical, hospital, regional and national health databases and repositories. Conventional approaches to healthcare information management are not able to support advanced health information systems of the future that will be able to take advantage of the increasing amount of health data being generated in order to radically improve healthcare decision making and practice. Indeed, traditional approaches to managing healthcare information that met the needs of healthcare professionals and organizations in past decades have not scaled well to the current information needs of modern healthcare (Shortliffe & Cimino, 2006).

In response to this need, a wide range of information technologies have been designed and deployed, ranging from systems designed to support retrieval of basic patient data to physician order entry systems designed to support ordering of medications by healthcare workers (Borycki & Kushniruk, 2005). However, despite the promise of information technology for improving healthcare, much of the current healthcare system worldwide continues to be based on outmoded traditional models for information management and exchange. Furthermore, studies examining the potential benefits of the introduction of healthcare technology are mixed and some studies have indicated that information technology that is not designed or deployed properly may lead to little or no benefit (Chaudhry, Wang, Wu, Maglione, Mojica, Roth, et al., 2006). This is a consequence of a range of difficulties encountered in attempting to modernize healthcare using information technology, both technical and non-technical. From a technical perspective many advances have and continue to be made. However experience is indicating that integration of technological innovation with human work and social activity in healthcare is problematic.

Over the past several decades it has become increasingly recognized that perhaps the most serious barriers to achieving widespread improvement in healthcare using information technology are related to human and social aspects of healthcare information systems. These include issues related to understanding and optimizing the complex interaction between people (e.g. healthcare professionals, patients and laypeople) and computer systems, organizational issues surrounding understanding the impact of implementation of such systems in complex healthcare settings, as well as the legal, ethical and social issues surrounding the use and potentially widespread sensitive electronic dissemination of healthcare information. In order to address these issues a wide variety of researchers and practitioners from many disciplines have contributed both theoretical and methodological approaches in order to improve our understanding of barriers to successful use of information technology in healthcare. In this book we gather multiple perspectives on human and social aspects of healthcare information technology. The contributors to this book describe a variety of models, frameworks and empirical approaches to considering human and social aspects of health information systems.

BACKGROUND: THE EMERGENCE OF HEALTHCARE INFORMATION TECHNOLOGY AND THE ELECTRONIC HEALTH RECORD (EHR)

Over the past several decades, great strides have been made in technological developments in healthcare information technology. These have included improvements in approaches to digitally storing and retrieving textual data (e.g. descriptions of patient illnesses), advances in imaging data (e.g. digital X-rays and imaging systems), as well as advances in database technologies, networking and communication technologies. Foremost among new and emerging information technologies in healthcare is the electronic health record (EHR), which can be considered a "cognitive artifact" (i.e. a tool that enables people to reason and communicate) that will ultimately serve an integrating role for patient records and other emerging healthcare electronic technologies. In this book we refer to the EHR as the repository of information about an individual's health (including relevant medical and health information) that can be stored and retrieved electronically and ideally will exist not only within physician practices and hospitals but ideally will be maintained over an individual's lifetime (Shortliffe & Cimino, 2006). Such systems are designed to be integrated with other forms of computer support for healthcare such as clinical decision support systems, alerting and reminding systems and disease surveillance systems. While this ideal has not been fully achieved yet, a wide range of more limited electronic records have appeared and are deployed increasingly routinely in healthcare – including the EMR (electronic medical record), which is maintained by the health professional to store and retrieve electronic data about an individual or patient, the EPR (electronic patient record) which is maintained by a particular healthcare organization about a patient, and the PHR (personal health record), which is meant to be maintained and accessed directly by patients and laypeople themselves (Nagle, 2007).

Perhaps the greatest potential of modernizing healthcare through use of information technology will come from new functionality and capabilities that will emerge based on the initial conversion of paper-based records and data to electronic forms. For example, decision support systems will be capable of alerting physicians about problems in entering a medication due to a patient's drug allergies (or provide public health warnings about potential epidemics) and will also be capable of integrating data about a patient's genetic makeup to support physician selection of medications (Shortliffe & Cimino, 2006). Such systems are expected to become routinely integrated in future healthcare practice once healthcare data is widely stored and integrated in digital form. Such systems are envisaged to become commonly used to improve healthcare across a range of settings, including hospitals, clinics, health professional offices as well as home care. Other emergent benefits and potential functions resulting from widespread encoding, storage and retrieval of interchangeable healthcare data (both textual and image-based data) will likely emerge in an opportunistic manner and will in turn shape new functionality in repeated cycles of innovation (Patel & Kushniruk, 1998).

Despite these technological advances associated with EHRs and related information technologies (and their potential to shape modern healthcare), the penetration and success of information technologies in healthcare to date has be less than expected and efforts at implementing regional, national and international initiatives are currently facing numerous problems. For example, estimates of use of electronic health records within North America have remained relatively low (for example in Canada such system are used by considerably fewer than half of practicing physicians) and in countries reporting highest usage of such technology, a wide range of issues related to adoption and integration of these technologies remain (Protti, 2007). Indeed, the literature contains many examples of healthcare information system implementations that have failed to be implemented, have ended up not improving healthcare and in some cases that were completely abandoned (Chaudhry, Wang, Wu, Maglione, Mojica, Roth, et al., 2006). The issues surrounding problems in successful implementation of healthcare system are many and are complex. While technological developments and advances in healthcare information systems are by no means complete and work along these lines is ongoing, human and social aspects of developing and implementing healthcare information technology are proving to be perhaps the most challenging factors in the successful deployment of healthcare information technology. The objective of this book is to provide the reader with multiple perspectives on major human and social issues and possible solutions that are emerging in an attempt to improve healthcare using information technologies.

HUMAN AND SOCIAL ISSUES IN SUCCESSFUL DEPLOYMENT OF HEALTHCARE INFORMATION TECHNOLOGY

To address the challenges noted above a range of theories and methodologies emerging from a wide variety of disciplines have appeared and are embedded in health informatics. The field of health informatics can be defined as the interdisciplinary study of how information is processed, managed and communicated in healthcare and stands at the intersection among disciplines such as medicine, nursing, computer science, psychology and management (Shortliffe & Cimino, 2006). Health informatics is an evolving field that considers healthcare information technology at multiple levels of abstraction and complexity, ranging from analysis of the impact of healthcare information systems at the individual, organizational and the regional level.

Figure 1 presents a conceptual framework for considering the interaction between humans and healthcare information technologies. Starting at Level 1 the focus is on aspects of the interaction of users (e.g. health professionals, patients and others) directly with information systems. Here cognitive psychology and related disciplines can help improve the design of healthcare systems by providing knowledge about what users can and cannot be expected to do, identifying the nature and causes of problems users encounter in using healthcare information technology, as well as supplying modeling tools and methods to help build more effective healthcare information systems from the perspective of different types of users (e.g. physicians, nurses, healthcare professionals and patients). At this level human issues include the critical need for developing healthcare information systems that are "usable" – i.e. systems that efficient, effective and enjoyable to use from the perspective of the human user of such systems (Sharp, Rogers & Preece, 2007). The healthcare literature contains considerable research that indicates that one of the major problems (that has been implicated for the low adoption rate of many healthcare information technologies) is the lack of usability of healthcare systems (Kushniruk & Patel, 2004). There is no doubt that many of the EHR and related information technologies produced to data have had poor usability and users of such systems have not been able to adequately take advantage of system technical capabilities due to usability issues related problems experienced by users in attempting to interact with such systems.

Figure 1. Layers of human and social aspects of health information systems

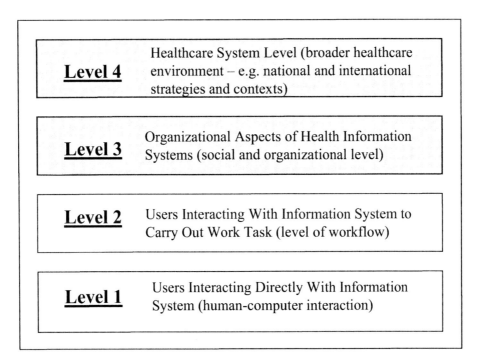

At the second level (Level 2) depicted in Figure 1 we consider issues in using and adopting healthcare information technology in the context of how such systems fit within the actual healthcare work activities and workflow they are designed to support. At this level systems can be considered in the context of how well they support complex human work activities, such as support of patient care by nurses or diagnosis of a patient's illness by a physician. One of the major criticisms of current healthcare information systems is a lack of appropriate integration of such technology within the routine work practices, decision making and reasoning processes of the users they are designed to support (Borycki & Kushniruk, 2005). Further work in understanding the complex interaction among humans, computers and collaborative healthcare work activity are explored at this level.

The third level (Level 3) in Figure 1 represents the organizational and social layer when considering health information technologies and their use by humans. At this level, application of knowledge from areas such as social psychology, organizational psychology and management science, as well as other related disciplines, can be brought to bear on improving healthcare information systems (Ash, Gorman, Lavelle, Lyman & Fournier, 2001; Kaplan, Dowling, Friedman & Peel, 2001). This includes providing improved knowledge about the context of use of such technology in complex social and organizational settings, identifying and explaining how healthcare professionals can work together to best support collaborative practice, as well as providing frameworks for modeling and evaluating the impact of health information technology. Such knowledge can be used to improve the design of healthcare information systems by identifying trouble spots in organizational and social processes, providing models for improved design of social and organizational structures and processes, and for supplying methods to support improved design and evaluation of technologies.

Moving up the next level of abstraction - Level 4, the impact of the broader environment and overall healthcare system (e.g. regional health authorities, national strategies, and international context) is brought to bear in considering health information technologies. Here strategic decisions that guide the deployment of such technology must take into account a range of social and political aspects of healthcare when for example deciding how to best deploy health information systems at the national level across regions (Protti. 2007). In addition, ethical issues begin to come to the fore when considering the complex interaction among individuals within the healthcare system as a whole, and dissemination of sensitive healthcare data using information technology. Finally, the dissemination of knowledge about health and healthcare practices across national and international boundaries (as well as across society from health professionals to patients to the general lay population) is becoming increasingly important through work in the area of knowledge translation, focusing on translating research knowledge to practical information to inform healthcare practice.

ORGANIZATION OF THE BOOK

The organization of this book reflects the multiple layers and varied interdisciplinary perspectives on human and social aspects of healthcare information systems described above. The perspectives span research that includes the consideration of human interaction with healthcare information systems from the level of individual user to the social, ethical and even the economic impact of health information systems on healthcare.

In Section I of this book we begin by considering issues around human-computer interaction, starting with a focus on the individual user of the system interacting with healthcare information systems (corresponding to Level 1 of the framework described in the previous section, focusing on users' interactions with systems). In Chapter I, Kushniruk, Borycki, Kuwata and Ho describe emerging approaches to evaluating the usability of healthcare information systems. The approaches discussed are aimed at providing feedback and input to designers and implementers to help improve the usability, effectiveness and adoption of health information systems by users, who may range from healthcare professionals to patients and lay people. In Chapter II, Price provides and overview of models of human-computer interaction, that have evolved historically from descriptions of individual user interactions with healthcare systems and analysis of cognitive aspects of computer use, to analysis of how healthcare information systems can be modeled in terms of cognition that is "distributed" amongst multiple healthcare professionals and computer systems.

In Section II of the book the impact of healthcare information systems on clinical work and practice is considered (corresponding to Level 2 of the framework described in the previous section, focusing on use of information technology to support healthcare workflow). In Chapter III Kuziemsky describes how the 'fit' (i.e. degree of match) of health information systems with the needs and information requirements of healthcare professionals can be enhanced through process supports and provides a case study of how this can be achieved. Nohr and Boye (Chapter IV) describe their work in monitoring the implementation process of electronic health records (EHRs) in Denmark and describe the development of a common conceptual model to support clinical processes when implementing healthcare information technologies. This is followed in Chapter V with a discussion by Boye of the vision of pervasive computing in healthcare whereby computer services are made widely available across varied settings and users, providing health information "anywhere and anytime". Issues and considerations associated with this vision are discussed from a human-societal perspective.

Section III of the book focuses on organizational and social aspects of healthcare information technology involving change management, best practices evaluation (corresponding to Level 3 – the organizational level, in the framework described in the previous section). In Chapter VI Day and Norris consider human aspects of change in healthcare information technology projects. They discuss how change management can be used to intervene and assist in the transition to health information technology. In Chapter VII Kucukyazici, Keshavjee, Bosomworth, Copen and Lai discuss best practices for implementing electronic health records and information systems. They introduce a multi-level, multi-dimensional meta-framework for successful implementations of electronic health records (EHRs) within organizations and discuss implications of the framework for improving the chance of effective implementation. In Chapter VIII Vimarlund introduces a framework to identify the areas within an organization that will be affected by use of health information systems and to provide a structure to evaluate how changes will affect key actors and the organization.

Safety and the reduction of error in healthcare are also becoming major issues as it is now recognized that healthcare information technologies have the potential to decrease human error in healthcare (through advanced features and capabilities such as alerting and remaindering) but may also introduce new errors if not appropriately designed. In Chapter IX Borycki and Kushniruk describe how "technology-induced" errors (i.e. unintended errors that occur as a consequence of introduction of technology) can be reduced through appropriate information gathering, diagnosis and system design processes. Anderson in Chapter X describes how regional patient safety initiatives involving use of information technology can be designed to reduce error and streamline healthcare processes at multiple levels. In Chapter XI Brender provides a description of range of evaluation methods that have appeared to monitor the success and failure of health information systems.

Section IV of the book discusses strategic approaches being implemented at the healthcare system level (corresponding to Level 4 in the framework described in the previous section). In Chapter XII Protti considers national and organizational strategies for implementation of electronic health records (EHRs) in three different countries – Canada, England and Denmark. The importance of this work is considerable given that huge monetary investments are being made by such countries in order to modernize their healthcare systems using information technology. Major roadblocks have been encountered by countries attempting to implement large-scale strategies for this type of change and much can be learned by comparing the journeys taken and lessons learned in different countries around the world. In Chapter XIII Kannry discusses the need to "operationalize" the science of health informatics within healthcare organizations in order to bridge the gap between academic work in the field of health informatics and real-life healthcare implementations. The benefits of this bridging will be considerable both for informing practical implementations with the latest research in order to improve chances of success, as well as to feedback lessons and experience learned from organizational implementations back to field of health informatics. In Chapter XVI Eisenstein discusses the important area of assessing the economic impact of health information systems and describes a framework for conducting economic analyses of health information systems. As Eisenstein argues, this is an area that is not yet well developed in healthcare but that will be essential in order to ensure the systems that are introduced do indeed have positive economic benefits for the healthcare system.

As information technology becomes a more central part of healthcare worldwide a number of complex legal, ethical and professional issues have come to the fore, which is the focus of Section V of the book. These include legal issues around ownership, privacy and confidentiality of electronic health data with the potential for widespread availability of health data using electronic health records. In Chapter XV Ries describes legal aspects in health information and electronic health records and argues that the reduction in patient control over personal information ought to be augmented with stronger security protections to minimize the risks of unauthorized access and fulfill legal obligations. Sarryeddine in Chapter XVI considers the potential for ethical benefits of health information systems in asking the questions "can health information systems make organizations more accountable, beneficent and more responsive to a patient's right to self determination?" Kluge extends this discussion in Chapter XVII by exploring why ethics matters in development of electronic health records and explores ethical implications of widespread use of health information systems.

In order to deploy information systems in healthcare that will provide users with information at the right time and place, the appropriate "translation" of knowledge via electronic media will become essential, which is the focus of Part 6. In Chapter XVIII Ho describes the rapidly emerging field of knowledge translation in healthcare. Given the rapid growth of health evidence and knowledge through research, health information technology will be key in integrating this knowledge and bringing it bear on health related decision making. Along these lines in Chapter XIX Doran and Di Pietro describe use of mobile computing technologies to improve knowledge translation in nursing practice through providing nurses decision support at the point-of-care. Finally, in Chapter XX Arocha and Hoffman-Goetz discuss improvement of Internet-based health knowledge through attention to literacy. This is an important area for improving the dissemination and uptake of useful healthcare information and evidence not only by health care professionals but also by patients and other consumers of health information.

REFERENCES

Ash, J., Gorman, P., Lavelle, M., Lyman, J., & Fournier, L. (2001). Investigating physician order entry in the field: Lessons learned a multi-centre study (pp. 1107-1011). *In Proceedings of MedInfo 2001.* North-Holland: New York.

Borycki, E., & Kushniruk, A.W. (2005). Identifying and preventing technology-induced error using simulations: Application of usability engineering techniques. *Healthcare Quarterly, 8,* 99-105.

Chaudhry, B., Wang, J., Wu, S., Maglione, M., Mojica, W., Roth, E., et al. (2006). Systematic Review: Impact of Health Information Technology on Quality, Efficiency, and Costs of Medical Care. *Annals of Internal Medicine, 144(10), 742-752.*

Kaplan, B., Brennan, P. F., Dowling, A. F., Friedman, C. P. & Peel, V. (2001). Towards an informatics research agenda: Key people and organizational issues. *Journal of the American Medical Informatics Association, 8*(3), 235-241.

Kushniruk, A. W. & Patel, V. L. (2004). Cognitive and usability engineering approaches to the evaluation of clinical information systems. *Journal of Biomedical Informatics, 37,* 56-57.

Nagle, L. M. (2007). Informatics: Emerging concepts and issues. *Nursing Leadership, 20*(2), 30-33.

Patel, V. L., & Kushniruk, A. W. (1998). Interface design for health care environments: The role of cognitive science. In C. Chute (Ed.) *Proceedings of the AMIA 98 Annual Symposium*, 29-37.

Protti, D. (2007).Comparison of information technology in general practice in 10 countries. *Healthcare Quarterly, 10(2):107-16.*

Sharp, H., Rogers, Y., & Preece, J. (2007). *Interaction design: beyond human-computer interaction* (2nd ed.). New York: John Wiley & Sons.

Shortliffe, E. H., & Cimino, J. J. (2006). *Biomedical informatics: Computer applications in health care and biomedicine* (3rd ed.). New York, NY: Springer.

Section I
Usability and Human–Computer Interaction in Healthcare

Chapter I
Emerging Approaches to Evaluating the Usability of Health Information Systems

Andre W. Kushniruk
University of Victoria, Canada

Elizabeth M. Borycki
University of Victoria, Canada

Shige Kuwata
Tottori University Hospital, Japan

Francis Ho
University of Victoria, Canada

ABSTRACT

It is essential that health information systems are easy to use, meet user information needs and are shown to be safe. However, there are currently a wide range of issues and problems with health information systems related to human-computer interaction. Indeed, the lack of ease of use of health information systems has been a major impediment to adoption of such systems. To address these issues, the authors have applied methods emerging from the field of usability engineering in order to improve the adoption of a wide range of health information systems in collaboration with hospitals and other healthcare organizations throughout the world. In this chapter we describe our work in conducting usability analyses that can be used to rapidly evaluate the usability and safety of healthcare information systems, both in artificial laboratory and real clinical settings. We then discuss how this work has evolved towards the development of software systems ("virtual usability laboratories") capable of remotely collecting, integrating and supporting analysis of a range of usability data.

Copyright © 2008, IGI Global, distributing in print or electronic forms without written permission of IGI Global is prohibited.

INTRODUCTION

A wide variety of health information systems have appeared in healthcare (Shortliffe & Cimino, 2006). Although, such innovation promises to revolutionize healthcare there are a number of critical problems and issues related to their development, deployment and acceptance by end users that are related to human-computer interaction (HCI). Usability of health information systems refers to the degree to which they are useful, effective, efficient and enjoyable (Sharp, Rogers, & Preece, 2007). Lack of system usability has been a major impediment to adoption of health information systems. Indeed, perhaps in no other field have issues related to HCI come more to the fore when attempting to introduce information technologies than in healthcare. It has been previously argued that issues of HCI may be the most serious barrier to successful implementation and adoption of information technologies in healthcare (Kushniruk & Patel, 2004). Strenuous demands are placed on healthcare professionals and end users of health information systems making the need for usable systems critical in healthcare. Health information systems must be designed to consider not only technical aspects but also the complex information needs, cognitive processing and limitations of human users of such systems.

One of the main areas of concern revolves around the following question: how can we ensure that the health information systems we develop are usable, meet user information, support work needs and are safe? The design of health information systems that are intuitive to use and that support human information processing is essential. This has become increasingly recognized as more and more complex software and hardware applications appear in healthcare. Furthermore, as the complexity and variety of healthcare situations in which this technology is deployed increases, issues related to ensuring that health information systems will support local work activities and practices in healthcare are becoming critical.

Closely related to issues of usability are issues related to healthcare safety, with the need to ensure that new devices and information systems increase patient safety and facilitate healthcare work. In addition, applications targeted to health consumers (e.g., patients and lay people) are also being developed at an increasing rate. It is essential that these systems be usable and that the information and advice they provide is both understandable and safe. Improved understanding of issues related to human cognitive processes that are part of human-computer interaction in healthcare is needed so that we can develop more effective health information systems.

In order to be able to determine if systems developed in healthcare are usable and safe methods of analysis are needed that can be used to characterize the information needs and processing of users of these systems. A wide variety of techniques and methods have appeared from applied psychology that can be used in health information system evaluation. One powerful method involves application of "think aloud" protocols. This involves the recording of subjects as they verbalize their thoughts while interacting with computer systems (Ericsson & Simon, 1993). In addition, video recordings of user interactions with systems can also be collected to provide a more complete picture of the interaction between humans and health information systems, as will be described in this chapter (Kushniruk & Patel, 2004). In addition to assessing the interaction with systems such methods can also be applied to assess the information needs of healthcare workers in order to form the basis for design of systems that better match both information needs and human information processing capabilities.

This chapter describes the evolution of our work in the development of practical and efficient approaches to assessing of the use and usability of new and emerging health information systems. This chapter begins with a discussion of cognitive aspects of human interaction with health information systems. This is followed by a discussion of an approach to rapid low-cost usability engineering that can be applied in the field to conduct studies of users interacting with health information systems in real settings. The approach has been used to evaluate a variety of healthcare information systems ranging from electronic health records (EHR) to Web-based information resources designed for use by both healthcare professionals and lay persons. We then follow this with discussion of our most recent work in extending the concept of usability testing to conducting studies of system usage and usability over the World Wide Web (WWW) remotely.

BACKGROUND

The Study of Human-Computer Interaction

The study of human-computer interaction (HCI) is concerned with the human, social, organizational, and technical aspects of the interaction between human and machines. It is a broad area of study that deals with a broad range of phenomena, including the design, evaluation and social implications of computer systems (Sharp, Rogers, & Preece, 2007). Research in HCI lies at the intersection of a number of disciplines including: cognitive and social psychology, computer science, anthropology, sociology, design sciences, and engineering. In this chapter we will illustrate how interdisciplinary perspectives to designing and evaluating healthcare information systems are needed in order to lead to healthcare systems that will be more effective and acceptable to their users.

Cognitive Aspects of HCI in Healthcare

There are a wide range of aspects of health information systems that are related to cognition and human information processing. One may ask "why study cognitive aspects of health in-

formation systems?" In answering this we must consider that the user interface to healthcare information systems can be defined as being the component of the overall man-machine system responsible for communication with the user of the system. Thus, HCI can be considered to be largely cognitive in that it involves processing of information by humans, in close conjunction with computer systems. Therefore, the application of ideas, theories and methods emerging from the field of cognitive psychology are highly relevant to the design and implementation of more effective healthcare information systems from the perspective of human users, for whom systems are designed to support and serve. There are a number of ways in which knowledge of human cognitive processing is important for improving healthcare information systems. These include the following: (a) providing knowledge about what typical users of systems can and cannot be expected to do, (b) identifying and explaining the nature and causes of user problems, (c) characterizing the problem solving and decision making processes of healthcare workers, (d) assessing the cognitive needs of users in designing systems and user interfaces, (e) feeding input back into system re-design and improvement, and (f) providing models and frameworks for conducting HCI research in healthcare.

TOWARDS A FRAMEWORK FOR HCI IN HEALTHCARE

In this chapter we take a broad perspective on HCI which encompasses the first three levels of human, social, and organizational aspects of health information systems, as outlined in the preface of this book: (1) Level 1—the level of the individual user interacting with a system in isolation, (2) Level 2—the level of the user interacting with an information system in order to carry out real work tasks, and finally (3) Level 3—the social and organizational level, where the interaction with an information system is considered in the context of its impact and effect on the organization as a whole. This characterization of the use of new information technologies in healthcare builds on a multi-level model of HCI which provides a useful framework for considering the complex problem of understanding how to best design, test and deploy innovative healthcare information technologies (adapted from Eason, 1991). Using this model, we can consider problems in acceptance of new technology at each of the three levels. For example, the goal of successful adoption of a health information system may fail at Level 1 if the design of the computer screens and instructions are such that users cannot easily learn how to use the system to enter patient data. Even if a system is designed to work well at Level 1, problems may occur once the system is inserted into the complex day-to-day activities and workflow of healthcare work practices, which may involve a variety of team members, contexts, environments, levels of urgency and complexity of tasks. However, careful analysis and adjustments made to provide effective systems at Level 2 does not guarantee uptake and acceptance of a new healthcare information technology, since the effect and impact of deploying such a technology at the organizational level (i.e., Level 3) may be an issue. For example, in the context of a patient record system, privacy and confidentiality issues at an organizational or political level may restrict the deployment of this technology within an organization such as a hospital. Nowhere in healthcare may careful consideration of each of these three levels of HCI be more germane than in consideration of barriers to adoption of health information systems. Health information systems span the levels of individual users of systems, from application of new technology within complex work roles and activities to issues that emerge with the increased possibilities for widespread

access and dissemination of patient information along with the resulting organizational concerns regarding privacy and confidentiality.

Another perspective from which to consider health information systems relates to the extent of interaction of human users with the system. Thus, we can consider user interaction with health information systems in healthcare along a continuum from applications which require continual focus of user attention on the information technology, to applications where the technology is "invisible" or interacts to a very limited extent with the user. For example, the user interfaces of many hand-held applications typically represent an extension of conventional desktop user interfaces to mobile applications. With these types of applications, users must focus considerable attention on the user interface [e.g., to enter medical values into a PDA (personal digital assistant)] at particular periods in time and explicitly insert its use within their work activities. Thus, the introduction of the technology must be understood in how it changes the work activity of the user and many aspects of human factors from the study of conventional user interfaces are applicable. However, many new applications of health information systems, including remote monitoring devices and wearable computing, are designed to be used ubiquitously *while* the user carries on their work activities (i.e., without switching their focus of attention to interacting with the technology). The implications of this new type of user-system interaction include the following (Lukowicz, Kirstein, & Troster, 2004): (1) interaction of the system with the environment is through a variety of modes that are appropriate for different contexts of use (2) the system may need to be operated with minimal cognitive awareness and effort on the part of the user, and (3) a wide range of tasks may need to be performed by the system with varying degrees of human-system interaction.

USABILITY ENGINEERING METHODS FOR IMPROVEMENT OF HEALTH INFORMATION SYSTEMS

Usability engineering is a rapidly emerging area in the field of human-computer interaction and has provided a set of methodologies for analysis of complex human interactions with computer-based systems. In this section, we will describe some of the main methods that may be employed for gaining insight into detailed aspects of HCI in the study of health information systems (Nielsen, 1993). These approaches can be considered along a continuum from experimental laboratory-based studies to the study of use of systems in naturalistic real-world settings. There is also a category of study of HCI that falls between pure experimental approaches that involves use of realistic simulations of real settings and contexts where information technologies may be used. For example, the laboratory study of a handheld application for entering medical prescriptions might involve subjects coming to a usability laboratory where their interactions with the application are recorded as they respond to artificial medical cases (e.g., they might be asked to verbalize their thoughts as they enter prescriptions from paper into the device). A simulation-based study of the same application might involve subjects (e.g., physicians) interacting with a "simulated patient" (i.e., a research collaborator playing the role of a patient) while the subject conducts an interview of the "patient." A naturalistic study of the same application might involve remote logging and tracking of user interactions with a device as the users carry out actual day-to-day activities in a medical clinic (as will be described later in this chapter). It should be noted that in-depth analysis of HCI in healthcare may involve iteration from laboratory study of user interaction with a device or application, that then lead to testing under simulated conditions and then finally in naturalistic settings. Analysis of HCI aspects of health information systems may require initial testing in artificial settings, followed by analysis involving simulated conditions, where conditions may be controlled for evaluation purposes.

USABILITY INSPECTION

Usability inspection is a cost-effective methodology adapted from study of HCI to healthcare that has emerged for improving the usability of health information systems (Nielsen & Mack, 1994; Zhang, Johnson, Patel et al., 2003). Usability inspection involves a usability analyst or inspector stepping through or "walking through" use of an interface or system in the context of some real task or activity. For example, an approach known as the cognitive walkthrough, involves the analyst (or a team of analysts) stepping through the activities that might involve use of a new health information system while recording their goals, actions, system responses and potential problems (Kushniruk & Patel, 2004). To guide such analyses, sets of principles emerging from HCI are considered. As another example, the methodology known as heuristic evaluation involves the identification of violations of principles of human factors design when a system is used to carry out a task. Jacob Nielsen (1993) has outlined a set of principles or rules to consider when conducting such analysis which include the following: (1) visibility of system status—this principle states that the state of system's processing should visible to users of a system when they so desire that information, (2) matching the system to the real world—this principle states that real world language and conventions should be used in user interfaces, (3) user control and freedom—users should feel like they are in control, (4) consistency and standards—the user interface and system operations should be consistent, (5) error prevention—designers should design interfaces to prevent errors, (6) minimize memory load—systems should support recognition (e.g., using menus) rather than recall, (7) flexibility and efficiency of use—systems should allow for customization and adaptability, (8) aesthetic and minimalist design—often the simplest and most minimal designs are the best, (9) help users recognize, diagnose and recover from errors, and (10) help and documentation—help should be available to users when needed.

These principles can be extended when considering health information systems, in particular system designed to be integrated into complex healthcare work activities. In our current work, we have developed the following heuristics for evaluation of such pervasive health information system applications: (1) unobtrusiveness—direct interaction of a user with a health information system should be limited to only parts of the task where such interaction is necessary (i.e., allowance for visibility when required), (2) privacy and security—use of a health information system must not violate privacy and security restrictions under normal conditions of use, (3) ability to provide emergency override capability—under exceptional conditions, security and access restrictions may need to be overridden, however such exceptional cases need to be identified and logged for subsequent audit, (4) appropriate context-awareness—health information systems must be able to track the context of use and respond to differing contexts in an appropriate manner, (5) failure backup—failure of a health information system or its supporting network should be made apparent to the user through some form of notification, (6) allowance for recovery and alternative modes of user interaction during failure periods, (7) information and altering prioritization—the system should appropriately prioritize and display alerting or remaindering information only at essential points in user workflow to avoid cognitive overload, (8) user control in the absence of traditional interface cues, (9) Selection of appropriate mode for system-user interaction, (10) consistency across modes of interaction, and (11) allowance for seamless modal switching.

Heuristics, such as those presented previously can be applied in a principled manner in both designing and evaluating health information systems. For example, analysts may step through the use of an information system, recording violations of any of the heuristics mentioned during such testing. In addition, the same heuristics can be used to guide the analysis of data collected from study of subjects interacting with systems under artificial conditions, simulations or naturalistic settings. These types of heuristics essentially form the basis for coding and quantifying problems observed by analysts and investigators in reviewing video data obtained from recordings of user interactions. Used in this way, the heuristics provide categories for identifying interaction problems in coding the resultant video recordings of user interactions, as will be illustrated later in this chapter.

USABILITY TESTING IN HEALTHCARE

One of the most powerful methods for understanding and analyzing usability of health information systems is known as usability testing (Nielsen, 1993). Usability testing refers to the evaluation of information systems through the in-depth analysis of user interactions with the system (under artificial or realistic conditions). Subjects in such studies are asked to carry out tasks for which the system or device was designed to support. For example, physicians may be observed while they carry out tasks that may use of a system to remotely access patient records. Typically this may involve video recording the entire interaction of users with the system (e.g., the screens of a computer application, or logs of the system's behavior as well as the physical and verbal behavior of subjects as they interact with others in their work environment and with a health information system). Usability testing may be conducted under artificial laboratory conditions, simulations, or in real-life settings. Under artificial conditions, subjects may be asked to "think aloud" while interacting with a device or carrying out a task that involves the use of an information system (e.g., interacting with a EHR system remotely while carrying out emergency procedures), while under simulated conditions use of the device might be recorded while the subject interacts with patients in a simulated clinical environment. In either case, the resultant audio and video recordings of the interaction can then be analyzed using methods involving the coding and classification of user problems, as will be described in a subsequent section.

Usability testing is closely related to on an approach to analysis of HCI known as cognitive task analysis (CTA). Cognitive task analysis emerged from the fields of cognitive science and psychology and involves the detailed analysis of humans as they carry out complex reasoning and decision making tasks (Gordon & Gill, 1997). In healthcare, CTA is concerned with characterizing the decision making, reasoning skills, and information processing needs of users (e.g., doctors, nurses, patients) of health information systems. An essential part of conducting a cognitive task analysis is to initially identify the essential tasks, or work activities, that an information system under study has been designed to support. For example, tasks might include entering a medication order into a health information system or accessing patient information about drug allergies from a health information system. Once tasks of interest have been identified, CTA typically involves observing subjects of varying levels of expertise as they carry out the tasks, identifying the skills, knowledge and problems encountered by subjects.

Our approach to usability testing, which we term "rapid low-cost usability engineering" (Kushniruk & Borycki, 2006) builds on CTA as well as usability testing and involves the following stages (Kushniruk & Patel, 2004; Kushniruk, Patel, & Cimino, 1997):

- **Stage 1.** Identification of testing objectives: As a first step the objectives of the usability test must be identified. The objectives might for example consist of testing a new health information system in order to determine what specific aspects of the user interface design might be adversely affecting its adoption by physician users.
- **Stage 2.** Selection of test subjects and computer application: Data is typically collected from a representative sample of users (e.g., physicians, nurses, patients) of the system under study. This often involves testing 10-20 representative users of a system (Kushniruk & Patel, 2004). It is important that subjects selected for the testing are representative of real users of the system under study (e.g., physician users of a patient record system).
- **Stage 3.** Selection of representative experimental tasks: Usability testing of healthcare information systems typically involves selection of several key representative tasks (that the system under study is designed to support) that will be used in the testing. For example, in analyzing the interaction of physicians with a medication order entry system, representative tasks might include the entry of specific medications into the system by physicians.
- **Stage 4.** Selection of an evaluation environment: The actual environments where usability testing will take place may vary from a fixed usability laboratory (under artificial laboratory conditions) to the recording of users interacting with real systems under real conditions (e.g., evaluation of users interacting with a health information system in an operating room or hospital ward). The approach described in this chapter is based on a portable and low-cost approach to usability engineering, where the equipment required can be brought into any healthcare environment.

- **Stage 5.** Observation and recording of users' interaction with the health information system under study: This is the stage where the users' interaction with the system under study are observed and recorded. For example, physicians may be instructed to interact with a new patient record system while "thinking aloud." The resulting interaction is typically recorded in its entirety, for example, all computer screens are typically recorded using screen recording software, the users' physical interactions are video recorded and all verbalizations are also audio recorded (using methods that will be detailed following).

- **Stage 6.** Analysis of usability data: The data collected in Stage 5 can be analyzed using a variety of methods. In our consulting work this has often involved simply "playing back" the recordings of users interacting in order to visually illustrate type of issues and problems that users of their systems may be encountering. From our experience this can often provide extremely useful to designers of healthcare systems that will suggest improvements and modifications that might greatly improve adoption. More detailed forms of analysis (which will be described) can also be conducted. Typically, this involves coding the resultant data (which may consist of screen recordings, video recordings and transcripts of any audio recordings) to precisely identify the occurrence, type and frequency of user problems encountered. This type of in-depth analysis can also be used to characterize the cognitive processes of users of health information systems (e.g., reasoning and decision making strategies of healthcare professionals as they interact with computer technologies).

- **Stage 7.** Interpretation of findings and feedback into system improvement redesign: The ultimate objective of our work in conducting usability testing of health information

systems is to understand the complex interaction between healthcare workers and computer systems in order to improve the usability of health information systems. This typically involves feeding back results obtained from the analysis of usability data (as described in Stage 6) to designers and implementers of such systems in the form of recommendations for system improvement. In general we have found that the earlier in the development cycle of health information systems that results from usability can be fed back into design, the better (Kushniruk, 2002).

We have used the approach to analyze a wide range of healthcare information systems. For example, in a recent study of a medication order entry system, subjects were asked to enter prescriptions as accurately as possible into the system. By recording their activities in doing so, we were able to identify aspects of the user interface ranging from content issues that needed to be changed to allow for accurate data entry (e.g., changing the default dosages provided to users to match dosages actually used in their hospital) to issues related to lack of consistency in the user interface (e.g., multiple ways to exit a screen leading to confusion for new users).

RAPID LOW-COST USABILITY ENGINEERING IN HEALTHCARE

In this section of the chapter we will describe our approach to usability engineering that can be applied in any type of setting (ranging from hospital rooms to the home setting) to study the use of health information systems by end users (e.g., healthcare professionals or patients). This approach to rapid usability engineering has so far been used for a number of projects, ranging from the study of nurse's information needs to the evaluation of a range of new and emerging health information systems including medication administration record systems, which are designed to allow for electronic ordering of medications (Borycki & Kushniruk, 2005; Kushniruk & Borycki, 2006).

Figure 1 shows an example of a typical user (a nurse) interacting with a health information system under study during usability testing. In this example, the subject is interacting with the system within a hospital, obtaining information about a specific patient. The subject is being video recorded while doing so. Our typical studies carried out in naturalistic clinical settings involve asking subjects (e.g., nurses or physicians) to interact with systems to carry out real tasks (e.g., to enter medications for patients or access patient reports). In many of our studies, we also ask subjects to "think aloud" while carrying out the task (which is audio recorded). The recordings of subject's "thinking aloud" while using a system can be analyzed using methods from protocol analysis (Ericsson & Simon, 1993; Kushniruk & Patel, 2004). The subject's overt physical activities are recorded using a video camera (i.e., a mini-DVD camcorder) as shown in Figure 1. In addition to recording physical activities and audio of think aloud, the actual computer screens are also recorded as digital movies (with the audio portion of each movie corresponding to subject's verbalizations). In order to do this we are currently using a screen recording program called Hypercam© which allows one to record all the computer screens (and verbalizations) as a user interacts with the system under study, and stores the resultant digital movie for later playback and in-depth analysis of the interaction.

The equipment we are currently using for many of our usability studies of health information systems is both low-cost and portable. In summary, this typically includes: (1) a computer to run the system under study on, (2) screen recording software which allows the computer screens to be recorded as movie files (with audio input of subject's "thinking aloud" captured using a standard microphone plugged into the computer), and (3) a digital DVD camcorder on a tripod or a ceiling mounted camera to video record user's physical interactions.

Figure 1. User interacting with a health information system while being video-recorded

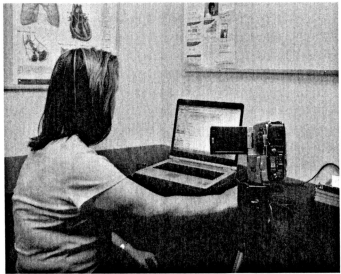

ANALYSIS OF USABILITY DATA

As previously mentioned, the analysis of the data collected varies from informal analysis (which consists of simply playing back the recordings of user interactions) to identifying specific usability problems and issues. The analysis can involve systematically annotating the recordings of interactions using software such as Transana© (a video annotation program that allows analysts to "mark up" and time stamp movies of user interactions with a system) as described in Kushniruk and Patel (2004). The typical result of carrying out such analyses includes identification of specific usability problems (often in a meeting setting with system developers, customers, and hospital or management staff present). For example, our work in the analysis of use of electronic health record systems has identified the following categories of problems with many health information systems we have studied: problems with lack of consistency in the user interface, lack of feedback provided by the system to the user about the status of the system, user problems in understanding information or terms displayed by the system, as well as user problems in entering information into the system in a timely and effective manner (Kushniruk, 2002).

As noted, the intent of our work is to provide feedback to system designers and implementers about system usability in order to provide useful information to improve systems. Our most recent projects have involved applying usability engineering methods to identify potential errors that may be caused by a system (e.g., inappropriate medication defaults in an order entry system), or "induced" by poor design of a user interface *prior* to release of the system in real clinical settings (Borycki & Kushniruk, 2005). This has involved conducting simulations of user interactions with systems under study as will be described below. We have also employed a similar approach to detecting and correcting potential user problems and preventing medical error in a range of systems.

This has included analysis of handheld prescription writing software designed to run on handheld devices to allow physicians to record medications and obtain recommended guidelines about their use (Kushniruk, Triola, Borycki et al., 2005). More recently, we have employed a methodology based on rapid usability engineering and use of simulations of clinical activities to determine how medical workflow may be inadvertently affected by introduction of a medication order entry system, described in the case study below (Borycki, Kushniruk, Kuwata, & Kannry, 2006).

In the early stages of our work and early experimentation with usability engineering in healthcare, we employed a number of different approaches to conducting usability testing including setting up a considerably more expensive "fixed" usability laboratory (where users would interact with systems in a fixed "wired" room while being observed through one-way mirrors). However, our experience has indicated that this approach does not allow us to easily and rapidly collect data at the site where the software under study is actually installed—which often ends up being at a location that is not readily accessible (e.g., due to security restrictions) from a fixed usability laboratory. In addition, for many of our studies it is essential that we test information systems in the actual environment in which the system under study is being used (i.e., in order to determine how aspects of a particular environment may be affected and how users interact with a system) which is not realistically possible without employing a portable approach. With the advent of inexpensive screen recording software and high quality portable digital video cameras, the costs have decreased for conducting such studies along with an increase in the portability of the equipment that can be taken into any hospital or clinical environment, which also simplifies the entire process.

Based on our experiences, the approach to rapid usability engineering in healthcare typically involves the following steps: (1) familiarizing oneself with the techniques and approaches that are possible (see Kushniruk & Patel, 2004, for details) in healthcare, (2) setting up a low-cost portable usability laboratory, (3) choosing a project area that is of significance (e.g., to identify the major usability problems that users of a patient record system may be encountering), (4) working closely with clinical informatics staff, designers and management to show how system usability can be improved in an effective and cost-beneficial manner, and (5) making alterations to the information system based on feedback.

EXAMPLE: EVALUATING THE UNINTENDED CONSEQUENCES OF A MEDICATION ADMINISTRATION RECORD SYSTEM

In the example described in the following, a rapid usability engineering approach (employing simulations of realistic healthcare situations) was used to assess the impact of a new medication administration system about to be deployed in a teaching hospital in Japan. The system was designed to allow users (e.g., physicians and nurses) to obtain information and instructions about medications to give to patients and to record the administration of the medication in a computer system. Thus the system is similar to many systems currently being deployed in hospitals around the world. The computer component of the medication administration system was also integrated with bar-coding technology that allows the doctor or nurse to scan the wrist band of the patient to identify the patient and to also scan the labels on medication bags. The study set up involved asking subjects to obtain information from the medication order entry system and administer medications while being video recorded (physical activities were recorded using a camcorder on a tripod, while all computer screens were automatically recorded using screen recording software).

Sixteen subjects, consisting of doctors and nurses were given written instructions for entering medications for a list of simulated patients. The subjects interacted with both the computer system as well as the "patient," which consisted of a dummy (i.e., a mannequin) with a bar coded wrist band (as shown in the bottom left-hand side of Figure 2). A typical computer screen from the system is shown on the right-hand side of Figure 2. Figure 2 shows the two video views from subject #14—the video of the subject's interaction with the patient in one window while the screen recordings of interactions with the computer system are shown in another window (supporting analysis of both "views" to identify subject actions both on and off the computer). In the study, subjects were specifically instructed to interact with the computer system and the dummy patient (e.g., to hang intravenous medication bags) just as they would be doing in a real situation. In order to record the use of the system in the study, we employed a digital video camera on a tripod to record the interactions of the subject with both the computer system and the patient.

In summary, the study design included full video recording of the subjects' interaction with the system while subjects were asked to use the computer application to enter the patient's name, obtain the list of medications to give the patient, to administer the medication (to the dummy patient) and to then record the administration in the computer application. All computer screens were recorded while subjects interactions with a dummy patient (a mannequin) were recorded using the portable camcorder. At the end of the session the subjects were also interviewed about their experience in using the system (and the interviews audio recorded).

In order to analyze the data collected, first the audio portion of the recorded sessions were transcribed in their entirety (including the interviews at the end of each session—see Figure 3 for the transcripts from one nurse subject) and then annotated by the experimenters by reviewing

Figure 2. Video playback of 2 recorded views: the subject's physical interactions (lower left window) and the computer screens (right window)

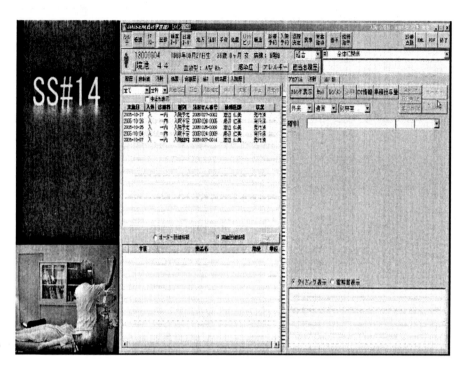

the video recordings of the computer screens and subjects' physical activities (e.g., actually hanging medication bags). In Figure 3 the numbers on the left hand side refer to the video counter corresponding to the actual actions of the subject. The latter portion of Figure 3 also contains the transcript of the interview with the subject (a nurse) conducted immediately following completion of the simulation task

From analysis of this data a range of usability problems were identified including the following: difficulty in physically scanning the medication bags and scanning the patient's wrist band, inability to record administration of a medication when the patient's record is "locked out" by other users of the system (who are accessing the system at the same time as the nurse or doctor is attempting to administer medication), and issues related to the slow speed of the system particularly when there were many medications to be administered. In addition to identifying potential

sources of specific problems that would arise from implementation of the new system, it was also observed that introduction of the computer actually generally led to a major change in the *process* of medication administration. This was characterized by a serialization of the workflow process that could not be deviated from, for example, as shown in the annotated transcript in Figure 3, the physician or nurse would have to administer one medication at a time, first accessing the computer, physically moving to the patient, scanning the patient identification band on their wrist, moving back to the computer for details, then back to the patient to administer that drug and finally back to the computer to record the administration prior to administering the next medication (which is repeated each time for each medication). As compared to the previous workflow (i.e., the workflow before the system involving paper records), it was discovered that the new system imposed a relatively rigid order

Figure 3. Transcript of a Subject (a Nurse) Administering a Medication (followed by post-task interview)

MEDICATION ORDER INFORMATION OBTAINED BY NURSE
00:14 NURSE SEARCHES FOR PATIENT ON THE COMPUTER
00:45 NURSE VIEWS ORDER LIST ON THE SCREEN
00:51 NURSE SELECTS MEDICATION ORDER FROM LIST
00:55 VERIFICATION SCREEN APPEARS

NURSE WALKS OVER TO PATIENT TO CHECK IDENTIFICATION
00:59 NURSE TALKS TO PATIENT - "Nice to meet you. I will now give you an IV drip"
01:09 NURSE SCANS PATIENT IDENTIFICATION (FROM PATIENT'S WRIST BAND)
01:10 VERIFICATION SCREEN AUTOMATICALLY UPDATES

NURSE WALKS BACK TO COMPUTER
01:25 NURSE VIEWS EXECUTION INFORMATION ON THE COMPUTER

NURSE WALKS OVER TO PATIENT AND SETS MEDICATION BAG

NURSE WALKS BACK TO COMPUTER
03:15 NURSE CONFIRMS ADMINISTRATION OF MEDICATION ON THE COMPUTER

POST-TASK INTERVIEW:

Experimenter: Did you find any difficulty with the task ?

Subject: I'm used to this operation, but sometimes it is hard to use the barcode reader when the barcode is not clearly printed.

Experimenter: What difficulties did you have with the barcode reader?

Subject: There are no problems when we have both a printed order and a label on the bottle (we can use either of them, because there are the same barcodes on both). But if the barcode is only on the bottle with its rough surface, I have often pushed its surface to flatten it, and scan it many times until I can read the barcode correctly.

Experimenter: Do you find any difficulty during the workflow process?

Subject: Sometimes I could not open the record of the patient whom I was giving a medication to because another nurse or doctor was opening the record at the same time

---

of activities for medication entry that could not be deviated from. Under normal conditions, this could lead to increased safety in medication entry by providing a structured and standardized procedure for medication entry. However, from our simulations it was also clear that under certain conditions (e.g., need to administer a number of medications under time-constrained conditions) the new computer-based system could also potentially result in cognitive overload leading to the need for complete bypass of the system by users under emergency or stressful situations. It should be noted that such potential unintended consequences of implementation of the system were not anticipated by the designers of the medication order entry system and that applying an approach to usability testing where users of health information systems are recorded as they participate in simulations of real clinical activity we were able to anticipate user problems prior to implementation of the system (Borycki & Kushniruk, 2005).

TOWARDS REMOTE USABILITY ANALYSIS OF WEB-BASED INFORMATION SYSTEMS

This section describes our most recent work in extending rapid usability engineering to the development of methods and approaches that will allow for remote usability testing of health information systems. The remote evaluation of the use and usability of Web-based healthcare information systems and resources is becoming recognized as being a critical area within health informatics. Many new health information system applications are being targeted towards use by not only health professionals but also by patients and lay people in an ever increasing variety of physical locations. Web sites containing digital libraries of on-line clinical information and guidelines, which provide health professionals with guidance and current evidence about the treatment and management patient cases, have appeared widely over the World Wide Web (WWW). In addition, many reputable healthcare organizations are providing similar type of information adapted to patients and lay people over the WWW. For example, the Canadian Medical Association provides guidelines on the treatment of Breast Cancer which are publicly accessible through their Web site. The assessment of such applications by varied end users (patients, physicians, nurses, etc.) from varied locations is challenging and has led us to a complementary line of work in developing and extending portable usability testing to the remote distance analysis of large numbers of users (e.g., healthcare providers or patients) interacting with health information system applications from any number of physical locations over the WWW.

As noted above, the evaluation of the use, usability and effectiveness of Web-based health information systems by end users who may vary greatly in terms of education, computer expertise and motivation, has become a major issue (Nielsen, 2000). However, the distributed nature of these systems leads to a number of challenges for system designers and evaluators. As a result in recent years an attempt has been made to conduct remote usability evaluations over the WWW. Such evaluation can involve collection of a variety of data, including remotely collecting on-line recordings of patients' and physicians' use of systems, telephone interviews, and in-depth video analysis of users interacting with systems. An example of this is a distance evaluation approach we have termed "televaluation" (Kushniruk, Patel, Patel, & Cimino, 2001). Cimino et al. (2002) describe the application of this approach to assess the use of a patient clinical information system (that allowed patients to access their own patient data from home over the WWW) based on remote logging of all user interactions with the system. This work built on and extended the work of Felciano and Altman (1996) in development of methods for remote tracking of Web users (using a program known as 'Lamprey'). By employing such a remote Web-based tracking component at the core of an evaluation system (Kushniruk et al., 2001; Kushniruk & Ho, 2004; Owston, Kushniruk, Pitts & Wideman, 2005; Kushniruk, Owston, Pitts et al., 2007) this line of work went on to extend the data collection to include results from online questionnaires and other sources of data (including remote recordings of computer screens), in an attempt to relate detailed usage logs from Web tracking with other types of data, such as user demographics, patient records etc. In the following, we describe experiences in extending the approach for evaluating a range of Web-based systems and information resources. The objective of this most recent work has been to develop an automated system to support the collection, integration and analysis of a range of remotely collected data and more specifically to extend the approach to the evaluation of Web-based information resources and health information systems targeted to both healthcare providers and patients.

METHODOLOGICAL APPROACH

Our approach to developing an evaluation tool for conducting remote usability evaluations has to involved the creation and integration of the following interacting system components (see Figure 4) to form the basis for an evaluation tool known as the virtual usability laboratory or "VULab":

1. A central tracking component, residing on an evaluation server (i.e., a computer located in our facilities), was designed for remotely tracking and analyzing use of Web-based information systems located at remote sites. This component can provide a customized record of all accesses by users to a system under study. For example, it can provide a log file of what Web pages within a site are accessed, the order of browsing and a time-stamped record of the users' activities in accessing a remote site. In addition, this component has recently been extended to allow for remote recording of users' computer screens (and audio) as digital movies stored on a central evaluation server allowing usability data (similar to the type of data collected described in the first part of this chapter) to be collected remotely.

2. A second component was designed for controlling the automatic presentation of online forms and questionnaires to users in order to assess the usability of Web sites remotely at point of use. The triggering of such online questionnaires can be based on a user profile created for each user of a site being evaluated. By redirecting requests for access to a Web site under evaluation through our evaluation server we are able to write programs that can trigger prompts for user information (e.g., about user satisfaction with information provided or usability) to appear at points when users enter or leave parts of a Web site of interest. For example, on first entry into a system under study a

demographic questionnaire can be triggered to appear and later, when the user accesses a page of interest, e.g., a Web page containing clinical guidelines in a health Web site, an online questionnaire can also be triggered to appear automatically to query the user (e.g., about why the page is being accessed, satisfaction with information provided, perceived educational value of the content provided, etc.).

3. A database component was designed for collecting and integrating the results of remotely tracking users, screen recordings and questionnaires in an integrated database containing other information about users including demographic and illness information (using relational database tables to store and interrelate data). For example, a database table can be created containing the results of logging of users' interactions with a Web site. This type of information can be linked to other data including information about user demographics, results of pre and post test online questionnaires (that may be triggered to appear just before or after a user enters a Web page being analyzed).

4. A researcher user interface component was designed that allows evaluators of a health Web site to easily set up a remote evaluation. For example, a researcher may specify what site will be evaluated, what type of questions should appear to users (by adapting or editing questions contained in a questionnaire bank) and indicating when questionnaires/logging is to be triggered. To facilitate this process, the researcher can choose from and modify questionnaires and prompts contained in a template bank, or alternatively choose to create their own. Finally, the researcher is prompted to indicate what type of data analysis they would like by selecting from a list of built-in types of statistical analyses. In addition, we are currently working on making a variety of data

Figure 4. Overall VuLab architecture

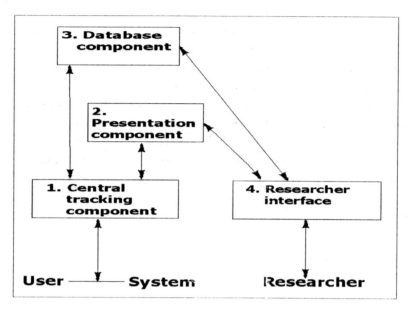

mining and knowledge discovery algorithms available to the researcher to select from in order to support computer-based automated analysis of use and usability data collected from many system users remotely (Han & Kamber, 2001).

REMOTE USABILTIY ANALYSES: EXPERIENCES TO DATE

The VULab is currently being tested and deployed for a number of projects examining the use of innovative health information resources and information systems. This has included the evaluation of a Web site designed to filter patient and provider requests for health information, as well as on-going application of the approach for a project involving remote analysis of use of advanced simulation software for health education purposes. We have found that the collection of varied forms of usage data remotely is not only feasible, but additionally by storing data in consistent database format the integration and

querying of varied forms of usage data can be supported for practical purposes.

A current application of the VULab is in the area of assessing the use and usability of Web-based applications and clinical guidelines designed to support physician decision making about cancer. To illustrate its use, a researcher studying use and usability of Web-based breast cancer guidelines might wish to set up a series of questions that are triggered to appear whenever a user of a system (e.g., a physician browsing through the guidelines) enters a particular part of a Web site or information system (including specifying what type of questions will be asked of users as they enter specific sections of a system under study, for example, "why are you interested in breast cancer guidelines?"). Specifically, the researcher may wish to understand when and why physicians access the breast cancer guidelines. To do this, the VULab can be set up by the investigators to automatically trigger presentation of a pop-up questionnaire to users whenever they click on the page containing the guideline (in this case the user would be queried as to why she is interested in breast cancer guidelines—see the pop-up question in Figure 5). It should be noted that this type of subjective information at point of user (regarding use, usability or usefulness of information presented) can be integrated with the logging data which records all Web pages the user had browsed through during his/her interaction with the site. Therefore we can interrelate logging data to subjective user data collected right at point of use (this combination of different types of data can be fed into data mining and knowledge discovery methods—see Han & Kamber, 2001).

In summary, the researcher interface allows the researcher/investigator to specify: (1) when and where in a remote web site questions should be automatically presented to the user, (2) what the question should be (e.g., in the example, "Why are you interested in breast cancer guidelines?"), and (3) in what format they would like user logging data to be stored. The results from the questionnaires are automatically stored in the database component of the VULab and collated with results from other users, to create a statisti-

cal summary of system usage. In addition, this information can be merged with results from other forms of data collection, such as responses from users to online demographic questions regarding their health status, as well as remotely collected screen recordings.

Another current application of the VULab is its use as a central component for evaluation in a cross Canadian network of researchers studying advanced gaming and simulation software for educational purposes—the SAGE project (Wideman, Owston, Brown et al., 2007). The objective of this line of research is to identify and assess key aspects of games and simulations that could be incorporated in educational software, evaluate learning as a result of use of such software, and analyze use and usability of emerging gaming and simulation components being developed as part of the SAGE project. Specifically, the VULab is being used to automatically collect and collate data on usage of Web-based collaborative, and other forms of educational games and simulations

Figure 5. Screen shot of the pop-up question as it appears to a user as she enters a specific Web page (within an on-line clinical guideline)

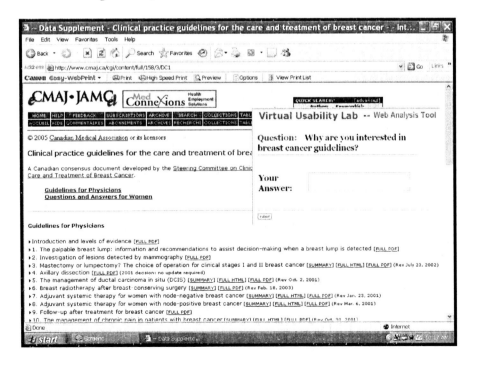

aimed at improving awareness and understanding of health issues. Data being collected includes what parts of games are accessed, how often along with information about specific user impressions and results from on-line questionnaires and quizzes presented to users. In one study of users of an educational simulation, the approach was able to identify and tease apart a variety of usability problems with the software under study, ranging from technical problems with scripting to problems of usability and understandability of user instructions.

CONCLUSION

In this chapter, we discussed our work in the development and evolution of methods for the analysis of health information systems by end users. As we have described, this work has evolved from development of low-cost rapid usability engineering approaches for conducting usability testing in both laboratory and real settings (which we continue to employ to study a wide range of health information systems) to the design and development of a "virtual" usability laboratory for the analysis of use and usability of health related Web-based information systems, resources and sites. Our work has been employed for improving healthcare information systems in Canada, the United States and internationally. Using these approaches we have been able to feed valuable information back to both designers and implementers of health information systems about what aspects of the system work from the end user's perspective and what aspects need to be modified to ensure usability. From our work we have found that is essential for dissemination of these approaches that we strive to develop methods that are both practical and cost-effective. The argument for the need for such analyses extends not only to providing input to improve and refine usability of health information systems and Web applications but also to ensuring patient safety. Indeed,

based on studies indicating that poorly designed healthcare systems may actually facilitate medical error we must ensure not only system usability but also equally as important we must ensure the safety of healthcare information systems. In this context, we have successfully used the approach to predict errors and problems that will occur from human-computer interaction *prior* to releasing the system for general use (Kushniruk et al., 2005). With the rapid increase in deployment of health information systems, continual development and refinement of new methods for conducting such analyses of human-computer interaction in healthcare will become even more critical.

FUTURE RESEARCH DIRECTIONS

There are a variety of future research directions in the area of usability engineering in healthcare. These include: (a) research into application of methods described in this chapter throughout the development cycle of health information systems, from system selection through to design, implementation and system testing, (b) further extension of usability engineering methods to data collection and analyses conducted remotely over the WWW, (c) development of experimental study designs that can be used to assess use of systems and cognitive issues involved in using system in real clinical conditions, (d) extension to use in the study of new and emerging health information systems, including mobile applications, (e) extension of approaches from usability engineering to include advanced simulation methods, and (f) automated analysis of usability data and application of data mining and knowledge discovery methods.

The application of scientific methods for analysis of health information system usability have been shown to be usefully applied throughout the entire process of developing health information systems. Kushniruk (2002) describes how the approach can applied from the earliest stages of system development, even including applying usability testing to assess different health information systems prior to selecting them, to the analysis of early system prototypes to provide early feedback to designers about features of systems that may enhance or decrease usability. As described in this chapter work in developing methods for remote analysis of a large number of users of systems is another area where ongoing research is being conducted, including work on tools such as the VULab. Also, the application of new study designs, incorporating aspects of ethnography and portable recording techniques, will be important to move usability engineering from being conducted in only a few fixed usability laboratories to widespread application throughout the healthcare industry. This will lead to study of new and emerging applications, including pervasive healthcare information systems, such as wearable computing and hand-held computing devices (Kushniruk & Borycki, 2007). Further work will also include incorporation of methods of simulation from other domains such as aviation and nuclear power to improve the identification and prediction of usability errors before systems are released for real use in healthcare (Borycki & Kushniruk, 2005). Finally, the application of methods from the field of data warehousing and mining will provide designers, implementers and health decision makers with improved knowledge about use and usability of health information systems.

REFERENCES

Borycki, E., & Kushniruk, A.W. (2005). Identifying and preventing technology-induced error using simulations: Application of usability engineering techniques. *Healthcare Quarterly, 8*, 99-105.

Borycki, E., Kushniruk, A.W., Kuwata, S., & Kannry, J. (2006). Use of simulation approaches to the study of user needs and error in biomedical informatics. *Proceedings of the 2006 Annual AMIA Conference* (pp. 61-65).

Cimino, J.J., Patel, V.L., & Kushniruk, A.W. (2002). The patient clinical information system (PatCIS): Technical solutions for and experiences with giving patients access to their electronic medical records. *International Journal of Medical Informatics, 68*(1-3), 113-127.

Eason, K.D. (1991). Ergonomic perspectives on advances in human-computer interaction. *Ergonomics, 34*, 721.

Ericsson. K.A., & Simon, H.A. (1993). *Protocol analysis: Verbal reports as data* (2nd ed.). Cambridge, MA: MIT Press.

Felciano, R.M., & Altman, R.B. (1996). Lamprey: Tracking users on the World Wide Web, *Proceedings of the 1996 AMIA Annual Fall Symposium* (pp. 757-761).

Gordon, S.E., & Gill, R.T. (1997). Cognitive task analysis. In C.E. Zsambok & G. Klein (Eds.), *Naturalistic decision making* (pp. 131-140). Mahwah, NJ: Lawrence Erlbaum Associates.

Han, J., & Kamber, M. (2001). *Data mining: Concepts and techniques.* New York: Morgan Kaufman Publishers.

Kushniruk, A.W. (2002). Evaluation in the design of health information systems: application of approaches emerging from usability engineering. *Computers in Biology and Medicine, 32*(3) 141-149.

Kushniruk, A., & Borycki, E. (2006). Low-cost rapid usability engineering: designing and customizing usable healthcare information systems. *Healthcare Quarterly, 9*(4), 98-100, 102.

Kushniruk, A., & Borycki, E. (2007). Human factors and usability of healthcare systems. In J. Bardram & A. Mihailidis (Eds.), *Pervasive computing in healthcare.* New York: CRC Press.

Kushniruk, A.W. & Ho, F. (2004, May). The virtual usability laboratory: Evaluating web-based health systems. *Proceedings of e-Health 2004*, Victoria, B.C.

Kushniruk, A., Owston, R., Ho, F., Pitts, K., Wideman, H., Brown, C., et al. (2007). Design of the VULab: A quantitative and qualitative tool for analyzing use of on-line health information resources. *Proceedings of ITCH 2007*.

Kushniruk, A.W., & Patel, V.L. (2004). Cognitive and usability engineering methods for the evaluation of clinical information systems. *Journal of Biomedical Informatics*, 37, 56-76.

Kushniruk, A.W., Patel, V.L., & Cimino, J.J. (1997). Usability testing in medical informatics: Cognitive approaches to evaluation of information systems and user interfaces. In D. Masys (Ed.) *Proceedings of the 1997 AMIA Fall Symposium*, 218-222.

Kushniruk, A.W., Patel, C., Patel, V.L. & Cimino, J.J. (2001). Televaluation of clinical information systems: An integrative approach to assessing web-based systems, *International Journal of Medical Informatics*, 61, 45-70.

Kushniruk, A.W., Triola, M., Borycki, E., Stein, B., & Kannry, J. (2005). Technology induced error and usability: The relationship between usability problems and prescription errors when using a handheld application. *International Journal of Medical Informatics*, 74, 519-526.

Lukowicz, P. Kirstein, T., & Troster, G. (2004). Wearable systems for healthcare applications. *Methods of Information in Medicine*, 43, 232-238.

Nielsen, J. (1993). *Usability engineering.* New York: Academic Press.

Nielsen, J. (2000). *Designing web usability.* Indianapolis: New Riders Press.

Nielsen, J., & Mack, R.L. (1994). *Usability inspection methods.* New York: John Wiley & Sons.

Owston, R., Kushniruk, A., Ho, F., Pitts, K., & Wideman, H. (2005). Improving the design of Web-based games and simulations through usability research. *Proceedings of Ed-Media 2005*.

Sharp, H., Rogers, Y., & Preece, J. (2007). *Interaction design: beyond human-computer interaction* (2nd ed.). New York: John Wiley & Sons.

Shortliffe, E. H., & Cimino, J. J. (2006). *Biomedical informatics: Computer applications in healthcare and biomedicine* (3rd ed.). New York: Springer.

Wideman, H.H., Owston, R., Brown, C., Kushniruk, A., Ho, F. & Pitts, K. (2007). Unpacking the potential of educational gaming: A new tool for gaming research. *Simulation & Gaming*.

Zhang, J., Johnson, T.R., Patel, V.L., Paige, D.L., & Kubose, T. (2003). Using usability heuristics to evaluate patient safety of medical devices. *Journal of Biomedical Informatics*, 36(1-2), 23-30.

ADDITIONAL READINGS

Beuscart-Zephir, M.C., Brender, J., Beuscart, R., & Ménager-Depriester, I. (1997). Cognitive evaluation: How to assess the usability of information technology in healthcare. *Computer Methods and Programs in Biomedicine*, 54, 19-38.

Beuscart-Zephir, M.C., Elkin, P., Pelayo, S., & Beuscart, R. (2007). The human factors engineering approach to biomedical informatics projects: state of the art, results, benefits and challenges. *IMIA Yearbook of Medical Informatics, Methods of Information in Medicine*, 46 (Supplement 1), 109-127.

Borycki, E., & Kushniruk, A.W. (2005). Identifying and preventing technology-induced error using simulations: Application of usability engineering techniques. *Healthcare Quarterly, 8,* 99-105.

Cimino, J.J., Patel, V.L., & Kushniruk, A.W. (2001). Studying the human-computer-terminology interface. *Journal of the American Medical Informatics Association, 8*(2), 163-173.

Elkin, P.L., Mohr, D.N., Tuttle, M.S., Cole, W.G., Atkin, G.E., Keck, K., et al. (1997). Standardized problem list generation, utilizing the Mayo canonical vocabulary embedded within the Unified Medical Language System. *Proceedings of the AMIA Annual Fall Symposium* (pp. 500-504).

Hackos, J.T., & Redish, J.C. (1998). *User and task analysis for interface design.* New York: John Wiley & Sons.

Han, J., & Kamber, M. (2001). *Data mining: Concepts and techniques.* New York: Morgan Kaufman Publishers.

Hix, D., & Hartson, H.R. (1993). *Developing user interfaces: ensuring usability through product & process.* New York: John Wiley & Sons.

Horsky, J., Kaufman, D.R., Oppenheim, M.I., & Patel, V.L. (2003). A framework for analyzing the cognitive complexity of computer-assisted clinical ordering. *Journal of Biomedical Informatics, 36*(1-2), 4-22.

Jaspers, M.W., Steen, T., Van den, B.C., & Geenen, M. (2004). The think aloud method: a guide to user interface design. *International Journal of Medical Informatics, 73*(11-12), 781-195.

Kaufman, D.R., Patel, V.L., Hilliman, C., Morin, P.C., Pevzner, J., Weinstock, R.S., et al. (2003). Usability in the real world: assessing medical information technologies in patients' homes. *Journal of Biomedical Informatics, 36*(1-2), 45-60.

Kushniruk, A.W. (2001). Analysis of complex decision making processes in healthcare: Cognitive approaches to health informatics. *Journal of Biomedical Informatics, 34*(5), 365-376.

Kushniruk, A. W. (2002). Evaluation in the design of health information systems: Applications of approaches emerging from systems engineering. *Computers in Biology and Medicine, 32*(3), 141-149.

Kushniruk, A., & Borycki, E. (2006). Low-cost rapid usability engineering: designing and customizing usable healthcare information systems. *Healthcare Quarterly, 9*(4), 98-100, 102.

Kushniruk, A.W., Kaufman, D.R., Patel, V.L., Levesque, Y., & Lottin, P. (1996). Assessment of a computerized patient record system: A cognitive approach to evaluating an emerging medical technology. *M.D. Computing, 13*(5), 406-415.

Kushniruk, A.W., & Patel, V.L. (2004). Cognitive and usability engineering approaches to the evaluation of clinical information systems. *Journal of Biomedical Informatics, 37,* 56-57.

Kushniruk, A.W., Patel, V.L., & Cimino, J.J. (1997). Usability testing in medical informatics: Cognitive approaches to evaluation of information systems and user interfaces. In D. Masys (Ed.), *Proceedings of the 1997 AMIA Fall Symposium* (pp. 218-222).

Kushniruk, A.W., Patel, V.L., Cimino, J.J., & Barrows, R.A. (1996). Cognitive evaluation of the user interface and vocabulary of an outpatient information system. In J. Cimino (Ed.), *AMIA Fall Symposium Proceedings* (pp. 22-26). Philadelphia: Hanley & Belfus Inc.

Kushniruk, A.W., Patel, C., Patel, V.L., & Cimino, J.J. (2001). "Televaluation" of information systems: An integrative approach to design and evaluation of web-based systems. *International Journal of Medical Informatics, 61*(1), 45-70.

Kushniruk, A.W., Triola, M., Borycki, E., Stein, B., & Kannry, J. (2005). Technology induced error and usability: The relationship between usability problems and prescription errors when using a handheld application. *International Journal of Medical Informatics, 74,* 519-526.

Mayhew, D.J. (1999). *The usability engineering lifecycle*. San Diego: Academic Press.

Nielsen, J. (1993). *Usability engineering*. New York: Academic Press.

Nielsen, J., & Mack, R.L. (1994). *Usability inspection*. New York: John Wiley & Sons.

Preece, J., Rogers, Y., Sharp, H., Benyon, D., Holland, S., & Carey, T. (1994). *Human-computer interaction*. New York: Addison-Wesley.

Patel, V.L., Kushniruk, A.W., Yang, S., & Yale, J.F. (2000). Impact of a computer-based patient record system on data collection, knowledge organization and reasoning. *Journal of the American Medical Informatics Association, 7*(6), 569-585.

Patel, V.L., & Kushniruk, AW. (1998). Interface design for healthcare environments: The role of cognitive science. In C. Chute (Ed.), *Proceedings of the AMIA 98 Annual Symposium* (pp. 29-37).

Pearrow, M. (2000). *Web site usability handbook*. Rockland, MA: Charles River Media.

Rasmussen, J., Pejtersen, A.M., Goodstein, L.P. (1994). *Cognitive system engineering*. New York: John Wiley & Sons.

Rubin, J. (1994). *Handbook of usability testing: how to plan, design and conduct effective tests*. New York: John Wiley & Sons.

Shneiderman, B., & Plaisant, C. (2004). *Designing the user interface: strategies for effective human-computer interaction* (4th ed.). New York: Addison Wesley Longman.

Sharp, H., Rogers, Y., & Preece, J. (2007). *Interaction design: beyond human-computer interaction* (2nd ed.). New York: John Wiley & Sons.

Staggers, N. (1995). Essential principles for evaluating the usability of clinical information systems. *Computers in Nursing, 9*(2), 47-49.

Weiss, S. (2002). *Handheld usability*. New York: John Wiley & Sons.

Chapter II
A Bio–Psycho–Social Review of Usability Methods and their Applications in Healthcare

Morgan Price
University of Victoria, Canada
University of British Columbia, Canada

ABSTRACT

The purpose of this chapter is to provide the reader with an overview of several models and theories from the general HCI literature, highlighting models at three levels of focus: biomechanical interactions, individual-cognitive interactions, and social interactions. This chapter will also explore how these models were or could be applied to the design and evaluation of clinical information systems, such as electronic medical records and hospital information systems. Finally, it will conclude with how an understanding at each level compliments the other two in order to create a more complete understanding of the interactions of information systems in healthcare.

INTRODUCTION

The field of human computer interaction (HCI) is a fast growing field of research in computer science. It is interested in understanding how we use devices and how the usability of those devices can be improved. HCI sits between several disciplines including computer science, psychology, cognitive science, sociology, and anthropology. Although a young field, it offers a wealth of understanding into the use of systems. It provides a relatively rich col-

lection of quantitative and qualitative models and methods that have been applied to the design and evaluation of information systems (IS) in many domains (Carroll, 2003) Despite the advances in HCI to guide design and evaluate systems, their published impact in health information systems has been limited in scope—systems are still designed, evaluated, and selected without often formally considering issues of usability, cognitive load and fit. There is a need to better understand where models from HCI can assist in the design

Copyright © 2008, IGI Global, distributing in print or electronic forms without written permission of IGI Global is prohibited.

and adoption of clinical information systems in health care.

In medicine, a biomedical, reductionist view has been the prevailing perspective through the 20th century. It has led to a great number of advances in medical science: from Pasteur's experiments in microbiology that led to the popularization of the germ theory at the end of the 19th century (Ewald, 2004) through to the mapping of the human genome at the beginning of the twenty-first (Venter, Adams, Myers et al., 2001), the science of medicine has seen an explosion in information, in diagnostic options, and in the treatment of diseases. During this time, prominence and understanding of illness, the patient's experience of the disease, decreased. In 1977, George Engel proposed a new conceptual model for illness: The bio-psycho-social model. His approach expanded the biomedical model to include both the psychological and the social impacts of a disease. It was meant to aid in better understanding and management of a patient rather than simply treating a disease (Engel, 1977). In this model, Engel stresses that the reductionist biomedical model, while it is powerful and has moved our understanding of *disease* forward, is not sufficient to describe the impact of *illness* to a patient and their surroundings. Indeed, an illness typically has a biologic component, but it also has a psychological impact on the patient as well as a social impact on those around the patient.

In this chapter, we will review applications of HCI in health information systems development and evaluation and will propose a model that aligns with Engel's bio-psycho-social model.

Clinical Example

Throughout this chapter, the reader will be brought back to aspects of a common clinical example: electronic prescribing (e-prescribing).

Recent reports on healthcare in North America describe high error rates (Baker et al., 2004; Kohn, 2000). Recommendations to improve the processes of care delivery are often focused on the increased use of information technology, information systems and, specifically, electronic medical records (EMR) (Romanow, 2002) with the expectation that these systems will improve care and reduce errors (Bates et al., 2001; Wilcox & Whitham, 2003). Despite promise, however, the adoption of clinical information systems has been slow and problematic. There are many reasons for this and strategies to align systems to support the adoption of electronic tools to support delivery of better care (Middleton, Hammond, Brennan, & Cooper, 2005). One reason for failure of adoptions of clinical information systems, and the focus on this chapter, is the usability of systems (Walsh, 2004). Computerized provider order entry, and more specifically e-prescribing is complex and involves interactions between the computer system and the user (Horsky, Kaufman, & Patel, 2003) and between members of the care team, making e-prescribing a good example for this chapter.

Clinical Example: Prescriptions

These examples will use the example of writing a prescription for Ramipril. Ramipril is a commonly prescribed, but expensive, blood pressure medication. It will be used to highlight some of the strengths of methods described in this chapter. Different steps in prescribing will be used to highlight aspects of models presented as appropriate.

BIOMECHANICAL MODELS OF INTERACTION

Early work in human computer interaction stemmed from human machine interaction and focused on physical interaction between humans and computers. Nearly all computer interaction is through various forms of physical movement and control of input devices, such as keyboards, mice, and so on, so it makes sense to start here. Biomechanical models are useful as they can help to predict time taken to perform functions in the system. These estimated durations can be based on empirically or theoretically derived values of a user's ability to perform types of actions, combined with calculated number of keystrokes, the measured size and position of buttons, degrees of freedom for input devices, and delays in computation of a response. Models, such as Fitts' law, have had a significant impact on the design of systems that we use today. They have been used to predict potential positive and negative costs to changes in design of systems.

Fitts' Law

In 1954, decades before the personal computer and the mouse driven graphical user interface became common, Paul Fitts applied basic in-

formation theory concepts to measuring and predicting abilities of the human motor and sensory systems (Fitts, 1954). From some very simple experiments, such as reciprocal tapping (Figure 1), Fitts discovered that the ability to process information was essentially constant and that one could predict performance. Through his experiments he was able to describe that smaller objects that were further away took longer to accurately touch than closer or larger objects. More importantly, he could mathematically predict how size and distance impacted speed and accuracy. From these simple experiments, Fitts and others extended the research. Fitts' model, which later became know as "Fitts' law," has had a significant impact on the development of machines and computer systems and on HCI. It is considered to be one of the most complete and used models that describe movement (Ware, 2003). The reprint of his article in the Journal of Experimental Psychol-

Figure 1. Fitts' reciprocal tapping apparatus

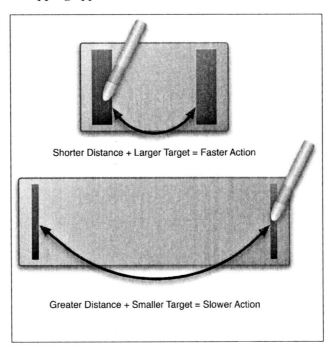

Shorter Distance + Larger Target = Faster Action

Greater Distance + Smaller Target = Slower Action

Note: Subjects were asked to alternately tap the plates (dark rectangles) on either side of the desk without missing. The size and position of the targets were adjusted. As target size decreased and distance between targets increased, responses were slower. The trials were repeated with varying target sizes and distances and resulting times were recorded and analyzed to generate the empirical model. (based on Fitts, 1992)

ogy (Fitts, 1992) has been cited over 1217 times by 2007 and the model has been adapted and extended to suit many applications including the design of graphical user interfaces on computers. Fitts' Law has had resurgence in recent years under the umbrella of ubiquitous computing as novel interfaces on mobile devices (phones and personal digital assistants) are being designed and developed (MacKenzie, 2002; Silfverberg, MacKenzie, & Korhonen, 2000).

As powerful as Fitts Law has been in human-machine interaction (including HCI) it is limited to the level of movement. It does not take into account other sources of variability of how to perform a specific task, learning, other cognitive processes, or other higher-level confounders. Despite these gaps, Fitts' Law is an important tool and provides us with some understanding into how to design systems to improve key aspects of the human computer interaction (MacKenzie, 1992).

Clinical Example: Fitts' Law

Writing a prescription is a common task in general practice. Fitts' law can predict that having a small "Rx" button near the top left corner of the screen on a menu bar may take more time for the user to accurately press the button than a larger button that is available near where the physician is already writing her clinical note.

Keystroke Level Model (GOMS)

The keystroke level model (KLM) is a simple model that can predict duration of tasks based on predefined duration of physical activities, such as mouse pointing, clicking, etc. KLM was derived from the GOMS model (GOMS stands for the four key elements of the framework: goals, operators, methods, and selection rules), which is one of the first cognitive models in modern HCI work. As KLM is simplified to focus primarily on the biomechanical and temporal aspects of task prediction it is best described here instead of with GOMS below. The KLM was developed

as a simple, quantitative, predictive model that could be used to calculate the duration of known tasks. It is a relatively low level model that can be used to compare task durations for different processes in a system during the design of a system or between systems.

The original KLM (Card, Moran, & Newell, 1980) uses a series of six primitive subtasks to estimate total time for activities. The primitives are: K (keystroke/button press), P (point to target), H (homing hands to different device, e.g., mouse to keyboard), D (draw line), M (mentally prepare for action), and R (system response). Table 1 provides experimentally derived time estimates for each primitive. As these are predefined estimates, evaluators and designers can use KLM without using the system.

The authors of the KLM acknowledge that the simplification of HCI to only these six primitives and the focus on interaction times does not take into account a variety of aspects, including: errors, learning, functionality, recall (e.g., remembering the name of a medication), concentration, fatigue, and acceptability. Despite these limitations, the KLM is a useful, inexpensive tool to estimate performance times of tasks and has been adapted by others to evaluate a variety of systems. It is particularly well suited when comparing data entry methods for routine actions.

Clinical Example: KLM

Deciding to treat someone's high blood pressure with Ramipril is a multi-step process. Broken down in a KLM model, these steps are illustrated in Table 2, along with the predicted duration for each step. This particular example sequence has a total predicted time of 6.7 seconds. The predicting would continue until the act of prescribing (selecting dose, frequency, duration, etc) was complete and a total estimated time could be calculated. Other design options could be reviewed and times compared to see which option has the shortest duration. A timesaving of 30 seconds means an additional 5 percent of a typical 10-minute visit

Table 1. Keystroke-level model

Operator	Description	Time (Range)
K	Keystroke or button press	0.08-1.2s
P	Point with mouse or other device	0.8-1.5s
H	Homing hands (from one device to another)	0.40s
D	Drawing lines (n_D = number of straight line segments and l_D = total length in cm)	$0.9n_D + 0.16l_D$
M	Mental preparation for executing physical action	1.35s
R(t)	Response of the system (provided by the developers as t in seconds)	t

Note: The six original subtasks for the keystroke-level model (KLM). The times described were based on the review of 1280 HCI scenarios in the original experiments. (Based on Card et al., 1980).

Table 2. KLM study: Selecting Ramipril KLM

Step	Time (s)
Mentally Decide on need for Medication	1.35
Home to Mouse	1
Point Mouse	1
Press Button	0.2
Decide on Ramipril	1.35
Home to Keyboard	1
Type ("Ram")	0.6 (3 x0.2)
Press Enter to Select Ramipril	0.2
TOTAL TIME:	6.7 seconds

Note: This table illustrates an example KLM evaluation of the predicted time to decide to treat a patient's high blood pressure with the medication Ramipril.

is spent interacting with the patient and not the computer, which is quite significant.

Ergonomics

Ergonomics, or human factors, considers the physical aspects of components, the type of components that are needed, and how the user's body is placed to reduce injury and strain. As medicine is increasingly computerized, physical factors are important to consider. However, these models will not be discussed in this chapter in any detail.

How Do These Physical Models Inform Health Informatics?

Human factors research and the application of Fitts' law to user interface design have an important role to play in the comparison of user interfaces. Ergonomics research in medicine is important as the application of technology into the clinical domain has a physical presence. The proper design and planning need to occur for the placement and physical design of systems to minimize user injury, but also reduce errors due to poor access and other performance problems (Stone & McCloy, 2004).

Biomechanical theories, such as Fitts' law, were important in the development of novel computer input devices, such as the mouse. They are still valuable today, particularly in the development in novel tools for procedures in healthcare and in developing smaller form factor tools for pervasive computing. For example, the improvement of endoscopic devices has an impact on "efficiency, safety and comfort" (Berguer, 1998). Development of new telepresence endoscopic surgical tools have benefited from the application of human factors research (Hill, Green, Jensen, Gorfu, & Shah, 1994; Hills & Jensen, 1998). personal digital assistants (PDAs) and other mobile computing devices are making their way into healthcare quite rapidly. With their smaller interfaces and data input methods, the application of Fitts' law may well be important in improving rapid entry of medical data into these systems, something that is currently quite challenging. The KLM model can also help designers refine small interfaces to reduce data entry time, a problem facing the use of PDAs, particularly in healthcare. A recent study showed that nursing ordering times were reduced (P < 0.0001) through a change in a user interface from text based to a GUI based interface, by changing some of the physical interaction aspects (Staggers & Kobus, 2000). The key limitation of these models is that they miss some key challenges in design that can impact decision-making and the context of care delivery. To address these issues we will first turn to individually focused models of HCI that look at cognitive usability and then to group focused HCI.

INDIVIDUALLY FOCUSED COGNITIVE MODELS

The application of the theories of cognitive psychology was seen as a significant step in the development of HCI as both a theoretical and applied discipline. In the 1970s-1980s the human information processor was the dominant model in cognitive psychology and its application moved the study HCI from the hands to the head of the individual users. This was a significant advance as it gave a framework for discussing, evaluating and predicting user actions based on internal goals and decision-making rules. Several key theories and methods were developed during this evolutionary phase of HCI. Most notably, the GOMS family of models, but also methods of cognitive task analysis, and cognitive walk through. As a compliment to these models, heuristic evaluation will also be discussed.

GOMS Models

The basis for the GOMS family of models began with some of the work of Xerox PARC in the 1970s. Key researchers began to explore the application of then modern psychological research to human computer interaction. From that work Card, Moran, and Newell published *The Psychology of Human-Computer Interaction* (Card, Newell, & Moran, 1983). In their book, the authors describe both the theoretical basis and the application of the human as information processor theory to HCI. Their primary computer application was text editing. They developed an engineering model that considers the user's **goals**, the system's **operators**, the **methods** (well defined sub-tasks) that the user is familiar with and how a user **selects** from the methods (GOMS).

GOMS was developed from the pervasive cognitive psychology paradigms of that time, the human as information processor. In this model, humans have three very high level processors: perceptual (which record stimuli through various senses), cognitive (which compare stimuli with internal working memories, long term memories and principles), and motor (which is triggered to respond). The model becomes more detailed and provides an established framework to explain observed phenomenon and to predict behavior. From this theoretical background, the authors developed a more streamlined engineering model that was applicable in HCI.

There are several reasons why one might chose to apply GOMS tools to evaluate systems (B. John, 1995). It can be used as a predictive tool to estimate: skilled-performance times, learning times, and error rates due to memory overload. From these, estimates can be made for training and the impact of errors can be assessed. Both of which can be factored into overall cost of systems deployment before development has occurred. Findings from a GOMS study can drive design changes as well direct the development of specific teaching materials where redesign is not possible or practical. The biomechanical models discussed previously cannot assess these aspects of a system.

Through the 1980s, the original GOMS model has been enhanced and extended. There are several major GOMS adaptations (John & Kieras, 1996) as well as many individualized applications. These different adaptations each address some of the shortcomings of the GOMS model including complexity of applying the method, ability to handle flexible workflows, and predicting tasks that can occur in parallel to other tasks.

One of the significant challenges of applying GOMS is the effort and time required to complete an analysis. It is often greater than what is available. This is particularly true for complex systems, such as clinical information systems (hospital systems, electronic records, etc.). Because of the detail level, a GOMS analysis can sometimes miss higher-level usability issues of information systems.

Clinical Example: Defining the "GOMS" for E-Prescribing Ramipril

- **Goals:** The goal is to "write Ramipril prescription" with sub-goals that include "select medication" "select dose" "select route," "select frequency," "select duration," and "print prescription."

- **Operators:** Operators of the system include button presses, keystrokes, and selecting an item from a list.
- **Methods:** Methods in this system include "prescribe new medication," "refill existing medication," and "prescribing from a favorites list."
- **Selection rules:** A user's selection rules might be to refill a medication if it exists and there is no change, use a favorite if it exists, prescribe new medication if no other option.

Cognitive Task Analysis

Task analysis is focused on understanding user's work activities (i.e. tasks) in a systematic manner and with sufficient detail to aid the design of functionality of systems. Task analysis can provide structure to the development of predictive requirements for systems. The process assists in the development of an understanding of what a user actually does in a manner that can be critically reviewed (Kieras, 1997). Task analysis can use a variety of methods from questionnaires, to interviews, to think aloud protocols that are video taped during user walkthroughs. Proponents of task analysis stress the need to consider tasks broadly as it is often not the design of the computer user interface that this the challenge, but the understanding of the tasks themselves and which to computerize (Goransson, Lind, Pettersson et al., 1986).

Cognitive task analysis (CTA) is a subset from the more general category of task analysis, which aims to yield information about the underlying complexity of the observed activities at the level of mental activity, knowledge, and processes required for a given task (Schraagen, Chipman, & Shalin, 2000). It is focused on internal tasks (e.g., thinking) instead of the external tasks (e.g., pressing buttons) that the lower level biomechanical models are focused on. CTA breaks down high-level tasks into hierarchical sets of detailed sub-tasks such that complex decision making processes can be mapped out prior to the evaluation (Zachary, Ryder, & Hicinbothom, 1998). Unlike GOMS, where the focus is on the end state goals, task analysis is more focused on the process. This provides some flexibility as some user tasks may not have an explicit goal. It allows analysis to occur about the "journey" along a task.

In general, there are three main approaches to CTA (Roth, Patterson, & Mumaw, 2001). First, a domain can be analyzed to reveal tasks that are then examined in detail for cognitive load. This is useful if the goals and processes are well described. Information can be gathered through interviews with subject experts to understand the detailed nature of tasks (Militello, 1998). Second, typical users can be studied in real or simulated work tasks in order to discover the activities they perform and strategies that they employ. This is useful for domains that are less well understood. It is also helpful when working with users with tacit expert knowledge that may not be able to articulate their own processes, such as can be the case with expert clinicians. The final approach is through computer modeling, which requires explicit descriptions of cognitive steps, but allows for simulated changes to be made easily, once the simulation is created.

Clinical Example: Cognitive Task Analysis

Based on user interviews and observations, the main steps are:
1. Determine if a patient requires the medication.
2. Decide if an existing medication that can be refilled or if it is a new prescription.
3. If it is a refill:
   a. Click the refill action
   b. Confirm the prescription
   c. Set the duration and repeats for the refill.

4. If it is not a refill:
   a. Pick the medication from the master formulary
   b. Decide on the dose, frequency, route, duration and repeats
5. Print and save the prescription.

The designer would then perform each step of the tasks that have been defined, this time with the system, assessing potential failure points and identifying correct actions from the user's perspective.

Inspection Methods

Inspection methods are procedures followed by a designer or evaluator to assess function of the user interface (Neilson & Mack, 1994). Walk-throughs and heuristic evaluation are examples of inspection methods. It is important to note that inspection methods can be theory based, as we see in cognitive walkthrough, or informally structured, as in heuristic evaluation.

Inspections and walkthroughs of software can be used early on in the design with paper prototypes or later after systems are completed. Experts select defined tasks of the system and the context they will be completed as well as any assumptions about the user. Then the task is stepped through, predicting how users would act.

Cognitive Walkthroughs

Cognitive walkthroughs are a structured version of a walkthrough from a cognitive view that designers can use to evaluate the system design (Polson, Lewis, Rieman, & Wharton, 1992). The cognitive walkthrough steps include: determining representative and important tasks to walk through; listing in a checklist the steps required to complete each task; identifying typical users and determining their goals and their expertise; assessing each user's goals for "correctness" against the application and determining if there are potential problems. Potential problems occur if there are difficulties identifying the actions associated with the goal, or if there are other difficulties performing the actions based on the user's knowledge and ability. Evaluation of each goal continues in an iterative fashion until all identified goals are completed (Blackmon, Polson, Kitajima, & Lewis, 2002).

Although cognitive walkthrough was not a direct descendant of GOMS, it shares roots in cognitive science and shares many similar characteristics with the GOMS model. Both are focused on the individual and both are applications of a goal-oriented model. Both GOMS and cognitive walkthroughs occur at a fine-grained level of analysis compared to other models discussed later in the paper. Walkthroughs are, typically, quicker to perform than a GOMS analysis. The walkthrough model does not deal well with the selection of representative tasks, which limits its usefulness with highly complex programs where it would only be possible to walk through a small set of tasks and task variants (Wharton, Bradford, Jeffries, & Franzke, 1992).

In the example fragment, checking to see if a patient needs a prescription renewal for Altace is the illustration of only one sub-goal, which is to check if the patient is taking that medication. Two users are selected for the task: a physician who is trained in pharmacology but is not familiar with computers and an MOA (medical office assistant) who is computer literate but has a limited training in names of medications. Assume that the electronic record is open to a patient's summary screen that includes a window with current medications listed.

Clinical Example: Cognitive Walkthrough

SUBGOAL: Review patient's medication profile (Physician).

Action 1: View list of current medications.
   Potential Problem: If window is too small, the details of each prescription might not be completely shown.
Action 2: Identify medication on list
   Potential Problem: User may not realize that medication profile is larger than list on screen and requires scrolling.
   Resolution: Train user.

SUBGOAL: Review patient's medication profile. (MOA)

Action 1: View list of current medications.
   Potential Problem: None noted, the user would scroll the list if needed.
   Action 2: Identify medication on list
   Potential Problem: The MOA may not be aware that Ramipril is equivalent to Altace.
   Resolution: Display both brand and generic names in summary.

Heuristic Evaluation

Heuristic evaluation is another method in use in HCI. Heuristic evaluation, as described by Nielson and others, is a useful collection of "rules of thumb" (see Table 3 for an example). Although not a theoretical construct, designers have adopted Heuristic evaluation to varying degrees, when developing computer systems (Nielson, 1994). It is typically easier to adopt than many of the formal methods described.

In heuristic evaluation, the evaluator moves through the software, often through a planned process covering all screens or by tasks, and looks to see how well each screen adheres to the "rules," such as consistency of button placement, speaking the users language and providing feedback to the user. The evaluator documents and ranks any errors (e.g., cosmetic (1), minor (2), major (3), and catastrophic (4)) observed during their review for each screen and provide recommendations on how to improve the system.

Table 3. Nielson's usability principles

Principle	Description
Simple and natural dialogue	Dialogue should be a terse as possible as redundant information detracts from the relevant information. Natural flow of information should be achieved.
Speak the users' language	System oriented terms should be avoided; instead terms that users are familiar with should be used.
Minimize the users' memory load	The system should not require the user to remember information as they move from screen to screen. Instructions should be embedded into the design.
Consistency	Instructions should be consistent. Buttons that perform the same action should not be named or placed differently from screen to screen.
Feedback	The system should provide feedback to the user about activities within a reasonable time.
Clearly marked exits	Users need to have easily marked back up options if they have entered an area by mistake.
Shortcuts	Accelerators should be available for expert users to speed up common tasks.
Good error messages	Error messages should explain the errors in an understandable manner and suggest a solution.
Prevent errors	Good design prevents errors before they can occur.
Help and documentation	Good help is tailored, focused, searchable, and provides concrete instructions for the user's tasks.

Note: These principles are used as rules of thumb in heuristic evaluation (Based on Nielson, 1994)

Observational Methods

To complement inspection methods, usability practitioners may also use observational methods to assess the usability of information systems. Methods, such as the think aloud protocol analysis, allow the investigator to capture an externalization of the users thoughts as they are observed performing actions in the system (Ericsson & Simon, 1993). Think aloud is often used today in usability testing in the laboratory setting. Usability testing refers to the analysis of the process of use of the system by representative subjects performing representative tasks, for example: a physician entering a medication into the system. These interactions are captured on video/audio and mapped to the recording of the user's actions, allows the study to capture a more rich collection of data than retrospective interviews or surveys could. New problems are elucidated using this technique fairly quickly. Think aloud protocols are often used with scenarios chosen by the designer to find cognitive friction in the system. Users' challenges may well be quickly found through thinking aloud that are not easily predicted by models or by designers, nor would the user be aware of them when responding in post-evaluation interviews and questionnaires.

How do These Models Inform Health Informatics

The study of medical cognitive science, outside of HCI and informatics, has a long history. Medical decision-making, learning, and development of expertise, have all been influenced by cognitive science (Patel, Arocha, & Kaufman, 2001). High error rates in medicine are seen, in part, to be a cognitive problem (Graber, Franklin, & Gordon, 2005; Zhang, Patel, & Johnson, 2002). Not surprisingly, there is a call to apply cognitive science to health informatics (Patel & Kaufman, 1998a). The psycho-cognitive models have been applied to the evaluation of clinical information systems more so than the biomechanical or social models. There has been a growing body of work that focuses on the cognitive methodology of usability evaluation in healthcare (Kushniruk & Patel, 2004). This section will review some example applications of the above model in healthcare evaluation.

In one case study, QGOMS (a variant of GOMS) was applied to CT (computed tomography) software design (Beard, Smith, & Denelsbeck, 1996). QGOMS effectively compared various potential CT viewing setups, comparing number of monitors and resolution of monitors to traditional setup costs. They were able to, with reasonable accuracy, predict the impact of using different designs to the radiologist's review of CT films and selected a design that provided both cost and time savings.

Video and audio taped user walkthroughs and patient encounters show that the presence of an EMR effects the way physicians collect information and organize that information, that is the EMR affects the cognitive process of medical decision-making (Patel, Kushniruk, Yang, & Yale, 2000). Cognitive task analysis has been used to study decision making in anesthesia, with a focus on high risk, non-routine events (Weinger & Slagle, 2002).

With the increasing focus on safety in healthcare, several studies have looked at how EMR systems reduce or promote potential errors in practice. Heuristic evaluation has been used to evaluate patient safety with medical devices (Zhang, Johnson, Patel, Paige, & Kubose, 2003) as well as telemedicine systems. Likely, there are more informal heuristic evaluations in medical software development than are reported in the literature.

One group has actively discussed the role of cognitive theories in health informatics. In 1998, the work of Patel and Kaufman (Patel & Kaufman, 1998b) and Patel and Kushniruk (Patel & Kushniruk, 1998) formally set the stage for this discussion. There has been follow up with their primer of cognition in medicine with Arocha (Pa-

tel, Arocha, & Kaufman, 2001) and more recent discussions on cognitive methods in evaluation (Kushniruk & Patel, 2004).

One of the benefits of using clinical information systems is the sharing of information between providers. To address the usability of systems used by more than one person, health information science can turn to models that incorporate social interaction into HCI.

SOCIALLY AWARE HCI MODELS

Historically, HCI has focused on the interaction of a single user with the computer system. Today, however, much of the computer work involves interacting with other people through or with the computer. Inserting a computer into a clinical encounter (reviewing charts, entering orders, printing handouts, etc) places it into the provider-patient relationship, therefore, understanding how it can impact the dynamic of that relationship is important. Socially aware HCI models can help us improve the computer's role in those interactions.

Groupware has become increasingly common as computers become more ubiquitous and more connected. Still, the definition of groupware is elusive (Baecker & Baecker, 1992). For the purposes of this chapter, the definition for groupware will be taken (Ellis, Gibbs, & Rein, 1991) as: *"computer-based systems that support groups of people engaged in a common task (or goal) and that provide an interface to a shared environment."* This definition is useful for the discussion of clinical information systems. It includes use of the computer system, a focus on common goals (e.g., the delivery of care) and discusses a shared environment (that, for example, contains clinical data). What it excludes is also useful: it does not restrict the group size or how the group may interact, as both of these can vary significantly in the delivery of care. Limiting to small groups or to real time groupware would be unrealistic as care delivery can include larger groups of people that span both distances (e.g., telehealth) and time (e.g., throughout a patient's life).

In this section, two socially aware HCI models will be examined. First, computer supported cooperative work (CSCW) will be reviewed. It is more of an umbrella term covering several models. One of those models, articulation work and common information spaces, will be explored as an example from the collection of CSCW models as it might have particular application in healthcare. Second, distributed cognition is reviewed a model that takes the cognitive framework discussed in the previous section and moves it into a shared space. These theories have developed from the common need to better understand the use of systems in context, but have developed relatively independently of each other (Kaptelinin et al., 2003).

Computer Supported Cooperative Work (CSCW)

Grief and Cashman coined the term computer supported cooperative work (CSCW) in 1984, as part of a workshop on how computers could better support the work of people working together. It was an important step in more formally understanding the requirements for group work. It was started by technologists in order to learn from a wide array of disciplines including social psychology, sociology, anthropology, economics and education (Grudin, 1994). With this diverse background, rich discussions have been had on what "computer supported" and "collaborative work" mean to different researchers.

Schmidt and Bannon reviewed CSCW as a field of study and published in the first issues of "CSCW: An international Journal" (Schmidt & Bannon, 1992). This work grew from previous papers by both authors (Bannon & Schmidt, 1991), and focused on the definition of the terms in the acronym to be the fulcrum for defining a model to explain the problem space. The term

"computer support" acknowledges the focus of CSCW on the design of computer tools to support work. "cooperative work" is defined in a neutral sense rather than a positive, non-competitive way. Their definition includes "mutual dependency in work" between members in a group and does include both positive and negative aspects of mutual dependency including division of labor and competing individual goals. It explicitly excludes the interdependence from simply sharing resources (e.g., CPU cycles, storage), and rather focuses on the more complex issues of members of the group relying on the quality and timeliness of each other's work to achieve a common goal, the work at hand.

In general, CSCW has been described as having two interrelated goals: to improve a *traditional group* interaction and to allow a *distributed group* to function as well as a traditional group (Kraut, 2003). The study of CSCW is more often focused on the human-human interaction and reflecting on how the computer intermingles with that process. Accordingly, CSCW has drawn more on sociology than psychology as we have seen individually focused models. CSCW applications can be categorized by describing the interactions between users in two axes: time and space. Geographically, users can be co-located or they can be distributed. Similarly, users may interact in a synchronous manner or asynchronously (Rodden, 1991). This is a simple and effective way of conceptually categorizing CSCW applications. The resulting two-by-two table (see Table 4) is populated with our ongoing e-prescribing clinical example.

The methods adopted by CSCW researchers are grounded in the context of the groups and organizations being studied. With the CSCW influences of sociology and anthropology, ethnography has a prominent position in gathering information. As a design focused discipline, much attention has been given to understanding requirements for systems from those ethnographic studies. Experimental design can also be used to

Table 4. CSCW application categorization

		TIME	
		Synchronous	Asynchronous
SPACE	Co-located	Reviewing current medication list with a patient in the exam room, showing drug side effects.	Documenting a prescription in the patient record to be referred to by the nurse the next week.
	Distributed	Videoconference discussion with a specialist in picking the most effective medication.	Secure transfer of a prescription to a pharmacist, to be processed the next day.

Note: Two-by-two table showing one categorization of CSCW applications through the comparison of users geographical and chronological cooperation. The table has been populated with examples, or representative artifacts.

test CSCW aspects of software. Usability labs have been expanded to include the ability to test groups of users.

In the development of computer systems in the past thirty years, it is hard to deny the need to better understand the support that computers can provider to collaborative work. What has been in debate is the usefulness of a specific theoretical model to support CSCW. In this chapter, we will look at articulation work and common information spaces as one example.

Articulation Work and Common Information Spaces

Bannon and Schmidt have looked at the "articulation work" that is required to dynamically manage the mutual dependencies within a group of people working together. In order to support the articulation work, they propose two key areas for understanding during the design approach: (a) the support and management of dynamic and changing workflows for the group and (b) the development and understanding of "common information spaces" where groups are able share what is known.

(Bannon & Bødker, 1997) further describe common information spaces as the combination of physical or external elements—the information, events, objects that are mutually accessible—and the work required to interpret these elements by each human actor involved in the overall process. Common information spaces may be physically and temporally created, such as in a patient examination room or an operating room, or they may be more abstract and span both distance and time, such as a longitudinal patient record that is accessed by people in different locations over a person's life. It is through these information spaces that articulation work occurs. The concept of articulation work was developed from empirical observations and through the review of CSCW literature to describe the additional work needed to work with others in the shared information space.

Distributed Cognition

Distributed cognition offers a different approach to socially aware HCI evaluation through the application of cognitive science models to groups instead of individuals. It takes the same premise of the information processor as used in GOMS and other cognitive models discussed previously; however, it describes a larger functional unit than the individual. In distributed cognition (DCog), the functional unit is the collection of actors *and artifacts* that is required to complete a specific goal or task. The model describes the flow of information and actions on that data between actors and between artifacts in the system in order to complete the goal. Distributed cognition takes the stance that individual cognition, no matter how detailed, cannot account for the interactions between individuals and the environment. Therefore, DCog adapts the cognitive model to groups (Hutchins, 1995b). This is different from other socially oriented models in HCI, which have tended to leave cognitive science to the domain of individual HCI and instead adapt sociology and anthropology models to CSCW and groupware (Rogers & Ellis, 1994).

Unlike GOMS, distributed cognition maintains that the context of cognition is key. There are many social aspects of work environments that contribute to the achievement of goals and these must be examined *in situ*. The concepts of inputs, processes, representations and outputs of cognition are still present, but they are assumed by the whole system. This includes artifacts within the system, which can receive input, perform processing, and generate output. In distributed cognition, it is the interactions between elements have a greater impact than the cognition that each piece does independently. The detailed micro-

evaluation of GOMS is overshadowed by the external processes that occur between elements in the system in context (Perry, 2003). Comparison of Figures 2 and 3 highlight the similarities and differences between individual cognition and distributed cognition models.

Key to the distributed cognition model is understanding that objects in the system can perform cognitive acts and can affect the subsequent cognitive activities in the system. For example, a clinical information system may be able to store physical measurements and lab results for a patient. It can then display a composite graph showing average blood sugars over time as they relate to changes in patient weight. This processing changes the representation of the data to something more immediately accessible to the users. It changes the cognitive processing required of the clinician and patient who then use this information in the next step of the episode of diabetic care. The artifacts are, in essence, accomplishing cognitive work, permitting the human actors to leverage that work and focus on other aspects of work.

With the focus on the larger system, the methods used to develop an understanding of

Figure 2. Human information processor model

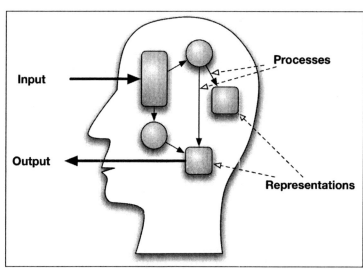

Note: *Human information processor model from cognitive science, as used in GOMS and other cognitive HCI models. (Based on Perry, 2003)*

Figure 3. Distributed cognition model

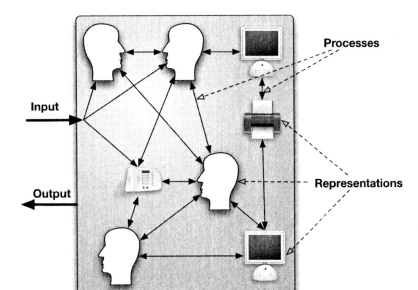

Note: The model of distributed cognition, as proposed by Hutchins, to describe cognitive processes between actors and external objects in a coordinated system. (Based on Perry, 2003)

distributed cognition within a system or domain are also largely ethnographic (Hollan, Hutchins, & Kirsh, 2000). This has been effective in developing detailed descriptions of how a cognitive process works in complex group environments such as ship navigation (Hutchins, 1995a) and in commercial airline cockpits (Hutchins & Klausen, 1996). Through the inclusion of experimental design with ethnography, a more complete model has been developed that iterates through a design cycle: first, an ethnography study discovers cognitive gaps and areas for improvement. Experimental testing of a new design is performed and, if successful, is incorporated into workplace studies that are reevaluated through further ethnographic study.

DCog extends cognitive science, with its deep roots in medical education and key place in usability engineering in healthcare, to the integrated dynamic of group work, which is central to the delivery of care.

How Do These Social Models Inform Health Informatics?

"The patient-physician relationship is central to the role of the family physician." (Canada, 2006)

The group, in healthcare, is traditionally a confidential dyad made up of the patient and their provider. However, the evolving landscape of healthcare is increasingly team focused with multiple providers supporting patient care in multiple locations over time. These teams are dynamic, with roles and responsibilities changing based on uniqueness of individuals and over time (Patel, Cytryn, Shortliffe, & Safran, 2000). Application of new artifacts into these environments can easily disrupt (positively or negatively) the evolved processes and the intricate interactions between providers, patients and the physical environment.

It is argued that the fit of systems needs to be considered, observed, and explained in the application of clinical information systems in order to enhance the likelihood of successful adoption (Berg, 1999; Sjöberg & Timpka, 1998).

The CSCW literature has tools that can help highlight the needs and challenges that clinical groups face. As the processes of medicine are collaborative and variable, CSCW methods may have a considerable amount to offer to our understanding of the requirements for clinical information systems (Pratt, Reddy, McDonald et al., 2004). Application of CSCW models have aided in the understanding of the complexity of tightly coordinated clinical areas such as medical wards (Bossen, 2002). As care becomes more coordinated and more distributed, particularly in the delivery of outpatient care where face-to-face meetings are not always possible between care providers (for example the patient's GP and the home care nurse), CSCW may well help to shape and improve integrated care delivery in both primary care and community care. There is an increasing awareness that the lens that CSCW provides can help deal with the challenges of design of distributed electronic records. There is a lack of evaluation of the application of groupware tools in healthcare (Househ & Lau, 2005). Application of CSCW has been applied to small group learning in primary care (Timpka & Marmolin, 1995; Timpka et al., 1995) as well as other group activities, such as telehealth (Ganguly & Ray, 2000; Kaplan & Fitzpatrick, 1997; Weerakkody & Ray). These can have an important part to play in the coordination of care and the learning from CSCW in other domains can aid in the effective application of these tools.

Bannon and Schmidt's model of CSCW with articulation work and common information spaces may have particular interest in healthcare. The approach fits with the processes we see in health care. A strong focus on common information spaces, that is a patient's longitudinal record, being the primary repository in the coordination of work and sharing of information in healthcare. Also, with articulation work being variable and dynamic fits with what we see in the complex processes in healthcare.

Distributed cognition, as a model to apply in health care, has aided in the design of clinical information systems and their deployment into the environments of healthcare (Xiao, 2005; Zhang et al., 2004), context-sensitive clinical coding (Bång, Eriksson, Lindqvist, & Timpka), and it can enhance the understanding of how physical artifacts are used by clinicians to support memory and collaboration as we transition the paper records to electronic systems (Bång & Timpka, 2003). Distributed cognition's view that external artifacts are actively involved in the cognitive process has an appeal when considering that electronic records have the ability to dramatically change how different users access patient data and medical knowledge to support the delivery of evidence-based care. Understanding that electronic records can be much more active in supporting both provider and patient decision making may help improve quality of decision making and reduce errors.

DISCUSSION: INTEGRATING HCI THEORIES IN HEALTH INFORMATICS

Engel's bio-psycho-social model has found particular resonance in management of complex chronic illness and provision of longitudinal care delivered in primary care and family medicine. It has been incorporated into the working descriptions of both. Considering the impact at each level is important in understanding the impact that an illness can have. In parallel, the study of HCI has included three levels of analysis: the biomechanical, the psychological/cognitive, and the social. Considering the interactions at all three levels is important in understanding potential impacts of the adoption of clinical information systems in the delivery of care and can help design more effective systems.

Biomechanical HCI, such as Fitts' Law and KLM can help us to design more efficient user interfaces, minimizing time for data entry and improving navigation. Human factors and ergonomics can help us understand physical requirements for the use of information systems and tools for procedures. Cognitive models can help us design systems that support a user to find what they are looking for, make the systems easier to learn, and support better decision making. Understanding what users need and do not need to make decisions is important in healthcare where so much of health is decision making—diagnosing, selecting treatments, and so forth. Decision support, in particular, could see benefits from understanding the cognitive needs and limits of users. This may help reduce problems such as "alert fatigue" and help decrease the errors in healthcare. Social models can aid in the understanding of broader interactions of health care teams, focusing more how to support human-human interactions, which is central to the delivery of care. Each level of HCI offers something to the design and evaluation of clinical information systems. However, as with Engel's model, it is the integration at all three levels where significant benefit might be seen.

Application of Complimentary Bio-Psycho-Social HCI Methods

Before concluding this chapter, let us revisit the clinical example of e-prescribing and observe how the use of tools in all three levels can help compare two systems. We will be selecting between two hypothetical e-prescribing systems: a best of breed, e-prescribing application that does not interface with your existing clinical information system (Alone-Rx) and one that can be tightly integrated into the existing system (Integrate-Rx). We have the opportunity to observe both in real practices as well as walk through the system with the designers. For our bio-psycho-social evaluation, we do not have a lot of time, so will use two inspection methods and one, short observational study. First, a KLM (keystroke level model) walkthrough of selecting a patient for a prescription; then a cognitive walk through of selecting an appropriate medication; and concluded with a brief observational study of prescription renewals that is reviewed through a distributed cognition lens.

First, selecting a patient. Alone-Rx appears to have a streamlined process for finding a patient—the search box is available on every screen. The predicted time for finding a patient in Alone-Rx is 4.7 seconds, the details are shown in Table 5. In contrast, searching for a patient in Integrate-Rx does not appear to be as streamlined and requires moving to the scheduling screen and then using a menu to get the search for a patient window. This appears to be much more cumbersome and would take a predicted 12.7 seconds just to find the patient (not shown). However, in routine work, Integrate-Rx does not require searching for the patient for each prescription written. As it is integrated to the scheduler, the office's patient scheduler displays the patients that are being seen that day. This has a positive impact on the time it takes for a provider to find a typical patient, reducing the predicted time to 3.7 seconds (Table 6).

Here we can see that there is a time improvement for Integrate-Rx. Admittedly a small difference, but measurable. Further KLM studies may show more time savings for one product or the other depending on the design.

Next, choosing an appropriate medication. A key part of prescribing is selecting a medication that is safe for the patient. Adverse drug events are common and can be serious. Many are preventable. Performing a cognitive walkthrough we can see how they can help avoid drug interactions. We have already developed the key goals and actions with a physician working group. One of the sub goals is to determine if a medication would be contraindicated for the patient. Let us use that

Table 5. KLM study for fictional "Alone-Rx" to select a patient

Step	Time (s)
Place hand on mouse	0.4
Point to search box	1.0
Click mouse	0.1
Place hands on keyboard	0.4
Mentally determine spelling of patient's name	0.5
Type "s m i t h" <enter>	0.6 (0.1x 6 keys)
Home hands on mouse	0.4
Point to correct Smith	1.0
Click mouse to open prescription screen	0.1
TOTAL TIME:	4.5 seconds

Note: Use of the KLM model to predict the time it takes a typical user to reach for a patient using the fictional stand alone e-prescribing tool "Alone-Rx."

Table 6. KLM study for fictional "Integrate-Rx"

Step	Time (s)
Place hand on mouse	0.4
Point to schedule button	1.0
Click mouse	0.1
Mentally determine which patient	0.5
Point to schedule button	1.0
Click mouse	0.1
TOTAL TIME:	3.1 seconds

Note: Use of the KLM model to predict the time it takes a typical user to reach for a patient using the fictional e-prescribing tool "Integrate-Rx," which is part of a complete clinical system and can leverage the existing schedule list of patients.

sub goal with its five key actions to illustrate the differences between the two provider order entry systems, see Table 7. Here we see that Integrate-Rx can potentially support the decision making process more effectively as it can draw on more of the patient's medical history from the central database that a standalone prescription writing tool (Alone-Rx) cannot; however, Integrate-Rx's implementation of alerts is not as clear as Alone-Rx, requiring the user to remember interaction severity.

Finally, completing our three-pronged illustrative, fictional evaluation, we look at the social interactions of e-prescribing. For this fragment we look at prescription renewals. Approval of a prescription renewal is a coordinated effort between patient, pharmacy, office staff, and physician. To understand the processes, we can place an observer in the office and watch the interactions. During a typical day, a physician's office will have many prescription renewal requests come in by phone. A prescription renewal occurs often enough that

Table 7. Cognitive walkthrough example

Sub Goal: Determine if there are any significant drug interactions	Alone-Rx	Integrate-Rx
Action 1: Determine if the patient is allergic to the medication.	Provides alerts when selecting medications that the patient is allergic to. Displays allergies on the patient screen during prescribing.	Provides alerts when selecting medications that the patient is allergic to. Displays allergies on the patient screen during prescribing.
Action 2: Determine if there are any interactions between the selected medication and the medication that the patient is currently taking.	Provides detailed drug: drug interaction alerts and ranks alerts by potential severity, making it easy to see which need to be focused on and avoided and which are less likely to cause serious problems.	Contains drug: drug interaction checking. This is displayed in pair wise listing in alphabetical order, not ranked by severity. Both pairs are displayed (A interacts with B as well as B interacting with A) increasing the burden on the user to review all duplicates.
Action 3: Determine if the patient has a diagnosis that interacts with the medication.	Does not provide drug: disease checking as diagnoses are not available to Alone-Rx. Must be remembered or looked up in the drug monograph.	Provides drug: disease checking integrated with the other interaction checking.
Action 4: Determine if the patient may have any abnormal lab values that may be exacerbated by the use of this medication.	Does not provide drug: lab checking as labs are not available to Alone-Rx.	Does not provide drug: lab checking, although labs are integrated into the system. NOTE: Users might assume that the system checks.
Action 5: Decide if any interactions are significant for this patient	Alone-Rx provides an easy way for the user to see severity—ranking and color coding. Details can be gathered from reading the alerts.	Integrate-Rx does not provide an easy way to support assessing severity of an interaction. The user either needs to remember the serious reactions or review the summaries for each interaction, which requires clicking each element on the list.

Note: A sample cognitive walkthrough comparison of the two fictional e-prescribing applications "Alone-Rx" and "Integrate-Rx."

several can be observed in a mini-ethnographic study lasting only one morning.

In an office using Alone-Rx, the observed workflow proceeds along these lines: the medical office assistant (MOA) receives a phone call from the pharmacy requesting a renewal. The MOA confirms the patient is part of the practice and writes a note to the MD with the renewal request information (date, patient name, medication, dose, etc.) in the existing clinical information system. When the MD is free, she looks through her inbox and, seeing the renewal, searches for the patient in Alone-Rx, sees that the prescription is appropriate, and documents the renewal in Alone Rx. Exiting Alone-Rx and re-entering the EMR, she then responds to the note to the MOA, who then phones the pharmacy back with verbal approval. If the renewal request is wrong (not appropriate, not from this office, wrong patient, etc.) the office performs the same steps until the MD reviews the medication list in Alone-Rx.

In the office using Integrate-Rx, the overall process is similar; however, we observe some of the steps are streamlined. For example, as the MOA speaks to the pharmacist, she searches for the patient and confirms the medication exists in the system. The MOA is able to handle erroneous requests at the first point of contact, not several hours later. While on the phone, the office assistant creates a message to the physician and links directly to the details of the prescription. When the physician checks the electronic inbox, she sees a message and opens up the renewal request, which is already populated, reducing errors, and so forth. As Integrate-Rx is part of the clinical record, the physician notes that the patient is overdue for a blood pressure check and, after approving the renewal, adds a note back to request that the patient come in for a visit. This is all documented in the chart as part of the work-flow. We see that the integrated system is able to help perform information processing at several key points where Alone-Rx cannot. It supports decision making of appropriateness of renewal requests at the first point of contact in the office with the MOA, reducing the number of erroneous requests interrupting the doctor (and then having to be re-handled by the MOA). It also reviews the patient's care record during a renewal request and can determine when the office might need to call in a patient for follow up.

Admittedly, this example is brief, is not a detailed methodological description, and has chosen two systems in order to highlight differences for discussion. One can quickly see that using tools at each level provides a richer picture of the applications strengths and weaknesses than any one approach alone.

FUTURE RESEARCH DIRECTIONS

Clinical information systems are, in some ways, analogous to complex chronic illnesses. CIS implementations are long-term (i.e., chronic) pursuits that affect the physical mechanics of daily life, change how we think about certain activities, and impact our social interactions. By considering HCI models through the bio-psycho-social model of care, this chapter has explored representative work from the broad domains of published HCI literature and has reflected on how aspects of each level can inform where systems succeed and fail. With recent calls for use of mix-methods and methodological plurism for healthcare evalu-

ation (Kaplan, 2001), it is very appropriate that HCI in health informatics make known what it can provide for systems design and evaluation, from the biomechanical, the cognitive, and the social levels.

Considering the breadth of discussion of theories in the literature of HCI and CSCW, of which we have only scratched the surface of here, there is a relative dearth of discussion of HCI theory in medicine. While case studies include reference to some of these theories, discussions of formal adoption and adaptation of CSCW and HCI methods into the design and evaluation of healthcare systems have been relatively rare in health informatics literature. Some have begun the discussion around application of cognitive usability and others have encouraged the adoption of CSCW perspectives in healthcare. Formal discussions of composite HCI frameworks in health informatics are difficult to find. This discussion is an important as part of the further establishment of the discipline within health informatics.

In general, broad frameworks are needed to evaluate the impact of clinical information systems; frameworks that address issues at many levels, including the system, the individual, the group and organizational levels (Delpierre et al., 2004; Kukafka, Johnson, Linfante, & Allegrante, 2003) HCI can offer methods at each of these levels. Which methods are selected from the three levels may vary depending on need, resources, and so forth. Several models have particular application to healthcare, such as cognitive walk through, common information spaces and articulation work, distributed cognition, as examples. Many have overlap with other theories and methods that you have read about in other chapters of this text. Applying models of HCI into health information science introduces our domain to a rich collection of tools that support the design, development, and evaluation of better clinical information systems that fit the context of healthcare.

REFERENCES

Baecker, R. M., & Baecker, R. M. (1992). *Readings in groupware and computer-supported cooperative work: Assisting human-human collaboration.* Morgan Kaufmann.

Baker, G. R., Norton, P. G., Flintoft, V., Blais, R., Brown, A., Cox, J., et al. (2004). The Canadian adverse events study: The incidence of adverse events among hospital patients in Canada. *Cmaj, 170*(11), 1678-1686.

Bång, M., Eriksson, H., Lindqvist, K., & Timpka, T. (1999). *A framework for context-sensitive terminology support.* AMIA 1999 Annual Symposium.

Bång, M., & Timpka, T. (2003). Cognitive tools in medical teamwork: The spatial arrangement of patient records. *Meth Inf Med, 42*, 331-336.

Bannon, L., & Bødker, S. (1997). Constructing Common Information Spaces. *Proceedings of the Fifth European Conference on Computer Supported Cooperative Work* (pp. 81-96).

Bannon, L. J., & Schmidt, K. (1991). CSCW: Four characters in search of a context. In *Proceedings of the First European Conference on Computer Supported Cooperative Work* (pp. 358-372). Gatwick, London.

Bates, D. W., Cohen, M., Leape, L. L., Overhage, J. M., Shabot, M. M., & Sheridan, T. (2001). Reducing the frequency of errors in medicine using information technology. *Journal of the American Medical Informatics Association, 8*(4), 299.

Beard, D. V., Smith, D. K., & Denelsbeck, K. M. (1996). Quick and dirty GOMS: A case study of computed tomography interpretation. *Human-Computer Interaction, 11*(2), 157-180.

Berg, M. (1999). Patient care information systems and health care work: A sociotechnical approach. *International Journal of Medical Informatics, 55*(2), 87-101.

Berguer, R. (1998). Surgical technology and the ergonomics of laparoscopic instruments. *Surgical Endoscopy, 12*(5), 458-462.

Blackmon, M. H., Polson, P. G., Kitajima, M., & Lewis, C. (2002). Cognitive walkthrough for the web. *Proceedings of the SIGCHI conference on Human factors in computing systems: Changing our world, changing ourselves* (pp. 463-470).

Bossen, C. (2002). The parameters of common information spaces:: the heterogeneity of cooperative work at a hospital ward. *Proceedings of the 2002 ACM conference on Computer supported cooperative work,* (pp. 176-185).

Canada, C. o. F. P. o. (2006). Four principles of family medicine. Retrieved January 27, 2006, from http://www.cfpc.ca/English/cfpc/about%20us/principles/default.asp?s=1

Card, S. K., Moran, T. P., & Newell, A. (1980). The keystroke-level model for user performance time with interactive systems. *Communications of the ACM, 23*(7), 396-410.

Card, S. K., Newell, A., & Moran, T. P. (1983). *The psychology of human-computer interaction.* Lawrence Erlbaum Associates.

Carroll, J. (2003). *Hci models, theories, and frameworks: Toward a multidisciplinary science.* Morgan Kaufmann.

Delpierre, C., Cuzin, L., Fillaux, J., Alvarez, M., Massip, P., & Lang, T. (2004). A systematic review of computer-based patient record systems and quality of care: More randomized clinical trials or a broader approach? *International Journal for Quality in Health Care, 16*(5), 407-416.

Ellis, C. A., Gibbs, S. J., & Rein, G. L. (1991). Groupware-some issues and experience. *Communication of the ACM, 34*(1), 38-58.

Engel, G. L. (1977). The need for a new medical model: a challenge for biomedicine. *Science, 196*(4286), 129.

Ericsson, K. A., & Simon, H. A. (1993). *Protocol analysis: Verbal reports as data.* MIT Press.

Ewald, P. W. (2004). Evolution of virulence. *Infect Dis Clin North Am, 18*(1), 1-15.

Fitts, P. M. (1954). The information capacity of the human motor system in controlling the amplitude of movement, J. of Exp. *Psychology, 47,* 381-392.

Fitts, P. M. (1992). The information capacity of the human motor system in controlling the amplitude of movement. *Journal of Experimental Psychology: General, 121*(3), 262-269.

Ganguly, P., & Ray, P. (2000). Software interoperability of telemedicine systems: A CSCW perspective. *Proceedings of the 7th International Conference on Parallel and Distributed Systems (ICPADS'00)* (pp. 349-354).

Goransson, B., Lind, M., Pettersson, E., Sandblad, B., & Schwalbe, P. (1986). The interface is often not the problem. *Proceedings of the SIGCHI/GI Conference on Human Factors in Computing Systems and Graphics Interface* (pp. 133-136).

Graber, M. L., Franklin, N., & Gordon, R. (2005). Diagnostic error in internal medicine. Am Med Assoc.

Grudin, J. (1994). CSCW: History and focus. *IEEE Computer, 27*(5), 19-26.

Hill, J. W., Green, P. S., Jensen, J. F., Gorfu, Y., & Shah, A. S. (1994). Telepresence surgery demonstration system. *Robotics and Automation, 1994. Proceedings, 1994 IEEE International Conference* (pp. 2302-2307).

Hills, J. W., & Jensen, J. F. (1998). Telepresence technology in medicine: Principles and applications. *Proceedings of the IEEE, 86*(3), 569-580.

Hollan, J., Hutchins, E., & Kirsh, D. (2000). Distributed cognition: Toward a new foundation for human-computer interaction research. *ACM Transactions on Computer-Human Interaction (TOCHI), 7*(2), 174-196.

Horsky, J., Kaufman, D. R., & Patel, V. L. (2003). The cognitive complexity of a provider order entry interface. *AMIA Annu Symp Proc, 2003* (pp. 294-298).

Househ, M. S., & Lau, F. Y. (2005). Collaborative technology use by healthcare teams. *Journal of Medical Systems, 29*(5), 449-461.

Hutchins, E. (1995a). *Cognition in the wild.* MIT Press.

Hutchins, E. (1995b). How a cockpit remembers its speeds. *Cognitive Science, 19*(3), 265-288.

Hutchins, E., & Klausen, T. (1996). Distributed cognition in an airline cockpit. In D. Middleton and Y. Engeström (Eds.), *Cognition and Communication at Work* (pp. 15-34). Cambridge University Press.

John, B. (1995). Why GOMS? *Interactions, 2*(4), 80-89.

John, B. E., & Kieras, D. E. (1996). The GOMS family of user interface analysis techniques: Comparison and contrast. *ACM Transactions on Computer-Human Interaction, 3*(4), 320-351.

Kaplan, B. (2001). Evaluating informatics applications-some alternative approaches: Theory, social interactionism, and call for methodological pluralism. *Int J Med Inform, 64*(1), 39-56.

Kaplan, S. M., & Fitzpatrick, G. (1997). Designing support for remote intensive-care telehealth using the locales framework. *Proceedings of the conference on Designing interactive systems: processes, practices, methods, and techniques,* (pp. 173-184).

Kaptelinin, V., Nardi, B., Bødker, S., Carroll, J., Hollan, J., Hutchins, E. et al. (2003). Post-cognitivist HCI: second-wave theories. *Conference on Human Factors in Computing Systems* (pp. 692-693).

Kieras, D. E. (1997). Task analysis and the design of functionality. *The Computer Science and*

Engineering Handbook. Boca Raton, CRC Inc (pp. 1401-1423).

Kohn, L. T. (2000). *To err is human.* National Acad. Press.

Kraut, R. E. (2003). Applying social psychological theory to the problems of group work. In J.M. Carroll (Ed.), *HCI models, theories and frameworks: Toward a multidisciplinary science* (pp. 325-356).

Kukafka, R., Johnson, S. B., Linfante, A., & Allegrante, J. P. (2003). Grounding a new information technology implementation framework in behavioral science: A systematic analysis of the literature on IT use. *Journal of Biomedical Informatics, 36*(3), 218-227.

Kushniruk, A. W., & Patel, V. L. (2004). Cognitive and usability engineering methods for the evaluation of clinical information systems. *Journal of Biomedical Informatics, 37*(1), 56-76.

MacKenzie, I. S. (1992). Fitts' law as a research and design tool in human-computer interaction. *Human-Computer Interaction, 7*(1), 91-139.

MacKenzie, I. S. (2002). Introduction to this special issue on text entry for mobile computing. *Human-Computer Interaction, 17*(2), 141-145.

Middleton, B., Hammond, W. E., Brennan, P. F., & Cooper, G. F. (2005). *Accelerating US EHR adoption: How to get there from here. Recommendations based on the 2004 ACMI Retreat.* Am Med Inform Assoc.

Militello, L. G. (1998). Applied cognitive task analysis (ACTA): A practitioner's toolkit for understanding cognitive task demands. *Ergonomics, 41*(11), 1618-1641.

Neilson, J., & Mack, R. (1994). *Usability inspection methods.* NY: John Wiley & Son. Usability Sciences Corporation (1994) Windows, 3.

Nielson, J. (1994). *Usability engineering.* Morgan Kaufmann.

Patel, V. L., Arocha, J. F., & Kaufman, D. R. (2001). *A primer on aspects of cognition for medical informatics.* Am Med Inform Assoc.

Patel, V. L., Cytryn, K. N., Shortliffe, E. H., & Safran, C. (2000). The collaborative health care team: The role of individual and group expertise. *Teaching and Learning in Medicine, 12*(3), 117-132.

Patel, V. L., & Kaufman, D. R. (1998a). Medical informatics and the science of cognition. *Journal of the American Medical Informatics Association, 5,* 493-502.

Patel, V. L., & Kaufman, D. R. (1998b). Science and practice. *Journal of the American Medical Informatics Association, 5,* 489-492.

Patel, V. L., & Kushniruk, A. W. (1998). Interface design for health care environments: the role of cognitive science. *Proc AMIA Symp, 2937.*

Patel, V. L., Kushniruk, A. W., Yang, S., & Yale, J. F. (2000). Impact of a computer-based patient record system on data collection, knowledge organization, and reasoning. *Journal of the American Medical Informatics Association, 7,* 569-585.

Perry, M. (2003). Distributed cognition. *HCI models, theories and frameworks: toward a multidisciplinary science* (pp. 193-223). San Francisco: Elsevier Science,.

Polson, P. G., Lewis, C., Rieman, J., & Wharton, C. (1992). Cognitive walkthroughs: A method for theory-based evaluation of user interfaces. *International Journal of Man-Machine Studies, 36*(5), 741-773.

Pratt, W., Reddy, M. C., McDonald, D. W., Tarczy-Hornoch, P., & Gennari, J. H. (2004). Incorporating ideas from computer-supported cooperative work. *Journal of Biomedical Informatics, 37*(2), 128-137.

Rodden, T. (1991). A survey of CSCW systems. *Interacting with Computers, 3*(3), 319-353.

Rogers, Y., & Ellis, J. (1994). Distributed cognition: An alternative framework for analysing and explaining collaborative working. *Journal of Information Technology, 9*(2), 119-128.

Romanow, R. J. (2002). Commission on the future of health care in Canada. *Building on Values: The Future of Health Care in Canada-Final Report,* 75-90.

Roth, E. M., Patterson, E. S., & Mumaw, R. J. (2001). Cognitive engineering: Issues in user-centered system design. *Encyclopedia of Software Engineering* (2nd ed.) New York: Wiley-Interscience, John Wiley & Sons.

Schmidt, K., & Bannon, L. (1992). Taking CSCW seriously. *Computer Supported Cooperative Work (CSCW), 1*(1), 7-40.

Schraagen, J. M., Chipman, S. F., & Shalin, V. L. (2000). *Cognitive task analysis.* Lawrence Erlbaum Associates.

Silfverberg, M., MacKenzie, I. S., & Korhonen, P. (2000). Predicting text entry speed on mobile phones. *Proceedings of the SIGCHI conference on Human factors in computing systems* (pp. 9-16).

Sjöberg, C., & Timpka, T. (1998). Participatory design of information systems in health care. *Journal of the American Medical Informatics Association, 5,* 177-183.

Staggers, N., & Kobus, D. (2000). Comparing response time, errors, and satisfaction between text-based and graphical user interfaces during nursing order tasks. *Journal of the American Medical Informatics Association, 7*(2), 164.

Stone, R., & McCloy, R. (2004). *Ergonomics in medicine and surgery.* Br Med Assoc.

Timpka, T., & Marmolin, H. (1995). Beyond computer-based clinical reminders: Improvement of the total service quality by small-group based organizational learning in primary care. *Medinfo, 8*(Pt 1), 559-563.

Timpka, T., Sjoberg, C., Hallberg, N., Eriksson, H., Lindblom, P., Hedblom, P., et al. (1995). Participatory design of computer-supported organizational learning in health care: Methods and experiences. *Proc Annu Symp Comput Appl Med Care, 800,* 4.

Venter, J. C., Adams, M. D., Myers, E. W., Li, P. W., Mural, R. J., Sutton, G. G., et al. (2001). *The sequence of the human genome.*

Walsh, S. H. (2004). The clinician's perspective on electronic health records and how they can affect patient care: Br Med Assoc.

Ware, C. (2003). Design as applied perception. In J.M. Carroll (Ed.), *HCI models, theories, and frameworks: Towards a multidisciplinary science.* San Franscisco: Morgan-Kaufmann.

Weerakkody, G., & Ray, P. (2003). CSCW-based system development methodology for health-care information systems. *Telemedicine Journal and E-Health, 9*(3), 273-282.

Weinger, M. B., & Slagle, J. (2002). Human factors research in anesthesia patient safety techniques to elucidate factors affecting clinical task performance and decision making. *Journal of the American Medical Informatics Association 2002, 9*(90061), S58-S63.

Wharton, C., Bradford, J., Jeffries, R., & Franzke, M. (1992). Applying cognitive walkthroughs to more complex user interfaces: experiences, issues, and recommendations. *Proceedings of the SIGCHI conference on Human factors in computing systems* (pp. 381-388).

Wilcox, R. A., & Whitham, E. M. (2003). Personal Viewpoint Reduction of medical error at the point-of-care using electronic clinical information delivery. *Internal Medicine Journal, 33*(11), 537-540.

Xiao, Y. (2005). Artifacts and collaborative work in healthcare: Methodological, theoretical, and technological implications of the tangible. *J Biomed Inform, 38*(1), 26-33.

Zachary, W., Ryder, J. M., & Hicinbothom, J. H. (1998). Cognitive task analysis and modeling of decision making in complex environments. *Making decisions under stress* (pp. 315-344) Washington, DC: APA.

Zhang, J., Johnson, T. R., Patel, V. L., Paige, D. L., & Kubose, T. (2003). Using usability heuristics to evaluate patient safety of medical devices. *Journal of Biomedical Informatics, 36*(1/2), 23-30.

Zhang, J., Patel, V. L., & Johnson, T. R. (2002). Medical error: Is the solution medical or cognitive? *Journal of the American Medical Informatics Association, 9*(90061), 75.

Zhang, T., Aranzamendez, G., Rinkus, S., Gong, Y., Rukab, J., Johnson-Throop, K. A., et al. (2004). An information flow analysis of a distributed information system for space medical support. *Medinfo, 2004,* 992-998.

ADDITIONAL READINGS

For an excellent general overview of HCI, see:

Carroll, J. (2003). *HCI models, theories, and frameworks: Toward a multidisciplinary science*: Morgan Kaufmann.

Additional Useful Readings:

Biomechanical:

Fitts, P. M. (1992). The information capacity of the human motor system in controlling the amplitude of movement. *Journal of Experimental Psychology: General, 121*(3), 262-269.

Individual Psycho- Cognitive:

Card, S. K., Newell, A., & Moran, T. P. (1983). *The psychology of human-computer interaction.* Lawrence Erlbaum Associates.

Horsky, J., Kaufman, D. R., & Patel, V. L. (2003). The cognitive complexity of a provider order entry interface. *AMIA Annu Symp Proc, 2003,* (pp. 294-298).

Kushniruk, A. W., & Patel, V. L. (2004). Cognitive and usability engineering methods for the evaluation of clinical information systems. *Journal of Biomedical Informatics, 37*(1), 56-76.

Patel, V. L., Arocha, J. F., & Kaufman, D. R. (2001). *A primer on aspects of cognition for medical informatics.* Am Med Inform Assoc.

Zhang, J., Johnson, T. R., Patel, V. L., Paige, D. L., & Kubose, T. (2003). Using usability heuristics to evaluate patient safety of medical devices. *Journal of Biomedical Informatics, 36*(1/2), 23-30.

Social:

Bannon, L. J., & Schmidt, K. (1991). CSCW: Four characters in search of a context.

Berg, M. (1999). Patient care information systems and health care work: A sociotechnical approach. *International Journal of Medical Informatics, 55*(2), 87-101.

Grudin, J. (1994). CSCW: History and focus. *IEEE Computer, 27*(5), 19-26.

Hollan, J., Hutchins, E., & Kirsh, D. (2000). Distributed cognition: Toward a new foundation for human-computer interaction research. *ACM Transactions on Computer-Human Interaction (TOCHI), 7*(2), 174-196.

Hutchins, E. (1995a). *Cognition in the wild.* The MIT Press.

General:

Kaplan, B. (2001). Evaluating informatics applications-some alternative approaches: Theory, social interactionism, and call for methodological pluralism. *International Journal of Medicine Information, 64*(1), 39-56.

Section II
Supporting Healthcare Work Practices

Chapter III
Enhancing 'Fit' of Health Information Systems Design Through Practice Support

Craig E. Kuziemsky
University of Ottawa, Canada

ABSTRACT

The design and implementation of healthcare information systems (HIS) is problematic as many HIS projects do not achieve the desired outcomes. There exist a number of theories to enhance our ability to successfully develop HIS. Examples of such theories include 'fit' and the sociotechnical approach. However, there are few empirical studies that illustrate how to understand and operationalize such theories at the empirical level needed for HIS design. This chapter introduces a practice support framework that bridges the gap between the theoretical and empirical aspects of HIS design by identifying specific process and information practice supports that need to be considered to actively produce fit of an HIS within a healthcare setting. The chapter also provides an empirical case study of how practice support was used to develop a computer based tool in the domain area of palliative care severe pain management.

INTRODUCTION

The design and implementation of healthcare information systems (HIS) is problematic as many HIS projects do not achieve the desired outcomes. It has been reported that up to 30-50 percent of implemented HIS fail (Anderson, Aydin, & Jay, 1994) and in fact we may not know the true rate of failure of HIS due to the disincentives to publish about failures (Pratt, Reddy, & McDonald, 2004).

Part of the problem is that a HIS needs to reconcile the complexity of both a healthcare domain area and an information system. Introducing a technical artifact such as a HIS will impact workflow, communication and other clinical tasks. Having some understanding about user requirements to achieve those clinical tasks will enhance our ability to design and implement HIS that meet user needs.

Copyright © 2008, IGI Global, distributing in print or electronic forms without written permission of IGI Global is prohibited.

The concept of 'fit' refers to the need to establish fit between HIS and the organizational context where it is being implemented. 'Fit' was first introduced by Southon, Sauer and Dampney (1997) and further described by Kaplan (2001). Aarts, Dooreward, and Berg (2004) suggest that fit is not a passive process but rather needs to be actively produced between the HIS and organization where the HIS is being implemented. Although the citations on 'Fit' have acknowledged its importance to HIS design there are few empirical studies that illustrate how to understand and operationalize fit at the detailed level needed for HIS design. Fit requires methodological rigor through qualitative research methods for understanding how HIS implementation impacts healthcare settings and for actively constructing fit between a HIS and a healthcare setting. However, the range of analysis that is possible in qualitative studies can be an obstacle as it can be difficult to determine how to study a healthcare setting to establish fit.

This chapter extends existing research on 'fit' by introducing a framework called practice support. Practice support refers to the need to understand all perspectives of how a HIS will impact healthcare providers when implemented in a healthcare setting. The chapter will describe existing theories and models related to fit of HIS and outline some of the limitations in the theories and models. It will then introduce the practice support framework and methodology, and provide a case study illustrating how the practice support framework was used to construct fit of a computer-based tool for palliative care severe pain management.

BACKGROUND

Theories and Models Related to 'Fit' of HIS

There exist a number of theories and models to explain the fit of HIS with healthcare providers and settings.

Berg describes the sociotechnical approach, which refers to increasing our understanding of how information systems or other communication techniques are developed, introduced and become a part of social practices (Berg, 1999). Sociotechnical approaches emphasize the inter-relation between information systems and the social environment where they are used (Berg, Aaarts, & van der Lei, 2003). HIS design from a sociotechnical perspective is about finding the synergy between the particularities of healthcare and information and communication technologies (Berg, 2003). The sociotechnical approach is also about designing interactions between users and technology such as interfaces and information retrieval not from the view of the technology but rather from the view of the agents that work with the technology and the work practices where the technology is embedded (Coeira, 2003). However Berg, Aarts, and van der Lei (2003) subsequently point out that there is no actual sociotechnical per se, but rather it has many roots including methods such as participatory design and fields such as computer supported collaborative work.

The concept of 'fit,' which refers to the need to establish fit between the HIS and the organizational context where it is being implemented, has been discussed by Southon, Sauer, and Dampney (1997) and Kaplan (2001). Kaplan (2001) summarizes studies about fit that identify a number of dimensions as being part of fit including clinical workflow (Kaplan, 1995; Safran, Jones, Rind et al., 1998; Sicotte, Lehoux, & Denis, 1998), healthcare providers level of expertise (Sicotte et al., 1998), organizational setting and cultures (Kaplan, 1988; Massaro, 1993), communication patterns (Aydin, 1994) and cognitive processes (Patel, Allen, Arocha, & Shortliffe, 1998). An important consideration is that Aarts et al. (2004) suggest that establishing fit is not a passive process but rather fit needs to be actively produced between the technology and the practice where the technology is being implemented.

As the HIS discipline has evolved so has the appreciation for conducting studies within an interpretative framework. Interpretative studies have shown to be valuable for "producing an understanding of the context of the information system, and the process whereby the information system influences and is influenced by the context" (Walsham 1993, pp. 4-5). Interpretive research does not predefine dependent and independent variables, but focuses on the full complexity of human sense making as the situation emerges (Kaplan & Maxwell, 1994).

Although quantitative methods have historically been the predominant methods used to capture data for HIS design and evaluation the limitations of relying solely on quantitative methods has been shown. Qualitative research methods are valuable for studying how HIS intersect with healthcare providers and for providing answers to the how and why questions about HIS usage that quantitative methods cannot provide (Ash & Berg, 2003). Kaplan and Duchon (1998) conducted a joint qualitative-quantitative evaluation of a laboratory information system and advocate using mixed methods because qualitative-based interviews, observations, and open-ended questions revealed a number of significant human and contextual findings about the system that were not identified through a quantitative based survey.

Models also exist from the behavioral science and management information systems (MIS) disciplines and such models have been applied to HIS research. Examples of such models include the technology acceptance model (TAM) from the behavioral sciences and DeLone and McLean's information system (IS) success model from the MIS discipline. TAM purports that user behavior with technology is dependant on intention to use technology, which is derived from the attitude towards usage, perceived ease of use and perceived usefulness of the technology (Kukafka et al., 2003). In healthcare, Chismar and Wiley-Patton (2002) used TAM to study internet and information technology usage in pediatric care.

DeLone and McLean's IS success model, which was originally published in 1992 and revised in 2003, contains six concepts used to measure IS success (DeLone & McLean, 1992, 2003). The six concepts are system quality, information quality, service quality, user satisfaction, intention to use and net benefits. DeLone and McLean's IS model has been applied in healthcare for telehealth evaluation (Hebert, 2001).

How to Operationalize 'Fit'?

The previous section advocated the need for fit and sociotechnical based approaches for understanding the social, behavioral and human contexts of HIS usage but there is a gap between such approaches and the means of operationalizing them. Empirical details are needed about the elements that comprise fit in order to inform HIS design. As stated in the previous section there is no actual sociotechnical approach but rather it is a combination of methods, frameworks and theories to support an understanding of the social and technical aspects of HIS implementation. Further, fit was defined as a concept that needs to be actively produced in each unique healthcare setting as opposed to a cookbook approach that applies to multiple settings.

The need to embrace qualitative methods and interpretative approaches is critical to studying and understanding the context of how HIS are developed and used in specific clinical settings. However, a challenge lies in how to apply qualitative methods to understand and establish fit. Qualitative research methods, particularly interpretative studies, provide a wide range of opportunities to study and analyze healthcare settings. Combine that with the complexity and unstable nature of healthcare and it can be difficult to determine what factors to consider for establishing fit. The literature in the previous section identified a number of studies that provided multiple dimensions of fit and those dimensions are certainly not exhaustive of the dimensions of fit. It would enhance our ability to establish fit if there was a methodological approach to studying fit coupled with a framework for understanding fit of an HIS within a healthcare setting.

Models such as TAM and DeLone and McLean's IS success model have value for understanding HIS usage but there are two shortcomings to such models. First, much of the application of these models has been to evaluate HIS usage with less research being conducted to identify critical factors for HIS design. Outcome based studies often do not provide sufficient detail about the processes that lead to the outcomes. It would be more useful to open up the black box outcome concepts into specific variables that can be used to inform subsequent HIS design revisions. DeLone and McLean's IS success model uses information quality as one outcome measure but how do we define information quality with respect to HIS design? Second, models such as TAM and DeLone and McLean's IS success model are from the general IS domain and thus they are intended for use in multiple settings. Therefore there is the need to operationalize the models for use in healthcare settings. Concepts such as perceived usefulness from TAM or intent to use a system from DeLone and McLean's model are both very broad and need to be articulated in the context of healthcare delivery.

CASE STUDY

A case study will be used as the basis for the remainder of the chapter. The case study will introduce the domain of palliative care severe pain management (SPM) and the desire for a computer based SPM tool. It will then describe the research methods and data sources used in the study. The practice support concept and framework will be presented as a means of understanding 'fit' of a healthcare setting. An empirical example will then be illustrated of how practice support was used to design a computer based SPM tool.

Palliative care is care provided to patients with terminal illness when curative therapy is not an option. Palliative care has only been established as a formal discipline of medicine since the 1960s and is still an emerging field. However as our population ages and people live longer with chronic illnesses the need for palliative services will increase. A central aspect of palliative care is relief of symptoms, particularly pain. Severe pain is pain scored as 8, 9, or 10 on a 10 point numeric rating scale. When a patient reports severe pain they are saying they have the worst pain imaginable and thus prompt interventions are required. However, pain is a complex entity that has physical, psychosocial and spiritual dimensions and an episode of severe pain needs to be understood in the context of all of those dimensions. Further, using an inappropriate intervention for pain can cause undesirable side effects, which can actually make the pain worse.

To enhance our understanding of severe pain management (SPM) a group of palliative care providers developed a paper based severe pain tool called clinically applied pain information tool (CAPIT). CAPIT contains 11 categories that outline why a patient may report severe pain and each category contains a listing of signs, symptoms, interpretations and strategies for relief (Downing, 2006). CAPIT also contains a set of fundamental considerations to understand the unique aspects of pain for each individual including impact of disease trajectory and ethical and cultural elements of pain. The palliative care providers who developed the paper based CAPIT also wanted a computer-based SPM tool as they recognized that the paper based CAPIT was limited in functionality. The need for a comprehensive understanding of the SPM domain suitable for design of the computer based SPM tool was the motivation for this study.

A METHOD FOR UNDERSTANDING 'FIT'

Understanding fit requires a methodological approach to understanding the processes that take place in a healthcare setting, the users who conduct the processes and the information required to support those processes. A grounded theory-participatory design (GT-PD) hybrid approach was conceived for understanding the processes that take place in a healthcare setting and the information required to support those processes (Kuziemsky, 2007). The hybrid approach was chosen to provide a means of capturing user requirements through PD and then analyzing and developing theory from the user requirements through GT. The goal of PD is not only to design a product but rather to ensure the usability and utility of the product by engaging end users in design (Shrader, Williams, Lachance-Whitcomb et al., 2001).The extensive user involvement of PD allowed interaction between the palliative care providers to get different perspectives on how severe pain is managed and what support is needed in different situations to assist with SPM.

The data obtained through PD was coded using principles of GT in order to establish concepts and categories that became the practice support requirements. GT is a means of developing theory through coding of empirical data. The hallmark of GT is three coding cycles: open, axial and selective coding (Straus & Corbin, 1998). Open coding establishes concepts and categories from the data which are connected in axial coding based on similarities. Selective coding involves final refinement of the multiple concepts and categories that emerge from axial coding. The resulting analysis is both rich and concise as it emerges from multiple coding cycles.

The GT-PD approach draws out the strength of both methods. PD provides the means of user engagement to obtain a rich perspective on clinical practice and how HIS need to be designed to support such practice. GT develops concepts and categories from the data to develop empirically based understanding about the data. The GT-PD approach emphasizes the methodological approach of capturing and understanding both the content and context of the data that is being used.

Data Sources for Understanding Fit

Three data sources were used with the GT-PD approach to understand fit: practice experience, patient charts and research literature. Each is described below.

- **Practice experience:** Consists of two sources. First is 150 hours of meetings with 12 palliative care providers (three physicians, three nurses and three counselors) to discuss and model how severe pain gets managed. The second source is clinical observations where a researcher spent 40 hours doing qualitative observation and documentation of pain management on the clinical ward of a 17-bed inpatient hospice.
- **Patient charts:** A chart audit was done of 88 retrospective patient cases with at least one severe pain episode. Data collected included medical data (such as current and past disease), severe pain episode (such as onset, duration, location, quality) and interventions (both pharmacological and non-pharmacological).
- **Research literature:** A literature search was done on severe pain in palliative care as well as general pain management. 30 relevant pieces of literature brought in current evidence on severe pain management such as randomized controlled trials on medication, conceptual models on pain management and educational resources on assessment, diagnosis and management of different types of pain. The screening and identification of relevant literature was done by the palliative care providers.

The three data sources were used to provide different perspectives of fit from the view of different palliative care providers (physicians, nurses, and counselors) and also to allow cross validation of the data. It was possible to compare what providers described in meetings with what was observed in day to day practice on the clinical ward. Research literature was used to identify opportunities for incorporating literature into practice settings as a means of knowledge translation of research findings. Patient charts provided information on how patient cases are charted and communicated across different providers, and the vocabulary that is used in charting. Patient charts also provided a baseline for how data is currently charted and communicated around patient cases, which allows comparison with the level of data collection desired through practice experience meetings.

Practice Support

The practice support concept is based on the principle that a HIS is often designed to support a specific clinical task (i.e., decision support or physician order entry). However, in the context of clinical practice it stands to reason the task does not occur in isolation but rather it will interact with other processes both before and after its completion. A clinical decision support system (CDSS) can help establish a diagnosis but it will require patient data to be collected both before and after the diagnosis has been made. Further, once a CDSS helps establish a diagnosis there will usually be clinical tasks such as treatment and follow up care that need to be provided. Practice support also considers issues related to different contexts of HIS use such as levels of clinical expertise, needs of different types of healthcare providers (i.e., physician or nurse) and location of care delivery (i.e., acute care centre or community based care).

The practice support framework is the summation of the results of applying the GT-PD approach

to the three data sources to actively construct fit of the computer-based SPM tool. The data acquired through PD were used to develop concepts and codes through GT. As the coding became more refined and relationships were established between the codes a set of core codes were identified that became the practice support framework for HIS design. The practice support framework is not meant to be another model that explains the fit of healthcare providers and HIS usage, but rather it is meant to operationalize the use of theories such as fit and the sociotechnical approach by providing empirical approaches to those theories. Practice support also provides the means to operationalize some of the models described in the review section. The information quality concept in the DeLone and McLean IS success model is operationalized through the practice support framework by providing specific details on the different types of information support needed for HIS design.

HIS Practice Support Framework

Figure 1 shows the HIS practice support framework. The practice support framework has two sections to it, the domain specific healthcare delivery needs shown on the left side of figure 1 and the practice support requirements shown on the right side of Figure 1. The practice support requirements were categorized into two types: process and information support. The rationale for the two categories is that in order to provide practice support for healthcare providers we not only need to define the processes that are done, the information needed and the relationships between the processes and information. Identifying a process done as part of clinical practice (i.e., a diagnosis) without the necessary information to support that process (i.e., supporting and contrasting information to support different types of diagnoses) will not provide the necessary practice support for a given clinical task.

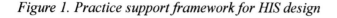

Figure 1. Practice support framework for HIS design

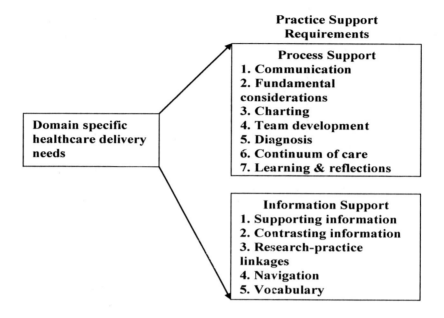

The process and information supports from the practice support framework are described in the following two sections.

Process Supports

Seven process supports were identified. The seven process supports are listed out in the following.

1. **Communication:** Effective communication needs to be promoted between all healthcare providers such as between physicians and nurses or between multiple nurses during shift change. Communication is also needed to support the ongoing care of a patient given that different providers may take part in patient care and care may take place in multiple settings.

2. **Fundamental considerations:** Cultural, social and ethical factors need be considered with respect to the patients receiving care as well as the healthcare providers and setting where a HIS is being used. Edwards and Roelofs (2006) showed that the domain of healthcare organizations, which included communication and monitoring and reporting mechanisms, varied across cultures and countries.

3. **Charting:** HIS need to ensure that all requisite data is charted about a patient case to facilitate other processes. Diagnoses, communication, team development and continuum of care all depend on requisite data being available.

4. **Team development:** As more patient care is provided from an interdisciplinary team perspective HIS will need to promote team development and team practices.

5. **Diagnosis:** Different types of diagnostic processes are used in healthcare and the different processes require different support. The identification of reasoning strategies used by clinicians may be critical to the optimal design of CDSS (Arocha, Wang, & Patel, 2005).

6. **Learning and reflections:** The level of expertise between users of an HIS will vary. Because of the ability of an HIS to store and retrieve information it can be used as a teaching tool for students and new staff

to learn about processes such as diagnosis or team development. HIS can also support reflective practice, which is how *individual* professionals address uncertain and non-routine, yet repetitive, problems in practice. Reflective practice has been described as a vehicle for learning by intertwining practice and theory (Schon, 1983).

7. **Continuum of care:** Healthcare delivery is not a one time occurrence and continuous communication and monitoring of patient cases are needed to support ongoing patient care. Once a patient has a diagnosis confirmed by a CDSS they may receive treatment or require diagnostic tests that will require follow-up.

The key aspect for each of the processes for practice support is to understand how the functionality of an HIS can implement the processes. Reflective practice is encouraged as a means of helping healthcare providers improve their practice. However, because reflective practice is removed from routine day to day clinical tasks such as charting and provision of medications, it is not something healthcare providers routinely think of doing. Using HIS to provide the means of doing reflective practice one computer screen away from the charting screen is a way of incorporating and encouraging reflective practice as part of routine practice.

Information Support

The second part of the practice support framework provides specific details on the types of information that can be structured in an HIS to support different elements of practice. The information support is broken down into five specific categories.

1. **Supporting information:** Supporting information provides a 'show me how' or 'help me do this' functionality. Waitman

and Miller (2004) emphasize that healthcare providers often take a 'show me' stance with respect to CDSS and therefore want both a recommended intervention and detailed steps involved in its implementation.

2. **Contrasting information:** Contrasting information is used to provide information to support diagnostic processes where more than one option exists. A patient may have signs or symptoms present in two or more disease conditions and contrasting information provides a 'show me why' functionality for differentiating the diagnostic options.

3. **Navigation:** As HIS get more complex and make available more information so must our ability to provide guidance for using such information. Part of the fit of information is navigation that provides the right information at the right time as well as ensuring that screens and interfaces have a flow that fits with the practice setting where the HIS is being used.

4. **Common vocabulary:** Part of interdisciplinary care is promoting common vocabulary between different health care providers. Healthcare providers all have their own vocabularies and if HIS are to facilitate interdisciplinary practices then the vocabulary must be acceptable to all providers.

5. **Research/practice linkages:** Because HIS have the ability to store and retrieve information they can be used to promote research-practice linkages as a means of knowledge translation.

APPLICATION OF THE PRACTICE SUPPORT FRAMEWORK TO PALLIATIVE SPM

A specific example of how the practice support framework was used to operationalize fit will be illustrated using the case example of the computer based SPM tool. The sections below illustrate how fit was established for each of the process and information supports from the practice support framework.

Charting and Communication Processes

While collecting the design requirements for the computer-based SPM tool the charting and communication processes were identified as crucial processes for nursing practice. The paper-based CAPIT is a comprehensive knowledge base of palliative SPM and acts as a reference about different etiologies of severe pain. However the paper based CAPIT is not specific to any patient. At the first practice experience meeting with nurses they very adamantly questioned how a computer-based SPM tool would help them if they had a patient in severe pain? Nurses felt the lack of specificity of the paper based CAPIT to a patient case takes away from its utility as nurses do a large amount of the patient charting. Nurses would be more likely to use the computer tool if it could be made specific for a patient by enabling a patient case to be charted. Nurses did not want to use a computer tool to view details about severe pain and then have to go to another application (either paper or computer-based) to chart the patient case. The computer-based SPM tool would provide practice support if they could view the information from the computer based tool and then develop and chart the patient's case directly in the computer based SPM tool.

Further emphasis of the importance of fit between the charting and communication processes was described as nurses stated that it is not uncommon for a patient to have more than one type of severe pain and each type will have its own clinical details such as signs and symptoms. However, the nurses also said that all requisite information about a patient case does not always get effectively communicated across different palliative care providers, which can adversely affect patient care. The charting component of

HIS design should not be just an afterthought as charting provides the data that feeds the communication processes around patient care. It is critical to understand the intricate details of patient cases to ensure appropriate charting is supported and to use reminders to ensure charting is actually completed.

Continuum of Care Process

Another process that was identified by physicians and nurses was continuum of care, which is the ability to support ongoing care for a patient. It was pointed out that palliative SPM is not a one time event and often takes place over hours, days, and even weeks. Further, many of the management strategies such as supporting counseling, screening for clinical depression or reduction of neuropathic pain can take days to complete and it is important that such strategies are followed up to monitor their effectiveness. The initial design of the computer tool was a 'one shot' process where a patient case was developed and not revisable unless all the data was reentered. However that 'one shot' functionality would not fit with the context of palliative practice given the ongoing nature of care. Once the computer tool is used to help assess, diagnosis, and recommend a management strategy for a patient's pain there will be follow up care that needs to be monitored. The ability to add progress notes to a previously developed case was devised as a solution to enable continuum of care to be supported.

Team Development Process

Another key process of SPM is team practices. Much of palliative care is done in the context of an interdisciplinary team consisting of two or more types of palliative care providers. Part of the team development process is ensuring that the vocabulary for information used in the computer based SPM tool is appropriate for the different types of healthcare providers (physicians, nurses, and counselors) that will be using the tool. Team development is more complex in instances where an interdisciplinary team is not co-located such as a remote area where there is only a family physician or homecare nurse. In such situations it is important that healthcare providers do not ignore the need to think from an interdisciplinary perspective. Therefore, practice support information resources should be made available to help a palliative care provider consider a team perspective when no team is available. One means of doing that is to have links to websites that offer both information resources about team functionality and in some cases real time interactions such as messaging with other healthcare providers to act as a virtual team. In essence the computer tool becomes the team when no team is available.

Diagnostic Process

In the practice support framework it was described that the fit of the diagnostic processes are important for acceptance of an HIS. The GT-PD approach was helpful for obtaining depth of detail about the diagnostic reasoning support needed in palliative SPM. One of the concepts in the paper based CAPIT is an 'interpretation.' When palliative care providers were queried as to what an interpretation consists of it was articulated that it is two types of diagnostic reasoning, a differential diagnosis and a provisional diagnosis. A provisional diagnosis is when a palliative care provider is relatively sure of the category of severe pain the patient is experiencing but they need some additional information to confirm the diagnosis. A differential diagnosis is when a sign or symptom is present in multiple categories of severe pain and the care provider needs help determining the correct category. Therefore provisional diagnostic reasoning needs to go top down, from an etiology to an explanation of signs and symptoms whereas differential diagnostic reasoning needs to go bottom up, from signs and symptoms to an etiology of severe pain. Those two types of diagnostic

reasoning also dictate how information support needs to be structured. Supporting information provides depth for drilling down about a concept (during a provisional diagnosis) whereas contrasting information provides breadth to support decision making across different options (during a differential diagnosis).

Learning and Reflection Process

Although the computer based SPM tool was designed to support specific aspects of palliative care (assessment, diagnosis, and management) during the GT-PD sessions palliative care providers described how some of the knowledge needed for SPM comes from general pain management and palliative care knowledge that is not contained in the paper based CAPIT. If a student or junior clinician is using the computer tool they may not have the background knowledge about pain or palliative care and thus would need access to educational resources. Supporting information about pain and palliative care needs to be made available.

Fundamental Consideration Process

One issue with designing a HIS is that it may be looked at as mitigating the human factor of patient care. To emphasize the importance of the human factor one practice support process is fundamental considerations. Fundamental considerations draw attention to factors such as the social and cultural issues of HIS usage. When the concept of the computer-based SPM tool was first discussed there was concern, particularly from the counseling staff, that the computer tool may slot a patient into a physical etiology of pain while ignoring the psychosocial dimensions of care. Palliative care is a branch of medicine that emphasizes all dimensions of care including physical, psychosocial, and spiritual dimensions and for a computer tool to be accepted in palliative practice it needs to represent all those dimensions. A number of specific fundamental considerations were derived that need to be considered as part of palliative care delivery. Those fundamental considerations include disease trajectory (i.e., how sick the patient is), cultural and ethnical aspects of care such as how pain perception and subsequent treatments may differ across cultures and ethnicities, and the context and meaning of both the illness and the severe pain based on the individual uniqueness of each patient. Alerts and checklists were devised as part of the computer tool to ensure the fundamental considerations are incorporated and charted as part of a patient's case.

Systems Design and Implementation of Computer-Based SPM Tool

Following the capture of all the requirements of fit for the computer-based SPM tool an architectural diagram was developed for the tool. The architectural diagram is based on the practice support requirements for SPM that were detailed in the previous section. Figure 2 shows the architectural diagram consisting of three sections: processes, functions and databases.

The information practice support requirements were used to design the database tables. The functionality of the computer-based SPM tool is achieved through the data query, data entry

and reminder functions. For example there are database tables to store supporting and contrasting information, which can retrieved through a data query. There are also database tables to store patient cases, which can be developed via data entry functions or retrieved and viewed through a data query function. During data entry there are reminders to ensure that requisite data is collected about a patient case and to ensure the fundamental considerations such as cultural elements of care are assessed and charted.

Figure 3 shows the physical implementation of the computer-based SPM tool. The processes and functions from the architectural diagram became the screens of the computer-based SPM tool to allow the entry and query of information. Figure 3 shows the data entry functionality that illustrates many of the practice support requirements that were described in the previous section. Figure 3 shows how specific patient cases can be entered including progress notes for continuum of care and checkboxes for completion of assessments on interdisciplinary teams and the fundamental considerations. There are 'info' buttons next to the interdisciplinary team and fundamental consideration checkboxes in case the palliative care provider needs supporting information about those concepts. Figure 3 also shows a reminder box pointing out that some requisite data has not

Figure 2. Architectural diagram of computer-based SPM tool

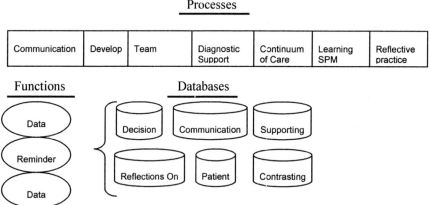

Figure 3. Screen shot of computer-based SPM tool

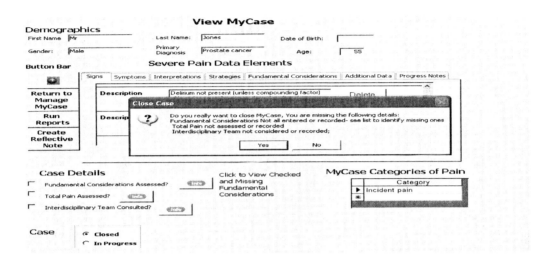

been charted, which was identified by palliative care providers as a requirement needed to support the communication process.

The other practice support requirements such as provisional and differential diagnostic support, the ability to engage in learning and reflective practice about palliative SPM and real time interdisciplinary team support are available through other screens of the computer-based SPM tool.

DISCUSSION

This chapter has presented a practice support framework and a methodological approach for establishing fit of a HIS. The practice support framework identified seven process supports and five information supports that should be considered as part of establishing fit of an HIS in a healthcare setting. The chapter also provided a case study illustrating how the practice support framework was used to operationalize fit in order to design a computer-based SPM tool.

The practice support framework is meant to extend existing theories and models by providing the means to operationalize them. Theories such as the sociotechnical approach or fit, and models such as the technology acceptance model are valu-

able for understanding fit of an HIS, but because clinical practice takes place at an empirical level we need the means of understanding the fit of a HIS in its practical usage. The practice support framework bridges the gap between theoretical and empirical by identifying specific process and information supports that need to be considered to actively produce fit of an HIS within a healthcare setting.

The practice support framework and other research on human and social issues described in this textbook have implications for students and systems designers of HIS. Education implications include illustrating the scope of practice support that is needed in an HIS as well as the need to educate healthcare providers to engage critically in the design of HIS. In the past, the design and implementation of HIS have often been portrayed as two different processes where design takes place in a laboratory and implementation takes place in a healthcare setting. Separating design and implementation leads to issues of weakened communication, lack of reflection and inability to track the continuum of care. Many of the practice support requirements in the case study were not part of the paper based CAPIT and were only identified after extensive engagement and in some cases criticism by the palliative care providers. It was the nurses' criticism of the lack of case specificity in the paper-based CAPIT that led to that function being designed for the computer-based SPM tool. Similarly it was the counselors fear that the computer-based SPM tool would dehumanize palliative practice that led to the development of specific fundamental considerations and reminders to ensure they are assessed and documented. If the paper-based CAPIT had been implemented as a computer-based SPM tool without the practice support enhancements such as enhanced charting and reminders it would have failed because of human and work practice issues.

System design implications include providing methodological guidance and a framework for engaging in qualitative and interpretative based HIS research. Although systems design is often taught using traditional approaches such as the system development lifecycle (SDLC) studies have shown that such approaches are problematic. Brender (1999) describes a paradox in systems development in that traditional approaches, such as the SDLC, do not consider that requirements change during the design process. The practice support framework and accompanying GT-PD approach provide a different perspective on HIS design through a qualitative based method for understanding the richness of detail of what practice support is needed for an HIS. Greater use of qualitative methods and interpretive research would help us understand the social, human, and work practice issues associated with designing and implementing HIS.

FUTURE RESEARCH DIRECTIONS

Despite the existing theories and models about 'Fit' and the findings presented in this chapter there is still much future research needed to help us understand and implement fit in different healthcare settings. Although this chapter described the importance of qualitative and interpretive research methods such methods are still under-

utilized in healthcare settings. Chiasson, Reddy, Kaplan, and Davidson (2007) point out that medical informatics as a field uses research methods that are primarily quantitative and experimental. This chapter emphasized that the sociotechnical approach has roots in different research methods and approaches including participatory design and computer supported collaborative work (Berg et al., 2003). Continued research is needed to explore methodological approaches to understand and implement perspectives of fit and the sociotechnical approach. Despite its utility for involving users in HIS design and for helping system designers to understand the users perspective there are few studies that empirically illustrate how to use methods such as participatory design in practice settings. Research is also needed to explore using hybrid methodologies such as the GT-PD approach presented in this chapter. Methods for qualitative analysis such as grounded theory or content analysis are a useful means of making sense of data to enable a comprehensive understanding of how technology and clinical practice intersect. Perhaps most importantly, further research is needed at developing the means of implementing concepts of fit, the sociotechnical approach and other user centered models into the HIS design phase. Relying on models to evaluate failure after the fact does not make full use of their potential. Fit and the sociotechnical approach need to do more than just describe how HIS are used. They must inform the design of the functionality of HIS including interfaces and data entry, retrieval, and decision support functionality.

CONCLUSION

Practice support encourages HIS designers, users and educators to think about the range of processes and information that form healthcare practice. Practice support includes traditional HIS functions such as decisions support and information management and it also encourages us to think about those functions in light of different practice settings, social norms and cultures of system use.

REFERENCES

Aarts, J., Doorewaard, H., & Berg, M. (2004). Understanding implementation: The case of a computerized physician order entry system in a large Dutch university medical center. *Journal of the American Medical Informatics Association, 11*, 207-216.

Anderson, J.G., Aydin, C.E., & Jay, S.J. (1994). *Evaluating health care information systems: methods and applications.* Thousand Oaks, CA: Sage Publications.

Arocha, J.F., Wang, D., & Patel, V.L. (2005) Identifying reasoning strategies in medical decision making: A methodological guide. *Journal of Biomedical Informatics, 38*, 154-171.

Ash, J., & Berg, M. (2003). Report of conference track 4: Sociotechnical issues of HIS. *International Journal of Medical Informatics, 69*, 305-306.

Aydin, C. (1994). Computerized order entry in a large medical center: evaluating interactions between departments. In J.G. Anderson, C.E. Aydin, & S.J. Jay (Eds.), *Evaluating health care information systems: Approaches and applications* (pp. 260-275). Thousand Oaks, CA: Sage.

Berg, M. (1999). Patient care information systems and health care work: A sociotechnical approach. *International Journal of Medical Informatics, 55*, 87-101.

Berg, M. (2003). The search for synergy: Interrelating medical work and patient care information systems. *Methods of Information in Medicine, 42*(4), 337-344.

Berg, M., Aarts, J., & Van der Lei, J. (2003). ICT in healthcare: Sociotechnical approaches. *Methods of Information in Medicine, 42*(4), 297-301.

Brender, J. (1999). Methodology for constructive assessment of IT-based systems in an organisational context. *International Journal of Medical Informatics, 56*, 67-86.

Chiasson, M., Reddy, M., Kaplan, B., & Davidson, E. (2007). Expanding multi-disciplinary approaches to healthcare information technologies: What does information systems offer medical informatics? *International Journal of Medical Informatics, 76*, (Supplement 1), S89-S97.

Chismar, W.G., & Wiley-Paton, S. (2002) Test of the technology acceptance model for the Internet in pediatrics. *Proc. AMIA Symp*, 155-159.

Coiera, E. (2003). Interaction design theory. *International Journal of Medical Informatics, 69*(2-3), 205-222.

DeLone, W.H., & McLean, E.R. (1992) Information systems success: The quest for the dependent variable, *Information Systems Research, 3*(1), 60-95.

DeLone, W.H., & McLean, E.R. (2003). The DeLone and McLean model of information systems success: A ten year update. *Journal of Management Information Systems, 19*(4), 9-30.

Downing, G. M. (Ed.). (2006). *Medical care of the dying* (4th ed.). Victoria Hospice Society Learning Centre for Palliative Care.

Edwards, N., & Roelofs, S. (2006). Developing management systems with cross-cultural fit: assessing international differences in operational systems. *International Journal Health Planning Management, 21*, 55-73.

Hebert, M. (2001). Telehealth success: Evaluation framework development. *Medinfo, 10*, 1145-1149.

Kaplan, B. (1988). Development and acceptance of medical information systems: An historical overview. *Journal of Health Human Resource Administration, 11*(1), 9-29.

Kaplan, B. (1995). Information technology and three studies of clinical work. *ACM SIGBIO Newsl, 15*(2), 2-5.

Kaplan, B. (2001). Evaluating informatics applications: Some alternative approaches: theory, social interactionism, and call for methodological pluralism. *International Journal of Medical Informatics, 64*, 39-56.

Kaplan, B., & Duchon, D. (1998). Combining qualitative and quantitative approaches in information systems research: A case study. *Management Information Systems, 12*(4), 571-586.

Kaplan, B., & Maxwell, J.A. (1994). Qualitative Research Methods for Evaluating Computer Information Systems. In J.G. Anderson, C.E. Aydin, & S.J. Jay (Eds.), *Evaluating health care information systems: Methods and applications* (pp. 45-68). Thousand Oaks, CA: Sage.

Kukafka, R., Johnson, SB., Linfante, A., & Allegrante, J. P. (2003). Grounding a new information technology implementation framework in behavioral science: A systematic analysis of the literature on IT use. *Journal of Biomedical Informatics, 36*, 218-227.

Kuziemsky, C.E. (2007). A grounded theory-participatory design approach for capturing user requirements for health information systems design. *Proceedings of Information Technology and Communications in Health (ITCH) 2007.*

Massaro, T.A. (1993). Introducing physician order entry at a major academic medical center: 1. Impact on organizational culture and behavior. *Academic Medicine, 68*(1), 20-25.

Patel, V.L., Allen, V.G., Arocha, J.F., & Shortliffe, E.H. (1998). Representing clinical guidelines in GLIF: individual and collaborative expertise. *Journal of the American Medical Informatics Association, 5*(5), 467-483.

Pratt, W., Reddy, M.C., McDonald, D.W., Tarczy-Hornoch, P., & Gennari, J. W. (2004). Incorporating ideas from computer support collaborative work. *Journal of Biomedical Informatics, 37,* 128-137.

Safran, C., Jones, P. C., Rind, D., Bush, B., Cytryn, K. N., & Patel, V. L. (1998). Electronic communication and collaboration in a health care practice. *Artificial Intelligence in Medicine, 12*(2), 137-151.

Schon, D. (1983). *The reflective practioner: How professionals think in action.* New York: Basic Books.

Shrader, G., Williams, K., Lachance-Whitcombe, J., Finn, L.-E., & Gomez, L. (2001). Participatory design of science curricula: The case for research for practice. Paper presented at the annual meeting of the American Educational Research Association, Seattle, WA.

Sicotte, C., Denis, J.L., & Lehoux, P. (1998). The computer based patient record: A strategic issue in process innovation. *Journal of Medical Systems, 22*(6), 431-443.

Southan, F.C.G., Sauer, C., & Dampney, C.M.G. (1997). Information technology in complex health services: Organizational impediments to successful technology transfer and diffusion. *Journal of the American Medical Informatics Associatio, 4,* 112-124.

Strauss, A., & Corbin, J. (1994). Grounded Theory Methodology: An Overview. In N.K. Denzin & Y.S. Lincoln (Eds.), *Handbook of qualitative research* (pp. 273-285). Thousand Oaks: Sage.

Waitman, L.R., & Miller, R.A. (2004). Pragmatics of implementing guidelines on the front lines. *Journal of the American Medical Informatics Association, 11*(5), 436-438.

Walsham, G. (1993). *Interpreting information systems in organizations.* Chichester: Wiley.

ADDITIONAL READINGS

Ash, J.S., Sittig, D.F., Seshadri, V., Dykstra, R.H., Carpenter, J.D., & Stavri, P.Z. (2005). Adding insight: A qualitative cross-site study of physician order entry. *International Journal of Medical Informatics, 74*(7-8), 623-628.

Ash, J.S., Berg M., & Coiera E. (2004). Some unintended consequences of information technology in health care: The nature of patient care information system-related errors. *Journal of the American Medical Informatics Association, 11*(2), 104-112.

Davidson, E. (2006). A technological frames perspective on information technology and organizational change. *The Journal of Applied Behavioral Science, 42*(1), 23-39.

Heeks, R. (2006). Health information systems: Failure, success and improvisation. *International Journal of Medical Informatics, 75,* 125-137.

Balka, E., Kahnamoui, N., & Nutland, K. (2007). Who is in charge of patient safety? Work practice, work processes and utopian views of automatic drug dispensing systems. *International Journal of Medical Informatics, 76*(Supplement 1), S48-S57.

Campbell, E.M., Sittig, D.F., Ash, J.S., Guappone, K.P., & Dykstra, R.H. (2006). Types of unintended consequences related to computerized provider order entry. *Journal of the American Medical Informatics Association, 13,* 547-556.

Chiasson, M.W., & Davidson, E. (2004). Pushing the contextual envelope: Developing and diffusing IS theory for health information systems research. *Information and Organization, 14,* 155-188.

Coeira, E. (2007). Putting the technical back into socio-technical systems research. *International Journal of Medical Informatics, 76S,* S98-S103.

Effken, J.A. (2002). Different lenses, improved outcomes: a new approach to the analysis and design of healthcare information systems. *International Journal of Medical Informatics, 65,* 59-74.

Goulding, C. (1998). Grounded theory: The missing methodology on the interpretivist agenda. *Qualitative Market Research: An International Journal, 1*(1), 50-57.

Harteloh, P.P.M. (2003). Quality systems in health care: A sociotechnical approach. *Health Policy, 64*(3), 391-398.

Hartswood, M.J., Procter, R.N., Rouchy, P., Rouncefield, M., Slack, R., & Voss, A. (2003). Working IT out in medical practice: IT systems design and development as co-realisation. *Methods of Information in Medicine, 42,* 392-397.

Johnson, C.M., Johnson, T.R., & Zhang, J. (2005). A user-centered framework for redesigning health care interfaces. *J Biomed Inform, 38,* 75-87.

Klein, H.K., & Myers, M.D. (1999). A set of principles for conducting and evaluating interpretive field studies in information systems. *MIS Quarterly, 23*(1), 67-93.

Kuziemsky, C.E., Downing, G.M., Black, F.M., & Lau, F. (2007). A grounded theory guided approach to palliative care systems design. *International Journal of Medical Informatics, 76S,* S141-S148.

Lamb, R., & Kling, R. (2003). Reconceptualizing users as social actors in information systems research. *MIS Quarterly, 27*(2), 197-235.

Lenz, R., & Kuhn, K.A. (2004). Towards a continuous evolution and adaptation of information systems in healthcare. *International Journal of Medical Informatics, 73*(1), 75-89.

Lorenzi, N.M., & Riley, R.T. (2003). Organizational issues = change. *International Journal of Medical Informatics, 69,* 197-203.

Luna-Reyes, L.F., Zhang, J., Gil-Garcia, J.R., & Cresswell, A.M. (2005). Information systems development as emergent socio-technical change: A practice approach. *European Journal of Information Systems, 14*(1), 93-105.

McDonald, C.J., Overhage, J.M., Mamlin, B.W., Dexter, P.D., & Tierney, W.M. (2004). Physicians, information technology, and health care systems: A journey, not a destination. *Journal of the American Medical Informatics Association, 11*(2), 121-124.

Mingers, J. (2001) Combining IS research methods: Towards a pluralist methodology. *Information Systems Research, 12*(3), 240-259.

Nykanen, P., & Karimaa, E. (2006). Success and failure factors in the regional health information system design process. *Methods of Information in Medicine, 45*, 85-89.

Reddy, M., Pratt, W. P., Dourish, P., & Shabot, M.M. (2003) Sociotechnical requirements analysis for clinical systems. *Methods Information in Medicine, 42*, 437-44.

Rose, A.F., Schnipper, J., Park, E., Poon, E.G., Li, Q., & Middleton, B. (2005). Using qualitative studies to improve the usability of an EMR. *Journal of Biomedical Informatics, 38*, 51-60.

Stockdale, R., & Standing, C. (2006). An interpretive approach to evaluating information systems: A content, context, process framework. *European Journal of Operational Research, 173*, 1090-1102.

Samaras, G.M., & Horst, R.L. (2005). A systems engineering perspective on the human-centered design of health information systems. *Journal of Biomedical Informatics, 38*, 61-74.

Sjoberg, C., & Timpka, T. (1998). Participatory design of information systems in health care. *Journal of the American Medical Informatics Association, 5*(2), 177-183.

Zhang, J.J. (2005). Human-centered computing in health information systems Part 1: Analysis and design. *Journal of Biomedical Informatics, 38*(1), 1-3.

Zhang, J.J. (2005). Human-centered computing in health information systems Part 2: Evaluation. *Journal of Biomedical Informatics, 38*(3), 173-175.

Chapter IV
Towards Computer Supported Clinical Activity:
A Roadmap Based on Empirical Knowledge and some Theoretical Reflections

Christian Nøhr
Aalborg University, Denmark

Niels Boye
Aalborg University, Denmark

ABSTRACT

The introduction of electronic health records (EHRs) to the clinical setting has led healthcare professionals, policy makers, and administrators to believe that health information systems will improve the functioning of the healthcare system. In general, such expectations of health information system functionality, impact, and ability to disseminate have not been met. In this chapter the authors present the findings of three empirical studies: (1) the structured monitoring of EHR implementation processes in Denmark from 1999–2006 by the Danish EHR observatory, (2) a usability study based on human factors engineering concepts with clinicians in artificial but realistic circumstances—a "state of the art (2005)" for Danish CPOE (computerized physician order entry system), and (3) user reactions to a conceptual "high level model" of healthcare activities—the Danish G-EPJ model in order to better understand the reasons for health information system failures and to suggest methods of improving adoption. The authors suggest that knowledge handling as a science seems immature and is not in line with the nature of clinical work. The prerequisites for mature knowledge handling are discussed in the second part of this chapter. More specifically, the authors describe one way of improving knowledge handling: the development of a more true digital representation of the object of interest (OOI) or the virtual patient/citizen that interacts with computer based healthcare services on behalf of and for the benefit of the citizen's health.

Copyright © 2008, IGI Global, distributing in print or electronic forms without written permission of IGI Global is prohibited.

INTRODUCTION

In 1968, the Danish journal of engineering science "Ingeniøren" published an article about a hospital-based computer system. The article described a computer system that was being used to support administrative and clinical tasks at the largest hospital in Denmark "Rigshospitalet." The article provided the reader with a picture of a desk with a computer terminal and a telephone. The text under the picture read: *"This is how the doctor's desk will look in a few years: No paper, the patient's record will be retrieved on the computer screen within fractions of a second"* (see Figure 1) (Jda, 1968). Almost 40 years later we are able to retrieve patient data, but not the entire record, and the predicted response time suggested in the article remains wishful thinking. The Danish example is not an exception. International studies report that up to 75 percent of all large IT projects in healthcare fail (Littlejohns, Wyatt, & Garvican, 2003), and according to Michael Rigby, evaluation is still a "Cinderella science" where information and communication technology (ICT) is concerned (Rigby, 2001).

A commonly held notion among the international electronic health record (EHR) community is that the failure of numerous IT projects is due to instances of bad programming and poor implementation that can be easily avoided the next time around (Wears & Berg, 2005). Results from a number of studies in Denmark, which the authors have been involved in, indicate that the difficulties associated with implementing ICTs in healthcare or health information systems (HIS) can be traced back to the perspectives and theories that computer scientists and systems developers hold about medical work and how these theories influence HIS development and implementation processes.

In this chapter the authors will present the results from a number of Danish studies involving a group of ICTs (i.e., HIS). The studies do not evaluate the promised benefits of HIS in terms of their outcomes. Instead, they focus on the practical use of HISs in clinical work situations. Based on our cross-study experiences, the authors then examine the future merits of information technology (IT) from a clinical point of view. Prior to beginning our discussion, they will first provide some background information about the Danish healthcare system to provide the context for our research work.

Figure 1. Perception of how a doctor's office would look from 1968

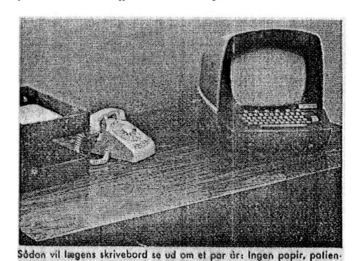

Sådan vil lægens skrivebord se ud om et par år: Ingen papir, patientens journal hentes frem på dataskærm i løbet af brøkdele af et sekund.

BACKGROUND

In the Danish healthcare system, policy making is the responsibility of the Ministry of Health and Prevention. Decision making involving healthcare system functioning is a county level activity. Until January 1, 2007 Denmark had 14 counties which now are merged into five regions that are responsible for healthcare system decision making. Health coverage is public and is tax-financed. Overall health expenditures in Denmark are 9.2% of gross national product (GNP) (in 2004) (USA 15.3%) (Source: OECD health data). Currently, health coverage is provided to approximately 4.2 million people for the price of 200 € a month per citizen. Dental services, physiotherapy and some pharmaceutical costs are not covered. These costs average 50 € a month (250 € ≈350 US$). Citizens can also obtain additional health coverage from private insurance companies in order to obtain faster access to treatments in private clinics. Private insurers provide faster access to treatment in private clinics. Alternatively, the private sector provides only a relatively small number of hospital beds (i.e., 1-2%) to the citizens of Denmark.

EMPIRICAL STUDIES

The empirical studies that are presented in this chapter include the following:

1. The EHR-Observatory study in which the authors monitored the EHR implementation process in Denmark over a six year period.
2. A usability study involving a medication module.
3. A study of users' reactions to common conceptual domain models for Danish EHRs (GEPJ).

THE EHR-OBSERVATORY: SIX YEARS OF MONITORING THE IMPLEMENTATION PROCESS OF EHRS IN DENMARK

Since 1996 a national strategy has guided Danish EHR-projects in the development and implementation of EHRs (Danish Ministry of Health, 1996). Denmark's national EHR strategy has been revised a number of times. The 1999 version of the strategy initiated the formation of an independent monitoring group, "the EHR-Observatory," with participants drawn from research institutions: Aalborg University, Danish Institute for Health Services (until 2001), Center for Health Telematics (until 2003) and a consultancy company "MEDIQ" (Danish Ministry of Health, 1999).

The purpose of the EHR-Observatory is support the advancement of Denmark's national HIS strategy by monitoring and assessing the development, implementation and application of EHR systems in Danish hospitals. Since 1999, the Observatory has collected data on various aspects of national EHR work including the following:

1. Implementation and dissemination issues:
   - Diffusion and diffusion rates of EHR systems.
   - Experience gained among the different stakeholders.
   - Factors that increase diffusion and use of EHR-systems.

2. Issues related to a common frame of reference for EHR systems:
   - Differences and compatibilities between regional data models.
   - Communication consequences of using incompatible data models.
   - Institutional demands for a common frame of reference.

In Denmark, it is the responsibility of the Ministry of Health, through the Danish National Board, to issue guidelines and common standards for EHRs. The Ministry of Health also publishes national strategies and revises the Danish national strategy every two to four years. The Danish National Board of Health houses an office for clinical information systems use and implementation that offers advice to county (regional) administrations about EHRs. Over the past five years, the Ministry of Health has worked on the development of a common conceptual domain model for Danish EHRs, which is expected to be implemented in Denmark in the next few years. County administrations are the "owners" of public hospitals, and have the political and administrative responsibility for running hospitals in Denmark. The implementation and financing of EHRs is the responsibility of the counties.

The EHR-Observatory has sent survey questionnaires each year for the last five years (i.e., 2001-2006) to each of the county administrations (n = 15) in order to monitor EHR work. The results of these surveys are reported annually (in Danish) (Andersen, Nøhr, Vingtoft, et al., 2002; Bernstein, Rasmussen, Nøhr et al., 2001, 2006; Bruun-Rasmussen, Bernstein, Vingtoft et al., 2003; Nøhr, Andersen, Vingtoft et al., 2004; Vingtoft, Bruun).

Rasmussen, Bernstein et al., 2005). Survey questionnaires are sent to county administrations electronically in April of each year (one electronic reminder is provided in addition to the original electronic invitation to participate). Response rates have been close to optimal (see Table 1).

The questionnaire itself consists of a kernel of 12 questions. Survey questions address general aspects of EHR strategy, diffusion, economy, benefits, and barriers. These questions have remained the same throughout the 6 year period during which survey has been conducted. The survey questionnaire also asks a number of detailed questions that focus on specific topic areas.

Table 1. Response rate

Year	Responses	Response rate
2001	12	80,0%
2002	15	100,0%
2003	14	93,3%
2004	15	100,0%
2005	14	93,3%
2006	15	100,0%

These questions vary from year-to-year and have specific themes.

There are several survey questions that focus on diffusion. Diffusion questions ask county administrations about the number of beds in their hospitals and the number of people covered by their EHR system (i.e., clinical documentation and medication). Furthermore, counties are asked to provide information about the number of beds that they are planning to cover with the EHR in the upcoming three years (these questions were not asked in 2001 as the counties were asked for the amount of beds covered at that point in time).

Data from the survey on actual and expected national EHR diffusion appears in Figure 2. The data clearly shows that the number of beds covered by an EHR system is steadily increasing and will continue to increase over the next few years, but that expectations show a systematic overestimation of expected EHR bed coverage by county administrators.

County estimates for the year immediately following the survey are reasonably accurate—counties overestimate by only a few per cent. Alternatively, county estimates about EHR coverage become more optimistic with projections into the future. This finding is consistent with optimistic EHR policies at the national level. Such a tendency to be optimistic about EHR implementation or coverage is also present internationally. In a publicly financed healthcare system, to a large extent controlled by politics, there will always

Figure 2. Actual and expected national EHR diffusion

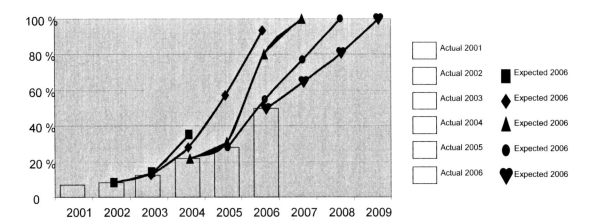

be a tendency to adhere to policy goals, even if they seem unrealistic.

The hospital administrators were also asked what they perceived as barriers to implementing EHRs. The responses to these questions are shown in Figure 3. (Each respondent could choose three barriers).

The 2001-2006 data suggest there are no trends in terms of perceived barriers to EHR implementation. It must be noted that county administrations have not systematically surveyed for EHR barriers. However, the belief among county administrators is that users are resisting change and this resistance has increased significantly over the last three years (see Figure 3). Unfortunately, the questionnaire does not explore this finding further.

County administrators identify that poor integration and missing or lack of EHR standards are the second largest barriers to EHR implementation (as illustrated in Figure 3). The issue of lack of EHR standards must be understood in terms of the local, Danish context. The National Board of Health and The Ministry of the Interior and Health have not subscribed to any international EHR standards, for example, HL7. Instead, the government's strategy has been to develop a national, basic EHR structure (GEPJ) for all the counties to follow (briefly mentioned in the

introduction to this section as the Danish common conceptual model, and further explained in Figure 4). This policy has given rise to widespread discussions about the relevance and robustness of developing a basic EHR structure independent to international standards such as HL7.

Poor EHR integration has also emerged as an issue. Poor EHR integration is linked to missing or a lack of EHR standards. For example, a single sign-on as a standard EHR implementation principle is absent in systems that have been implemented.[1] The absence of a single sign on has created a number of practical problems for local IT departments. It has also fueled users' dissatisfaction with the EHR. Anecdotal user reports suggest clinical staff are spending up to 20 minutes of every morning logging or "signing on" to various HIS and applications they plan to use to do their work during the course of a typical day.

The questionnaire also asks hospital administrators about how they evaluated their EHR implementations and what specific variables were measured as part of those evaluations. The majority of county administrations stated they evaluated their HIS implementations, but when asked about how they evaluated their implementations. Answers were remarkably unclear, leaving researchers with the impression that evaluation is

Figure 3. Barriers to implementing EHR in Danish hospitals in percent of the total responses

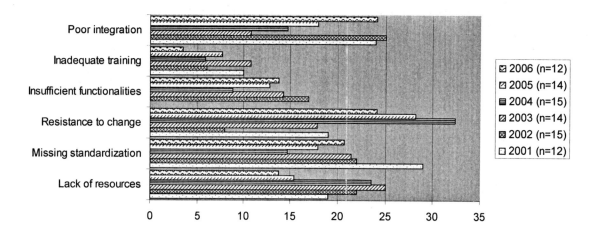

a "want-to-do issue." For example, one of the chief information officers (CIO) in a county replied that the hospital was undertaking continuous formative evaluation. The hospital had built in continuous formative evaluation into their internal meetings, as a standing point in their meeting agendas (i.e., meeting participants were asked to report on EHR developments since their last meeting).

The EHR-Observatory is a monitoring project. It does not perform any evaluation of local EHR progress. The consequence is that EHR evaluation at the county level is not possible and therefore there is little data available that could possibly be used to fully understand the possible reasons for continuous delays in EHR implementation plans and the constant tendency to be overly optimistic in terms of county ability to implement EHRs. The EHR-Observatory has only been able to establish the fact that there are delays in EHR implementations, overly optimistic beliefs about county capacity to implement EHRs, and the presence of barriers in the form of user resistance to change and poor integration of HIS systems.

A USABILITY STUDY OF A CPOE MODULE

Some of the reasons for user dissatisfaction could be explained by usability issues. However, most usability tests performed in traditional usability laboratories do not adequately replicate the complexities associated with HIS use in the clinical setting. Also, due to ethical issues traditional field studies cannot be carried out in the clinical setting. The study outlined in the following describes the advantages associated with using a combination of a traditional laboratory and field study approach. In the usability study we undertook, we retained a large degree control over the setting while at the same time creating a realistic, rich, clinical situation and context (Lilholt et al., 2006). The components of the study include: "think aloud," video recording, screen capturing, and debriefing. These study components were selected because they provided the authors with experimental data that could be triangulated to validate the results.

Study Materials and Methods

The usability studied employed "think aloud." The *think aloud* method is a simple method of collecting the users' immediate thoughts and reflections throughout a test. The user simply verbalizes his thoughts and reflections while using the system. The think aloud method was considered vital for later data analysis. *Video recording* of the contextual work situation as well as *screen capture* of the computerized physician order entry (CPOE) system[2] under study was used as a method for collecting data from the test. These recordings are essential as they provide documentation of the occurrence of usability problems during the test. Directly after the test, a *debriefing* with the user was conducted, to obtain additional information about the test. Since the main objective of the study was to evaluate usability using a number of methods and not to conduct a full usability evaluation, only two CPOE, experienced physicians participated as users. A scenario was scripted based on an authentic, complex patient trajectory to ensure the use of a wide range of functionalities of the CPOE system. The scenario consisted of a 39-year-old female patient suffering from cancer, admitted to a long-term medical treatment. The case involved several health professional stakeholders and multiple drug prescriptions. In the evaluation laboratory, Skej-Lab, at the Aarhus University Hospital, Skejby Sygehus, a hospital ward was simulated (i.e., hospital room and office). The hospital room consisted of a bed, table, chair, and medicine chest and various other accessories. In addition to the hospital room, an office was set up with a computer from which the user could access the CPOE system.

An actress played the role of the patient, partly due to ethical issues, but also to secure a consistent patient simulation for each test. Since the test facility was physically located at the hospital, it was possible to use a normal production IT-system instead of a test version of a prototype. This contributed to the realism of the test exposing the user to such authentic EHR system attributes as system response time. After the usability test, the video and screen recordings were analyzed and log files were prepared. These log files were then analyzed with the purpose of identifying usability problems. The data analysis of the log files identified a number of usability problems. These were classified according to Molich's rating scale for classifying the severity of a usability problem

Table 2. The classification scheme, the number of occurrences of a problem and in brackets the number of work functions where the problem occurred

	Response time	GUI Design	Functionality	Procedure	Error Message
Cosmetic	Response time of a few seconds and/or it occurs often. 1 (1)	The GUI design annoys or does not help the user. The user does not make any failure and/or is aware of which failure it can bring. 6 (3)	The functionality causes temporary problems but it is possible to perform the function, taking a few seconds extra. 3 (2)	The system gives rise to a complicated procedure taking extra time from the user. 3 (1)	The error message does not misinform the user, but is not specific enough and causes a few seconds delay. 2 (2)
Severe	Response time of several seconds and/or it occurs often.	The GUI design annoys or does not help the user. The user makes a failure but identifies it.	The functionality is difficult to carry out, taking several seconds extra. The user makes a failure. 2 (2)	The system gives rise to an incorrect procedure. 2 (1)	The error message misinform the user, resulting in several seconds delay. 2(2)
Critical	Response time of more than one or several i minutes and it occurs often 8 (3)	The GUI design annoys or does not help the user. The user makes a failure and does not identify it. 1 (1)	The functionality is not possible to perform or a system crash occurs. 3 (1)	The system gives rise to an incorrect and critical procedure.	The error message misinform the user, resulting in several minutes delay.

using the following categories: cosmetic, severe, and critical (Molich, 2000).

Inspired by Skov and Stage (Skov & Stage, 2005) a diagram to assist with the quantification of usability problems according to Molich's rating scale was developed using an iterative process. The diagram shown in Table 2 is not generic, but specifically targeted at usability problems associated with the CPOE system.

An example of a serious problem regarding response time is the following: the time it takes to right click on a medication in a medication order list to the appearance of an ordering window that allows for medication prescribing takes anywhere from nine to 20 seconds to occur. This is a very frequently used function of CPOE. The wait time associated with this functionality creates a lot of user annoyance; hence it is classified as critical. The following is an example of a serious problem in graphical user interface (GUI) design: The user chose the wrong route of medication administration when ordering the drug "Fragmin" (Dalteparin, a low molecular weight heparin-analogue that almost exclusively is administered subcutaneously), because the default dosage in the system was not standard. The following is an example of a cosmetic functionality problem: The user finds it annoying that they must discontinue a drug and then order it again just to change the dosage.

During usability testing, one of the central servers went down. Several error messages appeared during the study on the users screen. When the database server controlling the drug database went down the user received an error message: "Error when accessing information about the drug." When the user clicked the "OK" button in the error window a new window popped up with the text: "No drug has been chosen." The two error messages appeared because there was a system error in a central computer. The user believed he had forgotten to choose a drug. As a result, he repeated the sequence several times. This was classified as a serious error because the user was delayed in their work by close to a minute. The

authors believe these usability problems arose because of the authenticity of the scenario (i.e., the usability testing was performed on a production system, instead of a test version of a prototype). The authors argue that the problems discussed above occurred because of limited developer insight into clinical reasoning and practice.

USERS' REACTIONS TO THE COMMON CONCEPTUAL DOMAIN MODEL FOR DANISH EHRS (GEPJ)

To comply with the objectives of the National Strategy for IT in Health Care, the Office for Clinical Information Systems Use and Implementation of the National Board of Health developed a Common Conceptual Domain Model for Danish EHR systems or GEPJ. The common conceptual domain model (GEPJ) will be implemented in the years to come in Denmark. Currently, GEPJ is present in version 2.2. It specifies the structure, relation, and formalization of data necessary to create a coherent clinical documentation system. GEPJ is a model that is: problem oriented, focuses on the patient, is used by differing health professionals, and promotes the interdisciplinary use of the EHR. GEPJ does not specify patient record composition, but rather it specifies the documentation process and the relation between patient information and the EHR system (Sundhedsstyrelsen (SeSI), 2005).

In GEPJ, clinical processes consist of four main processes: diagnostic considerations, planning, execution, and evaluation. The model is outlined in Figure 4. The circles represent processes in the model. Processes in the model lead to the creation of information elements (see the boxes between the circles in Figure 4). The information elements produce documentation elements, as illustrated by four text boxes in the corners of the Figure. The four clinical processes are outlined in greater detail:

Diagnostic Consideration

During the diagnostic consideration process the healthcare provider collects information about the patient's health condition in order to develop an understanding of the patient's health state. This process involves learning about the patient's expression of health and disease and evaluating all possible relationships between the patient and his or her health conditions. During the diagnostic consideration process, the health professional must document the patient's health condition and information associated with the health condition when using the EHR. The diagnostic considerations may also be further elaborated upon in a diagnostic note. The following documentation elements exist in GEPJ: focused information, applied guidelines, complicating healthcare activities, external causes, and diagnostic notes.

Planning of the Intervention

In the planning of the intervention process, the provider plans relevant healthcare activities for the patient. This includes the definition of specific plans for care, treatments, observations, diagnostic tests, and so forth. Simultaneously, the healthcare provider plans and sets out operational objectives and expresses these plans as expected outcome for the patient. Planning considerations can be further documented in a planning note. The following documentation elements exist in the planning of the intervention: healthcare objective, indication, applied guideline, and planning note.

Execution

In the execution process the health provider implements the plan. This activity should improve the patient's condition or produce new knowledge about the patient's health condition. The outcome is the result of the intervention. The outcomes should be clear, state exactly what has been done, for how long, by whom and what the exact result is. The following documentation elements exist for the process of execution: executed activity, applied guidelines, and execution note.

Figure 4. GEPJ model

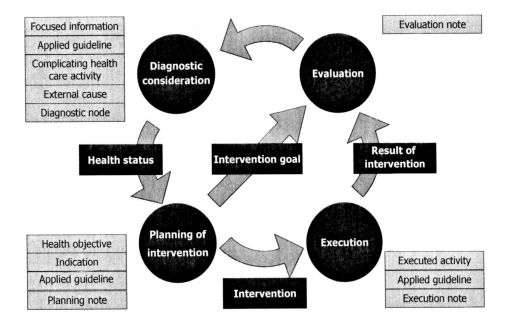

Evaluation

In the evaluation process the healthcare provider compares the expected and obtained results of the execution. Here, the healthcare provider evaluates whether the achieved outcome is acceptable. This process involves two sub-processes: comparison and new diagnostic considerations. The result of the evaluation can be used as focused information for documenting about a new health condition. The following documentation elements exist for evaluation: evaluation note.

Two prototype GEPJ based documentation systems were built for evaluation purposes. The systems were implemented in two different departments: a geriatric department at Amager Hospital in Copenhagen, and a department for internal medicine at Århus University Hospital. The process of building systems that were useful during daily, clinical routines turned out to be more complicated than expected (Vingtoft, 2004). The prototype systems never achieved an adequate level of practical, daily or routine use by healthcare providers. Hence, it was impossible to obtain data of an adequate quality to draw any significant conclusion. It was impossible to determine whether user statements about the prototype system were about its underlying domain model or the immature interface.

However, users made a number of significant, positive statements about the prototype when straightforward and uncomplicated cases were considered (i.e., cases where patients were suffering from trivial or well known problems). In contrast, users made more negative statements about the EHR when the situations or cases they had to deal with were complicated (i.e., patients with multiple diagnoses, or rare diseases).

The GEPJ model was intended to be used as a documentation model—a model that ensures coherence in the data gathered, by structuring the work procedures associated with health provider documentation (mainly doctors and nurses). However, when applied to health provider documentation practices associated with clinical work, the model heavily influenced work practices. Health providers found the model restrictive.

The core of the model promotes a hypothetical-deductive thinking process, which is quite common in scientific research, quality assurance, clinical work, and so forth. Hence, the model was easily recognized and understood by most clinicians. However, not all clinical work is performed using a hypothetical deductive thinking approach. Therefore, the authors will discuss the model in terms of computer-assisted clinical work and present some theoretical reflections on the model.

HUMAN CLINICAL REASONING: USING KNOWLEDGE IN AN INCONGRUENT CONTEXT

Biomedical research or the root of medical knowledge arises from the fields of applied biochemistry, genetics, physics, and mathematics (mathematics is also the "mother" of computer science). This means that ontologies and models in medicine are built upon concepts that arise from the domain of the natural sciences. During the provision of healthcare, health knowledge is applied or activated for the benefit of the individual patient. During this activation process, knowledge rooted in the human science domain is used by healthcare providers. In the human sciences scales are not as exact as those used in the domain of the natural sciences. The process of selecting and activating applied natural science knowledge in the human science domain is individual in nature and is probably the most unique and abstract feature of medical practice as compared to work in other domains. The foundations of clinical decision making are tangible and measurable, but they do not easily transform into proper or individualized health related decisions. Therefore clinical decisions are difficult to formalize using a digital system.

The patient record documents a patient's subjective and measurable problems, the signs and symptoms of their disease, and the procedures undertaken to alleviate the patient's health problems. The patient record may also contain patient specific considerations. Patient specific considerations appear as text in EHRs. The authors are not aware of any EHR research that has documented the EHRs ability to adequately formalize or extend clinical decision making. The EHRs inability to adequately formalize or extend clinical decision making may arise from the shared "genes" of bio-medical knowledge and computer-science, the historic reasons for record content (i.e., an indirect way of representing the subject/object of care), and a lack of a genuine formalization for clinical decisions. Overall, it makes the EHR a poor surrogate for the patient in a digital universe. The object of work, object of interest (OOI) or the patient is not truly represented in an operational manner in a clinical computer system. Therefore, case consideration is more easily undertaken using computer systems in other business domains than medicine (i.e., "an entry in the record is not a cure").

If one accepts the argument that "one is not cured by entries into medical records," how does one proceed towards real computer-supported clinical activity (CSCA)" while taking into account the dualistic nature of the natural and humanistic properties of clinical work? "Activity," instead of "work," occurs in the acronym CSCA for two reasons: (1) the acronym CSCW stands for computer-supported co-operative work (actually also an issue in clinical computer supported medicine), and (2) "activity" implies that professionals, patients, and relatives could benefit from computer support in care, self-care, and the care of their loved ones.

REPRESENTING OBJECTS OF INTEREST (OOI) IN THE COMPUTER SYSTEM

Every computer program has: (1) a primary mission (e.g., recoding or supporting clinical activity), (2) a conceptual model to represent the domain of interest (roles, organization and activities), and (3) models of the objects of interest. These three abstract components should fit with the reality (of clinical work), and together they should determine what a human operator can achieve using the software. "Killer applications" developed in the areas such as finance, airline booking, construction, architecture, and so forth can be characterized as having an evident fit between the three abstract components outlined above and therefore an ability to "do the job." Rich and adequate representations of objects of interest (e.g., money, passengers and seats, piping systems, houses, etc.) ensure there is a strong fit. We have seen no "killer applications" in healthcare as yet.

Currently, there are three different uses of computer power in connection with advanced clinical activities:

- Financial, administrative, logistic and communication purposes. This category of use also includes EHRs used in the general practitioner's office.
- Embedded in diagnostic and therapeutic equipment. This has probably been the most successful use of computer power in the clinical domain so far. The mission, (limited) domain model, semantics and representation of the OOI in the software supporting specific clinical hardware are always clear and relatively simple (mono-modal).
- General clinical use (mainly EHRs). EHRs typically record and quantify clinical activity. EHRs often use weak, incoherent, conceptual models, and the OOI can only be represented as within or close to—the natural sciences domain. Furthermore, the object

Table 3. Differences between office and hospital work

Office work (administrative purposes)	Hospital work (pure clinical purposes)
Desk situated	Nomadic
Quiet surroundings	Noisy surroundings
Long sessions on one case	Short interactions on individual cases
One person—one case; fixed teams	Many persons—many cases; changing teams
Predominantly sequential processing	Predominantly parallel processing
The object of interest (OOI) is represented sufficiently in the computer	The object of interest is not represented sufficiently in the computer-system

of interest is only indirectly represented though the signs, symptoms, measurements and acts carried out in relation to the patient's health status. The use of computer power for general clinical purposes demands multimodality, which in fact is a feature of the paper record that has not yet been mimicked by the EHR. This multimodality is based on a flexible formalization (as is currently possible). In the paper record this flexible, formalization provides room for narrative as well as arithmetic data entry and retrieval.

The construction of contemporary clinical software is based on the capabilities of the paper record combined with the main hard and software features of office automation, including the "personal computer" and sequential long sessions of desk-situated work as one "case" is executed by one logged-in human at a time. Often the model and representation of OOI in office automation software is advanced enough for the human operator to actually complete the tasks assigned. As outlined above the office context differs from clinical work. The clinical reality is that users are often nomadic and shifting, are involved in co-operative work with many disciplines, need to review several patient cases in parallel, and require their core professional functions to be supported not just recorded (Bardram & Bossen, 2005; Bossen, 2006). Some of these differences

are summarized in Table 3.

TOWARDS A NEEDED CONCEPTUAL THEORETICAL FRAMEWORK

The mission of future clinical software should be to clearly support all clinical activities not just tasks such as computerized physician order entry (i.e., CPOE) or acting as a "bridge" between clinical activity and administrative or financial systems. This would seem to be already implied in the EHR concept, but as shown empirically in the first part of this chapter, this seems to not be the case in real life. To approach a more coherent model and a better representation of the OOI in software development for general clinical use, one must understand the abstract nature of healthcare activity and of the OOI, including human (biological) and individual variation.

WHAT ARE THE COMPONENTS OF HEALTHCARE ACTIVITY?

An analysis of the components of healthcare activity supports the construction of computer-supported work that addresses four abstract components, which are rendered by an adaptation of a historical and artistic example displayed in Figure 5.

*Figure 5. Detail from a painting (1882) of Robert Hinckley showing the first public demonstration of anesthesia done on the 16th of October 1846 at Massachusetts General Hospital, Boston (Harvard Museum, Cambridge, Boston). Annotations are done by the authors showing the abstract components of the provision of healthcare. The three main components are: (1) technology utilization (in the example sulfur ether in a glass flask) (2) Manual skills and (3) Knowledge. The fourth component—teamwork—is present in many advanced healthcare organizations and "teamwork" will include the patient in the team. One could include **organization** as the fifth component in providing healthcare.*

The activities in the clinical domain consist of providing healthcare using the four components. In the next section the knowledge component is discussed.

KNOWLEDGE REPRESENTATION

The representation of knowledge remains an abstract art from a theoretical as well as clinical point of view. Other chapters in this book will deal with the challenges and methods associated with implementing knowledge representation schemes and decision supports using a computer system.

Medical knowledge can be stratified into three inter-dependent layers (Figure 6). At the top are abstract theories that form a coherent explanation and foundation for activity and research in the medical domain. The main theory in the medical domain is the patho-anatomical disease model. According to this model, every disease-entity has a specific lesion of anatomical, biochemical, genetic, microbiological, social, or psychological origins. Lesions give rise to symptoms, signs and problems and to some extent predict a "standard" disease course, trajectory or a general prognosis for a disease (i.e., This is sometimes referred to as the heuristic layer). Disease course or trajectory can be modified by an individual's own defense mechanisms, life-style and/or healthcare treatments or interventions.

When employing medical knowledge in clinical encounters healthcare professionals are intuitively aware of the stratification of health knowledge. Alternatively, computer systems are not. Currently, intuitive awareness of the stratifi-

Figure 6. The knowledge structure employed in the discussion

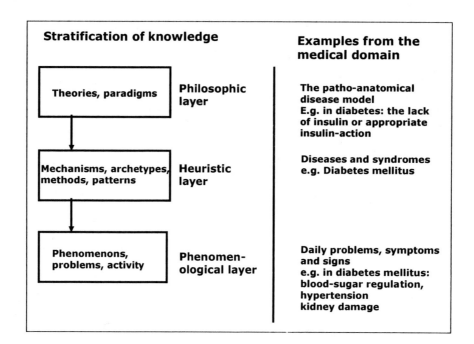

cation of health knowledge is not currently built into HISs. Instead, knowledge is only utilized in the phenomenological layer. We know that even in similar situations knowledge used in clinical decision making is different for differing individuals. We know that "clinically context sensitive" knowledge from the layers outlined in the diagram in Figure 6 are activated during clinical work. Therefore, it is essential that healthcare professionals have a deep understanding of the upper two layers of knowledge to be used in medical work (i.e., philosophical and heuristic). Informed patients may also benefit from such knowledge of their disease. For example, patient heuristic knowledge about the management of disease is necessary for the patient to engage in daily problem-solving in the phenomenological layer especially when managing a chronic disease or illness.

REPRESENTING THE OBJECT OF INTEREST (OOI)

As discussed previously, the OOI is only indirectly represented in the documentation model of EHRs. EHR documentation models are inherited from paper records. We need a documentation model that is clinically, context sensitive such as the "virtual patient" model. A "virtual patient" model should include knowledge about disease trajectory (thereby replacing the traditional chronology of the paper record). A "virtual patient" trajectory could be cross-sectional in nature, multi-stakeholder in content, and appear as a narrative, formatted record that balances health agonists and antagonists (as seen from the perspective of the patient) (Figure 7). The "virtual patient" model may to some extent replace the EHR. It could certainly replace *personal health records* that are currently found on the Internet. Health care organizations

Figure 7.Individual human related knowledge and information is represented as a trajectory in the virtual patient conceptual framework—a trajectory that is balanced between the health agonist and antagonist

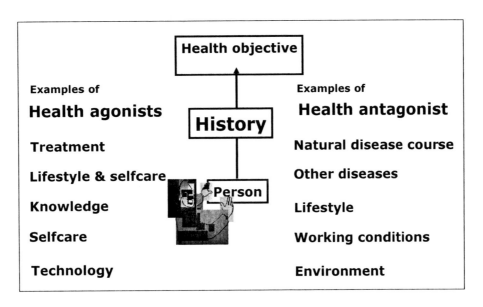

may choose to continue using their own corporate "bookkeeping" systems that are inter-operable with a collaborative health grid (as defined in the pervasive healthcare chapter). Alternatively, a "virtual patient" could be part of a health collaboration grid and a virtual trajectory could act as a digital knowledge proxi, thereby enabling the patient's ability to customize and operationalize abstract, general and specific knowledge to their own individual context.

CONCLUSION

In order to improve HISs, increase their adoption, usability, cross-societal diffusion as well as improve citizen use of such systems, we need to develop more coherent models of OOI in healthcare. The authors argue that the current lack of clinically context sensitive models such as the "virtual patient" may account for many of the adoption and dissemination issues described

in the first part of the chapter. Historically, the development of clinical systems has been modeled on the industrial and office automation paradigm. Clinical hardware and software need to be modeled after clinical work, decision making and patient disease processes to improve their clinical impact and enhance their dissemination speed. In the past, the focus of clinical hardware and software development has been on "manual" procedures and acts, which may not be equivalent to the knowledge content and individual service needs associated with those medical acts in the clinical setting.

Improvement in knowledge handling and a more "true" digital representation of patients or objects of interest should be developed. Health informaticians need to develop prerequisites for integrating digital health knowledge into societal activities that patients engage in. Furthermore, researchers need to explore the relationships between patient health related knowledge pervasive healthcare (as described in chapter 5 of this book).

ACKNOWLEDGMENT

The authors wish to thank the partners in the EHR-Observatory: Søren Vingtoft, Knut Bernstein, Morten Bruun Rasmussen and Stig Kjær Andersen for their contribution to the study on EHR diffusion in Denmark. This study was supported by The Ministry of the Interior and Health, The County Council, and The Copenhagen Hospital Cooperation.

REFERENCES

Andersen, S.K., Nøhr, C., Vingtoft, S., Bernstein, K., & Bruun-Rasmussen, M. (2002). *EHR-observatory annual report 2002*. Aalborg: EPJ-Observatoriet.

Bardram, J.E., & Bossen, C. (2005). Mobility work: The spatial dimension of collaboration at a hospital. *Computer Supported Cooperative Work (CSCW), 14*(2), 131-160.

Bernstein, K., Rasmussen, M.B., Nøhr, C., Andersen, S.K., & Vingtoft, S. (2001). *EHR observatory. Annual report 2001*. Odense: The County of Funen.

Bernstein, K., Rasmussen, M.B., Nøhr, C., Andersen, S.K., & Vingtoft, S. (2006). EHR Observatory. Annual Report 2006. Aalborg: EHR-Observatory.

Bossen, C. (2006). Evaluation of a computerized problem-oriented medical record in a hospital department: Does it support daily clinical practice? *International Journal of Medical Informatics, 76*(8), 592-600.

Bruun-Rasmussen, M., Bernstein, K., Vingtoft, S., Andersen, S.K., & Nøhr, C. (2003). *EHR-observatory annual report 2003*. Aalborg: EPJ-Observatoriet.

Danish Ministry of Health. (1996). *Action plan for electronic patient records—strategy report*. Copenhagen: Danish Ministry of Health.

Danish Ministry of Health. (1999). *National IT strategy for the hospitals 2000-2002*. Copenhagen: Danish Ministry of Health.

Jda. (1968, March 15). *Avanceret databehandlingsanlæg med "fjernsynsskærme" til Rigshospitalet*. Ingeniørens Ugeblad,

Lilholt, L.H., Pedersen, S.S., Madsen, I., Nielsen, P.H., Boye, N., Andersen, S.K., et al. (2006). Development of methods for usability evaluations of EHR systems. In A. Hasman, R. Haux, J. van der Lei, E. De Clercq, F. Roger-France (Eds.), *Ubiquity: Technologies for better health in aging societies* (pp. 341-346). Amsterdam: IOS Press.

Littlejohns, P., Wyatt, J.C., & Garvican, L. (2003). Evaluating computerized health information systems: hard lessons still to be learnt. *BMJ, 326*(7394), 860-863.

Ministry of Health and Prevention. (n.d.). Retrieved on February 11, 2008, from http://www.sum.dk

Molich, R. (2000). *Brugervenligt webdesign*. København: Teknisk Forlag.

Nøhr, C., Andersen S.K., Vingtoft S., Bruun-Rasmussen M., & Bernstein, K. (2004). *EHR-observatory annual report 2004*. Aalborg: EPJ-Observatoriet.

OECD. (2007). *OECD Health Data 2007*. OECD

Rigby, M. (2001). Evaluation: 16 powerful reasons why not to do it—and 6 over-riding imperatives. Medinfo 2001 10(Pt 2), 1198-1202.

Skov, M., & Stage J. (2005). Supporting problem identification in usability evaluations. In Proceedings of the Australian Computer-Human Interaction Conference 2005 (OzCHI'05). ACM Press.

Sundhedsstyrelsen. (SeSI). Beskrivelse af GEPJ-på begrebsniveau. (2005). Sundheds-styrelsen.

Vingtoft, S., Bernstein, K., Bruun-Rasmussen, M., From, G., Nøhr, C., Høstgaard, A.M., et al. (2004). *GEPKA-projektet. Klinisk afprøvning.* Aalborg: EPJ-Obseervatoriet.

Vingtoft, S., Bruun-Rasmussen, M., Bernstein, K., Andersen, S.K., & Nøhr, C. (2005). *EHR-observatory annual report 2005.* Aalborg: EPJ-Observatoriet.

Wears, R.L., & Berg, M. (2005). Computer technology and clinical work: Still waiting for Godot. *JAMA, 293*(10), 1261-1263.

ENDNOTES

[1] Single sign-on (SSO) is a method of access control that enables a user to authenticate once and gain access to the resources of multiple software systems i.e., booking module, lab. result system, medication system, etc.

[2] In general computerized physician order entry (CPOE), is a process of electronic entry of physician instructions for the treatment of patients. These orders are communicated over a computer network to the medical staff (nurses, therapists or other physicians) or to the departments (pharmacy, laboratory, or radiology) responsible for fulfilling the order. In the Danish context focus has been on the medication process as other proprietary systems have taken care of the communication to laboratories, radiology etc.

84

Chapter V
Pervasive Healthcare:
Problems and Potentials

Niels Boye
University of Aalborg, Denmark

ABSTRACT

Pervasive healthcare is a vision for the future of healthcare. Healthcare provisions can be delivered with high quality at low cost along with higher patient-experienced quality and satisfaction as a service on top of a pervasive computing infrastructure, which can be built by integrating communicating computer-power into industrial products and fixed structures in urban and rural spaces. For pervasive healthcare, integration with on body networks sensors and actuators may also be needed. This chapter discusses the prerequisites of this vision from a point of a healthcare professional. A number of parallel advances in concepts have to take place before pervasive healthcare (PH) is matured into a general method for delivering healthcare provisions. The contemporary, most widespread model of healthcare provisions as industrial products with consumer-goods characteristics has to mature into the concepts of welfare economics. New market models have to be developed for PH to pervade society and add value to the health aspects of an individual's life. Ethical and legal aspects must also be further matured. Maturation of technology is needed. This includes all the components of the "pervasive loop" from sensors to the central intelligence back to the actuators. The "virtual patient/healthy human" as an operational digital representation of the "object/subject of care" also has to be developed. Pervasive healthcare (or the European Union term: ambient assisted living) is a promising field, that has potential to integrate health considerations and health promoting activities for patients and non-patients in their everyday conduct and provide added value to life quality for individuals.

Copyright © 2008, IGI Global, distributing in print or electronic forms without written permission of IGI Global is prohibited.

INTRODUCTION

The author of this chapter will discuss, from the point of view of a person seeing patients every day (i.e., a health professional), the prerequisites and needs for successful implementation of a computer-supported, universal healthcare delivery system. The author will also suggest possible concepts for the future maturation of technology and services for the purpose of creating such a pervasive healthcare system. More specifically human aspects of pervasive healthcare computing are considered.

The topics discussed in this chapter will be more abstract than that of simply describing developed solutions and current research approaches; and it is not a comprehensive overview of "state of the art" in pervasive computing or pervasive computing for health. Future directions will be discussed briefly at the end of the chapter. There are three parts to this book chapter: the human-societal perspective, the clinical perspective on architecture and services, and briefly the future trends in pervasive healthcare.

Pervasive Computing

Pervasive computing is at present a vision for the future of healthcare. The word *pervasive* itself is derived from the Latin word *per vas* meaning to go through. Pervasive computing can be defined as a ubiquitous, computer-based service. Pervasive computing could be used to service both individuals and society as a backdrop for providing with information. Pervasive computing architectures are achieved by integrating, networking, and enabling communication between computers and humans, humans and computers, and between computers themselves. Such interactions could exist among (nearly) every industrial product and more fixed structures in the environment such as buildings, bus shelters, and poster stands used for advertising. Pervasive computing could also include *wearable computing* devices. Wearable computing is a term that describes *body area networks* (BANs) (or *PAN = personal area networks*). Here, computational power interacts with a pervasive infrastructure, the user, and/or his or her physiologic functions through on-body sensors and actuators. Intelligent textiles are also a part of this interaction network. Other terms, such as *ubiquitous computing* or the European Union's term for pervasive computing, *ambient intelligence*, have been used more or less synonymously with pervasive computing.

Pervasive Healthcare

"Pervasive healthcare" (PH) refers to the "invisible, omnipresent" networked, interoperable, computational power-structure that is employed for the purpose of adding to the quality of life and health and wellness of every citizen (whether they consider themselves healthy or not). Pervasive healthcare involves individualized interaction between health services layered "on top" of a pervasive computing infrastructure. In the future, pervasive healthcare could have a public health dimension as well, providing more general, invisible social science information via surveys and context sensitive advice and information aimed at prophylaxis and the collective health of groups of individuals. In European Union terms, pervasive healthcare is equivalent to the term "ambient assisted living."

In computer science, "context sensitivity" is a term that describes a computer system as being "aware" of a number of physical circumstances (the current user, the location, the task to be worked on... etc.). In order for pervasive healthcare to become a reality a health-oriented, individual, "intellectual, health context sensitivity" needs to be developed. This health or "clinical context sensitivity" will be discussed in a later chapter in terms of the current research and work in the areas of the object of work—or the object of interest (OOI).

SECTION ONE: THE HUMAN-SOCIETAL PERSPECTIVE

Societal Aspects of Healthcare

One of the main or fundamental pillars of a welfare society is its healthcare services. In welfare societies, healthcare services present as organized, industrial, institutions with a concentration of potentials, know-how, and technology grouped into hierarchical organizations. This mode of healthcare service organization and delivery of the provision of healthcare is in essence independent of how healthcare services are financed (i.e., public, private or by insurance).

Although modified by health maintenance organizations (HMO), governments or legislation, healthcare can be considered to be a basic and necessary function in a developed society, organized around citizen welfare principles (as some educational or social services are). Thus, healthcare could be regarded as a societal structure and not just a method of production that is used to address a market, consumer, or a customer need. This is in contrast to current approaches to the provision of healthcare services. Current approaches to providing healthcare view healthcare as an industrial product that is consumable by customers (i.e., patients) and subject to ordinary market economics. The English-Indian Nobel prize winner in economics in 1998, Amartya K. Sen, offers a further discussion of welfare economics and their relations to healthcare. He clearly demonstrates that healthcare provisions lack characteristics pivotal to consumer products This dilemma between the nature of healthcare provisions and our current industrial approach to delivering healthcare may be the main obstacle to the dissemination of pervasive healthcare. Even though pervasive computing supports Sen's view of healthcare as an omnipresent service that is provided to citizens by society in a developed welfare society or state.

A discussion about the societal aspects of welfare economics and the provision of healthcare may seem to be a distant one in a chapter on the use of ubiquitous computing in healthcare. Alternatively, pervasive healthcare (and pervasive computing) has not yet matured to the degree that it can be applied as a universal right or principle as part of healthcare delivery. Both in an immature and a more mature state, pervasive computing is an activity that has to be financed, and is of importance to the development of sustainable business models for the delivery of healthcare. Thus, short term financing of pervasive healthcare can be difficult to obtain, although long term societal and individual gains can be expected with its use. As different stakeholders become involved and models of healthcare are used it may not be possible to apply pervasive healthcare as a universal principle to a sufficient level from a clinical point of view using current healthcare business models and in the current healthcare context. It may even be necessary to make modifications to existing technical standards such as HL7 to ensure reference models use concepts that recognize the "roles of health professionals in participating in healthcare acts" (since one can bill for acts). Apart from sustainable business models the speed with which pervasive computing has matured in healthcare has been mitigated by user experiences both technical (and clinical[1]). User experiences include the richness and quality of service, size of service, "pervasiveness," the ubiquity of devices and the interaction possibilities associated with the use of pervasive healthcare.

Realistic Expectations on a Societal Level

Biological variability, the relative complexity of healthcare, the individual nature of the provision of healthcare combined with the level of maturity of current computer technologies has prompted health professionals and scientists in the field of pervasive healthcare to develop and use business cases with the expectation that pervasive healthcare will have a societal effect. More specifically, there will be a need to assess the "the (overall) impact factor" of PH. There will still be an ever increasing number of people that will demand traditional care, either due to the need for special technology, knowledge, and manual skills or because the patient is not able to join a PH group for some reason. On the other hand, for those individuals, that can engage in PH the added value in life quality and flexibility associated with using pervasive healthcare systems may have a significant impact on the individuals health and wellness (see the scenario later in this chapter). Pervasive healthcare will not be the savior of the healthcare system. There will likely be a large gap between the number of potential customers and actual or real customers that will benefit for pervasive healthcare. For example, the Center for Disease Control and Prevention (CDC) in Atlanta Georgia in the United States of America reported:

From 1980 through to 2004, the prevalence of diagnosed diabetes increased in all age groups. In general, throughout the time period, people aged 65-74 had the highest prevalence, followed by people aged 75 or older, people aged 45-64 years, and people less than 45 years of age. In 2004, the prevalence of diagnosed diabetes among people aged 65-74 (16.7%) was approximately 12 times that of people less than 45 years of age (1.4%).

In other words, this means that in a group of individuals 65 years of age and older, the frequency of diabetes is approaching 20 percent due to: (1) a real increase, and (2) another way of defining diabetes (which of course makes these new patients or "recruits" potential "customers" as well). A number of different diseases and stages of disease with different needs occur in conjunction with diabetes. Many diabetics are elderly and only a few of these individuals would likely use

information and communication technologies (ICT). Therefore, the real customers for PH are few in each "market-segment" of a disease.

Another factor to consider is that the majority of patients in this age group are type II diabetics. Although diabetes is their primary diagnosis, troublesome subjective symptoms that diabetic patients often note are not entirely associated with high blood glucose levels. These troublesome, subjective symptoms arise from the health issues associated with diabetes such as cardiovascular and kidney disease as well as the diseases of other organs (these organs are not in general connected to diabetes although complications may arise as a result of living with diabetes over the long-term). Therefore, a PH solution for type II diabetes in the elderly should address a far more complex and individual range of disease manifestations in order to have an impact upon the management of disease and to be able to "do the healthcare delivery job." There are nearly 15 million (known) diabetics in the United States and, of course, all of these individuals are potential customers for a diabetes PH setup, but all these individuals cannot be included in a business case or in a justification for a grant application.

Will PH Enable Societal Healthcare Services to Enter the Information Age?

Will pervasive computing provide more information to organizations and promote the function of healthcare well into the future? Will computer based pervasive healthcare induce changes in roles, acts, possibilities and responsibilities of health professionals and patients who work in and are a part of the provision of healthcare? The implementation of pervasive computing healthcare technologies should enable new actors and new business models to emerge as well as facilitate the use of conventional approaches to the provision of healthcare and actors to be distributed in other and more flexible ways. Unfortunately, such a situation is not "just around the corner." There is a need for an infrastructure to be built, software needs to mature, and technical standards need to be developed. Infrastructure, software and technical standards are well below what is needed and expected by healthcare services to address the complex, individualistic and mature needs of patients in the hyper-complex society (Qvortrup, 2003). The hyper-complex society is perceived as the current evolution of the information society.

Expectations and Values of the Post-Modernistic Patient

The human aspect of the hyper-complex society is the post-modernistic perspective of the individual, as an individual with unique values and expectations. Earlier the value for the single human was expressed more collectively through his or her membership of a society, a work-community, a religion, a family, or a tribe. The post-modernistic philosophic movement was rooted in France in the 1970s and 80s on top of the 1968-youth rebellion. It is an ideological showdown with the modern, industrial, and uniform society and that all problems have a "single solution." It is a promotion of complexity, individuality and lifestyle. The post-modernistic perspective of individuality creates expectations and values by the consumer of health that potentially could be fulfilled by PH. In brief, post-modernistic patients are taken care of by empowerment not by passive treatment.

In Conclusion: The Human-Societal Perspective

We are at present in a catch-22 situation. We lack the technical maturity to develop a new healthcare delivery system, and we also lack the financing needed to achieve technical maturation. This means that PH will be limited to disease, condition, and project oriented healthcare delivery and is dependent on technological drive from other markets that are dissimilar to healthcare. On the other hand, the only way to promote pervasive

healthcare is to demonstrate a return for society, for patients and/or healthcare professionals (or at least two of the three). Building the necessary PH infrastructure will demand a solid "business case" for every stakeholder, which for a number of reasons discussed above, is difficult to build, especially if healthcare provisions are perceived as being industrial products.

Healthcare delivery by computer-power will not be a universal principle until other factors are addressed, such as a lack of healthcare professionals, or when pervasive computing capabilities of sufficient maturity are built for other purposes. The total "project of pervasive healthcare" has yet to be completed, and as always for the purpose of scientific-based progress, there is a need for incremental, problem-specific, PH project-organized development (in this phase), with knowledge sharing of results and experiences which is generalizable and can be used to address people's needs and increase the collective wisdom of society in general.

Thus, healthcare is far from entering the information age and servicing the hyper-complex society with its post-modernistic inhabitants with pervasive services, due to industrial like business models and lack of maturity of soft and hardware. However, the evolution of PH will continue through project-organized research and development.

Experimental Computer Science as Social Science

As discussed previously, pervasive healthcare research and projects are dependent of a number of human and societal aspects, but there are aspects of experimental computer science in pervasive healthcare projects as well, although here experimental computer science has entered the domain of the social sciences. Therefore, there is a need to adapt the evaluation methods and scientific standards of the social sciences among other factors taking into account the biological range of human individuality. Experimental computer scientists cannot engage in "a proof of concept" in a laboratory setting alone. Instead, there is also a need for a clinical testing phase involving the proper use of qualitative and quantitative methodologies and evaluation using appropriate clinical endpoints.

Healthcare Provision Composition

An analytical breakdown of a healthcare provision may be of use in development of solutions that support ubiquitous delivery of health services. In the chapter by Nohr and Boye (2008), it is argued that the provision of healthcare is made up of four to five principle components (when analyzed for the purpose of computer support or complete computerization). These principle components include:

- Knowledge
- Teamwork—including the patient and their family
- Technology utilization—including the use of computer power
- Manual skills
- Organization (could be included as the fifth component)

Not every component may be present in every single provision of healthcare, but it should be possible to evoke all of the components when appropriate.

Knowledge as Power or a Shared Resource

In the industrial society "knowledge" was considered to be a source of power. Knowledge in the information society should now be considered as a universal distributed resource. This means, that power is attributed to those who have the ability to access, use, and filter knowledge. The ability to make knowledge become operational and useful is foremost important (i.e., the ability to "make

it work"). For example, you can use the Internet to acquire some knowledge of brain surgery, but not everybody is able to utilize that knowledge in a beneficial way. Knowledge activation or use (power) demands specific prior knowledge, special technology and/or skills.

Teamwork

In classical medicine patients are considered "the object of care." Patients are more so the subject of care today. Ideally, the patient is the most hard-working and valuable team member in his or her health-support-team. Pervasive healthcare will probably work best in cases where the patient (or their proxy) has the mental and cognitive abilities to participate actively in their care.

Technology Utilization and Manual Skills

At present, knowledge support and healthcare teamwork are the only fundamental components in a provision of healthcare that is electronically transportable. The computer-support for the components of technology utilization and manual work will be developed further through research in the next few years and when combined with the advantages associated with other technologies applied in healthcare (e.g., robotics, miniaturization, electronics, nanotechnology, and the use of composite materials), it has the potential to advance healthcare significantly.

SECTION TWO: THE CLINICAL PERSPECTIVE ON ARCHITECTURE AND SERVICES

Clinical Context Sensitivity

Currently there is no defined term for *clinical context sensitivity*. In the next few years it will be necessary to develop and define clinical context sensitivity for PH in order to elevate it to a more universal, clinical method of healthcare delivery. In this chapter *clinical context sensitivity* will be defined as a multi-axial, individual form of information space (MIIS) that communicates with a model framework such as "the virtual patient" or perhaps "the virtual healthy citizen" (to be discussed later in this chapter). The MIIS around each person issues automatic notifications, subscribes, filters, and applies (personal) weights to information. Hence, MIIS modulates and individualizes decision support for the patient. The MIIS is the patient stand-in in the PH-knowledge space.

There is a publication rate of around 6,000 biomedical papers on average each day. This means that the amount of available health information is huge, rapid changing, and for the single individual, on the whole, not of interest for the most part. To take advantage of the current medical knowledge each individual may benefit from pre-defined information filters defined by the scope of the PH-system and the nature and character of the patient's disease, state or condition.

Disease Stage Context

The American National Library of Medicine PubMed database, which indexes nearly all biomedical papers, defines the following categories for clinical queries: etiology (or aetiology—the study of causation), diagnosis, therapy, prognosis, and clinical prediction guides. Transferred to the personal information space, this could be expressed as the continuum that one (i.e., the patient) may pass through during the natural course of a chronic disease, from:

- Healthy
- Staying healthy
- Feeling ill
- Feeling sick
- Do I have a disease?
- Seeing your doctor (crossing the iatrotropic threshold)

- Before confirmed diagnosis
- Newly diagnosed
- Seeking second opinions
- Acute
- Prognosis
- Chronic ongoing
- Maintenance and compensatory measures (tertiary prophylaxis against late complications)
- Home care (devices for delivery of care or drugs)

Other categories along these axes could include general information about the condition, epidemiology, demography, and/or being a relative of the person diagnosed with the disease.

Competency and Resource Sensitivity

The terms "novice" and "expert" are used and defined in other chapters of this book. It is usually difficult to use these terms when assessing competencies in chronic patients. This is due to a natural lack of "academic distance" to ones own personal state of health. This lack of distance makes it difficult to utilize even expert knowledge about underlying disease mechanisms. The phenomenon is so general and human, that most doctors, when they contract a health condition (even in their own area of expertise) are unable to "cope" with the disease in an "expert-way." It could be that the expert shifts his usual decision pattern from forward reasoning to subjective, empathetic-reasoning; hence such an individual may say "this is not the case for me." Other chapters of in this book will provide more in-depth information about clinical reasoning and knowledge handling methods employed by individuals.

One of the great potentials for PH is its ability to provide a rational, academic distance and analytical perspective with arguments that minimize the empathy component in decisions on health. Therefore, PH allows the patient to obtain a "better, personal health understanding or reasoning." The virtual patient (see later) has to also include models having a very interesting synthesis of computer science, clinical reasoning, human factors, (clinical) knowledge handling, and cognitive psychology.

Self-Care as the Primary Healthcare Provision

The different needs of patients in "the disease stage context" have in a traditional, industrial society been sequential in nature and have been "matched" to differing types of provisions of healthcare. Conventional types of provisions of healthcare include the following acts: diagnosis, treatment, monitoring, training and rehabilitation, personal care, prophylactic treatment and life-style change or modulation. PH has the potential to combine some of these types of provisions of healthcare into a single "self-care (fused) provision." Replacing the current sequential approach to care with an information-society based approach, where acts are occurring in parallel. Furthermore, the continuum between health, wellness and compensatory measures for patients would be augmented by PH. PH would potentially help patients to maintain a feeling of healthiness despite having a disease.

The aim of society should be to make PH-supported self-care the primary method of providing healthcare. Society (or appointed representatives of the organization such as HMOs) are "topping up" with the necessary professional provisions including PH to complete the job of helping the patient to self-manage their disease.

Other Clinical perspective on architecture will be illustrated with a scenario (see Figure 1).

Scenario

Karen is seven years old and has been a diabetic for three months. She is now on holiday in a relatively remote tourist and fishing village at Skagen in Denmark, which is not her native country. Her parents were a little anxious to bring her, since her disease has not been stable, and the "family pool" of knowledge about diabetes is still not sufficient. Karen carries her MIIS-device in the physical form of a small teddy bear, which communicates with the PH-infrastructure, when she presses its nose. The MIIS organizes the information in different profiles, such as general characteristics, emergency information for paramedic use, information for healthcare professionals, food, physical activities, medications etc.....

The family decides to go to a restaurant and Karen approaches the sign outside. It reads her general profile of information, lowers to her height, and then displays the "children's diabetes menu." When inside and ordering an item from the menu—the "virtual patient" calculates the insulin-dose, and the corresponding physical activity advice relative to Karen's food intake and displays the different options on the menu in the restaurant for Karen and her parents to see and to help with their decision-making. The family wants to take a walk in the dunes after the meal. When the food arrives the "virtual patient" reprograms her insulin pump to deliver the appropriate dose of medication based on her current insulin sensitivity and her usual reaction to moderate physical exercise and the meal chosen from the menu.

Figure 1. Scenario illustrating the potential impact of pervasive healthcare

Comments about the Scenario

Since Karen is carrying a device, an insulin pump, it would be natural to integrate the MIIS-device in the pump that will act both as a sensor and an actuator in the PH-architecture.

From a human perspective there are several reasons that make it feasible for people to "control" their own information "physically," hence the teddy bear in the scenario. Someone could, of course, obtain the same by a distributed information architecture and identification, such as secure-RFID-tags or similar technology, but the personal dimension would be lost and the individual needs for interfacing the MIIS to any "personal gadget" (such as pedometers, bikes, exercise-monitoring devices,) for personal ways of collecting data may be more cumbersome. MIIS could be an enabling-technology of individual, personal paraphernalia—a gadget for patients and for the healthy—embedded in for example mobile phones, Swiss army knives, teddy bears, Gucci purses, Rolex watches, and so on.

A scenario may also illustrate the everyday gains associated with the use of PH. Karen's quality of life might improve as hopefully she will have fewer long-term complications associated with diabetes in 15 to 30 years. Karen could have received diabetic care without PH, but she might not have been able to go on holiday in another country so shortly after being diagnosed. This illustrates that gains of PH are mainly on the individual aspects of quality of life and care and the societal gain may be more difficult to demonstrate—at least in the near future. The near future societal gain of PH applications may be the ability to distribute healthcare services in times of need (e.g., natural disasters), given that a new and effective PH self organising infrastructures could be deployed in a short period of time

The "Virtual Patient:" "The Virtual Living and Staying Healthy Person"

For years, the following question has been asked: "why is healthcare so special, we use sophisticated computer technology to fly, fill, and maintain airplanes and space rockets, handle complicated financial transactions, and so forth so it must be the arrogance and resistance of health professionals to change, that makes it difficult to penetrate the healthcare market?" This maybe so, but there are some other reasons as well that prevent PH from being adopted:

- The expectations and values of the postmodernistic patient and the nature of disease processes.
- The current representation of the object of work or the object of interest (OOI).
- The nature of our current "models" of the OOI and data foundation problems.
- The specificity of sensors and actuators (especially in relation to PH).
- The participatory nature of health-decisions between caregiver, relatives, and objects/subjects of care.
- The non-algorithmic nature of health decisions (covered in other chapters of this book).
- The state of information technology maturity.

The Current Representation of the Object of the Work

We need a "virtual patient" to bring healthcare into the information age. Computer technology has developed from a tool that was used by the military and astronomers[2] to a tool that is now used everyday by many people in offices professionally and publicly. The most successful information technology applications represent "the object of work" in a constructive and productive manner to the office worker. This allows the office worker to *do* the work on the computer. Current electronic clinical systems represent the patient indirectly by some facts, considerations and descriptions of procedures done by healthcare professionals. *This is not a coherent and productive model of "the object of work" neither for the patient nor for the healthcare worker.* The patient's condition will not improve by an entry in his or her electronic patient record, cases are not considered to be done by entries in the record. Instead, the record is at present used as a necessary communication and memory aid, but not as a cure for disease. PH is concerned with healthcare interactions between the two (i.e., the patient and the healthcare worker) and in that sense closer to cure than to documentation, but would gain additional benefit by the development of "the virtual patient" as the digital representative of the patient.

"Models" of the Object of Work (or OOI)

Models are simplified representations of reality that may accentuate certain aspects of reality. They usually show relevant objects and describe the relationships between these objects.

There are two types of variation in the provision of healthcare: (1) *unwanted* variation due to lack of evidence, materials or methods, and (2) *wanted* individuality in the provision of healthcare arising from the very (post-modernistic) human nature of the patient and the provider. The overall aim of quality assurance in healthcare is to minimize the *unwanted* variation and promote the *wanted* variation arising from the individuality and uniqueness of the single patient. This is different from other industries (e.g., aviation) where there are attempts to reduce individuality, uniqueness and variation.

To minimize unwanted variation in medical practice and learning, models of the non-existent, average patient that has specific types of health

conditions are used in descriptions of best practices and standard operating procedures (SOP). Healthcare professional use their clinical knowledge to tailor and modify SOPs to the *individual* patient's needs and concurrent medical, social or other problems during the actual delivery of healthcare. Therefore, implicitly, it is not a good idea to transfer the restrictive nature of a standard SOP-average-patient model to a computer environment when creating a virtual patient. There is a need for a more "true" representation of a patient for use in PH decision support. A model framework needs to be developed. The virtual patient must be sensitive to the clinical context and to other human, and individual factors such as: decision modes, motivation, resources, concurrent health, social, and mental health problems. The model must also provide a linkage to "the back-office" platform and databases that have fundamental digital, genetic, biochemical, anatomical, physiological, and behavioral data, and be sensitive to information in the patient-MIIS (see Figure 2).

The virtual patient is linked to the front-end user and provides context sensitive data fused with "human data" (context sensitive "translations" and displays) of information that form the basis for end-user knowledge acquisition within a healthcare context. The end-users are health professionals, patients, healthcare professionals, family members and other interested parties. The presented information would probably require new ways of "browsing" complicated multi-axial information-structures in relation to each other (see Figure 2).

Data Foundation Challenges

As an example, let us examine genetic information about humans and micro-organisms in a virtual patient framework: a dream for the future.

In less than five years, the cost of documenting a near complete version of the human genome (i.e., DNA sequence) with its six-fold coverage may drop from $10-20,000,000 to $100-200,000.

Figure 2. A simplified diagram of a (clinical) PH-architecture

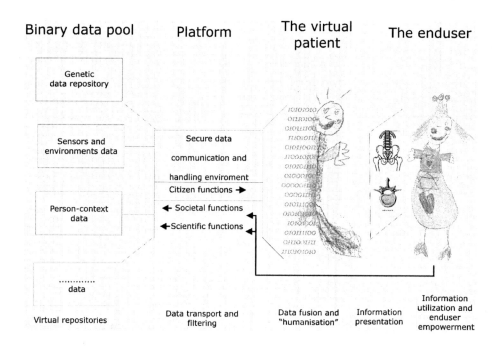

In 10-15 years, the cost may be as low as $1,000. Such dramatic advances will come through the use of novel, ultra-low cost sequencing (ULCS) techniques. Such prototypes are just starting to appear (Shendure, Mitra, Varma, & Church, 2004). Equally, predictable is the advancement of techniques for functional and structural characterization of the human genome.

The impact of ULCS on biomedical research and public health will be profound. When the costs for ULCS drop to below $100,000, human genomes and genotyping will probably be readily available to be used in large hospitals to provide quicker and more precise identification about genetic variations that cause disease. The ability to compare complete genomes for normal and neoplastic malignant cells will allow for cataloguing of cellular function perturbations that cause inappropriate transformations. This will be the first step towards finding specific cures for some disease. A $1,000 genome offers the potential for "individualized healthcare" in a clinic, including diagnosis, learning about prognoses for particular inherited diseases, risk assessments, prevention strategies, sensitivities to certain drugs, and the design of drugs for specific individuals. Epidemiological data could also be connected. Old samples (e.g., cancer biopsies) could be (re-)analyzed, and much more could be possible. This could form the basis for the development of a more specific body of knowledge about the transfer of information targeted towards providing advice about diseases with a genetic component while employing the distributed and counseling power of pervasive healthcare technology and it would provide the foundation for intelligent PH services beyond the capabilities of our current healthcare structures.

The same genetic information could be used to diagnose and fight diseases caused by microorganisms (which may be the case for some cancers) through the process of rapid sequencing. For example, in the future, one might see the use of rapid sequencing of bacterial RNA from a tissue sample as being used to give a precise diagnosis of an infection. This could probably be done in a few minutes rather than a few days as is currently the case (i.e., it takes several days to grow bacteria on agar-plates for the identification and functional characterization of bacteria as well as to determine the type of bacterial resistance that a bacteria has to different types of antibiotics). However, vastly improved genetic testing alone will not necessarily translate into great benefits for patients. For that to happen, the data have to be available, accessible, and consistent in various ways. Data has to be inter-connected, navigatable, and smoothly integrated with the many ways the user (e.g., clinician, patient) looks at the patient data It is far from clear at this point, which measures can and should be taken to ensure that new scientific and technical advances actually help with fighting disease. Pervasive infrastructure and technology alone are not an adequate prerequisite.

Data Issues

A number of questions or issues currently exist in the domains of clinical and biomedical informatics as well as the areas of practical genomic software and data integration. The following are some examples of questions and/or issues in these areas (there are undoubtedly several more examples):

1. Will more data create more inconsistency? A consequence of the widespread availability of cheap technology, there are many more sites that can afford to generate their own data, using separate names, protocols and formats. Therefore, the answer is probably yes. If so, what political, organisational and practical steps can be taken to prevent such additional chaos? Comment: *At this moment in time are we ready to begin proactive*

standardization of names, protocols and formats?

2. Will consistent, perhaps global, data repositories be needed? How critical will they be? In the future a doctor will be able to match a patient's genetic profile against profiles typical for certain diseases and receive a list of diseases to contrast with other clinical evidence. This will only occur if the data are consistent and comparable. A repository with consistent data will need to be in a well defined network locations, and will need to have at minimum high quality data. For example, consider the simple question "return all expression data for gene A, B, and C in a given tissue." Currently, this question is difficult to answer, since there are at least the following major sites with data:

1. Gene Expression Omnibus (NCBI, USA)
2. Stanford Microarray Database (Stanford University, USA)
3. ArrayExpress (European Bioinformatics Institute, England)
4. Whitehead Institute Center for Genome Research (Cambridge Massachusetts, USA)
5. Gene Expression Atlas (Novartis Research Foundation, Switzerland)
6. RNA Abundance Database (University of Pennsylvania, USA)
7. Public Expression Profile Resource (Children's National Medical Center, USA)

Some of the data sets appear in more than one of the collections listed. In some cases the same data are given different names, formats, and experimental protocols. As well, data names, formats and experimental protocols may change at any time without notice. This is clearly not the best situation. Several questions emerge when considering the above outlined issues: How much will it cost to make these changes? How much would it cost to avoid these issues (if at all possible)? Yet, there are still several single nucleotide polymorphism (SNP) repositories and many other kinds of not as yet coordinated data sites. Therefore, for example, one might instead want to ask a simpler question "what new bacterial genomes are out there?" and "how difficult is that to determine?" Two very difficult questions to answer.

GenBank and other major sites collect genomic data and save it in the most consistent ways. There is much more genomic data available in smaller sites, where the micro-organism's name, is not precise and/or consistent. There are many such examples of data that are "available but not accessible." This means that emerging genetic micro-organism detection methods will not be accessible for PH applications in the imminent future.

There are a number of obstacles that prevent genetic data from being connected to clinical observations. Today, genotype/phenotype relations are mostly found in journal articles. Therefore, researchers (or patients/relatives) must mine the research literature to find this data. This process is slow and error prone. There does not seem to be a well organized repository of genotype/phenotype data. Most of this essential data is described in other ways. Therefore, genetic databases will need to use high quality clinical annotations such as:

- Disease description (histology, physiology, etc.)
- Disease genotype, prognostic markers
- Experimental evidence for marker usefulness
- Literature and links for those genomic databases to be useful to patients, families and clinicians

Cancer is a good example of disease where genetic data are collected. The collection of genetic data in databases should provide information about complex as well as single-gene informa-

tion that causes disease. A genetic cancer data repository should support searches by disease, return information about the known markers of disease, and provide research based evidence for treatment so that there is some diagnostic value associated with collecting such information. As well, searches should return information about genes or genomic regions so that disease related information is returned along with information about associated markers.

Several other questions can also be asked: What are the most needed types of linkable data? Do nomenclature issues create critical disconnects? Such questions are important as linking expression data with disease phenotypes in a consistent nomenclature is critical. Presently, there are significant losses of information due to nomenclature issues and/or incomplete ontologies. Researchers also need to ask: How much genetic data is currently covered by ontologies? Are the ontologies of sufficient quality for practical use? Are there enough ontologies available? Are they freely (i.e., the ontologies) usable? Which database projects are the most critical to coordinate with? What data is proprietary and what would be the effect of making proprietary data public?

Software Design

Researchers need to address the issue of local versus remote data. At present, patient data cannot travel across the Internet to be analyzed at a few central servers on a routine basis due to confidentiality requirements and bandwidth limitations associated with handling such data. On the other hand, all the world's data that are relevant to a given "case" cannot reside on a local server. The solution is a combination approach. Here, data of local interest resides locally and general data centrally like the idea behind the MIIS. Researchers also need to determine who should decide where the data resides and how it should be monitored.

Scalable Viewers

If today's genomics user interfaces were used with a thousand times more data. The user would drown in the details. Viewers are needed that offer higher level views (i.e., that scale well). Growing desires to project patient data into a larger genomic context will definitely occur if it can be done in a seamless, confidential and secure way.

Ethical Issues

Before genetic information from repositories can be used to serve individual health issues in a PH structure, practical ethical organizational guidelines and responsibilities that protect the patient need to be established. For example, can an HMO demand a genetic profile and refuse to insure an individual for potential future genetic diseases? As well, can an employer use genetic or lifestyle information to refuse benefits, promotion or compensation to employees? Is the citizen bound to provide comprehensive genetic and health related (the MIIS) information to an HMOs, employers, or society?

The Specificity of Sensors and Actuators

The simplified architecture of PH forms a loop from sensor to a computer-supported "intelligent" environment, to an actuator giving an appropriate response to the condition sensed. The appropriateness of the corrective response by the PH is dependent upon:

- The specificity, sensitivity, and relevant response-characteristics of the sensor relative to the signal
- The specificity of the computer-supported "intelligence" relative to the signal
- The specificity and appropriateness of the actuator to correct the condition

- A proper balance between the three components giving a flexible and clinically relevant response to a range of possible conditions

One of the potential benefits of PH could be what the European Commission in its research programmes calls: "ambient assisted living (AAL)" which means that cognitive and physical impairments in specific patient populations (e.g., in elderly persons) are compensated for by technology and extend the patient's normal, active, independent lifestyle as long as possible.

Problems with PH are not limited to specific sensors with appropriate sensitivities and actuators for an appropriate response. Technology has not yet been developed to support the needs of a physically dependent, cognitively impaired elderly individual, living alone in their own home that forgets to turn off the stove on occasion.

Maybe an unspecific "behavioral" sensor could be constructed by fusing data inputs from a number of different types of sensors. Massachusetts Institute of Technology (MIT) has constructed a "living lab" in the form of a home that has several thousand sensors incorporated in its structures. People are invited to live in the home for a period. Sensors and actuators are tested to determine how data can be fused.

Since the specificity and sensitivity of sensors and actuators for the majority of potential PH applications is missing, it is difficult to construct a "computer-intelligence" that targets the patient's healthcare problem. Sensors are unspecific for a complex health condition such as Alzheimer's disease but specific to heartbeat and other distinct electrophysiological sources.

The Participatory Nature of Health-Decisions Between Caregivers, Relatives, and Object/Subjects of Care

As discussed in part one of this chapter, healthcare is a participatory process that takes place between a patient, their family and healthcare professionals. This process is fundamental and differs from built models of human behavior in other domains, where models in general do not leave room for participatory decision activity, second opinions, and alternative routes and plans between service providers and recipients of service.

Altered Production Settings in PH

The provision of healthcare is for the most part regarded as industrial production. This despite the fact that provision of healthcare does not have the usual characteristics of an industrial product that can be serially produced, stocked, transported, sold, and consumed independently.

Paradoxically, PH can bring healthcare into the information age (by means of "the virtual patient") and at the same time enable a more industrial like mode of production. PH has the potential to bring unique, on-demand, individually-produced provisions of healthcare based upon manufactured (computer-intelligence) of raw material (knowledge). This implies that PH can bring the provision of healthcare closer to the industrial product by de-coupling production and consumption and PH has the potential to stock and transport semi-manufactured provisions of healthcare for individual consumption (at a chosen time and place) by an individual citizen by means of a computer-supported self-care environment.

Infrastructure Discussion

Figure 3 gives a rough picture of the needed infrastructure for distributing the components in a provision of healthcare (as outlined previously and explained in more detail in Nohr's and Boye's chapter in this book).

PH-structure has three zones of influence: the delivery zone, the distribution zone and the knowledge zone ("raw materials for production"). The knowledge zone houses all the usual stakeholders of healthcare (e.g., physicians and nurses). It pro-

Figure 3. PH infrastructure

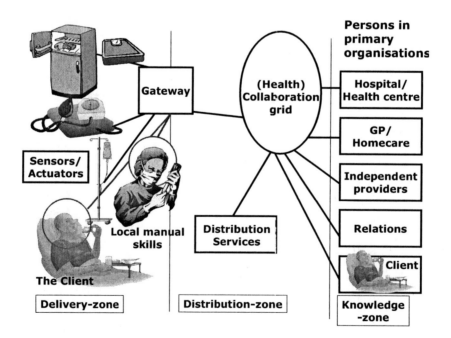

vides the healthcare stakeholders with an interface to the "ubiquitous" zones (i.e., the distribution and delivery zones). The client (patient, citizen) is present in both the knowledge zone and the delivery zone, since the primary PH-healthcare provision is self-care in a computer-supported context sensitive, knowledge intensive environment. It also underlines the participatory involvement of the patient in the healthcare team.

A universal distribution zone for PH with ambient facilities does not exist at present. Each PH project has so far constructed specific solutions for only the distributive aspect of PH. The predicted distribution zone incorporates "the virtual patient" (i.e., a universal model of health, behavior, reasoning, lifestyle-advice, compensatory and disease modifying mechanisms). The interaction between the model and the patient starts with the instantiation of the model within "the clinical context" using a MIIS-device and other relevant context information that is needed to produce a response. The PH healthcare-loop is established between the patient-proxy (MIIS), sensors, the intelligence, and actuators. The use of additional technology and manual skills to complete the provision of healthcare must be obtained from outside the general PH structure, but, ideally, those who provide healthcare should be able to communicate within the PH structure.

The "virtual patient-model" could be housed in a computer-supported teamwork system (i.e., software) (in Figure 3 this is called the "health collaboration grid"). Building, running and maintaining the "health collaboration grid" would be difficult. Building a health collaboration grid could have a similar impact upon healthcare, business, computer-methods, and secondary healthcare technology as putting a man on the moon had for the physical and astronomical sciences, materials, and communication (even though the mission would not be as spectacular as the endeavor for the moon!).

SECTION THREE: CURRENT TRENDS AND FUTURE RESEARCH DIRECTIONS

The history of scientific and clinical knowledge acquisition in medicine gives foundation for speculation about how the future maturation of PH might occur on a higher level of abstraction.

Medical knowledge started on the whole-body level observing disease and speculating on reasons for its occurrence. In different isolated parts of the world diverse disease-models were developed—a kind of "virtual," abstract patient. In China the model was build around the meridians in the body where energy was flowing, and disease was considered the result of wrong energy flows, which could be corrected by traditional Chinese medicine, including acupuncture. In the old world during the 16th and 17th century the Western Medical disease model was gradually formed by observing anatomy, physiology genetics and biochemistry gradually going into more and more detail. The search for details in bio-medicine is the basis of the rate of approximately 6,000 new publications in average a day. One could say: it is a "top-down approach" from gross anatomy and behavioral patterns to biochemistry and genetics.

In bio-informatics and model building for pervasive healthcare one starts with the details (i.e., in the algorithms, classifications, and gene-maps) and has to compile this massive amount of data into a coherent and balanced model in the virtual world of the object of interest (the human). It is a "bottom up approach" as complicated as the bio-medical research "top-down" approach.

State of the art of pervasive healthcare technologies (as of the year 2006) are coming mainly from a computer science perspective—described in a recent book edited by Bardram, Mihailidis and Dadong (2006). From this book it also appears—from a clinician's point of view—that PH is not yet a mature and general method to deliver well-defined health-care provisions. It is however still a promising and exciting experimental field where multi-disciplinary collaboration is producing the foundation that shows most potential. A distinction between telemedicine and pervasive healthcare has not been made and is maybe not possible. In the mind of the author "telemedicine" is more about monitoring and surveillance health and "pervasive healthcare" is more about computer-based servicing of health needs—intelligent—demonstrating the whole loop from sensor(s) via intelligence to an actuator responding to the sensed condition. Another distinction that arises is the following—who is in charge? One interpretation could be the following: in telemedicine it is the institution operating the system, in pervasive healthcare it is the team-member that is the object and subject of care, that is, the patient.

Research and development is occurring rapidly in the field and since the technology is still immature it is mostly very specific at this moment focused on single components of the information architecture. The Internet is the appropriate way to stay informed about industry research and products, conferences, and framework programs from national and international organizations and agencies. Since a regular overview will be outdated quickly some fields of study (that can be used as keywords for search) are listed thematically according to the components of the pervasive loop.

The Pervasive Loop

- **Sensors:** Sensors are a field of intensive research, ranging from study of materials in nanotechnology to incorporation in "intelligent band aid" and "intelligent textiles," to physiological response characteristics and algorithms (embedded software), to ways of transferring (coupling) the sensor signal to a network. Miniaturization is an important part of the efforts. Many sensors are currently built on electro-physiological principles sensing signals from the brain, nerves, heart or muscles, but other principles will be matured and developed and in the near future.

- **Network:** Major developments in recent years have been seen in body-area networks (BAN), personal-area-networks (PAN) components and power-supply, gateways and transmission, short-range-radiowave technologies (RFID, Bluetooth, Zigbee, others), security, and integration in structures and industrial products.

- **Intelligence:** This includes data fusion algorithms, information presentation (Virtual-reality), decision support models and methods, "the virtual patient" (starting with physiology) and other OOI-representations.

- **Actuators:** Very few actuators for pervasive healthcare have actually been developed and in the market. This is a field of great commercial potential although the rest of the "pervasive loop" must be in place for actuators to make a difference in any individual's life.

- **Integration in society:** There is still not sustainable business models developed for PH, as pointed out in the start of this chapter. Ethical and legal aspects are insufficiently developed for the concept to be marketable. Pervasive healthcare will need technical and semantic integration with other health related data repositories. As pointed out in the chapter with the example of genetic data, this is not a trivial exercise to carry out. Models and standardized vocabularies (e.g., SNOMED CT) and interface standards in healthcare (e.g., HL7) must be developed to maturity, where they may serve the needs of all the actors, including patients, professionals and organizations.

REFERENCES

Bardram, J.E.., Mihailidis, A., & Dadong, W. (2007). *Pervasive computing in healthcare* (1st ed.). New York: CRC Press.

Nohr, C., & Boye, N. (2008). Towards computer supported clinical activity: A roadmap based on empirical knowledge and some theoretical reflections. In A.W. Kushniruk & E. Borycki (Eds.), *Human, social and organizational aspects of health information systems.* Hershey, PA: IGI Press.

Qvortrup, L. (2003). *The hypercomplex society—Digital formations* (vol. 5). New York: Peter Lang Publishing.

Shendure, J., Mitra, R. D., Varma, C., & Church, G. M. (2004). Advanced sequencing technologies: Methods and goals. *Nat.Rev.Genet., 5,* 335-344.

ADDITIONAL READING

IEEE Pervasive Computing is a quarterly magazine, advancing research and practice in mobile and ubiquitous computing in a clear and accessible format. It is published by the IEEE computer society and has many papers dealing with health issues and occasional thematic volumes on health. Core technologies such as sensors, actuators and networks are covered.

A recent book that describes a range of aspects of pervasive computing in healthcare is the following:

Bardram, J.E., Mihailidis, A., & Dadong, W. (2007). *Pervasive computing in healthcare* (1st ed.). New York: CRC Press.

ENDNOTES

1   The term clinical will in this chapter be used of every healthcare related activity were a core provision is transferred from a system or person (including the patient) to a person or group of persons—despite the location and mode of transfer.

2   In 1943, the chairman of IBM said: "I think there's a world market for maybe five computers" – computers were something else at that time, but the quotation brings perspective to any prediction of the future (with computers) including this chapter.

Section III
Organizational Aspects:
Change Management, Best Practices, and Evaluation

Chapter VI
The Human Aspects of Change in IT Projects

Karen Day
University of Auckland, New Zealand

Tony Norris
Massey University, New Zealand

ABSTRACT

In this chapter we describe the transition phase (capability crisis) of the change process linked to health IT projects, indicate how it can be identified, and outline the ways in which we can use change management to intervene and assist people in their journey of change. Despite IT projects being considered a failure more often than not, we continue to implement IT innovations encapsulated in health information systems in healthcare services. These projects bring about considerable organizational change. Good project management includes the use of critical success factors such as change management in our attempts at ensuring success. The purpose of this chapter is to examine the ways in which we can identify (diagnose) the capability crisis and intervene (with change management) by means of learning, leadership, communication and workload management.

INTRODUCTION

The purpose of this chapter is to provide some insight into the way people transition from one way of working to another and the ways in which managers and leaders can assist in this transition. The principles of change are outlined from literature studies and from the events and experience of a major research project that charted the merging of the IT services of two large district health boards in New Zealand.

Health IT projects implement innovations which in turn are disruptive and result in changed organizational and individual processes, technology and relationships. In this chapter we outline the change process that most people follow and match

Copyright © 2008, IGI Global, distributing in print or electronic forms without written permission of IGI Global is prohibited.

it to the change journey people tend to follow from the simple, known and familiar to the complex, unknown, ambiguous and uncertain future and return as we master new processes, technology and relationships. An overview of change theory and complexity theory is provided as it relates to health IT projects. These projects are notorious for their failures—the reasons for failure are explored and critical success factors outlined.

The transition phase of the change process will be covered in depth in terms of its relationship to health IT projects. Recommendations on incorporating the management of this transition are provided in terms of change management practice.

THE COMPLEXITY OF CHANGE IN THE HEALTHCARE SYSTEM

Healthcare can be viewed as a complex adaptive system, in which many parts of the system interact interdependently in varying and unpredictable degrees with one another and their environment. The continuum of complexity ranges from simple and unambiguous with high degrees of perceived certainty, to chaos which extends beyond complexity, uncertainty and ambiguity. Within this context, the capability to perform well is potentially at its best in the "zone of complexity" (Fraser & Greenhalgh, 2001, p. 800), as shown in Figure 1, where change is most stimulating and best received, usually in a non-linear, or illogical manner. We usually function well in the position where most of our world is reasonably certain and predictable, fairly unambiguous, familiar, mostly known and knowable, and where interdependencies and relationships are fairly simple (Plesk & Greenhalgh, 2001).

While we are in the zone of complexity decisions are no longer simple: we are in a situation that is neither simple nor chaotic. Our natural tendency is to reduce ambiguity and uncertainty by attempting to create firm plans from which to work, seeking logic and simplicity, or to strip some of the paradoxes around us by simply ignoring them. Others have found that it may be more productive to work with ambiguity and uncertainty by being reflective, learning from the consequences of our actions as we go, or creating a cycle of plan, act, review and modify as used in action research (Brydon-Miller, Greenwood, & Maguire, 2003) and in quality improvement practice (Shin & Jemella, 2002). We tend to move in and out of

Figure 1. Change in a complex environment (after Tan, Wen, & Awad, 2005)

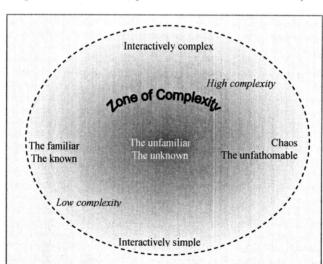

the zone of complexity as we work through the day, acting out agreements between ourselves and others, working according to habits and pre-existing accepted patterns of activity: however, often in healthcare we spend a high proportion of our time in the zone of complexity.

The introduction of an innovation in healthcare temporarily heightens complexity with accompanying increases in uncertainty and ambiguity. The implementation of such innovations usually removes us from our apparently less complex ways of working, where we have mastered our processes, knowledge, technology and relationships. The implementation of an innovation, such as an IT project, takes us on a journey through the zone of complexity and to the other side, sometimes as far as the cusp of chaos or even into chaos, as depicted by the curve in Figure 1. While we are there we are unable to predict with certainty the possible outcomes of our innovations, and uncertainty and ambiguity are more likely to cloud our capability than not. Such projects challenge what we know and have mastered, and in most instances take us to the place where many things are unknown where, as Flood (Barton, Emery, Flood et al., 2004) argues, many things are unknowable, and possibly should remain so. In addition, complexity is exacerbated by the emergence of unpredicted and unpredictable consequences of our actions within such a complex system as healthcare (Begun, Zimmerman, & Dooley, 2003). In some instances a small perturbance could result in a large change in the system (Glieck, 1987), for example, limiting the idle time of a computer to seven minutes before closing to secure access can disrupt a whole outpatients' clinic.

IT projects are an example of this shift to proximity with chaos: an innovation being implemented by a project is usually assessed from within our comfort zone with some shift into the zone of complexity to stimulate the development of innovations. However, the beginning of its implementation into an organization takes us to the zone of greatest complexity where the project

initially fundamentally challenges our capability to adapt. The old ways of working are juxtaposed against the innovation such that we can initially only conceptualize the changes, then attempt them, then return to our previous state of comfort as we master the new processes, technology and relationships. IT projects take us out of our comfort zone in the known, knowable, and perceived simplicity of our current work practices and relationships. Since the purpose of IT projects is to implement new information technology, we are wrenched out of our known world and stretched to the other side of the zone of complexity, and put at risk of drifting into chaos.

And so, we introduce information and knowledge management innovations in healthcare organizations by means of IT projects, many of which fail. The following section provides a background to the tendency of health IT projects to fail and the critical success factors that are usually employed to predispose such projects for success.

THE PARADOX OF HEALTH IT PROJECT FAILURES AND RESULTING SYSTEMIC CHANGE

Despite the tendency for IT projects to fail in healthcare organizations, we continue to implement knowledge management innovations such as the electronic health record. Between 50 and 80 percent of IT projects in general are considered failures (Shore, 2005). Descriptions of such failure range from outright failure (where a project is either abandoned before completion or an organization rolls back to the previous state after completion) to partial success (where core goals are not realized or outcomes are undesirable), or success (Cozijnsen, Vrakking, & van Ijzerloo, 2000; Keeling, 2000). There are replication failures (where the pilot cannot be replicated in a full implementation or a successful project cannot be replicated in a different setting or country), sustainability failures (where a project is successful only in the short term) and where the gap between the current and conceptualized future states is too big to traverse successfully (Heeks, Mundy, & Salazar, 1999). In some instances projects are considered to be a failure by some but not by others, making it hard to determine whether a project should be considered an overall success or not.

There are many reasons for project failures, most of which can be summarized in terms of scope, cost and time (Wateridge, 1998). Reasons for scope failure include a poorly defined concept that forms the basis of the project, ambitious goals, inadequate planning, unexpected, unavoidable or undesirable consequences of a project which then result in extension of the scope, poor feasibility assessment for the project, optimism of executives resulting in unrealistic decisions about innovations, and inadequately managed expectations (Heeks et al., 1999; Keeling, 2000). Where scope usually expands in failing projects, it is no surprise when time and costs do the same. Frequently, we hear project managers light-heartedly saying that there is "no time, no money, and no people to complete this project, so get on with it." The truth is that our projects fail for those reasons. When a project is not sufficiently aligned with an organization's strategy, budgets are frequently not adequate. Projects fail when management of project costs is inadequate. The easier signs to see of a failing project are time extensions, scope creep, and budget blowouts.

A project can still succeed under constrained scope, and limited budget and time if project management is good. Project management aspects that contribute to failure include inadequate risk management, sabotage from those resisting the project, poor relationship management, ineffective change management, lack of clarity around roles and responsibilities of those implementing the project and those affected by it (Turner & Muller, 2005). Other reasons for failure include inadequate identification of criteria for success at the outset, inadequate planning, failure to communicate the goals of the project to all those affected by its outcomes, ineffective learning of

new processes and technology, and poor project team development.

Add to this list of reasons for failure the complexity of implementing information technology and systems into the healthcare system. There are four components in the delivery of healthcare—clinical care, administration, research and education (Orr & Day, 2004). This means that many IT projects, even when they are not specifically clinical in nature, seem to overtly require clinical input in order to contribute to the probability of success. Clinicians traditionally left much of the administrative work to other personnel but the advent of real time data entry into electronic information systems has resulted in an increase in their administrative load. When we talk about IT projects in health we normally refer to components of the electronic health record, which is a lifelong, longitudinal record of all health and related data to be captured and stored and reused regardless of episode of care or service boundary (Orr, 2004). It is in this context that health IT projects are implemented, in order to contribute to health knowledge management systems. When health IT projects fail people's lives are at risk. In addition, health IT project success is linked to the way in which clinicians are enabled to provide care. Medical error is a serious issue in healthcare and unacceptable levels of error occur during the provision of clinical services. In some instances IT projects contribute to these errors in their very attempts at resolving them (Cosby, 2003).

Many IT projects are in businesses orientated to commercial profit and return on investment, while most health IT projects in national-based health systems such as those of New Zealand and the UK are in the public sector where the focus lies in making the most out of the resources available (Jeffcott & Johnson, 2002). This means that public sector health IT projects seek to add value in a different way from most IT projects in business. Even establishing an appropriate strategy has proved to be more difficult than expected as evidenced in the failure in the Wessex Region in the UK in the 1990s (Hackney & McBride, 2002) despite strong alignment with the nation's health strategy. It appears to be difficult to feed lessons learned from previous projects back into new policies and strategies (Jeffcott & Johnson, 2002). There is a need for risk assessment to incorporate technical, people, clinical and organizational aspects in order to reduce chances of IT project failure in the health context.

On the one hand there are reasons for failure and on the other we undertake to use critical success factors to predispose our projects for success. This forms a counterbalance to the predictable reasons for failure and even in a complex and mostly unpredictable system; sound project management practice requires their use.

CRITICAL FACTORS FOR PROJECT SUCCESS

IT projects bring about complex change, which means that we need to build success into a project from the outset. A successful, quality implementation project should deliver on time, and within agreed scope and allocated budget (Wateridge, 1998). Such success factors include strategic alignment orientated to meeting the organization's needs, customer and stakeholder satisfaction, usability of the new technology and processes, resulting in the realization of the project's benefits and delivery according to expectations. To achieve this end, effective project management and organizational leadership are essential (Turner & Muller, 2005). This includes finding the right project manager, one who exhibits characteristics of a strong management profile with relevant experience in the type of organization in which the proposed project will be implemented; leadership, communication and change management skills; team building capacity; business acumen; capacity to deal with uncertainty, ambiguity and paradoxes; and someone who is a pace setter and project process controller (Grundy & Brown, 2002). Although leadership does not appear to be a primary project management skill, organizational

leadership, project governance, sponsorship and champions are essential for project success. In the healthcare organization such leadership is complex as it is comprised of management and clinical leadership, which are often at odds with one another.

Such leadership requires early learning on the part of the leaders for whom IT is simply a tool for their clinical effectiveness. Projects usually implement something new and innovative, which in turn requires learning (Pinto, 2004). An array of users need to learn the new processes and technology as it is implemented, parallel to their performing tasks the old way until the cross-over to the new processes and technology. Project team members need to learn the new product and associated processes and also teach and support the users in the rest of their organization during the course of the project. Learning for project team members occurs on the two levels outlined by Argyris (1976)—single loop learning occurs where the person learns how to use the new product and processes, while project team members do double loop learning when they reflect on project progress, issues and risks and adjust the project activities accordingly in order to promote success.

This learning sets up the project team for complex change which includes adjustments to the planned change as well as mastery of the new processes, technology and the new relationships created by the project's outcomes. Since our health IT projects are delivered in "live" situations that could affect patient lives, and are disruptive by nature of changing the way we work, a change management programme is one of the most important critical success factors for a project in which a IT innovation is being implemented (Williams, 2005). Since change occurs on multiple levels in an organization (Moss Kanter, 2000) and we experience change on individual and collective levels as a process (Elrod & Tippett, 2002), we need to develop change management programmes that recognize the complexity of change in healthcare organizations.

THE CHANGE PROCESS

According to most change theorists, we progress through a process (Elrod & Tippett, 2002) when adapting to change, and on multiple levels when adapting to organizational change (Moss Kanter, 2000). This assumes that we generally follow a process of unbundling the old way of working, transitioning to the new way, and settling down into these new ways of working as described by Lewin's model of change (Lewin, 1951). However, in a complex adaptive system such as healthcare one could argue that we never achieve stasis that could allow us to freeze into the new ways of working (Dooley, 1997), as described in Lewin's model of unfreeze, change and refreeze.

Since innovations, large and small, with differing effects are constantly being absorbed in healthcare organizations, then one could argue that we are constantly looping through the change journey as shown in Figure 1. IT projects challenge us on multiple levels of technology, process, knowledge and relationships, on an organizational, group and individual level. However, it does appear that we follow a process as we journey through the zone of complexity and loop back to our comfort zone as we master new skills, technology and relationships with one another. This process has been best described for individual responses to change rather than on a collective level, as outlined by Elrod and Tippett (2002) in their comparison of theories of the change process as depicted by Figure 2: the process occurring during the journey through the zone of complexity and back again.

It appears that over time we move through a process of conceptually acknowledging a proposed change (or the change that is upon us), push it away, commit to it, make the transition from the old ways, and finally accommodate the changes in our daily activities following the curve in Figure 2, as our productivity and capability dip in the 'death valley of change' (Elrod & Tippett, 2002), and we adjust to the new ways. Schneider and Goldwasser (Schneider & Goldwasser, 1998) describe a period of transition in which we realize what we have undertaken after we embark on the journey to our goal. This transition is a landmark in the change process and how we manage it determines the success of health IT projects.

THE NEED FOR CHANGE MANAGEMENT IN COMPLEX HEALTHCARE SYSTEMS

Although there are several approaches to change management, there appears to be agreement

Figure 2. The process of change (Elrod & Tippett, 2002)

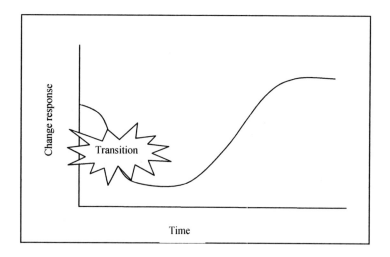

that change should be managed (Cao, Clarke, & Lehaney, 2003), especially in the context of health organizations as complex adaptive systems that are unpredictable and exhibit high levels of ambiguity and uncertainty. This approach is evident in project management methodology and is essential for the success of IT projects (Bentley, 1992; Project Management Institute, 2000). Since organizational change is multifarious, occurring on multiple levels, to multiple degrees and in multiple contexts (Moss Kanter, 2000), linear change management efforts are likely to fail (Cao et al., 2003): change management that addresses multiple components of a project on multiple levels is more likely to succeed, while at times positive change may even emerge without deliberate management (Smith, 2004). Some argue that a deliberate change management plan with a systemic focus is most effective (Cao et al., 2003), while others maintain that since change is continuous, change management can at best attempt to identify opportunities and steer organizations in the right direction as these opportunities arise in a complex environment (Dooley, 1997). Although such a change management program should be orientated to all aspects of change in a complex healthcare system, it is important to also address the individual and collective responses to change, especially the transition phase of the change process, which could be the turning point for most people involved in an IT project.

THE TRANSITION PHASE OF THE CHANGE PROCESS AS TURNING POINT

The transition step, as depicted in Figure 2, appears to be a key step in the change process and has to date been treated rather as a form of resistance to change than as an indicator of the occurrence of change. Those who have examined resistance to change, such as Mariotti, have explored ways in which people resist change (Elrod & Tippett,

2002), and Mabin, Forgeson, and Green (2001) have examined the paradox of using resistance to change for facilitating change. Reasons for resisting change include low tolerance for change, lack of readiness for change, perceptions of unacceptable loss, inability to see the usefulness of the change, desire to retain what is perceived to be valuable, and perceived loss of power resulting from role changes and organizational restructure (Kotter, 1996; Lu & Yeh, 1998; Moss Kanter, 1985; Teng, Grover, & Fiedler, 1996). With the idea of the utility of resistance to change and the key role of the process of change on an individual and collective level, we conducted research on change linked to health IT projects in the emergence of a shared services organization for two district health boards (DHB) in New Zealand described in detail elsewhere (Day & Norris, 2006c) and briefly here.

Change and the Emergence of a Shared Services Organization

Two DHBs in Auckland, New Zealand, established a shared services organization to share the provision of support services, such as finance, human resources and information services (IS). The aim of doing so was to make the total cost of ownership of these services transparent, to create savings by sharing services and to return those savings to the clinical budget of the two DHBs. The alignment of the IT infrastructure was one of the first objectives of the new, single IS department. Parallel to this multifaceted project, which involved radical technological and process changes, other health IT projects continued in both DHBs. This was typical of a complex adaptive healthcare system. The changes impacted mostly on the IT personnel but finally had an impact on every person who uses a computer in both DHBs and the shared services organization, when all computers were standardized as an expression of the planned project outcome of a single IT infrastructure for all three related service organizations.

We wove action research principles of participation, empowerment, cyclic action (plan, act, observe, reflect and modify the plan) (Brydon-Miller et al., 2003) into the change management program in order to simultaneously enhance the effectiveness of the program and conduct research. The goal of the research was to examine the transition phase of the change process to see how it could be used for future change management effectiveness. This transition step emerged as an important part of the change process and its relevance for a change management program.

TRANSITION, A FORM OF COMMITMENT RATHER THAN RESISTANCE TO CHANGE

The transition step of the change process occurs soon after commitment to planned change and initially appears as a sense of realization about what we have undertaken with the project in which we are currently involved (Schneider & Goldwasser, 1998). It occurs at a time when the impact of the project's goals is perceived to make a difference to an individual's daily working activities. This could occur at any point during the project for any individual, depending on at what point the project's changes impact on that individual's daily work activities. Although the transition occurs soon after commitment to the project at hand, it is at its height when we reach the cusp of chaos where our sense of ambiguity and uncertainty is strongest, as depicted in Figure 3.

The transition step is a form of capability crisis (Day & Norris, 2006c) that occurs for most participants in an IT project. People are working in the old ways whilst learning new ways of working, dealing with old relationships whilst developing new relationships, and in the project team itself, team members are helping others with this complexity while dealing with their own changing situation. There may be one or many of these crises, while some people claim that they don't have any. It appears that the person who initiates these projects does not have such a crisis, especially if they are involved on an executive level throughout the project duration (Day & Norris, 2006b). Others who may not have such crises seem to be able to avoid them by learning as much as they can about the proposed changes

Figure 3. Change process meets complexity in the capability crisis

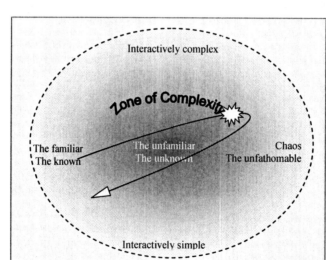

and treating continuing learning as a priority throughout the project's duration.

People feel their workload increases while resources for getting through all the work diminish. Too much is happening too soon. Although people consider communication to be crucial, they find it hard to take in information and use it appropriately. Everything seems uncertain and ambiguous. This crisis embodies a fundamental and scary moment for most people at a time when they seek leadership and find it either lacking, inappropriate or not where they expect to find it. Leadership is important for them to survive the project: they want their leaders to be everything for everyone but the leaders cannot fulfill this wish. The leaders themselves may be dealing with their own capability crisis as they cross over from known and familiar to the unknown and unpredictable. Predictions of failure emerge as people start to lack confidence in the project's success but paradoxically they continue to work on the project.

Superficially this crisis appears to be a form of resistance to change. On the contrary, it emerges as a marker of commitment to the goals of an IT project and indicates the beginning of real change on the part of those participating in the project. The success of a project could be said to hang on how we identify or diagnose this crisis and what we do with it as change managers. Knowing that people have a propensity to this type of crisis during planned change, managers and leaders can design and offer preventative interventions that reduce stress, shock and compromised capability linked to the realization of the implications of the project at hand.

USING THE TRANSITION AS A CHANGE MANAGEMENT TOOL FOR SUCCESS

When, as with most people, the crisis does occur, two overarching components of change manage-

ment emerge in this transition or crisis. When viewed from a manager's position, especially that of a project and change manager, it becomes clear that we need to predict and diagnose the nature and severity of the crisis in order to intervene and assist people in dealing with it so that effective change can occur without the pain and difficulty usually associated with health IT projects. People follow a process when changing and that process involves this transition step. We change in a complex system where we shift from our comfort zone through the zone of complexity to the cusp of chaos, change management programs should address the process and complexity of change simultaneously.

The capability crisis is usually followed by a dip in response to the change, and most people talk about dark times during and soon after the transition step when they feel that too much is happening too soon and they are frustrated that they are unable to perform in a manner to which they are accustomed. It is rare that people will flat line at the lowest ebb of the change process and not be able to emerge from it to complete their own change process. However, it is possible that they could stall at the cusp of chaos for too long and their mastery of the new processes, technology and relationships becomes compromised. This could account for some project failures when too many people are unable to take on the changes they confront. For most people, the crisis is short in duration, ranging from a momentary panic to months of stress. An extended crisis is frequently accompanied by a recent promotion, naïve management practice or novice leadership skills, or lack of project experience coupled with a senior project role. Regardless of experience and seniority, many people experience more than one crisis, depending on their ongoing role in an IT project and the milestones in which they are involved. It is possible to experience a crisis at the beginning of each milestone as we take in the meaning and impact of it in our daily work activities. Diagnosis of the capability crisis equips managers and leaders for an intervention that will predispose the people to change and the project to succeed.

Diagnosing the Capability Crisis

Since this capability crisis occurs for most people, the change manager, project manager and leaders should expect it to happen. The sign easiest to observe is the emergence of background chatter of predictions of failure. Some people will go so far as to call for the project or a particular milestone to be delayed, postponed or simply abandoned. There will be competition for resources with resultant perceptions of inequity, when those who do not get the full complement they expected, sense inequity when comparing their resource-to-workload ratio with that of others. There will also be calls for as much information as possible but paradoxically people will not be able to process it usefully.

There will be comments of how they have not been told about this, that, or another aspect of the project, and yet they have attended all meetings in which the information has been communicated. The need for simple, clear, brief, purposeful communication is heightened. Most people will confirm that they have a heightened sense of awareness of complexity, ambiguity and uncertainty. They find it hard to believe the information they are given about the project because it does not make sense to them in the way they expected it to at the beginning of the project. Interestingly, although this all sounds like resistance to change, people continue to act out their commitment to the project by attending training sessions, progressing through the project milestones and trying out the new processes and technology.

This is an intense experience, even for those whose capability crisis is momentary, and it compromises decision making, leadership capacity, and performance. For some it can be an extremely unpleasant experience in which they feel themselves floundering in their attempts at adapting to the changes brought about by the project simultaneous to ongoing business-as-usual activities. If we, as managers, project managers, change managers, leaders and colleagues, recognize that this capability crisis is characteristic of our attempts at the transition from the old to the new, then we will be able to assist one another in making that journey through the zone of complexity and return from the cusp of chaos in order to master the new and unknown that normally accompany the implementation of innovations. Such assistance should be built into a project's change management program.

Managing the Capability Crisis for Transition to New Ways of Working

The change management program that deals with the capability crisis in order to predispose the project for success, should include management of workload, resources and training; provide opportunities for learning; emphasize the role of useful communication, and develop a coalition of leadership.

Workload, Resources and Training

The capability crisis represents a time when workload disproportionately increases, when we are performing tasks and activities in the old way and will later abandon them once the new tasks and activities have been mastered (Day & Norris, 2006c). We are learning and performing new tasks parallel to the old tasks and yet are frustrated by our short-term failures to perform optimally. Our workload is temporarily disproportionate to the outcomes and in a complex healthcare organization there are few ways to support this load for any length of time before clinical care is at risk.

Bearing in mind that managers themselves are possibly experiencing their own capability crises, the change management program associated with an IT project should plan for this workload increase. Since decision making is compromised during the crisis, it is essential that important decisions regarding resource allocation and training are made during project planning stages so that those concerned are enabled to work with the best decisions about resources and workload that were available at the time. For example, training is frequently postponed during times of high stress in a team or department and it is training that is essential for a successful project if people are going to be using different processes and technology as a result of it. The change management program should include a detailed schedule for training so that if a manager or team leader is busy with their own capability crisis, they will be able to enact the earlier decisions without compromising their team's capacity to adapt to the changes.

Resources become a high priority and yet they appear to diminish as the need appears to grow. Again, the decisions regarding resource allocation should be worked through during project planning and in most cases they are (Pinto, 2004). However, it is characteristic for IT projects to demonstrate some degree of emergence common to complex adaptive systems and resources need to be reconsidered and matched to the need more closely as the project progresses. The change management program should provide opportunities for reflection (Day, Orr, Sankaran, & Norris, 2006), as in the action research process, on stages of the project to allow for adjustments to the project plan in order to fine-tune resources. However, if many people are experiencing a capability crisis simultaneously their capacity to reflect on progress and to adjust the project plan will be compromised, especially if they are participating in the background chatter of predictions of failure. In this instance, it would be advisable to make use of the community of practice that is common in projects (Garrety, Roberston, & Badham, 2004) in order to create an environment of mutual support and learning.

The Role of Learning in Managing the Capability Crisis

Not everyone who is faced with change experiences a capability crisis (Day & Norris, 2006c). There are those who embrace the change as a challenge or an opportunity to enhance their situation. These people use learning to turn the unfamiliar into the familiar while moving in and out of the zone of complexity in a complex and rapidly and unpredictably changing environment. It appears that a growing sense of ambiguity and uncertainty are stimuli for more learning, rather than an indication that there may be a problem as is the case with the capability crisis. The need to learn is juxtaposed against the time and resources needed to support the learning—however, if learning is prioritized there is a lowered risk of wasted resources thus lowering the risk of compromised capability due to an extended capability crisis. Project team members appear to learn on two levels as described by Argyris (1976) where they do single loop and double loop learning, building on their experiences in the project in order to develop their new skills, processes, technology and relationships. Opportunities for such learning should be built into the project process in order to minimize the impact of the capability crisis on project success.

The Role of Communication for Successful Transition

Communication is difficult during times of planned change. Sensitivity to information overload, the need for communication and the difficulty to assimilate it during this phase mean that key messages about the project should be relayed during times of reduced stress. Communication and learning become intricately linked such that the participants in a project are able to learn new skills and not lose sight of the project's expected outcomes (Elving, 2005). There is a need for crisp, brief, to-the-point, repetitive communication during the time when most people are busy with a capability crisis, at the cusp of chaos when it is hard to process information.

Communication for those in the capability crisis in complex healthcare services should make the most of multiple media, for example, intranet, e-mails, team and group discussions, and at the same time maintain a core message that is repeated so that people can hear the message when they are most unable to take it in (Elving, 2005). The change management program should incorporate information about the proposed change associated with an IT project and a learning program so that communication opportunities become learning opportunities (Day & Norris, 2006b). People are hungry for information, for a shared understanding of the project (Orr & Sankaran, 2005), for a community of practice, at a time when they are least able to achieve it. Multimedia communication is useful for people affected by the project in that they are able to absorb information in ways that resonate with their personal style of communication and learning. Later, they are able, after their own experience of the capability crisis, to refer to key written messages in order to continue with their change journey and mastery of the new processes, technology and relationships.

Leadership as a Capability Crisis Intervention

There is a mixed composition of leadership in most IT projects in that there are mandated leaders, for example, team managers, tangential leaders (mandated leaders who appear to have an agenda that does not support the project), leaders in other parts of the organization who are indirectly involved in the project, and informal leaders whose leadership emerges as a form of contingency leadership (Day & Norris, 2006a). Since people relate to different leadership forms from different people (Kouzes & Posner, 1990), it is useful to establish a leadership coalition for the purposes

of the project at hand. However, leaders may be grappling with their own capability crisis at the same time as everyone else. A new composite of leadership should be developed from all leaders available to people during the course of planned change. This leadership should be negotiated before the project is signed off for commencement so that during the time spent at the cusp of chaos leaders are able to enact their agreement while dealing with their own difficulties arising from increased complexity, working in the unknown and unknowable, and while they master their own changes (Day & Norris, 2006a). In the same way that the project team forms a community of practice it is recommended that the leadership affected by the project form a community of practice with a shared understanding of the project's goals, impact and benefits.

CONCLUSION AND RECOMMENDATIONS

In summary, this chapter provides an overview of change linked to health IT projects in the context of healthcare as a complex adaptive system. Health IT project usually introduce innovations and are thus disruptive, often resulting in complex changes to processes, technology and relationships in an organization. They challenge our familiar routines and shift us into the zone of complexity, causing changes that result in a journey to the cusp of chaos where we experience a transition that forms the turning point upon which we base our mastery of new processes, technology and relationships when things become familiar and comfortable again The transition is part of a change process we usually follow in which we commit to change, push it away, attempt adaptation and finally master the innovations implemented in health IT projects. The transition is expressed in most people's experience as a capability crisis in which we have a heightened sense of ambiguity, complexity and uncertainty, our workload increases disproportionately, we hunger for information but are unable to process what is communicated to us, resources seem too few and mismatched to need, leadership seems to be lacking and we cannot see how the project can succeed.

As we attempt to ensure project success, we should include the following components in the change management program in order to make the most of the capability crisis when it arises.

- The disproportionate increase in workload should be acknowledged and plans made to accommodate working simultaneously in old and new ways.
- Resource management is different in projects, especially in light of the competition for resources to accommodate the disproportionate increase in workload. A transparent resource plan to manage the rise and fall in workload, as well as standard project and operational workload should be established as part of the project plan.
- Communities of practice arise informally during a project. Two specific communities of practice should be established at the outset and require more research.
- A leadership coalition with negotiated key activities and approaches.
- A community of practice of project participants that is more than team building and outlives the project so that ongoing mutual support and connected competence form the foundation of changed work practices.

The capability crisis marks the transition from the old ways to the new and is a turning point in the change process in complex healthcare systems. It is potentially a powerful change management tool and, if incorporated in an IT project's change management program, is capable of enhancing our efforts to change in difficult, complex and apparently chaotic times.

FUTURE RESEARCH DIRECTIONS

The change process is well known as evidenced by the description of the 'death valley of change' by Elrod and Tippett (2002). Although the transition from before to after was identified by Schneider and Goldwasser (1998) it appears that no research has been conducted on what constitutes this transition (capability crisis) or its effect on how we adjust to organizational change in complex healthcare organizations. The complex adaptive systems theory has only recently been adopted as a way of understanding healthcare organizations. Finally, knowledge management is also relatively new to healthcare systems and as we continue to implement new information and knowledge initiatives in our healthcare services effective change management becomes a priority on the list of critical success factors for project managers. This leaves a gap for future research that includes the following.

- The use of action research principles (cycle of planning, action, reflection, modification and refinement of plans) as a foundation for change management in health IT projects in developing reflexive employees who are more capable of adapting to change.
- The application of complexity theory in understanding the use of critical success factors for health IT projects, over and above leadership and project management.
- The link between the project management process, and change as a process **and** a journey through complexity.
- The influence of the capability crisis amongst leaders when the demands on leadership from them are high during the course of a project.
- Resolving the 'problem of learning' during the course of a health IT project.
- The influence of communities of practice on project success linked to adaptation to

change, with special reference to experiencing the capability crisis during times of transition.

• The influence of a well-managed transition, that is, capability crisis, on health IT project success and its subsequent influence on the development of comprehensive knowledge management systems for a nation, community and/or individual.

As we continue to plan, implement and evaluate these initiatives opportunities for future research lie in each aspect of the associated projects. Complex healthcare systems change all the time—the opportunity to understand this change lies in every implementation of a health knowledge management implementation.

REFERENCES

Argyris, C. (1976). Leadership, learning and changing the status quo. *Organizational Dynamics, 4*(3), 29-43.

Barton, J., Emery, M., Flood, R. L., Selsky, J. W., & Wolstenholme, E. (2004). A maturing of systems thinking? Evidence from three perspectives. *Systemic Practice and Action Research, 17*(1), 3-37.

Begun, J. W., Zimmerman, B., & Dooley, K. (2003). Health care organizations as complex adaptive systems. In S. M. Mick & M. Wyttenback (Eds.), *Advances in health care organization theory* (Vol. 253-288). San Francisco: Jossey-Bass.

Bentley, C. (1992). *Introducing PRINCE*. Oxford: NCC Blackwell.

Brydon-Miller, M., Greenwood, D., & Maguire, P. (2003). Why action research? *Action Research, 1*(1), 9-28.

Cao, G., Clarke, S., & Lehaney, B. (2003). The need for a systemic approach to change manage-ment——A case study. *Systemic Practice and Action Research, 17*(2), 103-126.

Cosby, K. S. (2003). A framework for classifying factors that contribute to error in the emergency department. *Annals of Emergency Medicine, 42*(6), 815 - 823.

Cozijnsen, A. J., Vrakking, W. J., & van Ijzerloo, M. (2000). Success and failure of 50 innovation projects in Dutch companies. *European Journal of Innovation Management, 3*(3), 150-159.

Day, K., & Norris, A. C. (2006a, 9 August 2006). *Leadership in times of crisis during change due to health IT projects.* Paper presented at the Health Informatics New Zealand (HINZ), Auckland, New Zealand.

Day, K., & Norris, A. C. (2006b, 17 July 2006). *Supporting information technology across health boards in New Zealand: The role of learning in adapting to complex change.* Paper presented at the 11th International Sympsium on Health Information Management Research (iSHIMR), Halifax, Canada.

Day, K., & Norris, A. C. (2006c). Supporting information technology across health boards in New Zealand: Themes emerging from the develop-ment of a shared services organization. *Health Informatics Journal, 12*(1), 13-25.

Day, K., Orr, M., Sankaran, S., & Norris, A. C. (2006, 22 August 2006). *The reflexive employee: action research immortalised?* Paper presented at the 7th ALARPM (Action Learning, Action Research and Process Management Association) & 11th PAR (Participatory Action Research) World Congress, Groningen, The Netherlands.

Dooley, K. (1997). A complex adaptive systems model of organization change. *Nonlinear Dynamics, Psychology, and Life Sciences, 1*(1), 69-97.

Elrod, P. D., & Tippett, D. D. (2002). The 'death valley' of change. *Journal of Organizational Change Management, 15*(3), 273-291.

Elving, W. J. L. (2005). The role of communication in organizational change. *Corporate Communications, 10*(2), 129-139.

Fraser, S., & Greenhalgh, T. (2001). Coping with complexity: Educating for capability. *British Medical Journal, 323*(7216), 799-803.

Garrety, K., Roberston, P. L., & Badham, R. (2004). Integrating communities of practice in technology development projects. *International Journal of Project Management, 22*(2004), 351-358.

Glieck, J. (1987). *Chaos: Making a new science.* New York: Penguin Books.

Grundy, T., & Brown, L. (2002). *Strategic project management: Creating organizational breakthroughs.* London: Thomson Learning.

Hackney, R., & McBride, N. (2002). Non-implementation of an IS strategy within a UK hospital: observations from a longitudinal case analysis. *Communications of the AIS, 8*(8), 2-20.

Heeks, R., Mundy, D., & Salazar, A. (1999). *Why health care information systems succeed or fail. Information systems for public sector management. Working paper series 9.* Manchester: Institute for Development Policy Management.

Jeffcott, M. A., & Johnson, C. W. (2002). The use of a formalised risk model in NHS information system development. *Cognition, Technology & Work, 4,* 120 - 136.

Keeling, R. (2000). *Project management: An international perspective.* London: MacMillan Press Ltd.

Kotter, J. P. (1996). *Leading change.* Boston: Harvard Business School Press.

Kouzes, J. M., & Posner, B. Z. (1990). The credibility factor: what followers expect from their leaders. *Business Credit, 92*(5), 24-28.

Lewin, K. (1951). *Field theory in social science.* New York: Harper and Row.

Lu, H. P., & Yeh, D. C. (1998). Enterprises' perceptions on business process re-engineering: a path analytic model. *Omega, International Journal of Management Science, 26*(1), 17-27.

Mabin, V. J., Forgeson, S., & Green, L. (2001). Harnessing resistance: Using the theory of constraints to assist change management. *Journal of European Industrial Training, 25*(2-4), 168-191.

Moss Kanter, R. (1985). *The change masters: corporate entrepreneurs at work.* London: Unwin Paperbacks.

Moss Kanter, R. (2000). Leaders with passion, conviction and confidence can use several techniques to take change or change rather than react to it. *Ivey Business Journal, 64*(5), 32-38.

Orr, M. (2004). Evolution of New Zealand's health knowledge management system. *British Journal of Healthcare Computing and Information Management, 21*(10), 28-30.

Orr, M., & Day, K. (2004). Knowledge and learning in 'successful' IT projects: a case study. *Health Care and Informatics Review Online* Retrieved June 17, 2004, from http://www.enigma.co.nz/hcro/website/index.cfm?fuseaction=articledisplay&Feature

Orr, M., & Sankaran, S. (2005, 5-7 December). *Mutual emphathy, ambiguity and the implementation of electronic knowledge management within the complex health system.* Paper presented at the Systems Thinking and Complexity Science: Insights for Action. 11th Annual ANZSYS Conference: Managing the Complex, Christchurch, New Zealand.

Pinto, J. K. (2004). The elements of project success. In D. I. Cleland (Ed.), *Field guide to project management* (pp. 14-27). Hoboken, NJ: John Wiley & Sons.

Plesk, P. E., & Greenhalgh, T. (2001). Complexity science. The challenge of complexity in health care. *British Medical Journal, 323,* 625-628.

Project Management Institute. (2000). *A guide to project management body of knowledge (PMBOK Guide)* (2000 ed.). Newtown Square: Project Management Institute.

Schneider, D. M., & Goldwasser, C. (1998). Be a model leader of change. *Management Review, 87*(3), 41-45.

Shin, N., & Jemella, D. F. (2002). Business process reengineering and performance improvement. *Business Process Management Journal, 8*(4), 351-363.

Shore, B. (2005). Failure rates in global IS projects and the leadership challenge. *Journal of Global Information Management, 8*(3), 1-5.

Smith, A. C. T. (2004). Complexity theory and change management in sport organizations. *Emergence: Complexity & Organization, 6*(1-2), 70-79.

Tan, J., Wen, H. J., & Awad, N. (2005). Health care and services delivery systems as complex adaptive systems. Examining chaos theory in action. *Communications of the ACM, 48*(5), 37-44.

Teng, J. T. C., Grover, V., & Fiedler, K. D. (1996). Developing strategic perspectives on business process reengineering: from process reconfiguration to organizational change. *International Journal of Management Science, 24*(3), 271-294.

Turner, J. R., & Muller, R. (2005). The project manager's leadership style as a success factor on projects: a literature review. *Project Management Journal, 36*(2), 49-61.

Wateridge, J. (1998). How can IS/IT projects be measured for success? *International Journal of Project Management, 16*(1), 59-63.

Williams, B. (2005). Models of organizational change and development. *Futurics, 29*(3 & 4), 1-22.

ADDITIONAL READINGS

Ballard, D. (2005). Using learning processes to promote change for sustainable development. *Action Research, 3*(2), 135-156.

Baskerville, R. (1999). Investigating information systems with action research. *Communications of the Association for Information Systems, 2*(Article 19).

Baskerville, R., & Pries-Heje, J. (1999). Grounded action research: A method for understanding IT in practice. *Accounting, Management and Information Technologies, 9*(1), 1-23.

Bryman, A. (2004). Qualitative research on leadership: A critical but appreciative review. *The Leadership Quarterly, 15*, 729-769.

Grundy, T., & Brown, L. (2002). *Strategic project management: Creating organizational breakthroughs.* London: Thomson Learning.

Hammer, M., & Champy, J. A. (2001). *Reengineering the corporation: A manifesto for business revolution.* New York: HarperBusiness.

Hammer, M., Leonard, D., & Davenport, T. (2004). Why don't we know more about knowledge? *Sloan Management Review, 45*(4), 14.

McArdle, K. L., & Reason, P. (2006). Action research and organization development. In T. Cummings (Ed.), *Handbook of Organization Development.* Thousand Oaks: Sage Publications.

Pearce, C. L. (2004). The future of leadership: Combining vertical and shared leadership to transform knowledge work. *Academy of Management Executive, 18*(1), 47 - 57.

Reason, P. (2006). Choice and quality in action research practice. *Journal of Management Inquiry* Retrieved May 29, 2006, from http://www.bath.ac.uk/~mnspwr/

Sense, A. J., & Antoni, M. (2003). Exploring the politics of project learning. *International Journal of Project Management, 21*, 487-494.

Snowden, D. (2003). Complex acts of knowing: paradox and descriptive self-awareness. *Bulletin of the American Society for Information Science and Technology, 29*(4), 23-28.

Snowden, D., & Stanbridge, P. (2004). The landscape of management: Creating the context for understanding complexity. *Emergence: Complexity & Organization, 6*(1-2), 140-148.

Turner, J. R., & Muller, R. (2005). The project manager's leadership style as a success factor on projects: A literature review. *Project Management Journal, 36*(2), 49-61.

Chapter VII
Best Practices for Implementing Electronic Health Records and Information Systems

Beste Kucukyazici
McGill University, Canada

Karim Keshavjee
InfoClin Inc., Canada

John Bosomworth
University of Victoria, Canada

John Copen
University of Victoria, Canada

James Lai
University of British Columbia, Canada

ABSTRACT

This chapter introduces a multi-level, multi-dimensional meta-framework for successful implementations of EHR in healthcare organizations. Existing implementation frameworks do not explain many features experienced and reported by implementers and have not helped to make health information technology implementation any more successful. To close this gap, we have developed an EHR implementation framework that integrates multiple conceptual frameworks in an overarching, yet pragmatic meta-framework to explain factors which lead to successful EHR implementation, in order to provide more quantitative insight into EHR implementations. Our meta-framework captures the dynamic nature of an EHR implementation through their function, interactivity with other factors and phases, and iterative nature.

Copyright © 2008, IGI Global, distributing in print or electronic forms without written permission of IGI Global is prohibited.

INTRODUCTION: OVERVIEW OF THE ISSUE AND THE CHALLENGES

Advances in healthcare technology and the explosion of new therapies have outpaced the ability of healthcare systems, organizations, and professionals to cope. Healthcare costs have spiraled. Medical errors cause thousands of deaths each year and under-treatment is rampant (Institute of Medicine, 2001). Innovations take over 17 years to get from bench to bedside. Although information technology, such as electronic medical records (EMR), electronic health records (EHR) and computerized physician order entry (CPOE) systems, continue to evolve as technologies for use in clinical practice and show great promise, they are fraught with high implementation failure rates and sometimes cause even greater harm than previous paper systems (Koppel, Metlay, Cohen et al., 2005).

Typically, most of the investment of system implementation is born up-front both in terms of finances, and in time and energy. With increasing fiscal restraint and a greater demand by all stakeholders for demonstrated value, it is important to ensure that health information technology implementations are successful, yet, in spite of over three decades of experience with EHR implementation, the penetration of the EHR is still less than 20% in the United States and in Canada (Duke Clinical Research Institute, 2005). The failure rates of EHR and CPOE implementations are also consistently high at close to 50% (Centre for Health Policy and Research, 2006). As experience with implementations of technology in medical practice increases, new knowledge is gained on how to make those implementations more successful. The acceleration of EHR adoption and increasing success may depend in part on better understanding of the factors that influence the success and failure of EHR implementations (Studer, 2005). The existing empirical literature is beginning to reflect this knowledge in a series of case studies, limited randomized controlled trials, review articles and numerous qualitative studies exploring various factors and frameworks aimed at explaining how to best implement health record and information systems to achieve a successful outcome (Ash et al., 2003; Berg, 2001; Collins, 1998; Curtis et al., 1995; Golden & Martin, 2004; Rogers, 1995).

Existing implementation frameworks do not explain many features experienced and reported by users and have not helped to make health information technology implementation any more successful. To close this gap, we have developed an EHR implementation meta-framework that integrates the experiences of actual implementations and underpins those experiences using multiple conceptual frameworks from a variety of theoretical perspectives from the information technology (IT), business and EHR implementation literatures. This meta-framework is an overarching, yet pragmatic framework to explain the factors which are important in EHR implementations and how they interact in a dynamic and mutually reshaping manner which leads to successful EHR implementation.

BRIEF LITERATURE REVIEW

As experience with implementations of technology in medical practice increases, a cumulative literature of empirical support, in the form of case studies, limited randomized controlled trials, and numerous qualitative studies, has begun to emerge (Ash, 2003; Berg, 2001; Collins, 1998). The high failure rates seen in information systems implementation calls for a better understanding of the critical success factors necessary for EHR implementation (Somers et al., 2000). Listing 'success factors' has been the most popular approach in the literature for describing implementation approaches (Chiang & Starren, 2002, Chin, 2004; Saleem et al., 2005; Smith, 2003; Tape & Campbell, 2003; Weir et al., 1995), but has not been fully explanatory and predictive of success or failure (Kukafka et al., 2003; Studer, 2005). The factor approach however is too static to account for the evolving nature of EHR implementation experienced by implementers. Development of a more comprehensive framework which takes into account the dynamic, iterative and interactive aspects of EHR implementations is necessary to provide a sounder theoretical basis to underpin practical EHR implementations. Kukafka et al. (2003) confirm in their systematic review of the healthcare IT implementation literature that the integrative impact of multiple factors on implementations and indeed the development of multi-dimensional interventions is lacking (Kukafka et al., 2003). Several different factors and frameworks have been put forward in the literature for explaining how to best implement the EHR to achieve a successful outcome and to improve EHR diffusion and uptake. These include Rogers' diffusion of innovations model (Rogers, 1995), Collins' risk mitigation model (Collins, 1998) and Ash et al's success factor matrix model (Ash et al., 2003). More recently, Berg has described the socio-technical model (Berg, 2001) and Heeks describes a 'design-reality' gap model (Heeks, 2006). The technology acceptance model (TAM) of Davis and Wilder (1998) provides understanding of human behavior relative to potential technology uptake. However, most models explain only a small component of the complex interplay of factors that are inherent in an EHR implementation. Only Ash et al. (2003) take a comprehensive view of IT implementations, but they do not explain how the various factors interact nor do they underpin their framework with a theoretical base.

The success of information systems implementation and utilization depends on the integration of the information technology (IT) into an often complex organizational setting (Golden & Martin, 2004). In this context, EHR implementation should be understood in a much more complex framework (Curtis et al., 1995). Without addressing the full range of factors in an implementation

framework, EHR implementers run the risk of being ineffective because they fail to recognize the interdependencies between individual, organizational and technological factors (Kukafka et al., 2003). There are several features of EHR implementations that require frameworks from organization behavior and IT literature to fully explain what implementers observe and experience during an implementation. Golden's systems theory approach using his Strategic Star Model (Golden & Martin, 2004) provides a framework for organizational change which is rooted in the organizational behavior literature. The people-capability maturity model (P-CMM), which utilizes the people, process, and technology model (Curtis et al., 1995), is rooted in the IT literature. Kotter's model of change management which addresses change agent issues, change leadership, and change management is rooted in the business literature (Kotter, 1995).

DEVELOPMENT OF AN INTEGRATED BEST PRACTICES EHR IMPLEMENTATION FRAMEWORK

We integrated multiple conceptual frameworks from the EHR implementation, information technology, business and organizational behavior literatures in the process of developing our EHR implementation meta-framework. The EHR implementation meta-framework was developed through an iterative process of reading primary descriptions of implementations, identifying implementation-relevant factors and iteratively mapping those factors to the various conceptual frameworks we identified earlier. In this manner, we identified and filled gaps in the existing EHR implementation models and used the additional models to label new issues arising from the EHR implementation literature to create our meta-framework. Finally, we developed operational definitions for the factors in our implementation framework. This multi-theoretical, meta-framework for EHR implementation was recently presented and published in a conference proceeding (Keshavjee et al., 2006).

We applied our EHR implementation meta-framework retrospectively to 47 articles, which were primary descriptions of the experiences of EHR implementers obtained through a systematic search of the literature (Keshavjee et al., 2006). Each article was reviewed independently by two authors for whether a factor existed, whether it was correctly implemented and whether that factor had an impact, positive or negative, on the final outcome. Each author also provided a global outcome score for the article. Inter-rater reliability of the factors within the framework and use of the framework to analyze actual implementations will be reported elsewhere. All scores were resolved through consensus and the final scores were analyzed using logistic regression. Odds-ratios reported in this chapter are from this logistic regression analysis. Greater explanation of the methodology will be reported elsewhere and is out of the scope of the current article. This chapter takes a more pragmatic approach and presents a more nuanced discussion on the human and social aspects of EHR implementations.

INTEGRATED FRAMEWORK FOR EHR AND INFORMATION SYSTEMS

Figure 1 illustrates the meta-framework that integrates the theoretical frameworks and factors and is intended to guide multi-level EHR implementations. Key to this framework is its comprehensive and integrative nature for including various thematic threads such as people, process, and technology-related factors. In addition, our framework describes the implementation process as the journey of an EHR implementation through the healthcare system over time with respect to strategic and operational levels. The meta-framework describes three phases over which

EMR implementations occur: pre-implementation, implementation and post-implementation phases. Each phase has its specific conceptual 'tasks' or sets of activities that need to be done and 'deliverables' or outcomes that are expected before it can move on to the next phase.

People-Process-Technology

An implementation of a new information systems results in a complex set of interacting forces (Clegg et al., 1997). People and tasks in an organization undergo significant change, learning, adaptation and growth in response to the introduction of information technology (IT). The changes are often drastic and cause intra-organizational tensions (Kuruppuarachchi et al., 2002). For the success of the healthcare delivery institution, an integrated approach to organizational and technical change must be adapted. Our literature review has established that there are many factors influential to understanding the successful EHR implementation in an effective healthcare delivery organization. For these reasons, we have concluded that human factors as well as technology factors need to be taken into consideration. The conceptual bridge between human and technology sides, "process," also has an important contribution. It is the process components of an implementation that allow the people and technology factors to mutually influence and shape each other—the end-users changing and adapting as they learn about the technology and how it will impact their work and the technology changing as vendors and developers better understand the goals and needs of end-users. People, process, and technological issues have to be seen as inextricably linked as a triad for successful change to take place. The people-process-technology triad in each phase has its important tasks which, correctly implemented, lead to appropriate deliverables— both in terms of technology being ready to be implemented and in terms of readiness of people to move on to the next phase.

People

People are one of the most important elements of healthcare delivery systems (Ash et al., 2003). Workforce knowledge and skills are related concepts in explaining the effectiveness of EHR implementation. Human resources of the healthcare delivery organizations include decision makers, such as executives or managers; end users, such as physicians or nurses; and information technology specialists, such as systems or software related subordinates. Additionally, project leaders have a crucial role during the implementation efforts. We identify four groups of important people in an EHR implementation: (a) senior management, (b) project managers and project champions, (c) end users, (d) information technology specialists and/or vendors.

a. **Senior management:** Initiating an EHR implementation effort is a strategic decision for most organizations. It requires significant investment of organizational resources and energy and it commits the organization to a particular direction. Leadership, commitment, and participation of senior management are prerequisites for EHR implementations (Davis & Wilder, 1998; Laughlin, 1999; Oden et al., 1993; Sherrard, 1998). Senior management is responsible for analyzing and rethinking existing business directions and deciding on future directions for the organization. They also have to weigh integration of a new information technology system against other organization priorities and need to have a keen understanding of the benefits and risks of EHR in terms of operational costs, human resource capabilities and retraining and return on investment (Krupp, 1998; Umble et al., 2003).

b. **Project managers and project champions:** Successful information systems implementation requires skilled and experienced project management (Rosario, 2000). This includes a clear definition of objectives which are congruent with the strategic direction and vision of the organization, a work plan that tracks utilization of resources, continuous monitoring of project progress and management of risks (Bingi et al., 1999; Buckhout et al., 1999; Sumner, 1999). Initially, the scope of the project must be framed accurately, since the project will affect overall business processes (Holland et al., 1999; Rosario, 2000; Umble et al., 2003).

Project leadership encompasses two distinct roles: that of a project manager who has skills and experience in managing complex project implementations (Collins, 1998) and that of a project champion who has organizational credibility with clinicians (Ash et al., 2003; Chiang & Starren, 2002; Chin, 2004). Project leaders are responsible for all these planning and managing issues and play key role in successful management of the project. They bridge the strategic needs of senior management and the operational and tactical needs of end users by matching activities to strategic goals, creating an agreeable working climate, solving conflicts, coordinating and enhancing internal communication, managing risk and coordinating users and training of human resource of the organization.

c. **End users:** End-users have a crucial role in EHR system development, specifically in identifying and clearly articulating their needs and requirements and participating actively in designing and implementing new systems (Clegg et al., 1997). Although end-users are very important in implementation, they are rarely influential in designing new systems. End-user participation is usually limited in influencing the design of the technology and their participation is usually poorly managed. End-users need to have a much greater voice in implementations for them to achieve greater success (Clegg et al., 1997).

In many cases, system developers are still seen as the 'owners' of new technologies, where in reality, end-users are the real customers—those who will actually use the systems. The reason for this is believed to be technical orientation of system developers and the widespread failure to address human and organizational factors when designing technology (Clegg et al., 1997; Kuruppuarachchi et al., 2002).

d. **Information technology specialists and/or vendors:** Assistance to clinicians or primary users by detecting, solving and following up on problems that arise during implementation is essential for the success of the EMR experience. Continuous improvements and/or modifications of the system are important to achieve the expected outcomes. Changes may need to be made to applications for such components as basic configurations and workflows, custom templates, forms and shortcuts (Miller & Sim, 2004), to hardware and network components that are not functioning properly or to network architectures. In many cases, implementations have failed simply because of hardware problems that plagued implementers who had not planned for them; a simple recurring hardware problem that is not solved quickly can create havoc in a production environment and cause healthcare providers to quickly lose confidence in the technology. Vendors and technical support play a key role to assist in implementation. The assistance team, both vendor and technical support, needs to provide rapid and efficient service, or clinical users will stop calling and find some other way to access and record data (Keshavjee, et al. 2001). Implementation assistance should be available on-site initially (Aydin & Forsythe, 1997; Smith, 2003; Tonnesen, et al., 1999) and should be easily accessed throughout the implementation phase. Technical support also has a "bridger" role between end users and vendor (Chin, 2004).

Process

Organizational determinants such as complexity or connectedness to other organizations have a direct impact on the outcome of the implementation. The structure of the organization and existing operational processes also impact outcomes. If poorly handled, they can create significant conflict within the organization. Organizational complexity, which may be regarded as a basis for conflict, is related to the technology used within the organization (Killing, 1988). Healthcare is growing increasingly complex (Bates & Atul, 2003) and complex tasks can be a hindrance to the quality of healthcare delivery outputs.

In our meta-model, process is the arena and mechanism through which people engage with technology and through which each shapes the other along a journey toward a successful transformation of the organization. This is much clearer today than it has been in the past (Aarts & Berg, 2004).

Technology

Enormous improvements have been made in recent years in healthcare delivery technology. Although technological change has been very beneficial in various ways, it also causes many new problems that need to be addressed. These include redistribution of power, new types of errors and requirements for new skills and competencies and new scopes of practice; many of these are human resource, policy and regulatory issues which create friction within and outside the organization and manifest as resistance to change (Ash et al., 2006). In some cases, there is a mismatch between technology and organizational and end-user needs (Lawler, 1993; Massaro, 1993; Tonessen et al., 1999). The scale of health information and the complexity of using it properly make technology another important element for EHR implementations, especially since it is seen to be the vehicle through which the organization will meet its strategic goals.

Figure 1. Integrated meta framework

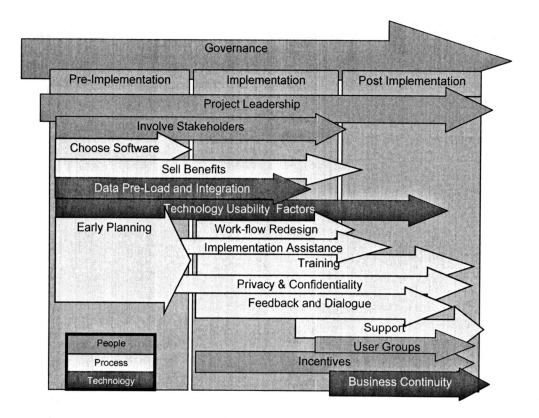

The increasingly complex technology, task scope, intensity and the number of tasks performed simultaneously by healthcare workers push organizations toward a requirement for coordination and integration and use of information technology (Hage, 1980; Schumaker, 2002). Paradoxically, it is precisely this task complexity and organizational complexity which makes implementation of technology so difficult and prone to failure.

BEST PRACTICES FOR EHR AND INFORMATION SYSTEMS IMPLEMENTATIONS

Implementation of the EHR is not only a technology application at the operational level, but also a major change in the business processes, organizational structure and organizational culture, which are directly related to the mission and vision of an institution. In this context, the decision of transferring the overall system of the healthcare setting from a paper-based environment to a new information system happens at the strategic level, which is followed by operative level management and execution activities (Poskela et al., 2005).

A key aspect of our meta-framework is that it models the time perspective which brings out the dynamic and interactive nature of EHR implementations. The time frame element is modeled as three major operational phases of an EHR implementation: pre-implementation phase, implementation phase and post-implementation phase activities. In each phase, related tasks or factors aggregate together due to similar time courses, functions, and outcomes. A factor can begin in one phase and end in another, but may spend most of its lifetime in a specific phase. It is to this phase that we allocated its primary relevance for the purposes of this framework. However, the strategic level is beyond these phases; the time frame of the strategic level activities starts before these operational phases and goes as long as EHR lives in that setting.

Strategic Level

The meta-framework factor ***governance*** speaks to senior management's activities or substantive personal interventions in the EHR implementation. It is concerned with mission, vision and senior management's behaviors related to pre-implementation, implementation and post-implementation phases of the EHR. Senior management support is a must for EHR implementation (Bingi et al., 1999; Buckhout et al., 1999; Fui-Hoon Nah et al., 2001; Sumner, 1999) and EHR must have a plausible chance of helping attain the strategic business goals (Sumner, 1999). Senior management must allocate valuable resources to the implementation efforts (Holland et al., 1999), including providing the needed people for the implementation (Roberts & Barrar, 1992). Management needs to announce the new system and structures regarding EHR implementation, provide the compelling rationale for taking the EHR pathway and support the key champions and project managers who will communicate the strategy and tactics for EHR implementation throughout the organization (Kotter, 1995). Senior management must create a sense of "urgency" for change, inspiring people to act, think, and make objectives real and relevant (Kotter, 1995). New roles and responsibilities should be established and policies should be set by senior management to suit the new systems in the company (Roberts & Barrar, 1992).

Top-down organizational support is one of the dominant factors associated with successful implementation of EHR. Project leadership must be "empowered to act" by removing obstacles and enabling support from senior management (Kotter, 1995). Our analysis indicates that implementations that had good governance were 6 [95% CI 1.3 to 27, p= 0.025] times more likely to succeed than implementations that had poor governance. Without real commitment from the top, stresses experienced during implementation can easily hinder EHR development (Townes et al., 2000). In some implementations which experienced failure, EHR implementation was either not sanctioned by senior management (Chiang & Starren, 2002; Townes et al., 2000) or senior management was diverted by other organizational priorities (Tonessen et al., 1999) at a crucial time in the EHR implementation. Without top level support, implementations, which hit a snag that requires additional resources to resolve, will quickly die on the vine.

Operational Level

Pre-Implementation Phase

The initial or pre-implementation phase is relatively the most important part of any IT initiative and should focus on activities that facilitate project success, such as goal setting, planning, and communication. Pre-implementation activities set the tone for all other phases of an IT implementation project, and it is important to recognize any potential progress impediments and be prepared to proactively address them (Rosenthal, 2002). The key outcomes of the pre-implementation phase are a consensus within the organization on which technology it will implement, that the technology is the right one for the organization and a willingness and excitement amongst clinician end-users to implement the technology.

Our factor ***project leadership*** combines two important roles in the EHR implementation. This factor runs through the entire implementation, from pre-implementation to post-implementation phases. The first role is that of the experienced and skilled project management. Much has been written about project management and we will not repeat it here. In an EHR implementation, the role of the project manager is to use the process factors of the implementation meta-framework as a series of activities that over time bring about the desired change within end-users and technology for a successful implementation to occur. Successful implementations also need champions who are able to influence operational level activities (Hauschildt, 1999). Physician champions are central in all phases of an implementation, acting as enabling advocates, selling benefits and engaging in a 'web' of communications with other clinician end-users. Championship, defined as the persistent and persuasive communication between strategic and operational levels, is a crucial instrument for senior management and appears to be an important middle management function (Floyd & Wooldridge, 1992). Our findings show its strong impact, with a 26-fold [95% CI 3 to 234, p = 0.004] increase in likelihood of success with strong project champions and experienced project managers working together to manage the people, process and technology aspects of an implementation.

One of the key activities in the pre-implementation phase is the software selection process, our factor *choose software carefully.* All of the pre-implementation activities and outcomes revolve around this process. It is the process through which end-users buy-in to the needs of the organization, the need for a software solution and the appropriateness of a particular technology to meet organizational needs. Project leaders, both project managers and project champions, need to help stakeholders within the organization to galvanize their commitment to the particular pathway chosen by senior management to achieve its strategic objectives and to put their own stamp on the implementation through participation in the selection process; after all, they will be the ones to live with the day to day consequences of their choices. Project managers also need to hold vendors and system developers accountable to meeting the needs of end-users. This factor is the key mechanism through which the mutual re-

shaping of end-users and technology takes place. Implementations which correctly implemented this process were 17 [95% CI 2-152, p = 0.011] times more likely to succeed than those that executed it incorrectly or did not use this process at all. User friendliness of the software and meeting users' requirements are important for user acceptance of the system and human related issues. The flexibility of the software and matches with the norms and values of the organization makes this factor crucial in terms of processes. In this context, choosing the software is a central activity that can unite an organization and generate excitement and a shared vision or can create deep divisions. Successful project managers and project champions are able to use a series of pre-planned activities to guide the organization and end-users toward a shared vision and a commitment to the EHR pathway. Unsuccessful project managers were more likely to have embarked on a journey to develop their own software after finding out that they couldn't find a suitable one on the market (Chiang & Starren, 2002) or followed a good process and then sabotaged it at the end because a 'new and improved' software came along "at the 11th hour" (Goddard, 2000).

Involvement of end users was one of the key factors mentioned by implementers as being essential for the implementation. It facilitates creating a better system that is integrated with the existing one and promotes user ownership (Clegg et al., 1997). This factor appears to provide a 4.5-fold [95% CI 0.98 to 20.5, p = 0.054] improvement in success. Although this factor did not achieve statistical significance in our study, a larger sample size might have allowed us to detect statistical significance. It is likely that the *choosing software carefully* incorporates this factor. Many failed implementations that did not involve end-users also did not choose their software carefully (Lawler, 1993; Massaro, 1993; Tonesson et al., 1999; Wager et al., 2001).

Selling benefits and addressing barriers leads to a 14-fold [95% CI 1.54 to 119, p=0.019] increase in the likelihood of the success. By selling benefits, the organization and actors of the system are prepared for change by identifying core values, understanding the broader organizational context and stakeholder concerns, understanding end-user needs, creating a vision and compelling need for change, and being sensitive and responsive to organizational stresses resulting from change (Kotter, 1995; Lorenzi & Riley, 1995). Physicians, nurses, and staff need to be constantly reminded of the benefits of EHR and need to feel confident that obstacles and barriers are being addressed. It is quite common for clinicians to misinterpret the chaos of implementation as incompetence of implementers and a sign of things going awry. End-users need to experience early and quick wins to maintain their confidence in the implementation process. Implementations that failed due to incorrect execution of this factor were more likely to assume that the benefits were self-evident and did not need to be sold or project champions were entirely absent from the implementation process (Chiang & Starren, 2002).

Early planning strategies encompasses early and extensive planning on how computers will be introduced and implemented into the organization. It is concerned with foreseeing and predictive risks and problems that may arise and planning for them. Plans for acquiring appropriate experts and support personnel to field concerns, anticipation of problems and development of plans to solve them, plans for process and workflow redesign, training plans and planning for the technology deployment are all required to ensure a successful implementation. Use of *early planning strategies* increases the likelihood of success by 10-fold [95% CI 1.8 to 56, p = 0.009]. Given the large number of factors that need to go right in the implementation phase and given that those factors are also potential points of failure, *early planning strategies* are crucial to the successful implementation of an EHR into actual practice. Unsuccessful project managers did not plan for unexpected contingencies. Given the fast-paced,

mission critical environment of healthcare, there is typically very little time or patience to deal with technology problems. Successful project managers made sure that a multi-disciplinary team was on-site or readily available during the early weeks of implementation to quickly manage problems that arose. Problems that arise during implementation are likely to span multiple disciplines, such as a hardware problem that exacerbates an existing process problem, causing chaos to ensue. If the problem is not fixed quickly, users are forced to go back to their old processes. If this is allowed to last too long, clinicians lose confidence in the implementers and will not go back to using the new technology (Chiang & Starren, 2002; Lawler, 1993). Quick, on-site support is crucial at these junctures.

Technology usability appears to be a very important factor, with a 96-fold [95% CI 9 to 999, p < 0.00001] increase in likelihood of success for overall system design including hardware and software and the system selection at the outset. Conversely, technology usability issues are ostensibly blamed for most failures, partial failures or even hiccoughs in implementation. This is likely to be an over-estimate of the actual impact of technology fit to the organization as it is easy for an organization to blame the system instead of pointing to themselves as the cause of implementation problems, but clearly the perception of its importance is high. New EHR technology will be implemented better if it is easy to use thereby helping derive its purported benefit, especially if it's real benefit closely fits end-user expectations. Essentially the EHR must perform as advertised and be a good match to the needs of the organization, without disrupting workflow and time to complete task expectations, and organizational culture so much that the organization cannot adapt to this change (Ash et al., 2003; Berg, 2001; Delone et al., 2003; Heeks, 2006; Kushniruk & Patel, 2004). The technology usability factor has two aspects to it. Initially, it is the organization's and stakeholder's perception of how usable the technology is and whether it will meet the needs of the end-users. This is modeled in Davis' technology acceptance model (TAM) (Davis & Wilder, 1998). Later, as the technology is implemented, the actual usability and fit within the organization becomes a crucial factor. Many implementations failed to make the transition from perceived usability to actual usability (Lawler, 1993; Massaro, 1993; Tonnesen et al., 1999). Most partial failures languish in a situation where the technology only partially supports the strategic and operational requirements of the organization—stuck in a limbo not of their own making (Aarts & Berg, 2004; Chiang & Starren, 2002; Poon et al., 2003; Tonessen et al., 1999; Wager et al., 2001; Williams, 2002). The reasons for failure in this factor can be attributed to: (1) a flawed EHR selection process that did not engage the appropriate stakeholders whose input was crucial to ensuring a good fit of technology to users (Massaro, 1993); (2) poor mapping between functionality of the software and needs of the organization (Aarts & Berg, 2004) and; (3) poor understanding that flaws in acquired technology requires organizational capacity to overcome them (Lawler, 1993).

Data pre-load and integration plays an important part in achieving success with EHR implementations (Ash et al., 2003; Smith, 2003; Townes et al., 2000). Data-preload and integration of systems before providers start to use the system decreases the requirement for initial data entry from previous documentation and from other systems. Getting data from other systems makes it easier for physicians to get started and decreases their on-going charting efforts. Digitization of paper charts into the new system is an example of decreasing the gap between the technology reality ("we allow you to document all encounters, as long as you do it our way") and expectation of end-users ("we need previous records to be easily accessible when we use the system") (Heeks, 2006), resulting in a better fit of the technology to the expectations of the organization. Previously used database formats

from legacy systems can be imported into the new system. Effective integration with other systems containing billing, lab results, reporting, scheduling, diagnostic imaging, referrals and reference sources can be achieved (Chin, 2004). Consideration can be given to scanning parts of the previous paper-based record provided the information can be effectively indexed for later retrieval. These integration and pre-load activities increase end user satisfaction and user acceptance of the new system.

Lack of data pre-load and integration can lead to duplicate paper and electronic documentation which leads to inefficiency, risk to patient safety and a cognitive burden which is difficult to overcome for most clinicians (Keshavjee et al., 2001).

In summary, the goals of the pre-implementation phase are to assist the clinicians within the organization to make the necessary mental and attitudinal changes to implement the EHR technology. This phase uses the EHR selection process as the central activity through which the transformation occurs and which leads to the selection of a particular software solution which will be implemented. At the end of this phase, the organization and its users are confident that the technology is usable and that it will meet their needs, they have a clear understanding of the risks and benefits associated with their choice of EHR software and have begun the planning process to take the organization into the implementation phase.

Implementation Phase

In the implementation phase the work of EHR activation begins. This is the true test of an organization's preparations made in the pre-implementation phase, and of the overall match of these success factors to the nature of its EHR implementation.

Workflow redesign speaks to the relationship between human factors, how people work, and technology. Critical to successful implementation is the fit of staff and physician work flow to that of the EHR functionality and usability design constrictions (Smith, 2003). If the EHR software fits into clinician workflow then it is more likely to be accepted (Wager et al., 2001). It is well documented that redesign of business process is important for technology to deliver on its promise. Automation of poor workflows only leads to faster chaos—an undesirable outcome (Keshavjee et al., 2001). Workflow redesign is a highly specialized field and requires skilled practitioners to guide clinicians in a process through which they can achieve superior productivity in their work. It is the role of the technology to support and enable the new, more efficient workflows to be implemented. Implementers who correctly executed *workflow redesign* experienced 36-fold [95% CI 4 to 333, p = 0.002] increases in the success of their implementations.

Training, implementation assistance and *feedback and dialogue*, all had relatively modest impacts on the success of implementations of between five and nine-fold. Proper *training* (nine-fold increase [95% CI 1.6 to 48, p = 0.013]) supports the smooth transition to a paperless patient care system. Hands on training sessions immediately prior to going live has great significance for accelerating the implementation and user acceptance of the new system (Halley et al., 1996; Swanson et al., 1997; Wager et al., 2001). Training of the end users on EHR should be both initial and on-going, as it is not possible to learn all the features of the EHR software during initial training. Many functions of an EHR are only used once a physician has climbed up the steep learning curve of using an EHR.

A successful implementation requires comprehensive *implementation assistance* (five-fold increase [95% CI 1.1 to 23, p = 0.037]) to be responsive to solving technical problems quickly. In addition, end-users need assistance in making system improvements and modifications and making necessary changes such as developing custom templates, forms and shortcuts (Miller & Sim, 2004; Swanson et al., 1997). Quick and competent support can come from a variety of resources. A strong vendor partnership (Swanson et al., 1997), the presence of "super-users" (Chin, 2004; Keshavjee et al., 2001; Pizziferri et al., 2005; Wager et al., 2001) and "bridgers" (Chin, 2004) and on-site technical teams can contribute significantly to provide proper assistance on time. EHR implementations are dynamic processes which evolve as learning occurs and new problems and opportunities are discovered. End-users who are learning while continuing to provide patient care require additional support to ensure a smooth transition to using technology in their practices.

Feedback and dialogue (nine-fold increase [95% CI 1.6 to 48, p = 0.013]) is essential for supporting the dynamic EHR implementation process by providing opportunities to end-users for discussing issues and problems, to vent their frustrations, to share problems they are experiencing and to recommend changes to the software or to workflows. This process gives project managers and project champions an opportunity to monitor and track the progress of the implementation and detect and resolve problems before they get out of hand (Ash et al., 2003; Chin, 2004; Swanson et al., 1997; Townes et al., 2000).

EHR implementations must meet requirements for *privacy and confidentiality*. Although this is usually stated as a 'top 3' requirement for clinicians and is an important component of information systems management, it did not achieve statistical significance as being a factor for implementation success (4.70-fold increase [95% CI 0.53 to 42, p=0.165]). It is easy to see that although privacy and confidentiality is unlikely to be a driver of success, its absence could be a factor which prevents success or hastens failure. In any case, no discussion of implementation can be considered complete without mention of privacy and confidentiality.

In summary, the goals of the implementation phase are to assist physicians in making a successful transition from existing paper-based processes to the new electronic process. Barriers to the transition must be quickly resolved lest users revert to previous practices. Ensuring that new workflows are logical and streamlined, that appropriate training has been provided, that users have a forum in which to provide feedback and that they get support in a timely manner is crucial for successful navigation through the implementation phase.

Post Implementation Phase

The goals of the post-implementation phase are to consolidate the gains of the implementation phase and to start the organization along the journey toward meeting the real goals of the organization: improved efficiency and improved patient care. This is done through providing incentives and support to clinicians and providing them with a forum in which to share best-practices and enhance their use of the system.

The post-implementation phase is the culminating activity of an IT implementation initiative (Rosenthal, 2002), but also the start of a new journey toward newer implementation activities (Chin, 2004). Despite very limited discussion in the literature on importance of *incentives* in the EHR literature, in our analysis implementation efforts that offer incentives to users were 70 times more likely to succeed [95% CI 7 to 705, $p < 0.001$). The identified benefits of an EHR including improved patient safety (Berner et al., 2006; Hippisley-Cox et al., 2003; Mekhjian et al., 2002), increased income and decreased costs (Cooper, 2004), increased efficiency of care (Hippisley-Cox et al., 2003; Mekhjian et al., 2002; Nordyke & Klikowski, 1998), faster access to clinical information at the point of care and more efficient outcomes assessment (Nordyke & Klikowski, 1998) need to be demonstrated to all users. Most incentives were professional and work related

incentives—increased efficiency, better patient care and more professional satisfaction, rather than monetary incentives.

Users groups and *business continuity plans* are two post-implementation phase factors that did not achieve statistical significance as drivers of implementation success. However, as with privacy and confidentiality, they can be interpreted as barriers to success rather than as a driver. Structured interactions of the users by scheduling meetings, *users groups* or discussion platforms provides a forum for ongoing training and facilitates a cooperative dynamic where end users can solve technical problems, write templates, and teach each other about software features (Berner et al., 2006). User groups can produce a greater user acceptance and satisfaction (Smith, 2003). A business continuity plan is also essential where there is provision for data protection and disaster recovery (Swanson et al., 1997).

EHR users require significant amounts of *support*, especially in the early phases after implementation. Myriad questions and issues arise which can lead to disenchantment and disillusionment if not handled appropriately (Keil et al., 1998; Massaro, 1993; Miller & Sim, 2004). *Support* did show some impact on the success of implementation; however the sample size was too small to reliably detect the magnitude of the impact.

Requirements of the new system and structures tend to change continuously even after the completion of the implementation phase. In this context, post-implementation activities are critical for the acceptance of new systems (Kuruppuarachchi et al., 2002) and for allowing the organization to grow and achieve its mission.

Overall, it appears that much of the success of EHR implementations can be explained by activities in the pre-implementation and implementation phase. Only the provision of incentives in the post-implementation phase has a large impact on success of implementations. However, the role of user groups and support should not be underestimated, as these are required for clinicians to meet higher order goals such as chronic disease management, preventive maintenance care and more evidence-based care. Although these higher order clinical goals may not be important to the 'technological success' of the project, they are important to help the organization meet its strategic goals for which it implemented the technology in the first place!

CONCLUSION

Despite remarkable advances in EHR, many systems still fall short of performance expectations (Centre for Health Policy and Research, 2006). A growing share of these implementation failures are due to non-technical factors (Clegg et al., 1997). This study has attempted to combine a large and diverse literature into a multi-level multi-dimensional meta-framework of successful implementations of EHR in healthcare organizations. Our meta-framework provides a comprehensive set of factors for assessing the EHR implementation literature. Our systematic review of the literature has provided support for this meta-framework by assessing impact on EHR implementation success.

The limitations of our research come from the relatively poor quality of case reports on EHR implementations. Most articles are written by implementers, not academics, who were probably asked to write about their experiences after a successful implementation. These articles are mostly experience reports, are generally incomplete and probably suffer from recall bias. There is also a publication bias in that the number of articles describing failed implementations is under-represented. Of the 47 articles we reviewed, only 10 described failures. Given the prevalence of failed implementations, we should expect to see many more articles describing failures. In addition, implementations in smaller clinic settings are

presently under-represented in the literature and need to be examined and reported upon.

Research aimed at validating this framework should include prospective usage of these factors in an EHR implementation and establishing key outcome measures of overall EHR success.

FUTURE RESEARCH DIRECTIONS

Although, our review affirmed well-described success factors in the literature, they add additional components which model the dynamic and evolving nature of EHR implementations. The complexity and multi-dimensional nature of EHR implementation makes it difficult to match a factor tightly to the phenomena in a real EHR implementation (Berg, 2001). Also, a gold standard model to assess and rate EHR implementations is still needed. We believe that our meta-framework can be used iteratively in future research efforts to refine these matches and design a more standardized framework to evaluate the success of implementations prospectively. Future research could benefit from improved data collection through more precise operational definitions and generation of checklists in an attempt to more precisely identify the presence of certain factors or concepts. Improved hypothesis generation could be achieved again by defining more precise operational definitions of success factors and further identifying component concepts that might be successful and unsuccessful. Further definition could be done of the weighting of different factors as they contribute to implementation success. Finally, knowledge translation and controlled trial research needs to be conducted to translate findings from this study into practical advice for project managers and project champions. The factors identified in this study need to be validated in actual implementations through systematic collection of data on a prospective basis from actual implementations.

ACKNOWLEDGMENT

The authors wish to acknowledge the generous support of CIHR and the CHPSTP project in providing funding and infrastructure to accomplish this research.

REFERENCES

Aarts, J., & Berg, M. (2004). A tale of two hospitals: a sociotechnical appraisal of the introduction of computerized physician order entry in two Dutch hospitals. *Medinfo, 11*(Pt 2), 999-1002.

Ash, J. S., Stavri, P. Z., Fournier, L. & et al. (2003). Principles for a successful computerized physician order entry implementation. *AMIA Annual Symposium Proceedings* (pp. 36-40).

Ash, J.S., Sittig, D.F., Dykstra, R.H., et al. (2006). An unintended consequence of CPOE implementation: Shifts in power, control, and autonomy. *AMIA Annual Symposium Proceedings.*

Aydin, C.E., & Forsythe, D.E. (1997). Implementing computers in ambulatory care: Implications of physician practice patterns for system design. *AMIA Annual Symposium Proceedings,* 677-681.

Bates, D.W., & Atul, A.G. (2003). Improving safety with information technology. *Engl J Med., 348,* 2526-2534.

Berg, M. (2001). Implementing information systems in healthcare organizations: myths and challenges. *Int J Med Inform., 64*(2-3), 143-156.

Berner, E.S., Houston, T.K. & et al. (2006). Improving ambulatory prescribing safety with a handheld decision support system: A randomized controlled trial. *J. Am. Med. Inform. Assoc., 13*(2), 171-179.

Bingi, P., Sharma, M.K., & Godla, J. (1999). Critical issues affecting an ERP implementation. *Information Systems Management,* 7-14.

Buckhout, S., Frey, E., & Nemec, J. (1999). Making ERP succeed: turning fear into promise. *IEEE Engineering Management Review,* 116-123.

Centre for Health Policy and Research. (2006). *Health information technology adoption in Massachusetts: costs and timeframe.* Retrieved March 13, 2006, from www.umassmed.edu/healthpolicy/uploads/eHealthInformation.pdf

Chiang, M.F., & Starren, J.B. (2002). Software engineering risk factors in the implementation of a small electronic medical record system: The problem of scalability. *Proceedings AMIA Annual Symposium* (pp. 145-149).

Chin, H. (2004). The reality of EMR implementation: lessons from the field. *Kaiser Permanente HealthConnect, 8*(4).

Clegg, C., Axtell, C., Damodaran, L., et al. (1997). Information technology: A study of performance and the role of human and organizational factors. *Ergonomics, 40*(9), 851-871.

Collins, P. (1998). Risky business. It takes a 'risk-balanced' team to implement a CPR. *Health. Inform., 15*(3), 85-88.

Cooper, J.D. (2004). Organization, management, implementation and value of EHR implementation in a solo pediatric practice. *Journal of Healthcare Information Management, 18*(3), 51-55.

Curtis, W., Hefley, W. E. & Miller, S. (1995). *Overview of the people capability maturity model. Prepared for the USA Department of Defense.* Pittsburgh, PA: Research Access, Inc.

Davis, B., & Wilder, C. (1998). False starts, strong finishes—companies are saving troubled IT projects by admitting their mistakes, stepping back, scaling back, and moving on. *Information Week, November 30,* 41-43.

Delone, W. H., & Mclean, E.R. (2003). The delone and mcLean model of information systems success: A ten-year update. *Journal of Management Information Systems, 19*(4), 9-30.

Duke Clinical Research Institute (2005). *FDA public meeting.* Retrieved March 13, 2006, from www.fda.gov/cder/meeting/ICHspring2005/Nahm.ppt

Floyd, S.W., & Wooldridge, B. (1992). Middle management involvement in strategy and its association with strategic type: A research note. *Strategic Management Journal, 13*, 153-167.

Fui-Hoon Nah, F., Lau J., & Kuang, J. (2001). Critical factors for successful implementation of enterprise systems. *Business Process Management Journal, 7*(3), 285-296.

Goddard, B.L. (2000). Termination of a contract to implement an enterprise electronic medical record system. *Journal of the American Medical Informatics Association, 7*(6), 564-568.

Golden, B.R., & Martin, R.L. (2004). Aligning the stars: Using systems thinking to (re)design Canadian healthcare. *Healthcare Quarterly, 7*(4), 34-42.

Hage, J. (1980). *Theories of organizational: Form, process, and transformation.* New York: John Wiley.

Halley, E.C., Kambic, P.M. & et al. (1996). Concurrent process redesign and clinical documentation system implementation: A 6-month success story. *Topics in Health Information Management, 17*(1), 12-17.

Hauschildt, J. (1999). Promotors and champions in innovations—development of a research paradigm. In K. Brockhoff, A. K. Chakrabarti & J. Hauschildt (Eds.), *The dynamics of innovation—strategic and managerial implications,*

Heeks, R. (2006). Health information systems: failure, success and improvisation. *International Journal of Medical Informatics, 75,* 125-137

Hippisley-Cox, J., Pringle, M., Cater, R. & et al. (2003). The Electronic patient record in primary care - Regression or progression? A cross sectional study. *British Medical Journal, 326,* 1439-1443.

Holland, P., Light, B., & Gibson, N. (1999). A critical success factors model for enterprise resource planning implementation. *Proceedings of the 7ᵗʰ European Conference on Information Systems, 1,* 273-297.

Institute of Medicine. (2001). *Crossing the quality chasm: A new health system for the twenty-first century.* Washington: National Academy Press.

Keil, M., Cule, P. E., Lyytinen, K., & Schimdt, R.C. (1998). A framework for identifying software project risk. *Communications of the ACM, 41*(11), 76-83.

Keshavjee, K., Bosomworth, J., Copen, J., et al. (2006). Best Practices in EMR Implementation: A Systematic Review. *iSHIMR Proceedings,* (pp. 233-246).

Keshavjee, K.S., Troyan, S., Holbrook, A.M., & Vandermolen, D. (2001). Measuring the success of electronic medical record implementation using electronic and survey data. *AMIA Annual Symposium Proceedings,* 309-313.

Killing, J.P. (1988). Understanding alliance: The role of task and organizational complexity. In F. Contractor & P. Lorange (Eds.), *Cooperative strategies in international business.* Lexington Books.

Koppel, R., Metlay, J., Cohen, A., et al. (2005). Role of Computerized Physician Order Entry Systems in Facilitating Medication Errors. *JAMA, 293,* 1197-1203.

Kotter, J. (1995). Leading change: Why transformation efforts fail. *Harvard Business Review, March-April,* 59-67.

Krupp, J. (1998). Transition to ERP implementation. *APICS—The Performance Advantage.*

Kukafka, R., Johnson, S.B., Linfante, A., & Allegrante, J.P. (2003). Grounding a new information technology implementation framework in behavioral science: A systematic analysis of the literature on IT use. *Journal of Biomedical Informatics, 36,* 218-227

Kuruppuarachchi, P.R., Mandal, P., & Smith R. (2002). IT project implementation strategies for effective changes: A critical review. *Logistics Information Management, 15*(2), 126-137.

Kushniruk, A.W., & Patel, V.L. (2004). Cognitive and usability engineering approaches to the evaluation of clinical information systems. *Journal of Biomedical Informatics, 37,* 56-62.

Laughlin, S. (1999). An ERP game plan. *Journal of Business Strategy.*

Lawler, F. (1993). Implementation and termination of a computerized medical information system–Editorial. *Journal of Family Practice, 42*(3), 233-236.

Lorenzi, N., & Riley, R.T. (1995). *Organizational aspects of health informatics: Managing technological change.* New York: Springer-Verlag.

Massaro, T. (1993). Introducing physician order entry at a major academic medical center: Impact on organizational culture and behavior. *Academic Medicine, 68*(1), 20-25.

Mekhjian, H.S., Kumar, R.R., Kuehn, L., & et al. (2002). Immediate benefits realized following implementation of physician order entry at an academic medical center. *J Am Med Inform Assoc., 9*(5), 529-539.

Miller, R.H. & Sim, I. (2004). Physicians' use of electronic medical records: Barriers and solutions. *Health Affairs, 23*(2), 116-126.

Nordyke, R.A., & Kulikowski, C.A. (1998). An informatics-based chronic disease practice: Case study of a 35-year computer-based longitudinal record system. *Journal of the American Medical informatics Association,* (5), 88-103.

Oden, H., Langenwalter, G., & Lucier, R. (1993). *Handbook of material and capacity requirements planning.* New York: McGraw- Hill.

Pizziferri, L., Kittler, A.F., Volk, L.A. et al. (2005). Primary care physician time utilization before and after implementation of an electronic health record: A time-motion study. *Journal of Biomedical Informatics, 38,* 176-188.

Poon, E.G, Blumenthal, D., Jaggi, T. et al. (2003). Overcoming the barriers to the implementing computerized physician order entry systems in U.S. hospitals: Perspectives from senior management. *AMIA Annual Symposium Proceedings,* 975.

Poskela, J., Dietrich, P., Berg, P. et al. (2005). Integration of Strategic Level and Operative Level Front-end Innovation Activities. *IEEE Conference Proceedings,* 197-211.

Roberts, H.J., & Barrar, P.R.N (1992). MRPII implementation: Key factors for success. *Computer Integrated Manufacturing Systems, 5*(1), 31-39.

Rogers, E. M. (1995). *Diffusion of innovations* (4th ed.). New York: Free Press.

Rosario, J.G. (2000). On the leading edge: Critical success factors in implementation projects. *BusinessWorld*

Rosenthal, D.A. (2002). Managing non-technical factors in healthcare IT projects. *Journal of Healthcare Information Management, 16*(2), 56-61.

Saleem, J.J., Patterson, E.S., Militello, L., et al. (2005). Exploring barriers and facilitators to the use of computerized clinical reminders. *J Am Med Inform Assoc., 12*(40), 438-447.

Schumaker, A.M. (2002). Interorganizational networks: Using a theoretical model to predict effectiveness. *Journal of Health and Human Services Administration, 25*(3/4), 371-380.

Sherrard, R. (1998). Enterprise resource planning is not for the unprepared. *ERP World Proceedings.* Retrieved January 1, 2007, from http://www.erpworld.org/proceed98

Smith, P.D. (2003). Implementing an EMR system: One clinic's experience. *Family Practice Management, 10*(5), 37-42.

Somers, T.M., Nelson, K., & Ragowsky, A. (2000). Enterprise resource planning for the next millennium: development of an integrative framework and implications for research. *Proceedings of the American Conference on Information Systems (AMCIS)* (pp. 998-1004).

Studer, M. (2005). The effect of organizational factors on the effectiveness of EMR system implementation—what have we learned? *Electronic Healthcare, 4*(2), 92-98.

Sumner, M. (1999). Critical success factors in enterprise wide information management systems projects. *Proceedings of the Americas Conference on Information Systems (AMCIS)* (pp. 232-235).

Swanson, T., Dostal, J., Eichhorst, B.,et al. (1997). Recent implementations of electronic medical records in four family practice residency programs. *Academic Medicine, 172*(7), 607-612.

Tape, T.G., & Campbell, J.R. (1993). Computerized medical records and preventive healthcare: success depends on many factors. *Am J Med., 94*(6), 619-625.

Tonnesen, A.S., LeMaistre, A., & Tucker, D. (1999). Electronic medical record implementation: Barriers encountered during implementation. *AMIA Annual Symposium Proceedings* (pp. 624-626).

Townes, P.G., Benson, D.S., Johnson, P. et al. (2000). Making EMRs really work: The Southeast Health Center experience. *Journal of Ambulatory Care Management, 23*(2), 43-52.

Umble, E.J., Haft, R.R., & Umble, M.M. (2003). Enterprise resource planning: Implementation procedures and critical success factors. *European Journal of Operational Research, 146,* 241-257

Wager, K.A., Lee, F.W., & White, A.W. (2001). *Life after a disastrous electronic medical record implementation: One clinic's experience.* Hershey, PA: Idea Group Publishing.

Weir, C., Lincoln, M., Roscoe, D. et al. (1995). Dimensions associated with successful implementation of a hospital based integrated order entry system. *Proceedings of AMIA Annual Fall Symposium,* 653-657.

Williams, R.B. (2002). Successful computerized physician order entry system implementation. Tools to support physician-driven design and adoption. *Healthc Leadersh Manag Rep., 10*(10), 1-13.

ADDITIONAL READINGS

Aaronson, J. W., Cassie, D. O., Murphy-Cullen, L. et al. (2001). Electronic medical records: The family practice resident perspective. *Medical Informatics, 133*(2), 128-132.

Ash, J. S., Sittig, D. F., Seshadri, V., et al. (2004). Adding insight: A qualitative cross-site study of physician order entry. *Proceedings of Medinfo* (pp. 1013-1016).

Ash, J. S., Stavri. P. Z., Fournier, L. et al. (2003). Principles for a successful computerized physician order entry implementation. *AMIA Annual Symposium Proceedings* (pp. 36-40).

Barlow S., Johnson J., & Steck J. (2001). The economic effect of implementing an EMR in an outpatient clinical setting. *Journal of Healthcare Information Management, 18*(1), 46-51.

Barrows, R. C., & Clayton, P. D. (1996). Privacy, confidentiality and electronic medical records.

Journal of the American Medical Informatics Association, 3(2), 139-148.

Bingham, A. (1998). Cost justification for computerized patient records. *Journal of Medical Practice Management, January/February,* 193-198.

Chin, H. L., Krall, M., et al. (1997). Implementation of a comprehensive computer-based patient record system in Kaiser Permanente's Northwest Region. *MD Computing, 4*(1), 41-45.

Churgin, P. G. (1994). Introduction of an automated medical record at an HMO clinic. *MD Computing, 11*(5), 293-300.

Dansky, K. H., Gamn, L. D., Vasey, J. J., & Barsukiewicz, C. K. (1999). Electronic medical records: Are the physicians ready? *Journal of Healthcare Management, 66*(6), 454-458.

Davis, F.D. (1989). Perceived usefulness, perceived ease of use, and user acceptance of information technology. *MIS Quarterly, 13*(3), 319-339.

Davis, F. D., Bagozzi, R. P., & Warshaw, P. R. (1989). User acceptance of computer technology: A comparison of two theoretical models. *Management Science, 35*(8), 982-1003.

Gadd, C. S., & Penrod, L. E. (2001). Assessing physician attitudes regarding use of an outpatient EMR: A longitudinal, multi-practice study. *Proceedings AMIA Annual Symposium* (pp. 194-198).

Hanson, S., & Schutzengel, R. (2004). Pioneers and perseverance: Implementing the HER in physician practices. *Journal of AHIMA, 75*(1), 38-43.

Hassol, A., Walker, J. M., et al. (2004). Patient experiences and attitudes about access to a patient electronic healthcare record and linked web messaging. *Journal of the American Medical Informatics Association, 11*(6), 505-513.

Holbrook, A., Keshavjee, K., Troyan, S., et al. (2003). Applying methodology to electronic medical record selection. *International Journal of Medical Informatics, 71,* 43-50.

Jarvenpaa, S. L., & Ives, B. (1991). Executive involvement and participation in the management information technology. *MIS Quarterly, 15*(2), 205-225.

Keshavjee, K. S., Troyan, S., Holbrook, A. M., & Vandermolen, D. (2001). Measuring the success of electronic medical record implementation using electronic and survey data. *Proceedings of the AMIA Symposium* (pp. 309-313).

Maxwell, M. (1999). EMR: Successful productivity tool for modern practice. *Health Management Technology, 20*(9), 48-9.

Mohd, H., & Mohamad, S. M. S. (2005). Acceptance model of electronic medical record. *Journal of Advancing Information and Management Studies, 2*(2), 75-92.

Packendorff, J. (1995). Inquiring into the temporary organization: new directions for project management research. *Scandinavian Journal of Management, 11*(4), 318-313.

Pennbridge, J., Moya, R., et al. (1999). Questionnaire survey of California consumers' use and rating of sources of healthcare information including the internet. *West J Med, 171,* 302-305.

Rind, D. M., Kohane, I. S., et al. (1997). Maintaining the confidentiality of medical records shared over the internet and the World Wide Web. *Annals of Internal Medicine, 127*(2), 138-141.

Smith, D., & Newell, L. M. (2002). A physician's perspective: Deploying the EMR. *Journal of Healthcare Information Management, 16*(2), 71-79.

Wang, S. J., Middleton, B., et al. (2003). A cost-benefit analysis of electronic medical records in primary care. *American Journal of Medicine, 114,* 397-403.

Chapter VIII
Health Informatics and Healthcare Redesign Using ICT to Move from an Evolutionary to a Revolutionary Stage

Vivian Vimarlund
Linköping University, Sweden

ABSTRACT

This chapter introduces a framework to analyze the pre-requisites to move from an evolutionary stage to a revolutionary one when using ICT in healthcare. It argues that the degree of transformation should be determined by the role ICT has in the organization when initiating the redesigning process, but also by the aims technology is supposed to achieve. The suggested framework can be used to identify preconditions and areas affected from the implementation and use of ICT providing a structure to evaluate how changes will affect key actors and the organization. The classification suggested to identify different steps of transformation should indicate stakeholders, healthcare personnel, and managers how to refocus their priorities to be able to built organizations that can be adapted to the revolutionary stage to obtain the same benefits that the industry has previously identified from the implementation of use of ICT.

INTRODUCTION

The use of information and communication technology (ICT) is becoming a self-evident part of the development and delivery of healthcare services.

In fact, predictions that collaboration and technology would become critical elements of the healthcare industry of the future have proven to be true as healthcare organizations have grappled with the interdisciplinary challenges of implementing

Copyright © 2008, IGI Global, distributing in print or electronic forms without written permission of IGI Global is prohibited.

and expanding ICT-systems and IS (information systems) for the support of caregivers.

From systems primarily designed to collect and process data in order to prepare the documents required by the personnel and stakeholders, there has now evolved many applications such as integrated financial functions, scheduling packages, decision-support functions, personnel management, billing functions, financial reporting and statistical reporting capabilities. How healthcare personnel actually manage the health information they search for and retrieve, where they are using these resources, or how they integrate health information systems and resources in their daily work activities are questions that are becoming more and more important in medical informatics research.

However, the more common approaches used to study these issues have been, to our best knowledge, socio-cognitive theories to guide the type of context to include, and the manner in which systematic application motivate individuals behaviors to use ICT and to achieve healthcare goals (Vimarlund & Olve, 2005). Approaches to design ICT systems and business process models to emphasize information-flow and afford insights to the role of health-information management in healthcare processes have often been used to explain the role of personal health-information management in the healthcare process. Activities, strategies, and consequences for the personnel that produce and deliver care services, the economic consequences of their work behavior and organizational pre-requisites that influence the acceptance of new work-routines and the use of ICT as complement at work, the consequences for the stakeholders, and the development of tools that allow to inform future development processes, have until today not accurate been discussed (Vimarlund, Timpka & Patel, 1999). It is therefore rational to argue that it is necessary to continue to pay attention to business processes, reengineering, and organizational transformation when planning and implementing systems in healthcare in order to allocate resources optimally.

In this chapter, we propose a framework to analyze the degree of transformation when moving from an evolutionary to a revolutionary level. We start out from the premise that ICT has a large potential to be useful in healthcare, much of it still untapped. While hospitals are now often equipped with advanced tools using digitized (computerized) analysis and embedded technology for operations etc., ICT based administrative tools used to coordinate activities and communicate knowledge have not yet been generalized.

However, new technology by itself is not a sufficient condition for changes to take place. The potential benefits from ICT are realized only when organizations adopt new patterns of behavior, exploiting new possibilities. In healthcare organizations such changes will involve a number of direct and indirect actors: healthcare personnel, technology suppliers, care centers, and branches of local or central government. Our framework can therefore be used to identify preconditions and areas affected from the implementation and use of ICT, and provide a structure for evaluation of how change will affect key actors and areas of importance for "business transformation." Without this type of analysis, promising technologies may fail because some actor lacks incentives to make needed investments in competences, technologies, or changed procedures, or does not trust new modes of operation because roles and responsibilities are unclear.

A FRAMEWORK TO IDENTIFY TRANSFORMATION: FROM EVOLUTIONARY TO REVOLUTIONARY HEALTHCARE

Much of the economic benefits from introducing ICT in industry during the past 40 years derive from 'reengineering' processes: changing tasks and who performs them. Faced with increasingly costly in healthcare, there are hopes for similar effects in the healthcare area. Using ICT support, it should be possible to reconfigure care in ways that allow us to live longer in our private homes, increase self-service, or substitute cheaper manpower for professional medical staff.

Another way of stating this is that ICTs value is not primarily in simplifying communication and information provision, or reducing their cost. Rather, its contribution is in *enabling* new ways of working. These, however, often require organizations to reconsider structures, roles, processes, and skill requirements. To realize ICTs potential, however, processes and ICT have to be redesigned together, and investments in reorganization, training and ICT timed to coincide.

Vice versa, changing processes and organizations should include an analysis of how ICT can enable new ways of working. New technical solutions are relevant to both social care and healthcare. National plans to make electronic health information more widely available in the United States and in Europe should be important for both, and proposed new tools for communicating medical data and advice between the different providers of healthcare will require the involvement of all involved actors. Increased specialization and investments, together with improved communications, mean that it will make sense to serve a larger geographical area.

Venkatraman (1994) identified five "levels of IT-enabled business transformation" (see Figure 1). Comparing them with the ambitions to transform contemporary healthcare, they may be interpreted as follows:

- **Level 1:** One or some care providers introduce new ICT-systems. Such intra-organizational use of ICT is already quite common.
- **Level 2:** Collaborating care providers share information to support their processes.
- **Level 3:** Here care integration extends to new practices, for instance introducing healthcare services at distance.
- **Level 4:** The equivalent of the "business network" in integrated care is the system of actors involved in the care processes. ICT-systems may enable new roles for service providers at different levels.
- **Level 5:** "Business scope" in this context could refer to the range of services offered. For instance, ICT could be used to provide some patients with social contacts and entertainment that have not been a part of the care provided.

Figure 1. Venkatraman's (1994) five levels of IT-enabled business transformation

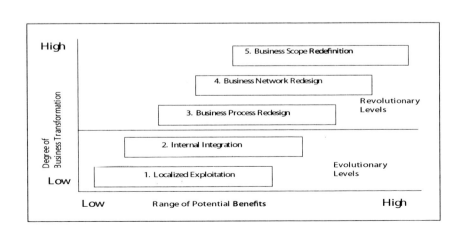

PRE-REQUISITES TO MOVE FROM EVOLUTIONARY TO REVOLUTIONARY HEALTHCARE

In organizations on level 2 (the evolutionary level) ICT is mainly used for administrative purposes: keeping records, ordering supplies, dealing with personnel issues. Electronic forms and standard formats are used as part of work procedures, for instance to place orders and receive confirmations as part of EDP systems. Healthcare organizations at this level use ICT for localized applications, and capital investments are mainly made to reduce costly time-consuming errors from manual data entry, and to increase system usability. Short-term returns result from reductions in transaction costs when administrative services can be rationalized (Vimarlund, Sjöberg, & Timpka, 2003). The use of ICT in evolutionary healthcare organizations is illustrated in Table 1.

Shared systems for patient information are now being developed in many countries. They will provide asynchronous, place-independent access to information. At the most basic level (far to the left, localized exploitations level in Figure 1), this will reduce information search and enable improved decision-making, which should result both in higher-quality care and eliminate unnecessary resource use. As a by-product, information that exists in the system may be shared with next-of-kin: reduces worry and need to contact care providers, as the relative is able to monitor that care activities take place, health condition, and so forth (to the extent that legal requirements are met).

INITIATING REVOLUTION

Organizations on level 3 (see Figure 1) are often developing less hierarchical ways of organizing work. Through new structures for interacting and new services they try to improve internal (mostly horizontal) integration. This involves decentralization, active use of e-mail and other modern means of communication, and a more active attitude to the management of information and knowledge, involving both healthcare personnel and administrators.

As incentives grow and the use of ICT increases, coordination throughout the workplace becomes easier as all use ICT systems actively (Vimarlund et al., 2003). A natural next step then is to adapt organizational structures to fit the new

Table 1. Characteristics used to describe the use of ICT in evolutionary healthcare organizations (Vimarlund, Sjöberg, & Timpka, 2003)

Area	Characteristic
Percentage of individuals who use ICT	> 25 %
Rationale for ICT investments	➢ To reduce costs ➢ To increase usability
For what is ICT used?	ICT is used for : Storage and ordering ➢ Administrative and personnel matters ➢ To develop new production processes
Means to transfer for person to person information and/or knowledge	➢ E-mail ➢ Internet

process technology. There may also be changes in formal responsibilities and incentive systems that reflect the new transaction patterns and *de facto* job contents. Gradually, ICT is used even more in service production, education, and purchasing. If the organization operates on several sites—for instance also in people's homes, or with close links to primary care centers—new ways of working together are tried out that go much further than the relatively simple access to data described previously. This means that over time, the information sharing discussed under level 2 in Figure 1 may result in process redesign that can be counted as a level 3 in Figure 1. With improved access to information, employees will develop new skills and adapt their tasks accordingly (if no regulations prevent this). The use of ICT in

healthcare organizations that initiate revolution is illustrated in Table 2.

REVOLUTIONARY HEALTHCARE ORGANIZATIONS

Revolutionary healthcare organizations work actively with the total design of organizational structure, and they regard their information management as an integral part of this. ICT plays a role similar to that older general-purpose technology like telephone and telegraph have done for a long time. Geographical location is rethought as part of new business models, and the revolutionary healthcare organization actively searches for innovative designs and develop of business networks

Table 2. Characteristics used to describe the use of ICT in healthcare organizations that initiate the revolutionary process (Vimarlund, Sjöberg, & Timpka, 2003)

Area	Characteristics
Percentage of individuals who use ICT	> 50 %
Rationale for ICT investments	➢ To reduce costs ➢ To increase usability ➢ To introduce new or change products and/or services ➢ To decentralize the organization
Percentage of individuals trained in how to use ICT	A minority of the employees have participated in ICT training program
For what is ICT used?	ICT is used for ➢ Storage and ordering ➢ Administrative and personnel matters ➢ To develop new production processes ➢ To develop and transfer educational material ➢ Process development
ICT Integration level	ICT allows to transfer data and information between some of the different levels in the organization
Means used for transfer person-to person information and/or knowledge	➢ E-mail ➢ Internet ➢ Network ➢ Electronic Conferences
Electronic Commerce	E-commerce is used for the purchase of goods and services.

that will explore and benefit from the new opportunities opening up. For instance, data entered by care personnel may be monitored automatically to identify deviations from normal values. An example is automatic alarms, programmed to react when the wearer's activity deviates from a normal level. Reacting to such signals may become the task of some new organization, or outsourced to some existing rescue organization.

The paradox of this organizational type is that the benefits from ICT become easier to appreciate, although the technology is now so interwoven in all activities that its contribution can no longer be analyzed separate from the general performance of the organization. This is because ICT has become

so powerful and complex that the organization cannot be imagined without it. This also means that ICT investments are accompanied by considerable changes in structures, work processes and competences—or even regarded as just a minor part of an organizational change, not as separate projects. The use of ICT in revolutionary healthcare organizations is illustrated in Table 3.

COMMENTS

A successfully revolutionary healthcare organization, however, requires more information than ten years ago, as new ICT has made it possible to

Table 3. Characteristics used to describe the use of ICT in revolutionary healthcare organizations (Vimarlund, Sjöberg, & Timpka, 2003)

Area	Characteristics
Percentage of individuals who use ICT	> 75 %
Rationale for ICT investments	➢ To reduce costs ➢ To increase usability ➢ To introduce new or change products and/or services ➢ To decentralize the organization ➢ To improve collaboration between companies ➢ To increase data security
Percentage of individuals trained in how to use ICT	A majority of the employees have participated in ICT training programme
For what is ICT used?	ICT is used for ➢ Storage and ordering ➢ Administrative and personnel matters ➢ To develop new production processes ➢ To develop and transfer educational material ➢ Process development in direct production
ICT Integration level	ICT allows to transfer data and information between all parts of production both within the workplace and the whole organization
Means used to transfer person-to-person information and/or knowledge	➢ E-mail ➢ Internet ➢ Network ➢ Electronic Conferences ➢ Common databases
Electronic commerce	Electronic commerce is actively used for purchase, distribution and sale of goods and services.
Telework or distance work	Distance work has increased and the personnel is allowed to work at home or at other geographically distant organizations

handle and benefit from more information. Ten years from now it is likely that even more will be required. Over time, organizations will adapt, and adopt new generations of ICT, new structures and ways of operating will make possible to reach the business scope re-definition stage identified by Venkatraman (see Figure 1). At the core of this will be information and the strategies for managing data and information will last longer and develop more gradually than the technical means of realizing the strategies. Healthcare organization should possess the ability to manage information dynamically and also to respond immediately to new needs and requirements through their capability of synchronizing their use of information and new networks of teams.

Existing ICT- systems are, however, often still incompatible, and for many years to come it is likely that data will have to be translated in new, add-on systems. Also, incentives may be lacking to transform organizations from evolutionary to revolutionary (Olve & Vimarlund, 2005). It is possible that may even exist disincentives as some organization does not trust the other, or have institutional incentives to form teams that transcend organizational boundaries.

Furthermore, investments in ICT systems are usually made based on expectations of improving organizational operations, reducing of costs, controlling resource allocation and achieving of a higher standard of quality (Clayton & van Mulligen, 1996; Timpka, 1994). People and work-processes however usually undergo unexpected changes when a new ICT system is introduced. This is due to the fact that changes associated with the introduction of ICT are often drastic and cause intra organizational tension (Kaplan, 2001). However, individuals are expected to be agents of change and to also contribute to the rapid adaptation to the changes that any new ICT system demands. Rules, demands, at both the external and internal level as well as differences

in goals, visions and opinions affect the introduction of ICT systems and the re-engineering of work processes.

Another important issue is that while researchers often express opinions of what it is important to focus upon when implementing a new ICT system, managers representing healthcare organizations are often focused on patient empowerment, clinic management and possibility of co-determination or patient empowerment. Issues such as organizational flexibility or how to obtain increase control over resources, increase autonomy and responsibility at work or cost efficiency of IT are not structured and defined.

Therefore, to succeed, and to move from the evolutionary stage to the revolutionary ones, it is necessary to change all stages combined with ICT and the aims technology is supposed to achieve. In addition to this, it is necessary beforehand to identify the social impacts that the forthcoming IT systems will have both for organizations, the personnel and the customer (Kaplan & Shaw, 2004).

There is today a good deal of wisdom and experience in ICT outside of health informatics area. However, when discussing pre-requisites to interact between organizations that provide healthcare, issues concerning process-reengineering, resource allocation, organizational issues and organizational and individual behavior and its consequences for inter-organizational collaboration are not taken into consideration. Often the introduction of ICT leads them to failures, resistance to use ICT or to a non-optimal use of the scarce recourses

The degree of transformation from evolutionary to revolutionary should therefore be determined by the role ICT will have in the organization when initiating the redesigning processes, but also in according to the work-procedures and competencies along the organization.

DISCUSSION

Healthcare capacity, such as hospitals, and competences, such as ability to handle ICT systems, all require investments in material and immaterial capital. These normally are meaningful only if they are to be used for several years. However, when we transform organizations and move them from an evolutionary stage to revolutionary ones the benefits are not any longer static. Some changes involves mostly rationalizations of existing procedures, while others invites us to explore new ways of organizing, new ways to interact with customers and suppliers and new ways to provide health care services.

This chapter suggests a framework to identify changes that is, from evolutionary to revolutionary as a consequence of the implementation and use of ICT. The classification of organizations in different steps of transformation indicates further that stakeholders, healthcare personnel, and managers will have to cooperate and refocus their priorities to be able to build healthcare organizations that can be adapted to revolutionary levels. This is due to the fact that the new breed of healthcare organization that is beginning to materialize today is an organization that purposely constructs cross-functional and process-oriented structures and strategies so as to enhance and maximize organizational resources. The transition from one organizational stage to another will not occur in all healthcare organizations simultaneously or in the same manner. This is because context and other important variables such as health service area, geographical location, legal status, number of workers, and degree of modernization as well as environmental, political and economic factors play important roles.

Even more important, to move from one level to another will need that collaborative solutions will work, but also the identification of long-term outcomes as for instance to highlight how information exchange (knowledge) can be used to gradually build trust between partners, what institutions are needed, and how all of these interact with each other. In designing responsibilities, a high level of trust will mean that less information or institutionalized rules will be required. Even if a manager has the legal responsibility to procure adequate information, what this means has to be interpreted, and prior knowledge and trust will be important in determining the amount and content of such information.

For a long time there were concerns that ICT did not lead to the benefits that were expected for enterprises. Some talked of a 'productivity paradox' (Solow, 1987), meaning the lack of proof that ICT investments provided value for money. Only recently has the general consensus become that ICT spending, correctly applied, is indeed profitable (Oz, 2005). Most writers now favor two explanations for the delayed proof of ICTs profitability. One is the time required to make concomitant changes in processes, organization and competences. They believe that most of the economic benefits from introducing ICT in industry during the past 40 years have in fact derived from 'reengineering' processes: changing tasks and who performs them. This leads to the second explanation. Many ICT investments have not been combined with the needed investments in (re)organization and training, and such investments are not always well timed with the introduction of new systems.

Faced with increasingly costly healthcare, there are hopes for similar effects and benefits in healthcare than the industry has reported. Using ICT systems, it should be possible to reengineering work processes, changing tasks and achieve the revolutionary level that contemporary enterprises has obtained, and at the same time, have the possibility to reconfigure healthcare in ways that allow us to deliver services that increase self-service, substitute cheaper manpower for professional medical staff, reduce costs and stimulate service production and educations as well as business transformation and cost-effectiveness of investments.

FUTURE RESEARCH DIRECTIONS

The next decade will offer many exciting challenges to healthcare, especially in areas such as elderly health- and homecare. However, in the past 25 years of implementing ICT and IS in healthcare, people, organizations and policies are the dominant forces 90% of the time and ICT is only 10% of the implementation (Saba & McCormick, 2005). In future research it would be interesting to pay more attention to productivity changes due to the implementation and use of ICT in healthcare setting. The development of indicators and measures that clearly indicate the monetary benefits and costs to move from one stage to another (from evolutionary to revolutionary) will be of essential relevance to decision makers and stakeholders. Decision-makers have to see the monetary value of their ICT investments. Models and methods to measure the economic effects of changes and how the changes that are produced will affect the actors involved should be essential as tools for decision-making and design of new proposals, but also for preparing for change, and monitoring of change processes.

REFERENCES

Clayton,P.D., van Mulligen, E. (1996, October 26-30). The Economic Motivation for Clinical Information Systems. In J.J. Cimino (Ed.), *Proceeding of Annual Fall Symposium* (pp. 660-668). Washington, DC.

Kaplan, B. (2001). Evaluating informatics applications? Social interactionism and call for methodological pluralism. *International Journal of Medical Informatics*, 64(1), 39-56.

Kaplan, B., Shaw, N. (2004). Future directions in evaluation research: People, organizational, and social issues. *Methods of Information in Medicine*, 43(3-4), 215-231.

Olve, NG., Vimarlund, V. (2005).Locating ICT's benefits in elderly care. *Medical Informatics and the Internet in Medicine*, 30(4): 297-308.

Oz, E. (2005). Information technology productivity: in search of a definitive observation. *Information and management* 42, 789-798.

Solow, R. M. (1987). We'd Better Watch Out. *New York Times Book Review*, July 12.

Saba, V., McCormick, K. (2005). *Essentials of Nursing Informatics*. McGraw Hill.

Timpka, T. (1994). Organizational learning in the continuo development of healthcare: Making use of information technology to increase the total service quality. *Human Factors in Organizational Development and Management, IV*, 505-510.

Venkatraman, N. (1994). IT-enabled business transformation: From automation to business-scope redefinition. *Sloan Management Review*, 35(2), 73-87.

Vimarlund, V., Olve, N.G. (2005). Economic analyses for ICT in elderly healthcare: Questions and challenges. *Health Informatics Journal*, 4(11), 293-305.

Vimarlund, V., Timpka, T., Patel, V. (1999).Information technology and knowledge exchange in health-care organisations. *Proceedings of AMIA'99, American Medical Informatics Association* (pp. 632-636). Philadelphia: Hanley & Belfus Inc.

Vimarlund, V., Sjöberg, C., Timpka, T. (2003). A theory for classification of healthcare organisations in the New Economy. *Journal of Medical Systems*, 27(5), 467-475.

Chapter IX
Where do Technology-Induced Errors Come From?
Towards a Model for Conceptualizing and Diagnosing Errors Caused by Technology

Elizabeth M. Borycki
University of Victoria, Canada

Andre W. Kushniruk
University of Victoria, Canada

ABSTRACT

Health information technology has the potential to greatly improve healthcare delivery. Indeed, in recent years many have argued that introduction of information technology will be essential in order to decrease medical error and increase healthcare safety. In this chapter we review some of the evidence that has accumulated indicating the positive benefits of health information technology for improving safety in healthcare. However, a number of recent studies have indicated that if systems are not designed and implemented properly health information technology may actual inadvertently result in new types of medical errors—technology-induced errors. In this chapter we discuss where such error may arise and propose a model for conceptualizing and diagnosing technology-induced error so that the benefits of technology can be achieved while the likelihood of the occurrence of technology-induced medical error is reduced.

Copyright © 2008, IGI Global, distributing in print or electronic forms without written permission of IGI Global is prohibited.

Every great mistake has a halfway moment, a split second when it can be recalled and perhaps remedied.

Pearl Buck – *U.S. novelist in China (1892 - 1973)*

INTRODUCTION

Today technology permeates almost every aspect of healthcare delivery from clinician to administrator to researcher and policy maker work (Shortliffe & Cimino, 2006; van Bemmel & Musen, 1997). Consequently, many health professionals, administrators, policy makers, and researchers have begun to take technology (i.e., computer software and hardware) for granted, believing that the technology provides information and integrates and executes processes correctly, consistently and accurately in a valid, reliable and useful manner. However, technology is developed, designed, implemented, and used by humans, who we know, are imperfect and prone to making mistakes. These human imperfections lead us to make errors in the design, development, customization, implementation, and use of complex technologies such as health information systems (Kaner, Falk, & Nguyen, 1999; Patton, 2001). These errors may in turn introduce or induce new types of errors into healthcare delivery processes (i.e., technology-induced errors).

Defining Technology-Induced Errors

Technology-induced errors can emerge during the software development lifecycle through to the implementation and operation of health information systems (Kaner et al., 1999; Patton, 2001). The notion of technology-induced errors is not new to the health information systems literature. Over the past several decades there have been many published occurrences involving the attributes of health software and hardware that induce er-

rors. These reports, although infrequent, have led to significant learning's and the redesign and improvement of healthcare technologies, their implementation and user training associated with their use (Koornneef & Voges, 2002; Vicente, 2003). As well, with the rise in the acuity and complexity of patients, health professionals are increasingly becoming more reliant upon technology (i.e., health information system software and hardware) to aid patients in the process of recovering, recuperating and managing severe patient illness and disease (Sandelowski, 2000). As the rate of technology use in healthcare continues to increase in response to changing demographic and healthcare needs of patients so does the potential for technology-induced error. Therefore, technology-induced error as a patient safety issue has become a source of increasing concern for system designers, developers, implementers and users. To better understand technology-induced error one must first understand the notion of medical error and how technology has been used to reduce medical error associated with the management of acutely ill, complex patients. Therefore, the purpose of this chapter will be to: (a) first define and describe traditional sources of medical error, (b) briefly describe the background, and introduction of technology (i.e., software and hardware) into healthcare for the purpose of medical error prevention, (c) define technology-induced error and differentiate this type of error from traditional sources of medical error, (d) review the possible sources of technology induced error across the technology design, development, implementation and operation continuum, and (e) propose a conceptual framework for diagnosing technology-induced errors.

TRADITIONAL SOURCES OF MEDICAL ERROR

As outlined earlier, before one can discuss technology-induced error, one must first understand what medical error is, how technology is believed to address medical errors as well as how technology can improve the quality of healthcare. In healthcare, medical error is a significant issue for the health professions. Research has revealed medical error is one of the leading causes of death and disability for healthcare consumers (Institute of Medicine, 1999). According to the Institute of Medicine's report To Err is Human a sizable number of patients are harmed in the United States each year as a consequence of medical errors (Institute of Medicine, 1999). Current estimates suggest approximately 44,000 Americans die each year due to medical errors (American Hospital Association, 1999). Similar studies have been conducted in other countries (i.e., Canada, Australia and New Zealand) with analogous results (Baker & Norton, 2004; Baker, Norton, Flintoft et al., 2004; Davis, Lay-Yee, Briant et al., 2001; Wilson, Runiciman, Gibberd et al., 1995). In these studies medical errors (i.e., adverse events) were defined as those events that lead to "an unintended injury or complication resulting in disability at the time of discharge, death or a prolonged hospital stay and that is caused by healthcare management rather than by the patient's underlying disease process" (Baker et al., 2004).

Medical error arises from health professionals' mistakes regarding diagnosis and treatment (e.g., incorrect decisions, lack of information and poor decision-making). Examples of such medical errors include medication errors in: dose, frequency, route, timing, substitution errors, errors in prescribing the wrong type of medication, errors in medication delivery and mismatches between the types of medication prescribed for treatment and a patients health condition and/or health history. Health professionals and the organizational environments where they work were the focus of these studies. Such organizational research effectively uncovered several differing types of medical errors that were occurring in healthcare settings (e.g., hospital and home care). This research documented the types of medical errors that occurred and the underlying work processes that could lead to medical errors. The intent of this research was to prevent future medical errors from occurring (Bates, Leape, Cullen et al., 1998; Baker et al., 2004; Evans, Pestotnik, Classen et al., 1998). Once documented, health professionals attempted to identify the sources and methods of reducing the likelihood of the most common types of medical errors from occurring.

HEALTH INFORMATION SYSTEMS IN HEALTHCARE AND THE BENEFITS ASSOCIATED WITH THEIR USE IN REDUCING MEDICAL ERRORS

The development of computers in the 1940s brought about the beginning of a technological hardware and software revolution. By the 1950s and 60s, the introduction of computers to healthcare led to the early use of technology in healthcare research, education and practice (Shortliffe & Cimino, 2006; van Bemmel & Musen, 1997). At first, computers were used in a limited number of healthcare settings (i.e., laboratory, diagnostic imaging, and billing departments). Computers were used to diagnose patients early in their disease process and to treat patients with complex medications and treatment regimens. As well, computers were used in the billing process. Others identified the potential of computerization to improve the quality and safety of healthcare, but it was not until the landmark report by the Institute of Medicine (1999), *To Err is Human,* that the full potential of health information systems and computers was recognized. More specifically, as a method of streamlining patient care processes, reengineering healthcare and supporting information seeking and decision making. The report led to increased dissemination of health information systems throughout healthcare (Hersh, Stavri, & Detmer, 2006; Kushniruk, 2002; McLaughlin & Kibb, 2006).

Healthcare administrators and clinicians attempted to harness the potential of health information systems to reduce medical error and tried to understand the implications of computerization for healthcare work (Institute of Medicine, 1999; Shortliffe & Cimino, 2006). Over the last several decades the healthcare industry saw the introduction and testing of many health information systems that could aid in improving the quality and safety of patient care (i.e., electronic health records and decision support systems could be used to reduce medical error rates) (Bates et al., 1998; Tierney, 2001). A number of demonstration studies concluded some types of health information systems (i.e., physician order entry could significantly reduce medical error rates) (Chaudry, Wang, Wu et al., 2006). As excitement grew about the potential role of health information systems, many healthcare organizations began the process of implementing health information systems. Research suggested that health information systems could reduce: length of stay, unnecessary laboratory testing, improve immunization rates (McDonald, Hui, Smith et al., 1984), and most importantly, reduce medication errors (Bates et al., 1998). This research culminated in the recommendation by the Institute of Medicine and the Leapfrog Group in the United States that health information systems (such as physician order entry) be implemented in healthcare facilities (Institute of Medicine, 1999; National Quality Forum, 2003). The United States was not alone in making these policy changes. Other countries such as Canada and England have also followed suit in integrating and implementing health information systems into healthcare processes (Canada Health Infoway, 2006; National Health Service, 2005).

As the healthcare industry identified some of the most common sources of medical error and attempted to address their systemic causes (i.e., processes) by streamlining and re-engineering healthcare processes through the use of health information systems and by identifying new technologically based methods of supporting health professional information seeking and decision-making (i.e., again to reduce medical error) (McLaughlin & Kibb, 2006; Shortliffe & Cimino, 2006). Healthcare activities and processes were modeled and incorporated into health information systems, increasing the number of activities that were executed by machines, improving the consistency and accuracy with which work activities could be carried out and reducing the likelihood that human activities could lead to medical error. Incorporating aspects of healthcare processes into health information systems successfully reduced some of the human sources of medical error (Bates & Gawande, 2003; Bates et al, 1998; Evans et al, 1998; McLaughlin & Kibb, 2006; Tierney, 2001). Health information systems were seen to be better able to perform some healthcare processes (e.g., such as the delivery of a physician order from a nursing unit to the pharmacy for fulfillment with better speed, accuracy and consistency) (McLaughlin & Kibbe, 2006; Savitz & Bernard, 2006).

In addition to streamlining and reengineered healthcare processes, health information systems were developed that could provide health professionals with information that could support health professional information seeking and decision making. Here, health information systems provided information at point of care in real time that could be used to support health professional work. By supporting these cognitive processes, researchers believed health information systems (i.e., decision support systems) would improve the quality of patient care decisions and reduce the likelihood of medical judgment errors (Hersh et al., 2006; Musen, Shahar, & Shortliffe, 2006). For example, if a decision support system was available in conjunction with a physician order entry system, a physician could be given additional information about the patient and the medications that would support their decision-making (e.g., physicians would be given alerts, reminders or warnings about drug-drug interactions, patient allergies to medications, and drug-food interactions for the patient). This would prevent prescribing errors and improve the quality of medical decisions (Institute of Medicine, 1999; Savitz & Bernard, 2006; Shortliffe & Cimino, 2006). Studies conducted by McDonald, Tierney and their colleagues have demonstrated that providing computer-based information about physician orders can lead to improved patient care and efficiency (McDonald et al., 1984; Tierney, McDonald, Martin et al., 1987; Tierney, McDonald, Hui, & Rogers, 1988; Tierney, Miller, & McDonald, 1990; Tierney, Miller, Overhage, & McDonald, 1993). Physician order entry and decision support systems were not the only types of systems that were identified as having a significant influence on medical error. Other health information system studies documented the value of point of care medication administration systems (i.e., systems that ensure medication is administered safely reducing medical errors such as errors of omission, incorrect time of administration and errors involving the wrong medication being given). Such point-of-care systems include those systems that use barcoding and scanning technology in conjunction with medication administration systems to prevent errors associated with patients being given the wrong medication, dose of medication, medication at the wrong time of day etc. (Cohen & Vaijda, 2005). As previously outlined, health information systems designers and researchers documented the benefits that were derived from integrating and using physician order entry, decision support and point of care medication administration systems in terms of reducing medical errors. Again, researchers have found integrating such hardware and software may introduce the potential for errors (Kushniruk, 2001; Patterson, Cook, & Render, 2002). For example, integrating medication administration software with bar coding technology may lead to nurse confusion during the medication administration process, decreased coordination of activities between physicians and nurses (Patterson et al., 2002), increased

cognitive load as previously parallel activities became serialized (Kushniruk et al., 2006) and increased complexity associated with performing medication administration tasks (Borycki et al., 2006). As a consequence, there is a need to use new methods and approaches to diagnosing such problems before systems are implemented to reduce the likelihood of error emerging from system use (Kushniruk et al., 2006).

In summary, much attention was given by researchers and health information system designers to the healthcare processes that may lead to medical error. Health information systems were used to streamline, and reengineer processes in order to reduce human sources of medical error. Based on the results of these studies (i.e., indicating the positive effect of specific health information systems in reducing error), many researchers, healthcare administrators and politicians concluded health information systems could be used to reduce the number of medical errors that were occurring in healthcare. However, as processes were changed opportunities to introduce new types of errors were also created (Han, Carcillo, Venkataraman et al., 2005; Koppel et al., 2005; Kushniruk, Triola, Stein et al., 2004; Kushniruk et al., 2006; Patterson et al., 2002). Little attention was given to the possible introduction of new types of errors associated with the streamlining, reengineering or adding new decision support tools used in patient care with the use of technology (Koppel, Metlay, Cohen et al., 2005).

THE EMERGENCE OF A NEW TYPE OF ERROR: TECHNOLOGY-INDUCED ERROR

Even as healthcare organizations were implementing systems, research began to emerge supporting the view that health information systems may lead to errors. In 2004 and 2005, several landmark publications suggested that the introduction of health information systems into patient care processes could lead to the emergence of a new type of error: technology-induced errors (Koppel et al., 2005; Kushniruk et al., 2004; Kushniruk et al., 2005). Here, health information systems in of themselves or the interactions between health information systems and humans were observed to in some cases facilitate technology-induced errors. Since the publication of these first works on technology-induced error, a number of studies have been conducted that have identified the unintended and pervasive nature of the consequences of health information systems where technologically-induced errors are concerned (e.g., Ash, Sittig, & Poon et al., 2007; Han et al., 2005; Horsky, Kuperman, & Patel, 2005). From these studies it has been shown that health information systems may induce or facilitate medical errors when they are not designed to take human cognitive limits and capabilities into account and when not tested. For example, Kushniruk and colleagues (2004, 2005) found that specific usability problems (e.g., lack of visibility on a PDA screen may influence the medication dosages that could be selected) in the user interface of an application designed to support physician entry of medications (Kushniruk et al., 2004). Other types of errors facilitated by poor human-computer interaction were identified by Koppel et al. (2005), including errors that occur due to an excessive number of computer screens required for entering a medication and unclear logon and logoff procedures.

Healthcare consumers and health professionals are now becoming increasingly more cognizant of the potential benefits and pitfalls of health information systems. One school of thought among leading health information system researchers supports the view that health information systems have: helped to make significant improvements to the quality of healthcare work, reduced some types of errors, created new opportunities to provide and verify information, support healthcare worker decision-making (e.g., ordering a medication that does not interact with a patients condition or other medications the patient may be taking). This per-

spective supports the view that more traditional forms of medical error can be mitigated by the implementation of health information systems in clinical environments (Bates et al., 1998; Institute of Medicine, 1999; Tierney, 2001). An alternative perspective on health information systems (i.e., that of another select group of researchers) suggests there is an increasing need to pay attention to, identify and address the types of errors that technologies can introduce or propagate, that is, technology-induced errors (Ammenwerth & Shaw, 2005; Ash et al., 2007; Kushniruk et al., 2004). These researchers have suggested that health information systems can reduce medical errors but they may also introduce new types of technology-induced errors and efforts need to be made to diagnose potential technology-induced errors before systems are deployed into healthcare environments. Diagnosing technology-induced errors before a health information system is implemented can prevent such errors from occurring. As most health information systems are modifiable, that is, the technology can be altered to eliminate the error. There is a need to develop methods and approaches for diagnosing technology-induced error so that such potential errors can be eliminated before reaching the real world (Kushniruk et al., 2006).

More recent publications in the health informatics literature have suggested that such an approach needs to be undertaken when designing, implementing and operating health information systems (Ammenwerth & Shaw, 2005; Horsky, Zhang, & Patel, 2005). Furthermore, researchers (e.g., Borycki et al., 2006; Kushniruk et al., 2004) are calling for the development and use of new methodologies for diagnosing and evaluating health information systems ability to introduce or propagate errors *prior* to systems release (using advanced simulation methods). Therefore, a significant and fundamental shift has taken place in the health informatics literature. Health informaticians are expecting systems that designers develop to not only reduce medical error, but to not introduce, induce or facilitate new types of errors as a result of their use (Ash et al., 2007; Borycki & Kushniruk, 2005; Koppel et al., 2005; Kushniruk et al., 2004). These researchers are also developing new methodologies for both predicting and for diagnosing newly emerged technology-induced errors so they can be diagnosed prior to implementation (e.g., Borycki et al., 2006; Borycki & Kushniruk, 2005; Kushniruk et al., 2005; Kushniruk et al., 2006; Kuwata, Kushniruk, Borycki, & Watanabe, 2006). Such a solution oriented approach is critical. Prevention (i.e., diagnosis) is needed early in the software development lifecycle and implementation and operation of systems.

TOWARDS AN ERA OF PREVENTING TECHNOLOGY INDUCED ERRORS

Before technology-induced errors can be diagnosed one must first identify where potential technology-induced errors come from. In reviewing the literature, it can be noted that technology-induced errors have a number of potential sources. They arise from: (a) the design and development of technology, (c) the implementation and customization of a technology and (d) the interactions between the operation of the new technology and the new work processes that arise from technology's use. In this section of this chapter we will discuss the potential sources of technology-induced.

ERRORS ARISING FROM THE DESIGN AND DEVELOPMENT OF HEALTH INFORMATION SYSTEMS

Traditionally, the field of software engineering has focused on developing methods for identifying errors in the design, specification and programming of code in the release of software (Patton, 2001;

Pressman, 2005). However, in healthcare, traditional software testing methods have been found to be lacking in that they have failed to adequately consider how complex healthcare information systems can interact with healthcare professionals as they carry out complex tasks in real world settings (Kushniruk, 2002; Patel, Kushniruk, Yang, Yale, 2000). We will outline the sources of error arising from the software engineering literature and discuss how traditional software testing methods have failed to adequately consider a health professional's use of health information systems in real life, complex environments. According to the software engineering literature, technology-induced errors involve those technology failures where the system did not function as it was intended to. These errors range in severity on a continuum from inconveniences at one end of the continuum (i.e., the technology does not work properly resulting in a hassle to the user), to catastrophic errors at the other (i.e., where there is injury or loss of life) (Koppel et al., 2005; Patton, 2001; Vicente, 2003).

Inadequate Requirements Specification as a Source of Error

In the software engineering literature, studies have shown that the majority of errors in completed systems can be traced back to one of three systems development lifecycle processes: requirements specification, design and programming (Kaner et al., 1999; Patton, 2001). Although each source of error contributes significantly to the final technology product (i.e., the health information system), studies have shown poor requirements specification contributes the most to these types of errors. In poor requirements specification (i.e., gathering), the designer fails to adequately specify what the system will do (i.e., its functions), "how it will act, and what it won't do" (Patton, 2001, p. 15). Poor requirements specification often emerges as a gap between user expectations, the purchasing organizations and the actual functionality of the product in the real world clinical environment. Poor requirements specification may lead to the software not being able to perform certain actions that were originally expected of the product at the time of purchase. In other cases, poor requirements gathering may lead to too much functionality being made available to the user—functionality that is not useful or usable (Kushniruk, 2002). For example, poor user requirements gathering may manifest as the inability to create and modify health information system's alerts and reminders that are representative of emerging trends in evidence based clinical practice. In such a case the health information system may have a set of built-in rules and reminders that are specific to guidelines published during one point in time (e.g., the 1990s). Generally, alerts and reminders are based on evidence based clinical guidelines. In such a case, if the guideline changes, so should the systems' alerts or reminders have the capacity to change to reflect the new or emergent guideline. If the alert or reminder cannot be altered to reflect the changes to guidelines, then the requirements specification failed to gather sufficient information about nature of evidence based guidelines (i.e., information about the fact that guidelines change over time as new research emerges and that this should be represented in the health information system in real time). Such a poor specification would lead to clinicians using outdated guidelines in their clinical practice and this may lead to errors.

Poor requirements specification not only influences software design and development, it can also affect specific downstream system development and programming activities. Consequently, if a specification is inadequate there may be a need for new specifications or the altering of existing ones to ensure the technology meets with end user needs. Furthermore, careful attention must be paid to understanding the "true" source of the error as requirements specification influences downstream system software development processes such as design, development and programming.

Errors in design and programming may have their origins in the requirements specification itself. Therefore, identifying and isolating the "true" source of technology-induced error is key to addressing the error and correcting aspects of the requirements specification that affect subsequent technology design and programming (Kaner et al., 1999; Patton, 2001).

Other indications of inadequate requirements specification or gathering that suggest a need for attention include: (1) the system does not perform what was outlined in the specifications, (2) the system does something that the specifications indicate it should not do, (3) the system does something that is not mentioned in the specifications, (4) the system requirements specifications do not allow the technology to meet the fundamental needs of end users and the environment where it will be deployed, (5) the system does not address the workflow practices of users in routine and non-routine situations, (6) the system is difficult to comprehend, not usable, slow and/or (7) viewed by the end user as not intuitively meeting their information needs and/or the demands of their work (Kaner et al., 1999; Patton, 2001). In summary, requirements specifications may lead to technology-induced errors when systems designers fail to adequately specify the requirements before is the technology is built, resulting in a gap between end users expectations about how the technology should work and what the technology actually does.

Inadequate Design as a Source of Error

Inadequate design can also be a source of error. System developers may fail to adequately blueprint the conceptual model of how the system components should work and integrate together (Pressman, 2005). For example, a system may provide the user with access to incorrect or inappropriate data sources, may require the user to re-enter data in two subsystems redundantly when they could have been integrated, (e.g., a physician enters a patient's allergies in the physician order entry system and then has to re-enter the same information into their admission notes). Here, failure to enter the allergy information in one of the systems would be considered an error of omission, yet such an error has its origins in poor systems design and integration. The systems components have not been integrated by the designer. In another example, a pharmacist receives a physician order via a physician order entry system, has to print off the order and then re-enter it into a pharmacy information system. Here, the two health information systems are not interoperable. The benefits of the physician ordering the medication and having it sent to the pharmacist directly are evident. It must be noted that the inability to interface the two systems adds work and introduces the possibility that transcription errors may occur while the pharmacist is transcribing orders from one system to another (Spencer, Leininger, Daniels et al., 2005).

Programming as a Source of Error

It must be noted that programmers are human. Therefore, they may make programming errors. For example, a programmer who is on a deadline that is working long hours is more likely to make an error when programming than a well-rested individual with reasonable time pressures. Similarly, novices may make more errors than experts (McKeithen, Reitman, Rueter, & Hirtle, 1981). Such errors may cause health information systems to perform in a ways they were not intended to (Patton, 2001).

There have been examples of cases where programming errors and the reuse of software code in the field of health informatics have lead to technology-induced errors. Some have lead to catastrophic consequences (Ammenwerth & Shaw, 2005). Many techniques in the field of software engineering have been developed to mitigate against such errors (Kaner et al., 1999;

Patton, 2001; Pressman, 2005). These include black box testing (i.e., testing of program code using test cases where computer inputs are varied to assess correctness of outputs without a detailed examination of the actual code) and white box testing (i.e., involving close visual inspection of the code itself) as described in the previous section. In mission critical industries such as aviation, strict additional standards and guidelines exist for programmers. Increasingly, there is an expectation among the user community in healthcare (i.e., physicians, nurses, and other health professional) that similar standards and guidelines need to be applied to the specification, design and development of health information systems. Here, users believe that like aviation systems, health information systems can have a significant impact upon health and human life and that careful scrutiny and testing of program code is required.

In summary, when considering the development of a technology, the software engineering research identifies several main sources of error: requirements specification, design and coding. Each type of error may be disruptive to health professional work, especially, when health professional, end user expectations and needs differ from those envisioned by designers. These types of errors can alter or disrupt clinician work, organizing and reasoning and therefore may lead to error.

ERRORS ARISING FROM IMPLEMENTATION AND CUSTOMIZATION OF HEALTH INFORMATION SYSTEMS

Once a technology's requirements have been specified, designed and programmed, the technology's implementation process can be a potential source of error. In the next section of this chapter we will discuss two phases of technology implementation: beta testing and customization as potential sources of technology-induced error. Both occur before a technology is formally deployed in a healthcare environment and influence the ultimate implementation and use of health information systems.

Inadequate Beta Testing as a Potential Source of Error

Beta testing occurs when a system is first deployed and tested in an organization. Prior to beta testing occurring, the company that develops the health information system and the healthcare organization that will be adopting the health information system work together to develop requirements specifications. This is followed by the development of a working version of the health information system. In beta testing the partnering healthcare organization or a representative organization is selected by the health information system development company. These two organizations work together to implement and essentially test the newly developed health information system in a real world environment. This is known as beta-testing. During beta-testing the representative healthcare organization and the health information systems development company fine tune or change the system in response to the health information systems ability to address user needs in a real world clinical settings (Denis & Wixom, 2003; Kushniruk & Patel, 2004).

In the area of health informatics, many companies that develop health information systems perform beta testing: (a) at the site where they collected their initial requirements specification, and (b) a few other representative sites (e.g., other hospitals). Most often beta testing takes place in the healthcare organization where the initial specifications were gathered. However, it is well known that sites chosen for beta testing may not be entirely representative or replicate all future sites where a system may be deployed. As a result, deployment to a new organization that is unlike the organization where the beta testing took place

may lead to a range of differences and gaps in work processes and activities that may lead to a range of errors associated with integrating the system into the new organization's work practices, processes, and information flows (Borycki et al., 2005; Koppel et al., 2005; Kushniruk et al., 2006). It must be noted that in beta testing there is an opportunity for the organization that developed the software to adjust it to meet user specific needs at the representative beta testing sites. Therefore, the potential for errors arising from the integration of the health information system with new organizational work practices may be higher initially but may decrease over time as the health information system's developers try to "fit" the software product to the new organization's work and information flows. As task-technology "fit" improves, potential technology-induced errors may also decrease significantly over time.

Customization of as a Potential Source of Error

Once a technology is developed and beta tested, other organizations will purchase and implement the health information system (Orlinkowski, 1992). This process may involve an extensive customization period where a health information system such as an electronic patient record is modified to replicate local practices, work, and information flows within the organization that purchased the health information system. Customization is often a complex process that may introduce new types of errors into the adopting organization if a gap exists between a technology's functions and the practices, work processes, information flows and expectations of end users (e.g., physicians, nurses and administrators) or if the software significantly differs from the organization on which the system was originally developed and tested. For example, the workflows embedded in a health information system may not be representative of the work and information flows of the new organization or the system's workflows may not be similar to the practice expectations of the new organization or the country where the system is now being deployed. Such gaps between technological and organizational practice, work and information flows have led to differences in the rates of adoption of health information systems (Southton, Sauer & Grant, 1997), users development of significant workarounds (Koppel et al., 2005; Kushniruk et al., 2006; Patterson et al., 2002;) and significant user changes in work and information flows that may, in turn, facilitate errors (Koppel et al., 2005).

INTERACTIONS BETWEEN THE OPERATION OF THE NEW TECHNOLOGY AND THE NEW WORK PROCESS

The operation of new technologies can also lead to new types of error. Just as the design, development and implementation of a new technology can introduce new types of error so can a health information system's day-to-day use lead to errors. According to Orlinkowski (1992), when technology designers develop an information technology (e.g., a health information system), they base their designs upon the policies and procedures, interaction patterns of workers as well as the institutional work and information flows (i.e., the structures) of the "model" organization. The information technology, once completed, represents the structures (e.g., interaction patterns of the actors or workers) in the "model" organization. The information technology, as a result, has certain rules or "structures" from the "model" organization that influence worker behaviors (e.g., work and information flows) (Dennis & Wixom, 2003; DeSanctis & Poole, 1994; Orlinkowski, 1992; Simon, 2001).

The adopting organization or the organization that purchases the technology chooses to incorporate these "structures" into their organization. As outlined earlier, the adopting organization

may need to alter the information system (i.e., through the process of customization) to better resemble or "fit" its own structures. Therefore, when the information system is deployed in the adopting organization, it is often a combination of the "model" and the "adopting" organization's structures (Dennis & Wixom, 2003; DeSanctis & Poole, 2004; Orlinkowski, 1992). When the information system (e.g., health information system) is implemented in the adopting organization, workers or actors apply these structures within the social context of the adopting organization. The information system's structures, in turn, constrain or facilitate the actor's or worker's level of knowledge, interpretation, intentionality, interactions, behaviors and social relations. These structures essentially influence the organizational workers subsequent use of the information system. For example, as nurses learn to use a new technology (e.g., a barcoding and medication administration system) they may accept the changes introduced by the new technology where their work is concerned or they may create and develop new methods and ways of interacting with the information system to overcome the its constraints and limitations (i.e., workarounds or methods of ignoring or bypassing system functions) (Ash et al., 2007; Campbell, Sittig, Ash et al., 2006; Koppel et al., 2005; Orlinkowski, 1992; Orlinkowski & Gash, 1994; Orlinkowski & Yates, 1994; Patterson et al., 2002). Researchers have found that such workarounds or bypassing of system functions occur when a new health information system does not integrate seamlessly with routine (Kushniruk et al., 1997; Koppel et al., 2005; Patterson et al., 2002), non-routine, complex or task urgent worker information and workflows as well as interaction patterns (Borycki et al., 2006; Kushniruk et al., 2006), or results in increased cognitive load (Kushniruk et al., 2006). Researchers such as Koppel et al. (2005) suggest that such complex workarounds and bypassing of system functions may facilitate technology-induced errors. Essentially, the creation and development of new interaction patterns to overcome health information system's constraints and limitations (as outlined in Orlinkowski's earlier 1992 work) may lead to the creation of new types of errors. Currently, many researchers are attempting to understand the types of unintended consequences that arise from such operation of systems (e.g., Ash et al., 2007; Koppel et al., 2005) Such work is key to diagnosing and addressing technology-induced errors. Other researchers are developing new and empirically based methodologies to diagnose such technology-induced errors in simulation environments prior to system release (e.g., Borycki et al., 2006; Kushniruk et al., 2004; Kushniruk et al., 2006; Kuwata et al., 2006). Health informatics researchers will need to develop new methods of diagnosing and investigating the source of technology induced errors before they occur as well as after health information systems have been implemented when adverse events occur much as the aviation industry has developed such investigative approaches and methodologies to develop technologies, processes and training approaches to prevent future occurrence of technology-induced error from system development through to implementation and operation of aircraft.

LIMITATIONS OF TRADITIONAL SOFTWARE TESTING METHODS

The range and diversity of situations in which healthcare information system ultimately becomes deployed makes the testing of such systems very difficult. Unlike systems developed in less complex domains where traditional testing methods may ensure that the system is adequately safe and free of error, in healthcare this has proven to be extremely difficult to achieve (Kushniruk, 2002). The two most widely known approaches to testing systems to ensure that they do not cause error are termed *white box* and *black box* testing (Patton, 2001, Pressman, 2005). White box testing focuses on the actual programming code that underlies

information systems, where the analyst/tester carrying out the testing may examine the code itself to see if it performs as expected (e.g., produces the appropriate outputs). With black box testing the tester only knows what outputs to expect given inputs to an information system (e.g., what result to be returned from a system when enquiring about a patient's laboratory results). In healthcare software development and deployment (i.e., during the phases of system development outlined in the previous section) both white box and black box testing are commonly employed. However, the complexity of use of health information systems in real clinical and hospital settings has indicated the need to test systems with a variety of users in a much more detailed and rigorous manner than is currently the norm. This type of testing is recommended to be take place in the actual context of healthcare work activities (e.g., testing for errors in a medication order entry system that might take place while a nurse or physician is also carrying out other normal activities, such as interacting with sick patients, hanging intravenous bags, being called away to emergency situations while in the middle of entering a medication etc.) (Kushniruk et al., 2005).

Indeed some authors have argued that simulation approaches need to be applied on a routine basis for testing health information systems and ensuring their safety. Simulation and usability engineering approaches focus on in-depth analysis of users' (e.g., physicians, nurses) interactions with systems while carrying out either real or highly realistic healthcare tasks (using clinical scenarios) within complex healthcare settings (e.g., Borycki & Kushniruk, 2005; Borycki et al., 2006; Kushniruk et al., 2006). Applying methods of simulation testing, subjects (e.g., healthcare professionals) are asked to interact with healthcare systems and their every action is recorded (typically using video recording), including all computer screens and verbalizations. In this way the complex context in which technology-induced errors arise can be captured and analyzed to precisely pinpoint and identify complex errors that may only arise in real system use *prior* to system release (i.e., diagnose the causes of the error) (Kushniruk et al., 2005). In healthcare such testing may be a necessary adjunct to traditional computer-centered testing of information systems (i.e., typical white box and black box testing) in order to ensure that systems do what they are expected to do and not inadvertently introduce error. In addition to development of new and refined testing methodologies, work is needed in developing a conceptual framework that takes into account the complexity of the healthcare domain when considering reduction of error involving use of technology. Toward this objective, in the next section of this chapter we will present a conceptual framework for understanding the potential sources of medical error.

MEDICAL ERROR: TOWARDS A CONCEPTUAL FRAMEWORK

In the early part of this chapter we discussed the potential sources of medical error. These sources of error have been significant and are well-known in to healthcare workers. We refer to them as "traditional medical errors" (i.e., error due to cognitive limitations of healthcare professionals as they work in traditional (typically paper-based) environments). We then illustrate that although health information systems may reduce error in healthcare, we identified a number of potential sources of "technology-induced errors" that can result from the complex interaction between human and computer once an information system is deployed in healthcare settings. We also discussed problems that may arise during the development of health information systems that can also be a source of potential error, "technology development errors" and implementation of systems errors (i.e., implementation errors). Each of these potential sources of error may increase the overall error rate in healthcare.

In summary, error in healthcare can arise from a number of sources: from the individual clinician (e.g., cognitive errors in making decisions or reasoning about patient cases), from the introduction of the information system (e.g., errors that arise from difficult to understand and use information systems) and the processes associated with information system development, implementation and operation.

Lastly, incompatibility between the adopting organization's practices, work and information flows and those of the adopting organization can further accentuate these types of errors (e.g., Koppel et al., 2005).

When we consider the impact of the introduction of health information systems into real healthcare settings (e.g., hospitals or clinics) we need to consider the total impact of the system on error. That is, when considering error after a technology is implemented (*total medical error*), we must consider the following: (a) the reduction of error that introduction of the system may be associated with (i.e., errors that it may be preventing), and (b) the potential for increase in or occurrence of new *error* due to the technology itself (i.e., errors that the new health information system and its processes may be actually causing). It should be noted that the studies cited in this chapter have generally focused on one or the other of these possibilities (i.e., either how health information systems reduce error, or alternatively how they might increase error) and little work has been conducted on understanding the complex balance between error reduction and facilitation in judging a system in order to ensure that its introduction results in a net benefit (i.e., an overall reduction of total error).

We must also consider the concomitant reduction or increase in error due to technology (i.e., from its development and implementation). Possible medical errors can arise from the clinician, technology development process, technology implementation, and operation process as previously outlined and illustrated in the formula here:

Total medical $_{error}$ = traditional medical $_{error}$ + technology-induced $_{error}$ (technology development *error* + *technology implementation* *error* + *technology operation* *error*)

As previously outlined, *technology development error* is composed of different types of errors; namely errors in requirements specification, design, programming, beta testing, customization, implementation and operation (i.e., during each of the phases in the standard system development lifecycle and implementation of systems, as described in Kushniruk, 2002).

Each source of error can be additive and may lead to an overall increase in the potential for medical errors to occur. Careful attention must be paid to ensure that a reduction in one source of error does not increase other sources of error. For example, the introduction of an order entry system in a hospital may reduce *traditional medical error* through the introduction of alerts and remindering functions (Bates & Gawande, 2003). However, the introduction of that very same technology may well lead to new categories of errors that are technology-induced or related to the technology's implementation as described in the previous section of this paper. In considering the *total* impact of technology upon errors, it is necessary for us to consider all of these broad categories of error (i.e., *medical, technology, implementation, and operation induced*) to ensure the cumulative impact of the system is positive in reducing errors as compared to before the system was implemented. Therefore, more detailed analysis of technology induced error is argued for in this paper and will be necessary to ensure the ultimate safety and reliability of healthcare information systems.

CONCLUSION

It has been argued by many researchers, administrators and politicians that use health information systems such as the electronic patient record can be equated with patient safety and a decrease of medi-cal errors. However, based on emerging research with health information systems of widely varying design approaches, testing, and implementation strategies and operation approaches, it is clear there is a variation in the attributes of healthcare information systems and their implementation (Ash et al., 2007). As a consequence, we feel that it is dangerous to argue that health information systems (e.g., the electronic health record) will reduce error as there is such a wide range of approaches and ideas regarding the development, design, testing, customization, and operation of the electronic health record (i.e., there is *no* one electronic health record, implementation or operation process, but rather there are many different systems and approaches each with its own strengths and limitations regarding safety and error) that need to be studied to identify attributes that reduce technology-induced error.

FUTURE RESEARCH DIRECTIONS

We feel there is a need to argue for a much more extensive evaluation within the framework of the systems development, implementation and operation lifecycle of *each* particular system we create and deploy to ensure its effectiveness, efficiency and safety and that standardized methods or guidelines be developed based on best practices from a health information industry perspective to reduce the likelihood of technology induced errors throughout the software development lifecycle and through to implementation much like the approach taken in the aviation industry. Such an approach would help to diagnose the origins of technology-induced errors as the systems development lifecycle and implementation process is lengthy and there is a need to identify error types in health information systems and to isolate these errors in each step of the process so they can be identified and addressed early on before they can have potentially catastrophic outcomes (i.e., addressing technology-induced errors in the systems specification, design, programming, beta testing, customization implementation and operational processes before a system is fully used in real world settings).

Work in the application of clinical and computer-based simulations in healthcare (see Borycki et al., 2005, Kushniruk et al., 2006; Kuwata et al., 2006 as borrowed from the field of healthcare usability engineering) promises to be an important trend since simulations of complex healthcare activity (involving use of new health information systems) can not only diagnose technology-induced errors before they occur, but more importantly they can be used to predict and prevent error from ever occurring in real world settings (i.e., by fixing such error *before* widespread release of a health information system occurs). Along these lines, much can be learned from work being conducted in other domains, such as aviation and nuclear power, where safety is also considered to be extremely important and where methods involving advanced simulations of use of systems are widely applied a part of technological testing

REFERENCES

Ash, J. S., Sittig, D. F., Poon, E. G., Guappone, K., Campbell, E., & Dykstra, R. H. (2007). The extent and importance of unintended consequences related to computerized provider order entry. *JAMIA, 14*(4), 415-423.

Ammenwerth, E., & Shaw, N.T. (2005). Bad health informatics can kill: Is evaluation the answer? *Methods of Information in Medicine, 44*, 1-3.

American Hospital Association. (1999). *Hospital statistics.* Chicago: American Hospital Association.

Baker, G. R., & Norton, P. (2004). Addressing the effects of adverse events: Study provides insights into patient safety at Canadian hospitals. *Healthcare Quarterly, 7*(4), 20-21.

Baker, G. R., Norton, P. G., Flintoft, V., Blais, R., Brown, A., Cox, J. et al. (2004). The Canadian adverse events study: The incidence of adverse events among hospital patients in Canada. *Canadian Medical Association Journal, 170*, 1678-1686.

Bates, D.W., & Gawande, A.A. (2003). Improving safety with information technology. *New England Journal of Medicine, 348*, 2526-2534.

Bates, D.W., Leape, L.L., Cullen, D.J., Laird, N., Petersen, L.A., Teich, J.M., et al. (1998). Effect of computerized physician order entry and a team intervention on prevention of serious medication errors. *Journal of the American Medical Association, 280*(15), 1311-1316.

Borycki, E., & Kushniruk, A.W. (2005). Identifying and preventing technology-induced error using simulations: Application of usability engineering techniques. *Healthcare Quarterly, 8*, 99-105.

Borycki, E. M., Kushniruk, A. W., Kuwata, S., & Kannry, J. (2006). Use of simulation in the study of clinician workflow. *AMIA Annual Symposium Proceedings* (pp. 61-65).

Campbell, E. M., Sittig, D. F., Ash, J. S., Guappone, K. P., & Dykstra, R. H. (2006). Types of unintended consequences related to computerized provider order entry. *JAMIA, 13*(5), 547-556.

Canada Health Infoway. (2006). *EHR: At the crossroads of success 2006-2007.* Toronto: Canada Health Infoway.

Chaudry, B., Wang, J., Wu, S., Maglione, M., Mojica, W., Roth, E. et al. (2006). Systematic review: Impact of health information technology on quality, efficiency and costs of medical care. *Annals of Internal Medicine, 144*(10), 742-752.

Cohen, M. R., & Vaijda, A. J. (2005). Point-of-care bar coded medication administration:

Experience in the United States. *Farm Hospitals, 29*, 151-152.

Davis, P., Lay-Yee, R., Briant, R., Schug, S., Scott, S., Johnson, et al. (2001). *Adverse events in New Zealand public hospitals: Principle findings from a national survey*. (Occasional Paper no. 3). Wellington: New Zealand Ministry of Health.

Dennis, A., & Wixom, B. H. (2003). *Systems analysis and design* (2nd ed.). Toronto: John Wiley & Sons.

DeSanctis, G., & Poole, M. (1994). Capturing the complexity in advanced technology use: Adaptive structuration theory. *Organizational Science, 5*(2), 121-147.

Evans, R.S., Pestotnik, S.L., Classen, D.C., Clemmer, T.R., Weaver, L.K., Orme, J.F. et al. (1998). A computer assisted management program for antibiotics and other antiinfective agents. *New England Journal of Medicine, 338*(4), 232-238.

Han, Y. Y., Carcillo, J. A., Venkataraman, S. T., Clark, R. S., Watson, R. S., Nguyen, T., et al. (2005). Unexpected increased mortality after implementation of a commercially sold physician order entry system. *Pediatrics, 116*(6), 1506-1512.

Hersh, B., Stavri, P., & Detmer. D. (2006). *Information retrieval and digital libraries* (pp. 660-697). In T. E. Shortliffe & J. J. Cimino (Eds.), *Biomedical informatics: Computer applications in healthcare and biomedicine* (3rd ed.). New York: Springer.

Horsky, J., Kuperman, G.J., & Patel, V.L. (2005). Comprehensive analysis of a medication dosage error related to CPOE. *Journal of the American Medical Informatics Association, 12*(4), 377-82.

Horsky, J., Zhang, J., & Patel, V.L. (2005). To err is not entirely human: Complex technology and user cognition. *Journal of Biomedical Informatics, 38*(4), 264-266.

Institute of Medicine. (1999). *To err is human: Building a safer health system*. Washington, DC: National Academy Press.

Kaner, C., Falk, J., & Nguyen, H.Q. (1999). *Testing computer software* (2nd ed.). New York: Wiley & Sons.

Koppel, R., Metlay, J. P., Cohen, A., Abaluck, B., Localio, A. R., Kimmel, S. E., et al. (2005). Role of computerized physician-order entry systems in facilitating medication errors. *JAMA, 293*(10), 1197-1203.

Koornneef, F., & Voges, U. (2002). Programmable electronic medical systems-related risks and learning from accidents. *Health Informatics Journal, 8*, 78-87.

Kushniruk, A. W. (2001). Analysis of complex decision-making processes in healthcare: Cognitive approaches to health informatics. *Journal of Biomedical Informatics, 34*, 364-376.

Kushniruk, A. W. (2002). Evaluation in the design of health information systems: Applications of approaches emerging from systems engineering. *Computers in Biology and Medicine, 32*(3), 141-149.

Kushniruk, A. W., & Borycki, E. M. (2006). Low-cost rapid usability engineering: Designing and customizing usable healthcare information systems. *Healthcare Quarterly, 9*(4), 98-100, 102.

Kushniruk, A. W., & Patel, V.L. (2004). Cognitive and usability engineering approaches to the evaluation of clinical information systems. *Journal of Biomedical Informatics, 37*, 56-57.

Kushniruk, A., Triola, M., Stein, B., Borycki, E., & Kannry, J. (2004). The relationship of usability to medical error: An evaluation of errors associated with usability problems in use of a handheld application for prescribing medications. *Proceedings of MedInfo—World Congress on Medical Informatics 2004* (pp. 1073-1076).

Kushniruk, A., Borycki, E., Kuwata, S., & Kannry, J. (2006). Predicting changes in workflow resulting from healthcare information systems: Ensuring the safety of healthcare. *Healthcare Quarterly, Oct, 9*(Spec No), 114-118.

Kushniruk, A.W., Triola, M., Borycki, E.M., Stein, B., & Kannry, J. (2005). Technology induced error and usability: The relationship between usability problems and prescription errors when using a handheld application. *International Journal of Medical Informatics, 74,* 519-526.

Kuwata, S., Kushniruk, A., Borycki, E., & Watanabe, H. (2006). Using simulation methods to analyze and predict changes in workflow and potential problems in the use of a bar-coding medication order entry system. *AMIA Annual Symposium Proceedings,* 994.

McDonald, C.J., Hui, S.L., Smith, D.M., Tierney, W.M., Cohen, S.J., Weinberger, M. et al. (1984). Reminders to physicians from an introspective computer medical record: a two year randomized trial. *Annals of Internal Medicine, 100,* 130-138.

McKeithen, K. B., Reitman, S. C., Rueter, H. H., & Reitman, S. C. (1981). Knowledge organization and skill differences in computer programmers. *Cognitive Psychology, 13,* 307-325.

McLaughlin, C. P., & Kibb, D. C. (2006). Information management and technology in CQI (pp. 243-278). In C. P. McLaughlin & A. D. Kaluzny (Eds.), *Continuous quality improvement in health care* (3rd ed.). New York: Jones & Bartlett.

Musen, M. A., Shahar, Y., & Shortliffe, E. H. (2006). Clinical decision-support systems (pp. 698-736). In T E.. Shorliffe & J. J. Cimino (Eds.), *Biomedical informatics: Computer applications in healthcare and biomedicine* (3rd ed.). New York: Springer.

National Health Service. *Direct business plan 2005-2006.* London: National Health Service.

National Quality Forum. (2003). *Safe practices for better healthcare: A consensus report.* Washington, DC: National Quality Forum.

Orlinkowski, W. J. (1992). The duality of technology: Rethinking the concept of technology in organizations. *Organizational Science, 3*(3), 398-427.

Orlinkowski, W. J. & Gash, D. C. (1994). Technological frames: Making sense of information technology in organizations. *ACM Transactions on Information Systems, 12*(2), 174-207.

Orlinkowski, W. J., & Yates, J. (1994). Genre repertoire: The structuring of communicative practices in organizations. *Administrative Science Quarterly, 39*(4), 541-574.

Patel, V.L., Kushniruk, A.W., Yang, S., & Yale, J.F. (2000). Impact of a computer-based patient record system on data collection, knowledge organization and reasoning. *Journal of the American Medical Informatics Association, 7*(6), 569-585.

Patterson, E. S., Cook, R. I., & Render, M. L. (2002). Improving patient safety by identifying side effects from introducing bar coding in medication administration. *JAMIA, 9,* 540-553.

Patton, R. (2001). *Software testing.* Indianapolis, IN: SAMS.

Poole, M. S., & DeSanctis, G. (2004). Structuration theory information systems research: Methods and controversies (pp. 206-249). In M. E. Whitman & A. B. Woszczynski (Eds.), *The handbook of information systems research.* London: Idea Group.

Pressman, R. (2005). *Software engineering: A practitioner's approach* (6th ed.). New York: McGraw Hill.

Sandelowski, M. (2000). *Devices and desires.* Chapel Hill: The University of North Carolina.

Savitz, L. A., & Bernard, S. L. (2006). *Measuring and assessing adverse medical events to promote patient safety* (pp. 211-225). In C. P. McLaughlin & A. D. Kaluzny (Eds.), *Continuous quality improvement in health care* (3rd ed.). New York: Jones & Bartlett.

Shortliffe, E. H., & Cimino, J. J. (2006). *Biomedical informatics: Computer applications in healthcare and biomedicine* (3rd ed.). New York: Springer.

Simon, J. C. (2001). *Introduction to information systems.* John Wiley & Sons.

Southton, F. C., Saur, C., & Grant, C. N. (1997). Information technology in complex health services: Organizational impediments to successful technology transfer and diffusion. *JAMIA, 4*(2), 112-124.

Spencer, D. C., Leininger, A., Daniels, R., Granko, R. P., & Coeytaux, R. R. (2005). Effect of a computerized prescriber-order-enry system on reported medication errors. *American Journal of Health System Pharmacy, 62,* 416-419.

Tierney, W.M. (2001). Improving clinical decisions and outcomes with information: a review. *International Journal of Medical Informatics, 62*(1), 1-9.

Tierney, W.M., McDonald, C.J., Hui, S.L., & Martin, D.K. (1988). Computer predictions of abnormal test results: effects on outpatient testing. *Journal of the American Medical Association, 259,* 1194-1198.

Tierney, W.M., McDonald, C.J., Martin, D.K., Hui, S.L., & Rogers, M. P. (1987). Computerized display of past test results: effects on outpatient testing. *Annals of Internal Medicine, 107,* 569-574.

Tierney, W.M., Miller, M.E., & McDonald, C.J. (1990). The effect on test ordering of informing physicians of the charges for outpatient diagnostic test. *New England Journal of Medicine, 322,* 1499-1504.

Tierney, W.M., Miller, M.E., Overhage, J.M., & McDonald, C.J. (1993). Physician inpatient order writing on microcomputer workstations: Effects on resource utilization. *Journal of the American Medical Association, 269,* 379-383.

van Bemmel, J.H., & Musen, M.A. (1997). *Handbook of medical informatics.* Bohn: Springer.

Vicente, K. (2003). *The human factor.* Toronto: Vintage Canada.

Wilson, R.M., Runciman, W.B., Gibberd, R.W., Harrison, B.T., Newby, L., & Hamilton, J.D. (1995). The quality of the Australian healthcare study. *Medical Journal of Australia, 163*(9), 458-476.

ADDITIONAL READING

Ash, J. S., Sittig, D. F., Poon, E. G., Guappone, K., Campbell, E., & Dykstra, R. H. (2007). The extent and importance of unintended consequences related to computerized provider order entry. *JAMIA, 14*(4), 415-423.

Borycki, E., & Kushniruk, A.W. (2005). Identifying and preventing technology-induced error using simulations: Application of usability engineering techniques. *Healthcare Quarterly, 8,* 99-105.

Han, Y. Y., Carcillo, J. A., Venkataraman, S. T., Clark, R. S., Watson, R. S., Nguyen, T. et al. (2005). Unexpected increased mortality after implementation of a commercially sold physician order entry system. *Pediatrics, 116*(6), 1506-1512.

Koppel, R., Metlay, J. P., Cohen, A., Abaluck, B., Localio, A. R., Kimmel, S. E., et al. (2005). Role of computerized physician-order entry systems in facilitating medication errors. *JAMA, 293*(10), 1197-1203.

Koornneef, F., & Voges, U. (2002). Programmable electronic medical systems-related risks and learning from accidents. *Health Informatics Journal, 8,* 78-87.

Kushniruk, A.W., Triola, M., Borycki, E.M., Stein, B., & Kannry, J. (2005). Technology induced error and usability: The relationship between usability problems and prescription errors when using a handheld application. *International Journal of Medical Informatics*, 74, 519-526.

Patel, V.L., Kushniruk, A.W., Yang, S., & Yale, J.F. (2000). Impact of a computer-based patient record system on data collection, knowledge organization and reasoning. *Journal of the American Medical Informatics Association*, 7(6), 569-585.

Patterson, E. S., Cook, R. I., & Render, M. L. (2002). Improving patient safety by identifying side effects from introducing bar coding in medication administration. *JAMIA*, 9, 540-553.

Patton, R. (2001). *Software testing.* Indianapolis, IN: SAMS.

Pressman, R. (2005). *Software engineering: a practitioner's approach* (6th edition). New York: McGraw Hill.

Shortliffe, E. H., & Cimino, J. J. (2006). *Biomedical informatics: Computer applications in healthcare and biomedicine* (3rd ed.). New York: Springer.

Tierney, W.M. (2001). Improving clinical decisions and outcomes with information: a review. *International Journal of Medical Informatics*, 62(1), 1-9.

Vicente, K. (2003). *The human factor.* Toronto: Vintage Canada.

Chapter X
Regional Patient Safety Initiatives:
The Missing Element of Organizational Change

James G. Anderson
Purdue University, USA

ABSTRACT

Data-sharing systems—where healthcare providers jointly implement a common reporting system to promote voluntary reporting, information sharing, and learning—are emerging as an important regional, state-level, and national strategy for improving patient safety. The objective of this chapter is to review the evidence regarding the effectiveness of these data-sharing systems and to report on the results of an analysis of data from the Pittsburgh Regional Healthcare Initiative (PRHI). PRHI consists of 42 hospitals, purchasers, and insurers in southwestern Pennsylvania that implemented Medmarx, an online medication error reporting systems. Analysis of data from the PRHI hospitals indicated that the number of errors and corrective actions reported initially varied widely with organizational characteristics such as hospital size, JCAHO accreditation score and teaching status. But the subsequent trends in reporting errors and reporting actions were different. Whereas the number of reported errors increased significantly, and at similar rates, across the participating hospitals, the number of corrective actions reported per error remained mostly unchanged over the 12-month period. A computer simulation model was developed to explore organizational changes designed to improve patient safety. Four interventions were simulated involving the implementation of computerized physician order entry, decision support systems and a clinical pharmacist on hospital rounds. The results of this study carry implications for the design and assessment of data-sharing systems. Improvements in patient safety require more than voluntary reporting and clinical initiatives. Organizational changes are essential in order to significantly reduce medical errors and adverse events.

Copyright © 2008, IGI Global, distributing in print or electronic forms without written permission of IGI Global is prohibited.

PATIENT SAFETY

For more than a decade, studies in the United States (Brennan et al., 1991; Gawande et al., 1999; Leape et al., 1991; Thomas et al., 2000) and other countries (Baker et al., 2004; Davis et al., 2002, 2003; Vincent et al., 2001; WHO, 2004; Wilson et al., 1995) have reported that adverse events in health care are a major problem. These studies estimate that anywhere from 3.2% to 16.6% of hospitalized patients in the United States and Australia respectively experience an adverse event while hospitalized. A recent Canadian study of hospital patients estimated a rate of 7.5 adverse events per 100 hospital admissions (Baker et al., 2004). Over 70% 0f these patients experience disability and 14% die as a result of the adverse event. The Institute of Medicine (IOM) report, *To Err is Human: Building a Safer Health System* (Kohn, Corrigan & Donaldson, 2001), estimated that between 44,000 and 98,000 deaths occur in the United States each year as a result of medical errors. In fact, there is evidence that morbidity and mortality from medical errors increased between 1983 and 1998 by 243% (Phillips & Bredder, 2002).

A significant number of these errors involve medications. A meta-analysis of 39 prospective studies indicated that adverse drug reactions from medication errors account for a significant proportion of these events in the U.S. (Lazarou, Pomeranz & Corey, 1998). One study of medication errors in 36 hospitals and skilled nursing facilities in Georgia and Colorado found that 19% of the doses were in error; seven percent of the errors could have resulted in adverse drug events (ADEs) (Barker et al., 2002). ADEs also occur among outpatients at an estimated rate of 5.5 per 100 patients. A recent analysis of hospital emergency departments in the United States, estimated that ADEs account for 2.4 out of every 1000 visits (Budnitz et al., 2006). Based on these studies the Institute of Medicine recommended that confidential voluntary reporting systems be adopted in all health care organizations (IOM, 2001).

Traditionally efforts to reduce errors have focused on training, rules and sanctions. Also, hospitals have relied on voluntary reporting of errors. Currently only 5-10% of medication errors that result in harm to patients are reported (Cullen et al., 1995). As a result little progress has been made since the IOM report five years ago (Leape & Berwick, 2005).

Data Sharing Systems

Studies have indicated that adverse events in health care settings primarily result from deficiencies in system design (Anderson, 2003). A study of adverse drug events in Utah and Colorado estimated that 75% of ADEs were attributable to system failures (Gawande et al., 1999; Thomas et al., 2000). Consequently, there is growing consensus that improvements in patient safety require prevention efforts, prompt reporting of errors, root-cause-analysis to learn from these errors and system changes to prevent the errors from reoccurring.

Currently only 5-10% of medical errors are reported (Cullen et al., 1995). Incident reporting represents a major strategy to address growing concerns about the prevalence of errors in healthcare delivery (Billings, 1998). The Patient Safety and Quality Improvement Act was signed into law in 2005. This act encourages health care providers to report medical errors to patient safety organizations that are being created. Patient safety organizations are authorized to analyze data on medical errors, determine causes of the errors, and to disseminate evidence-based information to providers to improve patient safety. Currently, over 24 states have mandated some form of incident reporting (Comden & Rosenthal, 2002). Also, there has been a steady increase in the number of regional coalitions of providers, payers, and employers working to improve patient safety (Halamka et al., 2005). These efforts are driven by the premise that the identification of unsafe conditions is an essential first step toward analyzing and remedying the root causes of errors. Such reporting systems often occur in the context of an infrastructure for inter-organizational sharing of these data. The emphasis on data-sharing is based on the premise that when organizations share such data about incidents and the lessons learned from them, it will lead to accelerated improvements in patient safety across the board. In other words, data-sharing is expected to result in community-wide learning. Indeed, patient safety centers in states that have created them are charged with facilitating such data-sharing. Not surprisingly, these data-sharing systems vary widely. They differ in the data that is shared (from specific processes/outcomes such as medication errors and/or nosocomial infections to a broad range of incidents); the participants (individual clinicians to entire healthcare organizations); geography (regional, state, and national); technology (paper-based to online); and regulatory expectations about participation (voluntary or mandatory) (Flowers & Riley, 2001; Rosenthal et al., 2004).

Despite such differences, data-sharing systems are typically based on the premise that threats to patient safety arise from the unwillingness/discomfort of healthcare providers to openly discuss errors and their resulting lack of awareness of the magnitude of the problem. The identification and reporting of unsafe conditions is a necessary first step in a systemic approach to revamping patient safety. But technological, psychological, cultural, legal, and organizational challenges pose formidable barriers to the blame-free identification and discussion of unsafe conditions. Whereas individual organizations by themselves may not be able to take on these challenges, participation in a data-sharing coalition provides a shared rationale and the subtle benefits of peer influence. Second, the data from increased reporting facilitates the diagnosis of systemic causes of unsafe conditions and the implementation of systemic solutions. So data-sharing, it is assumed, will accelerate the

identification of unsafe conditions, encourage analysis of the underlying causes, and enable continuous process improvement. Although different organizations may benefit differently from participating in a data-sharing system, a strong implicit assumption underlying these systems is that they will benefit the entire community of participating organizations.

To date, few studies have examined the anticipated benefits of medical error data-sharing systems. In the following, we report the results of a study of developmental trends in two indicators of the effectiveness of one regional data-sharing coalition. The indicators are the reported number of medication errors and the number of corrective actions taken by hospitals as a result of these errors. The objectives of the study were to examine whether hospitals that participated in medication error data-sharing consortium experienced increased reporting over time. The second objective was to determine whether error reporting resulted in organizational actions aimed at reducing future errors. A third objective was to explore organizational interventions designed to reduce mediation errors in hospitals.

The Pittsburgh Regional Healthcare Initiative (PRHI)

A consortium of providers, purchasers, insurers and other stakeholders in healthcare delivery in southwestern Pennsylvania was formed in 1997 (Siro et al., 2003). Its purpose was to improve patient care by working collaboratively, sharing information about care processes and their links to patient outcomes, and using patient-centered methods and interventions to identify rapidly solve problems to root cause at the point of care. Clinicians, 42 hospitals, four major insurers, several large and small-business healthcare purchasers, corporate and civic leaders, and elected officials make up the consortium.

In order to improve clinical practice and patient safety PRHI created a regional infrastructure for common reporting and shared learning. The consortium focuses on two patient safety goals, reducing nosocomial or hospital acquired infections and medication errors.

The organizational learning model that underlies the PRHI strategy is based on the science of complex adaptive systems (Plsek, 2001). Healthcare delivery systems are viewed as a collection of individual agents whose actions are not always predictable. At the same time, agents are interconnected so that the actions of one agent can change the organizational context for other agents. Accordingly sustainable system-wide improvements in patient safety require real-time error reporting and decentralized problem solving. PRHI has relied on several strategies to promote improvements. The system chosen for reporting of medication errors was the USP's Medmarx (Hicks et al., 2004). The system standardizes medication error reporting by using the National Coordinating Council for Medication Error Reporting and Prevention (NCCMERP) error categories. The Medmarx system is anonymous and voluntary. Health care providers can report medication errors online using a standardized format. The following information is collected on each reported order:

1. Inpatient or outpatient setting
2. Type of error
3. Severity
4. Cause of error
5. Location
6. Staff and products involved
7. Contributing factors
8. Corrective actions taken

Data reported by consortium members is analyzed and quarterly reports are provided to participating hospitals. These reports contain facility-specific regional and national data. The quarterly reports provided data on reporting volume reflecting the early strategic emphasis on increasing reporting. The reports also contain data on the corrective actions being reported by each hospital. These reports provided an opportunity to compare the trends in reporting of errors with reporting of corrective actions. It was hypothesized that growth in the reporting of medication errors reported through the data sharing system would predict growth in corrective actions taken by the hospitals in response to the reported errors.

Effectiveness of Data Sharing

We set out to examine the effects of data-sharing on the group of participating hospitals. The data analyzed consisted of approximately 17,000 reports of medication errors submitted over a 12-month period by 25 hospitals that are participating in PRHI. There were two outcome variables: the number of medication errors reported by each hospital each quarter and the ratio of corrective actions reported by each hospital to the number of errors reported each quarter. Control variables included the hospital's teaching status (i.e., teaching versus non-teaching), the hospital size in terms of the number of beds, and the latest JCAHO accreditation score. A latent growth curve analysis was used to examine longitudinal trends in error reporting and organizational corrective actions (Anderson, Ramanujam, Hensel, & Siro, 2007). This analysis permitted the investigators to determine whether statistically significant changes in error reporting and corrective actions occurred over time; whether these trends varied significantly among the hospitals; and whether hospital characteristics were associated with these trends.

Figure 1 shows the distribution of medication errors reported by severity. Fifty one percent of the events had the capacity to cause harm but did not affect the patient. Another 41% of the errors reached the patient but did not cause harm. The remaining medication errors caused patient harm and in two cases may have resulted in the patient's death.

Figure 2 shows the trends in error reporting and corrective actions over the four quarters. During

Figure 1. Percentage of medication errors reported by severity

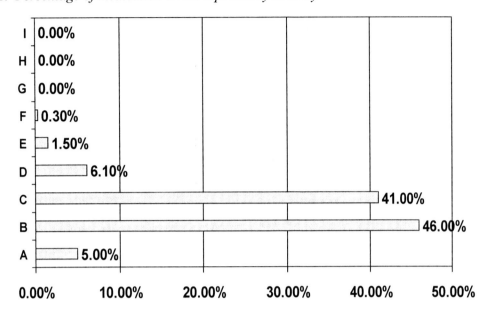

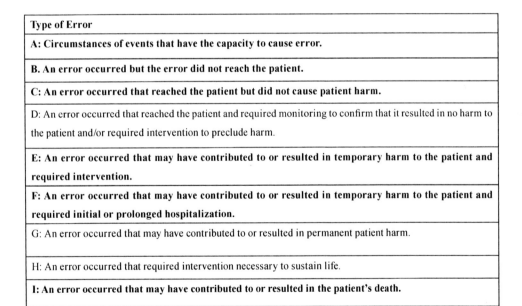

Type of Error
A: Circumstances of events that have the capacity to cause error.
B. An error occurred but the error did not reach the patient.
C: An error occurred that reached the patient but did not cause patient harm.
D: An error occurred that reached the patient and required monitoring to confirm that it resulted in no harm to the patient and/or required intervention to preclude harm.
E: An error occurred that may have contributed to or resulted in temporary harm to the patient and required intervention.
F: An error occurred that may have contributed to or resulted in temporary harm to the patient and required initial or prolonged hospitalization.
G: An error occurred that may have contributed to or resulted in permanent patient harm.
H: An error occurred that required intervention necessary to sustain life.
I: An error occurred that may have contributed to or resulted in the patient's death.

the first quarter, hospitals reported on average 45 medication errors. The number of errors reported rose steadily and had almost doubled by the fourth quarter. In contrast, the number of corrective actions taken by the hospitals in response to the errors remained fairly constant and, in fact, decreased slightly by the fourth quarter.

Furthermore, our analysis indicated that, although there were significant differences between hospitals in error reporting at the baseline, subsequent error reporting increased at similar rates among the hospitals. By contrast, while there were significant differences among hospitals in their base line reporting of corrective actions, the number of corrective actions reported per error

Figure 2. Medication errors and organizational changes reported over four quarters

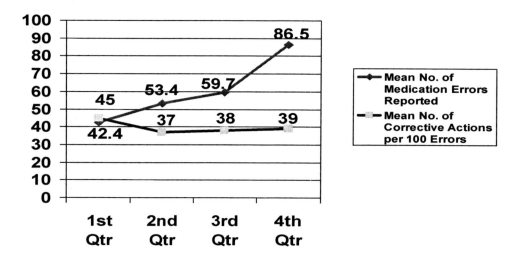

remained unchanged during subsequent quarters. The finding that the increase in reporting rates were similar across participating hospitals is consistent with the notion that data-sharing provides opportunities for organizations to observe others' actions and adjust their behaviors. This is especially likely because in focus groups conducted during this period, informants from eight of these hospitals stated that medication error reports were reviewed by senior managers and that their typical response was "how are we doing with respect to others?" If the response of participating hospitals was to initiate actions to increase the reporting rate in line with the regional trend, it would partly explain how the reporting trends across hospitals moved in tandem. This finding is important because our analysis controlled for differences in baseline reporting, hospital size, teaching status, and accreditation scores.

Corrective actions taken by hospitals as a result of medication errors indicate how important patient safety is to the institution. First-order interventions include individual interventions such as:

1. Informing staff who made the error
2. Informing other staff involved in the error
3. Providing education/training
4. Informing the patient's doctor
5. Informing the patient/caregiver
6. Instituting policies/procedures
7. Enhancing the communication process

Second-order interventions include system changes such as:

1. Computer software modified/implemented
2. Staffing practice/policy modified
3. Environment modified
4. Policy/procedure instituted
5. Formulary changed
6. Policy/procedure changed

First-order interventions are aimed at individuals and are likely to have short-term effects and thus are unlikely to be effective in preventing future errors from occurring. Second-order interventions involve system changes and are much more likely to prevent errors from reoccurring. Figure 3 shows the types of actions taken in response to reported medication errors. Eighty-five percent of the actions taken by the hospitals in response to reported errors involved individuals.

Figure 3. Number of organizational actions taken in response to 1,760 reported errors

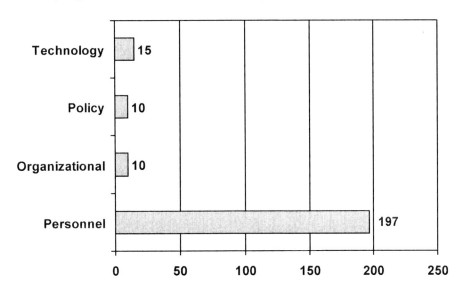

Only 15% of the organizational actions involved system changes.

A second analysis was based on a computer simulation model constructed to model medication error reporting and organizational changes needed to improve patient safety (Anderson et al., 2006). Several potential organizational interventions were simulated (Anderson et al., 2002; Anderson, 2004). First, baseline conditions were simulated. Intervention 1 involved introducing a basic computerized physician order entry (CPOE) system with minimal decision support for medication prescribing and administration. The second intervention assumed implementation of a CPOE system with decision support. Intervention 3 involved the inclusion of a clinical pharmacist on physician rounds who reviewed all medication orders. The fourth intervention assumed an organizational commitment to undertake root-cause analyses and system changes to prevent errors from reoccurring.

Figure 4 shows the results of the simulation. The model predicts that the introduction of a basic CPOE system will have little effect on the number of medication errors that could result in adverse drug events. Even the addition of decision support to the CPOE system is likely to result in only about a 20% reduction in medication errors. The inclusion of a clinical pharmacist on hospital physician rounds is like to reduce errors by only about 27%. Finally, the model predicts that when a commitment is made to root-cause-analysis of errors and system changes to prevent errors from reoccurring medication errors can be reduced by as much as 70% over time.

CONCLUSION

The results of this study carry implications for the design and assessment of data-sharing systems. Organizational actions taken in response to errors indicate how aggressive the organization is in responding to errors. Efforts that only affect individual staff and involve voluntary reporting and clinical initiatives are likely to have little effect in reducing errors long term. System-wide organizational changes are essential in order to significantly reduce medical errors and adverse events. In general, there is a mismatch between patient safety goals and hospital actions to reduce the risk of future medication errors. Hospitals increasingly recognize the need to implement error reporting systems. At the same time they

Figure 4. Estimated average number of medication errors that could have resulted in ADEs by quarter

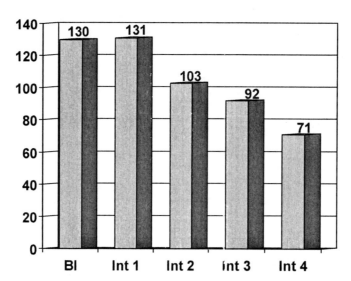

- [BL] Existing information system
- [Int 1] Computer-based physician order entry system
- [Int 2] Computer-based physician order entry system that provides dosing information about drugs at the time orders are written
- [Int 3] Pharmacists participation on physician rounds
- [Int 4] Pharmacists participation and organizational commitment to identify causes of errors and make system changes to improve patient safety

fail to implement organizational changes needed to improve patient safety. Actual error reduction will require organizational changes to be carefully institutionalized and integrated into long term plans.

Currently only 5-10% of medical errors are reported. There are a number of barriers that must be overcome in order to implement data-sharing systems designed to improve patient safety (Ferris, 2006; Rosenthal & Booth, 2004). First, competition inhibits provider participation. There is a lack of trust of other providers. Also, concerns about information ownership and reliability and privacy of data impede cooperation. Second, there is lack of a business case for patient safety. Healthcare delivery systems are complex. Implementation of information technology such as electronic medical records (EMR), electronic prescribing, clinical decision support, bar coding is expensive. Provid-

ers do not perceive a return on their investment in new technology such as electronic medical records and electronic prescribing.

Third, the culture of medicine presents significant barriers. Medicine is committed to individual professional autonomy. This results in a hierarchical authority structure and diffuses accountability. Furthermore, there is a culture of "blame and shame." The fear of malpractice litigation inhibits reporting of errors. Fourth, there are technical barriers to implementation of data-sharing. There is a lack of an accepted error reporting system and standards. Also, there is a lack of agreement of what constitutes an error. The difficulty in identifying problems, measuring progress and demonstrating improvement makes many healthcare institutions reluctant to participate in data-sharing coalitions. Moreover, voluntary reporting does not support comparative analysis of institutions on overall safety performance. What is more, the current reimbursement structure militates against improving safety.

Some of the steps that need to be taken to overcome these barriers to data-sharing include (Institute for Healthcare Improvement, 2006):

1. Diffusion of safe practices such as those identified by the National Quality Forum (NQF).
2. Training on safety and team work.
3. Implementation of error reporting systems.
4. Establishment of a National Patient Safety Agency similar to the one established in the UK.
5. Changes in reimbursement policies to provide incentives to hospitals and physicians for safe care.
6. Provision of disincentives for unsafe practices and adverse events (e.g., Minnesota's decision to stop paying hospitals for preventable adverse events).
7. Bringing together the Joint Commission on Accreditation of Healthcare Organizations (JCAHO), National Quality Forum (NQF), American Hospital Association (AHA), American Medical Association (AMA), Leapfrog Group, the Centers of Medicare/ Medicaid Services and major payers to set explicit goals for patient safety to include a 90% reduction in nosocomial infections, a 50% reduction in errors associated with medications, and a 100% elimination of errors on the NQF "never" list.

Leape and Berwick (2005) observed "The primary obstacles to achieving these [improved safety] results for the patients who depend on physicians and health care organizations are no longer technical; the obstacles lie in beliefs, intentions, cultures, and choices."

FUTURE RESEARCH DIRECTIONS

Despite a great deal of publicity concerning the 1999 IOM report, *To Err is Human*, little progress has been made in improving patient safety. Despite the implementation of error reporting systems it is estimated that less than 10% of errors are reported and relatively weak organizational actions are taken to prevent errors from reoccurring. Error reporting systems are important tools that can be used to educate providers and improve systems. However, in most instances, submission of reports fails to make a difference in patient safety. Major research efforts need to be directed at ways to overcome these barriers to improved patient safety. Also research is needed into new ways of translating error reports into meaningful organizational actions.

Information technology undoubtedly can help to improve patient safety. For example, electronic medical records, electronic prescribing, bar coding of medications and decisions support systems at the point of care can reduce medical errors. However, few physicians and hospitals have made major investments in information technology such as EMRs. It will be necessary to make a stronger business case for patient safety in order to overcome provider resistance to the required capital expenditures. At the same time, there are reports of system failures and errors introduced by IT systems. Research is needed into better ways of implementing IT systems in health care that avoid provider resistance and technology induced errors.

An important area for research involves the health care reimbursement system. The current reimbursement system does not provide incentives to hospitals and physicians to invest in patient safety. Errors can result in increased revenue under the present system. Furthermore, the economic interests of physicians and hospitals frequently are at odds. New models for reimbursement systems that promote patient safety are needed.

Finally, 24 states have passed legislation or regulations related to hospital reporting of adverse events. All but one are mandatory. To make significant improvements in patient safety, research is needed into improving the collection, analysis and feedback of the data collected by these state systems.

REFERENCES

Anderson, J. G. (2003). A system's approach to preventing adverse drug events. In S. Krishna, E.A. Balas, & S. A. Boren (Eds.), *Information technology business models for quality health care: An EU/US dialogue* (pp. 95-102). The Netherlands: IOS Press.

Anderson, J. G. (2004). Information technology for detecting medication errors and adverse drug events. *Expert Opinion on Drug Safety, 3*(5), 449-455.

Anderson, J. G., Jay, S. J., Anderson, M. M., & Hunt, T. J. (2002). Evaluating the capability of information technology to prevent adverse drug events: A computer simulation approach. *Journal of the American Medical Informatics Association, 9*, 479-490.

Anderson, J. G., Ramanujam, R., Hensel, D. J. Anderson, M. M., & Siro, C. A. (2006). The need for organizational change in patient safety initiatives. *International Journal of Medical Informatics, 75*(12), 809-817.

Anderson, J.G., Ramanujam, R., Hensel, D. J., & Siro, C. (2007). Reporting trends in a regional medication error data-sharing system (unpublished manuscript).

Baker, G. R., Norton, P. G., Flintoft, V., Blais, R., Brown, A., Cox, J., et al. (2004). The canadian adverse events study: The incidence of adverse events among hospital patients in Canada. *Canadian Medical Association Journal, 170*(11), 1678-86.

Barker, K.N., Flynn, E.A., Pepper, G.A., Bates, D. W., & Mikeal, R.L. (2002). Medication errors observed in 36 health care facilities. *Archives of Internal Medicine, 162*, 1897-1903.

Billings, C.E. (1998). Some hopes and concerns regarding medical event-reporting systems: Lessons from the NASA aviation safety reporting system. *Archives of Pathology & Laboratory Medicine, 122*(3), 214-5.

Brennan, T.A., Leape, L.L., Laird, N. et al. (1991). Incidence of adverse events and negligence in hospitalized patients: Results of the Harvard Practice Study. *New England Journal of Medicine, 324*(6), 370-7.

Budnitz, D.S., Pollock, D.A., Weidenbach, K.N., Mendelsohn, A.B., Schroeder, T.J., & Annest, J.L. (2006). National surveillance of emergency department visits for outpatient adverse drug events. *JAMA, 296*(15), 1858-1866.

Cullen, D.J., Bates, D.W., Small, S.D., et al. (1995). The incident reporting system does not detect adverse drug events: A problem for quality improvement. *Journal of Quality Improvement, 21*, 541-548.

Comden, S.C., & Rosenthal, J. (2002). *Statewide patient safety coalitions: A status report.* Portland. ME: National Academy for State Health Policy.

Davis, P., Lay-Yee, R., Briant, R., et al. (2002). Adverse events in New Zealand public hospitals I: occurrence and impact. *New Zealand Medical Journal, 115*(1167), U271.

Davis, P., Lay-Yee, R., Briant, R. et al. (2003). Adverse events in New Zealand public hospitals II: occurrence and impact. *New Zealand Medical Journal, 116*(1183), U624.

Ferris, N. (2006, October 17). Us vs. them: Regional health information exchanges require participants to dampen the urge to compete. But it's not clear yet whether collaboration is more powerful than competition, *Government Health*

IT. Retrieved October 17, 2006, from http://www.govhealthit.com/article96347-10-09-06-Print

Flowers, L., & Riley, T. (2001). *State-based mandatory reporting of medical errors: An analysis of the legal and policy issues.* Portland, ME: National Academy for State Health Policy.

Gawande, A. A., Thomas, E. J., Zinner, M. J., et al. (1999). The incidence and nature of surgical adverse events in Colorado and Utah in 1992. *Surgery, 126*(1), 66-75.

Halamka, J., Aranow, M., Asenzo, C., Bates, D., Debor, G., Glaser, J. et al. (2005). Healthcare IT collaboration in Massachusetts: The experience of creating regional connectivity. *Journal of the American Medical Informatics Association, 12*(6), 596-601.

Hicks, R.W., Santell, J.P., Cousins, D.D., & Williams, R.L. (2004). *MEDMARX 5ᵗʰ anniversary data report: A chartbook of 2003 findings and trends 1999-2003.* Rockville, MD: U.S. Pharmacopeia.

Institute for Healthcare Improvement. (2006). *Leadership guide to patient safety.* Cambridge, MA: Institute for Healthcare Improvement.

Institute of Medicine. (2001). *Crossing the quality chasm: A new health system for the 21ˢᵗ century.* Washington, D.C.: National Academy Press.

Kohn, K. T., Corrigan, J. M., & Donaldson, M. S. (Eds.). (1999). *To err is human: Building a safer health system.* Washington, DC: National Academy Press.

Lazarou, J., Pomeranz, B. H., & Corey, P. N., (1998). Incidence of adverse drug reactions in hospitalized patients: a meta-analysis of prospective studies. *Journal of the American Medical Association,* 279, 1200-1205.

Leape, L. L., & Berwick, D. M. (2005). Five years after 'to err is human:' What have we learned, *Journal of the American Medical Association, 293,* 2384-2390.

Leape, L.L., Brennan, T.A., Laird, N., et al. ((1991). The nature of adverse events in hospitalized patients: results of the Harvard Practice Study. *New England Journal of Medicine, 324*(6), 377-384.

Phillips, D. P., & Bredder, C. C. (2002). Morbidity and mortality from medical errors: An increasingly serious public health problem. *Annual Review of Public Health, 23,* 135-150.

Plesk, P. (2001). Redesigning health care with insights from the science of complex adaptive systems. In Institute of Medicine (ed.), *Crossing the quality chasm: A new health system for the 21ˢᵗ century* (pp. 309-322). Washington, DC: National Academy Press.

Rosenthal, J., & Booth, M. (October 2004). *State patient safety centers: A new approach to promote patient safety.* Portland, ME: National Academy for State Health Policy.

Siro, C. A., Segal, R. J., Muto, C. A., Webster, D. G., Pisowicz, V., & Feinstein, K.W. (2003). Pittsburgh regional healthcare initiative: A systems approach for achieving perfect patient care. *Health Affairs, 22*(5), 157-165.

Thomas, E. J., Studdert, D. M., Runchiman, W. B., et al. (2000). A comparison of iatronic injury studies in Australia and the USA I: context, method, case mix, population, patient and hospital characteristics. *International Journal of Quality in Health Care, 12*(5), 371-378.

Vincent, C., Neale, G., & Woloshynowych, M. (2001). Adverse events in British hospitals: preliminary retrospective record review. *British Medical Journal, 322,* 517-519.

Wilson , R.M., Runciman, W.B., Gibberd, R.W. et al. (1995). The Quality of Australian Health Care Study. *Medical Journal of Australia, 163,* 458-471.

World Health Organization. (2004). World Alliance for Patient Safety: Forward Programme 2005, Switzerland: WHO.

ADDITIONAL READING

Altman, D.E., Clancy, C., & Blendon, R.J. (2004). Improving patient safety: Five years after the IOM. *New England Journal of Medicine, 351*(20), 2041-2042.

Aspden, P., Wolcott J.A., Bootman, J.L., & Cronenwett (Eds.) (2007). *Preventing medication errors.* Washington, DC: National Academies Press.

Bates, D.W., & Gawanda, A.A. (2003). Improving safety with information technology. *New England Journal of Medicine, 25,* 2526-2534.

Bates, D.W., Evans, R.S., Murff, H., Stetson, P.D., Pizziferri, L., & Hripcsak, G. (2003). Detecting adverse events using information technology. *Journal of the American Medical Informatics Association, 10*(20), 115-128.

Berwick, D.M. (2003). Errors today and tomorrow. *New England Journal of Medicine, 348*(25), 2570-2572.

Bodenheimer, T. (1999). The movement for improved quality in health care. *New England Journal of Medicine, 340*(6), 488-492.

Classen, D.C., Pestotnik, S.L., Evans, R.S., Lloyd, J.F., & Burke, J.P. (1997). Adverse drug events in hospitalized patients: Excess length of stay, extra costs, and attributable mortality. *Journal of American Medical Association, 277,* 301-306.

Clinton, H.R., & Obama, B. (2006). Making patient safety the centerpiece of medical liability reform. *New England Journal of Medicine, 354*(21), 2205-2208.

Comden, S.C., & Rosenthal, J. (2002). *Statewide patient safety coalitions: A status report.* National Academy for State Health Policy.

Devers, K.J., Pham, H.H., & Liu, G. (2004). What is driving hospital's patient safety efforts? *Health Affairs, 23*(2), 103-115.

Doing what counts for patient safety: Federal actions to reduce medical errors and their impact. (2000). Rockville, MD: Agency for Health Care Research and Quality Report of the Quality Interagency Task Force (QuIC) to the President.

Enabling patient safety through Informatics. (2002). Selected works from the 2001 AMIA annual symposium and educational curricula for enhancing safety awareness. *Journal of the American Medical informatics Association, 9*(6), S1-S132.

Flowers, L. (2002). *State responses to the problem of medical errors: An analysis of recent state legislative proposals.* Portland, ME: National Academy for State Health Policy Report.

Greenfield, S., & Kaplan, S.H. (2004). Creating a culture of quality: the remarkable transformation of the Department of Veterans Affairs health care system. *Annals of Internal Medicine, 141*(4), 316-318.

Institute of Medicine. (2001). *Crossing the quality chasm.* Washington, DC: National Academy Press.

Leatherman, S., et al. (2203). The business case for quality: case studies and an analysis. *Health Affairs,* 22(2)17-30.

Leape, L.L., & Berwick, D.M. (2005). Five years after 'to err is human:' What have we Learned? *Journal of American Medical Association, 293,* 2384-2390.

Leape, L.L., Berwick, D.M., & Bates, D.W. (2002). What practices will most improve safety? Evidence-based medicine meets patient safety. *Journal of American Medical Association, 288*(4), 501-508.

Making Health Care Safer: A Critical Analysis Patient Safety Practices. Evidence Report/Technology Assessment: Number 43. Rockville, MD: AHRQ Publication No. 01-E058, July 2001. Agency for Healthcare Research and Quality, http://www.ahrq.gov/clinic/ptsafety/

McNeil, B.J. (2001). Hidden barriers to improvement in quality of care. *New England Journal of Medicine, 35*(22), 1612-1620.

O'Conner, P.J. (2006). Improving medication adherence: challenges for physicians, payers and policy makers. *Archives of Internal Medicine, 166,* 1802-1804.

Ortiz, E., & Clancy, C.M. (2003). Use of information technology to improve quality of health care in the United States, AHRQ Update. *Health Services Research, 38*(2), xi-xxii.

Romano, P.S. (2005). Improving the quality of hospital care in America. *New England Journal of Medicine, 353*(3), 302-304.

Wachter, R.M. (2004). The end of the beginning: Patient safety five years after "to err is human." *Health Affairs, W4,* 534-545.

Wachter, R.M., & Shojania, K.G. (2004*). Internal bleeding: The truth behind America's terrifying epidemic of medical mistakes.* New York: Rugged Land Press.

Chapter XI
Evaluation Methods to Monitor Success and Failure Factors in Health Information System's Development

Jytte Brender
University of Aalborg and Virtual Center for Health Informatics, Denmark

ABSTRACT

This chapter discusses the extent to which factors known to influence the success and failure of health information systems may be evaluated. More specifically, this is concerned with evaluation of such factors—for screening, diagnostic or preventive purposes—by means of existing evaluation methods designed for users. The author identifies that it is feasible to identify evaluation methods for most success factors and failure criteria. However, there is a need for situational methods engineering as the methods are not dedicated to answering the precise information needs of the project management. Therefore, demands are being placed on the evaluators' methodical and methodological skills, when evaluating health information systems. The author concludes the chapter by pointing at research needs and opportunities.

INTRODUCTION

"Evaluation is the act of measuring or exploring properties of a health information system (in planning, development, implementation, or operation), the result of which informs a decision to be made concerning that system in a specific context." (Ammenwerth et al., 2004, p. 480)

Many times health informatics professionals have suggested verbally that there are not enough evaluation methods that can be used to evaluate health information systems. A review of the evaluation literature regarding biases in assessment of medical IT-based solutions (Brender, 2006a, pp. 243-323) indicates that the general level of

Copyright © 2008, IGI Global, distributing in print or electronic forms without written permission of IGI Global is prohibited.

knowledge among evaluators is insufficient, that is, such methods and their assumptions are not appropriately known to their target users. This was also discussed among a group of key evaluation researchers and journal editors gathered in 2003 on the topic "New Approaches to the Systematic Evaluation of Health Information Systems" (HIS-EVAL), sponsored by the European Science Foundation (ESF) (see Ammenwerth et al., 2004). The outcome of this workshop was a number of recommendations as regards the future of health information systems evaluation, also called the Innsbruck Declaration. Among others, the declaration suggests promotion of reports on methodological and methodical evaluation studies, and that evaluation studies should be grounded on scientific theory and rigorous approaches.

The above implicitly indicates that the literature on evaluation of health information systems is far from robust. Recent publications of textbooks, such as the *Handbook of Evaluation Methods* for *Health Informatics* (Brender, 2006a; a Danish version was published in 2004), have demonstrated that there exists a substantive number of evaluation methods applicable within health informatics. This handbook has the nature of an encyclopedia, since it takes a (critical) meta-view on an extensive list of evaluation methods while focusing on their areas of application, assumptions for application, tacit built-in perspectives as well as their perils and pitfalls, rather than putting emphasis on detailed cookbook prescriptions for application.

Therefore, the purpose of this chapter will be: (1) to verify whether there exist appropriate evaluation methods for the assessment of factors known to influence the success and failure of IT-based solutions, and (2) to identify potential needs as regards further development of evaluation methods, be it innovation or refinement of existing methods. More specifically, this chapter will emphasize the assessment of IT-systems from a user perspective within organizational settings, that is, this chapter is concerned with methods addressing interactions between a technology

and its organizational, psychological and social components, as well as its effects. The methods in the handbook have been gathered from a variety of disciplines, ranging from psychology and social science to computer science and health informatics. Some of the methods are not designed as dedicated evaluation methods, but may be valuable as supportive means in an evaluation context. Thus, in such cases situational method engineering will be needed, thereby putting demands on the methodical and methodological skills of the evaluator.

There are two types of evaluation, constructive (or formative) and summative evaluation. Both types of evaluation serves the purpose of providing the (project) management with a decision-making basis in some context, cf. the definition given in the introductory citation. The difference is the overall context within which they each operate. For example, constructive assessment has the purpose of providing the foundation for identifying new or the need for altered directions with regard to subsequent development or implementation tasks. Alternatively, it can illuminate possible issues associated with specific problem situations. Since most IT-projects involve some compromises between an ideal solution and something realizable, controlled by local concerns, considerations and limiting factors, the role of constructive evaluation is to provide guidance to organizations in optimization of the dynamic health information systems development and/or implementation process.

The purpose of summative evaluation is to provide a concluding statement on properties of a health information system in a different kind of decision-making context. Examples of summative evaluation include: the evaluation of objectives fulfillment (i.e., assessing a health information system implementation in terms of its ability to fulfill organizational objectives), or assessing a system when it is delivered and one wants to ascertain that the system functions in accordance with the contractual agreement.

Some evaluation methods are retrospective in nature (like **root causes analysis** and **functionality assessment**). Others (like **balanced scorecard** and **delphi**) may guide the planning or revision of a health information systems development and thereby enable constructive evaluation. Still, other evaluation methods are not clearly prospective or retrospective in nature; rather they allow one to assess evolving situations.

BACKGROUND

The analysis of whether there exist appropriate evaluation methods for the assessment of known success and failure factor will be based on the union of factors identified within the literature. A huge number of studies of a single case have concluded on one or a few specific factors influencing the diffusion, penetration, or acceptance of IT-based systems, implying that the literature is a puzzle of findings. Consequently, we will take advantage of existing, significant reviews, based on different approaches.

Recently, Brender et al. (2006) conducted a delphi study where they identified a comprehensive list of success and failure aspects of health information systems development or implementation. The study was conducted as a follow-up initiative on the MIE2004 Special Topic Conference, in Munich, 2004, with the purpose of identifying success and failure characteristics of health informatics applications. Even though the study was conducted in the health informatics domain, its findings may also be valid for a number of other domains as well. In their work a total of 110 success factor and 27 failure criteria were identified and rated quantitatively for a number of different types of health information systems. These factors were organized in a hierarchical structure based on a number of categories, such as functional, behavioral, technical, managerial, cultural, and so forth; see the sample in Table 1. The reader is referred to Brender et al. (2006) for the complete

list of factors, or alternatively, almost all of them are included in the below discussion on methods to support the evaluation of such factors.

Within the delphi study, none of the aspects identified were concluded to be insignificant by the expert panel at the final quantitative rating. Therefore, none of the factors could be excluded from the list. Brender et al. (2006) suggest that the reason for including all of the success/failure factor arises as a consequence of the contextual nature of the factors themselves. If one uses this list of success and failure factor as a starting point only additional factors identified within literature reviews shall be included in the below analysis.

Three major case studies on IT systems' success and failure factor were reported in the 90s: Bikson and Eveland (1989), Crosswell (1991), based on quantitative and qualitative analysis of 55 and 39 cases, respectively. Lastly, Price Waterhouse (1997) conducted an extensive questionnaire survey of 500 cases worldwide. These three studies all indicate that there are a number of strong indicators of success and failure residing within the organizational context, from the beginning of the projects' lifecycle till full-blown operation. As compared to Brender et al.'s work (2006), one additional success indicator was reported by Bikson and Eveland (1989):

- Users' conception of their own status in terms of technological innovation

Croswell's work (1991) focused on obstacles and identified the following additional IT success and/or failure factors:

- Organizational coordination and conflicts
- Database structure and source materials
- Data communication and networking
- Software complexity/maturity

Croswell noted (with surprise) that there were few technical obstacles associated with IT failure. Nevertheless he observes more of this kind

Table 1. Examples of the hierarchy of success factor from Brender et al. (2006). The dots indicate that the list is continued at that particular place.

Functional success factor

1. Careful preparation of the User Requirements Specification to appropriate and balanced take into account and express users' requirements, needs as well as demands
    a) (in general)
    b) Fulfill the needs (whether stated or not) rather than only the requirements of the users
    c) Enable and allow ongoing extension, while carefully controlling the aspect of moving targets
2. Alignment of the role and design of the IT-system
    a) .....
    b) Semantic understanding of the application domain
    c) The socio-technical nature of health information systems is understood
    d) The functionality has to be compatible with the users' way of thinking (cognitive aspects)
    e) .....
3. Coping with the complexity
4. ......

Organizational success factor

1. Collaboration and cooperation
    a) .....
2. ......
3. Work from the workflow
    a) .....
    b) Planning of new procedures must appropriately take existing patterns of collaboration into account
    c) .....
    d) The users show a willingness to change practice
4. .....

---

of obstacles than the two other reviews. These technical obstacles are included implicitly in the analysis below.

Price Waterhouse (1997) identified a number of success factor in addition to the set outlined in Brender et al.'s delphi study (2006):

- Competing resource priorities
- Insufficient communication
- Long lead-time for IT solutions
- Initiative fatigue
- Poor integration of IT and non-IT aspects of change
- Lack of HR policy re-inforcement

A more recent report by Stavri and Ash (2003) used a review of narrative stories of success/ failures from a consensus conference on CPOE involving 13 experts. The study suggests that two additional factors (reported as success factor) are of relevance in our context:

- "When they say 'no way,' we asked 'what can you live with?'" and
- Change (goals, software, plans) based on lessons from pilot.

A recent, but smaller, literature review aimed at developing a better conceptual foundation for health information systems failure (and success), was presented by Heeks (2006). Heek's work identifies a couple of archetypes of IT failure that need to be added to the list of success/failure factor:

- Dominating design inscriptions—be they technological, managerial or medical—that incorporate particular cultural values, the failure arising when the stakeholder groups differ from the designer groups and/or includes different levels of formality and rationality

- Varying organizational conditions and cultures between private and public hospitals
- Differences in cultures between industrialized and developing countries, within and between countries of the latter type

These additional factors were included in the following analysis explicitly as separate factors or implicitly as part of the explanation of one or more given other factors.

In summary, the literature in general points to the presence of soft and organizational factors rather than hard-core technical factors as primary determinants of IT success and failure. Haimes and Schneiter (1996) reference the following definition of a 'system' (p. 483): "a system is all the components, attributes and relationships needed to accomplish an objective." With this definition of a system, the conclusion is not surprising: The soft human and organizational issues associated with a health information systems development and implementation range in complexity from addressing concerns about user interface aspects to the social nature of the employment and organizational context. The soft human and organizational issues also include the qualities and characteristics of the organization, its members as well as mutual interactions among individuals at every level (from a psychological, anthropological and sociological point of view to a legal and liability point of view). These factors all contribute to the shaping of organizations. Therefore, since the implementation of new IT systems inevitably induces changes in the organization as a whole, the mentioned soft human issues are not invariant factors. They will as primary or propagated effects influence the success or failure of IT-based solutions within the healthcare organization.

Delimitation

The primary objective of this study was to verify whether there exist appropriate evaluation methods for the assessment of each of the known success and failure factor. However, naturally, not all success factor and failure criteria need an explicit evaluation method for their assessment. For example, some forms of information need require simple 'yes/no' questions. Other types of success and failure factor, like 'evolution rather than revolution,' constitute (simple) project management aspects of a kind for which calling for a dedicated evaluation method would seem artificial. Furthermore, the study of political factors in general has another nature than those relevant in a pure evaluation context. All of these kinds are omitted from the below analysis, since space does not permit us to go detailed into each and every factor on the list.

There are a number of key themes that arise when one examines the success and/or failure of health information systems. For example, when one examines success/failure factor, one can see that some success factor are prerequisites for others. Therefore, these success factors have second or third order propagation effects upon the organization. For instance, senior management commitment is a prerequisite for strong, clear, and appropriate leadership, effective communication and resource allocation, but not for the ability to generate sustainable solutions. This was not taken into account in this chapter. As well, the issue of whether a given success/failure factor constitutes a root cause or a propagated effect was not addressed. They all represent the pattern of presentation of the success or failure much as a symptom is a part of a disease pattern.

In any case, it is the project management's responsibility to reduce the uncertainties as early as possible within the natural trajectory of a project—that is, to take into account the success/failure factor. This is where we perceive evaluation as a valuable means to timely address known symptoms. Preferably, one should look beyond the symptoms to the root cause. The project management should not merely tinker with problems (i.e., treat symptoms) but radically seek and address the root causes of problems. Such investment in evaluation during project management is necessary as only then will the chances of implementation success be dramatically increased. However, tinkering or not is not the issue of this contribution. In the following, there is merely a point to point correlation of an information need and candidate sources of information needed to ensure that a project succeeds. Some methods can dig deeper than others. Furthermore, evaluation methods can be combined and be used to explicitly address the root causes of identified problems; see for instance **root causes analysis** and **functionality assessment** in Brender (2006a).

CANDIDATE METHODS OF EVALUATING SUCCESS/FAILURE FACTOR

In the present section of this chapter IT success/failure factor will be matched to evaluation methods. One factor or criterion at a time will be analyzed for its overall meaning and then matched with the individual methods' application area, location in the life cycle, and assumptions for application, perspectives, and so on.

Note that within the sections following, the success/failure factor are indicated in Italics between apostrophes. Likewise, methods (as named in Brender, 2006a) are stated in bold. For ease of referencing the names from Brender (2006a) have been kept; however, since these are usually identical with the original authors' own naming of their methods or intuitively understandable the reader may easily find alternative descriptions in the literature. The structure of this entire section follows the framework suggested in Brender et al. (2006).

Note also, that it is the decision-makers within the organization that ultimately are the responsible (liable) for the final outcome of the information system development and/or implementation process when it concerns operation of and with an IT-based solution. The following shall be perceived by the readers as suggestions for instruments supporting an organization at the development and/or implementation of such systems. However, it is entirely up to the project management whether or not to monitor for given success/failure factor, and whether he or she finds the issues relevant or the suggested methods useful in their specific project context.

Suggestions on Methods Applicable for the Evaluation of Success Factor

Functional Factors

The first functional factor is *'careful preparation of the user requirements specification to appropriate and balanced take into account and express users' requirements, needs as well as demands.'* More specifically, this factor is concerned with fulfillment of needs (whether stated or not) rather than fulfilling users' explicit requirements alone. The method **requirements assessment** supported by the method **framework for assessment of strategies** may address issues like feasibility, verifiability, completeness, and alike. These methods may also address whether the solution described is the right one ('relevance'). However, user needs are to some extent tacit, and consequently, user requirements may be very difficult to fully and reliably assess. Requirements addressing a functionality that is characterized by tacit needs cannot be fully assessed, but input based on a combination of focuses may at least support such an assessment; see for instance, the above mentioned **framework for assessment of strategies** and the methods **analysis of work procedures**, **stakeholder analysis**, and **organizational readiness**, as well as **future workshop**.

Another functional factor is *'enable and allow ongoing extension, while carefully controlling the aspect of moving targets.'* This factor is a consequence of the indeterministic nature of system development projects and is aggravated by the long lead-time for IT solutions. Extensions and modifications of project plans are necessary among others to take into accounts unforeseen tacit requirements as well as to handle project encounters. Such work calls for a strong project vision, a clear project purpose, as well as a defined strategy. A strategy is necessary in order to accommodate for emergent project changes while maintaining project direction. In such cases the use of an evaluation method like the **balanced scorecard** may be helpful in handling strategic and directional aspects, while methods like **BIKVA** and **KUBI**[1] might be better as a means in the initial social process of deciding on the project direction.

The overall factor *'alignment of the role and design of the IT-system'* includes a number of issues of relevance for the IT success and/or failure. A first component factor is *'the functionality has to be compatible with the users' way of thinking.'* For example, in case of users performing repeated activities, users can be trained to operate a system in spite of its cumbersome functionality. However, for systems dedicated to supporting users' decision-making and work procedures (like the electronic healthcare record) the functionality has to comply with user tasks and user methods of operating within the work environment. Otherwise, dissatisfaction and human operational errors will arise. Awareness of the need to change work procedures when implementing a new system is necessary in order to limit the number of changes to user activities to what is feasible within a given organizational context or domain. Since alignment of user role and design of an IT system is clearly related to the cognitive aspects of work, several **usability** approaches may be applicable in this respect, prospectively and retrospectively. Methods such as **cognitive assessment, cognitive walkthrough, heuristic evaluation,** and **think aloud** may be useful when the study is assisted by cognitive psychologists. More research is needed in this area, since really effective assessment methods for addressing cognitive aspects are sparse at present.

The second component factor is *'the system has to be usable and useful, helping the user in his/her daily routine work.'* The issues here include the defined system's coverage of daily practice and whether it supports the accomplishment of the primary goal of user activities. For a prospective assessment of whether the system is usable and useful the **analysis of work procedures** may be a valuable source of input. For a retrospective assessment of whether a system is usable and useful the **functionality assessment** is valuable to identify deviations and explore causal relations.

The third component factor is *'the role and the design of the system have to comply with the organizational context, including structure, people, information flow and external links.'* Of course, organizations need to adapt to the new technology during their implementation of a new IT-based system, but the number, nature and seriousness of changes is an invariant factor that determines the degree of the system's success or failure. Therefore, prospective studies of organizational change should bear this factor in mind. The means is—as above—systems analysis methods, like different approaches for **Analysis of Work Procedures**.

The fourth component factor is *'the IT-system has to be compatible with the organization's daily practice.'* The issue and the means for addressing this factor are the same as for the previous factor.

The fifth component factor is *'semantic understanding of the application domain is necessary.'* The syntactic aspects (i.e., corresponding to work procedures) are addressed by systems analysis and design approaches. The semantic aspects are concerned with the profession-oriented culture of the domain, like determinant factors in decision-making. For example, in healthcare this may be illustrated by the tendency by healthcare staff to consider and treat all patients as unique cases, as opposed to the opposite and rational perspective that prescribes strict compliance to clinical protocols and guidelines. There is no need for dedicated evaluation methods in this respect, but there is a need for awareness from the designers and managers side, as the perspective of uniqueness implies a huge need for flexibility.

The sixth component factor is *'the socio-technical nature of health information systems needs to be understood.'* Socio-technical aspects of health information systems address people issues. The socio-technical perspective espouses the view that IT systems are more than technical constructs and that a flexible planning that balance social and technical effort is recommended. Consequently, there is a need to develop policies for handling the people issues. However, there are strong cultural differences in this respect, as discussed in Brender (2006a, part III; 2006b). Also this factor does not need an evaluation method, but has to be an integrated part of the systems development approach.

The final two component factors to the mentioned overall functional factor are: *'coverage of daily practice has to be sufficient, compared with the defined role of the IT-system'* and *'addressing a real, high-impact problem area rather than a borderline problem area.'* These two (sub-)factors are addressing the issue of attracting the attention of the users. It is important that the IT-system supports the users in accomplishing the primary goal of their activities to avoid competing activities. And again, a means (systems design and/or evaluation-wise) is systems analysis methods such as **analysis of work procedures**.

The overall factor *'coping with complexity'* comprises three factors, all of which have the nature of systems analysis/design rather than objects for formal evaluation:

- *'The implementation project should apply explicit means for coping with the complexity'*
- *'Keep it simple, but not simpler than needed'*
- *'Evolutionary or incremental development as an approach to cope with complexity, including the educational aspect.'*

The factor *'flexibility towards dynamic changes and changes in the organizational context'* is closely related to organizational readiness and may therefore be evaluated prospectively by means of the method **organizational readiness**. On the other hand, too many organizational changes or fluctuations may become a problem in itself. Methods like the **balanced scorecard** and **risk assessment** may be used as a means for organizations that are hyper-innovative and where change is a constant.

The final functional factor is *'added functionality are provided by the IT-system, enabling the user to provide new or better services.'* It is related to the users' motivation for engaging. The sub-theme of this factor, *'the incentive for the user (and stakeholders in general) must be clear and visible,'* in itself indicates the solution, namely to establish a clear and visible motivation. No formal evaluation method is dedicated to assess this issue. If user engagement turns out to be a project issue or one wants to prevent this then it is relevant prospectively to assess whether the incentive for the users is sufficient (or what is further needed) to motivate the user. Here, the methods **focus group interviews** or **delphi**, in combination with **social network analysis** or a **stakeholder analysis** might be useful.

Organizational Factors

The organizational factor *'Collaboration and cooperation'* concerns the delicate issue of social and other types of relations between elements in an organization. Such relations can be horizontal (i.e., across organizational units) and/or vertical (i.e., hierarchical). Evaluation of aspects related to collaboration and cooperation of relevance for the health information system success/failure may all be addressed prospectively by means of methods such as **social network analysis** and **stakeholder analysis**.

The organizational factor *'make implementation a transparent process within the organization'* has a sub-theme *'generally open for debate.'* These two factors address the question of balancing between two issues: transparency versus covertness, and decision-making versus decision-taking. Both are culturally influenced topics, and culture can here be understood in either the national respect and/or in the organizational respect that also includes the organization's prior history. By "decision-making versus decision-taking" is referred to the distinction between a hierarchical, top-managed approach for the development or implementation process (i.e., decision-taking) as opposed to a process that leads to a decision among relevant stakeholders (i.e., decision-making). Decision-making does not preclude the management from concluding on a decision, but implies that stakeholders' issues are openly discussed. So, the issue in reality is whether the decision approach taken is aligned with the needs and interests of the (involved) stakeholders. Methods like **focus group interviews**, alone or in combination with **social network analysis** or a **stakeholder analysis** might be valuable in providing insight into these aspects.

The organizational factor *'work from the workflow'* concerns among others the issue *'planning of new procedures must appropriately take existing patterns of collaboration into account.'* Radical changes to workflow and patterns of collaboration can be disruptive to the delicate social balance in an organization. Consequently, radical change bears the risk of all kinds of negative social reactions. The method **social network analysis** addresses the relations between elements within an organization (such as individuals, professions,

departments or other organizations). Therefore, this method may provide useful input into the design and other planning of health information systems development or implementation, and thus it constitutes the candidate evaluation method.

Behavioral Factors

The behavioral factor stating that *'the users are key'* is highly culturally dependent. In some cultures end users refrain from being involved at all due to their perception of the division of roles between the management and the employees, see the discussion in (Brender, 2006b). However, in the Western countries suitable involvement of employees is a significant success factor—that is, involvement of the right type, level, and scale of employees. Another relevant question here is whether the right competences are available and accessible—that is, a question of competing activities. **Stakeholder analysis** and **social network analysis** are valuable methods for assessing behavioral aspects related to the development or implementation process. Both of these approaches may provide input as to what users to involve and/or to involve in what situations.

The behavioral factor *'the personal attitude, engagement and commitment'* concerns end users, managers as well as other stakeholders. It addresses issues such as employee opposition, lack of middle management support, aspects of executive leadership, and managerial commitment. Employee opposition may be explored by means of **focus group interviews** throughout a project. Managerial commitment can be addressed indirectly, for example by conducting a situation analysis, such as using that of the **logical framework approach**. The success factor *'presence of sufficient motivational activities'* relates to all aspects of personal attitude, engagement and commitment.

The behavioral factor *'user conception of their own status as regards technological innovation'* was pointed out by one of the reviews as a motivating factor. User conceptions influence motivation and can be elicited by means of different kinds of individual **interviews** and/or **focus group interviews**. Both types of interviews are general methods and that are well suited towards illuminating individual' opinions, attitudes and perceptions regarding a phenomenon and observations (e.g., health information system implementation).

Cultural Factors

There are many types of cultures, ranging from national, over religious to professional cultures. The deeply rooted, tacit cultural factors in general are not factors that one should evaluate. They just are, and changes in this respect may not be a short term effort. For example, some national cultures perceive answering a question with a "no" as highly impolite. Therefore, imagine the potential bias in a questionnaire study or the effect of yes/no-buttons in a user interface when asking individuals with such cultural backgrounds to answer those yes/no questions. Hence, project management needs to understand how to take cultural factors into account, especially when transferring technologies and/or development methodologies or specific information systems from one culture to another.

More specifically, project management needs to be aware of a couple of factors related to the professional culture need awareness:

- *'Understand medicine and healthcare in general as a separate culture:'* The strong professional culture in healthcare implies that healthcare staff should be involved in the implementation process—if not being in the driver's seat. There may even be varying organizational conditions and cultures that are present between private and public hospitals. For example, Heeks (2006) suggests that accounting and billing procedures are less of an issue in publicly rather than privately funded hospitals. And certainly this

difference is pronounced between American IT solutions and the majority from the European countries. Differences of this kind may be identified by means of **analysis of work procedures.** Here, comparisons can be made between a system's business or enterprise model, and/or data models.
- *'Understand the local culture:'* Even within a given domain there may be islands of differing professional cultures. This factor may be addressed in the same way as the previous factor, but requires a finer level of analysis.

The cultural factor *'preparedness and willingness towards cultural change'* refers to the need for cultural changes, however, mainly related to the professional culture, for instance in work procedures. It includes a number of issues, such as:

- *'Awareness of the need for cultural change'*
- *'Readiness for a potential new business model'*
- *'Readiness for solutions not invented inhouse'*

Implementation of a (new) IT-based solution inevitably changes the organization. It is therefore important to nurture a new local culture for it to embrace the new technology. One problem may be that there is no perceived need for change by the local culture. Therefore, it is important to evaluate the readiness of an organization along with the factors outlined. **Organizational readiness** as an evaluation method was explicitly designed for prospective assessment in this respect. Unfortunately, the impression is that it is not yet a fully matured evaluation method. Alternatively, both the **field study** (screening and monitoring) and the **equity implementation model** (diagnostic) approaches may be useful as they allow for retrospective assessment of organizational context in terms of cultural success/failure factor.

Management Factors

The overall factor *'management support'* is mentioned in several of the reviews and hence it must be considered a significant success factor. Management support includes a number of sub-factors. However, some of these are yes/no aspects or belong under project management solely, and therefore, they are excluded here.

The first management factor is *'formulation and expression of a clear vision for the enterprise showing the IT-system as part of it.'* In most cases project management need not initiate an evaluation activity to assess the clarity of an organization's IT vision. In cases where an organization wishes to evaluate management factors such as clarity of organizational IT vision, a more formal evaluation approach can be taken. For example, the methods **balanced scorecard** and **framework for assessment of strategies** both require a clear and operational vision and strategy to be able to proceed smoothly in a development or implementation process. These two methods may therefore be valuable indirectly to assess the clarity of the vision specifically with respect to aspects of strategic relevance for implementing information technologies. Such evaluation may be carried out by performing the preparatory steps of either of these methods to see if the vision is sufficiently clear and operational.

There are a number of useful methods for assessing the management success factor *'Setting goals and courses'* (i.e. clarity of objectives), for example:

- **Framework for assessment of strategies** may be used prospectively to analyze the feasibility, timeline, risks, viability, and so forth, of the defined IT goals and courses.
- **KUBI** elicits a set of user or customer/client defined values, norms and objectives, and may provide an alternative set of goals and courses for comparison.

- **Balanced Scorecard** is a strategic project management approach based on goals and courses. These goals are used as a kind of measuring stick at decision making throughout the project. Applying **balanced scorecard** even as a desktop pilot may provide users and project team members with feedback on whether the established set of goals and courses are operational or defined in a useful way.

Regarding the management factor *'understanding the return of investment (whether material and/or immaterial benefits)'*: Beyond economic assessment of material benefits, a **delphi** investigation may reveal and characterize the immaterial benefits, other bottomline benefits, as well as the attitudes towards these both prospectively and retrospectively.

The management factor *'flexible planning'* includes the following themes:

- 'Enabling and allowing change of project plans and time tables'
- 'Realistic time lines'
- 'Understanding that implementation of an IT-based solution is a non-linear (indeterministic) process'
- 'Response to shortcomings is constructive'

These success factors are attitudinal in nature and are concerned with the project management itself and are also dependent upon the actual project management experience with the kind of activities in question. They are not topics that are meant for dedicated evaluation efforts. Should an organization wish to evaluate these attitudinal topics, one could prospectively evaluate these factors by means of methods such as **interview** using an external evaluator. Retrospectively, one could assess these IT success factor using **root causes analysis**, investigating the history, events and initiatives associated with the project to identify patterns of problems and possible subsequent actions.

The management factor *'prospective and proactive control'* includes a number of sub-factors, such as:

- 'Project management in general'
- 'A high degree of delegation and involvement combined with good coordination and communication'
- 'Sufficient communication,'
- 'Organizational coordination and conflicts'
- 'Stringent risk management'
- 'Cost-active control'
- 'Coordination'
- 'Appropriate action in response to unanticipated events'
- 'Sanction bottom-up signals as valuable input for steering'

Although this list is long, all of the items are related to good project management. One would not normally make these success factors the object of a formal and dedicated evaluation study in its normal sense. If a project is proceeding in ways that it should not and the project management is experiencing difficulties in diagnosing the causes, a **root causes analysis** could be carried out. Alternatively, if a **root causes analysis** is too difficult to undertake simpler approaches such as the situation analysis in **logical framework approach** would probably suffice in most cases.

The management factor *'consider IT implementation as a change process'* has four sub-factors related to IT success. These sub-factors can serve as guidelines for project management rather than requiring time taken away from project processes for the purpose of evaluation. These sub-factors include:

- *'Acknowledging that the IT-system represents a chance to support a change in the care delivery process'*
- *'Stepwise progression rather than reengineering everything'*

- *'Good supervision to enable a smooth and continuous change management'*
- *'Poor integration of IT and non-IT aspects of change'*

The essentials of the management factor *'change (goals, software, plans) based on lessons from pilot'* is that lessons from a pilot application should deliberately be used and taken action upon. Pilot studies allow the project management to find potential project flaws and to address those flaws prior to full IT implementation, irrespective of the nature or causal relation of the flaws. The **functionality assessment** method is perfectly suited for a retrospective investigation of problems and their causal relations. The principle within this method is that problems in the functionality (irrespective of cause) will reveal themselves in terms of unexpected or changed/changing work procedures—that is, resulting in observable, propagated actions and initiatives within the organization's work procedures (other than those that are planned or expected). Consequently, such emergent work procedures reflect the problems and therefore constitute candidates for subsequent exploration and potential action.

The factor *'coping with the impact of change'* concerns the ability to handle the necessary change processes. The method **organizational readiness** is an obvious candidate approach for prospective evaluation of the organization's ability to cope with the impact of change. The evaluation method **equity implementation model** can help in the retrospective assessment of users' reaction to the impact of implementing a new system, and thus this method may be valuable in understanding user behavior.

The factor *'user involvement'* (in general) is highly culturally dependent. **Stakeholder analysis**, as a user assessment strategy, allows one to determine if user involvement is appropriately being dealt with. **Stakeholder analysis** not only assesses who is involved, but how they are involved and engaged? Are they (i.e., the users) engaged in terms of representatives of stakeholder groups? Are users available? And in what way are users engaged: informed, consulted or actively engaged in the decision-making processes? The **stakeholder analysis** addresses these issues, taking into account the culture and existing organizational practice.

Another aspect of the *'user involvement'* factor is the sub-factor *'time must be freed or funding allocated for users to participate in the process.'* This aspect of IT success is closely connected to another sub-factor, *'competing resource priorities.'* These aspects of user involvement may prospectively be dealt with using a **risk assessment** approach, for instance by means of the concept of 'external factors' from the method **logical framework approach**. Retrospectively, user involvement may be explored in many ways, such as **interview** methods in general, **questionnaires**, or for instance, the situation analysis in **logical framework approach**.

One further management factor is *'when they say "no way," we asked "what can you live with?"'* This factor is concerned with the management approach to dealing with stakeholders' attitude. No formal evaluation method is needed to assess whether a given approach is the right solution for a given case, but the **balanced scorecard** and **KUBI** are two evaluation methods that can stimulate stakeholder-management dialogue in finding the way forward.

The factor *'strategy'* refers to the ability of an organization to formulate the foundation for all significant decisions and action plans (i.e., plans, methods, or series of maneuvers or stratagems for obtaining a specific goal or result). In terms of evaluation approaches organizational strategy can be evaluated using the method **framework for assessment of strategies**. The **framework for assessment of strategies** is a valuable method that can be used to assess an organizational strategy or to choose among alternative organizational strategies for instance with respect to feasibility, time lines and implicitly also sustainability.

A sub-factor where organizational strategy is concerned is *'synergy between initiatives.'* Synergy between IT initiatives may be assessed during the IT development and/or implementation by analysis of flows of information between relevant initiatives, combined with **stakeholder analysis** and/or **social network analysis**.

The last management success factor is *'handling the diversity within stakeholder goals.'* This includes the organization's capacity in the following respects:

- *'Awareness and mediation of diverging goals'*
- *'Handling of hidden agendas'*
- *'Initiative fatigue.'*

Evaluation in the context of an organization's ability to handle diverse stakeholder goals may be accomplished by using evaluation approaches such as **stakeholder analysis** and **organizational readiness analysis**. With respect to the first two of the listed issues, a **stakeholder analysis** may be useful in providing a rich picture of individual stakeholder goals and interests. **Stakeholder analysis** raises awareness and reveals the stakeholders who will benefit from as well as be victims of the new IT solution. *'Initiative fatigue'* implies the loss of organizational capability for change. Here, **organizational readiness** as an evaluation approach can be used to identify the severity of initiative fatigue.

Technical Factors

A number of the technical factors that affect IT success/failure were identified in the delphi study and the literature reviews mentioned in the background section. These technical factors are to a great extent of a nature that renders it obvious for them to be assessed as an integrated part of the **technical verification**. They will not be mentioned individually here. A factor such as *'integrated functionality and communication standards'* includes sub-factors like (1) *'integration with legacy system,'* (2) *'interoperability'* (connected systems logically and functionally co-operating in real-time), and (3) *'interconnectivity.'* From an IT evaluation perspective the previous mentioned technical factors are considered part of the **technical verification**, but may require special skills for their in-depth evaluation. Especially the technical interoperability of interconnected legacy systems may be challenging to assess in practice because of its dependency on timing for all kinds of transactions (requesting, cancelling, modifying, and reporting), to verify that timing is not an issue in practice. Technical verification may also involve determining if the system has semantic interoperability. Evaluating semantic interoperability requires special expertise and includes activities related to ensuring that the meaning of communicated data and information is the same when it appears in two different but interfaced systems. In today's practice, the latter involves aspects of communication and architectural standards, medical vocabularies, and the use of appropriate terminology servers (see for instance Blobel et al., 2006; Engel et al., 2006; Ingenerf, Reiner, & Seik, 2001).

The factor *'usability'* (i.e., the technical implementation of usability aspects) is also a critical IT success factor. A number of methods are dedicated to the evaluation of system usability, either constructive evaluation or summative evaluation: **cognitive assessment**, **cognitive walkthrough**, **heuristic evaluation**, **think aloud**, and **video-recording**.

Another technical factor is *'balance between flexibility and stability.'* IT flexibility enables variation in work procedures. However, flexibility can severely increase the complexity of an IT solution and therefore tends to counteract the stability. And consequently, finding the right balance between flexibility and stability is a dilemma for the project management. A limiting factor may be organizational readiness as regards change. Consequently, the method **organizational readiness** may be valuable here.

The last technical success factor is *'evolution rather than revolution'* in combination with a couple of its sub-topics: *'stepwise progress following functional needs as well as technological achievements and potentials'* and *'flexibility and adaptability, enabling future functional and technical changes.'* These factors are project management issues and will not be further dealt with here.

Strategy Factors

The overall factor *'strategy'* may be subdivided into three topics (see also *'strategy'* in the section on management factors): *'national,' 'regional,'* and *'organizational.'* There is a dedicated approach designed to assess alternative strategies, in particular aspects related to their feasibility and timing aspects: **framework for assessment of strategies**. Furthermore, **interviews** in general can help to elicit individuals' opinions, attitudes and perceptions regarding phenomena and observations, including those related to a strategy. And in particular, the **focus group interview** method is suited, when a model solution is discussed.

Another factor related to strategy is *'Accepted also at lower levels.'* Here, in particular the **focus group interview** method is well suited when addressing whether a given strategy is acceptable by the stakeholders.

Economy

An IT success factor related to economy is *'there has to be a return of investment (whether material or immaterial).'* The return of investment is concerned with the justification of the system prior to any decision to move forward on initiating a given IT project. Organizational arguments in favor or against an IT project have to be balanced against time, resources, and fiscal investments, as well as the inherent risks. If it's difficult to prospectively assess such justification, a **delphi** approach may get arguments on the table regarding the immaterial benefits. Retrospectively, **impact assessment** or a **field study** may be valuable to assess immaterial effects, but are themselves quite laborious, thereby indicating that their own return of investment may be questionable.

Education

The factor *'sufficient training'* in general points at two other factors: *'to make the best out of the daily operation'* and *'to provide an understanding of its limitations and future potentials.'* How much education employees need to use a system effectively depends on the actual system and its future organizational context. Unfortunately, the level of education and training users will need is not something one can fully assess prior to operating a system, but one can learn from the experiences of reference sites and other organizations. Moreover, one may get a good hint (prospectively) by means of one or more of the methods designed for **usability** assessment. In daily operation (retrospectively) one can follow up on deviations from desired operation in terms of user errors in the operation of a system. Here, for instance the **functionality assessment** method may be valuable. However, **functionality assessment** may be too stringent to use in all such cases.

User Acceptance

'User acceptance' is a factor, for which a number of dedicated tools and studies have been published in the health informatics literature. The approach applied is mainly **questionnaires**; see also **user acceptance and satisfaction**. However, also the **equity implementation model** and **focus group interviews** approaches may be valuable in this respect, depending on what precisely one wants to know. Of these, the latter may be applied prospectively, the others only retrospectively.

Suggestions on Methods Applicable for Evaluation of the Failure Criteria

Functional Criteria

The first functional failure factor is *'limitations in the way the user can express him or herself.'* Such limitations may be caused by either usability problems or by functional barriers. The usability may prospectively—or retrospectively—and constructively be dealt with by means of one or more of the **usability** evaluation approaches (human factors engineering). This can even be done as part of the selection among bids, see examples under **bids assessment** in Brender (2006a). If the problems are not (solely) of an ergonomic or cognitive nature, but are caused by an awkward functionality the organization may retrospectively analyze the IT system using the **functionality assessment** method.

The functional failure factor *'moving target'* is risky. It is risky but also inevitable because of the long lead-time for IT solutions, because it means that the project conditions, plans and directions may get out of control. For example, the technologies of healthcare organizations change rapidly as a function of the technological evolution and knowledge gain. Or the moving target may arise as a consequence of indecisiveness or of increased insight into the opportunities created by the new IT technology. If the moving target issue is considered a problem in a project one may use the **balanced scorecard** to assess each individual suggestion for change.

Organizational Criteria

The overall organizational failure factor *'not understanding the organizational context'* includes at least the below three topics.

The first of the three sub-factors is: *'not understanding or foreseeing the extent to which* the new IT-system affects the organization, its structure and/or work procedures.' This type of lacking insight is a bad foundation for the design or purchase of an IT-based solution and can be risky for the organization. The organization's commitment to forecasting the extent to which the work procedures will change is considered an obvious concern during planning activities. A **future workshop** may provide some input for the decision making in this respect. However, judging whether the organization is capable of making the necessary changes to the organizational structure and/or work procedures also requires assessment of **organizational readiness**.

The second sub-factor is *'too many changes of work procedures.'* Project management may overestimate the organization's capability for change. **Organizational readiness** as an evaluation method may help proactively but probably only partly to support assessment of organizational ability to accept and implement planned change. Presently, true organizational capability for change—that is, the number and severity of changes that an organization can cope with is still guesswork. Bearing such knowledge in mind the identification of a limited organizational readiness at evaluation is important prior to the preparation and assessment of the user requirements, as well as at bids assessment. Retrospectively, the method **equity implementation model** may be effective in understanding users' reaction to information systems by focusing on the impact that such a system brings about.

The third failure sub-factor related to organizational aspects is: *'Analysts dominate the development at the expense of those understanding the organizational context.'* Such cases may arise when stakeholder groups differ significantly from the designer groups and/or include different levels of formality and/or rationality. A **stakeholder analysis** would reveal those stakeholder characteristics and the relationship dynamics that influence IT implementation success. A stakeholder analysis normally has the purpose of identifying participants for the completion of a given task, problem solving activity or project, and thereby stakeholder analysis as a preventive action may lead to the best balance of the two parties in a project.

Behavioral Criteria

The behavioral failure factor *'overloading the user'* is concerned with planning and designing the functionality of a health information system. More specifically, designs that forces the user to remember too much (data or sub-tasks) in order for him or her to complete an activity may lead to an overload of the mental capacity of a user. Therefore, this factor is tightly connected to aspects dealt with by methods of **usability**. And consequently, differing types of usability studies that could be employed—for preventive and/or curative purposes—are: **cognitive assessment**, **cognitive walkthrough**, **heuristic evaluation**, **think aloud**, and **video-recording**.

The factor *'underestimating user acceptance'* is a complex issue. User acceptance is not only affected by usability but also by psychological aspects beyond the functionality of the IT system. For example, aspects may be grounded in the implementation process itself. Therefore, **user acceptance and satisfaction** evaluation approaches are important where there is a need to measure the level of user satisfaction retrospectively. Alternatively, the **equity implementation model** may provide a deeper understanding of the reasons behind potential IT system problems.

The last failure factor related to behavior is the factor *'resistance because of fear or loss of control of own job situation.'* Indications of resistance may be explored prospectively by means of **focus group interview** as well as **interview** methods in general, as these methods are particularly suited for elucidation of individuals' opinions, attitudes and perceptions regarding phenomena and observations.

Cultural Criteria

Two cultural failure factors are addressed here. The first is *'assuming that what works at one place also works somewhere else.'* Many managers tend to make the mistake of assuming that what works one place also works in their organization. Such mistakes are often made during the technology transfer between industrialized and developing countries (or vice versa), but they also occur at transfer of technologies between countries of the former type. Differences in legislation or legislative processes, in professional culture, in specialized equipment, and even in the profession-oriented terminology may hinder the transferability of an IT-based solution. This is well-known for knowledge-based systems, where even more invariant factors are present, such as the epidemiology; see (Nolan et al., 1991). Consequently, there is a need to study the transferability of a health information system to explore the system's applicability at new sites. Such transferability evaluation may involve almost any existing evaluation method. Presumably **analysis of work procedures** is the best general approach for preventive (prospective) purposes, while **functionality assessment** may fulfill the information need for curative, retrospective purposes.

The other failure factor addressed here is *'users have too high expectations.'* This failure factor may indeed be prevented by proactive evaluation of the expectations followed by communicative actions that focus at aligning or harmonizing expectations. Here, **interviews**, in particular **focus group interviews**, are suited as these methods may elicit individuals' opinions, attitudes and perceptions.

Technical Criteria

There are a number of technical failure factors, of which the first to be addressed is *'limitations in the way users can express themselves.'* This factor is parallel to the functional success factor

with the same name, see above. Project management need to be cognizant of the technical limitations of a system and discuss this with the user organization, including how a system affects users' expressions of themselves. However, the functional consequences of the technical barriers in the perspective of this factor compares to a needle in a haystack, if you do not know what to look for then the solution space is too big and too undetermined to even think of initiating an evaluation study.

Another technical failure factor is *'the technology is so restricted that it impacts design and implementation choices.'* According to the author's personal experience restrictiveness is usually correlated with the capabilities of analysts, designers, and implementers rather than the technology itself. Complexity as well as software immaturity may also influence technological restrictiveness. However, rather than being a topic specifically for evaluation technical restrictiveness is an issue for the project management to prevent and/or take action upon at an early point in the development process.

The factor *'response rate and other performance measures'* has two component aspects: a general one regarding the traditional technical performance (response times, throughput times, reliability, etc.) and a functional regarding *'the time needed to complete the users' tasks.'* The technical performance is normally evaluated as part of a **technical verification** provided that technical performance is specified as part of the contract. Technical verification normally takes place in an experimental set-up of a system within an organization, and it may require deep functional insight to define and establish the right evaluation set-up with realistic workloads and patterns of work activities. The second factor mentioned above (*'time needed to complete user tasks'*) compares to a kind of organizational response and throughput times, sometimes denoted service delivery times. An example is the time from a flight lands till the customers get their luggage, or the time from receipt of an order in an electronic healthcare system to the submission of the end result to the requester of the information. Service delivery times may be dealt with in a fashion similar to the technical counterparts. Evaluation of such service delivery times for user tasks requires before-and-after time-motion studies (time measurement for paradigm use scenarios and tasks: **prospective time series**). Some of the measures may be provided by the IT-system involved. Unfortunately, these measures may be more difficult to realistically evaluate in an experimental set-up in systems that are deeply interwoven or integrated with and dependent on other technologies and/or medical instruments. This is especially the case for some kinds of information systems (e.g., the production support part of laboratory information systems).

Another two technical failure factors are: *'vendor did not support the functionality quoted'* and *'insufficient verification of conformity with requirements specification.'* These factors are closely related. One has a small chance of realizing the former if the latter factor is present, and this may result in unpleasant surprises when the system is placed into daily operation. Even a trifle in the functionality that is not supported may have a great impact on organizational practices or resource consumption. The means for preventing this is to tenaciously and meticulously verify the delivery of the agreed functionality by means of **technical verification** using the contract (or other formalized agreement) as the frame of reference. The author recommends that the user evaluation in this respect takes the user organization's daily reality in terms of tasks and work procedures as the starting point and design test scenarios that mimic the daily work in all its details. Therefore, not only should prescribed organizational rules be tested, but the entire variation in organizational activities as well as exceptions to activities that arise in daily organizational work should be tested. This is the only way to prevent surprises during daily operation, but such an approach assumes

that the contract (the requirements specification) is an adequate frame of reference.

Educational Criteria

An educational failure factor identified is the *'visible discrepancy between successive versions of the IT-system.'* Obviously, visible discrepancy between successive system versions implies a need to provide users with continuous learning and support. No evaluation method that is dedicated to assess this criterion has been identified. If the discrepancies between versions of an information system are too large for the organization to deal with prior to operation the organization should recognize that there will be some temporary inefficiency that will arise in work procedures and that will be accompanied by operational errors involving the system. Problems associated with version changes and education may originate from a lack of communication, understanding or foreseeing the extent to which the version changes affect the organization, its structure and/or work procedures. Such lack of communication, understanding or foreseeing of the need for education may slow down proactive educational activities. As well, organizations must also recognize that such issues may arise from users' inability to cope with change (see this separately).

DISCUSSION

The first objective of this chapter was to verify the existence of appropriate evaluation methods for the assessment of known factors that influence the success and failure of health information systems. The chapter is based on a comprehensive set of IT success/failure factor synthesized from a number of literature reviews as well as a delphi study conducted by Brender et al. (2006). This approach leads the author to suggest that the list of success and failure factor itself is fairly complete. Therefore, the union of factors is a reasonably good instrument for analyzing whether adequate evaluation methods exist for monitoring or preventing given success and failure factor for health information systems. The author suggests it is feasible to identify suitable approaches for evaluating most of the IT success and failure factors.

There was one surprise that arose from the analysis: The author had expected risk management approaches with monitoring of risk factors to be high scoring as an approach particularly valuable for optimization with respect to the identified success and failure factor. It was not. This certainly does not rule out risk management as an integral part of best practice for systems development or implementation. It just shows that more is needed.

The top eleven methods referred to in the above are (in order of decreasing significance. However, some of the methods—like the bottom five methods—are ranked with the same significance):

- Stakeholder analysis
- Focus group interview
- Interview
- Social network analysis
- Analysis of work procedures
- Organizational readiness
- Framework for assessment of strategies
- Usability
- Equity implementation model
- Functionality assessment
- Balanced Scorecard

Almost all of these evaluation methods focus on the soft human aspects, such as who is affected by IT related decision-making, patterns of decision making, and management of change. The outcome of the present study simply reflects the fact that most of the factors identified in this work are related to the soft human factors outlined previously. Therefore, at least in the Western countries where most of the incorporated reviews originate, the organizational issue, as well as project management of information systems related issues are central: policy, commitment, and approaches.

FUTURE RESEARCH DIRECTIONS

The second objective of this chapter was to identify the potential needs as regards further development of evaluation methods. The main problem in many cases is that evaluation methods are not designed in a dedicated fashion to the assessment of those specific success factor and failure criteria. An example of this is **analysis of work procedures** approach, which has been adopted from the domain of systems analysis. Therefore, methods engineering is necessary.

Many places above a reference to a method is stated as "might be valuable"—or similar. This means that the method in question may not be dedicated to answer that specific information need. All of these evaluation approaches are obviously candidates for methods engineering and further evaluation research. Furthermore, evaluation methods need to be made more accessible to the common, organizational evaluator. Until then, practical application of such candidate evaluation methods requires methodological and methodical skills, imagination and flexibility in order to adapt the methods to a specific case, its conditions and its particular information need.

One method is explicitly mentioned as possibly needing more maturation as an evaluation method: **organizational readiness**. Organizational readiness is a very complex phenomenon, and relevant in connection with numerous success/failure factor. Organizational readiness ranges from the hospitality (openness) to solutions not invented in-house, to the capacity of organizations to invent efficacious IT-based responses to changes within the healthcare environment, to triggering the invention of such IT-based solutions, and to building the capacity to develop sustainable solutions.

Furthermore, several of the methods referred to in this chapter are designed to provide exhaustive and highly accurate information, bordering on scientific stringency. This implies that large investments of calendar time and/or resources are needed to undertake such evaluation studies—which may be out of the question in a practical evaluation setting. Therefore, in the practical context of a specific project, the challenge may be to modify or simplify a specific evaluation method to the practical needs of the organization, again, the situational methods engineering is required.

As Rigby emphasizes: "Adequately funded evaluation, based on proven sound techniques, is the means of moving forward to a credible discipline ..." (Rigby, 2006, p. 119). Implicitly, he says in his conclusion that there is a step ahead of us before the evaluation methods are sufficiently dedicated and matured for their application purpose. This conclusion is in agreement with the statement in the review by (Berghout & Remenyi, 2005, p. 88) that "... there has been only marginal improvement in the maturity in this field over the past eleven years." Implementation of IT-based solutions (and therefore also the implied evaluation needs) are somewhat indeterministic. However, the present study indicates that we do have a foundation of approaches valuable for most evaluation purposes. From this foundation of evaluation approaches we may adapt or develop and mature evaluation methods dedicated to the specific information needs. Still, major research efforts are needed.

Finally, according to Brender (2006b) there are a number of evaluation research challenges ahead of us: Research needs to focus on constructive evaluation of cognitive and work process-oriented aspects of IT-based solutions to cope with the full complexity. This full complexity includes the dynamics, the variation, and the evolution of the target domain—here health care. The analysis in the present contribution could not go into sufficient detail to confirm or reject this hypothesis.

CONCLUSION

Evaluation is perceived as a means to optimize the likelihood of success while minimizing the likelihood of failures of health information systems development and/or implementation. A list of success and failure factor identified within the literature was examined to identify candidate evaluation methods. It turned out being feasible to identify suitable approaches for most of the factors. However, there is a need to undertake situational methods engineering in many situations as the evaluation methods referred to in this chapter often are not dedicated to answering the precise information needs of an organization. This therefore, also points at the research needs and opportunities.

REFERENCES

Ammenwerth, E., Brender, J., Nykänen, P., Prokosch, H.-U., Rigby, M., & Talmon, J. (2004). Visions and strategies to improve evaluation of health information systems—Reflections and lessons based on the HIS-EVAL workshop in Innsbruck. *International Journal of Medical Informatics, 73*(6), 479-491.

Berghout, E., & Remenyi, D. (2005). The eleven years of the european conference on IT evaluation: Retrospectives and perspectives for possible future research. *The Electronic Journal of Information Systems, 8*(2), 81-98. Available online at www.ejise.com

Bikson, T. K., & Eveland, J. D. (1989). Technology Transfer as a Framework for Understanding Social Impacts of Computerization. In M. J. Smith & G. Salvendy (Eds.), *Work with computers: Organizational, management, stress and health aspects. Vol. 1.* (pp. 28-37). Amsterdam: Elsevier.

Blobel B. G., Engel K., & Pharow, P. (2006). Semantic Interoperability—HL7 Version 3 compared

199

to advanced architecture standards. *Methods of Information in Medicine, 45*(4), 343-53.

Brender, J. (2006a). *Handbook of evaluation methods for health informatics.* New York: Academic Press.

Brender, J. (2006b). Evaluation of health information applications—Challenges ahead of us. *Methods of Information in Medicine, 45*, 62-66.

Brender, J., Ammenwerth, E., Nykänen, P., & Talmon, J. (2006). Factors influencing success and failure of Health Informatics Systems, a pilot delphi study. *Methods of Information in Medicine, 45*, 125-136.

Crosswell, P. L. (1991). Obstacles to GIS implementation and guidelines to increase the opportunities for success. *URISA Journal, 3*(1), 43-56.

Engel, K., Blobel, B., & Pharow, P. (2006). Standards for enabling health informatics interoperability. In A. Hasman, R. Haux, J. van der Lei, E. De Clercq, & F.H. Roger France (Eds.), *Ubiquity: technologies for better health in aging societies, Procedings of MIE2006. Studies in Health Technology and Informatics 124*, 145-150.

Haimes, Y. Y., & Schneiter, C. (1996). Covey's seven habits and the systems approach: A comparative approach. *IEEE transactions on Systems, Man and Cybernetics, 26*(4), 483-487.

Heeks, R. (2006). Health information systems: Failure, success and improvisation. *International Journal of Medical Informatics, 75*, 125-137.

Ingenerf, J., Reiner, J., & Seik, B. (2001). Standardized terminological services enabling semantic interoperability between distributed and heterogenous systems. *International Journal of Medical Informatics, 64*, 223-240.

Nolan, J., McNair, P., & Brender, J. (1991). Factors influencing transferability of knowledge-based Systems. *International Journal of Biomedical Computing, 27*, 7-26.

Price Waterhouse (1997). *Without change there is no progress—Coping with chaos, a global survey.* London: Price Waterhouse.

Rigby, M. (2006). Evaluation—the Cinderella science of ICT in health. *IMIA Yearbook of Medical Informatics, 2006*, 114-120.

Stravri, P. Z., & Ash, J. (2003). Does failure breed success: narrative analysis of stories about computerized provider order entry. *International Journal of Medical Informatics, 72*, 9-15.

ADDITIONAL READINGS

(See also the extensive lists of annotated references and World Wide Web sites on evaluation methods and case studies in (Brender 2006a)).

Ammenwerth, E., Iller, C., & Mahler, C. (2006). IT-adoption and the interaction of task, technology and individuals: A fit framework and a case study. *BMC Medical Informatics and Decision Making 6(3)*. Retrieved July, 25, 2007 from http://www.biomedcentral.com/1472-6947/6/3

Coolican, H. (1999). *Introduction to research methods and statistics in psychology* (2nd ed.). London: Hodder & Stoughton.

Davidson, E.J. (2005). *Evaluation methodology basics: The nuts and bolts of sound evaluation.* Thousand Oaks: Sage Publications Inc.

DeLone, W.H., & McLean, E.R. (2003). The DeLeone and McLean model of information systems success: A ten-year update. *Journal of Management Information Systems 19(4)*, 9-30.

Friedman, C.P., & Wyatt, J.C. (2006). *Evaluation methods in biomedical informatics* (2nd ed.). Springer.

Fink, A. (2005). *Evaluation fundamentals: Insights into the outcomes, effectiveness, and quality of health programs* (2nd ed.). Thousand Oaks: Sage Publications Inc.

Kaplan, B., & Shaw, N. (2004). Future directions in evaluation research: People, organizational, and social issues. *Methods of Information in Medicine, 43*, 215-31.

Kushniruk, A.W., & Patel, V.L. (2004). Cognitive and usability engineering methods for the evaluation of clinical information systems. *Journal of Biomedical Informatics, 37*(1), 56-76.

van der Meijden, M.J., Tange, H.J., Troost, J., & Hasman, A. (2003). Determinants of success of Inpatient Clinical Information Systems: A literature review. *Journal of the American Medical Informatics Association, 10*(3), 235-243.

Murphy, E., Dingwall, R., Greatbatch, D., Parker, S., & Watson, P. (1998). Qualitative research methods in health technology assessment: A review of the literature. *Health Technology Assessment 2(16)*. Retrieved July 25, 2007, from http://www.ncchta.org

Neville, D., Gates, K., MacDonald, D., Barron, M., Tucker, S., Cotton, S. et al. (2004). *Towards an evaluation framework for electronic health records initiatives: A proposal for an evaluation framework.(pp. 82)*. Retrieved July 25, 2007, from http://www.nlchi.nf.ca/research_evaluations.asp

Patton, M.Q. (2002). *Qualitative research & evaluation methods* (3rd ed.). Thousand Oaks: Sage Publications Inc.

Schalock, R.L. (2002). *Outcome-based evaluation* (2nd ed.). New York: Kluwer Academic/Plenum Publishers.

Southon, G. (1999). IT, Change and evaluation: An overview of the role of evaluation in health services. *International Journal of Medical Informatics, 56*, 125-133.

Talmon, J.L. (2006). Evaluation and implementation: A call for action. *IMIA Yearbook of Medical Informatics, 2006*, 11-15.

ENDNOTE

[1]   The full name of the two methods are (in English translation): BIKVA "User involvement in Quality Development," and KUBI "Quality Development through User Involvement."

Section IV
Strategic Approaches to Improving the Healthcare System

Chapter XII
A Comparison of How Canada, England, and Denmark are Managing their Electronic Health Record Journeys

Denis Protti
University of Victoria, Canada

ABSTRACT

Healthcare is one of the world's most information-intensive industries. Every day, volumes of data are produced which, properly used, can improve clinical practice and outcomes, guide planning and resource allocation, and enhance accountability. Electronic health information is fundamental to better healthcare. There will be no significant increase in healthcare quality and efficiency without high quality, user-friendly health information compiled and delivered electronically. The growing use of information and communication technology (ICT) in the healthcare sector has introduced numerous opportunities and benefits to patients, providers and governments alike. Patients are being provided with tools to help them manage and monitor their healthcare, providers are able to seamlessly access up-to-date patient information, and governments are showing transparency to the public by reporting health data and information on their websites. There is mounting evidence that national, regional, and organizational e-health strategies are being developed and implemented worldwide. This chapter provides an overview of three different national e-health strategies, and identifies the lessons learned from the e-health strategies of Canada, England and Denmark.

Copyright © 2008, IGI Global, distributing in print or electronic forms without written permission of IGI Global is prohibited.

INTRODUCTION

Due to the ever increasing pressures and demands for healthcare services and the strain those services put on the economy, many nations have realized that they must develop a more sustainable, efficient and effective healthcare system. In doing this, there has been much investment in ICT. Information systems play a significant role in helping improve health outcomes and decision-making at the point of care, and the benefits don't stop there. There are a number of global themes that emerge regarding the use of health information systems (Figure 1). These themes include establishing electronic health records, developing clinical decision support tools and introducing Telehealth services to those in remote and rural areas often with a high incidence of chronic disease. Orchestrating the change from the paper-based world, to one with seamless and fluid information systems requires a great amount of coordination, time and funding and most importantly a comprehensive strategy.

The impact of the electronic health record (EHR) on patient care can be quite substantial (Infoway, 2006). Some of the potential benefits include:

- Improved communication between providers, and between providers and patients. In many countries, the flow of information has grown exponentially.
- In a number of countries, the implementation of the EHR among various professions has created momentum for working in teams. The EHR has been a catalyst for accelerating this key element of healthcare innovation widely supported at the policy level throughout the world.
- Patient empowerment. In Denmark, people have access to their EHR. They can review information such as laboratory results and prescriptions to improve self-care—particularly important for chronic disease management. They can see which providers have viewed their records, which allows them to monitor privacy.
- Improved adherence to preventive measures. The literature suggests that electronically generated reminders for screening and follow-up increases adherence by 10% to 15%.
- Improved delivery of recommended care for various conditions. The Vanguard group, in Boston, delivered recommended care about 60% of the time in a baseline study. It improved to over 90% by combining team-based practice with the EHR.
- Nation-wide implementation of the EHR in the USA, including e-prescribing with decision support tools built in, could reduce adverse drug events by two million annually, preventing 190,000 hospitalizations.
- According to the literature, introducing the EHR into the ICU reduces ICU mortality by 46% to 68%; complications by 44% to 50%; and overall hospital mortality by 30% to 33%.
- The use of e-prescribing in Denmark has reduced the medication problem rate from 33% to 14%, and laboratory systems have reduced tube labeling errors from 18% to 2%.
- A major touted benefit of the EHR is chronic disease management (CDM). Some believe the benefits have already been demonstrated and there is consensus that the EHR is a necessary, but perhaps not sufficient, tool to improve CDM.

CANADA'S JOURNEY

Canada has an e-health strategy that is committed to accelerating the implementation of electronic health information systems in Canada. Canada Health Infoway Inc., an independent, not-for-profit organization, created in 2000, is governed

Figure 1. Global themes in health information systems

Theme	Deliverables and Challenges
Electronic Health Records (EHRs)	• Conveys clinical information • Coordinates care for particular diseases or services • "Virtual concept" reliant on the network approach • Pulls data from multiple stores

Decision Support Tools	• Supports clinician decision making at the service (planning, peer reviews) and care level (care plans, individual clinical actions)
	• Uses include:
	   o Computerized Physician Order Entry (CPOE)
	   o Computerized Nurse Order Entry (CNOE)
	   o E-Prescribing
	   o Formularies

Unique Patient Identifiers	• Enable EHRs to span across the continuum of care • Manages patient visits and person data
Connectivity	• Online access demands create a need for greater bandwidth • Addressing security demands in order to ensure patient information is secure
Common Standards and Minimum Data Sets	• Detailed data sets lack consensus within and across countries • Consistent and standardized reporting is lacking, worldwide
Coordination of Care in General Practice	• Growing use of more sophisticated practice management systems • Opportunities for greater functionality including clinical uses • Individual care plans are supported • Increasing number of electronic interactions • Supports the global trend to focus on primary care as the main focus of health service delivery • IT vendors are focusing more research and development budgets in this area
Telehealth	• Delivers community and home-based services remotely • Potential to provide specialist services to rural and disadvantaged communities, from a distance • Opportunity to deliver care, monitor and manage chronic conditions remotely via the internet • Devices available for home use to capture vital signs and transmit to the care provider
Consumer Involvement	• Consumers are making informed decisions • Demand for health information and knowledge • Available information should be integrated into service delivery to better involve consumers • Demand for individually tailored care
Access	• Demands on the healthcare system has resulted in various initiatives which allows consumers access to the most appropriate care provider o Call centers, knowledge bases, nurse-based telephone triage

by Canada's 14 federal, provincial and territorial Deputy Ministers of Health. Infoway provides leadership by establishing a strategic direction for EHR implementation in Canada in collaboration with the provinces and territories.

Canada Health Infoway recently released an updated electronic health record Solution blueprint for Canada. This blueprint is meant to be a business and technical framework defining how health information is shared "between health services providers (physicians, specialists, nurses and pharmacists) across care settings (hospitals, emergency rooms, clinics and homecare settings) and across geographical distances."

Currently, a key focus in Canada is to develop a network of interoperable electronic health record solutions across Canada, through linking clinics, hospitals, pharmacies and other points of care, in order to help increase access to healthcare services, enhance the quality of care and make the healthcare system more productive. Canada is planning on accomplishing the goals of achieving a comprehensive integrated electronic health records solution, through nine investment programs.

The main areas of interest of Canada Health Infoway are interoperable EHRs and related telehealth and applications. Priority activities are defined and funded from an allocation of $1.2 billion from the federal government. Infoway acts as a "strategic investor"and aims to build on existing work in Canadian Provinces or explore new initiatives in collaboration with other partners, whether healthcare organizations or commercial IT suppliers.

There are nine Infoway programs:

- Interoperable EHR (including privacy and security architecture and standards)
- Infostructure— (architecture, standards to ensure interoperability of systems and support reuse)
- Registries—to provide electronic identification of patients and providers and provide basis of health record system
- Telehealth Diagnostic Imaging
- Drug Information Systems—medication profiles and eventually e-prescribing
- Lab Information Systems—to view lab results
- Telehealth—particularly for rural and remote settings
- Health Surveillance
- Innovation/Adoption

The main objective is to make interoperable electronic health records available for 50% of the population by 2009. However, Canada's healthcare system still manages information with old technologies and practices, some of which literally originated in the 19th century (94% of physician visits in Canada involve paper records; most prescriptions are handwritten). The production of information has grown exponentially, but the capacity to process, analyze, and deploy it to good effect has not kept pace.

Though there has been some progress towards the EHR, it was recently reported that Canada lags significantly on use of electronic medical records in physician's offices (Schoen, 2006). An international survey of more than 6,000 doctors in seven countries found that only 23% of Canadian physicians use electronic medical records, which is the lowest percentage and far behind the 98% level in The Netherlands. Primary care doctors in Australia, the Netherlands, New Zealand and the United Kingdom have the most widespread and multifunctional systems. The majority of doctors in these countries also reported routine use of electronic prescribing and electronic access to test results. Overall, fewer than one-in-five Canadian and U.S. primary-care doctors have access to robust information systems that provide a foundation to guarantee high-quality care.

In the four countries that report widespread EMR use, about 50 to as much as 90% of doctors routinely use computerized alerts to notify themselves of possible prescribing problems, reminder systems to notify patients about preventive or follow-up care, and prompt to advise patients of test results. In contrast, less than a quarter of Canadian and U.S. doctors have computerized systems for these tasks.

Canada has five priorities in healthcare (Infoway, 2006):

1. Reduced wait times, not only in high profile areas such as hip and knee replacements and cancer care, but also in access to primary and specialty care, and underserved areas such as mental health;

2. Primary healthcare, with interdisciplinary teams providing comprehensive, convenient care with an increased emphasis on health promotion and prevention.

3. Enhanced patient safety in the community and institutions.
4. Improved quality of care, particularly for people with chronic conditions.
5. Improved efficiency and better value for money.

The EHR could contribute to addressing them provided there is full-fledged implementation across the country. As the EHR becomes richer, with more elements and connectivity, the potential impact grows. In some areas, there is already solid evidence that the benefits can be realized. In others, the logical case appears persuasive, but there is a need for stronger empirical evidence.

ENGLAND'S JOURNEY

England journey is based on building on its success in the primary care computing arena. There are currently approximately 8,900 general practices (GP) in England, of which 97% have a GP clinical computer system. All practices use their systems for NHS acute prescribing (once only) and for repeat prescribing. Exceptions to this rule are those prescriptions generated during home visits or when prescribing controlled drugs which at present by law these must be hand written. Many practices are using electronic appointment systems and an increasing number of practices scan all hospital letters, reports etc which are then attached to the individual patient record. There are estimates of up to 30% of practices running 'paper-light' systems today.

All health systems such as England's NHS depend on successful handling of vast quantities of information to function safely and effectively. The National Programme for Information Technology in the NHS (NPfIT—now referred to as Connecting for Health—CfH) is a 10-year program which presents an unprecedented opportunity to use information technology (IT) to reform the way the NHS in England uses infor-

mation, and hence to improve services and the quality of patient care. The core of CfH will be the NHS Care Records Service, which will make relevant parts of a patient's clinical record available to whoever needs it to care for the patient. The national program also includes many other elements, including medical images accessible by computer, electronic transmission of prescriptions, and electronic booking of first outpatient appointments.

According to a recent National Audit Office report, in the past, individual NHS organizations procuring and maintaining their own IT systems and the procurement and development of IT within the NHS was haphazard. The Department of Health did not consider this approach to have been successful, and one of the aims of the national program has been to provide strong central direction of IT development, and increase the rate of take up of advanced IT. CfH is being delivered mainly through contracts negotiated by NHS Connecting for Health with IT service suppliers. Once systems have been developed by the suppliers, further action is needed to bring them into use, such as integrating with existing IT systems and configuring them to meet local circumstances, training staff to use them, and adapting ways of working to make the best of the solutions. Four local service providers are primarily responsible for organizing this work, but much work is needed by local NHS organizations—strategic health authorities, NHS Trusts and other providers working for the NHS, such as GPs and pharmacists.

The scope, vision and complexity of CfH is wider and more extensive than any ongoing or planned healthcare IT program in the world, and it represents the largest single IT investment in the UK to date. If successful, it will deliver important financial, patient safety and service benefits. The main implementation phase of CfH and the realization of benefits is mainly a matter for the future and it will therefore be some time before it is possible fully to assess the value for money, as this will depend on the progress made in developing and using the systems it is intended to provide.

CfH has not been without significant growing pains. An April 2006 open letter by 23 English academics to the Health Select Committee argued that the committee should be aware of the concerns of health professionals, technologists and professional organizations about the £6bn NHS National Programme for Information Technology (NPfIT). It pointed out that the NHS Confederation has said "the IT changes being proposed are individually technically feasible but they have not been integrated, so as to provide comprehensive solutions, anywhere else in the world."

The letter went on to point out that two of NPfIT's largest suppliers had issued warnings about profits in relation to their work and a third has been fined for inadequate performance. Various independent surveys show that support from healthcare staff is not assured. Concern was expressed that concrete, objective information about NPfIT's progress is not available to external observers. Reliable sources within NPfIT have raised concerns about the technology itself. Questions which the academics felt had not been answered included: Have realistic assessments been carried out about the volumes of data and traffic that a fully functioning NPfIT will have to support across the 1000's of healthcare organizations in England; need for responsiveness, reliability, resilience and recovery under routine and full system load?

As a result of the letter and a series of other documents and accounts—particularly about privacy and confidentiality of the national care record—a shift of responsibility for NHS IM&T in England from the center to local organizations was signaled in the service's new plan for 2007-2008 which was published on December 11, 2006.

The NHS in England: the operating framework for 2007-8 was launched by the NHS chief executive, who says in his foreword: "We are devolving power from the centre to the service in many ways, not least in how we allocate money, such as the unbundling of central budgets. Some of the key enablers of service transformation, such as the delivery of information technology, will also increasingly need to be driven and owned by the service rather than from the centre so that patients can get the full benefits as quickly as possible."

Plans will be required from NHS organizations showing not only how local but national priorities will be achieved including: implementation of GP Systems of Choice; preparing for the National Summary Care Record; the completion of picture archiving and communications rollout; implementation and benefits realization for the Electronic Prescriptions Service and further exploitation of e-booking. The framework also says plans should show how organizations will carry out the deployment and benefits realization for patient administration systems and order communications and results functionality, in line with existing commitments and targets set by each SHA, in the context of existing commercial arrangements.

The broad planning local NHS organizations will be required to do is set out, though the framework says more detailed guidance will be issued shortly. All NHS providers will have to have a forward looking IM&T plan which is "core to their business, exploits fully the NPfIT opportunity and thereby demonstrates migration to the NHS Care Record Service." Primary care trusts, as commissioners, will have their own comprehensive IM&T plan and work with all providers in their local health communities to align IM&T plans and enable patient-centered service transformation. Strategic health authorities will be charged with assuring that the local NHS has the capability and resources to deliver their plans.

From 2007/08 onwards, IM&T investment and exploitation will form part of mainstream NHS planning in support of health and service priorities and reform. With the shift to a self-improving system, the new accent is on local ownership and leadership—away from the centralized approach used by CfH—driving a local IM&T agenda which also meets a defined set of national expectations and exploits the National Programme for IT (NPfIT). Some have suggested that the direction of travel is reminiscent of the 1998 national health information strategy.

DENMARK'S JOURNEY

Denmark is perhaps the most advanced nation in the world when it comes to the use of information technology in healthcare (Protti & Johansen, 2003). Virtually all Danish GPs, and as of January, 2007 (all specialists as well), use their computers to electronically send and receive clinical messages such as prescriptions, lab results, lab requests, discharge summaries, referrals, and so forth. Sixty standardized messages (up from 32 in 2002), including their "One letter solution," have been implemented in approximately 100 computer systems, including physician office systems, hospital systems, laboratory systems and pharmacy systems. The national network is used by over three quarters of the healthcare sector, altogether more than 5,000 different organisations. All hospitals, all pharmacies, all laboratories and general practices take part. As of January, 2006, all private physiotherapists (1,750 in 550 clinics) and all private dentists (2,800 in 1,600 clinics) were also connected to the network. By the end of 2006, all 240 private chiropractor clinics and all 675 private psychologists will also be part of the electronic network. The majority of specialists and all of the local authority health visitor services now participate in the electronic communication via the healthcare data network. Over 90% of the country's clinical communications in the primary sector are exchanged over Denmark's national network. This high level of connectivity means that most Danish physicians run paper-light offices.

GPs enter all medications themselves. They access a drug database that is maintained centrally by the national Danish Drug Agency. The Agency automatically updates the physician office systems every 14 days. Physicians are required to use the lowest cost drug unless a "no substitution" order is given. Most systems provide some decision support in terms of drug-drug interaction, warnings concerning pregnant patients, etc. After the physician selects the patient's pharmacy from a pull down menu, the prescription is sent electronically to the specific pharmacy. At this time, over 85% of prescriptions are sent electronically to pharmacies. All 332 pharmacies with four different IT systems are able to receive electronic prescriptions. As of 2006, all dispensed medications are in a central database which is accessible via the health portal to both physicians and patients who have a digital signature (Johansen, 2006).

Thirty-five percent of Danish hospitals have electronic patient record (EPR) systems, a figure higher than most of Western Europe. EPR penetration in Denmark is expected to rise to 100% during the next two years. Ninety-eight percent of general practitioners (GPs) and a large percentage of specialists use electronic medical record (EMR) systems—a level similar to the UK, The Netherlands, and the other Nordic countries.

MedCom, Denmark's coordinating organization for healthcare IT was founded in 1994 to address these problems. By 2002, it had developed national standards for electronic data interchange (EDI) communication and ensured their widespread adoption in primary care. MedCom is funded 50% by the Ministry of Health, 35% by the Association of County Councils, with the remainder of the funding coming from municipalities, the Danish Pharmacy Association, and other organizations. MedCom has a staff of approximately 15 and a budget of three million euros per year.

MedCom created standard EDI forms for the six principal information flows in primary care for which paper forms were used: lab orders and results; prescriptions ordered by GPs; referrals from GPs to specialists; radiology orders and results; community (home care) messages; and insurance claims submissions and reimbursements. It disseminated these standards through local projects funded by the counties. To encourage adoption, MedCom published on its Web site the number of messages sent in each county, and the progress of vendors in modifying their applications to become compliant with the standards. The main problem was that the standards were too ambiguous. Focus groups involving clinicians, IT professionals and vendors resulted in more-precise versions of the standards.

Since 2002, MedCom has:

- Formed a health data network by linking existing local and regional secure healthcare networks and the value-added network services of counties, hospitals, vendors and other organizations to a central hub via a virtual private network (VPN). The VPN is used for transferring messages, as well as for videoconferencing, conducting teledermatology, accessing digital images, and accessing the standardized extracts of patient data (SUP) system and the national portal.
- Developed a tool to convert EDI messages to XML. One of the goals is to facilitate the transition from existing administrative and clinical applications to applications based on the new EPR data model.
- Developed standards for hospital-to-hospital discharge letters, patient referrals, correspondence messages and clinical biochemistry laboratory results. MedCom paid vendors to modify their applications to incorporate these standards.
- Developed messages for GPs and hospitals to communicate with local authorities and home care providers. This is particularly important in the care of senior citizens, who are frequently transferred between hospital and home care.

- Has been certifying all supplier systems since 2000. Currently suppliers do not have to pay for certification, which entails not only messaging standards but also presentation formats, functionality, ability to change, etc. Suppliers are certified for life unless they introduce major changes (e.g., convert their operating system from DOS to Windows). There are currently 11 suppliers who support 16 different physician office systems, with the major products being either local install or through an Internet service provision. Three suppliers have 57% of the market. Overall, there are some 60 vendors with over 100 software systems using the MedCom network.

The Danish central government contributes to healthcare IT through the National Board of Health (Edwards, 2006).

The board has created a EPR data model known as the basic structure for electronic health records. The board plans to bring the data model into compliance with the health level seven (HL7) version 3 reference information model (RIM) during the next few years. The data model specifies the functionality that every EPR system in Denmark should contain. It is being used as the basis for the tenders that counties are issuing for EPR systems. The board is also completing the development of a national terminology server, including a translation of systematized nomenclature of human medicine (SNOMED) into Danish.

The purpose of the SUP project, which was designed by two counties and three vendors and was implemented by MedCom, is to make data held by Danish hospitals available to clinicians and patients across the country. SUP is currently supplied with data on 16% of the population. Three counties are contributing data. The SUP metadata model contains the data common to the main administrative and clinical applications used in Danish hospitals. Every 24 hours, the data from local applications is copied into an XML file, which is transferred to the SUP database. Clinicians can only view the data; they cannot download it into their own applications.

Once vendors adopt the EPR data model and hospitals implement upgraded EPR applications, the SUP metadata model will be updated, which is expected to enable data extracts every one to two hours. It is likely that SUP will become an EHR covering the entire country.

Since year-end 2003, Denmark has had a healthcare portal, Sundhed.dk, which is funded by the same organizations as MedCom. The portal was developed by IBM Acure and runs on an IBM WebSphere portal server, WebSphere application server and DB2 database. The portal cost 15 million euros to set up. Its annual cost is 4.5 million euros: 3 million euros for IT operations and 1.5 million euros for administration. The content is contributed by the stakeholders (principally the counties and local authorities).

The portal enables patients to:

- View their data from the SUP database (to go into effect in August 2006).
- View their medicine profiles.
- Renew prescriptions.
- View summaries of their medical histories (as of September 2005).
- View a shared care pregnancy record.
- Purchase prescription drugs from pharmacies.
- View information on medical conditions, preventive medicine, and health laws and regulations.
- Specify their organ donation preferences.
- Book appointments with GPs, view a calendar containing their appointments and set up appointment reminders.
- Have electronic consultations with GPs, which are reimbursed according to nationally agreed fees. The Danish GP association has agreed that, by year-end 2007, all GPs will offer electronic consultations.

- View a directory of healthcare organizations, with information on waiting times, quality and accessibility.

Clinicians can view the same information as patients. In addition, they can view clinical knowledge (the Cochrane Library), job listings, laboratory test results (a pilot project) and guidelines for referring patients to hospitals. The portal uses a public-key infrastructure (PKI) for security. Access by patients requires a digital signature; 650,000 have been issued to date. Patients store the digital signatures on their personal PCs and can also transfer them onto thumb drives if they wish to access the portal from another PC. There are approximately 175,000 unique patient visits to the portal per month.

Access by clinicians or pharmacies requires special security certificates. Patients can view the name of the person viewing their data, the date and time of the access, and the action taken. In theory, Danish patients have to give explicit consent each time data is shared, they are allowed to choose which clinicians can access their medical records, and they are allowed to restrict access to data on mental and sexual health. In reality, patients are encouraged not to exercise these powers. Consent to share data is requested only when the patient changes physicians or hospitals.

Studies have concluded that MedCom has produced financial benefits (Gartner). A cost-benefit analysis conducted in 2006 by the market research firm Empirica estimated that the cumulative present value cost of MedCom prior to year-end 2005 was 536 million euros, and the benefit was 872 million euros. Empirica estimated that a typical GP, serving 1,300 patients, saves 30 hours per week of secretarial work by using the MedCom standards.

Higher quality and higher throughput by individual GPs due to the use of EMRs and electronic communication have been shown. On average, GPs have experienced a 20% increase in number of consultations after beginning use of EMRs and electronic communications. Other outcomes include reduced cost of medications and a lower mortality rate due cervical cancer. There are less smear samples and a reduction in cervical cancer (62 in 1988 down to 18 in 2004) and in deaths (29 in 1988 down to 12 in 2001).

Though there is little hard evidence of clinical benefits, soft evidence includes more effective communications (clear, accurate, complete and consistent), more-efficient communications (rapid and lower-cost), and more widespread communications. GPs and hospitals spend less on administrative processing and get reimbursed faster. Local authorities spend less on handling transfers of patients between hospital and home care. Patients benefit from more-efficient delivery of health services, better and more rapid communication of patient data, and access to information about their health.

LESSONS LEARNED

Canada embarked on its particular EHR journey for a number of reasons. One was because at the time when Canada started with EHRs there was not a proliferation of EMRs in doctors' offices. Since healthcare is a provincial responsibility, moving that agenda forward is based on the provinces negotiating with their doctors to install computers in their offices. Secondly, national statistics suggested that the system errors, the adverse effects occur in hospitals, in emergency departments. Infoway wanted to make medication history, lab results and diagnostic imaging data available at that front line.

Lesson learned from the Canadian journey include:

- Secured funding from the federal government
- Facilitated unprecedented federal/ provincial/territorial cooperation

- Enabled a broad language of acceptance around the need for and expected benefits of EHRs
- Established standards
- Secured some early implementation successes (e.g., registries)
- Achieved savings from national procurement initiatives

Despite the investments of funding, planning, goodwill and achievements to date, some feel that the current process for building an electronic infrastructure for the Canadian healthcare system faces a very real danger of delivering a fragmented system that may provide less value to patients in terms of providing better care, and alienates the majority of physicians expected to embrace these new tools (Pascal, 2006). Pascal argues that without serious re-evaluation of our investment priorities and the timing of those investments, as well as how best to involve and support frontline healthcare workers—especially physicians—in meaningful ways throughout this process, Canada is at risk falling far short of our goal of improving healthcare outcomes through the effective application of ICT. He argues that the current approach is seriously impairing the achievement of an adequate return on value (ROV—return on value is the assessment of quantitative and qualitative costs and benefits from IT investments in the healthcare sector; ROV is richer than ROI which only deals with the quantification side of the equation).

According to Pascal (2006), as Canada Health Infoway, provincial and regional jurisdictions go about their work concentrating on the acute sector; there is growing concern within the medical community about how the process is unfolding without their involvement. The greatest gains in healthcare outcomes occur in the community care as over 80% of care originates and is delivered in community settings. Pascal questions why the concentration on the construction of large data bases when physicians and other healthcare workers have little or no connectivity to neither this information, nor the electronic capabilities in their offices to capture or display it? One of the goals of the Canada Infoway e-health strategy is was to have the right information, at the right place, with the right provider, at the right time to provide the best care possible. To do this there has to be connectivity between points of care and the necessary technologies available at them when the encounter occurs. The majority of health information that will make up an EHR or that will be shared among providers to support the care of a patient will be generated at the community level and captured in physician's EMRs.

The lessons learned from England were recently addressed by the British Computer Society who suggested that in order for the national program to succeed the following changes are required:

- Provide a business context for CfH owned at national and local level
- Focus on local implementations at Trust and provider unit level, for example, hospitals, diagnostic and treatment centers, community and mental health trusts, and practices. Providing specialty, service-specific and niche systems will encourage clinical involvement and give quicker benefits
- Persuade local NHS management that informatics is an essential part of business solutions and service transformation. Provide explicit additional funds for business change and service transformation. Embed informatics in trust business targets with realistic target dates.
- Adopt a truly patient-centered approach at the local health community level.
- The strategy should be evolutionary, building on what presently works and encouraging convergence to standards over time, rather than revolutionary.
- Given a heterogeneous set of systems, there needs to be a greater emphasis on standards

to enable systems to interoperate effectively, rather than focusing on relatively few monolithic systems.
- Establish basic informatics elements that are standard across the UK to enable coherent treatment of patients irrespective of their movement across home country borders. Ensure that other facets of the English strategy support this coherence.
- Fully implement GP system choice at practice level.
- There needs to be an accreditation process for all new and existing systems, both against the chosen standards and functionality requirements that does not stifle innovation.
- Revisit and reallocate roles and responsibilities of the NHS at each level, NHS CFH nationally and locally, and system suppliers.
- Transform NHS CFH into an open partnership with NHS management, users, the informatics community, suppliers, patients and their careers that is based on trust and respect.
- There are major issues about the sharing of electronic patient data which need to be resolved whatever the shape of future informatics in the NHS. These must not be hijacked by technical issues, and informed patient consent should be paramount.
- Information sharing between care professionals should initially be by messaging using the Spine TMS service pending further work on information governance and the National Care Record Service.
- Clearly define what the NHS Care Record Service (NHS CRS) is. A virtual service offering views of the distributed records available for a patient would seem appropriate.
- Put implementation of the personal spine information system (PSIS) on hold.
- Consider developing the equivalent of the Scottish Emergency Care Summary. Gen-

eral practice systems could provide this on demand.

- The clinical professions, NHS management and informaticians should collaborate to provide clear and comprehensive guidance for all sectors on good informatics practices, such as record keeping and information management—clinical and other—and embed this in undergraduate and post-graduate training. The NHS should facilitate the take-up of this guidance.
- More appropriately skilled/qualified staff is likely to be needed. The approximate volumes need to be agreed, and their supply enabled. The process of professionalizing informatics staff should continue.
- Data quality is critical to reaping the benefits of the raised investment in IT. The improvement of general practice patient data across England has been the subject of work for some years. The same needs happen in all care sectors, including private and voluntary care providers, and to be extended to data other than patient data.

The lessons learned from Denmark are many and include:

- Support to adopt MedCom standards is paid for by counties. Project coordinators at hospitals involve staff in determining the data to be communicated electronically and develop new procedures for handling electronic messages. Data consultants, paid for by the counties, train physicians and their staff on how to use electronic communications. Physicians are paid to help hospitals communicate better with physician practices.
- Precise standards. MedCom did not just create standards; it worked with clinicians to define the precise content of the standards. This process, though time-consuming, resulted in more-accurate communications

and was critical in educating clinicians about the value of IT. Vendors are actively involved as well in setting standards.

- Peer pressure through public monitoring of participation. The MedCom Web site displayed a running total of electronic messages sent, participating counties and compliant vendors.
- Gradual approach with realistic time frames. There is an acceptance by all parties that the adoption of electronic communication takes many years and should not be rushed. Danes start simple and keep it as simple as possible. It is tempting to take on many projects at once, but increasing the level of complexity does not bring a corresponding increase in benefits.
- Financial incentives to physicians to adopt EMR systems. Physicians in Denmark are independent contractors who make independent decisions about IT. Physicians who adopted EMR systems and used the MedCom standards received faster reimbursement.
- Incentives to vendors. No one requires healthcare organizations to use a particular vendor. Counties encourage vendors to upgrade their applications to the MedCom standards by committing to purchase the upgraded applications.
- Culture of consensus. MedCom is funded by many different stakeholders and is viewed as an impartial organization. There is an appropriate balance between central coordination and local leadership
- Project-based approach. Approximately half of MedCom's budget is spent on permanent employees and overhead. The rest is devoted to projects. MedCom believes that this approach has given it more flexibility.
- The Danish Act on Processing of Personal Data (July 2000) was amended in 2004 to permit physicians to have access to medication data. Prior to the change, it was against the law to have access to medication profiles

without patients' consent. In terms of patient consent, the current legislation is based on an 'opt-in' model which means that the patient has to give his or her verbally or written consent to let a health professional have access to this/her data. Danish law forbids the interconnection of IT systems across sectors (e.g., health and taxation).

CONCLUSION

No healthcare jurisdiction, other than perhaps the Veteran's Administration in the United States, has achieved a fully automated, comprehensive EHR for its entire population. Hence there are no definitively proven strategies for problem-free implementation. However, a number of insights are beginning to emerge from the countries leading the way, including:

- The transition period is invariably difficult. The initial preferences of users (e.g., text-based rather than structured data entry) may change over time. Flexibility is therefore essential.
- Moving to an EHR in its fullest form is not just a technical innovation; it is a cultural transformation. Change management is vital, and failure to build in processes for effecting the transformation will reduce both uptake and impact. Providers and managers need to complete the transition from resistance to electronic information (historical position) to acceptance (current position) to addiction (cannot function without it).
- Implementation takes time, but can be accelerated once adoption and proven successes have reached a critical mass, or tipping point. At these stages, policy can drive faster change, for example, by making certain resources available only through electronic portals.

- The data elements are the core of any system, and spending time and resources on standardizing definitions and usage will go a long way toward creating information systems that yield valid and reliable measures of quality and performance.
- There will be far greater acceptance of provider-level information technology (IT) if workflow is modified accordingly to gain improvements.
- Creating secure networks for communicating information in any form has proven to be hugely appealing to providers in almost every country. E-mail use grows very rapidly and is an effective vehicle for introducing providers to the world of electronic information.
- It is very important to structure contracts so that risks are appropriately shared, and purchasers do not pay for systems that do not work. The National Health Service (NHS) in England has taken a firm stance, and while it incurred delays because it changed a principal vendor, it did not take a huge financial hit.
- Leadership at all levels—including the very top—is crucial. Clinician leadership is essential but cannot be effective in isolation.
- Helping family doctors use the data generated by the EHR to analyze and improve their own practices will increase uptake. In Denmark, the counties fund data consultants who visit each practice 1-2 times per year to troubleshoot and help produce usable quality-oriented information on treatment patterns, and so forth.
- If providers perceive "early wins" in the process, they will be more likely to invest their own money and agree to standards.
- Some strategies to enhance adoption among providers include clinical stories, peer-to-peer training, demonstration clinics, mentorship, and protected time.

As stated in the Infoway findings at Montebello, the EHR by itself cannot guarantee improved performance. The culture must also change, and all health system stakeholders, including users of services, must be inclined and trained to convert the potential of health information into concrete improvements in quality and efficiency. The benefits of the EHR grow over time as providers in particular exploit its potential to enhance communications, improve safety and quality by using decision support tools, expand the network of trusted colleagues, and generate valid performance measures and comparisons. In other words, however indifferent the initial reaction and despite the inevitable pain of the transition phase, over time the human and capital investment generates a high rate of return. No one ever goes back to paper world once exposed to an EHR.

FUTURE RESEARCH

A common frustration in all nations is determining the true cost of information technology in healthcare. One of the problems is that there is little consistency across healthcare organizations as to what is to be included in the IT domain—let alone the information management (IM) domain. As part of a course taught at the University of Victoria, 28 Canadian healthcare CIOs were interviewed and asked to describe the departments they were responsible for. The survey found that the CIOs were heading divisions that had 17 different names, with 'information management' leading the way—used in four sites. To say that our Canadian healthcare CIOs are responsible for a diverse set of departments would be an understatement. The areas of responsibility range from the usual IM&T areas to others areas such as networks, health records, decision support, telecommunications, biomedical engineering services, switchboard and information desk,

library services, privacy, and so forth. The areas that the CIOs were responsible for generated a list that was two pages long! Little wonder it is difficult to find a common set of measurements as what the IT investment really is.

The conundrum of measuring the IT function is that:

- Efficiency (doing things right) is easier to measure than effectiveness (doing the right things)
- Since effectiveness ("doing the right things") and innovation ("doing new things") can not be readily quantified in terms of traditional outputs, improvements are not usually reflected in economic efficiency statistics
- New systems are intended to change difficult to measure actions
- Strategic systems elude measurement
- Infrastructure investments cannot be cost justified on a ROI basis

As with any infrastructure, IT infrastructure does not provide direct business performance. Rather it enables other systems that do yield business benefits. ICT infrastructure is strikingly similar to other public infrastructures such as roads, hospitals, sewers, schools, etc. They are all long term and require large investments. They enable business activity by users that would otherwise not be economically feasible. They are difficult to cost-justify in advance as well as to show benefits in hindsight. They require a delicate investment balance—too little investment leads to duplication, incompatibility, and suboptimal use; while too much discourages user investment and involvement and may result in unused capacity.

Further research is required to determine whether or not ICT in healthcare, i.e. the EHR, is very much about infrastructure. If so, a new way of thinking of the investment and the return on investment is needed.

REFERENCES

Edwards, J. (2006). *Case study: Denmark's achievements with healthcare information exchange.* Gartner Industry Research.

Infoway. (2006). *Beyond good intentions: Accelerating the electronic health record in Canada.* Canada Health Infoway Montebello Policy Conference.

Johansen, I. (2006). *What makes a high performance health care system and how do we get there?* Paper presented at the Commonwealth Fund. Washington, DC.

Pascal, B. (2006). *Investment in health IT: Heading down the wrong road? HCIM&C, XV*(1), 6-7.

Protti, D.J., & Johansen, I. (2003). Further lessons from Denmark about computer systems in physician offices. *Electronic Healthcare,* 2(2), 36-43.

NHS. (2006*). The NHS in England: The operating framework for 2007/08. Guidance on preparation of local IM&T plans.* Department of Health.

Schoen, C., Osborn, R., Huynh, P. T., Doty, M., Peugh, J., & Zapert, K. (2006). On the front lines of primary care doctors office systems, experiences, and views in seven countries. *Health Affairs,* Web Exclusive, P. w555, 2.

ADDITIONAL READINGS

Adair, C., Simpson, E., & Casebeer, A. L. (2006). Performance measurement in healthcare. *Healthcare Policy,* 2(1)

Anderson, A., Vimarlund, V., Timpka, T. (2002). Management demands on information and communication technology in process-oriented healthcare organizations. *Journal of Management in Medicine,* 159-169.

Brigl, B., Ammenwerth, E., Dujat, C., Gräber, A., Große, A., Jostes, C., & Winter, A. (2005). Preparing strategic information management plans for hospitals: A practical guideline; SIM plans for hospitals: a guideline. *International Journal of Medical Informatics, 74*(1), 51-65.

Carr, N.G. (2003, May). IT doesn't matter. *Harvard Business Review, 81*(5), 41-49.

Clark, F.C., & Kimmerly, W. (2002). Strong IT governance: Don't even think about not doing it! *HIMSS Proceedings, Session 28.*

Dario, A, Giuse, K., & Kuhn, A. Health information system challenged: The Heidelberg conference and the future. *International Journal of Medical Informatics,* 105-114.

Deloitte. (2003). Clinical transformation: Cross-industry lessons for health care. Deloitte Research.

DIRAYA. (2006). Diraya—More than a medical record. Servizio Andaluz de Salud.

Dufner, D. et al. (2002). Can private sector strategic information systems planning techniques work for the public sector? *Communications of the Association for Information Systems, 8,* 413-431.

Edwards, J. (2006). Case study: Denmark's achievements with healthcare information exchange. Gartner Publications.

Feld, C.S., & Stoddard, D.B. (2004). Getting IT right. *Harvard Business Review, February.*

Gibson, M. (2007).Using technology to improve patient care—The POSP experience. ITCH 2007 Presentation. February.

Glaser, J. (2006). Information technology strategy: Three misconceptions. *Journal of Healthcare Information Management, 20*(4)

Grimson, J. (2001). Delivering the electronic healthcare record for the 21st century. *International Journal of Law and Medicine,* 111-127.

Gunasekaran, S., & Garets, D.E. (2003). Business value of IT: The strategic IM&T planning process. *Journal of Healthcare Information Management, 17*(1), 31.

Healthcare Information and Management Systems Society. (2000). The 11th Annual HIMSS Leadership Survey Sponsored by IBM: Trends in Healthcare Information and Technology Final Report. June 2000, [http://www2.himss. org/survey/2000/2000Final.pdf].

Leung, G, Yu, P., Wong, I., Johnston, J., & Tin, K. (2003). Incentives and barriers that influence clinical computerization on Hong Kong: A population-based physician survey. *Journal of the American Medical Informatics Association,* 201-211.

Luftman, J., et al. (1999). Enablers and inhibitors of business-IT alignment. *Communication for the Association of Information Systems, 1,* Article 11.

McAfee, A. (2006). Mastering the three worlds of information technology. *Harvard Business Review,* 141.

McConnell, H. (2004). International efforts in implementing national health information infrastructure and electronic health records (pp. 33-

40). UK: World Hospitals and Health Services, The Federation..

Protti, D. (2005). The benefits of a single 'national' health record has been demonstrated. http://www. npfit.nhs.uk/worldview/ March

Sanders, D. (2002). Designing, developing, and supporting an enterprise data warehouse (EDW) in healthcare. *Intermountain Healthcare.*

Rippen, J. (2003). Building support for heath information technologies. *Studies in health technology and informatics* (pp. 103-108). Netherlands: IOS Press.

Terry, N. (2004). Electronic health records: International structural and legal perspectives. *International Journal of Law and Medicine,* 26-39.

United States Government Accountability Office. (2004). HHS's efforts to promote health information technology and legal barriers to its adoption. Government Accountability Office, United States, pp.12. Retrieved August 13, 2004, from http:// www.gao.gov/new.items/d04991r.pdf

Wood, J., & Aceves, R. (2005). Five steps to electronic health record success. *Healthcare Financial Management,* 56-61.

Chapter XIII
Operationalizing the Science:
Integrating Clinical Informatics into the Daily Operations of the Medical Center

Joseph L. Kannry
Mount Sinai Medical Center, USA

ABSTRACT

Healthcare IT (HIT) has failed to live up to its promise in the United States. HIT solutions and decisions need to be evidence based and standardized. Interventional informatics is ideally positioned to provide evidence based and standardized solutions in the enterprise (aka, the medical center) which includes all or some combination of hospital(s), hospital based-practices, enterprise owned offsite medical practices, faculty practice and a medical school. For purposes of this chapter, interventional informatics is defined as applied medical or clinical informatics with an emphasis on an active interventional role in the enterprise. A department of interventional informatics, which integrates the science of informatics into daily operations, should become a standard part of any 21ˢᵗ century medical center in the United States. The objectives of this chapter are to: review and summarize the promise and challenge of IT in healthcare; define healthcare IT; review the legacy of IT in healthcare; compare and contrast IT in healthcare with that of other industries; become familiar with evidence based IT: Medical informatics; differentiate medical informatics from IT in healthcare; distinguish medical, clinical, and interventional informatics; justify the need for operational departments of interventional informatics.

Copyright © 2008, IGI Global, distributing in print or electronic forms without written permission of IGI Global is prohibited.

INTRODUCTION: THE PROMISE AND CHALLENGE OF INFORMATION TECHNOLOGY IN HEALTHCARE

The promise has always been that healthcare information technology (HIT) should be able to deliver rapid, relevant, and accurate information to clinical providers thereby providing greater efficiencies in patient care, facilitating excellence in patient care, and making improvements in patient safety possible (Bates & Gawande, 2003; Chaudhry et al., 2006; Millenson, 1997; Pizzi, 2007). Healthcare is an information intense industry (Stead, 1999) and by its very definition information technology "...specializes in the delivery and the management of information" (*IT Definition*, 2007). Not surprisingly HIT is frequently cited as the solution to all that ails healthcare (Coye, 2005; Institute of Medicine (U.S.) Committee on Improving the Patient Record, Dick, & Steen, 1991; Institute of Medicine (U.S.) Committee on Improving the Patient Record, Dick, Steen, & Detmer, 1997; Marchibroda & Gerber, 2003).

This belies a repeated inability of industry vendors to fully deliver on that promise as noted in a 1997 panel in Healthcare IT. In 1997 a panel of CEOs from Cerner, Eclipsys, HBOC and MedicaLogic noted only 60 percent of implementations of stable clinical products occurred on time and in budget, only 50 percent of available clinical function is used (Kuperman, Leavitt, McCall et al.,1997). There is general agreement that implementation problems stem from inability to integrate projects into existing workflow (Stead, 1999; Stead, Miller, Musen, & Hersh, 2000). This author and Ms. Kristin Myers have similarly noted that its process, people and workflow integration that are the key and not technology (Kannry, Mukani, & Myers, 2006; "Thinking About...Implementing the EMR," 2006).

At the same time there is general agreement that healthcare in the United States is in crisis whether it be due to the cost of healthcare, the lack of standardization and delivery of best practices, or issues of patient safety. Healthcare is an information intense domain (Kleinke, 2005) and clearly needs the efficiencies that IT can deliver. If information technology should be good at one task that task is managing information.

A frequent rejoinder by industry regarding the Internet around the turn of the century was that the Internet was providing information "just in time" which is defined as arriving just as needed (Strategos Inc.). For example, manufactured goods would arrive in the store based on information on sales, stock, and so on and thus reduce holding and storage costs (Wikipedia). In healthcare, where clinical information is a mission critical commodity, this could mean that when a test is ordered, the results of all previous tests of the same time are presented just in time to perhaps avoid re-ordering of the test. However, just in time information and applications never reached the shores of healthcare.

Few would disagree that IT in the rest of the world (ROW) seems to achieve efficiencies that HIT cannot. For purposes of this chapter, ROW is broadly defined as IT in any domain except healthcare meaning business, banking, industry, etc. A significant portion of this disparity between ROW IT and HIT can be traced to the beginning and evolution of healthcare IT. The earliest applications of information technology in healthcare were designed for support of financial transactions. In the later 1950s and early 1960s HIT began in earnest in response to a U.S. Government request to provide documentation for reimbursement. In the early 1990s, before the advent of managed care, sending just enough information to meet federal reimbursement requirements was good enough. Clinical information had little or no cost as tests could be re-ordered if lost or done at another center. Clinical applications such as computerized order entry, electronic medical records, and clinical repositories were just being developed and deployed with only one famous exception which dates back to the late 1970s TDS/Eclipsys 7000 (Bukunt, Hunter, Perkins et al., 2005).

Why is information technology so different in ROW when compared to HIT? There are several reasons: inherent mobility, multiple handoffs, data entry, security, information needs, information intensity and perhaps cost. Mobility is the rule and not the exception in the health care. Physicians, nurses, medical technicians (i.e., the workers) are, frequently mobile and untethered. Caring for patients requires healthcare professionals and employees to go to patients whether it is at the hospital bedside, in the nursing home, in the emergency room, and so forth. These settings of care have no formal fixed offices in which for example, physicians sit at desks all day. When physicians sit down to write a note in the hospital it is at a semi-public space in a healthcare setting. Even in the one setting which is most analogous to a business office, the private practitioner's office, the physician is only at any one location there for parts of each day. In contrast, ROW mobility is extremely desirable but most ROW employees are not mobile 95 percent of the time in contrast to physicians seeing patients, and so forth.

Particularly in academic centers, there are multiple handoffs regarding the same patient as teams of doctors' care for the patient. For example, patient Sally Smith is seen in the hospital by an attending physician Dr. Able, a resident Dr. Baker, and an intern Dr. Calloway. At night and weekends, each of these three doctors will have physician coverage. These multiple handoffs can and do cause medical errors (*Are handoffs too 'automatic'? QI experts fear errors could rise*, 2006; Gandhi, 2005; Greenberg et al., 2007; *JCAHO to look closely at patient handoffs*, 2006; Petersen, Orav, Teich et al., 1998; Streitenberger, Breen-Reid, & Harris, 2006) In contrast, in industry there are handoffs but not as frequently and not regarding information that is both complex and critical. SignOut is a process in which medical information is transferred each night regarding all patients, and it is difficult to find a comparable process in ROW. Anecdotally this author was once asked by Information Technology staff if they could use the (medical) SignOut System (Kan-

nry & Moore, 1999; Kushniruk, Karson, Moore, & Kannry, 2003) because there no software or analogous process for IT coverage at night and on weekends.

Entry of business data is another area of difference. In ROW business data entry usually involves the lowest paid and least skilled to entering business data. In contrast in healthcare IT the personnel entering clinical (i.e., the business of health care is patient (clinical) data) are among the healthcare field's most highly trained, skilled and paid personnel, the providers.

ROW information needs are role based, do not change often, and the characteristics of the data change even less. The chief executive officer (CEO), whose role is to run the company, is not going to need detailed information regarding elevator repair unless his business is elevator repair. The information needs of the CEO will not vary dramatically day-to-day so that one day the CEO needs the schedule of workers in the factory and the next day blueprints of the corporate office in Zurich, and on the next day information on corporate sanitation. Finally a CEO who measures corporate success will not measure profit and loss one day in dollars and cents and another day using shoe size.

In contrast, information needs in health care IT vary significantly by role, change often, and the characteristics of the data can vary significantly. For example, one physician may have many roles. A physician can be primarily responsible for the patient and require extensive information or consult on the patient requiring limited information set specific to the question being asked. The information needs change often as patients present with different diseases. What the physician needs to know about a patient with asthma and a patient with diarrhea are generally different.

Data characteristics vary widely by and within medical specialty and by patient. Medical specialties are subject domains that require and recognize specialized knowledge, diagnostic procedures, examinations, test interpretation, and therapeutic procedures including invasive procedures such as surgery. Examples of medical specialties include general medicine (entire adult patient), cardiology (heart), pulmonary (lung), obstetrics gynecology, general surgery, and so forth. For example, a general internist may deal with 17 different groupings of organ systems whereas a cardiologist may focus on one, the heart. The cardiologist though will want a great deal more information on the heart though than the internist. Within a specialty, a physician may have differing needs because of patients with different diseases. For example, a cardiologist may see one patient with congestive heart failure and need the echocardiogram and may see another patient who just suffered a heart attack and the physician needs to see the results of a cardiac catheterization.

Information intensity as defined by this author refers to that volume of information sent and received. The information intensity in ROW is relatively fixed with anecdotal reports of five to 30 data elements required per banking transactions. Contrast this with a portion of the data elements in HIT that may be contained in a routine progress note for a follow-up visit. The physical exam and review of systems which are only a part of the progress note alone may contain up to 34 elements with one to six pieces of data per element.

Finally, there are significant differences in cost between ROW IT and HIT. The total federal budget for IT is $66 billion in the 2008 proposed budget (Budget, 2007). In contrast, HIT costs are significantly higher. Ideally, there would be one national health information network (NHIN) in the United States so all relevant clinical information for any patient was available at any site of care (Stead, Kelly, & Kolodner, 2004; Walker et al., 2005; Yasnoff et al., 2004). In other words, the NHIN would be the realization of THE EMR defined by the Institute of Medicine over a decade ago. This definition says THE EMR is "all electronically stored information about individual's outpatient lifetime health status and health care" (Institute of Medicine (U.S.). Committee on Improving the Patient Record. et al., 1991; Institute of Medicine (U.S.). Committee on Improving the Patient Record.

et al., 1997). The estimated cost of a NHIN varies from $156 billion to $287 billion with maintenance from 16 billion to 48 billion per year (Hillestad et al., 2005; R. Kaushal et al., 2005; Walker et al., 2005). Savings range from $21 to $81 billion per year but depending on the analysis does not kick in until several years into the project (Hillestad et al., 2005; Walker et al., 2005).

However, an NHIN begs the question of connecting what to what. It is estimated that two thirds of the cost of the NHIN will be purchasing and implementing EMRs (Kaushal et al., 2005). Separate analyses, which looked at the cost of a nationwide implementation of EMR(s) without a nationwide network (i.e., no NHIN), estimated cost at $100 billion in the United States (Hillestad et al., 2005; Quinn, 2004). Hillestad et al. (2005). One of the $100 billion estimates assumed an existing EMR penetration of 20 percent before implementation which is either higher or lower than existing estimates of EMR penetration (Ash, Gorman, Seshadri, & Hersh, 2004; Bates, Ebell, Gotlieb et al., 2003; Kemper, Uren, & Clark, 2006; Miller & Sim, 2004; Simon et al., 2007) depending on definition of EMR (i.e., inpatient, outpatient or both), setting (i.e., individual office practices or large enterprises), medical specialty (e.g., pediatrics) or state (e.g., Massachusetts). It is beyond the scope of this chapter to determine whether estimated HIT costs are from years of under funded investments, the complexity described above, or combination of both. The author suspects both.

Despite differences in HIT and ROW described above, arguments continue to be made that that healthcare is as easy to automate as other industries such as finance (Walker, 2003). This needs to change.

MEDICAL INFORMATICS AND HIT: DEFINITIONS, MODELS, AND RELATIONSHIPS

One approach to improve the current state of affairs in healthcare information technology would be to employ the vast evidence based storehouse of medical informatics. The field of medical informatics can best be defined an interdisciplinary science of information management in support of patient care education, and research (Greenes & Shortliffe, 1990; Shortliffe, 2001). The medical informatics literature contains 30 plus years of scientific findings from numerous studies (Shortliffe, 2001).

How does medical informatics differ from healthcare information technology (HIT)? Unfortunately there is a great deal of confusion over the differences between the two domains with both terms being used mistakenly and interchangeably. Healthcare IT is a division of the business dedicated to deliver a service, while for information technology (*IT Definition*, 2007) the objective is to develop and maintain solutions for the enterprise. The enterprise for purposes of this paper is the (aka, the medical center) which includes all or some combination of hospital(s), hospital based-practices, enterprise owned offsite medical practices, faculty practice and a medical school. Directions are set by senior management, institutional funding, and some user input. User input is frequently used to reaffirm or support decisions that have already been made. In contrast the goal of informatics is to expand scientific frontiers and disseminate scientific knowledge. Directions are set by the state of research field, research interests, institutional and research funding and user experience/input. Frequently, health informaticists are practitioners and users as well.

Contrasting solution methodology also highlights the difference. HIT is a service that uses a methodology which centers around a business approach with standardized tools sets and proven solutions preferred. HIT may develop solutions internally when needed. In contrast informatics may play a service role but the informatics methodology is the scientific approach, builds what is needed, prefers cutting edge, and in some places develops solutions. The enterprise need for informatics research and innovation is quite high (Glaser, 2005). Evaluation methodology differs

in that HIT focuses on system performance, and overall user satisfaction with usage monitoring and interviews. As a result as projects are completed and users become accustomed to system, complaints become less focal and a form of silent dissatisfaction can develop (Kannry, 2007; Murff & Kannry, 2001). Post implementation there is less incentive to make changes as it requires going out to the users and asking what's wrong or in a sense looking for trouble. Additionally, there may be little budget especially if these changes require custom development work. In contrast, informatics uses scientific analysis, scientific instruments and looks at endpoints as improvements in healthcare. Informatics has actually lead the way at looking at issues that occur post implementation (Bates et al., 1999; Han et al., 2005; Horsky, Kuperman, & Patel, 2005; Hsieh, Gandhi, Seger et al., 2004; Kannry, 2007; Koppel et al., 2005). For example, Koppel's study of a CPOE (computerized physician order entry) system post implementation found that the system lead to decreased patient safety. Hsieh's study of drug allergy alerts in a CPOE system found that one in 20 overrides lead to and adverse drug event and that while the overrides were clinically justifiable, the alerts needed greater specificity to be effective. Murff and Kannry identified significant dissatisfaction among house staff after a CPOE implementation at one site and this dissatisfaction lead to a process to optimize the system in which over 200 changes were made (Kannry, 2007; Murff & Kannry, 2001).

There are many models of medical informatics and information technology partnerships ranging from an onsite physician champion to CMIOs (chief medical information officers) to divisions of informaticists and informaticist-CIOs (Gardner, Pryor, & Warner, 1999; Halamka, 2006; McDonald et al., 1999; Miller, Waitman, Chen, & Rosenbloom, 2005; Murray et al., 2003; Safran, Sands, & Rind, 1999; Slack & Bleich, 1999; Teich et al., 1999). This section will focus on models involving physicians.

The classic physician champion is a physician who serves as a vehicle of communication between IT and the physician community. If a system is implemented, it is the physician champion's job to champion the system to users and address their concerns. There is one problem, however, and that is the physician serves as advisor. There is no fiscal responsibility, limited authority over personnel and in some cases limited input on and control of strategy and direction.

The chief medical information officer (CMIO) CMIO is an executive position in which the physician champion is formally recognized and given responsibility to advice and on all clinical IT matters and at times makes final decisions. In a study of five CMIOs by Leviss et al. (Leviss, Kremsdorf, & Mohaideen, 2006) CMIOs have influence over policy making, served an advocacy role for important HIT initiatives, served as HIT consultant internally to their respective organizations and in some circumstances had limited budgetary authority. This is similar to the author's own experience and knowledge of similar positions. However, Leviss found the position to be one of a physician executive with informatics knowledge and not that of a "highly trained informaticist with secondary management expertise or support." In some organizations a new structure is emerging in which the informatics reports to the CMIO who reports to the CIO.

Unfortunately CIOs may not find CMIOs to be a valuable addition to the management team. A study by CHIMES (the College of Physician Health Executives) found that healthcare CIOs were either unsure of the need for a CMIO or were in no rush to hire one. The CHIMES survey found that 34 percent of respondent CIOs had a CMIO, a number essentially unchanged form 2002. However, 24 percent of CIOs stated that a CMIO was necessary but they did not have one and 23 percent of CMIOs stated that CMIOs are not necessary which means 47 percent. Of CIOs either did not have a CMIO nor wanted one. The author has no further information as CHIMES is a closed (members only organization) and did not publish the survey results. These findings are consistent with a survey reported by Leviss in which 23 percent of CIOs identified heavy involvement of physicians in clinical information systems.

Neither the Leviss nor the CHIME study identified CMIOs routinely having full budgetary authority over clinical IT, responsibility for setting strategic directions, personnel, authority to make decisions for all of clinical IT. This again is consistent with the authors experience (Leviss et al., 2006). The author would also note that CMIO is the one C (e.g., chief operating officer, chief financial officer, chief quality officer, and so on) that routinely reports to another C such as the CIO or CMO (chief medical officer).

Units, divisions and departments of medical informatics are frequently constructed as research entities which must seek their funding from external sources such as the National Institute of Health, National Library of Medicine, AHRQ, and so on (Cimino, 1999; Frisse, 1992; Murray et al., 2003; Talmon & Hasman, 2002). However, research entities whose research focused on applied medical informatics frequently found their innovations diffusing into and even leading clinical IT initiatives (Chessare & Torok, 1993; Gardner et al., 1999; Halamka, Osterland, & Safran, 1999; McDonald et al., 1999; Miller et al., 2005; Safran et al., 1999; Slack & Bleich, 1999). For example, research on CPOE lead to the development of institutional CPOE systems at Brigham and Womens, Beth Israel Boston, Intermountain Health System, Vanderbilt, and hospitals affiliated with Indianapolis University School of Medicine. In almost all of these examples, informatics worked closely with IT. In some of these examples, informatics successes lead to informatics either running clinical IT or all of clinical IT.

It should also be noted that the development work and lessons learned done at the informatics sites also lead to commercial partnerships with companies which wished to incorporate and build upon the innovation. Clinical decision support systems (CDSS) are computerized generation of patient-specific assessments or recommendations for clinicians (Hunt, Haynes, Hanna, & Smith, 1998; Randolph, Haynes, Wyatt et al., 1999). The CDSS developed at Brigham and Womens as part of their CPOE was licensed/purchased by Eclipsys. The work done at Intermountain Health Systems was licensed/purchased by 3M and transformed into a commercial portable data dictionary.

There are clear examples in which recognized informaticists are CIO. These examples include Vanderbilt, Beth Israel-Boston and Columbia (Cimino, 1999; Halamka et al., 2005; Miller et al., 2005). In the vast majority of these circumstances enterprise IT is part of larger informatics entity, informatics is integrated into daily operations, and there is a distinct academic unit if informatics.

For purposes of this chapter we will look at a case study from Mount Sinai Medical Center in NY, NY.

CLINICAL INFORMATICS AND MEDICAL INFORMATICS: A BRIEF WORD

For purposes of this chapter, the terms medical informatics and clinical informatics are used interchangeably. Clinical informatics is a part of the broader scientific field of medical informatics which includes both basic and applied science. Clinical informatics focuses on applied investigation and science (Shortliffe, 2001).

CASE STUDY OF THE RELATIONSHIP BETWEEN CLINICAL INFORMATICS AND HIT

At the time of this writing the division of clinical informatics is part of the information technology division and to date informatics personnel have been practicing physicians who have academic appointments. Mount Sinai Medical Center consists of The Mount Sinai Hospital 1,136-bed tertiary

care hospital, Mount Sinai Hospital of Western Queens, and the Mount Sinai School of Medicine. The Mount Sinai School of Medicine has one university affiliation, NYU (New York University). The Department of Information Technology serves the entire enterprise and informatics is division of IT. Informaticists were practicing physicians as practice provides credibility satisfaction and reality. Practice also gave the Informaticists the ability to relate problems and solutions to actually patient care experiences and was source of problem identification and problem solving. We will focus on examples of informatics work that partnered with IT but also employed cutting edge research or informatics knowledge, which in some cases lead to diffusion of innovation into operations. The examples will range the gamut from analysis to operational use.

An example of analysis would be the determination of the characteristics of the ideal notification device for healthcare. Numerous discussions and some experimentation with IT lead to the following list which actually ruled out the use of Blackberry as a notification device for housestaff. These characteristics are : rugged, cheap, rechargeable (since addressed by blackberry) but detachable power source, role based assignment to individual devices, confirmation of message delivered without reply, failure results in escalation algorithm on server, confirmation message, received/read, forwarding/rerouting, easy answer, loud (alarms), and integrates with existing paging system.

Over a decade ago this author identified a fundamental problem in the hospital where there was inconsistent identification of the attending of record (i.e., the physician primarily responsible for the patients care during their hospitalization). This observation lead to development of the SignOut System which was essentially a prototype application drafted into a production system (Kannry & Moore, 1999; Kushniruk et al., 2003; Moore & Kannry, 1997). A SignOut System allows housestaff (i.e., physician trainees such as residents and fellows) to generate patient lists and include information relevant to the on-call coverage team. Although two subsequent studies demonstrated that the SignOut had superior accuracy in identifying the attending of record as the information comes from the physicians, an operational decision was made not to use SignOut information to correct the attending of record in other hospital systems (Kannry & Moore, 1999). The SignOut system at Mount Sinai was subsequently redesigned in a partnership between informatics and IT as an enterprise IT system and critical source of clinical information (Kannry, Moore, & Karson, 2003; Kushniruk et al., 2003). An interesting anecdote was at one point someone in IT asked "Do we have to do this?" Two versions of this system are now in operation at two different medical centers that used to share one IT Department: Mount Sinai and NYU. At Mount Sinai there are over 700 users and an estimated 75 percent of all discharged patients pass through the SignOut system. The system is now considered a critical inpatient system at Mount Sinai.

The Signout System at Sinai was designed to also facilitate the creation and completion of Discharge Summaries. Informatics, anticipating the problems with continuity of care between inpatient and outpatient care developed interim discharge summaries (Kannry & Moore, 1999; Kannry et al., 2003; Moore & Kannry, 1997) developed interim discharge summaries. These summaries were designed to fill gaps between time of discharge and summary completion. The interim discharge summaries eventually lead to informatics development of institutionally approved and compliant discharge summaries. These summaries are now sent to the medical records where attendings can edit and electronically sign the summaries. The discharge summary functionality had been anticipated and built four years prior to a critical need. Most of the requirements for a full summary were already completed minus a few fields and the development of an interface to medical records. When the institution was faced with a costly and unwieldy manual program to solve the problem, informatics had a solution in hand and

was able to gain the support to operationalize the project. The discharge summary component of the SignOut System was so successful the SignOut System is now known as the SignOut and Discharge Summary System. Without the informatics solution, the institution might still be faced with significant issues regarding the timely completion of discharge summaries by housestaff.

However, partnership has its challenges. Informatics frequently faces the dilemma of not controlling budget resources, no to little direct control over and no ability to hire technical IT resources such as programmers, and, an uneven ability to introduce innovation into operations at Mount Sinai. This results in well received projects being aborted or not developed. One such instance is DocFind, an application that was designed to provide attending providers with easy to understand and accurate identification of patient specific housestaff coverage. This application was a prototype production system that was never further developed despite extensive use and very positive and vociferous user feedback.

Another example demonstrates informatics contribution from operations to operations. Operations had been fascinated by the use of RFID (Radio Frequency IDentification) tags which involves placing a tag on people and equipment that permits location tracking of people and supplies. Informatics knew from the literature that RFID was frequently an expensive technology that required significant infrastructure (i.e., wireless, robust networking) software etc. but with little scientific proof of efficacy in clinical settings. Informatics had observed that patient discharge would be an ideal to test small scale RFID and observes significant differences in time of discharge recorded versus RFID. Operations requested that the experimentation stop prematurely as the case had been made and that project planning begin immediately (Kannry, Emro, Blount, Ebling, & 2007).

Finally, application of informatics science into an operational process can be seen in selection and implementation of an EMR. The "Division

226

of Clinical Informatics had been following, analyzing, and reviewing the EMR literature for several years with particular focus on Ambulatory EMRs." Literature from several informatics research sites in regards to Ambulatory EMRs was cited including: Beth Israel-Boston OMAR (Hsieh, Gandhi et al., 2004; Rind & Safran, 1993; Safran et al., 1999; Sands, Libman, & Safran, 1995; Slack & Bleich, 1999), Brigham and Womens BICS and LMR (Poon et al., 2003; E. G. Poon, Wang, Gandhi, Bates, & Kuperman, 2003), Regenstrief (McDonald et al., 1999), Stanfords Pen and Ivory (Poon & Fagan, 1994; Poon, Fagan, & Shortliffe, 1996) and LDS' HELP (Gardner et al., 1999) and comprehensive analyses such as those written by Astrid M. van Ginneken (2002) and David Bates (Bates et al., 2003). A subsequent literature review was conducted to ensure being current state of knowledge as well as to answer any additional queries that occurred as the selection process evolved. Over 75 papers were identified that significantly shaped the selection process, resulted in identification of achievable goals, and created appropriate level of expectations breaking a 10 year paralysis on deciding to implement and select an ambulatory EMR (Kannry et al., 2006). One of the findings noted was the close partnership with the project manager IT) resulted in the success the combined the science and professional IT portions. Yet, there are challenges in the partnership as formal informatics analysis and research is unfunded mandate on the project.

RECOMMENDATION: OPERATIONAL DEPARTMENT OF CLINICAL INFORMATICS

For informatics to be effective and make a substantive contribution to the enterprise, there is a need to think differently about the role clinical informatics in medical center operations. Otherwise informatics methodology and results will never become a routine part of enterprise operations and decision making. The models previously described, while starting to become more commonplace, are unfortunately the exception and not the rule. Informatics needs to become an operational department in the enterprise.

One innovative model worth noting is the one at Partners in Boston. Dr. John Glaser, CIO at Partners describes a partnership between informatics and HIT in which .25 percent of the HIT budget (though not an insignificant amount in dollars) is spent on informatics to fund hardware, software, and time of existing personnel (Glaser, 2005). However, he notes and the author concurs that this is also partly the result of the culture at his institution, informatics personnel already in place or associated with the institution, and the long track record of informatics success at his institution including the building of the present and still in use CPOE system.

It this author's contention that clinical informatics needs to be a distinct operational department at each medical center. This department of informatics would have as its cornerstone the scientific knowledge and methodology unique to informatics and apply this science to operations of the medical center. The shape and scope of this department could take many forms depending on whether the department was designed to be an analysis and research department, research and development, or in charge of clinical information systems. The department could be responsible for conducting informatics research of value to operations such as the role of new technologies such as RFID, and questions about existing technologies such as effective use of clinical decision support in drug allergy checking. However, the department would need the authority, budget, and personnel to ensure diffusion of innovations and addressing questions as they arose during projects. The department could play a key or leading role in strategic decisions making about HIT as well as selection, implementation, and post implementation processes.

The greater the range and integration of informatics the greater the potential benefit to the enterprise. For example, informatics could analyze and assist in evaluation of utilization of clinical decision support. Yet, informatics might not be involved in the re-design of clinical decision support suggested by informatics findings. Such a structure would limit the utility and effectiveness of the science as the hypotheses can never be tested or implemented.

Unfortunately an operationally integrated informatics department is the exception and not the rule today. The majority of exceptions can be found in the discussion on models of informatics organization. Contributing to this state of affairs is little understanding from the multiple constituencies in need of informatics guidance whether it is in the form of research, application development, evaluation. As a result, many thoughtful articles have explored the need to define how informatics could be integrated into operation and real world HIT setting (Bakken, 2001; Glaser, 2005; Hersh, 2006; Lorenzi, Gardner, Pryor, & Stead, 1995; Stead, 1999; Stead & Lorenzi, 1999) and provide guidance on exactly what informatics does or why it is necessary at all. Comments from the IT, vendor and physician communities regarding informatics topics or participation range from "Doctors should do what they do best…doctoring, Doc….you can leave…..this is the IT portion of the presentation, informaticists are what I say they are, nobody here knows what informatics is and it would not get funding, we need to have the vendors socialize with the executives to demonstrate CPOE value, all I need to know about clinical decision support is in a book at home, and there is no informatics research budget for the EMR." It is this author's assertion that no constituency: physicians, IT, vendors etc is not in its own way contributing to the confusion over, the poor allocation of, or misuse of informatics in the enterprise.

Not so surprisingly penetration rates are low for electronic medical record (EMR) and computerized physician order entry (CPOE) (Ash, Gorman, & Hersh, 1998; Ash, Gorman et al., 2003; Ash et al., 2004; Bates et al., 2003; van Ginneken, 2002). CPOE is defined as the part of HIS (hospital information system) that handles the physician and nursing orders sent to the laboratory, radiology, pharmacy, and other ancillary departments (Bemmel, Musen, & Helder, 1997) and an EMR is defined as all electronically stored information about individual's outpatient lifetime health status and health care" (Institute of Medicine (U.S.). Committee on Improving the Patient Record. et al., 1991; Institute of Medicine (U.S.). Committee on Improving the Patient Record et al., 1997). It is this author's suspicion that the biggest barrier to diffusion is not cost but qualified people. There is a shortage of qualified informaticists with the expertise to make the case, demonstrate success, and identify post implementation problems (AMIA, 2006). For example, this author has previously stated that the errors identified by Koppel (Koppel et al., 2005) could have been preventable with a process called optimization (Kannry, 2007). Yet, despite the informaticist shortage, there are proposals to fund nationwide implementation of EMRs and the NHIN for hundreds of billions of dollars with no linkage to increasing the number of informaticists and operational departments of informatics.

The recommendation for an operational informatics department at each medical center assumes that there is an affiliation with an academic unit or department or the group. It is beyond the scope of this chapter to discuss possible relationships between such groups as this would require an extensive discussion of the organization and function of academically housed informatics groups. However, it should be noted that the cross fertilization of personnel and research between two groups would benefit the academic as well as the operational group.

The need for operational departments of clinical informatics only grows with each passing day while at the same time there is a continually worsening shortage of informaticists (AMIA, 2006). It is the author's belief that government and market forces would lessen this shortage if there was a place for these newly trained personnel to go to; an operational department of informatics.

A BRIEF WORD ABOUT CLINICAL AND INTERVENTIONAL INFORMATICS

The author would like to formally introduce the term Interventional informatics which is a term suggested to him by Dr. Charles Safran. While interventional and clinical informatics are essentially one and the same, Interventional informatics emphasizes that informatics is an active part of the enterprise that both informs and intervenes ultimately changing the enterprise for the better.

SUMMARY

In summary, healthcare is an information intense field. Yet HIT which should be able to go a long way in addressing information management which is under funded with reports of three to five percent of budget spending on IT compared to industry (ROW) rates of at least 5-10 percent (Andriole, 2005; Presidential Advisory Commission on Consumer Protection and Quality in Health Care Industry, 1998). One article notes that any company that funds investment in IT at a four percent or lower rate essentially views IT as a service and cost leader and not a source of innovation and transformation (Andriole, 2005). In a financially strapped environment with insufficient budget there is very little margin for error and repetition of mistakes and in particular the NIH/NDH (not invented here/not done here) syndrome. In this syndrome mistakes are repeated because the organization has never experienced the mistakes firsthand.

The solution to avoid mistakes in, leverage resources for, and bring innovation on demand to HIT is to create an operational department of interventional informatics. Such a department should be a standard operational department at each medical center much the way there are departments of medical records, compliance, risk management, quality improvement/assurance,

and so forth. Interventional informaticists who work in such a department should be a cadre of EMPOWERED and formally trained experts capable of analysis, development, implementation, and evaluation with an ability to know when to use standardized tools sets architectures.

HIT needs to become like the rest of healthcare; that is, scientifically grounded and evidence based. An operational department of intervention informatics with budgetary authority, personnel, and institutional responsibility would be a very important step in bridging the evidence gap between HIT and the rest of health care. Every medical center in the 21st century should have an operational department of interventional informatics.

FUTURE RESEARCH DIRECTIONS

Recent extramural funding for studies in clinical informatics has significantly decreased from its heyday of the mid-late 80s and 90s. Yet there is a growing need for clinical informatics research particularly regarding clinical information systems. This need is especially acute at the operational level as questions are asked on a daily basis that the informatics literature has yet to fully explore and in some instances answer. For instance it is difficult to find qualitative let alone quantitative studies on a fundamental operational topic such as enterprise master patient index (EMPI) (Arellano & Weber, 1998; Lenson, 1998; Mercer, Widmer, Prada, Grogan, & Tresnan, 1995; Mills, 2006). The EMPI assures that every patient has one medical record number irrespective of the number of registration systems any one medical center or integrated health delivery systems (e.g., multiple hospitals) might have. Studies of EMPI need to quantitate before and after states, impact on workflow, and so forth. Research on EMPI might give insight into the challenges of creating inter-institutional and national patient identifiers which will require the merging of multiple medical record numbers (Arellano & Weber, 1998; Mills, 2006).

Many of the lessons and benefits demonstrated by 30 years of informatics studies have yet to be replicated in commercial systems. At the same time there has been an increasing number of studies demonstrating either harm or no benefit from clinical information systems and in particular commercial CPOE and EMR systems (Gesteland, Nebeker, & Gardner, 2006; Han et al., 2005; Horsky et al., 2005; Koppel et al., 2005; Murray et al., 2004; Potts, Barr, Gregory, Wright, & Patel, 2004). Research is needed to further examine which lessons learned can be extrapolated to commercial systems as well as what factors affect replication of benefits.

Even informatics developed systems have not been immune to studies demonstrating adverse events caused by CPOE and EMR systems (Gesteland, Nebeker, & prokosch, 2006; Hsieh, Kuperman, Jaggi et al., 2004; Nebeker, Hoffman, Weir et al., 2005). This raises some broader questions regarding unintended consequences of CPOE and EMR systems.

Previous studies demonstrating the benefits of EMR have recently been called into question. Two newly published studies looking at ambulatory EMRs, found that EMRs were neither associated with improvements in care quality, enhancements in patient safety nor reductions in cost of care (Eslami, Abu-Hanna, & de Keizer, 2007; Linder, Ma, Bates, Middleton, & Stafford, 2007; Welch et al., 2007). Further research is clearly needed for both informatics and commercial systems to explore what factors lead to successful implementation and realization of benefits in clinical information systems and particularly those systems with clinical decision support systems (CDSS).

Future studies would benefit greatly from the participation of multiple sites in the same study. There is a need to be able to eliminate variables and control for factors by studying the same aspect of the same system whether it be the VA's Vista System (Brown, Lincoln, Groen, & Kolodner, 2003) or the same commercial system and studies conducted at multiple sites would address that need. Such studies might be able to highlight organizational factors such as culture, leadership etc that affect

implementations for the better or worse (Ash, Stavri, & Kuperman, 2003). One such attempt to study one system at multiple sites found differences in user satisfaction with the same version of the same CPOE system in the same specialty at two different sites (Kannry, 2007). The differences in satisfaction were attributable to differences in the functionality used (i.e., at one site physicians directly placed orders while at the other site clerks placed orders for physicians) though the study could not rule out other external factors as well. There is also need to compare implementations and outcomes within an institution to identify intra-institutional factors such as the study that looked at two practices with the same EMR (O'Connell, Cho, Shah et al., 2004).

Operationally, informatics is faced with a plethora of questions regarding implementation process and decision making as well as training. There are few investigations that focus on training of users and particularly one of the largest segments of users, housestaff (Aaronson, Murphy-Cullen, Chop, & Frey, 2001; Chessare & Torok, 1993; Gamm, Barsukiewicz, Dansky, & Vasey, 1998; Hier, Rothschild, LeMaistre, & Keeler, 2005; Keenan, Nguyen, & Srinivasan, 2006; Retchin & Wenzel, 1999; Swanson et al., 1997).

While a great deal of thought has been given and published on lessons learned and requirements for successful implementation and potential factors, there is limited research on the implementation process itself. Further research is needed to create a framework for laying out step to a successful implementation and the relative contributions of those steps to successful outcome.

There is little in the way of systematic analysis or studies of ROI (return on investment) on enterprise clinical information system (Frisse, 2006; Grieger, Cohen, & Krusch, 2007; Kaushal et al., 2006; Miller, West, Brown et al., 2005; Piasecki et al., 2005; Wang et al., 2003; Welch et al., 2007; Zaroukian & Sierra, 2006). Studies need to place greater emphasis on revenue enhancement as opposed to cost avoidance. Revenue enhancement looks at real dollars while cost avoidance estimates dollars that would have been lost or spent but may not have been.

Two examples are illustrative of the need for further research on the ROI of enterprise clinical information systems. Avoidance of medical errors may save millions but that does not translate to millions actually saved (Kannry, 2007). Prior studies of the ROI for ambulatory EMRs attribute significant savings to reduced chart pulls, eliminating the chart filing (i.e., medical records room), and reducing or eliminating medical records personnel. Chart pulls are defined as pulling the chart for each patient visit and the cost of chart pulls is frequently estimated as the cost of personnel and the amount of time spent on pulling the chart. These cost savings may be true for individual or small to medium size practices but do not seem applicable at the enterprise level where such savings are a negligible portion of the millions allocated for the EMR and personnel reduction/elimination does not occur as readily. In the authors' experience at the enterprise level reducing chart pulls and eliminating the chart filing room do not contribute to significant savings and reducing/eliminating personnel is difficult. If anything the medical records personnel whose previous responsibilities were to file and pull charts need to be re-deployed to scanning the many paper documents still produced. For example, private consultants may send patients to the medical center and these consults need to be scanned into the EMR. For example, research consents may need to be scanned into the chart. The fully paperless office is along ways away from reality. Preliminary analysis by the author of ROI for an Ambulatory EMR at a large academic medical center, found revenue enhancements that neither depends on chart pulls, personnel reductions, or elimination of chart filing rooms.

Significant challenges and questions remain regarding the link between clinical information systems and clinical research systems (Boers, van der Linden, & Hasman, 2002; Embi, Jain, Clark, & Harris, 2005; Gerdsen, Mueller, Jablonski, & Prokosch, 2005; Goldstein et al., 2004; Green, White, Barry et al., 2005; Hanzlicek, Zvarova,

& Dostal, 2006; Platt, 2007; Powell & Buchan, 2005; Tilghman, Tilghman, & Johnson, 2006). For example, EMRs do not easily, if at all, link to clinical research systems (Sim, Olasov, & Carini, 2003; Sim, Owens, Lavori, & Rennels, 2000; Sim, Wyatt, Musen, & Niland, 1999). More studies need to be done to better identify problems with and solutions for linking commercial clinical information systems and commercial (research) trial management systems.

Subject accrual (i.e., the recruitment and enrollment of human subjects) in clinical trials is critical to the success of clinical trials and there are only a handful of studies looking at using EMR for subject accrual (Embi et al., 2005; Embi et al., 2005). Much work still needs to be done creating and testing portable models for subject accrual that can be used in any commercial EMR.

Translational research is research that "the clinical application of scientific medical research, from the lab to the bedside" (USC/Norris Comphrehensive Cancer Center, 2007). Clinical application of scientific research will require linking discoveries to the bedside through the use of clinical information systems. For example, a new study linking treatment of disease y to gene x would ideally require alerting the physician to the fact that disease y and gene y have a relationship, obtaining a genetic sample from the patient, sending the findings back to the physician and recommending treatment based on the genetic analysis. Translational research would benefit from research on how best to use and link to clinical information systems (Martin-Sanchez, Maojo, & Lopez-Campos, 2002).

It is difficult to find peer reviewed studies that specifically examine patient satisfaction with physician use of enterprise EMRs, yet, this is of vital interest to operations (Gadd & Penrod, 2000; Garrison, Bernard, & Rasmussen, 2002; Legler & Oates, 1993; Rouf, Whittle, Lu, & Schwartz, 2007; Solomon & Dechter, 1995). If investigations could demonstrate increased patient satisfaction with physician use of EMRs, institutions with EMRs could potentially differentiate their delivery of patient care in competitive markets.

However, investigations are first needed to identify which aspects of physician use of EMRs translate into in increased patient satisfaction. For example, are patients happier with physicians who use EMRs because physicians always have the patient's chart, now possess comprehensive knowledge of their illnesses and medications, get test results quicker, spend more time on them as opposed to hunting for documentation etc.

Finally, there is a need to study the role and impact of clinical informatics itself on operational processes. Specifically, what role does clinical informatics have in the success and failure of clinical information systems? Is there any relationship between organizational success with HIT and informatics? There are tantalizing hints (O'Connell et al., 2004) though anything conclusive has yet to be proven. The effect of informatics itself has yet to be the focus of investigation and definitive studies have yet to be done.

REFERENCES

Aaronson, J. W., Murphy-Cullen, C. L., Chop, W. M., & Frey, R. D. (2001). Electronic medical records: the family practice resident perspective. *Fam Med, 33*(2), 128-132.

AMIA, A. A. (2006). *Building the work force for health information transformation.*

Andriole, S. (2005). *10 questions you should be able to answer.* Retrieved January 20, 2007, from http://itmanagement.earthweb.com/columns/bizalign/article.php/3574421

Are handoffs too 'automatic'? QI experts fear errors could rise. (2006). *Healthcare Benchmarks Qual Improv, 13*(1), 1-4.

Arellano, M. G., & Weber, G. I. (1998). Issues in identification and linkage of patient records across an integrated delivery system. *Journal of Healthcare Information Management, 12*(3), 43-52.

Ash, J. S., Gorman, P. N., & Hersh, W. R. (1998). Physician order entry in U.S. hospitals. *Proceedings of AMIA Symp*, 235-239.

Ash, J. S., Gorman, P. N., Lavelle, M., Payne, T. H., Massaro, T. A., Frantz, G. L., et al. (2003). A cross-site qualitative study of physician order entry. *Journal of American Medical Information Association, 10*(2), 188-200.

Ash, J. S., Gorman, P. N., Seshadri, V., & Hersh, W. R. (2004). Computerized physician order entry in U.S. hospitals: results of a 2002 survey. *Journal of American Medical Information Association, 11*(2), 95-99.

Ash, J. S., Stavri, P. Z., & Kuperman, G. J. (2003). A consensus statement on considerations for a successful CPOE implementation. *Journal of American Medical Information Association, 10*(3), 229-234.

Bakken, S. (2001). An informatics infrastructure is essential for evidence-based practice. *Journal of American Medical Information Association, 8*(3), 199-201.

Bates, D. W., Ebell, M., Gotlieb, E., Zapp, J., & Mullins, H. C. (2003). A proposal for electronic medical records in U.S. primary care. *Journal of American Medical Information Association, 10*(1), 1-10.

Bates, D. W., & Gawande, A. A. (2003). Improving safety with information technology. *New England Journal of Medicine, 348*(25), 2526-2534.

Bates, D. W., Teich, J. M., Lee, J., Seger, D., Kuperman, G. J., Ma'Luf, N., et al. (1999). The impact of computerized physician order entry on medication error prevention. *Journal of American Medical Information Association, 6*(4), 313-321.

Bemmel, J. H. V., Musen, M. A., & Helder, J. C. (1997). *Handbook of medical informatics.* AW Houten, Netherlands; Heidelberg, Germany: Bohn Stafleu Van Loghum; Springer Verlag.

Boers, G., van der Linden, H., & Hasman, A. (2002). A distributed architecture for medical research.

Stud Health Technol Inform, 90, 734-738.

Brown, S. H., Lincoln, M. J., Groen, P. J., & Kolodner, R. M. (2003). VistA—U.S. Department of Veterans Affairs national-scale HIS. *International Journal of Medicine Information, 69*(2-3), 135-156.

Bukunt, S., Hunter, C., Perkins, S., Russell, D., & Domanico, L. (2005). El Camino Hospital: using health information technology to promote patient safety. *Jt Comm J Qual Patient Saf, 31*(10), 561-565.

Chaudhry, B., Wang, J., Wu, S., Maglione, M., Mojica, W., Roth, E. et al. (2006). Systematic review: Impact of health information technology on quality, efficiency, and costs of medical care. *Ann Intern Med, 144*: E-12-E22.

Chessare, J. B., & Torok, K. E. (1993). Implementation of COSTAR in an academic group practice of general pediatrics. *MD Comput, 10*(1), 23-27.

Cimino, J. J. (1999). The Columbia medical informatics story: From clinical system to major department. *MD Comput, 16*(2), 31-34.

Coye, M. J. (2005). No more procrastinating. Industry must eschew excuses and move fast on electronic health records. *Mod Healthc, 35*(7), 32.

Embi, P. J., Jain, A., Clark, J., Bizjack, S., Hornung, R., & Harris, C. M. (2005). Effect of a clinical trial alert system on physician participation in trial recruitment. *Arch Intern Med, 165*(19), 2272-2277.

Embi, P. J., Jain, A., Clark, J., & Harris, C. M. (2005). Development of an electronic health record-based Clinical Trial Alert system to enhance recruitment at the point of care. *AMIA Annu Symp Proceedings* (pp. 231-235).

Eslami, S., Abu-Hanna, A., & de Keizer, N. F. (2007). Evaluation of outpatient computerized physician medication order entry systems: A systematic review. *J Am Med Inform Assoc, 14*(4), 400-406.

Frisse, M. E. (1992). Medical informatics in academic health science centers. *Acad Med, 67*(4), 238-241.

Frisse, M. E. (2006). Comments on Return on Investment (ROI) as it applies to clinical systems. *Journal of American Medical Information Association*, M2072.

Gadd, C. S., & Penrod, L. E. (2000). Dichotomy between physicians' and patients' attitudes regarding EMR use during outpatient encounters. *Proceedings of AMIA Symp* (pp. 275-279).

Gamm, L. D., Barsukiewicz, C. K., Dansky, K. H., & Vasey, J. J. (1998). Investigating changes in end-user satisfaction with installation of an electronic medical record in ambulatory care settings. *Journal of Healthcare Information Management, 12*(4), 53-65.

Gandhi, T. K. (2005). Fumbled handoffs: one dropped ball after another. *Ann Intern Med, 142*(5), 352-358.

Gardner, R. M., Pryor, T. A., & Warner, H. R. (1999). The HELP hospital information system: Update 1998. *International Journal of Medicin Information, 54*(3), 169-182.

Garrison, G. M., Bernard, M. E., & Rasmussen, N. H. (2002). 21st-century health care: The effect of computer use by physicians on patient satisfaction at a family medicine clinic. *Fam Med, 34*(5), 362-368.

Gerdsen, F., Mueller, S., Jablonski, S., & Prokosch, H. U. (2005). Standardized exchange of medical data between a research database, an electronic patient record and an electronic health record using CDA/SCIPHOX. *AMIA Annu Symp Proc*, 963.

Gesteland, P. H., Nebeker, J. R., & Gardner, R. M. (2006). These are the technologies that try men's souls: common-sense health information technology. *Pediatrics, 117*(1), 216-217.

Glaser, J. P. (2005). Facilitating applied information technology research. *Journal of Healthcare Information Management, 19*(1), 45-53.

Goldstein, M. K., Coleman, R. W., Tu, S. W., Shankar, R. D., O'Connor, M. J., Musen, M. A., et al. (2004). Translating research into practice: organizational issues in implementing automated decision support for hypertension in three medical centers. *Journal of American Medical Information Association, 11*(5), 368-376.

Green, L. A., White, L. L., Barry, H. C., Nease, D. E., Jr., & Hudson, B. L. (2005). Infrastructure requirements for practice-based research networks. *Ann Fam Med, 3 Suppl 1,* S5-11.

Greenberg, C. C., Regenbogen, S. E., Studdert, D. M., Lipsitz, S. R., Rogers, S. O., Zinner, M. J. et al. (2007). Patterns of communication breakdowns resulting in injury to surgical patients. *Journal Am Coll Surg, 204*(4), 533-540.

Greenes, R. A., & Shortliffe, E. H. (1990). Medical informatics: An rmerging academic fiscipline and institutional policy. *JAMA, 263*(8), 1114-1120.

Grieger, D. L., Cohen, S. H., & Krusch, D. A. (2007). A pilot study to document the return on investment for implementing an ambulatory electronic health record at an academic medical center. *Journal of the American College of Surgeons, 205*(1), 89-96.

Halamka, J. (2006). Early experiences with e-prescribing. *Journal of Healthcare Information Management, 20*(2), 12-14.

Halamka, J., Overhage, J. M., Ricciardi, L., Rishel, W., Shirky, C., & Diamond, C. (2005). Exchanging health information: Local distribution, national coordination. *Health Aff (Millwood), 24*(5), 1170-1179.

Halamka, J. D., Osterland, C., & Safran, C. (1999). CareWeb, a web-based medical record for an integrated health care delivery system. *International Journal of Medicine Information, 54*(1), 1-8.

Han, Y. Y., Carcillo, J. A., Venkataraman, S. T., Clark, R. S., Watson, R. S., Nguyen, T. C. et al. (2005). Unexpected increased mortality after implementation of a commercially sold computerized physician order entry system. *Pediatrics, 116*(6), 1506-1512.

Hanzlicek, P., Zvarova, J., & Dostal, C. (2006). Information technology in clinical research in rheumatology domain. *Stud Health Technol Inform, 124,* 187-192.

Hersh, W. (2006). Who are the informaticians? What we know and should know. *Journal of American Medical Information Association, 13*(2), 166-170.

Hier, D. B., Rothschild, A., LeMaistre, A., & Keeler, J. (2005). Differing faculty and housestaff acceptance of an electronic health record. *International Journal of Medicine Information, 74*(7-8), 657-662.

Hillestad, R., Bigelow, J., Bower, A., Girosi, F., Meili, R., Scoville, R. et al. (2005). Can electronic medical record systems transform health care? Potential health benefits, savings, and costs. *Health Aff (Millwood), 24*(5), 1103-1117.

Horsky, J., Kuperman, G. J., & Patel, V. L. (2005). Comprehensive analysis of a medication dosing error related to CPOE. *Journal of American Medical Information Association, 12*(4), 377-382.

Hsieh, T. C., Gandhi, T. K., Seger, A. C., Overhage, J. M., Murray, M. D., Hope, C. et al. (2004). Identification of adverse drug events in the outpatient setting using a computerized, text-searching monitor. *Medinfo, 2004*(CD), 1651.

Hsieh, T. C., Kuperman, G. J., Jaggi, T., Hojnowski-Diaz, P., Fiskio, J., Williams, D. H. et al. (2004). Characteristics and consequences of drug allergy alert overrides in a computerized physician order entry system. *Journal of American Medical Information Association, 11*(6), 482-491.

Hunt, D. L., Haynes, R. B., Hanna, S. E., & Smith, K. (1998). Effects of computer-based clinical decision support systems on physician performance and patient outcomes: A systematic review [see comments]. *Jama, 280*(15), 1339-1346.

Institute of Medicine (U.S.). Committee on Improving the Patient Record., Dick, R. S., & Steen, E. B. (1991). *The computer-based patient record: an essential technology for health care.* Washington, D.C.: National Academy Press.

Institute of Medicine (U.S.). Committee on Improving the Patient Record., Dick, R. S., Steen, E. B., & Detmer, D. E. (1997). *The computer-based patient record : An essential technology for health care* (Rev. ed.). Washington, DC: National Academy Press.

IT Definition. (2007). Retrieved January 15, 2007, from http://www.webopedia.com/TERM/I/IT.html

JCAHO to look closely at patient handoffs. (2006). *Hosp Case Manag, 14*(1), 9-10.

Kannry, J. (2007). CPOE and patient safety: Panacea or pandora's box? In K. Ong (Ed.), *Medical informatics: An executive primer.* Chicago: HIMSS.

Kannry, J., Emro, S., Blount, M., Elbing, M., & (2007). *Small-scale testing of RFID in a hospital setting: RFID as bed trigger.* Paper presented at the AMIA Fall Symposium 2007, Chicago, Ill.

Kannry, J., & Moore, C. (1999). MediSign: using a web-based SignOut system to improve provider identification. *Proceedings AMIA Symp,* 550-554.

Kannry, J., Moore, C., & Karson, T. (2003). Discharge communique: Use of a workflow byproduct to generate an interim discharge summary. *AMIA Annu Symp Proc,* 341-345.

Kannry, J., Mukani, S., & Myers, K. (2006). Using an evidence-based approach for system selection at a large academic medical center: lessons learned in selecting an ambulatory EMR at Mount Sinai Hospital. *Journal of Healthcare Information Management, 20*(2), 84-99.

Kaushal, R., Blumenthal, D., Poon, E. G., Jha, A. K., Franz, C., Middleton, B. et al. (2005). The costs of a national health information network. *Ann Intern Med, 143*(3), 165-173.

Kaushal, R., Jha, A. K., Franz, C., Glaser, J., Shetty, K. D., Jaggi, T. et al. (2006). Return on investment for a computerized physician order entry system 10.1197/jamia.M1984. *Journal of American Medical Information Association, 13*(3), 261-266.

Keenan, C. R., Nguyen, H. H., & Srinivasan, M. (2006). Electronic medical records and their impact on resident and medical student education. *Acad Psychiatry, 30*(6), 522-527.

Kemper, A. R., Uren, R. L., & Clark, S. J. (2006). Adoption of electronic health records in primary care pediatric practices. *Pediatrics, 118*(1), e20-24.

Kleinke, J. D. (2005). Dot-gov: Market failure and the creation of a national health information technology system. *Health Aff (Millwood), 24*(5), 1246-1262.

Koppel, R., Metlay, J. P., Cohen, A., Abaluck, B., Localio, A. R., Kimmel, S. E. et al. (2005). Role of computerized physician order entry systems in facilitating medication errors. *Jama, 293*(10), 1197-1203.

Kuperman, G. J., Leavitt, M. K., McCall, C. W., Patterson, N. L., & Wilson, H. J. (1997). *Panel: Integrating informatics into the product: The CEO's perspective.* Paper presented at the 1997 AMIA Annual Fall Symposium, Nashville, TN.

Kushniruk, A., Karson, T., Moore, C., & Kannry, J. (2003). From prototype to production system: lessons learned from the evolution of the SignOut System at Mount Sinai Medical Center. *AMIA Annu Symp Proceedings,* 381-385.

Legler, J. D., & Oates, R. (1993). Patients' reactions to physician use of a computerized medical record system during clinical encounters. *J Fam Pract, 37*(3), 241-244.

Leviss, J., Kremsdorf, R., & Mohaideen, M. F. (2006). The CMIO—A new leader for health systems. *Journal of American Medical Information Association, 13*(5), 573-578.

Linder, J. A., Ma, J., Bates, D. W., Middleton, B., & Stafford, R. S. (2007). Electronic health record use and the quality of ambulatory care in the United States. *Arch Intern Med, 167*(13), 1400-1405.

Lorenzi, N. M., Gardner, R. M., Pryor, T. A., & Stead, W. W. (1995). Medical informatics: The key to an organization's place in the new health care environment. *J Am Med Inform Assoc, 2*(6), 391-392.

Marchibroda, J. M., & Gerber, T. (2003). Information infrastructure promises. Better healthcare, lower costs. *J Ahima, 74*(1), 28-32; quiz 33-24.

Martin-Sanchez, F., Maojo, V., & Lopez-Campos, G. (2002). Integrating genomics into health information systems. *Methods Inf Med, 41*(1), 25-30.

McDonald, C. J., Overhage, J. M., Tierney, W. M., Dexter, P. R., Martin, D. K., Suico, J. G. et al. (1999). The Regenstrief Medical Record System: a quarter century experience. *International Journal of Medicine Information, 54*(3), 225-253.

Millenson, M. L. (1997). *Demanding medical excellence: doctors and accountability in the information age: With a new afterword* (Pbk. ed.). Chicago: University of Chicago Press.

Miller, R. A., Waitman, L. R., Chen, S., & Rosenbloom, S. T. (2005). The anatomy of decision support during inpatient care provider order entry (CPOE): Empirical observations from a decade of CPOE experience at Vanderbilt. *J Biomed Inform, 38*(6), 469-485.

Miller, R. H., & Sim, I. (2004). Physicians' use of electronic medical records: Barriers and solutions. *Health Aff, 23*(2), 116-126.

Miller, R. H., West, C., Brown, T. M., Sim, I., & Ganchoff, C. (2005). The value of electronic health records in solo or small group practices. *Health Aff (Millwood), 24*(5), 1127-1137.

Moore, C., & Kannry, J. (1997). *Improving continuity of care using a web based signout and discharge.* Paper presented at the 1997 Annual Fall AMIA Symposium, Nashville, TN.

Murff, H. J., & Kannry, J. (2001). Physician satisfaction with two order entry systems. *Journal of American Medical Information Association, 8*(5), 499-509.

Murray, M. D., Harris, L. E., Overhage, J. M., Zhou, X. H., Eckert, G. J., Smith, F. E. et al. (2004). Failure of computerized treatment suggestions to improve health outcomes of outpatients with uncomplicated hypertension: Results of a randomized controlled trial. *Pharmacotherapy, 24*(3), 324-337.

Murray, M. D., Smith, F. E., Fox, J., Teal, E. Y., Kesterson, J. G., Stiffler, T. A. et al. (2003). Structure, functions, and activities of a research support informatics section. *Journal of American Medical Information Association, 10*(4), 389-398.

Nebeker, J. R., Hoffman, J. M., Weir, C. R., Bennett, C. L., & Hurdle, J. F. (2005). High rates of adverse drug events in a highly computerized hospital. *Arch Intern Med, 165*(10), 1111-1116.

O'Connell, R. T., Cho, C., Shah, N., Brown, K., & Shiffman, R. N. (2004). Take note(s): Differential EHR satisfaction with two implementations under one roof. *Journal of American Medical Information Association, 11*(1), 43-49.

Office of Management and Budget. (2007). *Budget of the United States Government Fiscal Year 2008.* Retrieved July 27, 2007, 2007, from http://www.whitehouse.gov/omb/budget/

Petersen, L. A., Orav, E. J., Teich, J. M., O'Neil, A. C., & Brennan, T. A. (1998). Using a computerized sign-out program to improve continuity of inpatient care and prevent adverse events. *Jt Comm J Qual Improv, 24*(2), 77-87.

Piasecki, J. K., Calhoun, E., Engelberg, J., Rice, W., Dilts, D., Belser, D. et al. (2005). Computerized provider order entry in the emergency department: pilot evaluation of a return on investment analysis instrument. *AMIA Annu Symp Proceedings*, 1081.

Pizzi, R. (2007). Healthcare IT a key aspect of physicians' reform principles. Retrieved Janaury 15, 2007, from http://www.healthcareitnews.com/story.cms?id=6165

Platt, R. (2007). Speed bumps, potholes, and tollbooths on the road to panacea: making best use of data. *Health Aff (Millwood), 26*(2), w153-155.

Poon, A. D., & Fagan, L. M. (1994). PEN-Ivory: the design and evaluation of a pen-based computer system for structured data entry. *Proc Annu Symp Comput Appl Med Care*, 447-451.

Poon, A. D., Fagan, L. M., & Shortliffe, E. H. (1996). The PEN-Ivory project: exploring user-interface design for the selection of items from large controlled vocabularies of medicine. *J Am Med Inform Assoc, 3*(2), 168-183.

Poon, E. G., Wald, J., Bates, D. W., Middleton, B., Kuperman, G. J., & Gandhi, T. K. (2003). Supporting patient care beyond the clinical encounter: three informatics innovations from partners health care. *AMIA Annu Symp Proc*, 1072.

Poon, E. G., Wang, S. J., Gandhi, T. K., Bates, D. W., & Kuperman, G. J. (2003). Design and implementation of a comprehensive outpatient Results Manager. *Journal of Biomedical informatics, 36*(1-2), 80-91.

Potts, A. L., Barr, F. E., Gregory, D. F., Wright, L., & Patel, N. R. (2004). Computerized physician order entry and medication errors in a pediatric critical care unit. *Pediatrics, 113*(1 Pt 1), 59-63.

Powell, J., & Buchan, I. (2005). Electronic health records should support clinical research. *J Med Internet Res, 7*(1), e4.

Presidential Advisory Commision on Consumer Protection and Quality in Health Care Industry. (1998). *Building the capacity to improve quality.*

Chapter Fourteen: Investing in Information Systems. Retrieved January 26, 2007, from http://www.hcqualitycommission.gov/final/chap14.html

Quinn, J. (2004). Vendor perspectives: Critical do's and dont's. In Spring AMIA 2004 (Ed.). Mc-Clean, Va.

Randolph, A. G., Haynes, R. B., Wyatt, J. C., Cook, D. J., & Guyatt, G. H. (1999). Users' guides to the medical literature: XVIII. How to use an article evaluating the clinical impact of a computer-based clinical decision support system. *Jama, 282*(1), 67-74.

Retchin, S. M., & Wenzel, R. P. (1999). Electronic medical record systems at academic health centers: advantages and implementation issues. *Acad Med, 74*(5), 493-498.

Rind, D. M., & Safran, C. (1993). Real and imagined barriers to an electronic medical record. *Proc Annu Symp Comput Appl Med Care*, 74-78.

Rouf, E., Whittle, J., Lu, N., & Schwartz, M. D. (2007). Computers in the exam room: Differences in physician-patient interaction may be due to physician experience. *J Gen Intern Med, 22*(1), 43-48.

Safran, C., Sands, D. Z., & Rind, D. M. (1999). Online medical records: a decade of experience. *Methods Inf Med, 38*(4-5), 308-312.

Sands, D. Z., Libman, H., & Safran, C. (1995). Meeting information needs: analysis of clinicians' use of an HIV database through an electronic medical record. *Medinfo, 8 Pt 1*, 323-326.

Shortliffe, E. H. (2001). *Medical informatics: Computer applications in health care and biomedicine* (2nd ed.). New York: Springer.

Sim, I., Olasov, B., & Carini, S. (2003). The trial bank system: Capturing randomized trials for evidence-based medicine. *AMIA Annu Symp Proc*, 1076.

Sim, I., Owens, D. K., Lavori, P. W., & Rennels, G. D. (2000). Electronic trial banks: A complementary method for reporting randomized trials. *Med Decis Making, 20*(4), 440-450.

Sim, I., Wyatt, J., Musen, M., & Niland, J. (1999). *Towards an open infrastructure for clinical trial development and interpretation.* Paper presented at the 1999 Fall AMIA Symposium, Washington DC.

Simon, S. R., Kaushal, R., Cleary, P. D., Jenter, C. A., Volk, L. A., Orav, E. J. et al. (2007). Physicians and electronic health records: A statewide survey. *Arch Intern Med, 167*(5), 507-512.

Slack, W. V., & Bleich, H. L. (1999). The CCC system in two teaching hospitals: A progress report. *International Journal Medicine Information, 54*(3), 183-196.

Solomon, G. L., & Dechter, M. (1995). Are patients pleased with computer use in the examination room? *J Fam Pract, 41*(3), 241-244.

Stead, W. W. (1999). The challenge to health informatics for 1999-2000: Form creative partnerships with industry and chief information officers to enable people to use information to improve health. *Journal of American Medical Information Association, 6*(1), 88-89.

Stead, W. W., Kelly, B. J., & Kolodner, R. M. (2004). Achievable steps toward building a national health information infrastructure in the United States. *Journal of American Medical Information Association.*

Stead, W. W., & Lorenzi, N. M. (1999). Health informatics: Linking investment to value. *Journal of American Medical Information Association, 6*(5), 341-348.

Stead, W. W., Miller, R. A., Musen, M. A., & Hersh, W. R. (2000). Integration and beyond: Linking information from disparate sources and into workflow. *Journal of American Medical Information Association, 7*(2), 135-145.

Strategos Inc. Lean Manufacturing History. Retrieved June 18, 2007, from http://www.strategosinc.com/just_in_time.htm

Streitenberger, K., Breen-Reid, K., & Harris, C. (2006). Handoffs in care—can we make them safer? *Pediatr Clin North Am, 53*(6), 1185-1195.

Swanson, T., Dostal, J., Eichhorst, B., Jernigan, C., Knox, M., & Roper, K. (1997). Recent implementations of electronic medical records in four family practice residency programs. *Acad Med, 72*(7), 607-612.

Talmon, J. L., & Hasman, A. (2002). Medical informatics as a discipline at the beginning of the 21st century. *Methods Inf Med, 41*(1), 4-7.

Teich, J. M., Glaser, J. P., Beckley, R. F., Aranow, M., Bates, D. W., Kuperman, G. J. et al. (1999). The Brigham integrated computing system (BICS): Advanced clinical systems in an academic hospital environment. *International Journal Medicine Information, 54*(3), 197-208.

Thinking About...Implementing the EMR [Electronic (2006). Version]. *Digital Office, Volume 1.* Retrieved January 15, 2007 from http://www.himss.org/Content/files/digital_office_enews/digitaloffice_200606.html

Tilghman, C., Tilghman, J., & Johnson, R. W. (2006). Integration of technology in a clinical research setting. *Abnf J, 17*(3), 112-114.

USC/Norris Comphrehensive Cancer Center. (2007). USC/Norris>Glossary. Retrieved August 3, 2007, from http://ccnt.hsc.usc.edu/glossary/

van Ginneken, A. M. (2002). The computerized patient record: Balancing effort and benefit. *International Journal of Medicine Information, 65*(2), 97-119.

Walker, J. (2003). Clinical-information connectivity nationwide. Healthcare can use the model of success frontiered by banks. *Healthc Inform, 20*(10), 62-64.

Walker, J., Pan, E., Johnston, D., Adler-Milstein, J., Bates, D. W., & Middleton, B. (2005). The value of health care information exchange and interoperability. *Health Aff (Millwood).*

Wang, S. J., Middleton, B., Prosser, L. A., Bardon, C. G., Spurr, C. D., Carchidi, P. J. et al. (2003). A cost-benefit analysis of electronic medical records in primary care. *Am J Med, 114*(5), 397-403.

Welch, W. P., Bazarko, D., Ritten, K., Burgess, Y., Harmon, R., & Sandy, L. G. (2007). Electronic health records in four community physician practices: impact on quality and cost of care. *Journal of American Medical Information Association, 14*(3), 320-328.

Welch, W. P., Bazarko, D., Ritten, K., Burgess, Y., Harmon, R., & Sandy, L. G. (2007). Electronic health records in four community physician practices: Impact on quality and cost of care. *J Am Med Inform Assoc, 14*(3), 320-328.

Wikipedia. Just In Time. Retrieved June 18, 2007, from http://en.wikipedia.org/wiki/Just_In_Time

Yasnoff, W. A., Humphreys, B. L., Overhage, J. M., Detmer, D. E., Brennan, P. F., Morris, R. W. et al. (2004). A consensus action agenda for achieving the national health information infrastructure. *Journal of American Medicine Information Association, 11*(4), 332-338.

Zaroukian, M. H., & Sierra, A. (2006). Benefiting from ambulatory EHR implementation: Solidarity, six sigma, and willingness to strive. *Journal of Healthcare Information Management, 20*(1), 53-60.

ADDITIONAL READING

Abdelhak, M. (2007). *Health information: Management of a strategic resource* (3rd ed.). St. Louis, MO: Saunders/Elsevier.

Bemmel, J. H. V., Musen, M. A., & Helder, J. C. (1997). *Handbook of medical informatics.* AW Houten, Netherlands, Heidelberg, Germany: Bohn Stafleu Van Loghum; Springer Verlag.

Friedman, C. P., & Wyatt, J. (2006). *Evaluation methods in medical informatics* (2nd ed.). New York: Springer.

Glaser, J. (2002). *The strategic application of information technology in health care organizations* (2nd ed.). San Francisco, CA: Jossey-Bass.

Griffith, J. R., & White, K. R. (2006). *The well-managed healthcare organization* (6th ed.). Chicago: Health Administration Press.

Kannry, J. (2007). CPOE and patient safety: Panacea or pandora's box? In K. Ong (Ed.), *Medical informatics: An executive primer.* Chicago: HIMSS.

Kannry, J., Mukani, S., & Myers, K. (2006). Using an evidence-based approach for system selection at a large academic medical center: lessons learned in selecting an ambulatory EMR at Mount Sinai Hospital. *J Healthc Inf Manag, 20*(2), 84-99.

Murff, H. J., & Kannry, J. (2001). Physician satisfaction with two order entry systems. *Journal of American Medical Information Association, 8*(5), 499-509.

Ong, K. (Ed.). (2007). *Medical informatics: An executive primer.* Chicago: HIMSS.

Shortliffe, E. H., & Cimino, J. J. (2006). *Biomedical informatics: Computer applications in health care and biomedicine* (3rd ed.). New York, NY: Springer.

Wager, K. A., Lee, F. W., & Glaser, J. (2005). *Managing healthcare information systems: A practical approach for health care executives* (1st ed.). San Francisco: Jossey-Bass.

Chapter XIV
Health Information Technology Economic Evaluation

Eric L. Eisenstein
Duke Clinical Research Institute, USA

Maqui Ortiz
Duke Clinical Research Institute, USA

Kevin J. Anstrom
Duke University Medical Center, USA

David F. Lobach
Duke University Medical Center, USA

ABSTRACT

This chapter describes a framework for conducting economic analyses of health information technologies (HIT). It explains the basic principles of healthcare economic analyses and the relationships between the costs and effectiveness of a health intervention, and then uses these principles to explain the types of data that need to be gathered in order to conduct a health information technology economic evaluation study. A current health information technology study is then used to illustrate the incorporation of the framework's economic analysis methods into an ongoing research project. Economic research in the field of health information technology is not yet well developed. This chapter is meant to educate researchers about the need for HIT economic analyses as well as provide a structured framework to assist them in conducting these analyses.

Copyright © 2008, IGI Global, distributing in print or electronic forms without written permission of IGI Global is prohibited.

INTRODUCTION

In 2004, President George W. Bush established the Office of the National Health Information Technology Coordinator with the charge of developing a "health information technology infrastructure" that "reduces healthcare costs resulting from inefficiency, medical errors, inappropriate care and incomplete information"(Sidorov, 2006; White House, 2004). This charge came with the assertion that the adoption of electronic health record systems can, "reduce healthcare costs by up to 20 percent per year"(U.S. Department of Health and Human Services, 2007). The U.S. House of Representatives recently approved legislation that would provide $40 million over five years to help physicians purchase health information technology products (Heavy, 2006). The stated goal is to provide funding that will enable the widespread adoption of electronic health records, which may in turn improve quality of care and reduce medical errors. One republican congresswoman was moved to say, "Realistically, the government's not going to pay for this. The system's going to do it ... because it creates system efficiencies that pays the system back" (Heavy, 2006). Yet despite the near unanimous optimism among policy makers surrounding these technologies, the precise nature of their value propositions and the best methods for measuring these expected medical cost reductions and health benefit increases remain unclear (Chaudhry et al., 2006; Girosi et al., 2005). Further, there are as yet no proposed methods for physicians, hospitals, or the government to determine whether or not they are actually receiving the financial returns they anticipate from their investments in health information technologies.

This chapter will present a conceptual framework for the economic evaluation of health information technologies. It will then describe how this framework can be applied to determine the types of economic data that should be collected in a health information technology economic evaluation study, and how those data should be analyzed.

BACKGROUND

Much of the recent interest in health information technology by policy makers has been fueled by the introduction of application systems (i.e., computerized provider order entry and the electronic health record) that have shown potential for improving patient outcomes (Chaudhry et al., 2006). While various models have been developed that point to the potential benefits from these systems, the formal economic evaluation of these and other types of health information technologies is immature, and characterized by incomplete methodologies that are inconsistently applied. (Eisenstein, 2006; Kaushal et al., 2006; Kuperman & Gibson, 2003; Ohsfeldt et al., 2005; Walker et al., 2005). We believe that these shortcomings stem from fundamental misconceptions among health information technology investigators regarding what should be evaluated and how evaluations should be conducted.

Introduction to Health Economic Evaluation

Traditionally, most health information systems have been concerned with conventional business functions such as financial management (e.g., general ledger and accounts payable), resource scheduling (e.g., hospital rooms and medical equipment), inventory management (e.g., pharmaceuticals and surgical implants) and accounts receivable (e.g., billing for physician and hospital services). Attempts at health information technology economic evaluation have typically borrowed either general business models or models from other industries that have demonstrated competence in information technology evaluation (Frisse, 1999; Panko, 1999; Tuttle, 1999). However, these models do not account for the unique nature of the healthcare industry in which information technologies are playing a greater role in patient care and may even affect patient outcomes (Stead & Lorenzi, 1999; Tierney et al., 1994). In these situations, increased costs may be acceptable if they improve the quality of patient care. As Sidorov observes, "a considerable body of evidence suggests that widespread adoption of the EHR (electronic health record) increases healthcare costs" (Sidorov, 2006). This observation suggests that evaluators of health information technologies need to adopt methodologies that allow for the comparison of the incremental costs of these systems with their incremental benefits to patients.

Health Economic Evaluation Methods

Since the mid-1990s, a number of standards have been proposed for the economic evaluation of medical technologies. Of these, the U.S. Public Health Service's Panel on Cost-Effectiveness in Health and Medicine and the National Institute for Health and Clinical Excellence (NICE) have received the most attention (Gold et al., 1996; NICE 2007) The U.S. panel's recommendations include elements that define the theory and conduct of economic evaluations. At the heart of these analyses is the need to account for both differences in medical costs (including the costs of the intervention) and the benefits to patients that will accrue through the use of these products and services.

Economic analyses are concerned with determining the incremental value associated with the use of a new product or service versus its best alternative (Nagle & Holden, 2002). In most industries, value can be expressed solely in terms of the expected cash flows (inflows and outflows) associated with the use of a product or service. In these situations, the product or service with the highest net present value (the value of its stream of cash inflows less outflows after adjustment for differences in their timing) is considered the preferred investment. In this case the net present value of the cash flows associated with product J is given by the following formula:

$$NPV_J = \sum_{t=0}^{n} \frac{A_t}{(1+k)^t},$$

where A is annual net cash flow, t is the study year, n is the study duration and k is the discount rate. When comparing the net cash flows associated with products A and B, one merely needs to subtract their net present values ($NPV_A - NPV_B$). For those unfamiliar with discounting, this formula is merely the reciprocal of the compound interest formula (Eisenstein & Mark, 2004). Just as one would expect to accrue interest if funds are loaned in the present in anticipation of their return at a future date, so one also must discount future receipts of funds to account for the time between their future availability and the present. Essentially, discounting allows all cash flows to be treated as if they occur at time zero. This approach eliminates advantages that might occur through the acceleration or deferral of cash flows. In the United States, a discount rate of three percent is typically used for analyses performed from the societal perspective; however, higher discount rates are common when analyses are performed from other perspectives (Li et al., 2007).

As previously stated, healthcare differs from other industries in that its products and services may change the morbidity, mortality, and quality of life of patients. In order to be able to incorporate these health benefits into a net present value equation, one must be able to place monetary values on changes in morbidity, mortality, and quality of life. While there have been attempts to do just this, all are fraught with difficulties as they will inevitably place more/less value on the life of some vs. other member of society, or they will not adequately reflect those who contribute more/less to society. For this reason most health economists have given up on cost-benefit analyses (where health benefits are monetarized); instead it is more common to use cost consequences analyses, in which incremental medical costs and health benefits are listed separately; or cost-effectiveness analyses, in which health benefits are related to medical costs by means of a cost-effectiveness ratio. In either approach, one calculates the discounted health benefit stream associated with healthcare products and services using a formula similar to that presented above to calculate the net present value of cash flows. The only difference is that in this situation we are calculating the net present value of health benefits. As one would expect, there has been some controversy among health economists regarding the discounting of health benefits. Essentially, discounting would imply that a year of life now is worth more than a year of life in the future. This controversy was settled by what has become known as the Keeler-Cretin paradox (Keeler & Cretin, 1983). These authors argued that if health benefits are discounted at a lower rate than medical costs then the resulting ratio of health benefits to medical costs (representing the choice of doing something vs. doing nothing) can be improved by delaying initiation of the health intervention, a situation which is contrary to clinical experience.

In cost-consequences and cost-effectiveness analyses, comparisons are made between the incremental medical costs and health benefits associated with the use of two healthcare products or services. The difference is that in a cost-consequence analysis the incremental medical costs and health benefits are listed separately so that the reviewer can make his or her own determination as to whether or not the new intervention is an economically attractive alternative to the standard of care. In a cost-effectiveness analysis these relationships are formalized in a cost-effectiveness equation. The general form of the cost-effectiveness equation compares each of these components as discounted values

$$\frac{C_A - C_B}{B_A - B_B}.$$

In this equation, the incremental discounted medical costs of healthcare product A are compared with those for product B and the incremental

health benefits associated with the use of product A are compared with those for product B. While the cost-effectiveness equation shown above provides a guide to the collection of information for a health economic analysis, it is not always necessary to calculate the cost-effectiveness ratio. The cost-effectiveness denominator (difference in health benefits) drives this decision and can result in four potential outcomes (Figure 1).

First, if health product A is less effective than health product B, an economic analysis is not performed. In this case, the economic analysis would report differences in medical costs and health benefits between health products A and B, but would not calculate a ratio. Second, if there is no difference in health benefits between health products A and B, the problem is reduced to a comparison of medical costs (numerator of the cost-effectiveness equation). In this case, the analysis become a comparison of the net present value of health product A versus that of health product B. Third, if the use of health product A is associated with greater health benefits than health product B, there are two alternatives. If health product A also is associated with equal or lower medical costs, it is considered to be dominant versus health product B (i.e., product A is better on both dimensions) and no further analysis is required. In this case, the economic analysis will report differences in medical costs and health benefits; however, a cost-effectiveness ratio is not calculated. Lastly, when health product A is associated with greater health benefits and greater medical costs versus health product B, a cost-effectiveness ratio is calculated. This ratio essentially measures the incremental cost per unit of health benefit gained with the use of health product A versus B.

When assessing the results of an economic analysis, one clearly would not accept a new therapy when its use was associated with reduced health benefits versus the standard of care (case 1). And, one would logically accept a new therapy whose use was associated with no difference in

Figure 1. Cost and effectiveness relationships

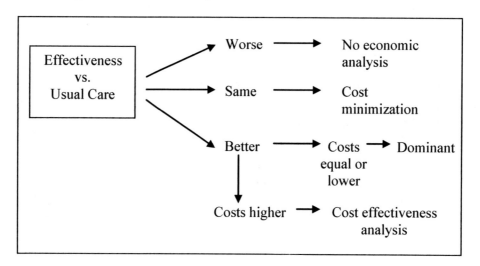

health benefit but did reduce medical costs (case 2). Similarly, one would always accept a new therapy when its use was associated with greater health benefits and lower medical costs (case 3). However, when a new therapy is associated with increased health benefits and increased medical costs, the analysis becomes complicated (case 4). That is because the natural question arising from a cost-effectiveness ratio is whether or not the resulting comparison represents a good value. Unfortunately, the answer to this question is ambiguous. Over the years several boundaries have been proposed to determine whether a new health technology is "cost-effective." Some have polled physicians; others have attempted to relate economic attractiveness to gross domestic product per capita; but perhaps the most straightforward is that proposed by Goldman et al. (Goldman et al., 1991). Since dialysis is the only medical therapy that is paid for by Medicare without regard to age, it represents a "willingness to pay" surrogate for United States society. In 2004, Medicare's End-Stage Renal Disease Program paid an average of $66,758 per dialysis patient year at risk (U.S. Renal Data System, 2006). Thus most health economists consider therapies costing <$50,000 per quality adjusted life year saved (QALY) to be economi-

cally attractive, those costing $50,000 to $100,000 per QALY to be marginally attractive, and those costing >$100,000 per QALY to be economically unattractive (Eisenstein & Mark, 2004).

Using the cost-effectiveness equation as a guide, we can now summarize the types of information we will need to collect in an economic analysis (Donaldson, Mugford, & Vale, 2002). Each component (health benefit and medical cost) can be divided into two elements, a measurement and a valuation placed on that measurement. For health benefits, the measurement is a clinical outcome and its valuation is the utility attached to that clinical outcome. If our measurement is life years saved and we use a time-tradeoff method to determine the patient's utility for life years saved, we will be able to calculate quality-adjusted life years saved. For medical costs, the measurement is resource use (e.g., intensive care days) and the valuation is the opportunity cost attached to those resources (i.e., their prices). By multiplying each resource by its unit price, we will be able to determine the costs of those medical resources consumed in treating a patient. Thus, the four information items required in an economic evaluation are: (1) change in clinical outcomes, (2) changes in resource use, (3) utility of clinical outcomes, and (4) opportunity cost of resources (Donaldson et al., 2002)

In addition to these four information items, we will also need knowledge of seven context factors that will serve to define the environment of the analysis. These seven context factors are: (1) details of interventions to be compared, (2) setting in which interventions are provided, (3) patient characteristics, (4) description of cost-generating events on the clinical pathway experienced by patients, (5) analysis perspective (reflecting key stakeholder interests), (6) time horizon of the intervention and its sequelae, and (7) the scale of the intervention (Mugford, 2001). These key information types and context factors provide a foundation for a more refined methodological framework that will be described in the remainder of this chapter.

Economic Analysis Methods

Each health information technology economic analysis should begin with the identification of a value proposition that hypothesizes how the use of the particular technology under evaluation will impact patient outcomes and medical costs. The subsequent economic analysis will then test this hypothesis. We use the framework proposed by Campbell et al., for the design and implementation of complex interventions in healthcare to introduce the value proposition concept, and we will use the methods of Donaldson et al. to illustrate the application of the value proposition concept in an economic analysis (Campbell et al., 2000; Donaldson et al., 2002). The value proposition defined by this framework will serve as a means for organizing the economic evaluation study. This framework's components will then serve as guides for determining what data needs to be collected within each of the four information types, and how the seven context factors will be described. Together, these components serve as inputs to our study design, data collection plan, and analysis plan.

HIT Value Case Study

Throughout this chapter we will use examples from the, "Showing health information value in a community network" study (HIT Value). HIT Value is a demonstration project funded by the Agency for Healthcare Research and Quality that is investigating three data-driven, asynchronous information interventions within an existing community health network. The Durham Community Health Network (DCHN) seeks to provide a community-oriented approach to coordinate healthcare delivery, and at any time serves approximately 17,000 Medicaid beneficiaries in Durham County, North Carolina. The network's partners include both hospitals located within the county, two emergency departments, three urgent care facilities, seven primary care clinics (including family medicine, one internal medicine, and obstetrics-gynecology), a federally qualified health center, the Durham County Health Department, the Durham County Department of Social Services, and a dedicated care management team.

The HIT value project builds upon an existing Web-based clinical database, community-oriented approach to coordinated healthcare (COACH), that has data entry interfaces with patients via kiosks at clinic sites and network clinicians via the Web. By incorporating system for evidence-based advice by simultaneous transmission of an intelligent agent across a network (SEBASTIAN), a clinical decision support system, COACH is able to provide an asynchronous, rule-based event notification system to its clinical users (Kawamoto & Lobach, 2005; Lobach et al., 2001; Lobach et al., 2004). This study's evaluation component will assess the relative value of three interventions targeted to different audiences. These interventions are prompted by missed tests and appointments, inappropriate use of the emergency room, and hospital admissions. They include e-mail alerts to case workers, mailings to patients, and periodic reports to outpatient clinics. Patients are randomized to one of the three interventions by household. While the content of the three interventions is essentially the same, there are differences in the mode of transmission, the frequency of transmissions, and the target audience. The primary aim of the HIT value evaluation component is to assess the clinical, organizational and financial value of these interventions in a community network from the societal perspective. Secondary aims include evaluations from the perspectives of specific stakeholder groups, including patients, providers, hospitals, payers, and purchasers. The HIT value economic evaluation will provide examples of how the concepts discussed in this chapter are being implemented.

Defining the Value Proposition

Most clinical trials are limited to the evaluation of single therapies (for example, beta blocker A versus beta blocker B). However, health information technologies differ from the typical mono-therapies investigated in clinical trials in that they generally have multiple, simultaneous interventions. The evaluation of these "poly-information therapies" becomes more difficult as the number of endpoints, processes, and inputs to the evaluation analysis increases. Campbell et al. use the term "complex intervention" to describe such evaluation problems (Campbell et al., 2000). These authors defined complex interventions as being "made up of various interconnected parts," and state that their evaluation "is difficult because of problems of developing, identifying, documenting, and reproducing the intervention." They also proposed a phase-approach, similar to the four phases of clinical trials, to guide health researchers in their evaluations. This approach has particular importance for health information technology researchers who need to be able to determine why and how their interventions work. We believe that this framework will be particularly useful for health information technology researchers contemplating an economic evaluation.

Campbell et al. begin with the observation that an incompletely defined and developed intervention is the source of many problems in the evaluation of complex interventions in healthcare (Campbell et al., 2000). We believe that this situation may easily occur in health information technologies where researchers typically emphasize the importance of the information intervention and ignore other components of the information system and its environment. Thus, we endorse the Campbell framework as a means to begin thinking about health information technologies and how they can best be evaluated. This framework begins with a preclinical phase during which the researcher seeks to find evidence that the proposed intervention might have a desired effect, and proceeds to a modeling phase during which the researcher uses simulation and other techniques to gain a better understanding of the intervention's components and their interrelationships. After these preliminary phases, the complex intervention is subjected to three testing phases during which the components of the replicable intervention and its evaluation are defined (exploratory trial phase), the fully defined intervention is evaluated using appropriate statistical power (definitive randomized controlled trial phase), and the intervention is replicated and evaluated in uncontrolled settings (long term implementation phase).

In preparation for the HIT value study, we conducted preliminary evaluations paralleling Campbell's first two phases. We began by asking how the proposed intervention might produce value for the DCHN and its constituent Medicaid patients in Durham County. We next hypothesized how the use of this intervention might result in changes in both components of the cost-effectiveness equation (health benefits and medical costs). In this theorizing, we postulated that, should the HIT Value interventions be successful, they would result in patients transitioning from inappropriate to appropriate modes of healthcare. We also postulated that patients would receive greater access to and improved utilization of the DCHN's healthcare resources. These two mechanisms (transitioning to appropriate care and greater access to and utilization of care) were the means by which we theorized that value would be derived through the HIT Value interventions. We then sought to identify potential "footprints" of our intervention. That is, to the extent that the HIT Value interventions were successful, how would we expect that the DCHN would be changed?

We began by developing a value chain for our community health network (Figure 2). Our value chain begins with Medicaid patients needing healthcare and ends with improvements in health for the community. We then defined a healthcare supply chain that is comprised of providers and payers; and a health benefits chain that represents the community. Within the provider component, resources/inputs go into the healthcare system, healthcare activities are performed, and health services are provided. The payer component then provides reimbursement for health services, while the health benefits accrue to individual patients and there is an overall impact upon the health of the community. We then hypothesized that transitioning patients from inappropriate to appropriate care would change/reduce certain types of emergency department visits (asthma, diabetes, and low severity) and some hospital encounters while increasing primary care en-

counters and reducing missed appointments. We also hypothesized that greater access to and improved utilization of care would be manifested as increases in follow-up appointments. These changes in turn would reduce payments for emergency department visits and hospitalizations while increasing primary care reimbursements as well as reimbursements for certain laboratory tests and other ancillary services. Thus, while we expected that our information interventions would change the mix of existing healthcare products and service consumed by Medicaid patients in Durham County, our analysis did not reveal the need to develop new products and services.

We then tested our hypothesized mechanisms by modeling potential medical cost savings that would accrue through reductions in low-severity emergency department visits. North Carolina Medicaid has defined a specific set of billing codes as constituting low-severity emergency department visits. They also determined that patients initiating these types of emergency department visits could best be served in the outpatient setting. Hence, transitioning these patients from emergency department to outpatient visits would constitute movement from inappropriate to appropriate care. Previous work by our group demonstrated that during a two-month test period there was an approximate 30 percent

Figure 2. Community health network value chain

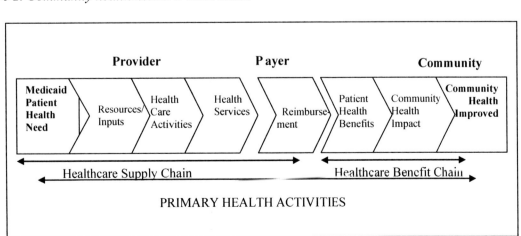

reduction in low severity emergency department visits after the implementation of e-mail alerts to DCHN case managers. We sought to determine whether this level of economic effect sustained over the SEBASTIAN system's lifecycle would be sufficient to pay for the costs of this information intervention. Two types of financial analysis were performed.

First, we performed a break-even analysis to determine what level of effectiveness would be required to achieve cost-neutrality (medical cost savings equal to the costs of the intervention). That is, the percent reduction in low-severity emergency department visits that would be required for the net present value of an investment in SEBASTIAN to be zero, assuming either a three or five year system lifecycle. We then conducted an anticipated effect analysis to determine what level of cost-saving is possible in the expected range of effectiveness, which was defined as the percent reduction in low severity emergency department visits. Both analyses were performed using a net present value format.

During the three month period of our study, 17,779 Durham County Medicaid patients were enrolled in the Community Care Program and they filed a total of 147,229 claims for $16,000,419 (Ta-

ble 1). Of these claims, 1,907 claims for $529,088 were for low-severity emergency room encounters at a cost to Medicaid of $227 per encounter.

Thus, the potential savings from conversion of low severity emergency department encounters to outpatient visits was $93,492 per month, or $9,349 per month for each 10 percent of low severity emergency encounters that are converted. The estimated development and implementation costs for SEBASTIAN would total $218,833, with $75,000 in maintenance and operating costs for the first year and $53,333 annually thereafter. In the break-even analysis the investment in SEBASTIAN would have a net present value of zero (pay for itself) if 11 percent of low severity emergency department encounters were converted to outpatient visits assuming a three-year system lifecycle and if 9 percent were converted assuming a 5 year lifecycle (Figure 3).

In the anticipated effect analysis, a 20 percent conversion of emergency department encounters to outpatient visits would result in a savings of $18,698 per month, $250,849 in net savings over a three-year lifecycle, and $554,830 in savings over a five-year lifecycle (Figure 4). If 30 percent are converted, there would be $28,048 savings per month, $572,917 net savings over a three-year

Table 1. Baseline economic data August-October 2004: Total Medicaid costs

COST TYPE	INDIVIDUAL CLAIMS		TOTAL CLAIMS
	N	Costs/Claim	Cost
Emergency Room Encounter	5,179*	$346	$1,791,038
Provider Encounter	108,853	$80	$8,739,608
Inpatient	405	$7,973	$3,229,011
Durable Medical Equipment	1,261	$152	$191,174
Drug Prescriptions	31,531	$65	$2,049,588
Total	147,229	$109	$16,000,419
*17,779 Durham County Community Care Patients			

Figure 3. HIT value break-even analysis

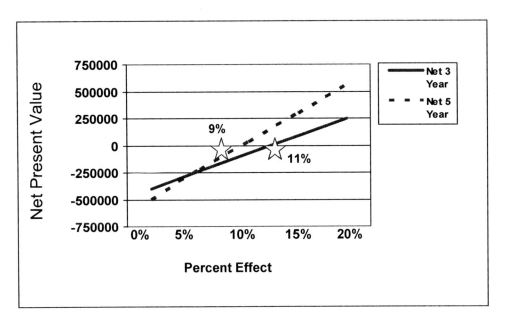

Figure 4. Medicaid claims and potential savings

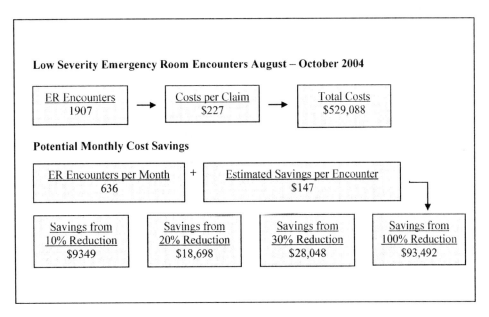

system lifecycle, and $1,076,280 over a five-year lifecycle.

Economic Data Collection Framework

The U.S. Public Health Service's panel on cost-effectiveness in health and medicine cost collection guidelines list five types of direct costs that are included in the numerator (as medical costs) of a cost-effectiveness ratio and two types of indirect costs that are reported in the denominator (as health benefits) (Luce, 1996). The costs in the numerator are termed direct costs because they are directly attributable to the information intervention and its associated treatment regimens. In contrast, indirect costs are costs that accrue through the use, or lack of use, of the information intervention but are not directly associated with the intervention or its associated treatment regimens. Typically, direct costs are collected, summarized, and reported in a net present value type of analysis; whereas, indirect costs are reported individually and separate from the health benefits. The direct costs types reported in the numerator are: (1) the costs associated with the intervention, (2) costs of other healthcare resources, (3) costs of non-healthcare resources associated with the intervention's use, (4) the value of informal caregiver time, and (5) the value of patient time while receiving treatment. The indirect cost types associated with the denominator are: (1) intrinsic value of improved health and (2) the value of changes in a patient's production output. We will discuss each of these cost types and give examples of their use. When collecting cost data, it is important to remember that all costs associated with the current use and future consequence of a health information technology intervention must be accounted for in the cost data collection plan even if it is not feasible to collect them.

Direct cost identification frequently begins with the information intervention and will include all costs associated with its development

or procurement, maintenance, and operations. These costs are typically collected using an ingredients approach in which all resources used in delivering the information intervention are enumerated and assigned prices (Lairson et al., 2006; Levin & McEwan, 2000; Miller & West, 2007). The major cost categories to be included are: personnel, hardware, software, miscellaneous supplies, and overhead. In many organizations the costs for these items will be available through internal financial management systems. When seeking to identify the direct costs associated with an information intervention, it is useful to think of the cost-generating events on the clinical pathway experienced by patients. In the inpatient setting, these will include emergency room visits, stays in observation units, acute care admission to hospitals, admissions to rehabilitation facilities, and admissions to nursing homes. Each of these inpatient episodes of care will also have various professional services with their associated fees. In the outpatient setting, cost-generating events will include technical services (such as laboratory medicine tests and radiology imaging), different types of professional services (include physician visits, test administration, and physical or occupational therapy), medical supplies, durable medical equipment, and pharmaceuticals. With each inpatient or outpatient episode, there may also be direct non-healthcare costs (such as child care costs for patients and care givers attending treatments, dietary prescriptions, and transportation to and from the treatment setting). Lastly, there will be costs associated with the use of informal caregiver time (even if uncompensated) as well as costs associated with the time a patient is receiving treatment.

Although indirect costs are considered part of the health benefit associated with the use of an information intervention, they are increasingly being reporting in economic analyses separately from the direct medical costs which are included in a cost-consequences or a cost-effectiveness analysis. Two productivity costs that may be included are those due to changes in morbidity (costs associated with reduced ability to work or engage in leisure activities) and mortality (such as costs due to lost wages). Because productivity costs are frequently driven by events occurring after the end of the study period (e.g., lifetime earnings), they are typically captured in models and their values are often considered somewhat speculative.

Economic Collection Example

We developed a direct cost collection protocol as a part of the overall HIT Value project evaluation plan (Figure 5). In developing this protocol we wanted to collect medical cost data at a sufficient level of detail to detect the hypothesized changes. However, as data collection can be time and re-source intensive, we did not want to collect cost data that would be of marginal value. In the HIT Value study, both of the hypothesized mechanisms are at the 'episode of care' level.

First, by migrating patients from inappropriate to appropriate care we assumed patients would change from one type of episode (e.g., low severity emergency department visit) to another type of episode (e.g., outpatient visit). Second, increas-ing access to care also increases the number of events at the episode of care level. Had we said we were going to reduce intensive care length of stay, this would have been at the 'resource unit' level and would have required a more detailed cost collection plan.

In our cost collection protocol, we identified categories of costs, the methods by which they would be captured and the sources of informa-tion required. This information will be gathered for medical costs incurred by patients and their families, and by the healthcare providers that are involved in their care. Although patient co-pays are classified as transfer payments and are not included with the medical costs of providing healthcare goods and services, they are an ex-pense for patients. We will estimate the costs of

Figure 5. Patient care costs

Category	Method	Source
Patients and Families		
Co-Pay	Ingredient	Estimate from rates
Out-of-pocket		Not available
Transportation	Ingredient	Distance estimate
Treatment time	Ingredient	Time estimates
Unpaid caregivers	Ingredient	Time estimates
Outpatient		
Professional	Medicare Standard Costs	Medicaid reimbursement
Technical	Medicare Standard Costs	Medicaid reimbursement
Hospitals		
Emergency room	Ratio of cost to charges	Departmental charges
Inpatient care	Ratio of costs to charges	Departmental charges
Other Outpatient		
Pharmaceuticals	Ingredients	Medicaid reimbursement (AWP)
Durable medical equipment	Ingredients	Medicaid reimbursement

co-payments from billing information describing the type of encounter and standard Medicaid co-pay rates within our network. Although it would be informative to include out-of-pocket medical expenses such as over the counter medications, it is not feasible to collect this information in our study. Since we do have patient and provider addresses in our system, we will be able to estimate distances traveled for medical care. These data will allow us to assign a standard price for the mileage and generate estimates for the time patients and their unpaid care givers spend traveling to/from and receiving treatment. However, it is not feasible to collect time estimates for unpaid caregivers.

In our project, provider cost information is available in an automated form. Hence we would be able to obtain billing codes for all outpatient services and then estimate their costs using the North Carolina Medicare Fee Schedule. This method of cost estimation is reasonable because Medicare is a resource-based reimbursement system that seeks to reflect the value of actual resources consumed in the provision of medical care. We proposed to estimate hospital costs (emergency room and other forms of inpatient care) using information from actual patient bills. Costs will be estimated using charge summaries for each hospital department and ratios of charges to costs (RCC) in each hospital's annual Medicare cost report. RCCs are reported for each hospital department, and give the ratio of each department's charges as listed on their bills to the actual costs of providing those services. Thus, the use of hospital billing information and RCCs allows us to estimate costs from charges. Lastly, we will estimate the costs of pharmaceuticals and durable medical equipment from actual Medicaid reimbursements for these products.

Economic Analysis Contextual Factors

Although it is frequently assumed that the economic attractiveness of a healthcare intervention is the same in all settings, this assumption is not the case because characteristics of the context in which the intervention is delivered will influence the economics of the intervention (Mugford, 2001). Earlier in this chapter, we listed seven context factors that will influence the economics of a health information technology intervention. In this section, we will discuss how they might affect the results of our HIT Value study and the economic returns in other communities.

1. **Details of interventions compared:** Our HIT Value study compares three methods of information intervention in three audiences (e-mail to care managers, mailings to patients, and periodic reports to clinics). Each of these interventions is generated by the SEBASTIAN clinical decision support system. However, we expect that the clinical and economic outcomes associated with these three information interventions may be different. Thus, the route of administration will be expected to influence the economic attractiveness of an information intervention.

2. **Setting in which interventions are provided:** Costs are inherently local, and medical costs will primarily be determined by local wage rates. Thus, it is conceivable that an intervention may be economically attractive in one community with certain prices for medical goods and services and economically unattractive in another community with a different cost structure.

3. **Patient characteristics:** Patient characteristics may influence the economic attractiveness of an information intervention in a number of ways. First, more severely ill patients tend to consume more resources. Thus, it is conceivable that the same information intervention may be economically attractive in an elderly population but not in a pediatric population. Other patient characteristics with potential impact are size of

the affected population and the population's adherence rate. For example, the economic attractiveness of an information system for managing congestive heart failure patients would be dependent upon the number of patients treated by the system, as well as upon the patients' level of adherence to the system's recommendations.

4. **Description of cost-generating events on the clinical pathway experienced by patients:** Clearly, the type of information available for an economic analysis will influence the quality of a study's results. In the HIT value study, provider economic information is already being collected through Medicaid's reimbursement mechanisms. Had this level of information not been available, our study's economic results would be less precise.

5. **Analysis perspective (reflecting key stakeholder interests):** All analyses should be performed from the societal perspective, with secondary analyses from other perspectives as warranted. The societal perspective establishes whether the particular information intervention is a good deal for society as a whole. However, just because an intervention is a good deal for society does not necessary mean that all stakeholders share equally in this value. For example, a hospital alert system may succeed in preventing serious medical complications. While the hospital that pays for this system may receive some financial benefit from reduced costs associated with lower complication rates, there may be other cost savings to society from reductions in subsequent medical expenses. To the extent that the hospital paying for the alert system does not share in these financial benefits, they are being under compensated for their efforts and other stakeholders (such as payers) may be reaping undue economic benefits. While

the misallocation of economic returns in this example has no effect on the overall economic attractiveness of the information intervention from the societal perspective, it may negatively impact the intervention's acceptance should hospitals feel that they are not being properly reimbursed for the costs of their information intervention services.

6. **Time horizon of the intervention and its sequelae:** As shown in our example, assuming a three versus five year system lifecycle will influence the potential economic attractiveness of our HIT value interventions. Similarly, the time horizon of an economic analysis will also influence the economic attractiveness of an outpatient disease management system in which changes in patient outcomes may occur gradually over an elongated time period.

7. **Scale of the intervention:** Economies of scale may influence the economic attractiveness of information interventions. A medical alert may be clinically and technically sound; however, if it is infrequently used, the health benefits may not justify the medical costs.

CONCLUSION

As healthcare costs continue to rise, policy makers are looking to health information technologies as a means of managing or reducing medical costs. However, until the medical informatics community adopts rigorous methods for economic analysis, it will not be possible to determine whether these expectations are being realized. In this chapter, we have given a brief overview of health economics and how some of these principles may be applied to the economic evaluation of health information technology interventions. We hope that this work will cause medical informaticians to begin thinking about how they can include economics into their evaluation studies.

FUTURE RESEARCH DIRECTIONS

Agenda

Many health policy makers believe that health information technology will be a key element in their efforts to improve quality while reducing healthcare costs. Yet, they have little substantive clinical and economic research to serve as a guide for making sound investment decisions. Work by our group and others have demonstrated the paucity of even moderate quality economic research among health information technology evaluation studies (Chaudhry et al., 2006; Eisenstein et al., 2006). For this reason, we propose a three pronged agenda to (1) educate medical informatics researchers about economic evaluation standards, (2) address research methods that are particularly important for medical informatics researchers, and (3) provide a portfolio of research which policy makers and other purchasers can use in making their health information technology investment decisions.

- **Standards adoption and education:** Numerous standards have been proposed for the economic evaluation of medical technologies (Drummond & Jefferson, 1996; Gold et al., 1996; NICE 2007a). Yet, the medical informatics community is largely ignorant of this work. Since the differences between these standards are minor, we propose that medical informatics researchers adopt the standard advocated by their particular governmental bodies. We also propose that medical informatics and other journals adopt as a standard method for organizing and presenting health information technology economic evaluation studies the STARE-HI guidelines (standards for reporting on evaluation studies in healthcare), which were developed by the European Federation for Medical Informatics' Working Group for Assessment of Health Information Systems

(EFMI 2007b). Once there is general agreement on guidelines for gathering data and reporting methods, there are a number of texts that can be used to train health informatics researchers in the details of economic evaluation methods (Donaldson et al., 2002; Gold et al., 1996; NICE 2007a; Levin & McEwan P, 2000; Mugford, 2001).

- **Creation and extension of methods:** Although health informatics researchers can benefit from previous work in the economic evaluation of medical technologies, there are areas in which they may be uniquely qualified to make methodological contributions. An example of this is in the area of complex interventions. While a general framework for the design and evaluation of these interventions has been proposed and some work has been conducted on their economic evaluation, much critical methodological work remains to be done (Byford & Selton, 2003; Campbell et al., 2000). Since many health information technologies function as complex interventions in the healthcare system, we believe that medical informatics researchers may be able to play a pivotal role in the understanding and evaluation of these systems, and in the development of tools and methods for this work.

- **Application of economic evaluation methods:** Although there are many areas in which medical informatics researchers can contribute to the economic evaluation of health information technologies, we believe that guidelines implementation will be among the most fruitful. Whether through EMR or CPOE, guidelines implementation is a natural application for information technology. Yet, work to date has not been uniformly successful (Eccles et al., 2002; Grimshaw & Eccles, 2004). Nonetheless, there is ample opportunity for medical informatics researchers to augment current efforts in this area and to play key roles in multi-disciplinary project teams.

ACKNOWLEDGMENT

The authors acknowledge and appreciate support of part of the work described in this chapter from the Agency for Healthcare Research and Quality, grant R01 HS15057.

REFERENCE

Byford, S., & Sclton, T. (2003). Economic evaluation of complex health and social care interventions. *National Institute Economic Review, 186,* 98-108.

Campbell, M., Fitzpatrick, R., Haines, A., Kinmonth, A. L., Sandercock, P., Spiegelhalter, D., & Tyrer, P. (2000). Framework for design and evaluation of complex interventions to improve health. *British Medical Journal, 321*(7262), 694-696.

Chaudhry, B., Wang, J., Wu, S., Maglione, M., Mojica, W., Roth, E. et al. (2006). Systematic review: impact of health information technology on quality, efficiency, and costs of medical care. *Annals of Internal Medicine, 144*(10), 742-752.

Donaldson, C., Mugford, M., & Vale, L. (2002). Using systematic reviews in economic evaluation. In *Evidence-based health economics. From effectiveness to efficiency in systematic review.* London: BMJ Books.

Drummond, M. F., & Jefferson, T. O. (1996). Guidelines for authors and peer reviewers of economic submissions to the BMJ. The BMJ Economic Evaluation Working Party. *British Medical Journal, 313*(7052), 275-283.

Eccles, M., McColl, E., Steen, N., Rousseau, N., Grimshaw, J., Parkin, D., & Purves, I. (2002). Effect of computerized evidence based guidelines on management of asthma and angina in adults in primary care: Cluster randomized controlled trial. *British Medical Journal, 325*(7370), 941.

Eisenstein, E. L. (2006). Conducting an economic analysis to assess the electrocardiogram's value. *Journal of Electrocardiology, 39*(2), 241-247.

Eisenstein, E. L., & Mark, D. B. (2004). Cost effectiveness of new diagnostic tools and therapies for acute coronary syndromes. In E.J.Topol (Ed.), *Acute Coronary Syndromes* (3rd ed., pp. 723-745). New York: Marcel Dekker.

Frisse, M. C. (1999). The business value of healthcare information technology. *Journal of the American Medical Informatics Association, 6*(5), 361-367.

Girosi, F., Melli, R., & Scoville, R. (2005). Extrapolating evidence of health information technology savings and costs. *RAND Corporation.* Retrieved December 01, 2006 from http://www.rand.org/pubs/monographs/MG410/index.html)

Gold, M. R., Siegel, J., Russell, L., & Weinstein, M. (1996). *Cost-effectiveness in health and medicine.* New York: Oxford University Press.

Goldman, L., Weinstein, M. C., Goldman, P. A., & Williams, L. W. (1991). Cost-effectiveness of HMG-CoA reductase inhibition for primary and secondary prevention of coronary heart disease. *Journal of the American Medical Association, 265*(9), 1145-1151.

Grimshaw, J. M., & Eccles, M. P. (2004). Is evidence-based implementation of evidence-based care possible? *Medical Journal of Australia, 180*(6 Suppl), S50-S51.

Heavy, S. R. (2006). House approves health data technology bill. Retrieved August 1, 2006, from http://news.yahoo.com/s/nm/20060728/hl_nm/congress_health_technology_dc

Kaushal, R., Jha, A. K., Franz, C., Glaser, J., Shetty, K. D., Jaggi, T., et al. (2006). Return on investment for a computerized physician order entry system. *Journal of the American Medical Informatics Association, 13*(3), 261-266.

Kawamoto, K., & Lobach, D. F. (2005). Design, implementation, use, and preliminary evaluation of SEBASTIAN, a standards-based web service for clinical decision support. *AMIA Symposium 2005*, 380-384.

Keeler, E. B., & Cretin, S. (1983). Discounting of life-saving and other nonmonetary effects. *Management Science, 29*, 300-306.

Kuperman, G. J., & Gibson, R. F. (2003). Computer physician order entry: Benefits, costs, and issues. *Annals of Internal Medicine, 139*(1), 31-39.

Lairson, D. R., Chang, Y. C., Bettencourt, J. L., Vernon, S. W., & Greisinger, A. (2006). Estimating development cost for a tailored interactive computer program to enhance colorectal cancer screening compliance. *Journal of the American Medical Informatics Association, 13*(5), 476-484.

Levin, H., & McEwan, P. (2000). *Cost-effectiveness analysis: Methods and applications.* Thousand Oaks, CA: Sage Publications.

Li, J. S., Eisenstein, E. L., Grabowski, H. G., Reid, E. D., Mangum, B., Schulman, K. A., et al. (2007). Economic return of clinical trials performed under the pediatric exclusivity program. *Journal of the American Medical Association, 297*(5), 480-488.

Lobach, D. F., Kawamoto, K., & Hasselblad, V. (2004). Development of an information system to support collaboration for population-based healthcare for Medicaid beneficiaries. TOP Project Evaluation Report. *Technology Opportunities Program.* Retrieved December 01, 2006, from http://ntiaotiant2.ntia.doc.gov/top/docs/eval/pdf/376099007e.pdf)

Lobach, D. F., Low, R., Arbanas, J. A., Rabold, J. S., Tatum, J. L., & Epstein, S. D. (2001). Defining and supporting the diverse information needs of community-based care using the web and hand-held devices. *Proceedings of the AMIA Annual Symposium*, 398-402.

Luce, B. (1996). Estimating costs in cost-effectiveness analysis. In M.R.Gold, J. Siegel, L. Russel, & M. C. Weinstein (Eds.), *Cost-effectiveness in health and medicine* (pp. 176). New York: Oxford University Press.

Miller, R. H., & West, C. E. (2007). The value of electronic health records in community health centers: Policy implications. *Health Affairs, 26*(1), 206-214.

Mugford, M. (2001). Using systematic reviews for economic evaluation. In M. Egger, G. Davey Smith, & D. G. Altman (Eds.), *Systematic reviews in health care: Meta-analysis in context.* London: BMJ Books.

Nagle, T. & Holden, R. (2002). *The strategy and tactics of pricing: A guide to profitable decision making.* Upper Saddle River, NJ: Prentice Hall.

National Institute for Health and Clinical Excellence (2007a). Retrieved December 01, 2006, from http://www.nice.org.uk/

Ohsfeldt, R. L., Ward, M. M., Schneider, J. E., Jaana, M., Miller, T. R., Lei, Y., & Wakefield, D. S. (2005). Implementation of hospital computerized physician order entry systems in a rural state: feasibility and financial impact. *Journal of the American Medical Informatics Association, 12*(1), 20-27.

Panko, W. B. (1999). Clinical care and the factory floor. *Journal of the American Medical Informatics Association, 6*(5), 349-353.

Sidorov, J. (2006). It ain't necessarily so: The electronic health record and the unlikely prospect of reducing healthcare costs. *Health Affairs, 25*(4), 1079-1085.

Stead, W. W., & Lorenzi, N. M. (1999). Health informatics: Linking investment to value. *Journal of the American Medical Informatics Association, 6*(5), 341-348.

Tierney, W. M., Overhage, J. M., & McDonald, C. J. (1994). A plea for controlled trials in medical informatics. *Journal of the American Medical Informatics Association, 1*(4), 353-355.

Tuttle, M. S. (1999). Information technology outside healthcare: What does it matter to us? *Journal of the American Medical Informatics Association, 6*(5), 354-360.

U.S.Department of Health and Human Services (2007). Office of the National Coordinator for Health Information Technology. Retrieved December 1, 2006, from http://www.hhs.gov/healthit/

U.S. Renal Data System (2006). *U.S.RDS 2006 annual data report. Atlas of end-stage renal disease in the United States.* Bethesda, MD: National Institutes of Health, National Institute of Diabetes and Digestive and Kidney Diseases.

Walker, J., Pan, E., Johnston, D., Adler-Milstein, J., Bates, D. W., & Middleton, B. (2005). The value of healthcare information exchange and interoperability. *Health Affairs, Supplemental Web Exclusives*). Retrieved December 01, 2006 from http://content.healthaffairs.org/cgi/content/abstract/hlthaff.w5.10v1 percent20

White House. (2004). *Transforming healthcare: The President's health information technology planG.* Retrieved April 27, 2006, from http://wwwwhitehouse.gov/infocus/technology/economic_policy200404/chap3.html

Working Group for Assessment of Health Information Systems of the European Federation for Medical Informatics (EFMI) (2007b). Retrieved June 01, 2007, from http://iig.umit.at/efmi/

ADDITIONAL READINGS

Evaluation Methods

Campbell, M., Fitzpatrick, R., Haines, A., Kinmonth, A. L., Sandercock, P., Spiegelhalter, D. et al (2000). Framework for design and evaluation of complex interventions to improve health. *British Medical Journal, 321*(7262), 694-696.

Eisenstein, E. L., Ortiz, M., Anstrom, K. J., Crosslin, D. R., & Lobach, D. F. (2006). Assessing the quality of medical information technology economic evaluations: room for improvement. *AMIA 2006 Annual Symposium Proceedings* (pp. 228-234).

Iezzoni, L.I. (Ed.). (1997). *Risk adjustment for measuring healthcare outcomes.* Chicago: Health Administration Press.

Rossi, P.H., Lipsey, M.W., & Freeman, H.E. (2004). *Evaluation: A systems approach.* Thousand Oaks, CA: Sage Publications.

Economic Evaluation Guidelines

National Institute for Health and Clinical Excellence. (2007). Retrieved December 01, 2006, from *http://www.nice.org.uk/*

Drummond, M. F., & Jefferson, T. O. (1996). Guidelines for authors and peer reviewers of economic submissions to the BMJ. The BMJ Economic Evaluation Working Party. *British Medical Journal, 313*(7052), 275-283.

Gold, M. R., Siegel, J., Russell, L., & Weinstein, M. (1996). *Cost-effectiveness in health and medicine.* New York: Oxford University Press.

Economic Evaluation Methods

Byford, S., Drummond, M., Eisenstein, E.l., Knapp, M., Mallender, J., McDaid, D. et al. (in press). Incorporating economic evidence. In J. Higging & S. Green (Eds.), *Cochrane handbook for systematic reviews of interventions.* Chichester: John Wiley & Sons.

Byford, S., & Selton, T. (2003). Economic evaluation of complex health and social care interventions. *National Institute Economic Review, 186,* 98-108.

Donaldson, C., Mugford, M., & Vale, L. (2002). Using systematic reviews in economic evaluation. In *Evidence-based health economics. From effectiveness to efficiency in systematic review.* London: BMJ Books.

Eisenstein, E. L., & Mark, D. B. (2004). Cost effectiveness of new diagnostic tools and therapies for acute coronary syndromes. In E.J. Topol (Ed.), *Acute coronary syndromes* (3rd ed., pp. 723-745). New York: Marcel Dekker.

Levin, H., & McEwan, P. (Eds.). (2000). *Cost-effectiveness analysis: Methods and applications.* Thousand Oaks, CA: Sage Publications.

Mugford, M. (2001). Using systematic reviews for economic evaluation. In M. Egger, G. Davey Smith, & D.G. Altman (Eds.), *Systematic reviews in healthcare: Meta-analysis in context.* London: BMJ Books.

Evaluation Studies

Ammenwerth, E., & de Keizer, N. (2005). An inventory of evaluation studies of information technology in healthcare trends in evaluation research 1982-2002. *Methods of Information in Medicine, 4*(1), 44-56.

Chaudhry, B., Wang, J., Wu, S., Maglione, M., Mojica, W., Roth, E. et al. (2006). Systematic review: Impact of health information technology on quality, efficiency, and costs of medical care. *Annals of Internal Medicine, 144*(10), 742-752.

Eisenstein, E. L. (2006). Conducting an economic analysis to assess the electrocardiogram's value. *Journal of Electrocardiology, 39*(2), 241-247.

Eisenstein, E.L., Anstrom, K.J., Marci, J.M., Crosslin, D.R., Johnson, F.S., Kawamoto, K. et al. (2005). Assessing the potential economic value of health information technology interventions in a community-based health network. AMIA *2005 Annual Symposium Proceedings,* 221-225.

Eisenstein, E.L., Ortiz, M., Anstrom, K.J., Crosslin, D.R., & Lobach, D.F (2006). Assessing the quality of medical information technology economic evaluations: room for improvement. *AMIA 2006 Annual Symposium Proceedings,* 234-228.

Kaushal, R., Jha, A. K., Franz, C., Glaser, J., Shetty, K. D., Jaggi, T. et al. (2006). Return on investment for a computerized physician order entry system. *Journal of the American Medical Informatics Association, 13*(3), 261-266.

Kuperman, G. J., & Gibson, R. F. (2003). Computer physician order entry: Benefits, costs, and issues. *Annals of Internal Medicine, 139*(1), 31-39.

Lairson, D. R., Chang, Y. C., Bettencourt, J. L., Vernon, S. W., & Greisinger, A. (2006). Estimating development cost for a tailored interactive computer program to enhance colorectal cancer screening compliance. *Journal of the American Medical Informatics Association, 13*(5), 476-484.

Ohsfeldt, R. L., Ward, M. M., Schneider, J. E., Jaana, M., Miller, T. R., Lei, Y. et al. (2005). Implementation of hospital computerized physician order entry systems in a rural state: Feasibility and financial impact. *Journal of the American Medical Informatics Association, 12*(1), 20-27.

Sidorov, J. (2006). It ain't necessarily so: The electronic health record and the unlikely prospect of reducing health care costs. *Health Affairs, 25*(4), 1079-1085.

Tierney, W. M., Overhage, J. M., & McDonald, C. J. (1994). A plea for controlled trials in medical informatics. *Journal of the American Medical Informatics Association, 1*(4), 353-355.

Section V
Legal, Ethical, and Professional Issues

Chapter XV
Legal Issues in Health Information and Electronic Health Records

Nola M. Ries
University of Alberta, Canada
University of Victoria, Canada

ABSTRACT

This chapter discusses key legal issues raised by the contemporary trend to managing and sharing patient information via electronic health records (EHR). Concepts of privacy, confidentiality, consent, and security are defined and considered in the context of EHR initiatives in Canada, the United Kingdom, and Australia. This chapter explores whether patients have the right to withhold consent to the collection and sharing of their personal information via EHRs. It discusses opt-in and opt-out models for participation in EHRs and concludes that presumed consent for EHR participation will ensure more rapid and complete implementation, but at the cost of some personal choice for patients. The reduction in patient control over personal information ought to be augmented with strong security protections to minimize risks of unauthorized access to EHRs and fulfill legal and ethical obligations to safeguard patient information.

INTRODUCTION

Healthcare providers have long observed an ethical imperative to respect privacy of patient information. For physicians, this ethical duty originates in the Hippocratic oath, which states:

Whatsoever things I see or hear concerning the life of man, in any attendance on the sick or even apart therefrom, which ought not to be noised abroad, I will keep secret thereon, counting such things to be as sacred secrets (quoted in Rozovsky & Inions, 2002, p. 86).

Copyright © 2008, IGI Global, distributing in print or electronic forms without written permission of IGI Global is prohibited.

In the past, individuals often had a longstanding relationship with a very small number of care providers and health records were maintained in paper files and seldom shared with other health practitioners, or even the patient. Contemporary healthcare is much more complex. Highly mobile individuals seek healthcare in different geographical locations and, with the growth in collaborative, multidisciplinary care, patients are treated not only by family physicians, but by medical specialists and complementary and alternative care providers. Care is delivered in a wide range of settings: practitioners' offices, walk-in clinics, acute care hospitals, long-term care facilities, and home care situations. To provide appropriate services, patient information must be shared among a wider range of care providers working in different locations. Additionally, many patients take a more active approach to their healthcare and seek access to their records.

Health information technology—including electronic health records (EHR)—can facilitate sharing of information in all these ways to the benefit of both patients and professionals. As a longitudinal record of an individual's healthcare history, EHRs may include summaries of physician visits and care provided in hospital or other facilities, medical test results, x-ray images, prescription drug histories, immunization history, and known allergies. One commentator asserts that EHRs "will transform the purpose of the medical record from a record of information generated by health professionals primarily for their own reference into a shared resource produced and used by all concerned with the process of care" (Cross, 2006b, p. 656). However, the ease with which information can be handled electronically compels special attention to matters of privacy, confidentiality and security. Advances in modern healthcare heighten this responsibility. Novel diagnostic and testing procedures reveal highly sensitive information about patients (e.g., genetic predisposition to a serious disease) and a growing range of pharmaceuticals and proce-

dures are used to treat conditions about which the patient may feel ashamed or embarrassed (e.g., sexual/reproductive health, mental health). Patients are likely to have special concern about safeguarding information that would reveal a stigmatizing medical condition.

EHRs attract particular concern about unauthorized access and disclosure of personal information contained in the records. Although electronic records have the potential to be more secure than paper records with implementation of sophisticated technical safeguards, they also have potential to reveal vast detail about an individual's health history. Unauthorized access may occur intentionally or accidentally by persons internal or external to an organization. A major New York City hospital reportedly "thwarted 1,500 unauthorized attempts by its own employees to look at patient records of a famous local athlete" (Freudenheim & Pear, 2006, p. 1). Hackers may also infiltrate EHR systems for nefarious purposes, such as identity theft. Canada's federal privacy commissioner articulates these concerns:

Until relatively recently, privacy was protected pretty much by default. As long as information about us was in paper records, and scattered over a whole lot of locations, someone would have to go to a lot of trouble to compile a detailed dossier on any individual. But now the move to electronic record-keeping is eating away at the barriers of time, distance, and cost that once guarded our privacy. (Privacy Commissioner of Canada, 2001)

This chapter discusses key legal issues raised by the contemporary trend to managing and sharing patient information via EHRs. Concepts of privacy, confidentiality, consent, and security are defined and considered in the context of EHR initiatives in several jurisdictions, including Canada, the United Kingdom and Australia. As this chapter concentrates on legal issues in health information and EHRs, the following questions are addressed:

Do patients have a right to withhold consent to have information collected and/or shared via EHRs? Do laws impose special security requirements for EHRs? Do legal rules hinder or impede the implementation of EHRs and the ability to realize benefits attributed to EHRs? These benefits and challenges are summed up in the following statement: "Most people agree that patient centred care requires comprehensive information to be available wherever and whenever care is provided. There is less agreement, however, on how patients should consent to use of electronic health records and how the data can be kept secure" (Watson & Halamka, 2006, p. 39).

ELECTRONIC HEALTH RECORD INITIATIVES

Many countries are investing significant resources in EHR initiatives. In Canada, Canada Health Infoway was launched in 2001 as a not-for-profit organization comprised of deputy ministers of health from the 14 federal, provincial and territorial jurisdictions in the country. Infoway receives funds from the national government, which it then invests in EHR projects, and aims to support interoperable networks across Canada. Its funding agreement mandates that it address personal health information protection in accordance with relevant laws and privacy principles. Each Canadian jurisdiction has its own personal information protection laws, which can pose challenges in ensuring EHR initiatives comply with multiple legal regimes (University of Alberta, 2005).

Beginning in 2002, the UK Health Department allocated £18 billion (US$32 billion) for National Health Service (NHS) information technology (Chantler, Clarke, & Granger, 2005). The NHS aims to implement the National Programme for Information Technology to "connect over 30,000 GPs in England to almost 300 hospitals and give patients access to their personal health and care in-formation, transforming the way the NHS works" (National Health Service, 2005a). This initiative includes several elements: the care records service, the national EHR initiative; electronic prescription transmission; the secondary uses service, which will de-identify patient data to make it available for research; and GP2GP, an initiative to support transfer of patient electronic records from one general practice to another when a patient registers with a new practice. The U.K. Programme "is attempting to create the most comprehensive electronic health records infrastructure of any healthcare system, in which multimedia records compiled at the point of care are made available to authorized users in primary, secondary, tertiary, and community care" (Cross, 2006a, p. 599). The care records service EHR will eventually encompass a comprehensive healthcare history for each patient. A national database, referred to as the "spine" of the system, will contain basic patient information such as name, birth date, allergies, adverse drug reactions, and NHS number. Local EHRs, linkable to the national spine, will contain more detailed information, including medication records, test results, and disease history.

A National Electronic Health Records Taskforce for Australia was established in 1999 to bring "a coordinated approach to electronic health record systems and to avoid the potential for duplication and incompatible systems" (National Electronic Health Records Taskforce, 2000, p. 6). Similar to Canada Health Infoway, the Australian national, state and territorial governments created a not-for-profit organization, the National E-Health Transition Authority (NEHTA), to develop e-health standards and infrastructure requirements for the national EHR initiative. A nationally interoperable shared EHR will allow healthcare providers to use a standardized format to create and store a summary each time a patient receives healthcare, including information such as test results, diagnosis, care plan, medication, and referrals to other care providers.

PRIVACY, CONFIDENTIALITY, CONSENT, AND SECURITY

The concepts of privacy, confidentiality, consent and security are all fundamental to handling of personal health information and EHRs raise important questions about how to operationalize these requirements in the development of systems for collecting and sharing patient information across various healthcare settings. The concept of privacy refers to an individual's right to control access to and use of their personal information and the concept of confidentiality refers to another individual's duty to safeguard information disclosed to them (Marshall & von Tigerstrom, 2002). To obtain healthcare services, patients voluntarily relinquish a degree of privacy by sharing personal details with care providers. However, patients generally do so with the expectation that the healthcare practitioner will keep the information confidential.

The concept of consent is also important in the healthcare context. It is a fundamental legal and ethical rule that healthcare providers must obtain informed consent from patients before administering treatment (subject to limited exceptions in, for example, emergency and health situations). Similarly, patients have certain rights to consent in regard to collection, use and disclosure of their personal information. Privacy and consent are interrelated concepts since privacy interests in one's personal health information are respected if one has an opportunity to exercise some control over it by consenting to, or withholding consent for, various uses or disclosures.

Consent may be given explicitly in writing or orally, or it may be implicit. For instance, if a patient visits her family physician and blood work is required, the doctor will collect and send a blood sample to a lab for analysis. The lab will then send the test results back to the medical office. This sharing of the patient's information is generally done on the basis of implied consent. In seeking care, the patient implicitly agrees to the sharing of her personal medical details between her physician's office and the testing lab. An example of explicit consent occurs when a patient signs a written form agreeing that researchers may review and extract identifiable information from his healthcare records. In this circumstance, the patient would make a consent decision after receiving sufficient information about how her information will be used and protected and those who will have access to it.

The concept of security is important as security measures are a means by which healthcare providers fulfill their duties of confidentiality. Security measures include technical, physical and administrative measures that guard against unauthorized access to information. In regard to electronic data, these may include password protections, encryption mechanisms and audit trails to monitor access. Security measures for paper records include storage in locked cabinets and shredding documents prior to disposal. As discussed later, privacy laws typically impose a legal obligation on organizations to adopt reasonable security measures to safeguard records over which they have control.

LEGAL PROTECTIONS FOR HEALTH INFORMATION

Various legal instruments provide privacy protections for health information, including legislative enactments and professional codes of conduct. Privacy laws are often enforced by independent agencies or commissioners with authority to investigate alleged violations, attempt to resolve complaints through mediation, recommend or order changes to policies or practices to prevent future breaches, and, in some circumstances, impose fines or terms of imprisonment. Healthcare providers may be sanctioned by their professional regulatory bodies for failure to comply with codes of conduct.

The past 15 years have witnessed remarkable growth in the number of laws regulating privacy in public, private and health sectors. The enactment of these laws indicates that legislators are taking privacy seriously, but a sensitive balance must be struck between protecting personal privacy and delivering healthcare. Indeed, stringent legal rules can hinder implementation of EHR initiatives; at the same time, appropriate legal frameworks may bolster patient and professional support for and trust in EHRs. One commentator observes:

EHRs, which facilitate sharing of information by a wide network of people, potentially conflict with privacy principles unless patients control how the record is shared and appropriate security measures are in place. A coherent legal framework to appropriately protect the privacy and confidentiality of personal health records is therefore an essential first step for successful EHRs. (Cornwall, 2003, p. 18)

In countries with multiple levels of government—national, state/provincial and local levels— several layers of legislation may apply to personal information contained in EHRs and add complexity for healthcare organizations and providers in understanding rules for lawful collection, use and sharing of patient information. The situation in Canada and Australia demonstrates the complexity of compliance with statutes enacted by various levels of government.

Beginning in the 1990s, many Canadian provinces began enacting privacy protection and information access laws applicable in the public sector. These laws generally applied to government health departments and publicly funded hospitals, but did not regulate private healthcare practices. By the late 1990s, several provinces had developed legislation to regulate health information directly and some adopted specific rules governing EHRs (Ries & Moysa, 2005). In 2001, the federal government adopted a personal information protection law to apply to commercial

activities and this legislation was extended to the health sector in 2004. Several provinces enacted their own private sector privacy laws, which allowed them to be exempt from regulation under the federal law. This patchwork of legal regimes has generated criticism, including concern that it may impede EHR implementation. For example, a 2002 Senate report on the Canadian healthcare system observed:

Currently, there is significant variation in privacy laws and data access policies across the country that poses a challenge for EHR systems that are dependent on inter-sectoral and inter-jurisdictional flows of personal health information. Differences in rules on how the scope of purpose is defined, the form of consent required, the conditions for substitute decision-making, the criteria for non-consensual access to personal health information, periods for retention of data and requirements for destruction, to name but a few, must be seriously addressed in order to enable the development of EHR systems. (Canada, Standing Senate Committee on Social Affairs, Science and Technology, 2002, section 10.4)

Like Canada, Australia has both federal and state privacy laws that apply to various healthcare entities (National Health and Medical Research Council, 2004). Federal bodies such as the national health department have been regulated under federal privacy legislation since 1988. This statute was extended to the private health sector in 2001, encompassing physicians, pharmacists and federal private hospitals. State-run organizations are governed by local legislation or, in the absence of legislation, codes of practice. The National E-Health Transition Authority has noted the challenges of navigating this legislative intricacy:

Privacy is regulated by a complex amalgam of Commonwealth, State and Territory privacy legislation combined with administrative instructions.

Requirements relating to the collection or handling of personal information can also be found in other non-privacy legislation ... The picture is further complicated by the increased use of outsourcing by Australian governments, and the need to ensure privacy protection follows the outsourced data, as well as the development of independent privacy schemes, particularly in the area of health privacy at the state/territory level. (National E-Health Transition Authority, 2006, p. 10)

Alongside the enactment of laws regulating health information, some health professional organizations have adopted codes of conduct that stipulate guiding principles relevant to privacy, consent, confidentiality and security. The Canadian Medical Association Health Information Privacy Code (1998) elaborates on the significance of the right to privacy in the professional-patient relationship:

The right of privacy is fundamental in a free and democratic society. It includes a patient's right to determine with whom he or she will share information and to know of and exercise control over use, disclosure and access concerning any information collected about him or her. The right of privacy and consent are essential to the trust and integrity of the patient-physician relationship. Nonconsensual collection, use, access or disclosure violates the patient's right of privacy.

If codes of conduct impose strict rules about patient control over health information, care providers may have difficulty complying with these rules during EHR implementation. Indeed, professional codes of conduct may create more onerous requirements than privacy laws. For example, the Canadian Health Information Privacy Code states that physicians can infer that patients consent to use and disclosure of health information for their therapeutic benefit. However, the code elaborates that "consent to collection, use, disclosure and access for longitudinal primary purposes must

be express unless the provider has good reason to infer consent" (Principle 5.5) and further, "implied consent does not deprive the patient of the right to refuse consent ..." (Principle 5.8). If patient information will be included in an EHR for the purpose of providing longitudinal care, then, according to the privacy code, the physician must obtain the patient's consent to include information on the EHR. Even if patient consent were implied, a right to revoke consent remains. Obtaining specific consent to opt-in to an EHR may be impractical to implement and, as discussed below, some privacy legislation has been revised to eliminate this requirement.

REGULATING COLLECTION, USE AND DISCLOSURE OF INFORMATION IN ELECTRONIC HEALTH RECORDS

In developing EHR systems, various strategies may be adopted to respect privacy rights of individuals and ensure healthcare providers can meet their confidentiality obligations. These include:

- Giving patients a choice to opt in or opt out of EHR systems
- Giving patients a choice to request that specified information be "masked" within the EHR system with limited access to certain healthcare providers
- Restrict levels of access to EHRs on a "need to know" basis
- Regular monitoring and auditing of access to EHRs
- Implement state-of-the-art security measures

While it is uncontroversial that rigorous administrative and security measures should be implemented to protect EHRs from unnecessary and unauthorized access, tampering and disclosure, the issue of patient consent to participation in EHR initiatives has generated much debate and some differences in approaches among jurisdictions (Cornwall 2003; Ries, 2006; Ries & Moysa, 2005). Many privacy protection principles and professional codes of conduct emphasize the importance of obtaining patient consent for collection, use and sharing of identifiable health information. Should this principle apply to require individual patient consent before a care provider records information in an EHR, or shares that information with others involved in the patient's care? Under an opt-in model, healthcare providers would need to obtain explicit, informed consent from patients before their health information would be put onto an EHR system. With an opt-out approach, patient information would be included in the EHR unless the individual specifically instructs the care provider not to collect or share the information electronically.

In the United Kingdom, development and implementation of the Care Records Service EHR has been dogged by privacy concerns; critics argue "the scale and proposed content of the electronic health record threatens medical privacy and, potentially, other human rights" (Cross, 2006a, p. 599). The British Medical Association (BMA) has also criticized the government for lack of sufficient consultation with the U.K. medical profession (Powell, 2004). Much confusion has erupted over whether patient participation in the EHR will be voluntary or compulsory and, if compulsory, whether patients may still exercise some control over personal information included in the EHR, such as "lock boxes" on sensitive details a patient may not want generally accessible to anyone who opens their EHR.

To remedy this confusion, the National Health Service issued a "care record guarantee" that describes patient rights and health provider obligations in regard to privacy and confidentiality of healthcare records. This guarantee assures patients that the EHR will hold their personal health details "securely, making them available to the right people where and when they are needed for your healthcare, while maintaining your confidentiality" (National Health Service, 2005b). The guarantee is premised on compulsory participation in the Care Records Service, so patients do not have the option of withholding consent for collection of their information electronically. However, the guarantee allows patients the right to limit sharing of their information: "Usually you can choose to limit how we share the information in your electronic care records which identifies you. In helping you decide, we will discuss with you how this may affect our ability to provide you with care or treatment, and any alternatives available to you." This guarantee suggests that "UK doctors will be expected to spend time in every consultation discussing with patients what information about them is shared across NHS computers" (Cross, 2005, p. 1226). Canadian and Australian experiences discussed below suggest that it may be very time-consuming and costly to expect physicians to have detailed conversations with patients about consent for sharing information electronically.

Despite the potential burdens on physicians, the British Medical Association supports an opt-in model for patient participation in the national EHR scheme:

It is the BMA view that patients should be asked for consent explicitly before any clinical information is shared onto a central system. Doctors feel that some patients may be unhappy about having their personal data uploaded onto a central system and a more gradual approach will allow patients to fully consider what information is contained in their records and whether they wish this information to be shared. Their view is that uploading clinical data without explicitly asking the patient could jeopardise the trust and relationship between doctors and patients, as well as violating a patient's right to confidentiality. (British Medical Association, 2006)

In Australia, a privacy framework is being developed for the national EHR initiative. The initial Business Architecture Plan stated that patient participation would be voluntary and individual consent would be required to authorize collection, use and disclosure of personal information via the system (Ries, 2006, p. 703). At each clinical interaction, patients would have a choice of having information recorded in the EHR and who would be authorized to access that information in the future. However, experience from pilot EHR trials in the Australian state of Tasmania demonstrated that care providers often did not obtain informed consent from patients before adding information to the system and such a requirement would be administratively burdensome (McSherry, 2004). The consent model Australia will adopt remains undecided and a December 2006 privacy consultation document states:

Consent in the health context has proved to be one of the most intractable policy and legal issues faced by Australian e-health initiatives. Numerous debates about the respective merits of 'opt in' v. 'opt out'; confusion about the plethora of privacy laws in operation in Australia; and the risk of failing to meet all relevant compliance requirements (particularly meeting the test of 'informed consent') have deeply affected the debate to date. (National E-Health Transition Authority, 2006, p. 23)

In Canada, legislators in some jurisdictions have amended privacy legislation to eliminate requirements to obtain individual patient consent before information is disclosed through an EHR. For example, when the province of Alberta enacted the Health Information Act in 2001, it contained rules that required a healthcare provider to explain a number of details to a patient to obtain permission to share health information electronically, including: the reason for disclosing the information; an explanation of why the information is needed; the risks and benefits of

granting or refusing consent; and the right of a patient to withdraw consent at any time. As with the experience in Tasmania, implementation of these conditions proved difficult in practice. In a pilot project for a pharmaceutical information network, "doctors were taking more than 30 minutes to explain the system, driven by concerns about professional liability" (Cornwall, 2003, p. 22). The Alberta Information and Privacy Commissioner (2003) noted that "getting consent ... was going to be difficult and costly" and conceded that the drawbacks of obtaining consent outweighed the benefit. The government revised the legislation in 2003 to remove the consent requirement.

However, some provincial health information protection laws may give patients the right to request limits on disclosure of their personal information. For example, legislation in the provinces of Ontario (Personal Health Information Protection Act, 2004, s. 22(2)) and Manitoba (Personal Health Information Act, 1997, s. 38(1)) permit a patient to refuse consent for disclosure of information to other healthcare providers. Under Ontario's law, if a healthcare provider does not have consent to release all patient information to another professional that may be relevant to the patient's care, this limitation on disclosure must be communicated to the other professional (s. 20(3)).

Canadian health information laws impose a legal duty to implement appropriate security safeguards to protect personal information from unauthorized handling. Information that is stored and transferred electronically is viewed as having greater risk of security breach, so additional security measures are generally required for electronic systems. For instance, Manitoba regulations require that security procedures for electronic health systems ensure regular monitoring and auditing of user activity (Personal Health Information Regulation, s. 4). The record of user activity must specify whose information was accessed, by whom, when, and if information from the electronic record was subsequently disclosed.

LEARNING FROM EXPERIENCE

As experiences from Canada, Australia and the United Kingdom show, legislators, policy-makers and EHR system designers must confront legal issues related to patient privacy and confidentiality of personal health information. Debate about patient control over information in EHRs is heightened as "[c]omputerized databases of personally identifiable information may be accessed, changed, viewed, copied, used, disclosed, or deleted more easily and by more people (authorized and unauthorized) than paper-based records" (Hodge, Gostin, & Jacobson, 1999, p. 1467). To sustain public trust in the healthcare system, patients must have confidence that their information will be secure if it is stored and shared through electronic networks. Patients do not have uniform views about whether EHR systems are based on opt-in or opt-out models; patients with sensitive medical histories may want to make a specific choice about opting in, but others may want governments to avoid further delay with EHR development. Indeed, a patient representative on the U.K. Care Record Development Board argues:

So does the advantage of opting in for a minority of patients with sensitive histories stack up against the disadvantage imposed on the majority if a flawed implementation process results in delays and frustration for patients and hard pressed practitioners? Certainly, an effective public information campaign is vital to fulfil the ethical and legal requirements for informed consent. But surely patients have a right to expect the NHS to positively harness technology, to reform the way it uses information, and hence to improve services and the quality of patient care? It would be unfortunate if an over-riding emphasis on the NHS's role as guardian of patient confidentiality resulted in an unworkable operating model for the implementation of the care record. (Wilkinson, 2006, p. 43)

Nonetheless, legal and ethical rules require attention to consent rights and confidentiality obligations. To mitigate problems of overlapping or conflicting privacy laws that may impede development of EHRs, cooperative efforts to develop best practices are useful. A national body in Canada has developed a health information privacy framework to recommend harmonized principles for collection, use and disclosure of personal health information across sectors. This harmonization initiative aims to "facilitate healthcare renewal, including the development of electronic health record systems...." (Pan-Canadian Health Information Privacy and Confidentiality Framework, 2005). Similarly, to address gaps in Australia's personal information protection practices, a National Health Privacy Working Group has promulgated a draft National Health Privacy Code, with three key goals: (1) provide consistent rules across jurisdictions and between public and private sectors; (2) address the impact of new technologies; and (3) safeguard privacy of personal health information (National Health Privacy Working Group, 2003). How this privacy code will apply to EHRs is a matter that remains unresolved.

Jurisdictions like Alberta and Tasmania that piloted EHR systems on the basis of an opt-in consent model have found this to be unworkable and it is foreseeable that other initiatives will face similar problems that it is time-consuming and complex for healthcare providers to explain the system, its features, risks and benefits to patients. If governments adopt an opt-out model, patients will be assumed to consent to having at least basic personal and medical information included in an EHR, but patients may refuse consent for collection and disclosure of specified information that is of particular sensitivity. If patients cannot opt-out entirely from an EHR system, then governments "must convincingly show that technical, organisational, and legal safeguards will be implemented in its information technology programme. These safeguards must include strict and transparent rules of access to health records, mechanisms of complaint, and open understandable information about the programme and its implications" (Norheim, 2006, p. 3).

CONCLUSION

Electronic health records promise important benefits for patients, healthcare providers, and those who plan and manage complex, modern health systems. Yet, EHRs raise special privacy concerns and an appropriate balance must be sought between personal information protection and systems that are reasonably comprehensive and not unduly cumbersome. Privacy principles and ethical standards often emphasize patient consent as fundamental to respect for autonomy and choice. However, if all patients must consent before their personal information is compiled onto an EHR and made available to others involved in their care and treatment, it is foreseeable that EHR implementation will be slow and costly. An opt-out model for EHR participation will ensure more rapid and complete inclusion of patient information, but at the cost of some degree of personal choice for patients. Governmental bodies responsible for developing EHR systems ought to engage in consultation with privacy commissioners, health practitioner groups, and the public on issues of privacy and confidentiality. A transparent approach to these contentious matters will help ensure that EHRs are implemented in ways that respect values and interests of all who have a stake in these major health information technology investments.

FUTURE RESEARCH DIRECTIONS

Additional research in two areas would assist in the development of appropriate privacy protections and consent models for EHR systems: (1) patient/citizen expectations and attitudes; and (2)

healthcare professional duties and behaviours. EHRs are adopted within social and professional contexts where patients and healthcare providers each have their own sets of expectations and concerns in regard to personal health information.

As this chapter discussed, some health professional codes of conduct may impose more stringent rules for handling of personal information than privacy laws. An important research question here, then, is how can professionals adopt and participate in EHR systems while meeting their fundamental ethical obligations to respect patient privacy? How prevalent and serious are conflicts between professional codes and privacy laws? Do healthcare professionals perceive there are conflicts and are they between the proverbial rock and a hard place, caught between professional ethics that dictate one behaviour (e.g., obtaining patient consent before including information on an EHR) and system-wide policies that dictate another (e.g., presumed consent for inclusion of information on EHRs)? How can competing principles be reconciled?

In addition to analyzing interrelationships between professional codes of conduct and privacy laws, further research is needed regarding health professionals' practices and behaviours in the context of EHR implementation. How do professionals manage issues related to privacy and patient consent? As discussed in this chapter, some experiences suggest it is very time-consuming for care providers to explain EHR systems to patients. Will this experience hold true in other contexts of EHR adoption? How will healthcare professionals explain patients' rights to them, such as a right to limit disclosure of personal information via an EHR? Will care providers offer the same explanation to all patients or will they only discuss these types of privacy protections with patients who have conditions perceived as stigmatizing? In other words, will a form of medical paternalism influence how professionals communicate with patients about EHRs?

Further, what are patient views about electronic health records? Is it making a mountain out of a molehill to constantly emphasize the sensitivity of personal health information? Citizen often guard other personal information very closely, such as details about income, investments and financial history, yet the banking industry is years ahead of the healthcare industry in many countries in the adoption of information technology. What can the healthcare sector learn from other sectors about adoption of information technologies in a manner that protects personal information and maintains client trust in organizations? For patients who express concerns about security of EHRs, what measures would make them more comfortable with the technology? What are patient preferences in regard to rights to opt in or opt out of EHR initiatives or to have information protected by lock boxes with the system? Do patients want electronic access to their records? What are their perceptions, preferences and expectations about EHRs?

Further investigation of these types of questions are critically important in informing further development and refinement of legal protections for personal health information in the context of EHR systems.

REFERENCES

Alberta Information and Privacy Commissioner. (2003). Commissioner's response to repeal of section 59 and introduction of section 60(2) of the *Health Information Act*. Press release retrieved December 20, 2006, from http://www.oipc.ab.ca/ims/client/upload/Repeal_of_s.59.pdf

British Medical Association. (2006). *BMA statement on Connecting for Health*. Retrieved January 25, 2007, from http://www.bma.org.uk

Canada, Standing Senate Committee on Social Affairs, Science and Technology. (2002). *The Health of Canadians—The Federal Role*, vol. 1-6. Ottawa: Standing Senate Committee on Social Affairs, Science and Technology.

Canadian Medical Association. (1998). *Health Information Privacy Code*. Retrieved December 1, 2006 from http://www.cma.ca/index.cfm/ci_id/3216/la_id/1.htm

Chantler C., Clarke, T., & Granger, R. (2006). Information technology in the English national health service. *Journal of the American Medical Association, 296*(18), 2255-2258.

Cornwall, A. (2003). Connecting health: A review of electronic health record projects in Australia, Europe and Canada. *Public Interest Advocacy Centre*. Retrieved December 1, 2006, from http://www.piac.asn.au/publications/pubs/churchill_20030121.html

Cross, M. (2005). UK patients can refuse to let their data be shared across networks. *British Medical Journal, 330*, 1226.

Cross, M. (2006a). Will connecting for health deliver its promises? *British Medical Journal, 332*(7541), 599-601.

Cross, M. (2006b). Keeping the NHS electronic spine on track. *British Medical Journal, 332*(7542), 656-658.

Freudenheim, M., & Pear, R. (2006). Health hazard: Computers spilling your history. *New York Times*, December 3, Section 3.

Hodge J.G., Gostin, L.O., & Jacobson, P.D. (1999). Legal issues concerning electronic health information: Privacy, quality, and liability. *Journal of the American Medical Association, 282*(15), 1466.

McSherry, B. (2004). Ethical issues in health*Connect*'s shared electronic record system. *Journal of Law and Medicine* 12,60.

Marshall, M., & von Tigerstrom, B. (2002). Health information. In J. Downie, T. Caulfield & C. Flood (Eds.), *Canadian health law and policy* (2nd ed.). Markham, Ont: Butterworths.

National E-Health Transition Authority. (2006). *Privacy blueprint—Unique healthcare identifiers, Version 1.0.* Retrieved February 1, 2007, from http://www.nehta.gov.au/

National Electronic Health Records Taskforce. (2000). *Issues paper: A national approach to electronic health records for australia.* Retrieved December 1, 2006, from www.gpcg.org/publications/docs/Ehrissue.doc

National Health and Medical Research Council. (2004). *The regulation of health information privacy in Australia.* Retrieved January 15, 2007, from http://www.nhmrc.gov.au/publications/_files/nh53.pdf

National Health Privacy Working Group of the Australian Health Ministers' Advisory Council. (2003). *Proposed National Health Privacy Code.* Retrieved December 1, 2006, from www.health.gov.au/pubs/nhpcode.htm

National Health Service. (2005a). *National Programme for IT in the NHS.* Retrieved December 1, 2006 from http://www.connectingforhealth.nhs.uk/

National Health Service. (2005b). *The Care Record Guarantee: Our Guarantee for NHS Care Records in England.* Retrieved January 12, 2007, from http://www.connectingforhealth.nhs.uk/crdb/docs/crs_guarantee.pdf

Norheim, O.F. (2006). Soft paternalism and the ethics of shared electronic patient records. *British Medical Journal, 333,* 2-3.

Pan-Canadian Health Information Privacy and Confidentiality Framework. (2005). Retrieved January 3, 2007, from http://www.hc-sc.gc.ca/hcs-sss/pubs/ehealth-esante/2005-pancanad-priv/index_e.html

Personal Health Information Act. (1997). *Continuing Consolidation of the Statutes of Manitoba,* chapter P33.5.

Personal Health Information Protection Act. (2004). *Statutes of Ontario,* chapter 3.

Personal Health Information Regulations, Manitoba Regulation 245/97, updated to Manitoba Regulation 142/2005.

Powell, J. (2004). *Speech from the Chairman of the IT Committee.* British Medical Association. Retrieved December 1, 2006, from http://www.bma.org.uk/ap.nsf/Content/ARM04chIT?OpenDocument&Highlight=2,john,powell

Privacy Commissioner of Canada. (2001). *Annual Report to Parliament, 2000-2001.* Retrieved December 15, 2006, from http://www.privcom.gc.ca/information/ar/02_04_09_e.asp

Ries, N.M. (2006) Patient privacy in a wired (and wireless) world: Approaches to consent in the context of electronic health records" *Alberta Law Review, 43*(3), 681-712.

Ries, N.M., & Moysa, G. (2005). Legal protection of electronic health records: Issues of consent and security. *Health Law Review, 14*(1), 18-25.

Rozovsky, L.E., & Inions, N.J. (2002). *Canadian Health Information* (3rd ed.). Markham, Ont: Butterworths Canada Ltd.

University of Alberta Health Law Institute and University of Victoria School of Health Information Science. (2005). *Electronic health records and the Personal Information Protection and Electronic Documents Act.* Retrieved December 12, 2006, from http://www.law.ualberta.ca/centres/hli/pdfs/ElectronicHealth.pdf

Watson, N., & Halamka J. (2006). Patients should have to opt out of national electronic care records. *British Medical Journal, 333,* 39-42.

Wilkinson, J. (2006). Commentary: What's all the fuss about? *British Medical Journal, 333,* 42-43.

ADDITIONAL READING

Advisory Committee on Information and Emerging Technologies. (2005). *Pan-Canadian Health Information Privacy Framework*. Ottawa, ON: Health and Information Highway Division, Health Canada. Available at: http://www.hc-sc.gc.ca/hcs-sss/pubs/ehealth-esante/2005-pancanad-priv/index_e.html

Bassinder, J., Bali R.K., & Naguib, R. (2006). Knowledge management and electronic care records: Incorporating social, legal and ethical issues. *Studies in Health Technology and Informatics, 121*, 221-227.

Blumenthal, D., & Glaser, A. (2007). Information technology comes to medicine. *New England Journal of Medicine, 356*(24), 2527-2534.

Buckovich, S.A., Rippen, H.E., & Rozen, M.J. (1999). Driving toward guiding principles: A goal for privacy, confidentiality, and security of health information. *Journal of the American Medical Informatics Association, 6*, 122-133.

Canada Health Infoway. (2007). *White paper on information governance of the interoperable electronic health record*. Montreal, QC: Canada Health Infoway.

Centre for Health Informatics and Multiprofessional Education. (1993). *The good european health record: Ethical and legal requirements*. Available at: http://www.chime.ucl.ac.uk/work-areas/ehrs/GEHR/EUCEN/del8.pdf

Cornwall, A. (2003). Connecting health: A review of electronic health record projects in Australia, Europe and Canada. *Public Interest Advocacy Centre*. Available at: http://www.piac.asn.au/publications/pubs/churchill_20030121.html

Fairweather, N.B., & Rogerson, S. (2001). A moral approach to electronic patient records. *Medical Informatics and the Internet in Medicine, 26*(3), 219-234.

Goldberg, I.V. (2000). Electronic medical records and patient privacy. *Healthcare Manager, 18*(3), 63-69.

Gritzalis, S. (2004). Enhancing privacy and data protection in electronic medical environments. *Journal of Medical Systems, 28*(6), 535-547.

Hillestad, R., Bigelow, J., Bower, A., et al. (2005). Can electronic medical record systems transform healthcare? Potential health benefits, savings, and costs. *Health Affairs, 24*, 1103-1117.

Kirshen, A.J., & Ho, C. (1999) Ethical considerations in sharing personal information on computer data sets. *Canadian Family Physician, 45*, 2563-2565, 2575-2577.

Kluge, E.H. (2000). Professional codes for electronic HC record protection: Ethical, legal, economic and structural issues. *International Journal of Medical Informatics, 60*(2), 85-96.

Kluge, E.H. (2003). Security and privacy of EHR systems—Ethical, social and legal requirements. *Studies in Health Technology and Informatics, 96*, 121-127.

Kluge, E. H. (2004). Informed consent and the security of the electronic health record (EHR): Some policy considerations. *International Journal of Medical Informatics, 73*(3), 229-234.

Lo, B. (2006). Professionalism in the age of computerised medical records. *Singapore Medical Journal, 47*(12), 1018-1022.

Nordberg, R. (2006). EHR in the perspective of security, integrity and ethics. *Studies in Health Technology and Informatics, 121*, 291-298.

Petrisor, A.I., & Close, J.M. (2002). Electronic health care records in europe: Confidentiality issues from an American perspective. *Studies in Health Technology and Informatics, 87*, 44-46.

Ries, N.M. (2006). Patient privacy in a wired (and wireless) world: Approaches to consent in the context of electronic health records" *Alberta Law Review, 43*(3), 681-712.

Roscam Abbing, H.D. (2000). Medical confidentiality and electronic patient files. *Medicine and Law, 19*(1), 107-112.

Sharpe, V.A. (2005). Privacy and security for electronic health records. *Hastings Center Report, 35*(6), 49.

Terry, N.P. (2004). Electronic health records: International, structural and legal perspectives. *Journal of Law and Medicine, 12*(1), 26-39.

University of Alberta Health Law Institute and University of Victoria School of Health Information Science. (2005). *Electronic health records and the Personal Information Protection and Electronic Documents Act.* Available at http://www.law.ualberta.ca/centres/hli/pdfs/ElectronicHealth.pdf

Wilson, P. (1999). The electronic health record—a new challenge for privacy and confidentiality in medicine? *Biomedical Ethics, 4*(2), 48-55.

Win, K.T., & Fulcher, J.A. (2007). Consent mechanisms for electronic health record systems: a simple yet unresolved issue. *Journal of Medical Systems, 31*(2), 91-96.

Chapter XVI
Accountability, Beneficence, and Self-Determination:
Can Health Information Systems Make Organizations "Nicer"?

Tina Saryeddine
University of Toronto, Canada
GTA Rehab Network, Canada

ABSTRACT

Existing literature often addresses the ethical problems posed by health informatics. Instead of this problem-based approach, this chapter explores the ethical benefits of health information systems in an attempt to answer the question "can health information systems make organizations more accountable, beneficent, and more responsive to a patient's right to self determination?" It does so by unpacking the accountability for reasonableness framework in ethical decision making and the concepts of beneficence and self-determination. The framework and the concepts are discussed in light of four commonly used health information systems, namely: Web-based publicly accessible inventories of services; Web-based patient education; telemedicine; and the electronic medical record. The objective of this chapter is to discuss the ethical principles that health information systems actually help to achieve, with a view to enabling researchers, clinicians, and managers make the case for the development and maintenance of these systems in a client-centered fashion.

Copyright © 2008, IGI Global, distributing in print or electronic forms without written permission of IGI Global is prohibited.

INTRODUCTION

Can health information systems make organizations more accountable, beneficent, and more responsive to a patient's right to self determination? In essence, can health information systems make organizations more ethical, "nicer" even?

This question is often implicit when decisions are made in practice settings, but it is seldom explicitly discussed in the context of health information systems. Rather, the field of "info-ethics" has arisen largely from the drive to explore and address ethical problems, rather than solutions, which result from health information systems (Fessler & Gremy, 2001). This chapter makes the case that health information systems can help organizations address issues related to beneficence, autonomy and accountability for reasonableness. It begins with a look at recent industry trends.

The evolution of health information systems can be conceptualized in terms of a number of shifts that have occurred over the past 2 years. These shifts include a movement from paper to electronic mediums and from alpha numeric to digital images; from being stationary to being ubiquitous and remote sensing; and from being departmental and local to system-wide and international. Shifts have also occurred in the manner in which health information systems are used. This includes a shift from the use of health informatics to compute and process information to their use in health planning, strategy and research (Haux, 2006). Finally, there are also two shifts that relate directly to the patient and consumer, the primary focus for this chapter. These include a shift from a professional end-user to a patient or consumer end-user and a shift from using the information to complement provider activities to health information systems which can replace patient care activity (Ibid).

Given the proximity of health information systems to the patient, standards of ethical practice performed by providers of healthcare services can also apply to health information systems.

The objectives of this chapter are to discuss three popular ethics-related concepts: accountability for reasonableness, autonomy, and beneficence. These concepts will be explored in terms of the extent to which they can be achieved through four different types of health information systems. Definitions, concepts, and an overview of the literature are provided in the next section, followed by a discussion of four different health information systems and the extent to which they succeed or fall short of enabling beneficence, respect for patient autonomy, and accountability. The chapter ends with a discussion of future and emerging trends, implications for clinicians and organizations, and possible opportunities for further investigation and research.

BACKGROUND

Health informatics is the development and assessment of methods and systems for the acquisition, processing and utilization of health information (Imhoff et al., 2001). Health information systems can be thought of in terms of the technologies of health informatics. These technologies include telemedicine, telecare and tele-health in which assessment, treatment, consultation and monitoring are done remotely; computer based patient records, electronic communication or electronic mail, personal digital assistants in which can enable point of care access to information, data warehouses or clinical repositories, and e-health which includes smart cards, computer-based video conferencing and Web sites (Layman, 2003).

The field of ethics involves systematizing, discussing, and recommending concepts of behavior (Feiser, 2006). There are three commonly accepted subject areas. The first is meta-ethics, which looks at the history of what we think is right or wrong; normative ethics, which takes on the practical task of regulating conduct; and applied ethics which looks at controversial issues (Ibid, 2006).

There are also various types of ethical theories. In ethical non-cognitivism, ethics are a matter of feelings about right or wrong. In ethical relativism, ethics are a matter relative to a particular point of reference. Finally, in ethical objectivism ethics are objective in nature (Kluge, 2005). The focus of this chapter is on three common concepts in normative objectivist ethics: beneficence, autonomy and accountability for reasonableness (Daniels & Sabin, 1998).

Accountability in the context of the allocation of scarce healthcare resources is commonly viewed from a market perspective (Daniels & Sabin, 1997). Such market accountability requires that the range of services and choices available to citizens be publicly available to enable free choice (Thiede, 2004). Market accountability however fails to get at issues of procedural justice when it comes to making rationing decisions about what will and will not be funded (Feiser, 2006). As such, Daniels and Sabin developed the concept of accountability for reasonableness with four tenets as a means by which to ensure procedural fairness in the allocation of resources (1997).

The accountability for reasonableness framework is considered to be one of the most important advances in the development of an ethical framework for resource allocation. Accountability for reasonableness proposes that for organizations to make legitimate and fair decisions, they have to meet four conditions. The first condition is that decisions and their rationales must be made accessible to clinicians, patients and citizens in a publicly administered system. The second is that grounds for such decisions must be ones that have face validity in terms of their relationship to the decision at hand. Third, there must be mechanisms to challenge and resolve limit-setting decisions. Finally, there must be some form of regulation to ensure that the other conditions are met (Daniels & Sabin, 1998; Singer, 2000).

The second ethical concept is self determination or respect for autonomy. According to

Beauchamp and Childress' 1994 framework for medical ethics, "respect for autonomy" is one of the factors that must be balanced against other ethical considerations in medical decision making. Respect for autonomy refers to not limiting the patient from exercising his or her own free will and stems from the theory of self determination which posits that individuals have an innate need to develop mastery of their own situation (Kluge, 2005; Ryan & Deci, 2000).

The concept of autonomy can be understood by considering a series of metaphors describing the patient-provider relationship. The first is a paternalistic relationship in which the provider assumes responsibility for the patient, as a parent would a child. The second is a partnership in which the provider and patient each have rights and responsibilities. The third metaphor is the rational contractor in which there are fixed roles for each of the patient and provider. The fourth metaphor is for the patient and provider to behave though they were in a friendship. The final metaphor is the provider as a technician, whose responsibility it is to fill tasks (Kluge, 2005).

As can be seen, each of these metaphors puts the patient in a different relationship to the provider and in a different role with respect to his or her own involvement in health care decision making. Respecting patients' needs for self determination or autonomy can also be thought of in terms of beneficence, the third ethical concept which will be discussed in the chapter. Under the principle of beneficence, healthcare practitioners, organizations, or individuals have a duty to be helpful to the patient (Kluge, 2005; Layman, 2003). Beneficence is defined as the duty to maximize the good. In order for this not to become paternalistic and compromise the patients' right to self-determination, "the good," must be defined by the other person (Kluge, 2005). This can become extremely complex when there is an asymmetry of information between the provider and the patient.

What types of health information systems could enable an organization to express these ethical interests? There are four types of examples that are currently commonly used in healthcare. The first includes Web-enabled inventories of programs and services that describe programs, services, how, and where-to access them. These enable a patient or provider to look up what types of service options there are in his or her region and determine whether or not he or she is an eligible candidate.

The second group that is commonly used includes health information systems designed to inform the patient of best practices and treatment options. These educational resources enable the patient to understand what will happen to them, what is expected of them, and what they can expect in the course of their treatment.

The third type of health information system that will be discussed through the lenses of accountability, autonomy and beneficence is a form of telemedicine. Through telecare technology, two-way communication is enabled between an elderly consumer in their home and a professional at healthcare organization through technology running through the phone line at the touch of a button worn in the form of a pendant or bracelet. Upon contact, the individual can request assistance if he or she can not reach a telephone. The professional responding to the call has a list of the user's friends, neighbors and family members, as well as data about his or her condition.

Finally, the electronic health record, perhaps the only health information system regulated by legislation will be discussed in light of the three ethical concepts. The next section discusses these technologies in more detail.

PUBLICLY ACCESSIBLE DIRECTORIES OF SERVICE

Publicly accessible listings and descriptions of available health programs and services function as directories and inventories. They are designed to describe services in a manner that is transparent and accessible. They usually contain not only a description and location of the service but also detailed descriptions of how to access the program and who is eligible for such access.

While such an inventory is not limited to Web-based technologies, paper format makes it inconvenient because of the cost of publication, updating, and distribution. In addition, making such criteria available in an electronic database or Web-based format provides the potential for searching the database. By making these inventories publicly available, in a publicly funded system, patients and providers have the ability to go onto these databases and search for programs that can match the patient's needs (Thiede, 2003).

The principle of beneficence is easily demonstrated here because the provider can assist the patient in finding the services that will meet the patient's healthcare needs. However, beneficence is reduced if the program description is incomplete, inaccurate or outdated. In order for such a listing of programs and services to lend itself to the principle of beneficence, it must be kept up to date and it must be accurate. Audits may need to be conducted on such systems to determine the extent to which they reflect practice. It should be noted, however, that posting an accurate listing and description of services not only benefits the patient, but also benefits the organization by providing a mechanism through which to market services.

Assuming that such a listing is accurate and publicly accessible, the patient can exercise a right to self determination or autonomy from three perspectives. First, the patient or consumer can review these listings and determine where he or she would like to receive services. This gives the patient or consumer choice. Second, the informational asymmetry that often exists in healthcare because of the professional knowing what the patient does not, is reduced. This gives the patient the opportunity to advocate for his or her own wishes. It changes the relationship from a paternalistic one to a partnership. Third, where access and eligibility criteria are listed, the patient is afforded the opportunity to meet the eligibility criteria where possible (Sang, 2004). For example, some programs require that a patient attend with a family member or friend. If a patient knows that this is a requirement for entry into the program, he or she may be deliberate about ensuring that the arrangement is made prior to the application being sent, in order to avoid being ineligible for the program for that reason.

In order for this self-determination to be possible however, it is necessary for the description to be available in lay language so that the patient can clearly and appropriately understand the description. This introduces a number of issues related to fairness and equity. To make information accessible to everyone means that individuals will need to have equitable access to computers and the Internet (Ibid). There also needs to be the consideration of language level. For example, it is known that joint replacement surgery and rehabilitation are utilized by individuals in higher education and income brackets because of their knowledge and awareness of the services available, which prompts them to ask (Thiede, 2003). However, making the knowledge available to patients and families will open the doors to more requests for services. This can become very costly and introduce other ethical issues.

The idea that criteria are transparent and accessible is very much related to the four requirements for accountability for reasonableness. Since the organization is being transparent about what it does and does not do, it can be accountable for the reasonable utilization of its resources. For example, organization X takes extremely complex surgery patients who require costly services. Organization Y takes patients of the same diagnoses, but whose complexity level is much lower. Without such a statement, the costs of care at the organization taking patients whose needs are complex and costly would be significantly but unexplainably

higher than organization Y. It is therefore in the interest of organization X to be very clear about the types of services it offers. Otherwise it may be perceived that there is poor cost control. The transparency of available services also affords community members, administrators, patients, and others to demonstrate need and use unmet requests as the case for opening new services.

WEB-BASED PATIENT EDUCATION PRODUCTS

The second type of health information system that can be discussed in terms of beneficence, autonomy, and accountability for reasonableness is Web-enabled patient education. Patient education Web sites often contain features that are not practical in other mediums. For example, some patient education Web sites come with audio-visual features, a message board which allows patients to communicate with each other, and in some cases, an evaluation mechanism which allows the creators to monitor use and quality of the information on the Web site.

There are three traditional models of interaction describing the patient relationship to the acquisition of health information. The ideal model is the health information sharing model in which there is a feedback loop between clinician and patient. The second is the dissemination of information model in which a professional provides information to a user. This model is contrary to adult learning principles because it does not optimize motivation. In the third model, the flow of information is initiated by the consumer who searches the Internet for information and is therefore an activated learner (Bruegel, 1998)

Although most Web sites cannot provide an effective feedback loop as in the ideal sharing model, many Web sites have the capacity for some form of feedback. Building surveys and message boards are one vehicle. The second is Web-traffic monitoring software, which has become a standard offering on patient education Web sites. These enable the provider or clinician to assess the utilization of the Web site without actively collecting data. The software monitors various statistics such as the number of sessions or series of hits by the same user on the Web site, the pages visited and the length of the session. It is also possible to monitor the keywords that consumers use to lead them from the search engine to the Web site. The information provides insight into special topics that patients are most interested in, providing valuable information to the provider.

Since the Internet is ubiquitous and enables multi-media, feedback, interaction, and choice, the consumer has the ability to determine his or her own level of interest and involvement with the material. The information can help to ease suffering, relax anxiety, encourage preparation, increase prevention and understanding of the procedure, thereby improving the provider's ability to promote beneficence and self-determination for the patient. The patient has choice in terms of how much of the site to read at once, when to read it, when to initiate discussions with others, and even has a means of evaluating the material that is presented. Web-based patient education with interactive forums is a form of patient empowerment because it enhances the ability of patients to actively understand and influence their health conditions. In some cases, consumers are empowered to assist each other. Information provides consumers with the ability to enter into meaningful conversations about their own care (Bruegel, 1998).

The potential problem with patient education Web sites, is that the information may be incomplete, inaccurate, out of date, or poorly reflective of actual practice. Perhaps the best known criteria for assessing the quality of a patient education Web site is presented by Charnock, (1998) in which 15 criteria are offered. These criteria include ensuring that the objectives of the site are clear and achievable; ensuring that the site information is

referenced in a transparent fashion and that dates of information and updates are posted; ensuring that the information is balanced and unbiased as well as reflective of the range of options that may be available. According to Charnock's criteria, the site must also describe what would happen if the treatment protocol were not followed and provide support for shared decision-making. These criteria raise a number of problems in practice, many of which are also related to the accountability for reasonableness framework (Charnock, 1998)

In the classic clinical decision making model (Haynes, 2004), evidence from the literature is considered in conjunction to patient preferences and the realities of the clinical practice setting in order to make a decision. When evidence and options from the literature, clinical context, and patient preferences are made available to patients, providers enable patients to take an active and participatory role in their own care. Appropriate and timely information has been shown to have positive effects on recovery, process satisfaction, outcomes and length of stay (Crowe & Henderson, 2003; Kelly & Ackerman, 1999). A lack of patient information has also been identified as an issue of concern to patients in client centered care (Cott et al., 2001).

It is this benefit of transparency that poses a dilemma. The educator can choose to present all options of care which are clinically relevant and evidence based, irrespective of whether or not the care will be offered within that organization or jurisdiction. If the patient is told about the possible options and demands these, problems of resource allocation may occur because the patient may request an option that is more expensive than what the organization or system can offer. On the other hand, if the patient really has no choice in the course of treatment options because of resource issues, should all of the options be presented in a patient education Web site?

This dilemma can be resolved by looking at the accountability for reasonableness framework, although the framework was not designed for the selection of patient education information. According to the accountability for reasonableness framework, the expectation would be that the rationale for the decision would be publicly available, reasonable, able to be appealed, and relevant. If patient education Web sites were to adhere to the accountability for reasonableness framework, they would also be closely aligned with Charnock's criteria for a quality patient education Web site.

In order to be accountable, the organization would have to undertake a systematic and transparent process for describing care and document the references, sources, and dates that would support effectiveness and then provide a publicly accessible rationale for that decision. This would enable not only education, but reassurance for patients and funders that evidence-based practice is being undertaken (Woolf et al., 2005).

As can be seen, the principles of beneficence, respect for autonomy, and accountability for reasonableness are achievable through Web-based patient education. There remains however the same problem of equity similar to that described for the Web-based service inventory. The problem with Internet enabled Web education is an equity problem in that not everyone has access to the Internet. Visual, cognitive or linguistic impairments may also pose barriers to the use of the Internet for health information. Canada is a world leader in the use of the Internet for health information and Canadians have an exceptionally high rate of Internet access in the home (Statistics Canada, 2002) as compared to other countries.

PATIENT OUTREACH AND MONITORING INFORMATION SYSTEMS

The third type of information system that can be discussed in light of the concepts of accountability, beneficence, and self determination are health information systems fits in the health informat-

ics framework of telemedicine. The concept of telemedicine took off in the 1960s (Currell et al., 2006). Over the past 20 years, companies have developed tele-monitoring services that connect an individual in their home with the appropriate assistance in an urgent or emergent situation.

This technology is typically made up of a bracelet or pendant worn by the client. In an event where help is required, a button on the bracelet or pendant is pushed which establishes two-way communications with an assistance center. The assistance centre has a database of the patients' conditions, informal caregiver contact number, and overall history. The two-way communication is initiated by speaker equipment running through the ordinary phone line. Once the patients' needs are identified, the assistance center contacts emergency services if appropriate, but can also contact an informal caregiver or neighbor. It is important to note here the difference between calling emergency services and calling a neighbor. In one study it was noted that up to 35 percent of hospital admissions among the elderly are social admissions related to social needs to the elder living alone in the home (Graham & Grey, 2005). In some cities, programs such as the telecare program have been initiated deliberately to reduce the utilization of 911 calls by involving family or informal caregivers in non emergent calls.

This technology poses an unconventional application of the accountability for reasonableness framework. Many healthcare organizations subsidize such systems in order to avert unnecessary pressures on ambulances and emergency departments for older individuals who can not pay for the technology on their own. Transparent criteria are usually offered to distinguish who are eligible for the service.

It is a much more interesting and complex example however of beneficence and respect for autonomy or self determination of the individual. Part of the complexity is due to the fact that this health information system benefits not only the patient or consumer who is using the system to summon help, but it is also of benefit to the informal caregiver, in part because it affects not only the patient, but the informal caregiver too. By giving elderly individuals security in their own homes, their right to autonomy is respected. They are able to remain in the home longer and be more independent. The value of beneficence is respected because of the physical and emotional support that can be offered to the individual when in need.

In Canada, over two million individuals provide informal support for a family member, neighbor, or friend (Health Canada, 2005). They play a significant role in sustaining the home health sector. However, caregiver burden in Canada is also high (Ibid). The health of caregivers, most of whom are women is often compromised because of emotional, physical, and economic burdens associated with their informal caregiving responsibilities. The ability to provide an elderly friend, neighbor or relative with technology that can monitor their condition and inform them when they are needed has the potential to reduce this burden. In this manner, the technology favors beneficence towards the informal caregiver as well as respecting the informal caregivers' right to autonomy by relieving the care burden he or she might ordinarily face. In addition, by harnessing the services of the informal caregiver when needed, the system is relieved from unnecessary expense.

This relates to the concept of social capital which was influenced initially by the work or Robert Putnam (Daniel, 2003). Social capital is a resource made up of social ties (Putnam, 2000). Social capital is demonstrated when individuals work together to achieve a goal, to earn trust, maintain a reputation, influence action, or even constrain behavior (Ibid). By linking consumers or patients to the informal caregiver, friend, family member or neighbor, technology is used to harness social capital. Social capital often functions to solidify norms. In this case the norm is to ensure that every older adult who is able to, can remain

longer in his or her home while preventing the informal caregiver from experiencing burnout.

ELECTRONIC MEDICAL RECORD

Unlike the other technologies described so far, the electronic medical record is a legislated information technology across most provinces in Canada. Like the paper-based health record, the primary purpose of the electronic medical record is one of accountability and communication. It allows providers participating in the patient's care to understand recent treatments and the status of the patient.

The electronic medical record must contain sufficient information to describe why the patient was seen on each visit, a clear record of the investigations, and the diagnoses. There should also be a ledger describing each professional's date, time, and type of involvement in patient care. Finally, the record often contains appointment sheets or a daily diary of the professional services rendered. Failure to complete a health record can be considered professional misconduct.

Since the electronic health record is a tool for communication and accountability, does it allow an organization to fulfill the criteria for accountability for reasonableness? The accountability for reasonableness framework with its tenets of public disclosure for reasonableness is not easily applied to the electronic health record. The electronic medical record is by private so it would not be subject to public scrutiny as would be the types of decisions that fall under the accountability for reasonableness framework. If data from multiple electronic medical records were to be aggregated at a system level however, it would be possible to use the aggregated results in accountability for reasonableness framework, since the relationship between treatment and outcome could be established, thereby facilitating resource allocation decisions. However, this would not be unique to electronic health records and would apply to any health database.

Like the other technologies discussed, the potential of the electronic health record to promote autonomy at the direct patient care level depends on how the record is implemented and utilized. The benefit of the electronic health record is that it is much quicker to access than a paper based health record. The immediacy of access facilitates utilization of the information in a timely fashion. However, the electronic medical record, like a paper-based medical record is the property of the hospital. If the hospital has not put structures and processes in place to facilitate access of the record, then it is unlikely to play a role in promoting beneficence above and beyond what is considered usual and expected care.

If, however, we expand the notion of the electronic health record from one which responds to professional standards to one which responds to the personal healthcare needs of the patient, re-termed as a "personal health record," the potential becomes much larger. If the electronic health record is a dynamic mechanism through which the patient can interact with his or her healthcare team and was presented in a format that was easily read with translation of professional jargon into language which was understood by the lay person. In this case, the record would empower the person to make 'informed' choices and judgments about personal health maintenance (Abadi & Goh, 2006).

FUTURE RESEARCH DIRECTIONS

The literature on how health information systems enable organizations to demonstrate the three ethics related concepts presented in this chapter is very sparse. In a search of major databases such as EMBASE, CINAHL, and MEDLINE, very few articles were found which addressed the manner in which health information systems promote beneficence, autonomy, and accountability for reasonableness. By contrast, hundreds of articles exist on the ethical issues presented by health information systems.

The benefits of thinking about the ethical issues that can be addressed through health information systems are twofold. First, from a patient care perspective, the more clearly the benefits of health information systems are understood, the more they can be leveraged to improve patient care. Second, the more that health information systems can be conceptualized in terms of these benefits, the easier it will be to conduct further research and evaluation and to prepare business cases.

The discussion of the four technologies presented in this chapter, showed how each could help to achieve the principles of beneficence, respect for autonomy and accountability for reasonableness. The caveat is in the manner in which the technology is implemented. In the case of patient education and service inventories, the information presented must be accessible, up to date, and accurate (Thiede, 2005). In the case of tele-health monitoring system for older adults, implementation of the technology must not be seen to be an invasion of privacy. In the case of the electronic medical record, the hospital must invest in the infrastructure needed to make the electronic medical record accessible to patients.

When we consider how these health information systems can achieve beneficence, respect for autonomy and accountability for reasonableness, it becomes possible to conceive that designing systems so that they deliver on their potential will become the norm. As norms evolve however, so does regulation. Law, like ethics, also has a normative role (Kluge, 2005) This opens the potential to a future healthcare organization which is compelled by regulatory standards to provide, for example, a public, transparent and accurate listing of all of its programs and services and how to access them or an accessible electronic medical record. If each organization did this, there would be much better capacity for system planning, resource allocation, and patient involvement in care.

The same holds true when we consider patient education. In an era in which both patients and providers are being bound by both rights and responsibilities, why shouldn't patients have a right to know what evidence upon which their treatment is based? Why should any organization or healthcare provider be able to produce patient education that does not meet a regulated standard? Regulating patient education products so that they are not released unless they meet a specified standard, is also a potential outcome that may result from clearly understanding how patient education can be used for beneficence, respect for autonomy and accountability for reasonableness.

As was noted earlier, conceptualizing health information systems in terms of their benefits to beneficence, respect for autonomy and accountability for reasonableness is not yet pervasive in the literature. Empirical studies should be conducted to measure the extent to which these health information systems can deliver on this potential. Cost benefit analysis should also present scope for future research.

Traditionally, funding decisions have put health information systems lower on the list of priorities than those regarded as necessary for patient care. However, human and social are at the heart of their very existence in patient care. As health information systems become more relevant to the encounter of the individual with the healthcare system, for example by promoting accountability, autonomy and beneficence, the potential to implement many of the systems already in existence will increase. Understanding the value of these systems from a patient perspective is an important opportunity for future normative research.

However, while the potential of public directories, Web-based patient education, tele-monitoring and the electronic medical record all have the potential of bringing beneficence, autonomy and maximizing accountability for reasonableness in resource allocation decisions, few studies have actually established empirically that this is the case. Future directions may therefore include developing approaches to empirically test this proposition. It may also be important to conduct normative and instrumental research to assist vendors in designing systems that better meet the needs of the public and providers when it comes to beneficence, autonomy and accountability for reasonableness.

Finally, the marriage of healthcare ethics and information systems has traditionally taken a problem-based approach in order to identify the ethical dilemmas that could arise. Technologies such as Web-based patient education, service inventories, home monitoring devices, and electronic medical records are by no means reflective of the technological advances of the future. Rather, they are common health information systems used in current practice. However, these health information technologies provide an excellent opportunity to advance the concepts of autonomy, beneficence, and accountability for reasonableness. This presents a new set of considerations for individuals designing or leading health information systems on how information systems can play a role very similar to that of providers in promoting beneficence, respect for the individual's autonomy and accountability for reasonableness.

REFERENCES

Beauchamp, T.L., & Childress, J.F. (1994). *Principles of biomedical ethics* (4th ed.). New York: Oxford University Press.

Bruegel, R.B. (1998). The increasing importance of patient empowerment and its potential effects on home health care information system s and technology. *Home Healthcare Management Practice, 10*(2), 69-75

Charnock, D. (1998). *The discern handbook: Quality criteria for consumer health information on treatment choices.* Radcliffe Medical Press.

Currell, R., Urquhart, C., Wainwright, P., & Lewis, R. (2001). Telemedicine versus face to face patient care: effects on professional practice and healthcare outcomes.

D'Alessandro, D., & Nienke, P. (2001). Empowering children and families with information technology. *Archives of Paediatrics and Adolescent Medicine,* 155(10), 1131-1136.

Daniel, B. (2003). Social capital in virtual learning communities and distributed communities of practice. *Canadian Journal of Learning and Technology,* 29(3).

Daniels N., & Sabin J., (1997). Limits to health care: Fair procedures, democratic deliberation, and the legitimacy problem for insurers. *Philosophy and Public Affairs,* 26.

Deci, E. L., & Ryan, R. M. (2000). The "what" and "why" of goal pursuits: Human needs and the self-determination of behavior. *Psychological Inquiry, 11,* 227-268.

Fessler, J.M., & Gremy, F. (2001). Ethical problems in health information systems. *Methods of Information in Medicine, 40*(4), 359-61.

Fieser, J. (2006). *Moral philosophy through the ages.* Mayfield Publishing Co.

Gostin, L.O., Lazzarini, Z., Neslund, V.S., & Osterholm, M.T. (1996). The public health information infrastructure. A national review of the law on health information privacy. *JAMA, 275(24),* 1921-7.

Haux, R. (2006). Health information systems: Past, present, future. *International Journal of Medical Informatics, 75(3-4 special issue),* 268-281.

Health Canada, Economic Impact of Health, Income Security and Labour Policies on Informal

Caregivers of Frail Seniors (2004). Retrieved from http://www.swc-cfc.gc.ca/pubs/pub-spr/0662654765/200103_0662654765_8_e.html

Imhoff, M., Webb, A., Goldschmidt, A. (2001). Health informatics. *Intensive Care Medicine.* 27(1), 179-86.

Jenkins, D. & Emmett, S. (1997). The ethical dilemma of health education. *Professional Nurse, 12*(6), 426-428.

Kluge, E.W. (2005). *Readings in biomedical ethics: A Canadian focus.*(3rd ed.). Prentice Hall.

Layman, E. (2003). Health informatics ethical issues. *Health Care Manager, 22*(1), 2-15.

Mysak, S. (1997). Strategies for promoting ethical decision-making. *Journal of Gerontological Nursing, 23*(1), 25-31.

Sang, B. (2004). Choice, participation, and accountability: Assessing the potential impact of legislation promoting patient and public involvement in health in the UK. *Health Expectations, 7,* 187-190.

Singer, P. (2000). Recent advances: Medical ethics. *British Medical Journal, 321,* 282-285.

Thiede, M. (2004). Information and access o health care: Is there a role for trust? *Social Science and Medicine, 61*(7), 1452-1461.

Thornicroft, G., & Tansella, M. (1999) Translating ethical principles into outcome measures for mental health service research. *Psychological Medicine, 29*(4), 761-767.

Woolf, S.H., Chan, E., Harris, R. Sheridan, B.C, Kaplan, R., Krist, A., et al. (2005). Promoting informed choice: Transforming health care to dispense knowledge for decision making. *Annals of Internal Medicine, 143*(4), 293-300.

ADDITIONAL READING

Abidi, S.S., & Goh, A. (2000). A personalised healthcare information delivery system: pushing customised healthcare information over the WWW. *Studies in Health Technology & Informatics, 77,* 663-7.

Amtmann, D., & Johnson, K.L. (1998). The internet and information technologies and consumer empowerment. *Technology and Disability, 8*(3), 107-13.

Bluml, B., Crooks, M., & G. M. (1999). Designing solutions for securing patient privacy—meeting the demands of health care in the 21st century. *Journal of the American Pharmaceutical Association, 39*(3), 402-7.

Bormark, S.R., & Moen, A. (2006). Information technology and nursing; Emancipation versus control? *Studies in Health Technology & Informatics, 122,* 591-5

Bormark, S.R., & Moen, A. (2006). Information technology and nursing; Emancipation versus control? *Stud Health Technol Inform, 122,*591-595.

Bruegel, R.B. (1998). The increasing importance of patient empowerment and its potential effects on home health care information systems and technology. *Home Health Care Management & Practice, 10*(2), 69-75.

D'Alessandro, D.M., & Dosa, N.P. (2001). Empowering children and families with information technology. *Archives of Pediatrics & Adolescent Medicine, 155*(10), 1131-1136.

Daniels, N. (2001). Justice, health, and healthcare. *American Journal of Bioethics, 1*(2), 2-16.

Daniels, N. (2000). Accountability for reasonableness. *British Medical Journal, 321*(7272), 1300-1301.

Daniels, N. (2001). Justice, health, and healthcare. *American Journal of Bioethics, 1*(2), 2-16.

Gibson, J.L., Martin, D.K., & Singer, P.A. (2005). Priority setting in hospitals: Fairness, inclusiveness, and the problem of institutional power differences. *Social Science & Medicine. 61*(11), 2355-62.

Hasman, A., &Holm, S. (2005). Accountability for reasonableness: Opening the black box of process. *Health Care Analysis, 13*(4), 261-73.

Kinney, L., & Piotrowski, Z.H. (2003). Internet access and empowerment: A community-based health initiative. *Journal of General Internal Medicine, 18*(7), 525-530.

Kupersmith, J., Francis, J., Kerr, E., Krein, S., Pogach, L., Kolodner, R.M., et al. (2007). Advancing evidence-based care for diabetes: Lessons from the Veterans Health Administration. *Health Affairs, 26*(2), 156-68.

Madden, S., Martin, D. K., Downey, S., & Singer, P.A. (2005). Hospital priority setting with an appeals process: a qualitative case study and evaluation. *Health Policy, 73*(1), 10-20.

Masi, C.M., Suarez-Balcazar, Y., Cassey, M.Z., Kinney, L. & Piotrowski, Z.H. (2003). Internet access and empowerment: A community-based health initiative. *Journal Gen Intern Medicine, 18*(7), 525-30.

Nelson, N. (2000). Can computer-mediated communication democratize the workplace? *Information Outlook, 4*(6), 18-22.

Remington Report. Jul-Aug; 5(4), 24-6, 28-9.

Renblad, K. (2000) Persons with intellectual disability, social interaction and video telephony. An interview study. *Technology and Disability, 13*(1), 55-65.

Ross, S., & Lin, C. (2003) A randomized controlled trial of a patient-accessible electronic medical record. *AMIA Annu Symp Proceedings,* 990.

Safran, C. (2003). The collaborative edge: Patient empowerment for vulnerable populations. *International Journal of Medicine Information, 69*(2-3), 185-189.

Chapter XVII
Electronic Health Records:
Why Does Ethics Count?

Eike-Henner W. Kluge
University of Victoria, Canada

ABSTRACT

The development of electronic health records marked a fundamental change in the ethical and legal status of health records and in the relationship between the subjects of the records, the records themselves and health information and healthcare professionals—changes that are not fully captured by traditional privacy and confidentiality considerations. The chapter begins with a sketch of the nature of this evolution and places it into the epistemic framework of healthcare decision-making. It then outlines why EHRs are special, what the implications of this special status are both ethically and juridically, and what this means for professionals and institutions. An attempt is made to link these considerations to the development of secure e-health, which requires not only the interoperability of technical standards but also the harmonization of professional education, institutional protocols and of laws and regulations.

INTRODUCTION

Archaeological evidence suggests that patient records have been an integral part of healthcare since the dawn of civilization. The history of health record keeping is usually presented as follows: In beginning records were made using materials such as clay (Marsiglia, 1966), wax (Brosius, 2003) or string (quipus) (Ascher & Ascher, 1997). Eventually, these were superseded by paper-based records, and in the second half of the 20th century electronic methods of recoding and storage were introduced and began to replace paper-based records. While electronic based records may never completely replace paper-based records, it seems fair to assume that because of their unparalleled

Copyright © 2008, IGI Global, distributing in print or electronic forms without written permission of IGI Global is prohibited.

power in facilitating data storage, handling and communication, electronic health records (EHR) will become the dominant form of health records in the future.

When the history of health record keeping is presented in this way, it portrays the development of EHRs as merely another step in the material evolution of the recording medium. It suggests that while EHRs may present an exponential increase in data storage, handling and communication capabilities, they are inherently no different from any of the previous technological developments except in scale. It thereby places EHRs squarely into the tradition of codes, conventions and traditions that have grown up around medical records in general, and it embeds them in a complex web of professional standards, administrative statutes and legal decisions that have been developed for their protection by the medical profession, the legislatures and the courts. This protective screen has traditionally been grounded in the nature of the physician-patient relationship and in the codes that regulate it and therefore has a sound professional basis.

This way of looking at EHRs is not without its attraction because it has the weight of tradition behind it. Historically, the interaction between physician and patient has been construed as quasi-religious in character and as something that should be shielded from prying eyes, and it has always been understood to include medical records. The roots of this tradition are ancient and universal. They go back to Imhotep in ancient Egypt, the Charaka School in ancient India (Chakraberty, 1923) and the Huangdi tradition in ancient China (McDougall & Hansson, 2002). It was taken up by Hippocrates in ancient Greece (Edelstein, 1923), was inherited by Roman and Arabic medical cultures, and survives today in various contemporary codes of medical ethics. The laws, codes, and protocols that have been developed on this basis, therefore, have a firm and universal foundation and make it readily understandable why there should be restrictions on what may be included

in EHRs, how access should be controlled, and why issues of security, privacy, communication, storage and manipulation should be considered important. It also makes it relatively easy to see how these restrictions affect the conduct of healthcare and health information professionals as well as of the institutions that may be in possession or in control of EHRs. From this perspective, therefore, ethical considerations are relevant for EHRs simply because they are medical records and as such are covered by the tradition of the physician-patient relationship, which is central to healthcare delivery itself.

However, attractive as this perspective may be, it has several drawbacks. First, it fosters the dangerous illusion that tradition can provide ethical guidance for all developments in medical record keeping. This is assumption is warranted only if the underlying logic of the tradition is sufficiently flexible to be able to deal with developments that were not even on the intellectual horizon when the tradition itself evolved. It is questionable whether this holds true for EHRs—to say nothing of developments like e-health which integrally depends on EHRs for its construction and implementation. In fact, given the rapid pace of developments in electronic record keeping, manipulation and communication and the inevitable lag-time between changes in the real world and changes in codes and traditions, a reliance on tradition virtually guarantees that the ethics of EHRs will fail when new developments arise.

Second, if the procedural and statutory provisions that protect records are defined by tradition, they become dependent on professional, legislative, and judicial interpretations of that tradition and on current perceptions of its validity. Therefore the web of protection that surrounds medical records in general and EHRs in particular becomes subject to political and pragmatic concerns that may proceed independently of ethical principles. The USA Patriot Act (2001, rev. 2005) is here a good example. In the post 9/11 climate, U.S. security concerns rose to such a pitch that pragmatic considerations were taken to trump ethics and traditions were re-interpreted so that all records—including those that previously had been protected by the tradition of medical secrecy—were allowed to be non-consensually and secretly accessed by U.S. security agencies on the mere suspicion that by inspecting the records, the work of the agencies would be facilitated. This made EHRs particularly ideal targets for security intrusions and privacy violations because of their eminently searchable nature.

Moreover, codes and traditions merely reflect what was traditionally accepted, not necessarily what is ethically correct, and statutes and court decisions merely record what persons find appropriate on the basis of political or juridical considerations. What is contained in them, therefore, may be quite unsupported by ethics. Reference has already been made to the *USA Patriot Act* in this regard. Another example is found within the medical tradition itself that deals with health records. Thus, physicians have traditionally claimed—and their codes have traditionally insisted—that physicians own not only the material on which the patient-relative health information is recorded but also the information that is contained in these records. As has since become abundantly clear, this position is ethically mistaken, tradition and historical roots notwithstanding (EU Directive 95/46 EC).

Most importantly, however, a traditionalist approach to EHRs radically misconstrues the true nature of EHRs. EHRs are fundamentally distinct from paper-based records. Not to put too fine a point on it, the development of EHRs marked the beginning of a fundamental change in health record keeping and healthcare decision-making structures because it turned the patient record from a mere material entity with epistemological implications into a patient analogue with meme-like metaphysical status in information and decision-space. As yet, this evolution is still in its infancy because EHRs are still relatively unsophisticated and incomplete and have not

been completely integrated into the all aspects of healthcare delivery and planning. Nevertheless, the process has been initiated, and to truly appreciate its import requires that we abandon the perspective of EHRs as merely a technological innovation over paper-based records and adopt a wholly new way of thinking.

In what follows, I shall outline the precise nature of this evolution, place it into the epistemic framework of healthcare decision-making and sketch some of its implications. The discussion will begin with a brief analysis of the relationship between data and information and relate this to the concepts of information and decision-space. This will then be followed by a brief discussion of how it applies to EHRs, why it results in a special status for EHRs both ethically and juridically, and why it means that professionals and institutions who are involved in the development, maintenance, communication, manipulation, storage and use of EHRs have special duties. One of the inferences that will be drawn from this analysis is that ethical considerations and provisions should not be mere add-ons to the technologically focussed IT development that deals with EHRs and to the protocols that govern their utilization. Instead, ethics should be integrated into the development of the technology itself and should be an important driver for usage protocols that are promulgated by institutions. Moreover, the training both of health informatics professionals and of healthcare professionals who engage with EHRs should be structured to take these considerations into account.

DATA, INFORMATION AND THEIR LOGICAL SPACES

Data and Information-Space

Considered from a purely information-theoretical perspective, data are entities that fulfil a symbolic function by standing for concepts or for distinguishable items in the real world. As symbols, they can be related to one another, where the nature of their relations *qua* symbols is functionally determined by the logically identifiable features of the entities for which they stand. For example, the data that are the result of X-ray scans of a particular piece of bone are only electronic impulses or patterns. However, they become data by being integrated into a programme or convention[1] that assigns to each of them certain values and that embeds each of them in a system of possible relations with other data, where the logic of these possibilities mirrors the logic of the bone's properties such as density, composition and size. Similarly, the data that result from an immunological assay of a given serum sample capture certain logically distinguishable aspects of the serum sample and allow them to be related to each other with respect to type, concentration, agglutination factors, and so forth. Each datum, therefore, can be understood as having both a value that gives it content and a logical form that defines its nature and that allows it to be related to those other data with which it is logically compatible.

Information, in turn, can be defined as data-in-relation, which is to say, as data that are related to each other by one of the relations that are possible given the logic of the data themselves. The precise nature of a given piece of information, therefore, will depend on the nature of the relation itself as well as on the value of the data that are being related to each other. Data can be related to each other at various levels. At the most primitive level, they can be related to each other within their own modalities, for instance temperature to temperature, serum agglutination levels to serum agglutination levels, and so forth, to provide comparative information within that particular modality. At a more sophisticated level, data can be related to each other across modalities (for example, temperature and serum agglutination levels can be related to each other) to provide more complex information at a higher level—for example, that the individual from whom

these data are taken is suffering from an infection. These involve higher-level logic functions. The limit of sophistication for data-in-relation, and thus the limit of the information that can be extracted from a given set of data, is a function of the complexity of the logical forms of the data themselves.

The totality of data that are contained in the record about a given individual constitutes the data-space of that record, irrespective of how the data have been derived. Analogously, the totality of possible relationships in which these data can be related are the information-space relative to that record. If there are different types of relations that can structure the data-space, then one and the same data-space can give rise to different information-spaces. This is well illustrated by the relationship between different disciplines in medicine. For example, both oncology and immunology use some of the very same data. However, the oncologist might use the data—more correctly, certain formal parameters of the data—to diagnose the probability of cancer, whereas the immunologist might use different formal parameters of some of the same data to diagnose the functioning of a patient's apoptosis mechanism at the cellular level.

Decisions and Decision-Space

Decisions are choices that are made between the options that exist at a particular point in time. Logically, it is possible to make a choice only if three conditions are met. *First*, there must be different options among which one can choose; *second*, one must be aware of them as options; and *third*, there must be some values that determine the direction of the choice itself (Darwall, 1983; Hodgkinson, 1996; Kluge, 2004). In other words, choice requires data that are significant as information, as well as values that motivate the selection from among the meaningful options that are presented. The totality of possible choices that can be based on a given piece of information (or on several pieces of information-in-relation) may be called the decision-space in which that piece of information is embedded.

We can distinguish further between logical decision-spaces, factual decision-spaces, and valuational decision-spaces. Logical decision-spaces are decision-spaces that contain all logically possible options that are open to a decision-maker at that point in time; factual decision-spaces are truncated versions of logical decision-spaces in that they contain all and only those possible decisions that the decision-maker could factually implement at that point in time, given the material state of affairs that obtains. Valuational decision-spaces, in turn, are all those decisions within factual decision-space that are open to the decision-maker given her or his values. It follows that valuational decision-spaces are subsets of factual decision-spaces and that factual decision-spaces are subsets of logical decision-spaces relative to a given set of information. Clearly, the very same information may be embedded in a series of distinct decision-spaces. However, if we ignore the differences between the various types of decision-spaces and focus solely on the totality of decisions that are possible relative to a given set of information and simply call that the decision-space, then we can say that each set of information is embedded in a complex decision-space.

EHRs, Patient Analogues and Patient Profiles

With this in mind, we can now turn to the notion of an EHR. An EHR may be viewed in two ways: materially and informatically. Materially, it is the medical record relating to the past, present or future physical and mental health or condition of a patient that resides in computers or other electronic devices that capture, transmit, receive, store, retrieve, link, and manipulate multimedia data for the primary purpose of providing healthcare and health-related services (ISO/TS 18308; ISO

20514). As such, it may be localized in a single setting or be spatially distributed. Informatically, it is the set of health data that have been generated about a given patient and that can be linked in virtue of the relational structure in which they are embedded.

Informatically, therefore, an EHR constitutes a patient-relative data-space. Of course, the number of data that are generated about a patient are not coextensive with the number of data that could in principle be generated, since what data are actually generated depends on the instrumentation and the investigative procedures that are employed (and, of course, on the investigative effort that has been expended) when examining the patient. Consequently the EHR data-space that is the foundation of the information-space relative to a particular patient is not strictly isomorphic with the patient considered as a totality of possibilities of distinction (Gremy, 1994). Nevertheless it can be argued that an EHR, as the total package of data that have been generated about a given patient, constitutes a patient analogue (Kluge, 1996).

The reason an EHR constitutes a patient analogue is that an analogue is something that can perform a similar function to, or that can be substituted for, that of which it is the analogue (Concise Oxford English Dictionary, 2004). An EHR functions precisely in this fashion in the healthcare setting. That is to say, it can function as the informatic and epistemic foundation of patient profiles that are developed by medical professionals and other healthcare professionals and that are used by them when making their respective diagnoses. Moreover, it can function as the basis of decision-making about the patient by the relevant healthcare decision-makers. In other words, it can function as the basis of the information-spaces and decision-spaces that are developed by healthcare professionals relative to the patient from whom the data are derived.

The point can also be approached somewhat differently by beginning with the notion of a patient profile itself. A patient profile is a collection of data that are selected and interrelated by a healthcare professional relative to a given patient. In other words, using the language developed a moment ago, a patient profile is an information-space that is traced by a healthcare professional through the patient-relative data-space by collecting and interrelating a subset of the total data that form the patient-relative data-space (Kay & Purves, 1996; Kluge, 1993, 1996, 2001). Since different healthcare professions emphasize different types of relationships among health data, and since individual healthcare professionals are even more distinctive in the types of relationships that they consider significant, patient profiles will constitute distinct information-spaces and vary not only relative to different healthcare professions and specialities but also from individual healthcare professional to individual healthcare professional. For example, the patient profile as drawn by a cardiologist will differ from that drawn by a haematologist, which in turn will differ from that of a psychiatrist or an oncologist. Moreover, the patient profile drawn by one cardiologist may differ from that drawn by another, and so on. At the same time, patient profiles may overlap, as will occur when different patient profiles constructed by different professionals share similar data and relate them in a similar fashion. This will be the case when the profile drawn by a general internist partially overlaps with the profile developed by an immunologist or a cardiologist.

A patient profile can be developed either on the basis of direct and immediate contact with the patient, indirectly by accessing and using the patient-relative data space (the EHR as an informatic entity) and interconnecting a subset of its data-points with the help of certain functional relations, or by involving both the EHR and the patient directly. Clearly, when the patient is directly involved, it is the patient that lies at the epistemic center of the undertaking. However, as soon as the patient profile is developed on the basis of the data-space that is the EHR, the EHR functions as patient analogue and the profiles

themselves are merely informatic versions of what, in material terms, would be called distinct views of the patient from distinct and particular professionally based epistemic perspectives. It is important to note that the patient who presents materially offers a much wider array of qualities or characteristics—in other words, presents with a much wider array of possibilities-of-distinction—than will actually be identified or used by the healthcare professional who examines the patient. The very same thing is true about the EHR that constitutes the patient analogue: Not all data within the data-space defined by the EHR will be used by a healthcare professional to generate a patient profile.

It is the analogue nature of EHRs that provides a sure and certain footing for the obligation to treat them in an ethically distinctive fashion irrespective of how traditions are understood or interpreted, and that grounds obligations relative to privacy and security that mirror, in informatic terms, analogous obligations towards patient themselves.

Patients, EHRs, Analogues and Isomorphs

However, before showing how this is the case, it may be useful to take a still closer look at the notion of EHRs as patient analogues and consider a possible objection. It is a rather technical objection but one that seeks to invalidate the thesis that an EHR functions as patient analogue in data- and information-space. The objection maintains that the EHR *qua* informatic entity is not strictly isomorphic with the patient whose analogue it is. Consequently, so goes the argument continues, the claim that the EHR *qua* informatic entity functions as patient analogue is fundamentally mistaken (Gremy, 1994).

The core of this objection is the concept of an analogue. It argues that two things are strictly isomorphic to each other only if they stand in a one-one relationship such that for every element in the one there is a corresponding element in the other and vice versa: in logical terms, if a one-to-one mapping of the one set onto the other set preserves the relations between all of the elements of the domains of the sets. There are many more elements—many more possibilities-of-distinction—in the set that is the material patient than there are in the EHR as developed within the limits of current technology. Absent a complete scan of the patient in all possible physical modalities and a complete analysis of the patient's psychology and socio-cultural embedding, nothing can be strictly isomorphic with the patient except the patient her/himself. Consequently, so that objection has it, the suggestion that the EHR functions as patient analogue fails.

However, while this objection is correct about the notion of an isomorph, it fails on two counts. *First*, it equates being an analogue with being an isomorph. While this may be considered a rather technical point, it is nevertheless central because it invalidates the logic of the objection itself. An analogue differs from an isomorph in that it does not necessarily stand in the strict one-one relationship that has been indicated. Instead, it is something that is similar in function to that of which it is an analogue because it shares certain crucial logical characteristics with it, but is of dissimilar origin. Therefore an EHR does not have to stand in a strict one-one correspondence with the patient whose record it is in order to function as patient analogue.

Second, the objection misses an important point about professional-patient encounters and about diagnosis and decision-making in healthcare. When a healthcare professional interacts directly with a physical patient, it is not the patient as a whole that functions as the basis of a healthcare professional's diagnosis and/or decision-making. Put it differently, it is not the total possibilities-of-distinction that constitute the psycho-social and material patient from a professional epistemic perspective that functions as the basis of the healthcare professional's epistemic actions. It is the patient as perceived by this particular healthcare professional with this particular training and outlook at this particular point in time.

That is to say, from the vantage-point of the healthcare professional and with respect to diagnosis and decision-making as epistemic undertakings, a patient is nothing more nor less than a totality of possibilities-of-distinction. However, even in the context of direct professional-patient interaction, the professional is aware of and selects only a subset of this totality. Therefore the set of possibilities-of-distinction that engage the professional epistemically is not an isomorph of the patient *qua* patient either, but an analogue. Consequently the fact that the EHR is not a strict isomorph of the patient does not detract from the fact that the EHR functions as patient analogue in information and decision-space *because that is precisely how the patient himself functions in real-life interactions*. The objection, therefore, fails.

PAPER RECORDS, EHRS, AND ANALOGUES

However, there is another possible objection that is much more serious. It goes to the very heart of the claim that because EHRs are fundamentally distinct from paper-based records (PBR), they deserve distinctive and special ethical consideration which, while in many ways similar to what is appropriate for PBRs, is radically different in origin and far wider in extent. The objection may be stated like this: Both EHRs and PBRs contain only a small subset of the data that would constitute a complete description of the patient; therefore both present only a reduced model of the patient in information-theoretical terms. Moreover, PBRs also function as the basis of decisions that are made about the patient, and only a small subset of the data that are contained in PBRs are used in constructing a patient profile or in making a patient-relative decision. Arguably, therefore, the difference between PBRs and EHRs is only technological, and to claim that the development of EHRs involved a change of quantum-like proportions and that different ethical considerations are appropriate is unjustified.

While this objection is correct in pointing to certain similarities between paper-based records and EHRs, it nevertheless fails. It fails because it ignores a fundamental difference between the logical natures of the two types of records. This difference is grounded in the different ways in which something becomes a datum for each kind of record. The data that are recorded in a PBR do not enter the record *as data*. To use the language of logical forms and data-space, the data-points in a PBR do not, as an integral part of their entry, enter embedded in the matrix of logical possibilities-of-combination that is their logical form. They enter the record as merely material entities—as marks on paper. Their identity as symbols with meaning—as entities with logical forms—and hence the data-space to which they give rise, are evanescent epistemic creatures that are contributed by and that are contained in the minds of the professionals who access the record and who, by seeing the material marks as having a certain significance, epistemically contribute the logical forms that turn them into data and make them combinable in certain ways.

It is precisely here that EHRs differ. The data that enter the EHR do not enter simply as electronic impulses to which the observer must contribute a logical form by seeing them as data-points that have certain significance (and hence as having certain possibilities of combination). Instead, the nature of an EHR as a piece of software is such that in order for something to enter as a data-point—which is to say, in order to be able to be a component of the EHR at all—it must enter as something that is embedded in (and therefore defined by) a logical matrix of possible combinations. It other words, it must enter as a logical object. Its logical form is not contributed by the observer.

Unless the logical possibilities-of-combination are part of its logical structure, it cannot enter the EHR. To use an information-theoretical term, unless data-points come embedded in a matrix of possibilities-of-connection, they will not be data but "noise."

This, of course, means that the data in an EHR necessarily have logical forms, where their very nature as data is defined by these logical forms.[2] And because these logical forms are integral to their nature as constituents of the EHR, they automatically give rise to a data-space that is observation-independent and whose nature is determined by their logical forms. Therefore, the data-space of an EHR is not an epistemic creature that depends on external observation. It is a metaphysically independent entity that is correlative with the existence of EHR itself. All that observation will do is identify distinct information-spaces, as we have seen before. This identification will initially be relative to the particular specialty of the professional observer, who will then particularize it on the basis of her or his expertise and training. The result is a patient profile which, as such, is a particular selection of data within the patient-relative information-space. However, the data-space and the possibility of information-spaces arise with the development of the EHR itself, and they grow in number and complexity commensurate with the increase in the number and kinds of data that make up the EHR itself.

This feature not only distinguishes EHRs from PBRs but also underscores the validity of the analysis of an EHR as a patient analogue. As has already been pointed out, one and the same patient will be viewed differently by different healthcare specialties, and different healthcare professionals can construct different patient profiles with respect to one and the same material patient. This is based on the fact that epistemologically speaking, patients present as totalities of possibilities-of-distinction. For any given patient, each specialty selects a subgroup from this totality of possibilities-of-distinction for its information-space, and each professional selects a further subgroup for the construction of a patient profile. Therefore, in the case of material patients, while the patient is existentially independent, the information-spaces and patient profiles that are developed by healthcare professionals are epistemically and metaphysically dependent on the presence of a viewer/observer. With due alteration of detail, the same thing holds true for EHRs. The data-space, which is defined by the EHR as informatic entity and which is the analogue of the patient, is also a totality of possibilities-of-distinction. Once the EHR is given, the data-space is given and it is independent of any epistemic stance that may be adopted by an observer. To be sure, both information-spaces and patient profiles will be metaphysically dependent because they are developed by external observers who adopt a particular epistemic stance with respect to it, but that is the same in the case of material patients.

Of course there is a basic difference between patients and EHRs that goes beyond their purely material or physical differences. Patients are existentially independent of healthcare professionals whereas EHRs, as material entities, depend on healthcare professionals for their very existence. However, that does not invalidate the claim that EHRs are patient analogues. *First*, all analogues are constructs that stand in a functional relation to that of which they are analogues. Therefore, the fact that they require material construction does not invalidate the claim that they are analogues. That is precisely what one would expect from something that is an analogue.

Second, any material entity is existentially dependent on something, and the patient is no exception. In the absence of parents and an appropriate material environment that allows them to survive, patients would not exist either. It is just that patients do not depend on healthcare professionals for their coming into being, whereas EHRs do. However, this merely highlights a difference

in the form of existential dependence, not the fact of existential dependence itself.

Third, given the material patient, the possibilities-of-distinction that are the patient from an information-theoretical point of view are given. The same thing is true about the EHR: given the EHR, the informatic entity that is the data-space defined by the EHR is also given. It does not depend on observation or anything else.

In fact, one could go further and argue that the EHR as patient analogue is a *meme*. A meme may be defined as an epistemic unit which, once it has come into being, can be transmitted from one context to another and to that extent has an independent metaphysical status that is non-material in nature because it is independent of the mode of expression. The notion of a meme was first explored by Dawkins (1976) in the context of evolution and genes and has lately been expanded by Dennett with respect to human consciousness (Dennett, 1991). Arguably, it is also applicable to EHRs. Their identity is a function of their informational content, and while they may share certain components with other records, it is the overall totality of data as a logically structured informatic entity (that reflects the logic of the individual patient) that differentiates them. Like memes, EHRs have an independent existential status not in the sense that they can exist independently of material instantiation but in the sense that whatever the substratum in which they are instantiated may be, they become *those specific entities* in virtue of their informatic content and structure. However, for present purposes it is unnecessary to pursue the point further.

SOME IMPLICATIONS: WHY ETHICS MATTERS

The preceding analysis lays the basis for the claim that ethical considerations should play a fundamentally different role when it comes to the treatment of EHRs as opposed to PBRs, in a word why, in the case of EHRs, ethics uniquely matters

Nature of EHRs

The clue is found in the concept of appropriate treatment. That is to say, the treatment of something is appropriate if and only if that treatment is in accordance with the nature of the entity in question. Thus, to treat a person like a piece of furniture or like a mere hunk of flesh is inappropriate because persons are more than mere pieces of matter: They are autonomous entities with rights and obligations, and as such their treatment is subject to ethical principles. This is not merely an artefact of Western culture but is globally recognized in the *Universal Declaration of Human Rights* and by the World Court in the Hague, as well as by various international declarations and conventions.

EHRs, as EHRs, are more than merely material entities. As the preceding has made clear, their very nature as logical entities and the role they play in decision-making marks them as patient-analogues in information and decision-space. Now, the treatment of an analogue is appropriate if and only if it functionally mirrors the treatment of that of which it is an analogue. It follows that the principles that should govern the treatment of EHRs insofar as they are EHRs must be informatic analogues of the principles that govern conduct towards patients themselves. It has long been recognized that the treatment of patients is subject to ethical analysis and must be in compliance with fundamental ethical principles. Consequently, the principles that should govern the treatment of EHRs as EHRs should be functionally analogous to the principles that govern ethical conduct towards the subjects of EHRs. As is clear from ethics in general and deontic logic in particular, ethical considerations are logically irreducible and *sui generis* (Brandt, 1959; Moore, 1903; von Wright, 1983). In other words, only ethical principles are ethical in nature. This means that the informatic analogues that should govern the appropriate treatment of EHRs insofar as they are EHRs must themselves be ethical in nature. It follows that in the treatment of EHRs ethics matters.

Clearly, the preceding considerations do not invalidate the claim that the treatment of PBRs is also subject to ethical considerations. However, it does highlight the fact that in their case the reason does not lie in their nature as records—because that is fundamentally distinct—but in something else. Specifically, it lies in the traditions that surround their development, in the nature of the physician-patient relationship and in the assumptions of confidentiality and security that have grown up around them. These conditions also apply to EHRs. After all, whatever else may be true about them, they are also records. However, because they are more than that—because they are patient analogues in information- and decision-space—ethical considerations apply to them with much greater force, and apply even when the traditions are reinterpreted.

Moreover, it is this special status of EHRs that allows one to see that certain questions that require an *ad hoc* decision when applied to PBRs receive a consistent and logical answer in the case of EHRs. Thus, the question who owns the information contained in an EHR is not subject to the legal wrangling that surrounds the treatment of health records as mere sensitive documents. It receives a straightforward answer because it is an analogue of the question of who owns the patient. The answer is that in both instances, the question is miscast as one of ownership. In each case, it is a question of control, and in each case control lies with the patients themselves. It is a matter of patient autonomy and its informatic analogue.(IMIA, 2002; *McInerney v. MacDonald*) And just as the patient's right to self-determination may be overruled by the equal and competing rights of others, so the patient's control of her or his analogue may also be overruled under similar circumstances. However, it may be overruled only for ethically defensible reasons, only with due process and only on the basis of considerations that find their basis in human rights. EHRs as merely sensitive records do not merit the protection of Articles 3 and 12 of the *Universal Declaration of Human Rights*, whereas EHRs as patient analogues fall under its protective umbrella. This becomes especially important in an era where genetic data are becoming increasingly important, and where there is a temptation to allow pragmatic considerations determine what is considered juridically permissible.

EHRs and E-Health

The preceding reflections are particularly important in light of the evolving informatic technology and the fundamental changes that are occurring in healthcare delivery itself. E-health, the application of information and communications technologies to the delivery of healthcare and healthcare administration, is rapidly transforming the face of healthcare delivery in many jurisdictions and, through its promise of improved system accessibility, quality and efficiency, has the potential of becoming a valued tool on a global scale both in the private and the public sector. To a large extent, e-health is predicated on the very nature and role of the EHR as patient analogue.

However, e-health is inter-jurisdictional by its very nature. Neither informatic nor healthcare professionals have to leave their jurisdictions to exercise their professions. The radiologist may be in Bangalore and the contracting hospital in Maine or Leeds, data input may occur in Glasgow and the data processing, storage and manipulation take place in Chennai, Hong Kong or West Virginia (Vijaya, 2004). These different jurisdictions have different legal and professional views on the legal status of medical records in general and of EHRs in particular. Unless there is a consistent understanding of the nature of EHRs, the treatment of EHRs will be subject to the vagaries of treaty negotiations, national laws and professional perspectives.

This becomes particularly difficult when even the minimal international ethical standards that exist—such as Article 12 of the *Universal Declaration of Human Rights*—are subordinated to the pragmatic interests of individual nation states. This is most glaringly illustrated by the USA Patriot Act. This Act, whose full title is *Uniting and Strengthening America by Providing Appropriate Tools Required to Intercept and Obstruct Terrorism Act*, allows U.S. intelligence agencies (and through them, all other affiliated intelligence agencies all over the world) to access the EHRs in the possession or under the control of U.S informatics professionals, corporations and institutions without the subject's consent or knowledge just as long as the agency believes that the subject of the EHR is in any way connected with their own intelligence mandate, and makes it a criminal offense to inform the subject of the EHR that such an invasion of privacy has occurred.

Such an abrogation of privacy rights would be difficult to sustain and defend if EHRs were to be recognized for what they really are, namely, patient analogues. The treatment of EHRs would then be moved under the protective umbrella of ethical principles and human rights. International regulations and standards could then be coordinated and it would be possible not merely to develop technically interoperable protocols for the delivery of e-health but also ethically and juridically consistent procedures.

CONCLUSION

The preceding has tried to show that there are several reasons why ethics matters for EHRs. EHRs are special both in their logical nature as well as in the roles they play as patient analogues in information and decision-space. To treat EHRs as merely sensitive instruments on the traditional model presented by PBRs and to consider them as adequately protected by the rules, regulations and laws that govern material records is not merely to misunderstand their true nature but is also to court disaster in a world where e-health is rapidly becoming a reality. The functional attraction of e-health lies in the fact that it allows consultation and expert medical interaction on a global scale; it allows outsourcing not only of book-keeping and record storing services to the most cost-effective venue but also of diagnostic services on a 24/7 basis, thereby advancing he very ideal of healthcare delivery itself. However, execution of this ideal requires consistent handling principles that do not vary across the geographic spectrum, that do not change as technical modalities are improved or replaced, and that do not encounter conflict of laws as the EHR passes from one jurisdiction to another. Recognizing the unique ethical nature of EHRs provides a consistent basis for the development of protocols and laws not merely within a given jurisdiction but also on an international scale.

REFERENCES

Ascher, M., & Ascher, R. (1997). *The code of the Quipu: A study in media, mathematics, and culture.* Ann Arbor: University of Michigan Press.

Brandt, R. B. (1959). *Ethical theory: The problems of normative and critical ethics.* Englewood Cliffs, NJ: Prentice Hall.

Brosius, M. (Ed.). (2003). *Ancient archives and archival traditions. Concepts of record-keeping in the ancient world. Oxford studies in ancient documents.* Oxford: Oxford University Press.

Chakraberty, C. (1923). *An interpretation of ancient Hindu medicine.* Calcutta: R. Chakraberty.

Soanes, C., & Stevenson, A. (2004). *Concise Oxford English dictionary* (11th ed.). Oxford: Oxford University Press.

Darwall, S. L. (1983). *Impartial reason.* Ithaca and London: Cornell University Press.

Dawkins, R. (1976). *The selfish gene.* Oxford: Oxford University Press.

Dennett, D. C. (1991). *Consciousness explained.* New York: The Penguin Press.

Edelstein, L. (1923). *The hippocratic oath.* Baltimore: Johns Hopkins Press.

EU Directive 95/46 EC. (1995). *On the protection of individuals with regard to the processing of personal data and on the free movement of such data.* Retrieved from http://www.cdt.org/privacy/eudirective/EU_Directive_.html

Gremy F. (1994). Comments on: Health information, the fair information principles and ethics. *Methods of Information in Medicine, 33,* 346-7.

Hodgkinson, C. (1996). *Administrative philosophy.* Oxford: Pergamon.

International Medical Informatics Association. (IMIA). (2002). *Code of ethics for health informatics professionals.* Retrieved from http://www.imia.org/code_of_ethics.html

ISO/TS 18308 (2003). *Requirements for an electronic health record architecture.*

ISO 20514 (2005) *Electronic health record—definition, scope and context.*

Kay, S., & Purves, I. (1996). Medical records and other stories: A narratological framework. *Methods of Information in Medicine, 35,* 72-88.

Kluge, E.-H. (1993). Advanced patient records: Some ethical and legal considerations touching medical information space. *Methods of Information in Medicine, 32,* 95-103.

Kluge, E.-H. (1996). The medical record: Narration and story as a path through patient data. *Methods of Information in Medicine, 35,* 88-92.

Kluge, E.-H. (2001). *The ethics of electronic patient records.* New York; Bern: Peter Lang.

Marsiglia, W. (1966). *Sumerian records from Drehem.* New York: AMS Press.

McDougall, B. S., & Hansson, A. (2002). *Chinese concepts of privacy.* Leiden, Boston; Tokyo: Brill.

McInerney v. MacDonald 93 DLR (4th) 415.

Moore, G. E. (1903). *Principia Ethica.* Cambridge: Oxford University Press.

United Nations. (1948). *Universal Declaration of Human Rights.* Retrieved from http://www.un.org/Overview/rights.html

USA Patriot Act. (2001, rev. 2005). *Uniting and Strengthening America by Providing Appropriate Tools Required to Intercept and Obstruct Terrorism Act,* HR 3162 revised as *USA Patriot Improvement and Reauthorization Act,* H.R. 3199.

Vijaya, K. (2004). Teleradiology Solutions: Taking expertise to hospitals in US. *Express Healthcare Management,* Issue dtd. 16th to 29th February 2004, from http://www.expresshealthcaremgmt.com/20040229/innews07.shtml

Von Wright, G. H. (1983). The foundation of norms and normative statement. In G.H. Von Wright, (Ed.), *Practical reason* (pp. 67-82). Basil Blackwell: Oxford.

ADDITIONAL READINGS

Anderson, J. G., & Goodman, K.W. (Ed.). (2002). *Ethics and information technology. A case-based approach to a health care system in transition.* New York: Springer.

British Computing Society Health Informatics Committee. (2003). *A handbook of ethics for health informatics professionals. Bristol.* British Computer Society. Retrieved from http://www.bcs.org/server.php?show=conWebDoc.1379

Goodman. K. W. (Ed.). (1998). *Ethics, computing, and medicine. Informatics and the transformation of healthcare.* Cambridge: Cambridge University Press.

IMIA Code of Ethics for Health Information Professionals. Retrieved from http://www.imia.org/code_of_ethics.html

Kluge, E-H. W. (2001). *The ethics of electronic patient records.* New York: Peter Lang.

ENDNOTES

[1]   Clearly, anything can be a datum just as long as it acquires a matrix of possibilities of combination with other data. From an information-theoretical point of view it is irrelevant whether it acquires this by a verbal (or other) convention, or whether it is assigned these possibilities automatically by software.

[2]   In arithmetic terms, the value of a datum in a record lies in its definition which specifies its logical relations to other data.

Section VI
Knowledge Translation in Healthcare

Chapter XVIII
Technology Enabled Knowledge Translation:
Using Information and Communications Technologies to Accelerate Evidence Based Health Practices

Kendall Ho
University of British Columbia, Canada

ABSTRACT

Because of the rapid growth of health evidence and knowledge generated through research, and growing complexity of the health system, clinical care gaps increasingly widen where best practices based on latest evidence are not routinely integrated into everyday health service delivery. Therefore, there is a strong need to inculcate knowledge translation strategies into our health system so as to promote seamless incorporation of new knowledge into routine service delivery and education to promote positive change in individuals and the health system towards eliminating the clinical care gaps. E-health, the use of information and communication technologies (ICT) in health which encompasses telehealth, health informatics, and e-learning, can play a prominently supportive role. This chapter examines the opportunities and challenges of technology enabled knowledge translation (TEKT) using ICT to accelerate knowledge translation in today's health system with two case studies for illustration. Future TEKT research and evaluation directions are also articulated.

Copyright © 2008, IGI Global, distributing in print or electronic forms without written permission of IGI Global is prohibited.

KNOWLEDGE TRANSLATION: INTRODUCTION

The tenet of modern healthcare practice is evidence-based, established from knowledge generated through medical research and proven practice patterns. Evidence-based practice takes time to evolve. It is estimated that incorporating advances advocated by current research into routine, everyday medical practice takes one to two decades or more (Haynes, 1998; Sussman, Valente, Rohrbach et al., 2006). The causes of this apparent lag time of translating evidence into routine health practice are multifactorial, including but not restricted to: explosion of research and generation of resultant evidence, ineffective continuing education for health professionals to propagate the knowledge, lack of adoption of the knowledge by health professionals after exposure and education, the complexity of health management strategies that commonly demand more than simple changes in treatment approaches, reduction in healthcare resources, a lack of mutual understanding and dialogue between researchers that generated the research and health practitioners and health policy makers who need to translate the research into routine practices, and the practitioners' and policy makers' own beliefs and experiences that influence how knowledge will ultimately be utilized in clinical situations and quality assurance initiatives. As a result, a clinical care gap occurs when the best evidence is not routinely applied in clinical practice (Davis, 2006; Grol & Grimshaw, 2003).

Definition

Canadian Institutes of Health Research (CIHR), one of the three members of the Canadian Research Tri-council and the guiding force in Canadian Health Research, defines knowledge translation as "the exchange, synthesis, and ethically-sound application of knowledge, within a complex set of interactions among researchers and users, to accelerate the capture of the benefits of research for Canadians through improved health, more effective services and products, and a strengthened healthcare system" (CIHR, 2007). The Social Sciences and Humanities Research Council of Canada (SSHRC, 2006), another member of the Tri-council with focus on humanities research, defines knowledge mobilization as "moving knowledge into active service for the broadest possible common good." SSHRC further contextually defines knowledge to be "...understood to mean any or all of (1) findings from specific social sciences and humanities research, (2) the accumulated knowledge and experience of social sciences and humanities researchers, and (3) the accumulated knowledge and experience of stakeholders concerned with social, cultural, economic and related issues" (SSHRC, 2006). Both definitions speak to the central principle of the need for not only discovering new knowledge through research, but also utilizing the resultant knowledge effectively and routinely in order to fully realize the benefits of the body of research. For the rest of this chapter, knowledge translation (KT) will be used to denote this core concept of effective knowledge application.

Strategic Considerations

Strategically, effective and sustainable KT requires synchronized efforts at several levels towards a common vision of evidence based practice (Berwick, 2003; Katzenbach & Smith, 2005; Senge, 1994): the **personal** level where individuals influence their own behaviors towards change, the **team** level where groups of individuals work together collaboratively and cooperatively to drive towards group-based change, and the **system** level where health organizations and policy making bodies evolve and innovate on policies and establish organizational patterns and cultures to motivate members towards change.

Driving forces to motivate change at the individual level include:

- Helping individuals to arrive at their own willingness and commitment to change
- Recognizing explicitly the contributions that individuals would make in carrying out the change
- Providing individuals with appropriate compensation, either monetary or otherwise, in making the change
- Sharing successful results with and giving feedback to the individuals after practice change has been instituted

Key factors to promote effective change at the team level include:

- Jointly owning a shared vision towards an important goal
- Having effective overall leadership of the team, and also distributive leadership of the various individuals in the team and corresponding power and responsibility to drive change
- Sharing mutual trust with and accountability to each other in carrying out the necessary work
- Having an effective conflict resolution mechanism to bring differences; respectfully to the table for understanding, discussion, and resolution
- Achieving and celebrating success together

Important change management levers at the system's level include:

- Creating and adjusting fair and appropriate recognition and reward systems
- Bringing understanding to the impact of change in healthcare service delivery pattern towards the social, economic, and population health context
- Cultivating the spirit of innovation to motivate individuals in the system to generate better evidence and pathways against current standards and practice patterns

- Promoting transfer of functions amongst individuals in the health system as effective division of labor and recognition of increasing competence through expansion of responsibilities
- Implementing routine system's level reflection for continuous quality improvement and iterative modifications towards excellence

Success in sustainable KT requires not only transformation at the various levels, but also the harmonization of efforts in the totality of all these levels towards the common vision. For example, the April 2003 Institute of Medicine report advocates five core competencies that the health professionals of the 21st century need to possess (Institute of Medicine, 2003): delivering patient-centered care; working as part of interdisciplinary teams; practicing evidence based medicine; focusing on quality improvement; and using information technology. As an illustration, let us examine the core competency of interdisciplinary team establishment. In order to translate the concept of interdisciplinary team into routine health practice, having research that demonstrates examples of successful team based practice is not enough to cause lasting change in practice patterns. These successful examples, or documented knowledge, need to be vivified in health professionals' own practice context so they and their own teams can visualize how they can model after these successful examples to replicate success (Ho et al., 2006). This type of education is necessary but not sufficient either; innovative policy translation by the policy makers to promote team based practice, patient and health consumer demand or preference for same, health system redesign and implementation by health administrators, and appropriate accreditation for the educational system to promote the values and transform the curriculum for health professional trainees should all occur in synchrony in order to bring about lasting change, that is, sustainable knowledge translation.

Finally, it is important to note that knowledge translation is not a straightforward and linear approach, but rather a complex and adaptive process based on common vision, solid principles, shared commitment at different levels, and human ingenuity in flexible adaptation.

Effective KT in Health

It is desirable and achievable to accelerate knowledge translation in health to expeditiously reap the benefits health research to realize optimal evidence-based care for patients. Known and tested KT pathways, such as the Model of Improvement developed by Associates in Process Improvement (API, 2007) and endorsed by The Institute for Healthcare Improvement (IHI, 2007), can lead to successful KT in health system transformation through the following sequence of steps:

- Setting aims to decide what accomplishments are to be achieved
- Establishing measure in order to assess positive change
- Selecting the key changes that will result in improvement
- Testing changes through the plan-do-study-act cycle
- Implementing changes after testing
- Spreading changes to other organizations

Each of these steps require not only systems based mind-shift, but also individuals in the systems changing their personal behaviors. Therefore, in the health system context, health research can and ideally should be synchronized with individual practice, education, and policy setting environments so as to accelerate KT towards expeditious evidence based healthcare delivery.

ICT IN HEALTH

Modern information and communication technologies (ICT), including computers, personal digital assistants, cellular phones, and an ever expanding list of imaginative electronic communication devices, are making unprecedented and innovative impact on healthcare service access, delivery, education and research (Ho, Chockalingam, Best, & Walsh, 2003). The rapid growth of affordable, interoperable ICTs that can facilitate seamless data communication and increase connectivity to the Internet are breaking down geographic and temporal barriers in accessing information, service, and communication. These advances are transforming the ways regional, national and global health services, surveillance, and education are being delivered.

Some of the clear advantages of using ICT in health service delivery and education, or commonly referred to as e-Health, include but not limited to (Health Canada, 2006; Miller & Sim, 2004; Shortliffe, 1999):

- Anywhere, anytime access to accurate and searchable health information for knowledge and clinical case exchange, such as the use of ePocrates to help health professionals in rapidly accessing drug information to promote safe medication prescribing
- Large capacity for information storage and organization for health surveillance, such as the World Health Organization's international health surveillance system to monitor infectious disease outbreaks in real time
- Ease of synchronous and asynchronous communication between health professionals in different geographic areas for health service delivery, knowledge exchange or consultations

Defining E-Health

When first introduced, the term "e-health" was used to signify health service delivery and activities on the Internet. Today, this term has been adopted to become an over-arching term to denote generally any use of ICT in healthcare (U Calgary Health Telematics Unit, 2005; Health Canada 2006), from health service delivery to health data storage and analysis to health education through ICT use.

E-health can be conceptually visualized to be supported by three distinct but inter-related pillars: *telehealth, health informatics*, and **e-learning** (Figure 1).

Telehealth commonly refers to "...the use of ICT to delivery health services, expertise, and information over distance" (U Calgary Health Telematics Unit, 2005). Whereas in the past, telehealth focused on the use of the videoconferencing medium as a distinguishing feature, today in many circles the emphasis is placed on the service delivery aspect of the definition. Therefore, telehealth can be either video-based through a closed network such as ISDN or fibre-optic videoconferencing, or Web-based through the use of the multimedia capabilities of the Internet. Telehealth can also be delivered either

synchronously where communication between individuals occur in real time, or asynchronously in a "store and forward" fashion where one individual can send the information and expecting a response from others in a delayed fashion (Ho et al., 2004). Ample examples of telehealth can be found in the literature ranging from tele-psychiatry to tele-dermatology, tele-ophthalmology, emergency medicine, nursing, physiotherapy, and usage by other health disciplines.

Health informatics (HI) have many definitions by different institutions, as documented on the University of Iowa Health Informatics Web site (U Iowa Health Informatics, 2005). One such typical definition of HI from Columbia University is "...the scientific field that deals with the storage, retrieval, sharing and optimal use of biomedical information, data, and knowledge for problem solving and decision making. It touches on all basic and applied fields in biomedical science and is closely tied to modern information technologies, notably in the areas of computing and communication." The emphasis on HI, then, is on the storage and utilization of information captured through ICT. Excellent examples of the application of HI in practice are electronic health records in clinics and hospitals in a regional scale, public health on line disease surveillance systems

Figure 1. E-health components

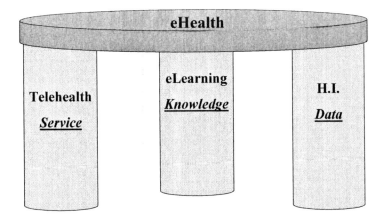

nationally (Public Health Agency of Canada, 2006) or the World Health Organization epidemic and pandemic alert and response (EPR) system (World Health Organization, 2007).

E-learning is commonly defined as "the use of electronic technology to deliver education and training applications, monitor learner performance, and report learner progress" (Sales, 2002). The distinguishing aspect of e-learning is the focus on the acquisition, utilization and evaluation of the knowledge captured by and synthesized through ICT. Examples of e-learning in health and their utility in changing health professionals' practice is well documented in the literature. A recent example of a randomized control trial demonstrating the equivalence of e-learning compared to face to face workshops in helping learners in knowledge retention, with a statistical significance favoring e-learning in helping learners to actually change their behaviours (e.g., Fordis, 2005).

While telehealth, health informatics, and e-learning have their own distinguishing features and pillars of pursuits, they also synergistically interact to offer maximal benefits to the health system as a whole. On the contrary, each pillar on its own can only have limited impact on the health system. For example, trans-geographic telehealth without capturing outcomes through health informatics and e-learning to teach and propagate the service delivery module might only lead to temporary adoption of telehealth without sustaining effects to the health system as a whole. Similarly, health data capturing would not be complete without considering the contextual elements of health service delivery and the accumulated practice knowledge to date in the communities from which the data was generated. It is also obvious that e-learning will be dependent upon accurate data and best practices models in health service delivery. Therefore, the exciting challenge and opportunity of e-health is indeed in the seamless and comprehensive and complimentary utilization of data, service and knowledge to drive the prospective transformation of health practices that are based on evidence, knowledge, and the needs of the health consumers and the communities (Figure 2).

TECHNOLOGY ENABLED KNOWLEDGE TRANSLATION

E-health is rapidly gaining momentum worldwide as a vital part of the healthcare system in and

Figure 2. Optimizing TEKT

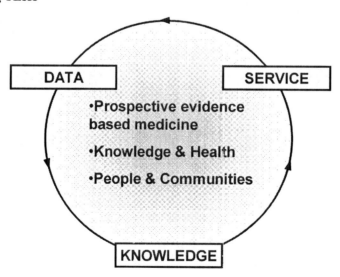

amongst nations. For example, National Health Services in the United Kingdom, in Australia, and Infoway in Canada are actively facilitating the establishment of infrastructure and implementation strategies in e-health to promote its entrenchment in health practices. Collaboration amongst different agencies and organizations is also evident in establishing emerging e-health networks in other countries such as the Africa Health Infoway (World Health Organization, 2006). Recognizing the potential, the UN General assembly categorically stated in its Millennium declaration that "… the benefits of new technologies, especially information and communication technologies … (should be made) available to all" (United Nations, 2000).

When considering e-health in practice, one needs to question not only "how do we augment or replace existing services with ICT," but also "how can ICT be innovatively used to best serve the health system that may not have any precedence?" This question can further be asked in two ways: "How can ICT be used to make current health service and education pathways more efficient, accessible, or higher quality?" and the companion question "How can ICT be used to provide unprecedented health service and educational models that were not possible in the past?" These questions guide us towards both adoption and innovation in e-health, and also properly consider ICT as serving the agenda of the health system, rather than using the latest and greatest technologies regardless of whether or not the usage actually improves health services and education.

TEKT Defined

Technology enabled knowledge translation (TEKT) is defined as the use of ICT to accelerate the incorporation of evidence and knowledge into routine health practices (Ho et al., 2003). By definition, TEKT is not only about using ICT to achieve one type of purpose, such as telehealth

for service delivery or health informatics for data storage and analysis. Rather, TEKT strategies **synchronize** and **coordinate** data, service, and knowledge capturing and utilization to synergistically cause a system's level change so as to translate evidence and health knowledge into routine practice and policy establishment.

ICT can play a pivotal role in the health system for knowledge synthesis, evidence-based decision-making, building shared capacity for knowledge exchange, and minimization of duplication of decision support systems. Various Web-based data and information repositories networked together can facilitate just-in-time clinical consultations, and support access to the latest management information on diseases, treatments, and medications. Instant sharing and exchange of knowledge by healthcare providers facilitated in these Internet portals as discussion groups or informal e-mail exchange can play an important role in team building. Remote access to centralized data repositories, such as electronic medical records via the Internet as well as intelligent information retrieval functionality and data pattern recognition are just some examples of the ways in which technologies can save time, eliminate laborious tasks, and interconnect to capture, disseminate, and help translate knowledge into practice in ways previously not possible.

Case Studies in TEKT

The following section highlights two case studies in TEKT to provide a qualitative illumination on best practices in TEKT. However, this discussion is not meant to be comprehensive or exhaustive, but rather illustrations to highlight and celebrate the innovation and ingenuity of the applications of ICT to facilitate TEKT and improved health outcome as they meet the challenges and needs of the healthcare system with existing and emerging technological solutions.

SARS (Srinivasan, McDonald, Jernigan et al., 2004; Marshall, Rachlis, & Chen, 2005; Wenzel, Bearman, & Edmond, 2005)

From late 2002 to 2003, the world was gripped by the emergence of a deadly and, up till then, unknown health threat sudden acute respiratory syndrome (SARS). This rapidly spreading infection with associated high mortality made its notorious impact worldwide into early 2003. In particular the South East Asian countries were most severely affected, with transmission to other continents due to mobility of infected populations. The eventual toll of SARS was recorded to be 8,098 cases worldwide, with 774 deaths.

During that period of outbreak, the many unknown features of SARS needed to be rapidly disseminated to health professionals and administrators around the world. Also, tracking of the spread of the infection, and patterns of spread to understand the modes of transmission and contact persons involved were paramount to bring effective control of this outbreak. SARS related infection control policies, criteria of diagnosis, education of health professionals and the general public, quality assurance activities were all vital information that were rapidly disseminated and exchanged through the use of ICT worldwide. Data repositories and electronic systems, together with Web-based information dissemination and consultations, were vital aspects of global SARS management and decision support for health professionals worldwide. The urgent and intensive efforts to disseminate information, sharing of best practices in infection control methods, and careful preparation of unaffected counties were key lessons learned, and ICT playing key roles in TEKT were pivotal in these activities. Also, as a result of SARS, great attention is paid in different countries and globally on disease monitoring and surveillance systems to prepare for future expected and unexpected outbreaks such as influenza, avian flu, or other diseases.

Medication Safety Surveillance (Bell et al., 2004; Graham, Campen, Hui et al., 2005; Leape & Berwick, 2005; Topol, 2004)

Non-steroidal anti-inflammatory drugs (NSAIDs) is a class of medications effective for pain management in patients with arthritis. However, NSAIDs are known to have substantial side effects in the gastroenteral system in causing ulcers and erosions. A new class of COX-II NSAIDs were introduced, the first one of which were rofecoxib (Vioxx®). Initial trials seemed to affirm that COX-II NSAIDs were effective for pain management and had lower gastrointestinal side effects compared to traditional NSAIDs. However, subsequent analysis of the data, with additional studies done by other groups, suggested the potential of increased cardiovascular side effects including myocardial infarctions and deaths.

Kaiser Permanente, an American Health Management Organization, wanted to clarify this controversy. It had an electronic health record system (HER) where, amongst a variety of health and administrative records, every doctor would track patient visits over time, medication prescriptions, and side effects. Using the California database of this EHR system, 2,302,029 person-years follow-up over a three year period where patients were exposed to rofecoxib were analyzed. The researchers found that there were 8,143 cases of serious coronary heart disease that occurred, with 2,210 cases (27.1 percent) where the patients died. This represented a more than three times risk (Odd ratio as high as 3.58) for the use of rofecoxib compared to another NSAID agent. This data, together with other studies, led to the company that made rofecoxib voluntarily withdrew the medication from the market in September 2004, and the Food and Drug Administration (FDA) officially recommending its withdraw in February 2005.

A very significant development in this medication surveillance was that, once Kaiser Permanente detected the significant cardiovascular side effect risk of rofecoxib, this information was passed onto physicians practicing in Kaiser, leading to a dramatic drop of rofecoxib prescription rate of four percent compared to the national average in United States of 40 percent, well before the medication was withdrawn from the market place.

This case demonstrates the power of EHR in not only being able to rapidly and prospectively track medication side effects so as to increase safety, but also disseminating the evidence to practitioners to influence practice outcome rapidly.

CHALLENGES AND OPPORTUNITIES IN TEKT

Barriers to ICT Uptake

Despite the potential and real benefits of ICT use in health, health professionals' uptake of ICT has been slow. Factors that impede the adoption of ICT tools include cost, lack of informatics platform standards, physicians' lack of time or technological literacy, the need for a cultural shift to embrace these necessary changes in medicine, and a lack of integration of various ICT methodologies into a cohesive deployment strategy.

For example, in a recent survey supported by The Commonwealth Fund (Schoen, Osborn, Huynh et al., 2006), the authors found that there was a wide variation of ICT uptake by primary care physicians amongst these seven countries, from as low as 23 percent to as high as 98 percent uptake in electronic patient medical records. This variation in electronic patient record uptake directly correlated with and underpinned issues related to quality and efficiency broached in this survey, such as coordination of care of patients, multifunctional capacity including automated alerts and reminders, or information sharing amongst interprofessional team members. Of note, both United States and Canada were lagging significantly behind the other five countries surveyed in terms of ICT uptake in practice. These variations were in large part due to the underlying policy choices of the different countries.

Therefore, in consideration as to how best to overcome barriers to technology uptake, it is important to not only focus on health professionals to increase their attitudes, knowledge and skills in ICT use, but also place emphasis on policy innovation to motivate the health systems towards quality and the adoption of ICT in support of this important vision of care.

FUTURE RESEARCH DIRECTIONS

As TEKT is an emerging field with a rapidly evolving environment, there is ample opportunity for research, innovation, and evaluation. Examples of dimensions of TEKT research could include but not restricted to:

- *Documentation* of best practices in TEKT to date
- Innovative *demonstrations* of ICT enabled models of knowledge translation, where ICT is used to either augment current approaches to evidence based knowledge translation or create unprecedented models
- Understanding the *human-technology interface* how ICT can be configured to optimize the utilization and practice of these tools in healthcare contexts
- Understanding and assisting in evidence based *e-health policy making*, as policy innovation is essential to guide the optimal use of ICT in the system's level
- *Integrating ICT into teams and communities* where human to human interactions and collaborations can be enhanced through ICT facilitation
- *Cost effectiveness and return on investment* evaluation as to how ICT can lead to increased capacity of the health system, cost avoidance or savings in health service delivery, or improved access and quality
- *Building capacity* in TEKT research over time

In order to accelerate the discipline of TEKT, it is important that efforts in this research and innovation be harmonized to enable cross study comparisons and standardized documentation of best practices. In this line of thinking, establishing a research evaluation framework towards TEKT would be an ideal approach (Ho et al., 2004).

CONCLUSION

ICT has tremendous potential to improve healthcare service delivery, and TEKT can help accelerate ICT adoption and change management to reap the corresponding benefits. Excellent literature based and practice based examples of TEKT have shone some best practice examples, and more innovative and effective models in the future are sure to come with the continuing improvement of technologies and practices. As a result, the practice of and research in TEKT are both timely and urgently needed to help achieve excellence in healthcare delivery.

REFERENCES

Associates in Process Improvement–API. (2007). *The model for improvement.* Austin, TX, Detroit, MI, Sacramento, CA, Washington, DC. Retrieved June 7, 2007, from http://www.apiWeb.org/API_home_page.htm

Bell, D. S., Cretin, S., Marken, R. S., & Landman, A. (2004). A conceptual framework for evaluating outpatient electronic prescribing systems based on their functional capabilities. *Journal of the American Informatics Association, 11,* 60-70.

Berwick, D. M. (2003). Disseminating innovations in health care. *Journal of the American Medical Association, 289*(15), 1969-1975.

Canadian Institutes of Health Research. (2007). Knowledge translation strategy 2004-2009: Innovation in action. Retrieved June 9, 2007, from http://www.cihr-irsc.gc.ca/e/26574.html#defining

Davis, D. (2006). Continuing education, guideline implementation, and the emerging transdisciplinary field of knowledge translation. *The Journal of Continuing Education in the Health Professions, 26*(1), 5-12.

Fordis, M., King, J.E., Ballantyne, C.M. et al. (2005). Comparison of the instructional efficacy of Internet-based CME with live interactive CME workshops: A randomized controlled trial. *Journal of the American Medical Association 294*(9), 1043-1051.

Graham, D. J., Campen, D., Hui, R., Spence, M., Cheetham, C., Levy, G., et al. (2005). Risk of acute myocardial infarction and sudden cardiac death in patients treated with cyclo-oxygenzse 2 selective and non-selective non-steroidal anti-inflammatory drugs: Nested case-control study. *Lancet, 365*(9458), 475-481.

Grol, R., & Grimshaw, J. (2003). From best evidence to best practice: Effective implementation of change in patients' care. *The Lancet, 362,* 1225-1230.

Haynes, R. (1998). Using informatics principles and tools to harness research evidence for patient care: Evidence-based informatics. *Medinfo, 9*(Pt 1 Suppl), 33-36.

Health Canada .(2006). *eHealth.* Retrieved on May 4, 2007, from http://www.hc-sc.gc.ca/hcs-sss/ehealth-esante/index_e.html

Ho, K., Chockalingam, A., Best, A., & Walsh, G. (2003). Technology-enabled knowledge translation: Building a framework for collaboration. *Canadian Medical Association Journal, 168*(6), 710-711.

Ho, K., Bloch, R., Gondocz, T., Laprise, R., Perrier, L., Ryan, D., et al. (2004). Technology-enabled knowledge translation: Frameworks to promote research and practice. *Journal of Continuing Education of the Health Professions, 24*(2), 90-99.

Ho, K., Karlinsky, H., Jarvis-Selinger, S., & May, J. (2004). Videoconferencing for Telehealth: unexpected challenges and unprecedented opportunities. *British Columbia Medical Journal, 46*(6), 285-289.

Ho, K., Borduas, F., Frank, B., Hall, P., Handsfield-Jones, R., Hardwick, D., et al. (2006). *Facilitating the integration of interprofessional education into quality healthcare: strategic roles of academic institutions.* Report to Health Canada Interprofessional Education for Collaborative Patient Centred Practice. October 2006.

Institute for Healthcare Improvement. (2007). How to improve: improvement methods. Retrieved on June 7, 2007 from http://www.ihi.org/IHI/Topics/Improvement/ImprovementMethods/HowTo-Improve/

Institute of Medicine of the National Academies. (2003). Health professions education: a bridge to quality. *Institute of Medicine April 8, 2003 Report.* Retrieved June 9, 2007, from http://www.iom.edu/CMS/3809/4634/5914.aspx

Katzenbach, J. R., & Smith, D. K. (2005 reprint). The discipline of teams. *Harvard Business Review 83*(7), 162-171.

Leape, L. L., & Berwick, D. M. (n.d.). Five years after 'to err is human': What have we learned? *Journal of the American Medical Association, 293*(19), 2384-2390.

Marshall, A. H., Rachlis, A., & Chen, J. (2005). Severe acute respiratory syndrome: responses of the healthcare system to a global epidemic. *Current Opinions in Otolaryngology, Head and Neck Surgery, 13*(3), 161-164.

Miller, R. H., & Sim, I. (2004). Physicians' use of electronic medical records: Barriers and solutions. *Health Affairs, 23*(2), 116-126.

Public Health Agency of Canada. (2006). Disease surveillance on-line. Retrieved June 7, 2007, from http://www.phac-aspc.gc.ca/dsol-smed/

Sales, G. C. (2002). *A quick guide to e-learning.* Andover, MN: Expert Publishing.

Schoen, C., Osborn R, Huynh, P. T., Doty, M., Peugh, J., & Zapert, K. (2006). On the front line of care: primary care doctors' office systems, experiences, and views in seven countries. *Health Affairs 25*(6), w555-w571. Retrieved June 9, 2007, from http://content.healthaffairs.org/cgi/content/abstract/hlthaff.25.w555?ijkey=3YyH7yDwrJSoc&keytype=ref&siteid=healthaff

Senge, P. M. (1994). *The fifth discipline: The art & practice of the learning organization.* New York: Doubleday.

Shortliffe, E. H. (1999). The evolution of electronic medical records. *Academic Medicine, 74*(4), 441-419.

Social Sciences and Humanities Research Council of Canada (2006). *Knowledge Impact on Society: A SSHRC Transformation Program.* Retrieved June 9, 2007, from http:// http://www.sshrc.ca/Web/apply/program_descriptions/knowledge_impact_e.asp

Srinivasan, A., McDonald, L. C., Jernigan, D., et al. (2004). Foundations of the severe acute respiratory syndrome preparedness and response plan for healthcare facilities. *Infection Control and Hospital Epidemiology, 25*(12), 1020-1025.

Sussman, S., Valente, T. W., Rohrbach, L. A., Skara, S., & Pentz, M. A. (2006). Translation in the health professions: Converting science into action. *Evaluation and the Health Professions, 29*(1), 7-32.

Topol, E. J. (2004). Failing the public health-Rofecoxid, Merck and the FDA. *New England Journal of Medicine, 351*(17), 1707-1709.

United Nations Millennium Declaration. (2000). Section III. 19 of the General Assembly resolution 55/2 of 8 September 2000. Retrieved June 9, 2007, from http://www.ohchr.org/english/law/millennium.htm

University of Calgary Health Telematics Unit. (2005). *Glossary of telhealth related terms, acronyms and abbreviations.* Retrieved June 7, 2007, from http://www.fp.ucalgary.ca/telehealth/Glossary.htm

University of Iowa Health Informatics. (2005). *What is Health Informatics?* Retrieved June 7, 2007 from http://www2.uiowa.edu/hinfo/academics/what_is_hi.html

Wenzel, R. P., Bearman, G., & Edmond, M. B. (2005). Lessons from severe acute respiratory syndrome (SARS): Implications for infection control. *Achieves of Medical Research 36*(6), 610-6.

World Health Organization (2006). *WHO Partnership—The Africa Health Infoway (AHI).* Retrieved June 7, 2007 from http://www.research-4development.info/projectsAndProgrammes.asp?ProjectID=60416

World Health Organization. (2007). Epidemic and pandemic alert and response (EPR). Retrieved June 7, 2007 from http://www.who.int/csr/en/

ADDITIONAL READING

Booz, Allen, Hamilton (2005). Pan-Canadian electronic Health record: Quantitative and qualitative benefits. Canada Health Infoway's 10-year investment strategy costing. *March 2005 Report.* Retrieved June 7, 2007 from http://www.infoway-inforoute.ca/Admin/Upload/Dev/Document/VOL1_CHI%20Quantitative%20&%20Qualitative%20Benefits.pdf

Bower, A. G. (2005). The diffusion and value of healthcare information technology. A RAND Report. Accessible at http://www.rand.org/pubs/monographs/MG272-1/

Canadian Institutes of Health Research. (2007). Knowledge Translation Strategy 2004-2009: Innovation in Action. Retrieved June 9, 2007, from http://www.cihr-irsc.gc.ca/e/26574.html#defining

eHealth ERA Report. (2007). eHealth priorities and strategies in European countries. European Commission Information Society and Media. Retrieved June 9, 2007, from http://ec.europa.eu/information_society/activities/health/docs/policy/ehealth-era-full-report.pdf

Fonkych, K., & Taylor, R. (2005). The state and pattern of health information technology adoption. A RAND report. Accessible at http://www.rand.org/pubs/monographs/MG409/

Institute for Healthcare Improvement. (2007). How to improve: Improvement methods. Cambridge, MA. Retrieved on June 7, 2007, from http://www.ihi.org/IHI/Topics/Improvement/ImprovementMethods/HowToImprove/

Ho, K., Chockalingam, A., Best, A., & Walsh, G. (2003). Technology-enabled knowledge translation: Building a framework for collaboration. *Canadian Medical Association Journal, 168*(6), 710-711.

Ho, K., Bloch, R., Gondocz, T., Laprise, R., Perrier, L., Ryan, D. et al. (2004). Technology-enabled knowledge translation: Frameworks to promote research and practice. *Journal of Continuing Education of the Health Professions, 24*(2), 90-99.

Schoen, C., Osborn R, Huynh, P. T., Doty, M., Peugh, J., & Zapert, K. (2006). On the front line of care: primary care doctors' office systems, experiences, and views in seven countries. *Health Affairs 25*(6), w555-w571. Retrieved June 9, 2007, from http://content.healthaffairs.org/cgi/content/abstract/hlthaff.25.w555?ijkey=3YyH7yDwrJSoc&keytype=ref&siteid=healthaff

Stroetmann, K. A., Jones T., Dobrev, A., & Stroetmann, V. N. (2006). eHealth is worth it: The economic benefits of implemented eHealth solutions at ten European sites. *A www.ehealth-impact.org report.* Retrieved June 7, 2007 from http://ec.europa.eu/information_society/activities/health/docs/publications/ehealthimpact-sept2006.pdf

Sussman, S., Valente, T. W., Rohrbach, L. A., Skara, S., & Pentz, M. A. (2006). Translation in the health professions: Converting science into action. *Evaluation and the Health Professions, 29*(1), 7-32.

Chapter XIX
Knowledge Translation in Nursing Through Decision Support at the Point of Care

Diane Doran
University of Toronto, Canada

Tammie Di Pietro
University of Toronto, Canada

ABSTRACT

With advances in electronic health record systems and mobile computing technologies it is possible to re-conceptualize how health professionals access information and design appropriate decision-support systems to support quality patient care. This chapter uses the context of nursing-sensitive patient outcomes data collection to explore how technology can be used to increase nurses' and other health professionals' access to patient outcomes information in real time to continually improve patient care. The chapter draws upon literature related to: (1) case-based reasoning, (2) feedback, (3) and evidence-based nursing practice to provide the theoretical foundation for an electronic knowledge translation intervention that was developed and tested for usability. Directions for future research include the need to understand how nurses experience uncertainty in their practice, how this influences information seeking behavior, and how information resources can be designed to support real-time clinical decision making.

INTRODUCTION

With the current explosion of accessible information and the continuing expansion of professional knowledge it is a challenge for nurses to regularly access information that is current and reliable. For example, being task-driven and coping with heavy workloads limits nurses' attention to and recognition of potential information needs and knowledge gaps (MacIntosh-Murray & Choo, 2005). McK-

Copyright © 2008, IGI Global, distributing in print or electronic forms without written permission of IGI Global is prohibited.

night observed critical care nurses' information seeking was limited to obtaining patient-specific information from patients and families, the chart, and other existing clinical information systems (McKnight, 2006). She also reported nurses' feelings that seeking and analyzing information from the Internet or other traditional information resources could be ethically wrong—taking time and focus away from patient care. Re-conceptualizing how nurses' access information and designing appropriate **decision-support systems** to facilitate timely access to information could be important to increase **research utilization** in such demanding work environments. For instance, Estabrooks and colleagues suggest that Internet use by nurses could be increased if the information available on the Internet was more dynamic and more contextually relevant, and if computer access was more conveniently available to them (Estabrooks, O'Leary, Ricker, & Humphrey, 2003). A clinical decision-support system that provides nurses (or other clinicians) with practice information automatically in response to patient-specific assessment information is suggested as a solution for increasing the utilization of research evidence in practice.

In this chapter, we review point-of-care clinical decision-support systems in nursing. We describe the development of a computerized handheld 'information gathering and dissemination system' (e-Volution in Outcomes-Focused Knowledge Translation™) that enables nurses to simultaneously: assess and record patient outcomes information through a wireless network using **personal digital assistants** (PDAs) and present information in summary format for case-based reasoning; experience real-time feedback of patient outcomes information; and reference practice information at the point of care, such as best-practice guidelines. We discuss its use in the Canadian context. We provide the theoretical background to this decision support system, specifically focusing on literature related to: (1) case-based reasoning, (2) feedback, (3) and **evidence-based nursing**.

We conclude the chapter with a presentation of the findings from our own program of research focusing on a usability evaluation of the decision-support system we have developed. General directions for further development of point-of-care decision support systems using **information technology** are discussed.

CLINICAL DECISION SUPPORT

Every activity involves **decision-making**. In medical science, physicians make decisions about the patient's clinical diagnosis and treatment. The typical methodological approach to obtain a diagnostic decision is the comparison of the patient's presenting signs and symptoms, 'data set,' with a similar 'reference' set of data, which represents the 'normal' condition. In nursing science, nurses seek to answer questions about the patient's current health status, how this health status is likely to change in the future, and what interventions will be appropriate to promote recovery, maintain health, or control symptoms.

Where nursing practice has been examined, wide variation in the care delivered has been observed (Cullum & Sheldon, 1996). Cullum and Sheldon noted variation in the nursing management of people with leg ulcers, infection control practices in high-risk areas, and the management of fever in children. Doran et al. found significant variation in the documentation of specific types of nursing interventions for the management of functional status, pain, nausea, dyspnea, fatigue, and pressure ulcers in acute hospitalized patients and long-term care residents (Doran, Harrison, Laschinger et al., 2006). Evidence-based nursing resources could address this kind of variation in nursing practice by providing nurses with reliable information about which nursing interventions are effective for particular patient concerns. There is good evidence to suggest that timely access to research evidence, especially if imbedded into the clinical processes of care, minimizes variation in clinical practice. For instance, a systematic review of clinical decision-support interventions found that computerized systems were significantly more effective than manual systems at improving practice (Kawamoto, Houlihan, Balas, & Lobach, 2005).

Computerized Clinical Decision Support

Computerized clinical decision-support systems (CDSS) are information systems designed to improve clinical decision-making. Finlay (1994) and others define a **decision-support** system as "a computer-based system that aids the process of decision-making" (Finlay, 1994). Turban (1995) defines it as "an interactive, flexible, and adaptable computer-based information system, especially developed for supporting the solution of a non-structured management problem for improved decision-making" (Turban, 1995). The goal of computer-aided therapy planning is to suggest suitable treatment strategies for a given patient (Macura & Macura, 1997). CDSSs provide several modes of decision-support, including alerts of critical values, reminders of overdue preventive health tasks, advice for drug prescribing, critiques of existing healthcare orders, and suggestions for various active care issues (Garg et al., 2005). In their systematic review of CDSSs, Garg et al. concluded that clinical **decision-support systems** that (a) provide decision-support automatically as part of clinical workflow, (b) deliver decision support at the time and location of decision making, (c) provide actionable recommendations, and (d) use a computer to generate the decision support are effective for improving clinical practice.

Computer decision-support systems (CDSS) are not new to nursing practice with one of the first systems, Creighton Online Multiple Modular Expert System (COMMES), introduced in the 1970s to assist nurses in patient care planning (Stagger, Thompson, & Snyder-Halpern, 2001). However, how systems are utilized in nursing practice over the years have changed from a focus

on tools that evaluate clinical decisions to tools that aid in the clinical decision process (Im & Chee, 2006). Unfortunately, a gap in full implementation and acceptance of CDSSs into clinical practice remains an issue. With technological advancements, new initiatives aimed at improving decision-support system use in clinical practice, including the use of point of care technology, has the potential to improve acceptance of CDSSs into clinical practice.

CDSSs support the clinical **decision-making** process of nurses by integrating real-time, clinical data with evidence-based clinical knowledge at the point-of-care (Snyder-Halpern, 1999). Based upon computer algorithms in statistical or clinical decision rules, the nursing decision process is mimicked (Finkelstein, Scudiero, Lindgren et al., 2005). Alerts, reminders, and intervention suggestions from evidence-based knowledge sources, such as practice guidelines, can be generated based upon individualized patient data entered into the system (Morris, 2002). Improvements to the quality of care delivered and a standardization of the clinical decision-making process ensues. By standardizing nurses' **decision-making** and utilizing patient data driven protocols, variations in clinicians' treatment and diagnoses choices are decreased, while preserving the individualized patient treatment plan (Clarke et al., 2005).

Currently, a small number of CDSSs have been developed for various clinical settings including: critical care (Apache Critical Care Series), home monitoring of pulmonary function for lung transplant recipients, oncology, wound care (The Wound and Skin Intelligence System (WSIS)), a Web-based intelligent oncological nurse advisor (PaSent), medication administration (Health Evaluation through Logical Processing (HELP)) and novice nursing (Novice Computer Decision Support (N Codes)) (Clarke et al., 2005; Finkelstein, Scudiero, Lindgren et al., 2005; Frize & Walker, 2000; Gustav Bellika & Hartvigsen, 2005; Im & Chee, 2006; Nelson, Evans, Samore, & Gardner, 2005; O'Neill, Dluhy, & Chin, 2005; Sakallaris, Jastremski, & Von Rueden, 2000).

The Apache system allows ICU nurses to collect and document chronic health and physiological items on a daily basis, trend the data and print a computerized daily report of individual patient deterioration or improvements. Apache identifies the impact of clinical decisions on length of stay, interventions and mortality that can be utilized by the multidisciplinary team at daily rounds (Sakallaris et al., 2000). Im and Chee (2000) developed a CDSS to aid in providing suggestions for nurses when assessing the effectiveness of cancer pain management based on sex and ethnicity. The WSIS, subsequently renamed "Solutions for Outcomes" assesses patient risks for pressure ulcers based on guidelines from the Agency for Healthcare Research and Quality and provides evidence-based prevention and treatment options for care planning. The system also provides audit and feedback information; resulting in improvements to nursing clinical practice (Clarke et al., 2005). The HELP system was designed to prevent medication administration errors by providing nurses with alerts, reminders and feedback information at the point-of-care (Nelson et al., 2005). O'Neill et al. (2005) identified novice nurses lack of clinical decision-making experience and in response developed N Codes to provide pertinent, reliable, clinical information to manage risk and support novice nurses in the decision-making process.

Though each of these CDSSs have a specialized clinical focus, the overall purpose of CDSS remains: to increase **research utilization** and facilitate the best available practice information in a timely fashion, at the **point-of-care**, such that the measurement and evaluation of patient outcomes data is obtained to improve patient outcomes, the quality of nursing care delivered and decrease the number of errors conducted in practice.

Case Based Reasoning

CDSSs also have the capacity to integrate other outcomes based decision-support tools, such as case-based reasoning (CBR), thereby further in-creasing **research utilization**, improving patient outcomes and the quality of nursing care provided. **Case-based reasoning** or "artificial intelligence" systems utilize past problems or patient cases stored in a database to solve or explain current patient problems (Bichindaritz & Marling, 2006; Frize & Walker, 2000). A case-based reasoning system (i.e., case-based reasoner) works by matching new problems to "cases" from an historical database. Successful solutions from past cases are then adapted to current problems (Watson, 1997). As human problem solving is based upon past learning experiences and the human mind is limited in its memory capabilities, the CBR is a beneficial tool in that it allows many more cases to be instantly retrieved from the memory base (depending on the size of the database); resulting in an increase ability of finding exclusive, similar cases (Frize & Walker, 2000).

The FLORENCE system (Bradburn, Zeleznikow, & Adams, 1993) is a case-based reasoning system for nursing. It is designed to model the reasoning processes of the expert nurse in the identification of nursing problems. Features (e.g., signs and symptoms) exhibited by a new client are compared to those of expected features in standard cases. The main purpose of FlORENCE is to advise in the identification of nursing diagnoses in a new client. It is built on a case-based reasoning paradigm. For instance, FLORENCE, learns by keeping records of salient features of new cases and using them to modify its case library. It classifies a new client as a standard case, or as an exception to a standard case, or as an unclassifiable unique case. A standard case is a collection of expected nursing diagnoses related to a medical condition (Bardburn, Zeleznikow, & Adams, 1993). In their description of the system, Bradburn et al. and Adams note that at the present the system does not provide guidance as to the selection of nursing actions, although this is a function that could be developed.

Bates et al contend that decision support tools must provide speedy application in real time, integrate easily into nurses current workflow with little, if any disturbance and suggest simple interventions (Bates et al., 2003). CBR systems that: (1) identify a current patient problem; (2) find and retrieve the closest past cases and rank them in order of similarity; (3) utilize cases retrieved to propose a solution to the current problem; (4) evaluate the current, proposed solution; and (5) update the CBR system by learning from this experience, meets all these criteria (Aamodt & Plaza, 1994). Though the benefits of CBR are realized, including the ability to propose a solution quickly and the avoidance of similar/previous errors, the actual implementation to clinical nursing practice is limited (Eshach & Bitterman, 2003). Currently, implementation of CBR systems have been initiated in the adult and neonatal ICUs through use of the Ideas for ICU and the Ideas for NICU in which current adult and neonate patient problems can be solved by reviewing 10 of the most similar matching, past cases and interventions instigated to improve length of stay, management strategies and mortality (Frize & Walker, 2000).

There are two groups of major difficulties in the application of case-based reasoning systems in complex medical situations. The first set concerns the difficulties in providing functions and values, because the input data must be available in a standardized form, something which is not always possible (Spyropoulos & Papagiunos, 1995). A recent initiative by the Ministry of Health and Long-Term Care of Ontario (MOHLTC) addresses this need through their Health Outcomes for Better Information and Care (HOBIC) policy initiative. HOBIC is part of the Ontario government's Information Management Strategy, which aims to produce better data, support accountability and quality improvement through performance measurement, and support evidence-based decision-making. Commencing April 2007, registered nurses (RN) and registered practical nurses (RPN) in acute, community, and long-term care healthcare facilities will begin to assess patients, clients and residents according to a pre-determined set of evidence-based outcome measures. The information will be useful to nurses in identifying patient/client/resident severity and needs when selecting nursing interventions, and in evaluating the effectiveness of care. Staff nurses will be trained to collect the outcomes using standardized tools and record their assessments as part of routine documentation. This Ontario initiative will highlight the importance of patient outcomes data and make it much more accessible to front-line providers of care in a standardized format to support clinical decision-making.

The second source of uncertainty, is the required evaluative calculus, in order to assign a relative importance to the items of information included in the knowledge base, since all the data concerning a case do not have equal weight in the diagnostic and treatment process (Spyropoulos & Papagiunos, 1995). Our research, is attempting to address this through the input of clinical experts.

To increase nurses' access to and use of research evidence for clinical decision-making, Doran and colleagues conducted a program of research, "Outcomes in the Palm of Your Hand," with the goal of developing an information gathering and dissemination prototype software system that would support **nursing-sensitive outcomes** data collection and evidence-based clinical decision-making at the point of patient care (Doran et al., 2007). Doran et al. contend that evidence-based information uptake in the form of CDSSs and **best practice guidelines** (BPGs) must be an integral component of the nursing process and available at the point-of-care to have any real impact on clinical practice. With this in mind, they built upon components of the promoting action on research implementation in health services model (PARIHS) (Kitson, 2002) and a redesigned version by Roycroft-Malone et al. (Rycroft-Malone et al., 2002) to develop the outcomes-focused knowledge translation framework (Doran & Sidani, 2007). In order to further refine this framework and evaluate its application in practice, a study was conducted with hospital and home-care based nurses. The study utilized focus groups and work sampling to identify information resources required by nurses for **point-of-care** decision-making (Doran et al.), and field testing to evaluate its usability in practice; resulting in the development of a prototype software for use with **personal digital assistants** (PDAs) titled "e-Volution in Outcomes Focused Knowledge Translation™."

E-VOLUTION IN OUTCOMES FOCUSED KNOWLEDGE TRANSLATION™

E-Volution in Outcomes-Focused Knowledge Translation™ is an electronic decision- support tool designed to increase nurses' use of evidence for clinical decision making (Doran & Sidani, 2007). It consists of four components: (1) patient outcomes measurement; (2) real-time feedback about these patient outcomes; (3) case-based reasoning, which involves benchmarking patient outcome achievement relative to similar patients; and (4) best-practice guidelines, imbedded in decision-support tools that deliver key messages in response to patient assessment data.

Outcomes Measurement

Outcomes, in a healthcare context, refer to patient responses to treatment. The Ministry of Health and Long-Term Care (MOHLTC) of Ontario and its expert panel on nursing health outcomes recommended the inclusion of the following **nursing-sensitive outcomes** in Ontario administrative databases: functional status, symptom control, therapeutic self-care, pressure ulcers, and falls (Pringle & White, 2002). In e-Volution in Outcomes-Focused Knowledge Translation™ we have incorporated the tools recommended by the MOHLTC Expert Panel for assessing patients' functional., symptom, self-care, pressure ulcer, and fall outcomes. Their psychometric proper-

ties were previously reported (Doran, Harrison, Spence-Laschinger et al., 2006). Nurses complete their patient outcomes assessments electronically, using hand-held computers PDAs, and the assessment data are transmitted through a secure wireless network.

Real-Time Feedback

Changing health professionals' practice usually involves feedback of performance data. **Feedback** is defined as the return of information about a product or service to its source. Feedback can be presented at the individual practitioner level, as aggregate data around groups of patients, as information on a single patient, or as aggregate data for groups of patients unified around a specific diagnosis or area of practice (Heffner, 2001). Content of feedback includes information about procedures, such as diagnostic tests, cognition, decisions, or outcomes. We have focused on outcomes feedback in our research.

As noted by Doran and Sidani (2007), outcomes feedback provides health professionals with knowledge of the results of their work; information that is essential for improving performance. Care that is provided in the absence of knowledge of its impact, even if based on the best available evidence, can be misdirected. For instance, practice guidelines based on the highest levels of evidence need to be evaluated for the specific patient population for whom the guidelines are used (DiCenso, 1999). Furthermore, practice guidelines established for specific diagnostic groups still need to be tailored to the needs of the individual patient and adapted based on the patient's response to treatment. Without appropriate outcomes feedback, clinicians are not able to make such modifications to their care.

When nurses complete their patient outcome assessments, using e-Volution in Outcomes-Focused Knowledge Translation™, they have the opportunity to view trends in the patient's outcome progress, thereby receiving **real-time** feedback about their patient's outcomes. This **feedback** serves as a decision aid, prompting the nurse to re-evaluate the plan of care if the patient's outcomes are not improving or changing at either the expected rate or in the expected direction.

Case-Based Reasoning

Cased-based reasoning means to use previous experience in the form of cases to understand and solve new problems. **Case-based reasoning** has been used to create numerous applications in a wide range of domains:

- **Diagnosis:** Case-based diagnosis systems try to retrieve past cases whose symptom lists are similar in nature to that of the new case and suggest diagnoses based on the best matching retrieved cases (Papagiunos & Spyropoulos, 1999). Diagnosis support systems are intended to integrate patient signs and symptoms, results from the laboratory tests and diagnostic procedures with the clinical context, to aid formulation of a diagnosis (Macura & Macura, 1997).
- **Outcome evaluation:** Previous cases are used to determine an achievable target for benchmarking (Doran, Mylopoulos, Kushniruk, et al., 2007).
- **Decision-support:** Interactive computer-based systems have been developed that help clinical decision-makers to utilize data from past cases to solve unstructured problems (Sprage & Carlson, 1982).
- **Medical education:** Computerized case-based teaching has been developed to provide students with access to the experience that is stored in a significant number of solved case problems (Macura & Macura, 1997).

Case-based reasoning is used when there is not high quality evidence to guide clinical decision-making. As such, it can be used to compliment **evidence-based resources** for clinical decision-making.

In case-based reasoning (CBR) systems expertise is embodied in a library of past cases. Each case typically contains a description of the problem (i.e., focus patient need), plus a solution and/or the outcome. To solve the current problem, the problem (i.e., focus patient) is matched against the cases in the case base, and similar cases are retrieved. The retrieved cases are used to suggest a solution which is reused and tested for success. CBR is liked by many people because they feel more comfortable with examples of similar cases rather than conclusions separated from their context.

In e-Volution in Outcomes Focused Knowledge Translation™ nurses are provided with the ability to **benchmark** their patient's outcome progress relative to similar patients. The system applies case-based reasoning to dynamically provide benchmarks for nursing-sensitive outcomes. The prototype system retrieves outcomes data for patients who are similar to the current patient and creates benchmarks from this data.

There are a variety of methods for organizing, retrieving, utilizing and indexing the knowledge retained in past cases. Retrieving cases starts with a problem description and ends when a best matching case has been found. The subtasks involve: identifying a set of relevant problem descriptors (in this example, patient status on functional, symptom, or therapeutic self-care outcomes); matching the case and returning a set of sufficiently similar cases. E-Volution in Outcomes Focused Knowledge Translation™ matches similar cases on the basis of age, gender, primary medical diagnosis, co-morbidities, and surgical procedure. The set of similar cases are selected based on a similarity threshold. In e-Volution in Outcomes-Focused Knowledge Translation™, we arbitrarily selected a similarity threshold of 50 percent match. Our research is seeking to validate both the criteria selected for identifying matching cases and the appropriate threshold. Specifically, we are interested in determining if a 50 percent similarity threshold is meaningful to nurses for clinical decision-making, or if a larger threshold (e.g., 80 percent) or if a less stringent threshold (e.g., 30 percent) is acceptable. The lower the similarity threshold the more efficient the system will be in identifying similar cases to guide clinical decision-making.

An overview of the CBR module is provided in Figure 1, and a sample screen shot in Figure 2.

Evidence-Based Practice/Best Practice Guidelines

Evidence-based medicine is "the conscientious, explicit, and judicious use of current, best evidence in making decisions about the care of individual patients" (Sackett, Richardson, Rosenberg, & Haynes, 1997, p.2). Resources to support evidence-based healthcare are rapidly evolving (Collins, Voth, DiCenso, & Guyatt, 2005). Those that are preprocessed resources could be the most practical source of current and

reliable information for front-line staff nurses. Preprocessed resources are literature that has been reviewed by someone and has been chosen based on methodological standards/criteria for inclusion (Collins, Voth, DiCenso, & Guyatt, 2005). "The sources are updated regularly—from months to a couple of years—with methodologically sound and clinically important studies" (Collins et al., p. 33). Collins and colleagues propose a hierarchy of preprocessed information and suggest information seekers should begin by looking at the highest-level resources available for the problem that prompted their search. At the top of the hierarchy, *systems* include practice guidelines, clinical pathways, or evidence-based textbook summaries. In our own work, we have focused on clinical practice guidelines. The Registered Nurses' Association of Ontario (RNAO) has developed best practice guidelines to direct clinical decision-making and intervention for a variety of patient conditions that nurses' encounter in their

Figure 1. Case-based reasoner model

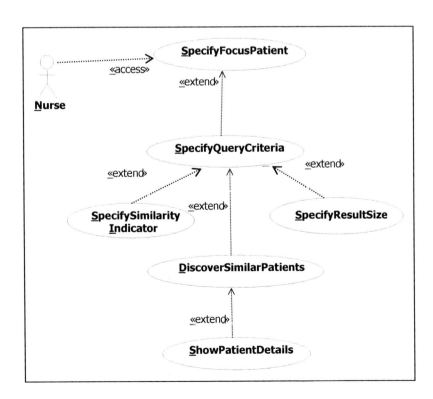

Figure 2. Compare functional status of patients

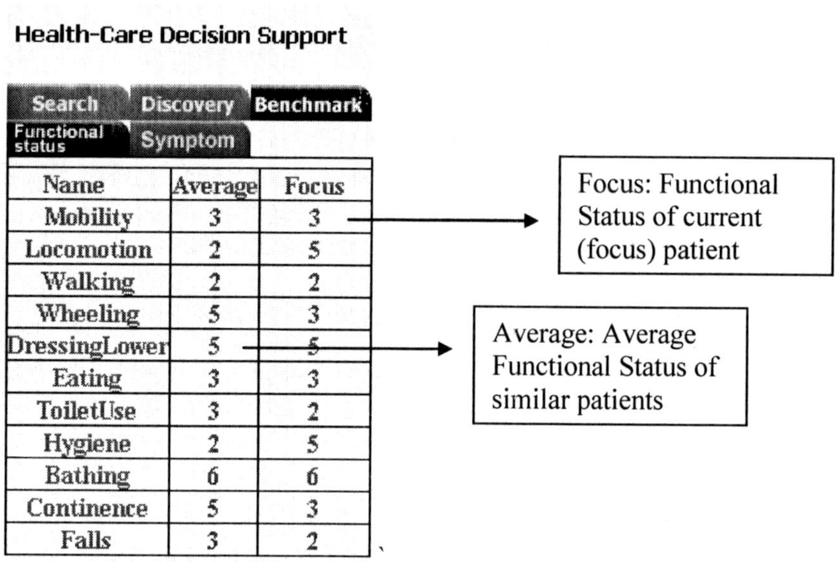

Health-Care Decision Support

Name	Average	Focus
Mobility	3	3
Locomotion	2	5
Walking	2	2
Wheeling	5	3
DressingLower	5	5
Eating	3	3
ToiletUse	3	2
Hygiene	2	5
Bathing	6	6
Continence	5	3
Falls	3	2

Focus: Functional Status of current (focus) patient

Average: Average Functional Status of similar patients

practice. The RNAO is the professional association representing nurses in Ontario. The RNAO cultivates knowledge-based nursing practice, quality of work life, and professional development. Some of the clinical guidelines that the RNAO has developed are directly relevant to the patient outcomes identified by the MOHLTC Expert Panel on Nursing Health Outcomes (Pringle & Doran, 2003) and incorporated into e-Volution in Outcomes-Focused Knowledge Translation™. **Best practice guidelines** (BPGs) have been developed by the RNAO for the assessment, prevention and treatment of pressure ulcers (RNAO Registered Nurses Association of Ontario, 2002), pain (RNAO Registered Nurses' Association of Ontario, 2005), dyspnea (Registered Nurses' Association of Ontario, 2005b), and falls (Registered Nurses' Association of Ontario, 2005a).

The e-Volution prototype system includes a guideline engine that determines when a recommendation is relevant to a given patient/client encounter by determining whether the patient outcomes data match the clinical scenario associated with the recommendation. The guideline engine is triggered when the nurse using the system completes an assessment. The guideline

engine presents brief summaries of relevant recommendations to the nurse who can chose to see the full details of the recommendation if they feel that it is valuable to do so. A sample of the user interface for the best practice guidelines component is shown in Figure 3.

USABILITY EVALUATION

The usability of the e-Volution in Outcomes-Focused Knowledge Translation™ prototype software was evaluated in a laboratory study, utilizing a randomized, cross-over design. Electronic resources and wireless data collection on PDAs was compared to data collection using laptop computers and clinical resources available in paper format

Nurses who consented to participate were randomly assigned to complete an outcomes assessment of a standardized patient (paid actor) and clinical decision-making task either first with the PDA prototype system with electronically-accessible resources, or a laptop computer and paper resources (i.e., drug compendium and RNAO best practice guideline paper tools). Nurse

322

Figure 3. Best practice guideline module

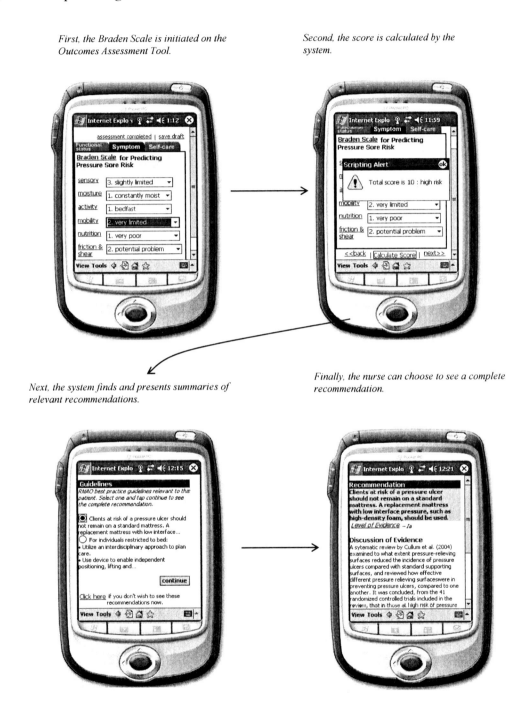

First, the Braden Scale is initiated on the Outcomes Assessment Tool.

Second, the score is calculated by the system.

Next, the system finds and presents summaries of relevant recommendations.

Finally, the nurse can choose to see a complete recommendation.

subjects were then crossed-over to complete the same assessment task with either the PDA or laptop, alternating the device used in the first assessment session. See Figure 4 for a diagram of the laboratory set-up.

Forty-two nurses participated in the laboratory study. It is noteworthy that nurses ranged in age from 26 to 72 years, with an average age of 44, and average of 16 years of nursing experience. The mean age of 44 is representative of the average age of Ontario nurses. There were 37 female (88 percent) and five male (12 percent) participants. Fifty-eight percent of the nurses worked in hospital settings and forty-two percent worked in a home care setting. Two participants had no past experience with a personal computer. Most participants had used e-mail (93 percent), searched the internet (93 percent), and had played computer games (62 percent).

Approach to Data Collection

Data collection involved video and audio recording of nurses as they entered patient assessment information and accessed best practice guidelines

and drug reference information using the PDA and the laptop. While the participants were using the PDA and the laptop computer for entering data, the screen of each device was audio and videotaped using the procedure published by Kushniruk (Kushniruk, Kaufman, & Patel, 1996; Kushniruk, Patel, & Cimino, 1997). In the majority of cases, the PDA was linked directly to a data projector, and the projected image on the wall was recorded. When this was not feasible, in approximately 25 percent of the cases, the video camera was placed on a tripod behind the participant and the screen of the device was videotaped directly. Immediately following each assessment session, nurses completed a usability questionnaire developed by Norman et al. at the University of Maryland (Norman, Slaughter, Schneidermn, & Harper, 1988). The time it took nurses to complete each assessment was recorded.

Data Analysis

Audio taping was transcribed and video taping was transferred to DVD recordings prior to data analysis and documented the nature and frequency

Figure 4. Usability lab setup

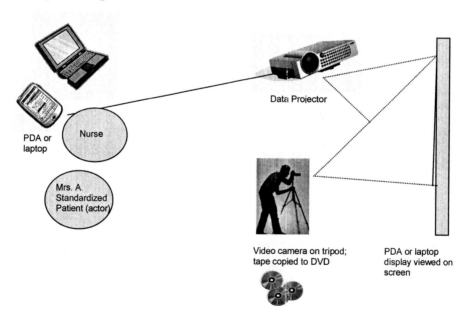

of data errors, time required to complete a task and usability. Descriptive statistics summarized participants' responses to the usability questionnaire. Paired t-tests were conducted to assess significant differences between participant's satisfaction with entering assessment information and accessing reference information using the PDA in comparison to the laptop. Independent t-tests were conducted to assess significant differences in participants' responses to usability questions depending on whether they completed the assessment task with the PDA or laptop first.

Results

Videotaping of the outcomes assessments by participants highlighted some usability issues using both the PDA and laptop. Visibility issues, such as failure to locate a button, were the same in both the laptop and PDA, as well as selecting a wrong answer and inadvertently skipping a question. The main usability differences between the PDA and laptop were noted in failures in clicking on a button, such as tapping errors; however this could be attributable to lack of expertise and comfort in using a stylus to tap or select answers. The usability questionnaires contained 44-question items and space for anecdotal comments. Differences between acute and home care nurses experiences and preferences in using a PDA and laptop were noted. Acute care nurses liked the ease of entering data and the sharpness of the PDA screen, but found the size of the screen and flexibility of entering data more difficult. Of the 44-question items, acute care nurses only rated two items higher on the laptop than the PDA; size and sequencing of the screen. Home care nurses rated five of the 44-question items higher on the laptop than on the PDA; size of characters, sharpness of image, screen size, power to enter patient information and system speed. Of note however, is the difference between network infrastructure for the home care arm of the study; as the PDA used a cellular network, while the laptop used a wired, broadband network. As cellular technology advances and continues to expand towards wireless, broadband cellular networks, improvements to the speed and power of the PDA will increase. Anecdotal comments indicated that participants found the PDA easier to use than the laptop. Participants also like the portability of the PDA and appreciated the ability to document while conducting an assessment, instead of having to rewrite in the chart. No differences were noted in response to usability questions related to the order of whether the PDA or laptop was used first. The time to complete clinical tasks using both the PDA and laptop were equivalent, but time to answer medication questions was greater when using the PDA than the laptop.

DISCUSSION

Data from the usability questionnaires indicated that participants were generally pleased with the PDA prototype system in comparison to the laptop. Videotaping data highlighted some usability issues. Though many nurses had used e-mail and the Internet previously, the majority of participants were novice PDA users, and PDA specific skills, such as how to appropriately use a stylus, "tap" the screen or move through data using a scroll bar, created additional teaching and learning needs. As the participants were representative of the general nursing population, it is anticipated that these teaching and learning skills will also need to be considered in the clinical setting so that nurses receive the technical and educational support necessary for a smooth transition in accessing evidence-based information in an electronic format. As a result of the usability evaluation, improvements in the application, particularly those related to ease of movement between questions and sections were made. As well, other items, such as radio buttons instead of drop down menus to reduce the number of taps required will be integrated at a future date. Though the time required to complete the medication task was greater in the PDA than the laptop, this may be under represented as participants had a drug dictionary readily available in the laboratory setting, and were also more familiar with researching a drug in the paper versus electronic format. This is, however, not the usual scenario in the clinical setting where clinical support resources, such as drug dictionary or best practice guidelines are kept in out of the way locations, separate from a patient's room.

CONCLUSION

e-Volution in Outcomes-Focused Knowledge Translation™ has the potential to improve nurses access to evidence-based information at the point of care. As participants represent the average nursing population, multiple teaching and support strategies will need to be implemented into the clinical setting to enhance the learning experiences of nurses using electronic devices, such as PDAs or laptops. Though the laboratory setting indicated potential benefits in the use of the PDA in clinical practice, further research using an acute care unit and home care setting is required to confirm the usability and feasibility of the device to improve nurses' ability to collect, utilize and communicate outcomes information and clinical decision-making skills.

Clinical decision-support tools, such as the example illustrated in this chapter, have three primary benefits. Firstly, they have the potential to impact the quality of care, as recommendations based on an individual patient's data can be delivered to the bedside in **real-time** for immediate action and any problems can be immediately identified and addressed. Secondly, by increasing the quality of care, they have the potential to improve patient outcomes and shorten patient stays, increasing patient turnover thereby reducing per patient costs. Thirdly, computer decision support systems and case-based reasoners

have the potential to increase nurses' **research utilization** in real time at the **point-of-care** and improve **clinical decision-making**. However, further research examining organizational and professional acceptance of the utilization of computer **decision-support systems** and case-based reasoning decision tools in clinical practice is warranted to identify potential barriers to adoption and strategies to improve this.

FUTURE RESEARCH DIRECTIONS

In order to expand on the research described in this chapter and to enhance future developments of decision-support systems for nurses, several directions for future research are suggested. First, there is a need to develop a deeper understanding of how nurses and other clinicians experience uncertainty in their practice and the influence this has on their information seeking behavior. Such knowledge will enable the design of information resources, such as case-based reasoners, that are suitable to nurses' information use and preferences. Second, there is a need to develop a better understanding of nurses' priorities for information resources at the point-of-care. Most of the previous work has not focused specifically on the use of information resources in real-time to facilitate clinical decision-making. With advancement of electronic healthcare record systems and mobile communication technologies, real-time use of electronic resources will become readily achievable. The research described in this chapter has taken a real-time approach to information use, however further research is needed to expand our understanding of how nurses use such information in **real-time** for patient care and what information resources are most important for real-time use. The decision- support application developed in this study supports the Ministry of Health and Long-Term Care Health Outcomes for Better Information and Care (HOBIC) initiative. The case-based reasoning application is designed to specifically address nurses' use of the HOBIC outcomes information at the point-of-care to inform clinical decision-making. The kind of use that was developed in this study is essential to meaningfully engage nurses in outcomes data collection. Future development needs to focus on expanded functionality, such as incorporating other outcome tools. In doing so, we need to work with nurses as the end-users to design case-based applications that support their work flow and clinical decision-making. The research described in this chapter involved a usability evaluation in a standardized laboratory setting. Information use could be very different in the context of a live healthcare environment where nurses and other clinicians face multiple competing demands on their time and on their cognitive load. Therefore, future research needs to evaluate the usability and effectiveness of a clinical decision-support system, such as the one describe in this chapter, within the context of a real practice setting. Only then will we build sound evidence on which to guide further developments of computerized clinical decision-support systems.

ACKNOWLEDGMENT

We gratefully acknowledge the Ministry of Health and Long-Term Care of Ontario, Ontario Centres of Excellence (OCE), Nortel, and Canadian Institutes of Health Research, for their funding of this research. The opinions, results and conclusions are those of the authors. No endorsement by the funding agencies/partners is intended or should be inferred.

REFERENCES

Aamodt, A., & Plaza, E. (1994). Case based reasoning: Foundational issues, methodological variations & system approaches. *AICom-Artificial Intelligence Communications, 7*(1), 39-59.

Bates, D. W., Kuperman, G. J., Wang, S., Gandhi, T., Kittler, A., Volk, L., et al. (2003). Ten commandments for effective clinical decision support: Making the practice of evidence-based medicine a reality. *Journal of the American Medical Informatics Association, 10*(6), 523-530.

Bichindaritz, I., & Marling, C. (2006). Case-based reasoning in the health and sciences: What's next? *Artificial Intelligence in Medicine, 36*(2), 127-135.

Bradburn, C., Zeleznikow, J., & Adams, A. (1993). FLORENCE: Synthesis of cased-based and model-based reasoning in nursing care planning system. *Computers in Nursing, 11*(1), 20-24.

Clarke, H. F., Bradley, C., Whytock, S., Handfield, S., van der Wal., R., & Gundry, S. (2005). Pressure ulcers: Implementation of evidence-based nursing practice. *Journal of Advanced Nursing, 49*(6), 578-590.

Collins, S., Voth, T., DiCenso, A., & Guyatt, G. (2005). Finding the evidence. In A. DiCenso, G. Guyatt & D. Ciliska (Eds.), *Evidence-based nursing: A guide to clinical practice* (pp. 20-43). St. Louis, MO: Elsevier Mosby.

Cullum, N., & Sheldon, T. (1996). Clinically challenged. *Nursing Management, 3*(4), 14-16.

DiCenso, A. (1999). Evidenced-based medicine, evidenced-based nursing. *Expert Nurse, 15*(12), 92-97.

Doran, D. M., Harrison, J. M., Spence-Laschinger, H., Hirdes, J., Rukhom, E., Sidani, S., et al. (2006). Nursing sensitive outcomes data collection in acute care and long-term care settings. *Nursing Research, 55*(2S), S75-S81.

Doran, D. M., Harrison, M. B., Laschinger, H. S., Hirdes, J. P., Rukholm, E., Sidani, S. et al. (2006). Nursing sensitive outcomes data collection in acute care and long-term care. *Nursing Research, 55*, S750S781.

Doran, D. M., Mylopoulos, J., Kushniruk, A., Nagle, L., Sidani, S., Laurie-Shaw, B. et al. (2007). Evidence in the palm of your hand: Development of an outcome-focused knowlede translation intervention. *Worldviews on Evidence-Based Nursing, 4*(2), 69-77.

Doran, D. M., & Sidani, S. (2007). Outcomes focused knowledge translation: A framework for knowledge translation and patient outcomes improvement. *Worldviews on Evidence-Based Nursing, 4*(1), 3-13.

Eshach, H., & Bitterman, H. (2003). From case-based reasoning to problem-based learning. *Academic Medicine, 78*(5), 491-496.

Estabrooks, C. A., O'Leary, K. A., Ricker, K. L., & Humphrey, C. K. (2003). The internet and access to evidence: how are nurses positioned. *Journal of Advanced Nursing, 42*(1), 73-81.

Finkelstein, S. M., Scudiero, A., Lindgren, B., Snyder, M., & Hertz, M. I. (2005). Decision support for the triage of lung transplant recipients on the basis of home monitoring spirometry and symptom reporting. *Heart & Lung, 34*(3), 201-208.

Finlay, P. N. (1994). *Introducing decision support systems.* Oxford, UK: Blackwell Publishers.

Frize, M., & Walker, R. (2000). Clinical decision support systems for intensive care units using case-based reasoning. *Medical Engineering & Physics, 22*(9), 671-677.

Garg, A. X., Adhikari, N. K. J., McDonald, H., Rosas-Arellano, M. P., Devereaux, P. J., Beyene, J., et al. (2005). Effects of computerized clinical decision support systems on practitioner performance and patient outcomes. *JAMA, 293*(10), 1223-1238.

Gustav Bellika, J., & Hartvigsen, G. (2005). The oncologocal nurse assistant: A web-based intelligent oncological nurse advisor. *Medical Informatics, 74*, 587-595.

Heffner, J. E. (2001). Altering physician behavior to improve clinical performance. *Topics in Health Information Management, 22*(2), 1-9.

Im, E. U., & Chee, W. (2006). Nurses' acceptance of the decision support computer program for cancer pain management. *Computers, Informatics, Nursing, 24*(2), 95-104.

Kawamoto, K., Houlihan, C. A., Balas, E. A., & Lobach, D. F. (2005). Improving clinical decision support systems: A systematic review of trials to identify features critical to success. *BMJ, 330*(7494), 765-792.

Kitson, A. (2002). Recognising relationships: Reflections on evidence-based practice. *Nursing Inquiry, 9*(3), 179-186.

Kushniruk, A. W., Kaufman, D. R., & Patel, Y. (1996). Assessment of a computerized patient record system: A cognitive approach to evaluating an emerging medical technology. *M. D. Computing, 13*(5), 406-415.

Kushniruk, A. W., Patel, V. L., & Cimino, J. J. (1997). *Usability testing in medical informatics: Cognitive approaches to evaluation of information systems and user interfaces.* Paper presented at the 1997 AMIA Annual Fall Symposium, Formerly SCAMC, Nashville, TN.

MacIntosh-Murray, A., & Choo, C. W. (2005). Informational behavior in the context of improving patient safety. *Journal of the American Society for Information Science and Technology, 56*(12), 1332-1345.

Macura, R. T., & Macura, K. (1997). Case-based reasoning: Opportunities and applications in healthcare. *Artificial Intelligence in Medicine, 9*, 1-4.

McKnight, M. (2006). The information seeking of on-duty critical care nurses: evidence from participant observation and in-context interviews. *J Med Libr Assoc, 94*(2), 145-151.

Morris, A. H. (2002). Decision support and safety of clinical environments. *Quality Safety Healthcare, 11,* 69-75.

Nelson, N. C., Evans, S., Samore, M. H., & Gardner, R. M. (2005). Detection and prevention of medication errors using real-time bed-side nurse charting. *Journal of the American Medical Informatics Association, 12,* 390-397.

Norman, K. L., Slaughter, L., Schneidermn, B., & Harper, B. (1988). *Questionnaire for user interface satisfaction (Version 7).* College Park, MD: Office of Technology Commercialization.

O'Neill, E. S., Dluhy, N. M., & Chin, E. (2005). Modeling novice clinical reasoning for a computerized decision support system. *Journal of Advanced Nursing, 49*(1), 68-77.

Papagiunos, G., & Spyropoulos, B. (1999). The multifarious function of medical records: Ethical issues. *Method Inform Med, 38,* 317-320.

Pringle, D., & Doran, D. M. (2003). Patient outcomes as an accountability. In D. M. Doran (Ed.), *Nursing-sensitive outcomes: State of the science* (pp. 1-25). Sudbury, MA: Jones and Bartlett.

Pringle, D. M., & White, P. (2002). Happenings. Nursing matters: The nursing and health outcomes project of the Ontario ministry of health and long-term care. *Canadian Journal of Nursing Research, 33,* 115-121.

Registered Nurses' Association of Ontario. (2005a). *Nursing care of dyspnea: The 6th vital sign in individuals with chronic obstructive lung disease (COPD).* Toronto, Canada: Registered Nurses' Association of Ontario.

Registered Nurses' Association of Ontario. (2005b). *Prevention of falls and fall injuries in the older adult (revised).* Toronto, Canada: Registered Nurses Association of Ontario.

RNAO Registered Nurses' Association of Ontario. (2005). *Nursing best practice guidelines shaping the future of nursing: Assessment and management of pain.* Toronto: Ontario.

RNAO Registered Nurses Association of Ontario. (2002). *Nursing Best Practice Guideline Shaping the future of nursing: Risk assessment & prevention of pressure ulcers.* Toronto, On: RNAO.

Rycroft-Malone, J., Kitson, A., Harvey, G., McCormack, B., Seers, K., Titchen, A., et al. (2002). Ingredients for change: Revisiting a conceptual framework. *Quality and Safety in Healthcare, 11*(2), 174-180.

Sackett, D. L., Richardson, W. S., Rosenberg, W. M., & Haynes, R. B. (1997). *Evidence-based medicine: How to practice teach EBM.* New York: Churchill Livingstone.

Sakallaris, B. R., Jastremski, C. A., & Von Rueden, K. T. (2000). Clinical decision support systems for outcome measurement and management. *AACN Advanced Critical Care, 11*(3), 351-362.

Snyder-Halpern, R. (1999). Assessing healthcare setting readiness for point of care computerized clinical decision support system innovations. *Outcomes Management for Nursing Practice, 3*(3), 118-127.

Spyropoulos, B., & Papagiunos, G. (1995). A theoretical approach to artifical intelligence systems in medicine. *Artifical intelligence in Medicine, 7,* 455-465.

Stagger, N., Thompson, C. B., & Snyder-Halpern, R. (2001). History and trends in clinical information systems in the United States. *Image: Journal of Nursing Scholarship, 33*(1), 75-81.

Turban, E. (1995). *Decision support and expert systems: Management support systems.* Englewood Cliffs, NJ. Prentice Hall.

ADDITIONAL READINGS

Abidi, S.S.R., & Manickam, S. (2002). Leveraging XML-based electronic medical records to extract experimental clinical knowledge: An automated approach to generate cases for medical case-based reasoning systems. *International Journal of Medical Informatics, 68,* 187-203.

Ammenwerth, E., Buchauer, A., Bludau, B., & Haux, R. (2000). Mobile information and communication tools in the hospital. *International Journal of Medical Informatics, 57,* 21-40.

Berge, M.S., & Thulin, L.B. (2006). The impact of computerized decision support systems on documentation skills. *Studies Health Technology & Informatics, 122,* 794.

Frize, M., Ennett, C.M., Stevenson, M., & Trigg, H.C.E. (2001). Clinical decision support systems for intensive care units: Using artificial neural networks. *Medical Engineering & Physics, 23,* 217-225.

Lyons, A., & Richardson, S. (2003). Clinical decision support in critical care nursing. *AACN Clinical Issues, 14*(3), 295-301.

Kushniruk, A. (2001). Analysis of complex decision-making processes in health care: Cognitive approaches to health informatics. *Journal of Biomedical Informatics, 34,* 365-376.

Kushniruk, A. (2002). Evaluation in the design of health information systems: Application of approaches emerging from usability engineering. *Computers in Biology and Medicine, 32,* 141-149.

Leckie, G.J., Pettigrew, K.E., & Sylvain, C. (1996). Modeling the information seeking of professionals: A general model derived from research on engineers, health care professionals, and lawyers. *The Library Quarterly, 66*(2), 161-193.

Montani, S., Bellazzi, R., Portinale, L., d'Annunzio, G., Fiocchi, S., & Stefanelli, M. (2000). Diabetic patients management exploiting case-based reasoning techniques. *Computer Methods and Programs in Biomedicine, 62,* 205-218.

Patel, V.L., Kaufman, D.R., Allen, V.G., Shortliffe, E.H., Cimino, J.J., & Greenes, R.A. (1999). Toward a framework for computer-mediated collaborative design in medical informatics. *Methods of Information Medicine, 38,* 158-76.

Rossille, D., Laurent, J.F., & Burgun, A. (2005). Modelling a decision-support system for oncology using rule-based and case-based reasoning methodologies. *International Journal of Medical Informatics, 74,* 299-306.

Schmidt, R., Montani, S., Bellazzi, R., Portinale, L., & Gierl, L. (2001). Case-based reasoning for medical knowledge-based systems. *International Journal of Medical Informatics, 64,* 355-367.

Chapter XX
Improving Internet–Based Health Knowledge Through Attention to Literacy

Jose F. Arocha
University of Waterloo, Canada

Laurie Hoffman-Goetz
University of Waterloo, Canada

ABSTRACT

This chapter presents a discussion and findings of health literacy and its relevance to health informatics. We argue that the Internet represents an increasingly important vehicle for knowledge translation to consumers of health information. However, much of the Internet-based information available to consumers is difficult to understand by those who need it the most. A critical factor to improve the comprehensibility, and therefore the quality, of health information is literacy. We summarize studies of various aspects of health literacy, such as readability and comprehensibility of risk information. We also point out ways in which the study of health literacy, including prose and numeric literacy, should inform researchers, health practitioners, and Web designers of specific ways in which consumer health information can be improved.

INTRODUCTION

The Internet has been increasingly replacing other mass media as the major source of health information for patients and the general public. The extensive malleability of information technology makes it an ideal vehicle for knowledge translation, dissemination, and exchange. However, part of the success or failure to develop knowledge translation strategies that are effective rests on creating understandable messages that serve as cues to action. Moreover, effective use of health

Copyright © 2008, IGI Global, distributing in print or electronic forms without written permission of IGI Global is prohibited.

information requires somewhat sophisticated cognitive skills, such as being able to search and find the necessary information, solving comprehension impasses, and discerning between reliable and unreliable health sources.

Health literacy, the "degree to which individuals have the capacity to obtain, process, and understand basic health information and services needed to make appropriate health decisions" (Ratzan & Parker, 2000), is a critical component in delivering and accessing health information effectively. Most published studies on health literacy have been concerned with issues of developing and testing assessment and readability instruments as well as with investigating factors associated with low literacy, such as aging and socio-economic factors, whereas some important aspects of health literacy, such as the ability to comprehend and to use numerical health information is much less understood.

Although there has been a great deal of research on various aspects of health literacy (and literacy in relation to health), its relationship to new emerging information technologies, such as the Internet, is just beginning to be explored (McCray, 2005). There are many research issues relevant to health literacy and information technologies that need to be examined in order to develop a systematic framework to evaluate associations between literacy and information technology utilization.

In this chapter, we present a discussion and empirical results from studies regarding the relevance of health literacy to knowledge translation strategies through the Internet. We first review the definition and characterization of knowledge translation and health literacy, including prose, and numeric literacy. We consider some of the major definitions of health literacy and its components, showing the concept's relevance to the design of health information systems. We then continue with representative empirical studies, which were designed to characterize the relation between readability assessment and comprehension of

health information on the World Wide Web, and to assess health numeracy skills of older adults when interpreting health information on cancer. We discuss the critical importance of literacy for the deployment of effective knowledge translation strategies in the context of information technologies. Finally, the last section is focused on health literacy as it relates to knowledge translation through health information technologies.

WHAT IS KNOWLEDGE TRANSLATION?

The concept of "knowledge translation" has gained popularity among health researchers as a way to promote the understanding and use of scientific evidence about health and disease to practitioners and consumers alike (Bowen & Martens, 2005; Choi, 2005; Davis, 2005; Davis et al., 2003; Pablos-Mendez, Chunharas, Lansang et al., 2005). Focusing on healthcare providers, the concept of knowledge translation has been defined by the Canadian Institutes of Health Research as "the effective and timely incorporation of evidence-based information into the practices of health professionals in such a way as to effect optimal healthcare outcomes and maximize the potential of the health system" (Canadian Institutes of Health Research). Similarly, attempts have been made to extend knowledge translation strategies to include the general public and community participation, incorporating people's cultural backgrounds and societal values (Bowen & Martens, 2005; McShane, Smylie, Hastings, & Martin, 2006; Saini & Rowling, 1997).

For practitioners, forms of knowledge translation involve the summarization and simplification of medical evidence in accessible and understandable formats (Choi, 2005). This may include critical appraisals of the medical literature, such as those presented in the American College of Physicians' ACP Journal Club, or timely systematic reviews of the research literature (Tugwell,

Robinson, Grimshaw, & Santesso, 2006), such as those generated by the Cochrane collaboration (Grimshaw, Santesso, Cumpston et al., 2006).

For consumers, knowledge translation involves the delivery of well-established and unambiguous scientific health knowledge, such that people can understand and make effective use of this information in their healthcare decisions. Improving health decisions with scientifically-supported health knowledge is done by disseminating patient and consumer-centered information through pamphlets, newsletters, patient guidelines, CD ROMS, and increasingly, the Internet.

With the growing acceptance of patient-provider shared decision making in healthcare, consumers are playing a more active role in influencing and managing their own healthcare needs and arriving at their own health decisions. Consumers' involvement in health decision making necessitates that patients and lay people be better informed about the health topics that matter to them. At the same time, more effective decisions by patients and lay people are more likely to occur if healthcare providers are able to communicate clear and easily understood health information (Safeer & Keenan, 2005).

A key component of knowledge translation consists of using the literacy levels of consumers of health information as a way to improve readability and comprehensibility of health information. Although health education is a fundamental approach for achieving better comprehension for all consumers (patients and providers alike), the readability of health messages needs to be stressed.

UNDERSTANDING HEALTH LITERACY

Health literacy has been defined in various ways. For instance, in their "Healthy People 2010" report, the U.S. Department of Health and Human Services defines the term as "the capacity to obtain, interpret and understand basic health information and services and the competence to use such information and services to enhance health" (U.S. Department of Health and Human Services, 2000). Similarly, the American Medical Association identifies health literacy as "a constellation of skills, including the ability to perform basic reading and numerical tasks required to function in the healthcare environment" (Ad Hoc Committee on Health Literacy for the Council on Scientific Affairs, 1999). Finally, the World Health Organization defines it more generally as "cognitive and social skills which determine the motivation and ability of individuals to gain access to, understand, and use information in ways that promote and maintain good health" (WHO Division of Health Promotion Education and Communications Health Education and Health Promotion Unit, 1998). Nutbeam (2000) has expanded these definitions of health literacy to include three core aspects: (1) functional health literacy, (2) interactive health literacy and, (3) critical health literacy. These levels of health literacy reflect increasing degrees of autonomy and empowerment, both individual and community focused.

Regardless of which of these definitions best captures the construct of health literacy, following Walker and Avant's (2005) framework for theory development, Speros (2005) has identified five defining components of health literacy suggested by these definitions, which might shed some light on the range of skills and knowledge types involved in the literacy process: (1) reading skills, which encompasses the ability to recognize words, to identify major ideas in text, to use text context to understand new terms, etc.; (2) numeracy skills, which involves the ability to understand numbers and statistical figures, and to perform basic mathematical operations; (3) comprehension, which involves the ability to use prior knowledge and contextual cues to assist reading; (4) capacity for decision making, which involves the ability to weight evidence and data to choose the best health options; and (5) successful functioning in healthcare consumer roles, which involves the effective deployment of social skills.

At the individual level, lower capability in any of the literacy component skills often has direct effects on the use of health services (Pathak, Ketkar, & Majumdar, 1981), including poorer screening for potential diseases and failure to adhere to prescribed treatments. Lower levels of health literacy also can negatively influence people's interactions with healthcare professionals, which may also lead to negative health outcomes (Schillinger et al., 2002). People with low health literacy have a limited health vocabulary, read health information slowly, skip over words, and fail to understand the benefits of screening or timely treatment (Davis et al., 2001).

At the population level, low literacy affects health more indirectly through interaction with other determinants of health status, such as age, socio-cultural backgrounds, and income. Indeed, low literacy appears to be a better predictor of health status than education (Lindau et al., 2002; Manly et al., 1999), economic status (Moore, Castillo, Richardson, & Reid, 2003), or cultural background (Parker, Ratzan, & Lurie, 2003; Williams, Baker, Parker, & Nurss, 1998).

Empirical research on health literacy has typically involved the study of both information and cognitive components of literacy. Studies looking at the information aspects have focused mostly on the readability of health information and the literacy skills of lay people as they interpret basic health questions. A consistent finding in the literature has been the almost universal high reading grade levels required by most educational materials and other information outlets, such as pamphlets, and Web-based pages devoted to patients and lay people.

A number of instruments, designed to assess reading difficulty of written materials, have been developed. The majority of these instruments are built on the assumption that word length and the number of syllables per word are accurate indica-

tors of reading difficulty. The more widely used standard readability tests are the Flesch-Kincaid, the SMOG, the FRY, and the FOG index, although other measures exist (Singh, 2003).

A typical finding is that popular health literature is written at the senior high school or college levels, in either printed form (Coey, 1996; Cooley et al., 1995; D'Alessandro, Kingsley, & Johnson-West, 2001; Davis et al., 1994; Forbis & Aligne, 2002; Mohrmann et al., 2000; Wilson & Williams, 2003; Zion & Aiman, 1989), or on the Internet (Boulos, 2005; Estrada, Hryniewicz, Higgs et al., 2000; Jaffery & Becker, 2004; Kaphingst, Zanfini, & Emmons, 2006; Smart & Burling, 2001), when the actual reading level of the population is about grades 7 or 8 (Barr-Telford, Nault, & Pignal, J. 2005; Boulos, 2005).

Aside from the evaluation of the reading difficulty of written information, other research aspects include the assessment of reading abilities of patients and health consumers. This research typically makes use of one or more standard instruments developed for the assessment of lay people's literacy. Most of these assessment tools consist of a series of items designed to assess the ability to read and understand prose and numeric health information. The more widely used tests are the Test of Functional Health Literacy, or TOFHLA (Parker, Baker, Williams, & Nurss, 1995), developed for assessing reading comprehension and numeracy of adult populations; the rapid estimate of adult literacy in medicine (REALM) (Davis et al., 1991), a test aimed at the quick screening of patients with low reading skills and estimating their reading ability; and a short version of the TOFHLA, known as the S-TOFHLA (Baker, Williams, Parker et al., 1999), which was developed as a more practically applicable measure of functional health literacy than the full TOFHLA. In order to improve practicality, a recently developed standard test, the newest vital sign instrument (NVS), was validated (Weiss et al., 2005). This brief instrument consists of information presented on a nutrition label and assesses both prose and numeracy comprehension skills. For a more complete review of readability and text comprehension instruments, the reader is referred to Friedman and Hoffman-Goetz (2006).

As standard readability formulas correlate with reading difficulty, they are the most popular methods for assessing the difficulty of Web-based information. However, these formulas leave out aspects of text information, such as coherence, that also influence reading difficulty. Thus, other models of text difficulty have been developed that are based on non-surface aspects of text difficulty. One such measure involves the use of propositional density, which is the number of idea units contained in a text unit, such as a phrase or a sentence. This measure is based on the theory of discourse comprehension developed by Kintsch (1998). The method assumes that the cognitive unit underlying thinking is the proposition (defined as a triplet composed of concept-relation-concept), which is usually expressed as a phrase. The ratio of number of propositions to a discourse segment, such as a sentence, is used as the indicator of text difficulty: the higher the number of propositions per discourse unit, the higher the difficulty of the text.

HEALTH LITERACY AND THE READABILITY AND COMPREHENSIBILITY CANCER INFORMATION ON THE INTERNET

Canadians are increasingly relying on the Internet as a major source of health information and usage has risen dramatically in Canada for online health-related searches, involving close to 60 percent of all Internet users in the country in 2001 (Crowley, 2002). Similarly, in the United States an estimated 41 million American used the Internet as a source of health information in the early 2000s (Fogel, 2003). Moreover, among all users of the Internet, older adults, especially those between 55 and 64 years old, are the fastest-growing user group (Peterson & Fretz, 2003).

Among adults, health information is highly searched for, with cancer being one of the top three diseases for which people search the Internet (Fogel, 2003). Unfortunately, people often encounter difficulties with Web-based health and cancer information, including being able to access comprehensible cancer prevention resources. Part of the difficulty may be that cancer prevention information on the Web is often written at very difficult reading grade levels, regularly requiring college education to read and understand skillfully (Berland et al., 2001; Friedman, Hoffman-Goetz, & Arocha, 2004, 2006).

We conducted a series of studies to investigate the readability and comprehensibility representative breast cancer, colon cancer, and prostate cancer Web sites and to determine the relationship that exists between readability and comprehensibility of breast, colon, and prostate cancer information (Friedman, Hoffman-Goetz, & Arocha, 2004, 2006). Web sites on breast cancer, colon cancer, and prostate cancer were selected based on their rankings on selected Internet search engines, such as Google and Yahoo, where various keywords (e.g., "colon cancer," "breast cancer") were entered. After applying several inclusion and exclusion criteria, fifty-five informational cancer Web sites were chosen for analysis. To assess readability of the selected pages, information on the Web sites was then analyzed using standard readability formulas, SMOG (McLaughlin, 1969), Flesch Reading Ease (Flesch, 1948) and Flesch-Kincaid. With the assistance of the local public library, a convenience sample of healthy older adults was recruited through advertising on message boards, periodicals, Web sites, and invitations at community health fairs.

The participants in the study were first given a workshop on how to search the Internet for cancer information (Hoffman-Goetz, Friedman, & Celestine, 2006) followed by a face-to-face interview. During the interview, they were asked to read three cancer Web pages selected from six Web pages, two on breast cancer, two on prostate cancer, and two on colon cancer. The Web sites from which the six Web pages were chosen included the total number of top-ranking Web sites on each of the three cancer types. The Web pages were selected from the top 15 Web sites across all search engines. The selected pages for testing focused solely on cancer prevention information, such as screening practices, diet, exercise, healthy lifestyle behaviors. Comprehension of participants was assessed through a modified version of the TOFHLA (Parker, Baker, Williams, & Nurss, 1995), which involves the deletion of every 7th or 8th word from the texts, for which multiple-choice selections are provided. Finally, four to five recall questions about the cancer pages were asked during the interview to probe further into the participants' comprehension.

Consistent with studies assessing Internet readability in other areas of health (D'Alessandro, Kingsley, & Johnson-West, 2001; Kaphingst, Zanfini, & Emmons, 2006; Smart & Burling, 2001), Friedman et al. (2004; Friedman, Hoffman-Goetz, & Arocha, 2006) showed that over 60 percent of the Web pages investigated were written at grade 12 or 13 or higher levels, according to the Flesch-Kincaid and SMOG readability tools. Breast cancer Web pages were written at lower reading levels than prostate and colorectal cancer pages. There was an increase in difficulty across all cancer types from the first paragraph and the last paragraph of text. The authors suggested that increasing difficulty of text readability across paragraphs could lead to a higher likelihood of text abandonment.

Aside from investigating readability using standard instruments, propositional density as indicator of text difficulty was also evaluated (Ta-Min, Arocha, & Hoffman-Goetz, 2007). Examining high and low readability Web pages (as measured through the Flesch-Kincaid and SMOG tools), it was shown that for colon and breast cancer information, high readability Web pages included a higher proposition density than the low readability Web pages, but this pattern

did not hold for the prostate cancer Web pages. Interestingly, readability scores for the SMOG and the Flesch-Kincaid did not agree: one page showed a higher score for one measure and a lower for the other measure, which suggests that more than one readability test should be used when assessing text difficulty with standard measures.

In addition to examining text coherence and readability of cancer information, verbal protocols of 16 healthy older adults were generated from the interviews using non-prompted general questions and prompted follow-up questions (Ta-Min, Arocha, & Hoffman-Goetz, 2007). Analysis of the verbal protocols revealed large, but expected individual differences for the kinds of information recalled, the types of inferences made, and the coherence of the study participants' mental models. Variations in background and personal interests appeared to influence whether superordinate or subordinate propositions were recalled. Another finding regarding comprehensibility was that the participants had more difficulty reading colorectal cancer Web pages than breast and prostate cancer Web pages independently of the actual readability level the pages. This finding can be interpreted as showing that poorer comprehension of colorectal cancer information may reflect the lack of public discourse about colon cancer, as compared to breast and prostate cancers, which have stronger advocacy and educational support.

HEALTH NUMERACY AND CANCER RISK UNDERSTANDING

A study was conducted (Donelle, Arocha, & Hoffman-Goetz, 2007, in press) with a sample older adults to investigate the people's understanding of cancer risk information. In the interview, demographic information was collected from the participants, after which assessments were conducted of functional health literacy, using the S-TOFHLA (Baker et al., 1999) general context numeracy (Schwartz, Woloshin, Black,

& Welch, 1997), health context numeracy (Lipkus, Samsa, & Rimer, 2001), and math anxiety (Hopko, Mahadevan, Bare, & Hunt, 2003), and risk comprehension.

Two different Web-pages about colorectal cancer prevention information were selected from the Canadian Cancer Society (CCS) Web site and matched in terms of the cancer type, font size, and readability. Among other criteria (three-page maximum length, less than 12 grade readability level), the Web-pages included numerical references in number or text form. Furthermore, the pages were chosen so that the content of the information was judged as either likely common (general prevention information such as information about diet and exercise) or uncommon (containing information about genetics and colon cancer) to a general audience. Participants' understanding of risk was assessed through multiple-choice questions based on the Web pages read.

The results of the study showed that the study participants possessed 'adequate' prose literacy and high numeracy ability, as measured by the S-TOFHLA, somewhat moderate levels of health context numeracy, as measured by a three simple question task (Schwartz, Woloshin, Black, & Welch, 1997) and moderate levels of math anxiety, but poor general context numeracy skill. Furthermore, there was a statistically significant difference between comprehension scores of 'common' (Mean: 9.14 vs. 11) and 'uncommon' (Mean: 7.64 vs. 11) Web-based colorectal cancer information. Overall, it was shown that math anxiety, level of formal education, numeracy, and prose literacy skills accounted for approximately 60 percent of the variation in participant comprehension scores.

Health context numeracy skill was shown to be the best "predictor" of risk comprehension scores of both common and uncommon online colorectal cancer Web pages. However, basic numeracy ability, as assessed by the S-TOFHLA tool, was a good "predictor" of participants' scores on the comprehension of 'common' cancer Web information. General context numeracy served as a robust "predictor" of risk comprehension of the 'uncommon' information. It appears that the numeracy portion of the S-TOFHLA is best to assess the very basic numeracy skill of number identification (Donelle, Arocha, & Hoffman-Goetz, in press). As pointed out elsewhere (Donelle, Arocha, & Hoffman-Goetz, 2007, in press), prior knowledge of a topic and risk comprehension ability have been shown to be related (Beier & Ackerman, 2005). Therefore, it is to be expected that prose health literacy skill contributed only to comprehension of 'uncommon' colorectal cancer information.

DESIGN OF HEALTH INFORMATION ON THE INTERNET

In order to improve the quality of health information on the Internet as a vehicle for knowledge translation, it is necessary to understand the many issues surrounding the generation, dissemination, and utilization of information. Chief among the many factors affecting these processes are design and psychological aspects. We can distinguish between three components: the information per se (e.g., language choices, document formatting), the medium of communication (e.g., technological aspects), and the user characteristics (e.g., knowledge, cognitive strategies, motivation). These components form the basis of the communication process of healthcare. Communication involves the matching of intentions and meaning between provider and user. By selectively targeting different users of information, understanding, and decision making can be improved. Described in the following lines are some of the psychological factors that need to be taken into account in the design and implementation of effective communication; these psychological factors are categorized in terms of format, content, and user factors.

Format aspects comprise textual and structural factors that affect user perception of the information. Much work has been carried out on these factors including delineation of typographical features of text that can be changed to improve understanding. At least for written materials on the Internet factors such as type and the size of the typeface (e.g., size and design) can make a difference in users' understanding and compliance (Morrow, Leirer, Andrassy et al., 1998). Other format factors which are more characteristic of Internet-based information include the use of multiple forms to represent health information, such as graphical and interactive components. Unlike paper-based information, the multiple modalities supported by information technology provide greater flexibility to the designers for adapting and personalizing information to consumers. The Internet, as a multimedia-competent technology, affords the support of textual information with dynamic modalities of information that have the potential of improving users' comprehension and decision making (Bodemer, Ploetzner, Bruchmüller, & Häcker, 2005; Wright, 1999). Multiple representations enable people to learn new information from different perspectives and by using different strategies (Seufert, 2003). This multiple representation is especially important when health education is one of the main goals: multiple representations of the same information increases retention and understanding (Patel, Branch, & Arocha, 2002). One particularly difficult form of information to understand, even for highly educated lay people, is evidence-based health information, which is often presented in a probabilistic manner (Patel, Branch, & Arocha, 2002). The use of multiple representations of the same information through other means than text, such as diagrams, or dynamical computer simulations, has been shown to help in user understanding (Ainsworth, 1999).

The concept of multiple representations is also important for designing information for different groups of users, so that the specific information format serves to support "natural" understanding. For instance, research (Garro, 1994; Patel, Arocha, & Kushniruk, 2002) has shown that lay people's model of disease is narrative, containing a sequence of events in story-like fashion. In contrast, physician's models are explanatory and often causal, generating a mismatch between physicians' and patients' models. Such mismatch may be a major obstacle to improving the quality of healthcare. Similarly, narrative, culturally relevant Web information about breast cancer was preferred by Aboriginal minority women in contrast to "evidence-based" scientific information (Friedman & Hoffman-Goetz, 2007).

Content factors include such aspects as the vocabulary used, and the word choices made when designing health information. Selection of appropriate word choices has also been responsible for improving understanding. For instance, in an early study (Patel, Eisemon, & Arocha, 1990) on the comprehension of instructions on pharmaceutical labels (an oral rehydration therapy solution package), it was found that, when interpreting the information on the original label, the users (consisting of rural and urban mothers) ignored the text and used their intuitions to understand the instructions. The use by some mothers of scientifically-based knowledge resulted in fragmentation of the information into a series of "facts" with little or no connection among them. However, when modifications were made to the words on the label that included culture-specific meanings, people's understanding of the information presented was greatly improved. There is much research supporting the need to adapt word choice to the population of interest (Wright, 1999).

Although improving the presentation of health information may suffice for bringing the attention of the user to important aspects of healthcare, educating the user so that he or she takes better care of his or her health requires a closer matching between user and provider models of health and disease (Morrow, Leirer, Andrassy et al., 1996). Suggestions for improving such matching can be found in social and cognitive research, which has emphasized the need for patient-centered communication and the similarity of knowledge and strategies for dealing with information between providers and consumers (Mead & Bower, 2000; Patel et al., 2002).

User factors include the use of heuristics and reasoning strategies for comprehending information, solving health problems, and making health decisions. A basic assumption about research on these issues is that people intuitively interpret information in terms of their own prior beliefs, backgrounds and assumptions, using reasoning heuristics that depart from well-justified forms of reasoning. Such intuitions are often at odds with scientifically acceptable knowledge. Being aware of the discrepancies between intuitive models and scientific information is especially important in understanding the ways people in which people assess health risk and, indeed, about risk in general (Patel, Arocha, & Kushniruk, 2002).

The seminal works by Tversky and Kahnemann (Kahneman, Slovic, & Tversky, 1982) have demonstrated that people display poor assessment for probabilistic events while making use of heuristics. These heuristics include availability bias (e.g., focusing on salient, well known features while ignoring others), representativeness bias (e.g., focusing on prototypical cases, disregarding atypical features), and anchoring (e.g., making estimates based on particular values known to the person while ignoring other values). Choices people make vary depending on whether the alternatives are framed as loss or gain, with choices representing prevention of loss given more emphasis than those aimed at gain. Health information systems would benefit from knowledge of the conditions under which such cognitive biases and heuristics are likely to be used, and especially as related to framing of health messages.

One of the more ubiquitous findings regards the misconceptions that people possess about the statistical information and the difficulty of evaluating inconsistent information. The ability to put aside prior beliefs when reasoning and

evaluating the quality of information has been traditionally considered a form of higher-order thinking displayed mostly by educated adults, more likely living in modern societies. The problem lies in that the interpretation of information is always done in the context of prior beliefs about the world. The main concern in the interpretation of inconsistent information is to decide whether the evidentiary information is strong enough to justify changing one's beliefs and accepting an alternative hypothesis that is supported by the evidence. This process requires separating evidence from belief, which amounts to using abstract reasoning, detached from the context of the task. Although the ability to distinguish between hypothesis and evidence is crucial for successful scientific reasoning, many adults are not capable of making such distinction. Frequently adults fail to see the difference between the two and interpret data and hypothesis interchangeably (Kendeou & Van Den Broek, 2005; Otero, 2002; Sinatra, Southerland, McConaughy, & Demastes, 2003).

Information technologies, such as the Internet, constitute important vehicles for bringing up-to-date information to lay people and patients. This can be beneficial as it promotes and reinforces patient-centered healthcare, with shared responsibility in maintaining health and preventing disease, based on the latest information available about prevention, screening, diagnostic and therapeutics (e.g., evidence-based medicine) through education about scientifically-based and psychologically motivating information. However, many users of health information from the Internet lack the adequate resources or the knowledge to understand this information unaided. Hence, the design and implementation of health information for consumers would benefit from attention paid to the psychological and cultural aspects involved in understanding and using information.

FUTURE RESEARCH DIRECTIONS

As health literacy is increasingly delivered through information technologies, such as the Internet, it becomes of growing importance to investigate Internet literacy as it relates to health in all of its aspects. We can think of at least two major areas of research that need to be explored: First, substantive issues regarding the processes of searching, understanding, and using health information, and the conditions that either foster or impede the effective utilization of such information. Among the conditions for use, we are exploring the role of multiple forms of representation, such as graphical, numerical, and textual formats, and how these representation formats affect the way lay people, patients, and care givers use information. Other substantive issues include technological literacy (i.e., the ability to make use technology to support health), and population factors associated with health information use, such as linguistic, ethno-cultural, and age differences in health information processing.

Second, methodological issues need to be investigated to develop new types of measurement and assessment. These issues include the development of better research tools to measure readability and comprehensibility of health information. Most readability tools, for instance, were developed many decades ago and may need to be revisited in light of current psycholinguistic and cognitive processing theories. Similarly, measurement tools of comprehension need to be generated that rely on a substantive theory of how people understand and makes use of health information.

The empirical research on literacy reported in this chapter is part of a long-range program of research on consumer and patient use of health information, including cancer information, on the Internet, including such questions as how such information affects consumer decision-making about cancer prevention, early detection, and treatment choices, and determination of the best channels for cancer information dissemination to reach diverse aging populations. Our research program focuses on identifying critical factors that make cancer information, available on the Internet, difficult to read and understand. Identifying such factors is especially important for enhancing health literacy and numeracy skills, and developing adequate health information that supports healthy action by community-dwelling older adults. Future plans for our research program include the expansion of the reported research to include comprehensively larger and more diverse samples of potential users in multiple settings.

REFERENCES

Ad Hoc Committee on Health Literacy for the Council on Scientific Affairs. (1999). Health literacy: Report of the council on scientific affairs. *Journal of the American Medical Association, 281,* 552-557.

Ainsworth, S. (1999). The functions of multiple representations. *Computers and Education, 33*(2-3), 131-152.

Baker, D. W., Williams, M. V., Parker, R. M., Gazmararian, J. A., & Nurss, J. (1999). Development of a brief test to measure functional health literacy. *Patient Education and Counseling, 38*(1), 33-42.

Barr-Telford, L., Nault, F., & Pignal, J. (2005). *Building on our competencies: Canadian results of the international adult literacy and skills survey* (Catalogue no. 89-617-XIE). Ottawa: Statistics Canada, Minister of Industry.

Beier, M. E., & Ackerman, P. L. (2005). Age, ability, and the role of prior knowledge on the acquisition of new domain knowledge: promising results in a real-world learning environment. *Psychology of Aging, 20*(2), 341-355.

Berland, G. K., Elliott, M. N., Morales, L. S., Algazy, J. I., Kravitz, R. L., Broder, M. S., et al. (2001). Health information on the internet: Accessibility, quality, and readability in English and Spanish. *Journal of the American Medical Association, 285*(20), 2612-2621.

Bodemer, D., Ploetzner, R., Bruchmüller, K., & Häcker, S. (2005). Supporting learning with interactive multimedia through active integration of representations. *Instructional Science, 33*(1), 73-95.

Boulos, M. N. (2005). British internet-derived patient information on diabetes mellitus: is it readable? *Diabetes Technology & Therapeutics S, 7*(3), 528-535.

Bowen, S., & Martens, P. (2005). Demystifying knowledge translation: Learning from the community. *Journal of Health Services Research and Policy, 10*(4), 203-211.

Canadian Institutes of Health Research. *Canadian Institutes of Health Research knowledge translation strategy 2004-2009*. Retrieved May 25, 2007, from http://www.cihr-irsc.gc.ca/e/26574.html#defining

Choi, B. C. (2005). Understanding the basic principles of knowledge translation. *Journal of Epidemiology and Community Health, 59*(2), 93.

Coey, L. (1996). Readability of printed educational materials used to inform potential and actual ostomates. *Journal of Clinical Nursing, 5*(6), 359-366.

Cooley, M. E., Moriarty, H., Berger, M. S., Selm-Orr, D., Coyle, B., & Short, T. (1995). Patient literacy and the readability of written cancer educational materials. *Oncology Nursing Forum, 22*(9), 1345-1351.

Crowley, D. (2002). Where are we now? Contours of the Internet in Canada. *Canadian Journal of Communication, 27*(4), 469-507.

D'Alessandro, D. M., Kingsley, P., & Johnson-West, J. (2001). The readability of pediatric patient education materials on the World Wide Web. *Archives of Pediatric and Adolescent Medicine, 155*(7), 807-812.

Davis, D. (2005). Quality, patient safety and the implementation of best evidence: Provinces in the country of knowledge translation. *Healthcare Quarterly, 8*, 128-131.

Davis, D., Evans, M., Jadad, A., Perrier, L., Rath, D., Ryan, D., et al. (2003). The case for knowledge translation: Shortening the journey from evidence to effect. *British Medical Journal, 327*(7405), 33-35.

Davis, T. C., Crouch, M. A., Long, S. W., Jackson, R. H., Bates, P., George, R. B., et al. (1991). Rapid assessment of literacy levels of adult primary care patients. *Family Medicine, 23*(6), 433-435.

Davis, T. C., Dolan, N. C., Ferreira, M. R., Tomori, C., Green, K. W., Sipler, A. M., et al. (2001). The role of inadequate health literacy skills in colorectal cancer screening. *Cancer Investigation, 19*(2), 193-200.

Davis, T. C., Mayeaux, E. J., Fredrickson, D., Bocchini Jr., J. A., Jackson, R. H., & Murphy, P. W. (1994). Reading ability of parents compared with reading level of pediatric patient education materials. *Pediatrics, 93*(3), 460-468.

Donelle, L., Arocha, J. F., & Hoffman-Goetz, L. (2007). *Colorectal cancer risk comprehension of older Canadians: Impact of health numeracy*. Paper presented at the ITCH: Today's Information for Tomorrow's Improvements, Victoria, BC Canada.

Donelle, L., Arocha, J. F., & Hoffman-Goetz, L. (in press). Colorectal cancer risk comprehension of older Canadians: Impact of health numeracy. *Chronic Diseases in Canada*.

Estrada, C. A., Hryniewicz, M. M., Higgs, V. B., Collins, C., & Byrd, J. C. (2000). Anticoagulant patient information material is written at high readability levels. *Stroke, 31*(12), 2966-2970.

Flesch, R. A. (1948). A new readability yardstick. *Journal of Applied Psychology, 32,* 221-233.

Fogel, J. (2003). Internet use for cancer information among racial/ethnic populations and low literacy groups. *Cancer Control, 10*(5 Suppl), 45-51.

Forbis, S. G., & Aligne, C. A. (2002). Poor readability of written asthma management plans found in national guidelines. *Pediatrics, 109*(4), e52.

Friedman, D. B., & Hoffman-Goetz, L. (2006). A systematic review of readability and comprehension instruments used for print and Web-based cancer information. *Health Education and Behavior, 33*(3), 352-373.

Friedman, D. B., & Hoffman-Goetz, L. (2007). Assessing cultural sensitivity of breast cancer information for older Aboriginal women. *Journal of Cancer Education, 22*(20), 12-18.

Friedman, D. B., Hoffman-Goetz, L., & Arocha, J. F. (2004). Readability of cancer information on the internet. *Journal of Cancer Education, 19*(2), 117-122.

Friedman, D. B., Hoffman-Goetz, L., & Arocha, J. F. (2006). Health literacy and the World Wide Web: Comparing the readability of leading incident cancers on the internet. *Medical Informatics and the Internet in Medicine, 31*(1), 67-87.

Garro, L. C. (1994). Narrative representations of chronic illness experience: Cultural models of illness, mind, and body in stories concerning the temporomandibular joint. *Social Science & Medicine, 38*(6), 775-788.

Grimshaw, J. M., Santesso, N., Cumpston, M., Mayhew, A., & McGowan, J. (2006). Knowledge for knowledge translation: The role of the cochrane collaboration. *Journal of Continuing Education in the Health Professions, 26*(1), 55-62.

Hoffman-Goetz, L., Friedman, D. B., & Celestine, A. (2006). Evaluation of a public library workshop: teaching older adults how to search the internet for reliable cancer information. *Journal of Consumer Health on the Internet, 10*(3), 29-43.

Hopko, D. R., Mahadevan, R., Bare, R. L., & Hunt, M. K. (2003). The Abbreviated Math Anxiety Scale (AMAS): Construction, validity, and reliability. *Assessment, 10*(2), 178-182.

Jaffery, J. B., & Becker, B. N. (2004). Evaluation of ehealth Web sites for patients with chronic kidney disease. *American Journal of Kidney Diseases S, 44*(1), 71-76.

Kahneman, D., Slovic, P., & Tversky, A. (1982). *Judgment under uncertainty: Heuristics and biases.* Cambridge, New York: Cambridge University Press.

Kaphingst, K. A., Zanfini, C. J., & Emmons, K. M. (2006). Accessibility of Web sites containing colorectal cancer information to adults with limited literacy. *Cancer Causes & Control, 17*(2), 147-151.

Kendeou, P., & Van Den Broek, P. (2005). The effects of readers' misconceptions on comprehension of scientific text. *Journal of Educational Psychology, 97*(2), 235-245.

Kintsch, W. (1998). *Comprehension: A paradigm for cognition.* Cambridge, New York, NY: Cambridge University Press.

Lindau, S. T., Tomori, C., Lyons, T., Langseth, L., Bennett, C. L., & Garcia, P. (2002). The association of health literacy with cervical cancer prevention knowledge and health behaviors in a multiethnic cohort of women. *American Journal of Obstetrics and Gynecology, 186*(5), 938-943.

Lipkus, I. M., Samsa, G., & Rimer, B. K. (2001). General performance on a numeracy scale among highly educated samples. *Medical Decision Making, 21*(1), 37-44.

Manly, J. J., Jacobs, D. M., Sano, M., Bell, K., Merchant, C. A., Small, S. A., et al. (1999). Effect of literacy on neuropsychological test performance in nondemented, education-matched elders. *Journal of the International Neuropsychological Society, 5*(3), 191-202.

McCray, A. T. (2005). Promoting health literacy. *Journal of the American Medical Informatics Association, 12*(2), 152-163.

McLaughlin, G. H. (1969). SMOG grading: a new readability formula. *Journal of Reading, 12*, 639-346.

McShane, K. E., Smylie, J. K., Hastings, P. D., & Martin, C. M. (2006). Guiding health promotion efforts with urban Inuit: A community-specific perspective on health information sources and dissemination strategies. *Canadian Journal of Public Health, 97*(4), 296-299.

Mead, N., & Bower, P. (2000). Patient-centredness: a conceptual framework and review of the empirical literature. *Social Science & Medicine, 51*(7), 1087-1110.

Mohrmann, C. C., Coleman, E. A., Coon, S. K., Lord, J. E., Heard, J. K., Cantrell, M. J., et al. (2000). An analysis of printed breast cancer information for African American women. *Journal of Cancer Education, 15*(1), 23-27.

Moore, D., Castillo, E., Richardson, C., & Reid, R. J. (2003). Determinants of health status and the influence of primary healthcare services in Latin America, 1990-98. *International Journal of Health Planning and Management, 18*(4), 279-292.

Morrow, D. G., Leirer, V. O., Andrassy, J. M., Hier, C. M., & Menard, W. E. (1998). The influence of list format and category headers on age differences in understanding medication instructions. *Experimental Aging Research, 24*, 231-256.

Morrow, D., Leirer, V., Andrassy, J., Tanke, E., & Stine-morrow, E. (1996). Medication instruction design: Younger and older adult schemas for taking medication. *Human Factors, 38*, 556-573.

Nutbeam, D. (2000). Health literacy as a public health goal: A challenge for contemporary health education and communication strategies into the 21st century. *Health Promotion International, 15*(3), 259-267.

Otero, J. (2002). Noticing and fixing difficulties while understanding science texts. In J. Otero, J. A. Leén, & A. C. Graesser (Eds.), *The psychology of science text comprehension* (pp. 281-307). Mahwah, NJ: Lawrence Erlbaum.

Pablos-Mendez, A., Chunharas, S., Lansang, M. A., Shademani, R., & Tugwell, P. (2005). Knowledge translation in global health. *Bulletin World Health Organ, 83*(10), 723.

Parker, R. M., Baker, D. W., Williams, M. V., & Nurss, J. R. (1995). The test of functional health literacy in adults: A new instrument for measuring patients' literacy skills. *Journal of General Internal Medicine, 10*(10), 537-541.

Parker, R. M., Ratzan, S. C., & Lurie, N. (2003). Health literacy: A policy challenge for advancing high-quality healthcare. *Health Affairs (Millwood), 22*(4), 147-153.

Patel, V. L., Arocha, J. F., & Kushniruk, A. W. (2002). Patients' and physicians' understanding of health and biomedical concepts: relationship to the design of EMR systems. *Journal of Biomedical Informatics, 35*(1), 8-16.

Patel, V. L., Eisemon, T. O., & Arocha, J. F. (1990). Comprehending instructions for using pharmaceutical products in rural Kenya. *Instructional Science, 19*(1), 71-84.

Patel, V. L., Branch, T., & Arocha, J. F. (2002). Errors in interpreting quantities as procedures: the case of pharmaceutical labels. *International Journal of Medical Informatics, 65*(3), 193-211.

Pathak, M., Ketkar, Y. A., & Majumdar, R. D. (1981). Perceived morbidity, utilisation of health services and factors affecting it in a rural area. *Health and Population: Perspectives & Issues, 4*(1), 79-89.

Peterson, M. W. & Fretz, P. C. (2003). Patient use of the internet for information in a lung cancer clinic. *Chest, 123*(2), 452-457.

Ratzan, S. C. & Parker, R. M. (2000). Introduction. *National Library of Medicine Current Bibliographies in Medicine: Health Literacy* Retrieved May 25, 2007, http://www.nlm.nih.gov/archive//20061214/pubs/cbm/hliteracy.pdf

Safeer, R. S., & Keenan, J. (2005). Health literacy: the gap between physicians and patients. *American Family Physician, 72*(3), 463-468.

Saini, F., & Rowling, L. (1997). It's more than literacy: The assimilation effect of the translation model. *Ethnicity and Health, 2*(4), 323-328.

Schillinger, D., Grumbach, K., Piette, J., Wang, F., Osmond, D., Daher, C., et al. (2002). Association of health literacy with diabetes outcomes. *Journal of the American Medical Association, 288*(4), 475-482.

Schwartz, L. M., Woloshin, S., Black, W. C., & Welch, H. G. (1997). The role of numeracy in understanding the benefit of screening mammography. *Annals of Internal Medicine, 127*(11), 966-972.

Seufert, T. (2003). Supporting coherence formation in learning from multiple representations. *Learning and Instruction, 13,* 227-237.

Sinatra, G. M., Southerland, S. A., McConaughy, F., & Demastes, J. W. (2003). Intentions and beliefs in students' understanding and acceptance of biological evolution. *Journal of Research in Science Teaching, 40*(5), 510-528.

Singh, J. (2003). Research briefs: Reading grade level and readability of printed cancer education materials. *Oncology Nursing Forum S, 30*(5), 867-870.

Smart, J. M. & Burling, D. (2001). Radiology and the Internet: A systematic review of patient information resources. *Clinical Radiology, 56*(11), 867-870.

Speros, C. (2005). Health literacy: concept analysis. *Journal of Advanced Nursing, 50*(6), 633-640.

Ta-Min, R., Arocha, J. F., & Hoffman-Goetz, L. (2007). Assessing readability and comprehensibility of Web-based cancer information. *Journal on information technology in healthcare, 5*(5), 300-312.

Tugwell, P., Robinson, V., Grimshaw, J., & Santesso, N. (2006). Systematic reviews and knowledge translation. *Bulletin World Health Organ, 84*(8), 643-651.

US Department of Health and Human Services. (2000). *Healthy people 2010: Understanding and Improving Health.* Retrieved December 12, 2006, http://www.healthypeople.gov/

Walker, L. O. & Avant, K. C. (2005). *Strategies for theory construction in nursing* (4th ed.). Upper Saddle River, N.J: Pearson/Prentice Hall.

Weiss, B. D., Mays, M. Z., Martz, W., Castro, K., Dewalt, D. A., Pignone, M. P., et al. (2005). Quick assessment of literacy in primary care: the newest vital sign. *Annals of Family Medicine, 3*(6), 514-522.

WHO Division of Health Promotion Education and Communications. (1998). *Health promotion glossary.* Retrieved May 31, 2007, http://www.who.int/hpr/NPH/docs/hp_glossary_en.pdf

Williams, M. V., Baker, D. W., Parker, R. M., & Nurss, J. R. (1998). Relationship of functional health literacy to patients' knowledge of their chronic disease. A study of patients with hypertension and diabetes. *Archives of Internal Medicine, 158*(2), 166-172.

Wilson, F. L., & Williams, B. N. (2003). Assessing the readability of skin care and pressure ulcer patient education materials. *Journal of Wound, Ostomy & Continence Nursing, 30*(4), 224-230.

Wright, P. (1999). Designing healthcare advice forward reasoning the public. In T. Durso (pp. 695-723). Chichester, UK: Wiley.

Zion, A. B., & Aiman, J. (1989). Level of reading difficulty in the American College of Obstetricians and Gynecologists patient education pamphlets. *Obstetrics and Gynecology, 74*(6), 955-960.

ADDITIONAL READINGS

Bailin, A., & Grafstein, A.(2001). The linguistic assumptions underlying readability formulae: A critique. *Language & Communication, 21*(3), 285-301.

Baker, D.W., Parker, R.M., Williams, M.V., Pitkin, K., Parikh, N.S., Coates, W.,.et al. (1996). The health care experience of patients with low literacy. *Archives of Family Medicine, 5*(6), 329-334.

Benigeri, M., & Pluye, P. (2003). Shortcomings of health information on the Internet. *Health Promotion International, 18*(4), 381-386.

Berland, G. K., Elliott, M. N., Morales, L. S., Algazy, J. I., Kravitz, R. L., Broder, M. S., et al. (2001). Health information on the Internet: accessibility, quality, and readability in English and Spanish. *Journal of the American Medical Association, 285*(20), 2612-21.

Biehl, M., & Halpern-Felsher, B. L. (2001). Adolescents' and adults' understanding of probability expressions. *Journal of Adolescent Health, 28*(1), 30-5.

Brennan, P. F. (1999). Health informatics and community health: support for patients as collaborators in care. *Methods of Information in Medicine, 38*(4-5), 274-278.

Bryant J. (2005). The Internet and the elderly. *Medical Informatics and the Internet in Medicine, 30*(1), 1.

Cline, R. J., & Haynes, K. M. (2001). Consumer health information seeking on the Internet: the state of the art. *Health Education Research, 16*(6), 671-92.

Davis, T. C., Williams, M.V., Marin, E., Parker, R. M., & Glass, J. (2002). *Health literacy and cancer communication, 52*(3),134-149.

Edwards, A., Elwyn, G., & Mulley, A. (2002). Explaining risks: Turning numerical data into meaningful pictures. *British Medical Journal, 6,324*(7341),827-830.

Eysenbach, G., & Diepgen, T. L. (2001). The role of e-health and consumer health informatics for evidence-based patient choice in the 21st century. *Clinical Dermatology, 19*(1), 11-7.

Eysenbach, G. (2000). Consumer health informatics. *British Medical Journal, 320*(7251), 1713-1716.

Fuller, R., Dudley, N., & Blacktop, J. (2001). Risk communication and older people-understanding of probability and risk information by medical inpatients aged 75 years and older. *Age & Ageing, 30*(6),473-6.

Kefalides, P.T. (1999). Illiteracy: The silent barrier to health care. *Annals of Internal Medicine, 130*(4 Pt 1), 333-336.

King, M. M., Winton, A. S. W., & Adkins, A.D. (2003). Assessing the readability of mental health Internet brochures for children and adolescents. *Journal of Child and Family Studies, 12*, 91-99.

Kreps, G.L. (2002). Evaluating new health information technologies: expanding the frontiers of healthcare delivery and health promotion. *Studies in Health Technology and Informatics, 80*, 205-12.

Lewis, D. (1999). Computer-based approaches to patient education: A review of the literature. *Journal of the American Medical Informatics Association, 6*(4),272-282.

Paasche-Orlow, M. K., Parker, R. M., Gazmararian, J. A., Nielsen-Bohlman, L. T., & Rudd, R. R. (2005). The prevalence of limited health literacy. *Journal of General Internal Medicine, 20*(2), 175-184.

Ratzan, S. C. (2003). Making sense of risk. *Journal of Health Communication, 8*(5), 399-400.

Rudd, R.E., Moeykens, B.A., & Colton, T.C. (2000). Health and literacy: A review of medical and public health literature. In J. Comings, B. Garner, & C. Smith (Eds.), *The Annual Review of Adult Learning and Literacy: Vol. 1* (pp. 158-199). San Francisco: Jossey-Bass.

Saranto, K., & Hovenga, E. J. (2004). Information literacy-what it is about? Literature review of the concept and the context. *International Journal of Medical Informatics, 73*(6), 503-513.

Thobaben, M. (2002). Technology and informatics. Accessibility, quality, and readability of health information on the internet: implication for home health care professionals. *Home Health Care Management & Practice, 14*(4), 295-6.

Turk-Charles, S., Meyerowitz, B. E., & Gatz, M. (1997). Age differences in information seeking among cancer patients. *International Journal on Aging and Human Development, 45*(2), 85-98.

Weinstein, N. D., Atwood, K., Puleo, E., Fletcher, R., Colditz, G., & Emmons, K. M. (2004). Colon cancer: Risk perceptions and risk communication. *Journal of Health Communication, 9*(1), 53-65.

Winker, M. A., Flanagin, A., Chi-Lum, B., White, J., Andrews, K., Kennett, R. L., et al. (2000). Guidelines for medical and health information sites on the internet: Principles governing AMA web sites. *Journal of the American Medical Association, 283*(12), 1600-1606.

Compilation of References

Aamodt, A., & Plaza, E. (1994). Case based reasoning: Foundational issues, methodological variations & system approaches. *AICom-Artificial Intelligence Communications, 7*(1), 39-59.

Aaronson, J. W., Murphy-Cullen, C. L., Chop, W. M., & Frey, R. D. (2001). Electronic medical records: the family practice resident perspective. *Fam Med, 33*(2), 128-132.

Aarts, J., & Berg, M. (2004). A tale of two hospitals: A sociotechnical appraisal of the introduction of computerized physician order entry in two Dutch hospitals. *Medinfo, 11*(Pt 2), 999-1002.

Aarts, J., Doorewaard, H., & Berg, M. (2004). Understanding implementation: The case of a computerized physician order entry system in a large Dutch university medical center. *Journal of the American Medical Informatics Association, 11*, 207-216.

Ad Hoc Committee on Health Literacy for the Council on Scientific Affairs. (1999). Health literacy: Report of the council on scientific affairs. *Journal of the American Medical Association, 281*, 552-557.

Ainsworth, S. (1999). The functions of multiple representations. *Computers and Education, 33*(2-3), 131-152.

Alberta Information and Privacy Commissioner. (2003). Commissioner's response to repeal of section 59 and introduction of section 60(2) of the *Health Information Act*. Press release retrieved December 20, 2006, from http://www.oipc.ab.ca/ims/client/upload/Repeal_of_s.59.pdf

American Hospital Association. (1999). *Hospital statistics.* Chicago: American Hospital Association.

AMIA, A. A. (2006). *Building the work force for health information transformation.*

Ammenwerth, E., & Shaw, N.T. (2005). Bad health informatics can kill: Is evaluation the answer? *Methods of Information in Medicine, 44*, 1-3.

Ammenwerth, E., Brender, J., Nykänen, P., Prokosch, H.-U., Rigby, M., & Talmon, J. (2004). Visions and strategies to improve evaluation of health information systems—Reflections and lessons based on the HIS-EVAL workshop in Innsbruck. *International Journal of Medical Informatics, 73*(6), 479-491.

Andersen, S.K., Nøhr, C., Vingtoft, S., Bernstein, K., & Bruun-Rasmussen, M. (2002). *EHR-observatory annual report 2002.* Aalborg: EPJ-Observatoriet.

Anderson, J. G. (2003). A system's approach to preventing adverse drug events. In S. Krishna, E.A. Balas, & S. A. Boren (Eds.), *Information technology business models for quality health care: An EU/US dialogue* (pp. 95-102). The Netherlands: IOS Press.

Anderson, J. G. (2004). Information technology for detecting medication errors and adverse drug events. *Expert Opinion on Drug Safety, 3*(5), 449-455.

Anderson, J. G., Jay, S. J., Anderson, M. M., & Hunt, T. J. (2002). Evaluating the capability of information technology to prevent adverse drug events: A computer simulation approach. *Journal of the American Medical Informatics Association, 9*, 479-490.

Anderson, J. G., Ramanujam, R., Hensel, D. J. Anderson, M. M., & Siro, C. A. (2006). The need for organizational change in patient safety initiatives. *International Journal of Medical Informatics, 75*(12), 809-817.

Copyright © 2008, IGI Global, distributing in print or electronic forms without written permission of IGI Global is prohibited.

Anderson, J.G., Aydin, C.E., & Jay, S.J. (1994). *Evaluating health care information systems: Methods and applications.* Thousand Oaks, CA: Sage Publications.

Anderson, J.G., Ramanujam, R., Hensel, D. J., & Siro, C. (2007). Reporting trends in a regional medication error data-sharing system (unpublished manuscript).

Are handoffs too 'automatic'? QI experts fear errors could rise. (2006). *Healthcare Benchmarks Qual Improv, 13*(1), 1-4.

Argyris, C. (1976). Leadership, learning and changing the status quo. *Organizational Dynamics, 4*(3), 29-43.

Arocha, J.F., Wang, D., & Patel, V.L. (2005) Identifying reasoning strategies in medical decision making: A methodological guide. *Journal of Biomedical Informatics, 38*, 154-171.

Ascher, M., & Ascher, R. (1997). *The code of the Quipu: A study in media, mathematics, and culture.* Ann Arbor: University of Michigan Press.

Ash, J. S., Gorman, P. N., & Hersh, W. R. (1998). Physician order entry in U.S. hospitals. *Proceedings of AMIA Symp*, 235-239.

Ash, J. S., Gorman, P. N., Lavelle, M., Payne, T. H., Massaro, T. A., Frantz, G. L., et al. (2003). A cross-site qualitative study of physician order entry. *Journal of American Medical Information Association, 10*(2), 188-200.

Ash, J. S., Gorman, P. N., Seshadri, V., & Hersh, W. R. (2004). Computerized physician order entry in U.S. hospitals: results of a 2002 survey. *Journal of American Medical Information Association, 11*(2), 95-99.

Ash, J. S., Sittig, D. F., Poon, E. G., Guappone, K., Campbell, E., & Dykstra, R. H. (2007). The extent and importance of unintended consequences related to computerized provider order entry. *JAMIA, 14*(4), 415-423.

Ash, J. S., Stavri, P. Z., & Kuperman, G. J. (2003). A consensus statement on considerations for a successful CPOE implementation. *Journal of American Medical Information Association, 10*(3), 229-234.

Ash, J. S., Stavri, P. Z., Fournier, L. & et al. (2003). Principles for a successful computerized physician order entry implementation. *AMIA Annual Symposium Proceedings* (pp. 36-40).

Ash, J., & Berg, M. (2003). Report of conference track 4: Sociotechnical issues of HIS. *International Journal of Medical Informatics, 69*, 305-306.

Ash, J.S., Sittig, D.F., Dykstra, R.H., et al. (2006). An unintended consequence of CPOE implementation: Shifts in power, control, and autonomy. *AMIA Annual Symposium Proceedings.*

Associates in Process Improvement–API. (2007). *The model for improvement.* Austin, TX, Detroit, MI, Sacramento, CA, Washington, DC. Retrieved June 7, 2007, from http://www.apiWeb.org/API_home_page.htm

Aydin, C. (1994). Computerized order entry in a large medical center: evaluating interactions between departments. In J.G. Anderson, C.E. Aydin, & S.J. Jay (Eds.), *Evaluating health care information systems: Approaches and applications* (pp. 260-275). Thousand Oaks, CA: Sage.

Aydin, C.E., & Forsythe, D.E. (1997). Implementing computers in ambulatory care: Implications of physician practice patterns for system design. *AMIA Annual Symposium Proceedings, 677-681.*

Baecker, R. M., & Baecker, R. M. (1992). *Readings in groupware and computer-supported cooperative work: Assisting human-human collaboration.* Morgan Kaufmann.

Baker, D. W., Williams, M. V., Parker, R. M., Gazmararian, J. A., & Nurss, J. (1999). Development of a brief test to measure functional health literacy. *Patient Education and Counseling, 38*(1), 33-42.

Baker, G. R., & Norton, P. (2004). Addressing the effects of adverse events: Study provides insights into patient safety at Canadian hospitals. *Healthcare Quarterly, 7*(4), 20-21.

Baker, G. R., Norton, P. G., Flintoft, V., Blais, R., Brown, A., Cox, J. et al. (2004). The Canadian adverse events study: The incidence of adverse events among hospital patients in Canada. *Canadian Medical Association Journal, 170*, 1678-1686.

Baker, G. R., Norton, P. G., Flintoft, V., Blais, R., Brown, A., Cox, J., et al. (2004). The canadian adverse events study: The incidence of adverse events among hospital patients in Canada. *Canadian Medical Association Journal, 170*(11), 1678-86.

Baker, G. R., Norton, P. G., Flintoft, V., Blais, R., Brown, A., Cox, J., et al. (2004). The Canadian adverse events study: The incidence of adverse events among hospital patients in Canada. *Cmaj, 170*(11), 1678-1686.

Bakken, S. (2001). An informatics infrastructure is essential for evidence-based practice. *Journal of American Medical Information Association, 8*(3), 199-201.

Bång, M., & Timpka, T. (2003). Cognitive tools in medical teamwork: The spatial arrangement of patient records. *Meth Inf Med, 42*, 331-336.

Bång, M., Eriksson, H., Lindqvist, K., & Timpka, T. A framework for context-sensitive terminology support.

Bannon, L. J., & Schmidt, K. (1991). CSCW: Four characters in search of a context.

Bannon, L., & Bødker, S. (1997). Constructing Common Information Spaces. *Proceedings of the Fifth European Conference on Computer Supported Cooperative Work* (pp. 81-96).

Bardram, J.E., & Bossen, C. (2005). Mobility work: The spatial dimension of collaboration at a hospital. *Computer Supported Cooperative Work (CSCW), 14*(2), 131-160.

Bardram, J.E.., Mihailidis, A., & Dadong, W. (2007). *Pervasive computing in healthcare* (1st ed.). New York: CRC Press.

Barker, K.N., Flynn, E.A., Pepper, G.A., Bates, D. W., & Mikeal, R.L. (2002). Medication errors observed in 36 health care facilities. *Archives of Internal Medicine, 162*, 1897-1903.

Barr-Telford, L., Nault, F., & Pignal, J. (2005). *Building on our competencies: Canadian results of the international adult literacy and skills survey* (Catalogue no. 89-617-XIE). Ottawa: Statistics Canada, Minister of Industry.

Barton, J., Emery, M., Flood, R. L., Selsky, J. W., & Wolstenholme, E. (2004). A maturing of systems thinking? Evidence from three perspectives. *Systemic Practice and Action Research, 17*(1), 3-37.

Bates, D. W., & Gawande, A. A. (2003). Improving safety with information technology. *New England Journal of Medicine, 348*(25), 2526-2534.

Bates, D. W., Cohen, M., Leape, L. L., Overhage, J. M., Shabot, M. M., & Sheridan, T. (2001). Reducing the frequency of errors in medicine using information technology. *Journal of the American Medical Informatics Association, 8*(4), 299.

Bates, D. W., Ebell, M., Gotlieb, E., Zapp, J., & Mullins, H. C. (2003). A proposal for electronic medical records in U.S. primary care. *Journal of American Medical Information Association, 10*(1), 1-10.

Bates, D. W., Kuperman, G. J., Wang, S., Gandhi, T., Kittler, A., Volk, L., et al. (2003). Ten commandments for effective clinical decision support: Making the practice of evidence-based medicine a reality. *Journal of the American Medical Informatics Association, 10*(6), 523-530.

Bates, D. W., Teich, J. M., Lee, J., Seger, D., Kuperman, G. J., Ma'Luf, N., et al. (1999). The impact of computerized physician order entry on medication error prevention. *Journal of American Medical Information Association, 6*(4), 313-321.

Bates, D.W., & Gawande, A.A. (2003). Improving safety with information technology. *New England Journal of Medicine, 348*, 2526-2534.

Bates, D.W., Leape, L.L., Cullen, D.J., Laird, N., Petersen, L.A., Teich, J.M., et al. (1998). Effect of computerized physician order entry and a team intervention on prevention of serious medication errors. *Journal of the American Medical Association, 280*(15), 1311-1316.

Beard, D. V., Smith, D. K., & Denelsbeck, K. M. (1996). Quick and dirty GOMS: A case study of computed tomography interpretation. *Human-Computer Interaction, 11*(2), 157-180.

Beauchamp, T.L., & Childress, J.F. (1994). *Principles of biomedical ethics* (4th ed.). New York: Oxford University Press.

Begun, J. W., Zimmerman, B., & Dooley, K. (2003). Health care organizations as complex adaptive systems. In S. M. Mick & M. Wyttenback (Eds.), *Advances in health care organization theory* (Vol. 253-288). San Francisco: Jossey-Bass.

Beier, M. E., & Ackerman, P. L. (2005). Age, ability, and the role of prior knowledge on the acquisition of new domain knowledge: promising results in a real-world learning environment. *Psychology of Aging, 20*(2), 341-355.

Bell, D. S., Cretin, S., Marken, R. S., & Landman, A. (2004). A conceptual framework for evaluating outpatient electronic prescribing systems based on their functional capabilities. *Journal of the American Informatics Association, 11*, 60-70.

Bemmel, J. H. V., Musen, M. A., & Helder, J. C. (1997). *Handbook of medical informatics.* AW Houten, Netherlands; Heidelberg, Germany: Bohn Stafleu Van Loghum; Springer Verlag.

Bentley, C. (1992). *Introducing PRINCE.* Oxford: NCC Blackwell.

Berg, M. (1999). Patient care information systems and health care work: A sociotechnical approach. *International Journal of Medical Informatics, 55*(2), 87-101.

Berg, M. (2001). Implementing information systems in healthcare organizations: myths and challenges. *Int J Med Inform., 64*(2-3), 143-156.

Berg, M. (2003). The search for synergy: Interrelating medical work and patient care information systems. *Methods of Information in Medicine, 42*(4), 337-344.

Berg, M., Aarts, J., & Van der Lei, J. (2003). ICT in healthcare: Sociotechnical approaches. *Methods of Information in Medicine, 42*(4), 297-301.

Berghout, E., & Remenyi, D. (2005). The eleven years of the european conference on IT evaluation: Retrospectives and perspectives for possible future research. *The Electronic Journal of Information Systems, 8*(2), 81-98. Available online at www.ejise.com

Berguer, R. (1998). Surgical technology and the ergonomics of laparoscopic instruments. *Surgical Endoscopy, 12*(5), 458-462.

Berland, G. K., Elliott, M. N., Morales, L. S., Algazy, J. I., Kravitz, R. L., Broder, M. S., et al. (2001). Health information on the internet: Accessibility, quality, and readability in English and Spanish. *Journal of the American Medical Association, 285*(20), 2612-2621.

Berner, E.S., Houston, T.K. & et al. (2006). Improving ambulatory prescribing safety with a handheld decision support system: A randomized controlled trial. *J. Am. Med. Inform. Assoc., 13*(2), 171-179.

Bernstein, K., Rasmussen, M.B., Nøhr, C., Andersen, S.K., & Vingtoft, S. (2001). *EHR observatory. Annual report 2001.* Odense: The County of Funen.

Bernstein, K., Rasmussen, M.B., Nøhr, C., Andersen, S.K., & Vingtoft, S. (2006). EHR Observatory. Annual Report 2006. Aalborg: EHR-Observatory.

Berwick, D. M. (2003). Disseminating innovations in health care. *Journal of the American Medical Association, 289*(15), 1969-1975.

Bichindaritz, I., & Marling, C. (2006). Case-based reasoning in the health and sciences: What's next? *Artificial Intelligence in Medicine, 36*(2), 127-135.

Bikson, T. K., & Eveland, J. D. (1989). Technology Transfer as a Framework for Understanding Social Impacts of Computerization. In M. J. Smith & G. Salvendy (Eds.), *Work with computers: Organizational, management, stress and health aspects. Vol. 1.* (pp. 28-37). Amsterdam: Elsevier.

Billings, C.E. (1998). Some hopes and concerns regarding medical event-reporting systems: Lessons from the NASA aviation safety reporting system. *Archives of Pathology & Laboratory Medicine, 122*(3), 214-5.

Bingi, P., Sharma, M.K., & Godla, J. (1999). Critical issues affecting an ERP implementation. *Information Systems Management*, 7-14.

Blackmon, M. H., Polson, P. G., Kitajima, M., & Lewis, C. (2002). Cognitive walkthrough for the web. *Proceedings of the SIGCHI conference on Human factors in computing systems: Changing our world, changing ourselves* (pp. 463-470).

Blobel B. G., Engel K., & Pharow, P. (2006). Semantic Interoperability—HL7 Version 3 compared to advanced architecture standards. *Methods of Information in Medicine, 45*(4), 343-53.

Bodemer, D., Ploetzner, R., Bruchmüller, K., & Häcker, S. (2005). Supporting learning with interactive multimedia through active integration of representations. *Instructional Science, 33*(1), 73-95.

Boers, G., van der Linden, H., & Hasman, A. (2002). A distributed architecture for medical research. *Stud Health Technol Inform, 90*, 734-738.

Borycki, E. M., Kushniruk, A. W., Kuwata, S., & Kannry, J. (2006). Use of simulation in the study of clinician workflow. *AMIA Annual Symposium Proceedings* (pp. 61-65).

Borycki, E., & Kushniruk, A.W. (2005). Identifying and preventing technology-induced error using simulations: Application of usability engineering techniques. *Healthcare Quarterly, 8*, 99-105.

Borycki, E., Kushniruk, A.W., Kuwata, S., & Kannry, J. (2006). Use of simulation approaches to the study of user needs and error in biomedical informatics. *Proceedings of the 2006 Annual AMIA Conference* (pp. 61-65).

Bossen, C. (2002). The parameters of common information spaces: The heterogeneity of cooperative work at a hospital ward. *Proceedings of the 2002 ACM conference on Computer supported cooperative work*, (pp. 176-185).

Bossen, C. (2006). Evaluation of a computerized problem-oriented medical record in a hospital department: Does it support daily clinical practice? *International Journal of Medical Informatics*.

Boulos, M. N. (2005). British internet-derived patient information on diabetes mellitus: is it readable? *Diabetes Technology & Therapeutics S, 7*(3), 528-535.

Bowen, S., & Martens, P. (2005). Demystifying knowledge translation: Learning from the community. *Journal of Health Services Research and Policy, 10*(4), 203-211.

Bradburn, C., Zeleznikow, J., & Adams, A. (1993). FLORENCE: Synthesis of cased-based and model-based reasoning in nursing care planning system. *Computers in Nursing, 11*(1), 20-24.

Brandt, R. B. (1959). *Ethical theory: The problems of normative and critical ethics.* Englewood Cliffs, NJ: Prentice Hall.

Brender, J. (1999). Methodology for constructive assessment of IT-based systems in an organisational context. *International Journal of Medical Informatics, 56*, 67-86.

Brender, J. (2006). *Handbook of evaluation methods for health informatics.* New York: Academic Press.

Brender, J. (2006). Evaluation of health information applications—Challenges ahead of us. *Methods of Information in Medicine, 45*, 62-66.

Brender, J., Ammenwerth, E., Nykänen, P., & Talmon, J. (2006). Factors influencing success and failure of Health Informatics Systems, a pilot delphi study. *Methods of Information in Medicine, 45*, 125-136.

Brennan, T.A., Leape, L.L., Laird, N. et al. (1991). Incidence of adverse events and negligence in hospitalized patients: Results of the Harvard Practice Study. *New England Journal of Medicine, 324*(6), 370-7.

British Medical Association. (2006). *BMA statement on Connecting for Health.* Retrieved January 25, 2007, from http://www.bma.org.uk

Brosius, M. (Ed.). (2003). *Ancient archives and archival traditions. Concepts of record-keeping in the ancient world. Oxford studies in ancient documents.* Oxford: Oxford University Press.

Brown, S. H., Lincoln, M. J., Groen, P. J., & Kolodner, R. M. (2003). VistA—U.S. Department of Veterans Affairs national-scale HIS. *International Journal of Medicine Information, 69*(2-3), 135-156.

Bruegel, R.B. (1998). The increasing importance of patient empowerment and its potential effects on home health care information system s and technology. *Home Healthcare Management Practice, 10*(2), 69-75

Bruun-Rasmussen, M., Bernstein, K., Vingtoft, S., Andersen, S.K., & Nøhr, C. (2003). *EHR-observatory annual report 2003.* Aalborg: EPJ-Observatoriet.

Brydon-Miller, M., Greenwood, D., & Maguire, P. (2003). Why action research? *Action Research, 1*(1), 9-28.

Buckhout, S., Frey, E., & Nemec, J. (1999). Making ERP succeed: turning fear into promise. *IEEE Engineering Management Review,* 116-123.

Budget, O. o. M. a. (2007). Budget of the United States Government

Budnitz, D.S., Pollock, D.A., Weidenbach, K.N., Mendelsohn, A.B., Schroeder, T.J., & Annest, J.L. (2006). National surveillance of emergency department visits for outpatient adverse drug events. *JAMA, 296*(15), 1858-1866.

Bukunt, S., Hunter, C., Perkins, S., Russell, D., & Domanico, L. (2005). El Camino Hospital: using health information technology to promote patient safety. *Jt Comm J Qual Patient Saf, 31*(10), 561-565.

Byford, S., & Selton, T. (2003). Economic evaluation of complex health and social care interventions. *National Institute Economic Review, 186,* 98-108.

Campbell, E. M., Sittig, D. F., Ash, J. S., Guappone, K. P., & Dykstra, R. H. (2006). Types of unintended consequences related to computerized provider order entry. *JAMIA, 13*(5), 547-556.

Campbell, M., Fitzpatrick, R., Haines, A., Kinmonth, A. L., Sandercock, P., Spiegelhalter, D., & Tyrer, P. (2000). Framework for design and evaluation of complex interventions to improve health. *British Medical Journal, 321*(7262), 694-696.

Canada Health Infoway. (2006). *EHR: At the crossroads of success 2006-2007.* Toronto: Canada Health Infoway.

Canada, C. o. F. P. o. (2006). *Four principles of family medicine.* Retrieved January 27, 2006, from http://www.cfpc.ca/English/cfpc/about%20us/principles/default.asp?s=1

Canada, Standing Senate Committee on Social Affairs, Science and Technology. (2002). *The Health of Canadians—The Federal Role*, vol. 1-6. Ottawa: Standing Senate Committee on Social Affairs, Science and Technology.

Canadian Institutes of Health Research. (2007). Knowledge translation strategy 2004-2009: Innovation in action. Retrieved June 9, 2007, from http://www.cihr-irsc.gc.ca/e/26574.html#defining

Canadian Medical Association. (1998). *Health Information Privacy Code.* Retrieved December 1, 2006 from http://www.cma.ca/index.cfm/ci_id/3216/la_id/1.htm

Canadian Institutes of Health Research. *Canadian Institutes of Health Research knowledge translation strategy 2004-2009.* Retrieved May 25, 2007, from http://www.cihr-irsc.gc.ca/e/26574.html#defining

Cao, G., Clarke, S., & Lehaney, B. (2003). The need for a systemic approach to change management—a case study. *Systemic Practice and Action Research, 17*(2), 103-126.

Card, S. K., Moran, T. P., & Newell, A. (1980). The keystroke-level model for user performance time with interactive systems. *Communications of the ACM, 23*(7), 396-410.

Card, S. K., Newell, A., & Moran, T. P. (1983). *The psychology of human-computer interaction.* Lawrence Erlbaum Associates.

Carroll, J. (2003). *Hci models, theories, and frameworks: Toward a multidisciplinary science.* Morgan Kaufmann.

Centre for Health Policy and Research. (2006). *Health information technology adoption in Massachusetts: costs and timeframe.* Retrieved March 13, 2006, from www.umassmed.edu/healthpolicy/uploads/eHealthInformation.pdf

Chakraberty, C. (1923). *An interpretation of ancient Hindu medicine.* Calcutta: R. Chakraberty.

Chantler C., Clarke, T., & Granger, R. (2006). Information technology in the English national health service. *Journal of the American Medical Association, 296*(18), 2255-2258.

Charnock, D. (1998). *The discern handbook: Quality criteria for consumer health information on treatment choices.* Radcliffe Medical Press.

Chaudhry, B., Wang, J., Wu, S., Maglione, M., Mojica, W., Roth, E. et al. (2006). Systematic review: Impact of health information technology on quality, efficiency, and costs of medical care. *Annals of Internal Medicine, 144*(10), 742-752.

Chessare, J. B., & Torok, K. E. (1993). Implementation of COSTAR in an academic group practice of general pediatrics. *MD Comput, 10*(1), 23-27.

Chiang, M.F., & Starren, J.B. (2002). Software engineering risk factors in the implementation of a small electronic medical record system: The problem of scalability. *Proceedings AMIA Annual Symposium* (pp. 145-149).

Chiasson, M., Reddy, M., Kaplan, B., & Davidson, E. (2007). Expanding multi-disciplinary approaches to healthcare information technologies: What does information systems offer medical informatics? *International Journal of Medical Informatics, 76,* (Supplement 1), S89-S97.

Chin, H. (2004). The reality of EMR implementation: lessons from the field. *Kaiser Permanente HealthConnect, 8*(4).

Chismar, W.G., & Wiley-Paton, S. (2002) Test of the technology acceptance model for the Internet in pediatrics. *Proc. AMIA Symp,* 155-159.

Choi, B. C. (2005). Understanding the basic principles of knowledge translation. *Journal of Epidemiology and Community Health, 59*(2), 93.

Cimino, J. J. (1999). The Columbia medical informatics story: From clinical system to major department. *MD Comput, 16*(2), 31-34.

Cimino, J.J., Patel, V.L., & Kushniruk, A.W. (2002). The patient clinical information system (PatCIS): Technical solutions for and experiences with giving patients access to their electronic medical records. *International Journal of Medical Informatics, 18, 68*(1-3), 113-127.

Clarke, H. F., Bradley, C., Whytock, S., Handfield, S., van der Wal., R., & Gundry, S. (2005). Pressure ulcers: Implementation of evidence-based nursing practice. *Journal of Advanced Nursing, 49*(6), 578-590.

Clayton,P.D., van Mulligen, E. (1996, October 26-30). The Economic Motivation for Clinical Information Systems. In J.J. Cimino (Ed.), *Proceeding of Annual Fall Symposium* (pp. 660-668). Washington, DC.

Clegg, C., Axtell, C., Damodaran, L., et al. (1997). Information technology: A study of performance and the role of human and organizational factors. *Ergonomics, 40*(9), 851-871.

Coey, L. (1996). Readability of printed educational materials used to inform potential and actual ostomates. *Journal of Clinical Nursing, 5*(6), 359-366.

Cohen, M. R., & Vaijda, A. J. (2005). Point-of-care bar coded medication administration: Experience in the United States. *Farm Hospitals, 29,* 151-152.

Coiera, E. (2003). Interaction design theory. *International Journal of Medical Informatics, 69*(2-3), 205-222.

Collins, P. (1998). Risky business. It takes a 'risk-balanced' team to implement a CPR. *Health. Inform., 15*(3), 85-88.

Collins, S., Voth, T., DiCenso, A., & Guyatt, G. (2005). Finding the evidence. In A. DiCenso, G. Guyatt & D. Ciliska (Eds.), *Evidence-based nursing: A guide to clinical practice* (pp. 20-43). St. Louis, MO: Elsevier Mosby.

Comden, S.C., & Rosenthal, J. (2002). *Statewide patient safety coalitions: A status report.* Portland. ME: National Academy for State Health Policy.

Cooley, M. E., Moriarty, H., Berger, M. S., Selm-Orr, D., Coyle, B., & Short, T. (1995). Patient literacy and the readability of written cancer educational materials. *Oncology Nursing Forum, 22*(9), 1345-1351.

Cooper, J.D. (2004). Organization, management, implementation and value of EHR implementation in a solo pediatric practice. *Journal of Healthcare Information Management, 18*(3), 51-55.

Cornwall, A. (2003). Connecting health: A review of electronic health record projects in Australia, Europe and Canada. *Public Interest Advocacy Centre.* Retrieved December 1, 2006, from http://www.piac.asn.au/publications/pubs/churchill_20030121.html

Cosby, K. S. (2003). A framework for classifying factors that contribute to error in the emergency department. *Annals of Emergency Medicine, 42*(6), 815 - 823.

Coye, M. J. (2005). No more procrastinating. Industry must eschew excuses and move fast on electronic health records. *Mod Healthc, 35*(7), 32.

Cozijnsen, A. J., Vrakking, W. J., & van Ijzerloo, M. (2000). Success and failure of 50 innovation projects in Dutch companies. *European Journal of Innovation Management, 3*(3), 150-159.

Cross, M. (2005). UK patients can refuse to let their data be shared across networks. *British Medical Journal, 330*, 1226.

Cross, M. (2006). Will connecting for health deliver its promises? *British Medical Journal, 332*(7541), 599-601.

Cross, M. (2006). Keeping the NHS electronic spine on track. *British Medical Journal, 332*(7542), 656-658.

Crosswell, P. L. (1991). Obstacles to GIS implementation and guidelines to increase the opportunities for success. *URISA Journal, 3*(1), 43-56.

Crowley, D. (2002). Where are we now? Contours of the Internet in Canada. *Canadian Journal of Communication, 27*(4), 469-507.

Cullen, D.J., Bates, D.W., Small, S.D., et al. (1995). The incident reporting system does not detect adverse drug events: A problem for quality improvement. *Journal of Quality Improvement, 21*, 541-548.

Cullum, N., & Sheldon, T. (1996). Clinically challenged. *Nursing Management, 3*(4), 14-16.

Currell, R., Urquhart, C., Wainwright, P., & Lewis, R. (2001). Telemedicine versus face to face patient care: effects on professional practice and healthcare outcomes.

Curtis, W., Hefley, W. E. & Miller, S. (1995). *Overview of the people capability maturity model. Prepared for the USA Department of Defense.* Pittsburgh, PA: Research Access, Inc.

D'Alessandro, D. M., Kingsley, P., & Johnson-West, J. (2001). The readability of pediatric patient education materials on the World Wide Web. *Archives of Pediatric and Adolescent Medicine, 155*(7), 807-812.

D'Alessandro, D., & Nienke, P. (2001). Empowering children and families with information technology. *Archives of Paediatrics and Adolescent Medicine, 155*(10), 1131-1136.

Daniel, B. (2003). Social capital in virtual learning communities and distributed communities of practice. *Canadian Journal of Learning and Technology, 29*(3)

Daniels N., & Sabin J., (1997). Limits to health care: Fair procedures, democratic deliberation, and the legitimacy problem for insurers. *Philosophy and Public Affairs, 26.*

Danish Ministry of Health. (1996). *Action plan for electronic patient records—strategy report.* Copenhagen: Danish Ministry of Health.

Danish Ministry of Health. (1999). *National IT strategy for the hospitals 2000-2002.* Copenhagen: Danish Ministry of Health.

Darwall, S. L. (1983). *Impartial reason.* Ithaca and London: Cornell University Press.

Davis, B., & Wilder, C. (1998). False starts, strong finishes—companies are saving troubled IT projects by admitting their mistakes, stepping back, scaling back, and moving on. *Information Week, November 30*, 41-43.

Davis, D. (2005). Quality, patient safety and the implementation of best evidence: Provinces in the country of knowledge translation. *Healthcare Quarterly, 8*, 128-131.

Davis, D. (2006). Continuing education, guideline implementation, and the emerging transdisciplinary field of knowledge translation. *The Journal of Continuing Education in the Health Professions, 26*(1), 5-12.

Davis, D., Evans, M., Jadad, A., Perrier, L., Rath, D., Ryan, D., et al. (2003). The case for knowledge translation: Shortening the journey from evidence to effect. *British Medical Journal, 327*(7405), 33-35.

Davis, P., Lay-Yee, R., Briant, R. et al. (2003). Adverse events in New Zealand public hospitals II: occurrence and impact. *New Zealand Medical Journal, 116*(1183), U624.

Davis, P., Lay-Yee, R., Briant, R., et al. (2002). Adverse events in New Zealand public hospitals I: Occurrence and impact. *New Zealand Medical Journal, 115*(1167), U271.

Davis, P., Lay-Yee, R., Briant, R., Schug, S., Scott, S., Johnson, et al. (2001). *Adverse events in New Zealand public hospitals: Principle findings from a national survey.* (Occasional Paper no. 3). Wellington: New Zealand Ministry of Health.

Davis, T. C., Crouch, M. A., Long, S. W., Jackson, R. H., Bates, P., George, R. B., et al. (1991). Rapid assessment of literacy levels of adult primary care patients. *Family Medicine, 23*(6), 433-435.

Davis, T. C., Dolan, N. C., Ferreira, M. R., Tomori, C., Green, K. W., Sipler, A. M., et al. (2001). The role of inadequate health literacy skills in colorectal cancer screening. *Cancer Investigation, 19*(2), 193-200.

Davis, T. C., Mayeaux, E. J., Fredrickson, D., Bocchini Jr., J. A., Jackson, R. H., & Murphy, P. W. (1994). Reading ability of parents compared with reading level of pediatric patient education materials. *Pediatrics, 93*(3), 460-468.

Dawkins, R. (1976). *The selfish gene.* Oxford: Oxford University Press.

Day, K., & Norris, A. C. (2006, 9 August 2006). *Leadership in times of crisis during change due to health IT projects.* Paper presented at the Health Informatics New Zealand (HINZ), Auckland, New Zealand.

Day, K., & Norris, A. C. (2006, 17 July 2006). *Supporting information technology across health boards in New Zealand: The role of learning in adapting to complex change.* Paper presented at the 11th International Symposium on Health Information Management Research (iSHIMR), Halifax, Canada.

Day, K., & Norris, A. C. (2006). Supporting information technology across health boards in New Zealand: themes emerging from the development of a shared services organization. *Health Informatics Journal, 12*(1), 13-25.

Day, K., Orr, M., Sankaran, S., & Norris, A. C. (2006, 22 August 2006). *The reflexive employee: action research immortalised?* Paper presented at the 7th ALARPM (Action Learning, Action Research and Process Management Association) & 11th PAR (Participatory Action Research) World Congress, Groningen, The Netherlands.

Deci, E. L., & Ryan, R. M. (2000). The "what" and "why" of goal pursuits: Human needs and the self-determination of behavior. *Psychological Inquiry, 11*, 227-268.

DeLone, W.H., & McLean, E.R. (1992) Information systems success: The quest for the dependent variable, *Information Systems Research, 3*(1), 60-95.

DeLone, W.H., & McLean, E.R. (2003). The DeLone and McLean model of information systems success: A ten year update. *Journal of Management Information Systems, 19*(4), 9-30.

Delpierre, C., Cuzin, L., Fillaux, J., Alvarez, M., Massip, P., & Lang, T. (2004). A systematic review of computer-based patient record systems and quality of care: More randomized clinical trials or a broader approach?

International Journal for Quality in Health Care, 16(5), 407-416.

Dennett, D. C. (1991). *Consciousness explained.* New York: The Penguin Press.

Dennis, A., & Wixom, B. H. (2003). *Systems analysis and design* (2nd ed.). Toronto: John Wiley & Sons.

DeSanctis, G., & Poole, M. (1994). Capturing the complexity in advanced technology use: Adaptive structuration theory. *Organizational Science, 5*(2), 121-147.

DiCenso, A. (1999). Evidenced-based medicine, evidenced-based nursing. *Expert Nurse, 15*(12), 92-97.

Donaldson, C., Mugford, M., & Vale, L. (2002). Using systematic reviews in economic evaluation. In *Evidence-based health economics. From effectiveness to efficiency in systematic review.* London: BMJ Books.

Donelle, L., Arocha, J. F., & Hoffman-Goetz, L. (2007). *Colorectal cancer risk comprehension of older Canadians: Impact of health numeracy.* Paper presented at the ITCH: Today's Information for Tomorrow's Improvements, Victoria, BC Canada.

Donelle, L., Arocha, J. F., & Hoffman-Goetz, L. (in press). Colorectal cancer risk comprehension of older Canadians: Impact of health numeracy. *Chronic Diseases in Canada.*

Dooley, K. (1997). A complex adaptive systems model of organization change. *Nonlinear Dynamics, Psychology, and Life Sciences, 1*(1).

Doran, D. M., & Sidani, S. (2007). Outcomes focused knowledge translation: A framework for knowledge translation and patient outcomes improvement. *Worldviews on Evidence-Based Nursing, 4*(1), 3-13.

Doran, D. M., Harrison, J. M., Spence-Laschinger, H., Hirdes, J., Rukhom, E., Sidani, S., et al. (2006). Nursing sensitive outcomes data collection in acute care and long-term care settings. *Nursing Research, 55*(2S), S75-S81.

Doran, D. M., Mylopoulos, J., Kushniruk, A., Nagle, L., Sidani, S., Laurie-Shaw, B. et al. (2007). Evidence in the palm of your hand: Development of an outcome-focused knowlede translation intervention. *Worldviews on Evidence-Based Nursing, 4*(2), 69-77.

Downing, G. M. (Ed.). (2006). *Medical care of the dying* (4th ed.). Victoria Hospice Society Learning Centre for Palliative Care.

Drummond, M. F., & Jefferson, T. O. (1996). Guidelines for authors and peer reviewers of economic submissions to the BMJ. The BMJ Economic Evaluation Working Party. *British Medical Journal, 313*(7052), 275-283.

Duke Clinical Research Institute (2005). *FDA public meeting.* Retrieved March 13, 2006, from www.fda.gov/cder/meeting/ICHspring2005/ Nahm.ppt

Eason, K.D. (1991). Ergonomic perspectives on advances in human-computer interaction. *Ergnomics, 34,* 721.

Eccles, M., McColl, E., Steen, N., Rousseau, N., Grimshaw, J., Parkin, D., & Purves, I. (2002). Effect of computerized evidence based guidelines on management of asthma and angina in adults in primary care: Cluster randomized controlled trial. *British Medical Journal, 325*(7370), 941.

Edelstein, L. (1923). *The hippocratic oath.* Baltimore: Johns Hopkins Press.

Edwards, J. (2006). *Case study: Denmark's achievements with healthcare information exchange.* Gartner Industry Research.

Edwards, N., & Roloefs, S. (2006). Developing management systems with cross-cultural fit: assessing international differences in operational systems. *International Journal Health Planning Management, 21,* 55-73.

Eisenstein, E. L. (2006). Conducting an economic analysis to assess the electrocardiogram's value. *Journal of Electrocardiology, 39*(2), 241-247.

Eisenstein, E. L., & Mark, D. B. (2004). Cost effectiveness of new diagnostic tools and therapies for acute coronary syndromes. In E.J.Topol (Ed.), *Acute Coronary Syndromes* (3rd ed., pp. 723-745). New York: Marcel Dekker.

Eisenstein, E. L., Ortiz, M., Anstrom, K. J., Crosslin, D. R., & Lobach, D. F. (2006). Assessing the quality of medical information technology economic evaluations: room for improvement. *AMIA 2006 Annual Symposium Proceedings* (pp. 228-234).

Ellis, C. A., Gibbs, S. J., & Rein, G. L. (1991). Group-ware-some issues and experience. *Communication of the ACM, 34*(1), 38-58.

Elrod, P. D., & Tippett, D. D. (2002). The 'death valley' of change. *Journal of Organizational Change Management, 15*(3), 273-291.

Elving, W. J. L. (2005). The role of communication in organizational change. *Corporate Communications, 10*(2), 129-139.

Embi, P. J., Jain, A., Clark, J., & Harris, C. M. (2005). Development of an electronic health record-based Clinical Trial Alert system to enhance recruitment at the point of care. *AMIA Annu Symp Proceedings* (pp. 231-235).

Embi, P. J., Jain, A., Clark, J., Bizjack, S., Hornung, R., & Harris, C. M. (2005). Effect of a clinical trial alert system on physician participation in trial recruitment. *Arch Intern Med, 165*(19), 2272-2277.

Engel, G. L. (1977). The need for a new medical model: a challenge for biomedicine. *Science, 196*(4286), 129.

Engel, K., Blobel, B., & Pharow, P. (2006). Standards for enabling health informatics interoperability. In A. Hasman, R. Haux, J. van der Lei, E. De Clercq, & F.H. Roger France (Eds.),*Ubiquity: technologies for better health in aging societies, Procedings of MIE2006. Studies in Health Technology and Informatics 124*, 145-150.

Ericsson. K.A., & Simon, H.A. (1993). *Protocol analysis: Verbal reports as data* (2nd ed.). Cambridge, MA: MIT Press.

Eshach, H., & Bitterman, H. (2003). From case-based reasoning to problem-based learning. *Academic Medicine, 78*(5), 491-496.

Estabrooks, C. A., O'Leary, K. A., Ricker, K. L., & Humphrey, C. K. (2003). The internet and access to evi-dence: how are nurses positioned. *Journal of Advanced Nursing, 42*(1), 73-81.

Estrada, C. A., Hryniewicz, M. M., Higgs, V. B., Collins, C., & Byrd, J. C. (2000). Anticoagulant patient information material is written at high readability levels. *Stroke, 31*(12), 2966-2970.

EU Directive 95/46 EC. (1995). *On the protection of individuals with regard to the processing of personal data and on the free movement of such data.* Retrieved from http://www.cdt.org/privacy/eudirective/EU_Direc-tive_.html

Evans, R.S., Pestotnik, S.L., Classen, D.C., Clemmer, T.R., Weaver, L.K., Orme, J.F. et al. (1998). A computer assisted management program for antibiotics and other antiinfective agents. *New England Journal of Medicine, 338*(4), 232-238.

Ewald, P. W. (2004). Evolution of virulence. *Infect Dis Clin North Am, 18*(1), 1-15.

Felciano, R.M., & Altman, R.B. (1996). Lamprey: Track-ing users on the World Wide Web, *Proceedings of the 1996 AMIA Annual Fall Symposium* (pp. 757-761).

Ferris, N. (2006, October 17). Us vs. them: Regional health information exchanges require participants to dampen the urge to compete. But it's not clear yet whether collabo-ration is more powerful than competition, *Government Health IT.* Retreived October 17, 2006, from http://www.govhealthit.com/article96347-10-09-06-Print

Fessler, J.M., & Gremy, F. (2001). Ethical problems in health information systems. *Methods of Information in Medicine, 40*(4), 359-61

Finkelstein, S. M., Scudiero, A., Lindgren, B., Snyder, M., & Hertz, M. I. (2005). Decision support for the tri-age of lung transplant recipients on the basis of home monitoring spirometry and symptom reporting. *Heart & Lung, 34*(3), 201-208.

Finlay, P.N. (1994). *Introducing decision support systems.* Oxford, UK: Blackwell Publishers.

Fiscal Year 2008. Retrieved July 27, 2007, from http://www.whitehouse.gov/omb/budget/

Fitts, P. M. (1954). The information capacity of the human motor system in controlling the amplitude of movement, J. of Exp. *Psychology, 47*, 381-392.

Fitts, P. M. (1992). The information capacity of the human motor system in controlling the amplitude of movement. *Journal of Experimental Psychology: General, 121*(3), 262-269.

Flesch, R. A. (1948). A new readability yardstick. *Journal of Applied Psychology, 32*, 221-233.

Flowers, L., & Riley, T. (2001). *State-based mandatory reporting of medical errors: An analysis of the legal and policy issues.* Portland, ME: National Academy for State Health Policy.

Floyd, S.W., & Wooldridge, B. (1992). Middle management involvement in strategy and its association with strategic type: A research note. *Strategic Management Journal, 13*, 153-167.

Fogel, J. (2003). Internet use for cancer information among racial/ethnic populations and low literacy groups. *Cancer Control, 10*(5 Suppl), 45-51.

Forbis, S. G., & Aligne, C. A. (2002). Poor readability of written asthma management plans found in national guidelines. *Pediatrics, 109*(4), e52.

Fordis, M., King, J.E., Ballantyne, C.M. et al. (2005). Comparison of the instructional efficacy of Internet-based CME with live interactive CME workshops: A randomized controlled trial. *Journal of the American Medical Association 294*(9), 1043-1051.

Fraser, S., & Greenhalgh, T. (2001). Coping with complexity: Educating for capability. *British Medical Journal, 323*(7216), 799-803.

Freudenheim, M., & Pear, R. (2006). Health hazard: Computers spilling your history. *New York Times*, December 3, Section 3.

Friedman, D. B., & Hoffman-Goetz, L. (2006). A systematic review of readability and comprehension instruments used for print and Web-based cancer information. *Health Education and Behavior, 33*(3), 352-373.

Friedman, D. B., & Hoffman-Goetz, L. (in press). Assessing cultural sensitivity of breast cancer information for older Aboriginal women. *Journal of Cancer Education.*

Friedman, D. B., Hoffman-Goetz, L., & Arocha, J. F. (2004). Readability of cancer information on the internet. *Journal of Cancer Education, 19*(2), 117-122.

Friedman, D. B., Hoffman-Goetz, L., & Arocha, J. F. (2006). Health literacy and the World Wide Web: Comparing the readability of leading incident cancers on the internet. *Medical Informatics and the Internet in Medicine, 31*(1), 67-87.

Frisse, M. C. (1999). The business value of healthcare information technology. *Journal of the American Medical Informatics Association, 6*(5), 361-367.

Frisse, M. E. (1992). Medical informatics in academic health science centers. *Acad Med, 67*(4), 238-241.

Frisse, M. E. (2006). Comments on Return on Investment (ROI) as it applies to clinical systems. *Journal of American Medical Information Association*, M2072.

Frize, M., & Walker, R. (2000). Clinical decision support systems for intensive care units using case-based reasoning. *Medical Engineering & Physics, 22*(9), 671-677.

Fui-Hoon Nah, F., Lau J., & Kuang, J. (2001). Critical factors for successful implementation of enterprise systems. *Business Process Management Journal, 7*(3), 285-296.

Gamm, L. D., Barsukiewicz, C. K., Dansky, K. H., & Vasey, J. J. (1998). Investigating changes in end-user satisfaction with installation of an electronic medical record in ambulatory care settings. *Journal of Healthcare Information Management, 12*(4), 53-65.

Gandhi, T. K. (2005). Fumbled handoffs: one dropped ball after another. *Ann Intern Med, 142*(5), 352-358.

Ganguly, P., & Ray, P. (2000). Software interoperability of telemedicine systems: A CSCW perspective. *Proceedings of the 7th International Conference on Parallel and Distributed Systems (ICPADS'00)* (pp. 349-354).

Gardner, R. M., Pryor, T. A., & Warner, H. R. (1999). The HELP hospital information system: Update 1998. *International Journal of Medicin Information, 54*(3), 169-182.

Garg, A. X., Adhikari, N. K. J., McDonald, H., Rosas-Arellano, M. P., Devereaux, P. J., Beyene, J., et al. (2005). Effects of computerized clinical decision support systems on practitioner performance and patient outcomes. *JAMA, 293*(10), 1223-1238.

Garrety, K., Roberston, P. L., & Badham, R. (2004). Integrating communities of practice in technology development projects. *International Journal of Project Management, 22*(2004), 351 - 358.

Garro, L. C. (1994). Narrative representations of chronic illness experience: Cultural models of illness, mind, and body in stories concerning the temporomandibular joint. *Social Science & Medicine, 38*(6), 775-788.

Gawande, A. A., Thomas, E. J., Zinner, M. J., et al. (1999). The incidence and nature of surgical adverse events in Colorado and Utah in 1992. *Surgery, 126*(1), 66-75.

Gerdsen, F., Mueller, S., Jablonski, S., & Prokosch, H. U. (2005). Standardized exchange of medical data between a research database, an electronic patient record and an electronic health record using CDA/SCIPHOX. *AMIA Annu Symp Proc*, 963.

Gesteland, P. H., Nebeker, J. R., & Gardner, R. M. (2006). These are the technologies that try men's souls: common-sense health information technology. *Pediatrics, 117*(1), 216-217.

Girosi, F., Melli, R., & Scoville, R. (2005). Extrapolating evidence of health information technology savings and costs. *RAND Corporation*. Retrieved December 01, 2006 from http://www.rand.org/pubs/monographs/MG410/index.html)

Glaser, J. P. (2005). Facilitating applied information technology research. *Journal of Healthcare Information Management, 19*(1), 45-53.

Glieck, J. (1987). *Chaos: making a new science*. New York: Penguin Books.

Goddard, B.L. (2000). Termination of a contract to implement an enterprise electronic medical record system. *Journal of the American Medical Informatics Association, 7*(6), 564-568.

Gold, M. R., Siegel, J., Russell, L., & Weinstein, M. (1996). *Cost-effectiveness in health and medicine*. New York: Oxford University Press.

Golden, B.R., & Martin, R.L. (2004). Aligning the stars: Using systems thinking to (re)design Canadian healthcare. *Healthcare Quarterly, 7*(4), 34-42.

Goldman, L., Weinstein, M. C., Goldman, P. A., & Williams, L. W. (1991). Cost-effectiveness of HMG-CoA reductase inhibition for primary and secondary prevention of coronary heart disease. *Journal of the American Medical Association, 265*(9), 1145-1151.

Goldstein, M. K., Coleman, R. W., Tu, S. W., Shankar, R. D., O'Connor, M. J., Musen, M. A., et al. (2004). Translating research into practice: organizational issues in implementing automated decision support for hypertension in three medical centers. *Journal of American Medical Information Association, 11*(5), 368-376.

Goransson, B., Lind, M., Pettersson, E., Sandblad, B., & Schwalbe, P. (1986). The interface is often not the problem. *Proceedings of the SIGCHI/GI Conference on Human Factors in Computing Systems and Graphics Interface* (pp. 133-136).

Gordon, S.E., & Gill, R.T. (1997). Cognitive task analysis. In C.E. Zsambok & G. Klein (Eds.), *Naturalistic decision making* (pp. 131-140). Mahwah, NJ: Lawrence Erlbaum Associates.

Gostin, L.O., Lazzarini, Z., Neslund, V.S., & Osterholm, M.T. (1996). The public health information infrastructure. A national review of the law on health information privacy. *JAMA, 275(24)*, 1921-7

Graber, M. L., Franklin, N., & Gordon, R. (2005). Diagnostic error in internal medicine. Am Med Assoc.

Graham, D. J., Campen, D., Hui, R., Spence, M., Cheetham, C., Levy, G., et al. (2005). Risk of acute myocardial infarction and sudden cardiac death in patients treated with cyclo-oxygenzse 2 selective and non-selective non-steroidal anti-inflammatory drugs: Nested case-control study. *Lancet, 365*(9458), 475-481.

Green, L. A., White, L. L., Barry, H. C., Nease, D. E., Jr., & Hudson, B. L. (2005). Infrastructure requirements for practice-based research networks. *Ann Fam Med, 3 Suppl 1*, S5-11.

Greenberg, C. C., Regenbogen, S. E., Studdert, D. M., Lipsitz, S. R., Rogers, S. O., Zinner, M. J. et al. (2007). Patterns of communication breakdowns resulting in injury to surgical patients. *Journal Am Coll Surg, 204*(4), 533-540.

Greenes, R. A., & Shortliffe, E. H. (1990). Medical informatics: An rmerging scademic fiscipline and institutional policy. *JAMA, 263*(8), 1114-1120.

Gremy F. (1994). Comments on: Health information, the fair information principles and ethics. *Methods of Information in Medicine, 33*, 346-7.

Grieger, D. L., Cohen, S. H., & Krusch, D. A. (2007). A pilot study to document the return on investment for implementing an ambulatory electronic health record at an academic medical center. *Journal of the American College of Surgeons, 205*(1), 89-96.

Grimshaw, J. M., & Eccles, M. P. (2004). Is evidence-based implementation of evidence-based care possible? *Medical Journal of Australia, 180*(6 Suppl), S50-S51.

Grimshaw, J. M., Santesso, N., Cumpston, M., Mayhew, A., & McGowan, J. (2006). Knowledge for knowledge translation: The role of the cochrane collaboration. *Journal of Continuing Education in the Health Professions, 26*(1), 55-62.

Grol, R., & Grimshaw, J. (2003). From best evidence to best practice: Effective implementation of change in patients' care. *The Lancet, 362*, 1225-1230.

Grudin, J. (1994). CSCW: History and focus. *IEEE Computer, 27*(5), 19-26.

Grundy, T., & Brown, L. (2002). *Strategic project management: Creating organizational breakthroughs.* London: Thomson Learning.

Gustav Bellika, J., & Hartvigsen, G. (2005). The oncologocal nurse assistant: A web-based intelligent oncological nurse advisor. *Medical Informatics, 74*, 587-595.

Hackney, R., & McBride, N. (2002). Non-implementation of an IS strategy within a UK hospital: observations from a longitudinal case analysis. *Communications of the AIS, 8*(8), 2-20.

Hage, J. (1980). *Theories of organizational: Form, process, and transformation.* New York: John Wiley.

Haimes, Y. Y., & Schneiter, C. (1996). Covey's seven habits and the systems approach: A Comparative Approach. *IEEE transactions on Systems, Man and Cybernetics, 26*(4), 483-487.

Halamka, J. (2006). Early experiences with e-prescribing. *Journal of Healthcare Information Management, 20*(2), 12-14.

Halamka, J. D., Osterland, C., & Safran, C. (1999). CareWeb, a web-based medical record for an integrated health care delivery system. *International Journal of Medicine Information, 54*(1), 1-8.

Halamka, J., Aranow, M., Asenzo, C., Bates, D., Debor, G., Glaser, J. et al. (2005). Healthcare IT collaboration in Massachusetts: The experience of creating regional connectivity. *Journal of the American Medical Informatics Association, 12*(6), 596-601.

Halamka, J., Overhage, J. M., Ricciardi, L., Rishel, W., Shirky, C., & Diamond, C. (2005). Exchanging health information: Local distribution, national coordination. *Health Aff (Millwood), 24*(5), 1170-1179.

Halley, E.C., Kambic, P.M. & et al. (1996). Concurrent process redesign and clinical documentation system implementation: A 6-month success story. *Topics in Health Information Management, 17*(1), 12-17.

Han, J., & Kamber, M. (2001). *Data mining: Concepts and techniques.* New York: Morgan Kaufman Publishers.

Han, Y. Y., Carcillo, J. A., Venkataraman, S. T., Clark, R. S., Watson, R. S., Nguyen, T., et al. (2005). Unexpected increased mortality after implementation of a commercially sold physician order entry system. *Pediatrics, 116*(6), 1506-1512.

Han, Y. Y., Carcillo, J. A., Venkataraman, S. T., Clark, R. S., Watson, R. S., Nguyen, T. C. et al. (2005). Unexpected increased mortality after implementation of a commercially sold computerized physician order entry system. *Pediatrics, 116*(6), 1506-1512.

Hanzlicek, P., Zvarova, J., & Dostal, C. (2006). Information technology in clinical research in rheumatology domain. *Stud Health Technol Inform, 124*, 187-192.

Hauschildt, J. (1999). Promotors and champions in innovations—development of a research paradigm. In K. Brockhoff, A. K. Chakrabarti & J. Hauschildt (Eds.), *The dynamics of innovation—strategic and managerial implications.*

Haux, R. (2006). Health information systems: Past, present, future. *International Journal of Medical Informatics, 75(3-4 special issue)*, 268-281.

Haynes, R. (1998). Using informatics principles and tools to harness research evidence for patient care: Evidence-based informatics. *Medinfo, 9*(Pt 1 Suppl), 33-36.

Health Canada .(2006). *eHealth*. Retrieved on May 4, 2007, from http://www.hc-sc.gc.ca/hcs-sss/ehealth-esante/index_e.html

Health Canada, Economic Impact of Health, Income Security and Labour Policies on Informal Caregivers of Frail Seniors: http://www.swc-cfc.gc.ca/pubs/pub-spr/0662654765/200103_0662654765_8_e.html

Heavy, S. R. (2006). House approves health data technology bill. Retrieved August 1, 2006, from http://news.yahoo.com/s/nm/20060728/hl_nm/congress_health_technology_dc

Hebert, M. (2001). Telehealth success: Evaluation framework development. *Medinfo, 10*, 1145-1149.

Heeks, R. (2006). Health information systems: failure, success and improvisation. *International Journal of Medical Informatics, 75*, 125-137

Heeks, R., Mundy, D., & Salazar, A. (1999). *Why health care information systems succeed or fail. Information systems for public sector management. Working paper series 9.* Manchester: Institute for Development Policy Management.

Heffner, J. E. (2001). Altering physician behavior to improve clinical performance. *Topics in Health Information Management, 22*(2), 1-9.

Hersh, B., Stavri & Detmer. D. (2006). *Information retrieval and digital libraries* (pp. 660-697). In T. E. Shortliffe & J. J. Cimino (Eds.), *Biomedical informatics: Computer applications in healthcare and biomedicine* (3rd ed.). New York: Springer.

Hersh, W. (2006). Who are the informaticians? What we know and should know. *Journal of American Medical Information Association, 13*(2), 166-170.

Hicks, R.W., Santell, J.P., Cousins, D.D., & Williams, R.L. (2004). *MEDMARX 5th anniversary data report: A chartbook of 2003 findings and trends 1999-2003.* Rockville, MD: U.S. Pharmacopeia.

Hier, D. B., Rothschild, A., LeMaistre, A., & Keeler, J. (2005). Differing faculty and housestaff acceptance of an electronic health record. *International Journal of Medicine Information, 74*(7-8), 657-662.

Hill, J. W., Green, P. S., Jensen, J. F., Gorfu, Y., & Shah, A. S. (1994). Telepresence surgery demonstration system. *Robotics and Automation, 1994. Proceedings, 1994 IEEE International Conference* (pp. 2302-2307).

Hillestad, R., Bigelow, J., Bower, A., Girosi, F., Meili, R., Scoville, R. et al. (2005). Can electronic medical record systems transform health care? Potential health benefits, savings, and costs. *Health Aff (Millwood), 24*(5), 1103-1117.

Hills, J. W., & Jensen, J. F. (1998). Telepresence technology in medicine: Principles and applications. *Proceedings of the IEEE, 86*(3), 569-580.

Hippisley-Cox, J., Pringle, M., Cater, R. & et al. (2003). The Electronic patient record in primary care - Regression or progression? A cross sectional study. *British Medical Journal, 326*, 1439-1443.

Ho, K., Bloch, R., Gondocz, T., Laprise, R., Perrier, L., Ryan, D., et al. (2004). Technology-enabled knowledge translation: Frameworks to promote research and practice. *Journal of Continuing Education of the Health Professions, 24*(2), 90-99.

Ho, K., Borduas, F., Frank, B., Hall, P., Handsfield-Jones, R., Hardwick, D., et al. (2006). *Facilitating the integration of interprofessional education into quality healthcare: strategic roles of academic institutions.* Report to Health Canada Interprofessional Education for Collaborative Patient Centred Practice. October 2006.

Ho, K., Chockalingam, A., Best, A., & Walsh, G. (2003). Technology-enabled knowledge translation: Building a framework for collaboration. *Canadian Medical Association Journal, 168*(6), 710-711.

Ho, K., Karlinsky, H., Jarvis-Selinger, S., & May, J. (2004). Videoconferencing for Telehealth: unexpected challenges and unprecedented opportunities. *British Columbia Medical Journal, 46*(6), 285-289.

Hodge J.G., Gostin, L.O., & Jacobson, P.D. (1999). Legal issues concerning electronic health information: Privacy, quality, and liability. *Journal of the American Medical Association, 282*(15), 1466.

Hodgkinson, C. (1996). *Administrative philosophy.* Oxford: Pergamon.

Hoffman-Goetz, L., Friedman, D. B., & Celestine, A. (2006). Evaluation of a public library workshop: teaching older adults how to search the internet for reliable cancer information. *Journal of Consumer Health on the Internet, 10*(3), 29-43.

Hollan, J., Hutchins, E., & Kirsh, D. (2000). Distributed cognition: Toward a new foundation for human-computer interaction research. *ACM Transactions on Computer-Human Interaction (TOCHI), 7*(2), 174-196.

Holland, P., Light, B., & Gibson, N. (1999). A critical success factors model for enterprise resource planning implementation. *Proceedings of the 7th European Conference on Information Systems, 1,* 273-297.

Hopko, D. R., Mahadevan, R., Bare, R. L., & Hunt, M. K. (2003). The Abbreviated Math Anxiety Scale (AMAS): Construction, validity, and reliability. *Assessment, 10*(2), 178-182.

Horsky, J., Kaufman, D. R., & Patel, V. L. (2003). The cognitive complexity of a provider order entry interface. *AMIA Annu Symp Proc, 2003* (pp. 294-298).

Horsky, J., Kuperman, G. J., & Patel, V. L. (2005). Comprehensive analysis of a medication dosing error related to CPOE. *Journal of American Medical Information Association, 12*(4), 377-382.

Horsky, J., Kuperman, G.J., & Patel, V.L. (2005). Comprehensive analysis of a medication dosage error related to CPOE. *Journal of the American Medical Informatics Association, 12*(4), 377-82.

Horsky, J., Zhang, J., & Patel, V.L. (2005). To err is not entirely human: Complex technology and user cognition. *Journal of Biomedical Informatics, 38*(4), 264-266.

Househ, M. S., & Lau, F. Y. (2005). Collaborative technology use by healthcare teams. *Journal of Medical Systems, 29*(5), 449-461.

Hsieh, T. C., Gandhi, T. K., Seger, A. C., Overhage, J. M., Murray, M. D., Hope, C. et al. (2004). Identification of adverse drug events in the outpatient setting using a computerized, text-searching monitor. *Medinfo, 2004*(CD), 1651.

Hsieh, T. C., Kuperman, G. J., Jaggi, T., Hojnowski-Diaz, P., Fiskio, J., Williams, D. H. et al. (2004). Characteristics and consequences of drug allergy alert overrides in a computerized physician order entry system. *Journal of American Medical Information Association, 11*(6), 482-491.

Hunt, D. L., Haynes, R. B., Hanna, S. E., & Smith, K. (1998). Effects of computer-based clinical decision support systems on physician performance and patient outcomes: A systematic review [see comments]. *Jama, 280*(15), 1339-1346.

Hutchins, E. (1995). *Cognition in the wild.* MIT Press.

Hutchins, E. (1995). How a cockpit remembers its speeds. *Cognitive Science, 19*(3), 265-288.

Hutchins, E., & Klausen, T. (1996). Distributed cognition in an airline cockpit. *Cognition and Communication at Work*, 15-34.

Im, E. U., & Chee, W. (2006). Nurses' acceptance of the decision support computer program for cancer pain management. *Computers, Informatics, Nursing, 24*(2), 95-104.

Imhoff, M., Webb, A., Goldschmidt, A. (2001). Health informatics. *Intensive Care Medicine. 27*(1), 179-86.

Infoway. (2006). *Beyond good intentions: Accelerating the electronic health record in Canada*. Canada Health Infoway Montebello Policy Conference.

Ingenerf, J., Reiner, J., & Seik, B. (2001). Standardized terminological services enabling semantic interoperability between distributed and heterogenous systems. *International Journal of Medical Informatics, 64*, 223-240.

Institute for Healthcare Improvement. (2006). *Leadership guide to patient safety*. Cambridge, MA: Institute for Healthcare Improvement.

Institute for Healthcare Improvement. (2007). How to improve: improvement methods. Retrieved on June 7, 2007 from http://www.ihi.org/IHI/Topics/Improvement/ImprovementMethods/HowToImprove/

Institute of Medicine (U.S.). Committee on Improving the Patient Record., Dick, R. S., & Steen, E. B. (1991). *The computer-based patient record: an essential technology for health care*. Washington, D.C.: National Academy Press.

Institute of Medicine of the National Academies. (2003). Health professions education: a bridge to quality. *Institute of Medicine April 8, 2003 Report*. Retrieved June 9, 2007, from http://www.iom.edu/CMS/3809/4634/5914.aspx

Institute of Medicine. (1999). *To err is human: Building a safer health system*. Washington, DC: National Academy Press.

Institute of Medicine. (2001). *Crossing the quality chasm: A new health system for the twenty-first century*. Washington: National Academy Press.

Institute of Medicine. (2001). *Crossing the quality chasm: A new health system for the 21st century*. Washington, D.C.: National Academy Press.

International Medical Informatics Association. (IMIA). (2002). *Code of ethics for health informatics professionals*. Retrieved from http://www.imia.org/code_of_ethics.html

ISO 20514 (2005) *Electronic health record—definition, scope and context*.

ISO/TS 18308 (2003). *Requirements for an electronic health record architecture*.

IT Definition. (2007). Retrieved January 15, 2007, from http://www.webopedia.com/TERM/I/IT.html

Jaffery, J. B., & Becker, B. N. (2004). Evaluation of ehealth Web sites for patients with chronic kidney disease. *American Journal of Kidney Diseases S, 44*(1), 71-76.

JCAHO to look closely at patient handoffs. (2006). *Hosp Case Manag, 14*(1), 9-10.

Jda. (1968, March 15). *Avanceret databehandlingsanlæg med "fjernsynsskærme" til Rigshospitalet*. Ingeniørens Ugeblad,

Jeffcott, M. A., & Johnson, C. W. (2002). The use of a formalised risk model in NHS information system development. *Cognition, Technology & Work, 4*, 120 - 136.

Jenkins, D. & Emmett, S. (1997). The ethical dilemma of health education. *Professional Nurse, 12*(6), 426-428.

Johansen, I. (2006). *What makes a high performance health care system and how do we get there?* Paper presented at the Commonwealth Fund. Washington, DC.

John, B. (1995). Why GOMS? *Interactions, 2*(4), 80-89.

John, B. E., & Kieras, D. E. (1996). The GOMS family of user interface analysis techniques: Comparison and contrast. *ACM Transactions on Computer-Human Interaction, 3*(4), 320-351.

Kahneman, D., Slovic, P., & Tversky, A. (1982). *Judgment under uncertainty: Heuristics and biases.* Cambridge, New York: Cambridge University Press.

Kaner, C., Falk, J., & Nguyen, H.Q. (1999). *Testing computer software* (2nd ed.). New York: Wiley & Sons.

Kannry, J. (2007). CPOE and patient safety: Panacea or pandora's box? In K. Ong (Ed.), *Medical informatics: An executive primer.* Chicago: HIMSS.

Kannry, J., & Moore, C. (1999). MediSign: using a web-based SignOut system to improve provider identification. *Proceedings AMIA Symp*, 550-554.

Kannry, J., Emro, S., Blount, M., Elbing, M., & (2007). *Small-scale testing of RFID in a hospital setting: RFID as bed trigger.* Paper presented at the AMIA Fall Symposium 2007, Chicago, Ill.

Kannry, J., Moore, C., & Karson, T. (2003). Discharge communique: Use of a workflow byproduct to generate an interim discharge summary. *AMIA Annu Symp Proc*, 341-345.

Kannry, J., Mukani, S., & Myers, K. (2006). Using an evidence-based approach for system selection at a large academic medical center: lessons learned in selecting an ambulatory EMR at Mount Sinai Hospital. *Journal of Healthcare Information Management, 20*(2), 84-99.

Kaphingst, K. A., Zanfini, C. J., & Emmons, K. M. (2006). Accessibility of Web sites containing colorectal cancer information to adults with limited literacy. *Cancer Causes & Control, 17*(2), 147-151.

Kaplan, B. (1988). Development and acceptance of medical information systems: An historical overview. *Journal of Health Human Resource Administration, 11*(1), 9-29.

Kaplan, B. (1995). Information technology and three studies of clinical work. *ACM SIGBIO Newsl, 15*(2), 2-5.

Kaplan, B. (2001). Evaluating informatics applications: Some alternative approaches: Theory, social interactionism, and call for methodological pluralism. *International Journal of Medical Informatics, 64*, 39-56.

Kaplan, B. (2001). Evaluating informatics applications? Social interactionism and call for methodological pluralism. *International Journal of Medical Informatics, 64*(1), 39-56.

Kaplan, B. (2001). Evaluating informatics applications-some alternative approaches: Theory, social interactionism, and call for methodological pluralism. *Int J Med Inform, 64*(1), 39-56.

Kaplan, B., & Duchon, D. (1998). Combining qualitative and quantitative approaches in information systems research: A case study. *Management Information Systems, 12*(4), 571-586.

Kaplan, B., & Maxwell, J.A. (1994). Qualitative Research Methods for Evaluating Computer Information Systems. In J.G. Anderson, C.E. Aydin, & S.J. Jay (Eds.), *Evaluating health care information systems: Methods and applications* (pp. 45-68). Thousand Oaks, CA: Sage.

Kaplan, B., Shaw, N. (2004). Future directions in evaluation research: People, organizational, and social issues. *Methods of Information in Medicine, 43*(3-4), 215-231.

Kaplan, S. M., & Fitzpatrick, G. (1997). Designing support for remote intensive-care telehealth using the locales framework. *Proceedings of the conference on Designing interactive systems: processes, practices, methods, and techniques*, (pp. 173-184).

Kaptelinin, V., Nardi, B., Bødker, S., Carroll, J., Hollan, J., Hutchins, E. et al. (2003). Post-cognitivist HCI: second-wave theories. *Conference on Human Factors in Computing Systems* (pp. 692-693).

Katzenbach, J. R., & Smith, D. K. (2005 reprint). The discipline of teams. *Harvard Business Review 83*(7), 162-171.

Kaushal, R., Blumenthal, D., Poon, E. G., Jha, A. K., Franz, C., Middleton, B. et al. (2005). The costs of a national health information network. *Ann Intern Med, 143*(3), 165-173.

Kaushal, R., Jha, A. K., Franz, C., Glaser, J., Shetty, K. D., Jaggi, T. et al. (2006). Return on investment for a computerized physician order entry system 10.1197/jamia.

M1984. *Journal of American Medical Information Association*, M1984.

Kaushal, R., Jha, A. K., Franz, C., Glaser, J., Shetty, K. D., Jaggi, T., et al. (2006). Return on investment for a computerized physician order entry system. *Journal of the American Medical Informatics Association, 13*(3), 261-266.

Kawamoto, K., & Lobach, D. F. (2005). Design, implementation, use, and preliminary evaluation of SEBASTIAN, a standards-based web service for clinical decision support. *AMIA Symposium 2005*, 380-384.

Kawamoto, K., Houlihan, C. A., Balas, E. A., & Lobach, D. F. (2005). Improving clinical decision support systems: A systematic review of trials to identify features critical to success. *BMJ, 330*(7494), 765-792.

Kay, S., & Purves, I. (1996). Medical records and other stories: A narratological framework. *Methods of Information in Medicine, 35*, 72-88.

Keeler, E. B., & Cretin, S. (1983). Discounting of life-saving and other nonmonetary effects. *Management Science, 29*, 300-306.

Keeling, R. (2000). *Project management: An international perspective*. London: MacMillan Press Ltd.

Keenan, C. R., Nguyen, H. H., & Srinivasan, M. (2006). Electronic medical records and their impact on resident and medical student education. *Acad Psychiatry, 30*(6), 522-527.

Keil, M., Cule, P. E., Lyytinen, K., & Schimdt, R.C. (1998). A framework for identifying software project risk. *Communications of the ACM, 41*(11), 76-83.

Kemper, A. R., Uren, R. L., & Clark, S. J. (2006). Adoption of electronic health records in primary care pediatric practices. *Pediatrics, 118*(1), e20-24.

Kendeou, P., & Van Den Broek, P. (2005). The effects of readers' misconceptions on comprehension of scientific text. *Journal of Educational Psychology, 97*(2), 235-245.

Keshavjee, K., Bosomworth, J., Copen, J., et al. (2006). Best Practices in EMR Implementation: A Systematic Review. *iSHIMR Proceedings*, (pp. 233-246).

Keshavjee, K.S., Troyan, S., Holbrook, A.M., & Vandermolen, D. (2001). Measuring the success of electronic medical record implementation using electronic and survey data. *AMIA Annual Symposium Proceedings*, 309-313.

Kieras, D. E. (1997). Task analysis and the design of functionality. *The Computer Science and Engineering Handbook. Boca Raton, CRC Inc* (pp. 1401-1423).

Killing, J.P. (1988). Understanding alliance: The role of task and organizational complexity. In F. Contractor & P. Lorange (Eds.), *Cooperative strategies in international business*. Lexington Books.

Kintsch, W. (1998). *Comprehension: A paradigm for cognition*. Cambridge, New York, NY: Cambridge University Press.

Kitson, A. (2002). Recognising relationships: Reflections on evidence-based practice. *Nursing Inquiry, 9*(3), 179-186.

Kleinke, J. D. (2005). Dot-gov: Market failure and the creation of a national health information technology system. *Health Aff (Millwood), 24*(5), 1246-1262.

Kluge, E.-H. (1993). Advanced patient records: Some ethical and legal considerations touching medical information space. *Methods of Information in Medicine, 32*, 95-103.

Kluge, E.-H. (1996). The medical record: Narration and story as a path through patient data. *Methods of Information in Medicine, 35*, 88-92.

Kluge, E.-H. (2001). *The ethics of electronic patient records*. New York; Bern: Peter Lang.

Kluge, E.W. (2005). *Readings in biomedical ethics: A Canadian focus*.(3rd ed.). Prentice Hall.

Kohn, K. T., Corrigan, J. M., & Donaldson, M. S. (Eds.). (1999). *To err is human: Building a safer health system*. Washington, DC: National Academy Press.

Kohn, L. T. (2000). *To err is human*. National Acad. Press.

Koornneef, F., & Voges, U. (2002). Programmable electronic medical systems-related risks and learning from accidents. *Health Informatics Journal, 8,* 78-87.

Koppel, R., Metlay, J. P., Cohen, A., Abaluck, B., Localio, A. R., Kimmel, S. E., et al. (2005). Role of computerized physician-order entry systems in facilitating medication errors. *JAMA, 293*(10), 1197-1203.

Koppel, R., Metlay, J. P., Cohen, A., Abaluck, B., Localio, A. R., Kimmel, S. E. et al. (2005). Role of computerized physician order entry systems in facilitating medication errors. *Jama, 293*(10), 1197-1203.

Kotter, J. (1995). Leading change: Why transformation efforts fail. *Harvard Business Review, March-April,* 59-67.

Kotter, J. P. (1996). *Leading change.* Boston: Harvard Business School Press.

Kouzes, J. M., & Posner, B. Z. (1990). The credibility factor: what followers expect from their leaders. *Business Credit, 92*(5), 24-28.

Kraut, R. E. (2003). Applying social psychological theory to the problems of group work. In J.M. Carroll (Ed.), *HCI models, theories and frameworks: Toward a multidisciplinary science* (pp. 325-356).

Krupp, J. (1998). Transition to ERP implementation. *APICS—The Performance Advantage.*

Kukafka, R., Johnson, S. B., Linfante, A., & Allegrante, J. P. (2003). Grounding a new information technology implementation framework in behavioral science: A systematic analysis of the literature on IT use. *Journal of Biomedical Informatics, 36*(3), 218-227.

Kukafka, R., Johnson, S.B., Linfante, A., & Allegrante, J.P. (2003). Grounding a new information technology implementation framework in behavioral science: A systematic analysis of the literature on IT use. *Journal of Biomedical Informatics, 36*, 218-227

Kukafka, R., Johnson, SB., Linfante, A., et al. (2003). Grounding a new information technology implementation framework in behavioral science: A systematic analysis of the literature on IT use. *Journal of Biomedical Informatics, 36*, 218-227.

Kuperman, G. J., & Gibson, R. F. (2003). Computer physician order entry: Benefits, costs, and issues. *Annals of Internal Medicine, 139*(1), 31-39.

Kuperman, G. J., Leavitt, M. K., McCall, C. W., Patterson, N. L., & Wilson, H. J. (1997). *Panel: Integrating informatics into the product: The CEO's perspective.* Paper presented at the 1997 AMIA Annual Fall Symposium, Nashville, TN.

Kuruppuarachchi, P.R., Mandal, P., & Smith R. (2002). IT project implementation strategies for effective changes: A critical review. *Logistics Information Management, 15*(2), 126-137.

Kushniruk, A. W. (2001). Analysis of complex decision-making processes in healthcare: Cognitive approaches to health informatics. *Journal of Biomedical Informatics, 34*, 364-376.

Kushniruk, A. W. (2002). Evaluation in the design of health information systems: Applications of approaches emerging from systems engineering. *Computers in Biology and Medicine, 32*(3), 141-149.

Kushniruk, A. W., & Borycki, E. M. (2006). Low-cost rapid usability engineering: Designing and customizing usable healthcare information systems. *Healthcare Quarterly, 9*(4), 98-100, 102.

Kushniruk, A. W., & Patel, V. L. (2004). Cognitive and usability engineering methods for the evaluation of clinical information systems. *Journal of Biomedical Informatics, 37*(1), 56-76.

Kushniruk, A. W., Kaufman, D. R., & Patel, Y. (1996). Assessment of a computerized patient record system: A cognitive approach to evaluating an emerging medical technology. *M. D. Computing, 13*(5), 406-415.

Kushniruk, A. W., Patel, V. L., & Cimino, J. J. (1997). *Usability testing in medical informatics: Cognitive ap-*

proaches to evaluation of information systems and user interfaces. Paper presented at the 1997 AMIA Annual Fall Symposium, Formerly SCAMC, Nashville, TN.

Kushniruk, A., & Borycki, E. (2006). Low-cost rapid usability engineering: designing and customizing usable healthcare information systems. *Healthcare Quarterly, 9*(4), 98-100, 102.

Kushniruk, A., & Borycki, E. (2007). Human factors and usability of healthcare systems. In J. Bardram & A. Mihailidis (Eds.), *Pervasive computing in healthcare.* New York: CRC Press.

Kushniruk, A., Borycki, E., Kuwata, S., & Kannry, J. (2006). Predicting changes in workflow resulting from healthcare information systems: Ensuring the safety of healthcare. *Healthcare Quarterly, Oct, 9*(Spec No), 114-118.

Kushniruk, A., Karson, T., Moore, C., & Kannry, J. (2003). From prototype to production system: Lessons learned from the evolution of the SignOut System at Mount Sinai Medical Center. *AMIA Annu Symp Proceedings*, 381-385.

Kushniruk, A., Owston, R., Ho, F., Pitts, K., Wideman, H., Brown, C., et al. (2007). Design of the VULab: A quantitative and qualitative tool for analyzing use of on-line health information resources. *Proceedings of ITCH 2007.*

Kushniruk, A., Triola, M., Stein, B., Borycki, E., & Kannry, J. (2004). The relationship of usability to medical error: An evaluation of errors associated with usability problems in use of a handheld application for prescribing medications. *Proceedings of MedInfo – World Congress on Medical Informatics 2004* (pp. 1073-1076).

Kushniruk, A.W. & Ho, F. (2004, May). The virtual usability laboratory: Evaluating web-based health systems. *Proceedings of e-Health 2004*, Victoria, B.C.

Kushniruk, A.W. (2002). Evaluation in the design of health information systems: application of approaches emerging from usability engineering. *Computers in Biology and Medicine*, 141-149.

Kushniruk, A.W., & Patel, V.L. (2004). Cognitive and usability engineering approaches to the evaluation of clinical information systems. *Journal of Biomedical Informatics, 37,* 56-62.

Kushniruk, A.W., Patel, C., Patel, V.L. & Cimino, J.J. (2001). Televaluation of clinical information systems: An integrative approach to assessing web-based systems, *International Journal of Medical Informatics, 61,* 45-70.

Kushniruk, A.W., Patel, V.L., & Cimino, J.J. (1997). Usability testing in medical informatics: Cognitive approaches to evaluation of information systems and user interfaces. In D. Masys (Ed.) *Proceedings of the 1997 AMIA Fall Symposium*, 218-222.

Kushniruk, A.W., Triola, M., Borycki, E., Stein, B., & Kannry, J. (2005). Technology induced error and usability: The relationship between usability problems and prescription errors when using a handheld application. *International Journal of Medical Informatics, 74,* 519-526.

Kuwata, S., Kushniruk, A., Borycki, E., & Watanabe, H. (2006). Using simulation methods to analyze and predict changes in workflow and potential problems in the use of a bar-coding medication order entry system. *AMIA Annual Symposium Proceedings*, 994.

Kuziemsky, C.E. (2007). A grounded theory-participatory design approach for capturing user requirements for health information systems design. *Proceedings of Information Technology and Communications in Health (ITCH) 2007.*

Lairson, D. R., Chang, Y. C., Bettencourt, J. L., Vernon, S. W., & Greisinger, A. (2006). Estimating development cost for a tailored interactive computer program to enhance colorectal cancer screening compliance. *Journal of the American Medical Informatics Association, 13*(5), 476-484.

Laughlin, S. (1999). An ERP game plan. *Journal of Business Strategy.*

Lawler, F. (1993). Implementation and termination of a computerized medical information system–Editorial. *Journal of Family Practice, 42*(3), 233-236.

Layman, E. (2003). Health informatics ethical issues. *Health Care Manager*, 22:1.

Lazarou, J., Pomeranz, B. H., & Corey, P. N., (1998). Incidence of adverse drug reactions in hospitalized patients: a meta-analysis of prospective studies. *Journal of the American Medical Association*, 279, 1200-1205.

Leape, L. L., & Berwick, D. M. (2005). Five years after 'to err is human:' What have we learned, *Journal of the American Medical Association*, 293, 2384-2390.

Leape, L.L., Brennan, T.A., Laird, N., et al. ((1991). The nature of adverse events in hospitalized patients: results of the Harvard Practice Study. *New England Journal of Medicine*, 324(6), 377-384.

Levin, H., & McEwan, P. (2000). *Cost-effectiveness analysis: Methods and applications*. Thousand Oaks, CA: Sage Publications.

Leviss, J., Kremsdorf, R., & Mohaideen, M. F. (2006). The CMIO—A new leader for health systems. *Journal of American Medical Information Association*, 13(5), 573-578.

Lewin, K. (1951). *Field theory in social science*. New York: Harper and Row.

Li, J. S., Eisenstein, E. L., Grabowski, H. G., Reid, E. D., Mangum, B., Schulman, K. A., et al. (2007). Economic return of clinical trials performed under the pediatric exclusivity program. *Journal of the American Medical Association*, 297(5), 480-488.

Lilholt, L.H., Pedersen, S.S., Madsen, I., Nielsen, P.H., Boye, N., Andersen, S.K., et al. (2006). Development of methods for usability evaluations of EHR systems. In A. Hasman, R. Haux, J. van der Lei, E. De Clercq, F. Roger-France (Eds.), *Ubiquity: Technologies for better health in aging societies* (pp. 341-346). Amsterdam: IOS Press.

Lindau, S. T., Tomori, C., Lyons, T., Langseth, L., Bennett, C. L., & Garcia, P. (2002). The association of health literacy with cervical cancer prevention knowledge and health behaviors in a multiethnic cohort of women. *American Journal of Obstetrics and Gynecology*, 186(5), 938-943.

Lipkus, I. M., Samsa, G., & Rimer, B. K. (2001). General performance on a numeracy scale among highly educated samples. *Medical Decision Making*, 21(1), 37-44.

Littlejohns, P., Wyatt, J.C., & Garvican, L. (2003). Evaluating computerized health information systems: hard lessons still to be learnt. *BMJ*, 326(7394), 860-863.

Lobach, D. F., Kawamoto, K., & Hasselblad, V. (2004). Development of an information system to support collaboration for population-based healthcare for Medicaid beneficiaries. TOP Project Evaluation Report. *Technology Opportunities Program*. Retrieved December 01, 2006, from http://ntiaotiant2.ntia.doc.gov/top/docs/eval/pdf/376099007e.pdf)

Lobach, D. F., Low, R., Arbanas, J. A., Rabold, J. S., Tatum, J. L., & Epstein, S. D. (2001). Defining and supporting the diverse information needs of community-based care using the web and hand-held devices. *Proceedings of the AMIA Annual Symposium*, 398-402.

Lorenzi, N. M., Gardner, R. M., Pryor, T. A., & Stead, W. W. (1995). Medical informatics: The key to an organization's place in the new health care environment. *J Am Med Inform Assoc*, 2(6), 391-392.

Lorenzi, N., & Riley, R.T. (1995). *Organizational aspects of health informatics: Managing technological change*. New York: Springer-Verlag.

Lu, H. P., & Yeh, D. C. (1998). Enterprises' perceptions on business process re-engineering: a path analytic model. *Omega, International Journal of Management Science*, 26(1), 17-27.

Luce, B. (1996). Estimating costs in cost-effectiveness analysis. In M.R.Gold, J. Siegel, L. Russel, & M. C. Weinstein (Eds.), *Cost-effectiveness in health and medicine* (pp. 176). New York: Oxford University Press.

Lukowicz, P. Kirstein, T., & Troster, G. (2004). Wearable systems for healthcare applications. *Methods of Information in Medicine*, 43, 232-238.

Mabin, V. J., Forgeson, S., & Green, L. (2001). Harnessing resistance: using the theory of constraints to assist change management. *Journal of European Industrial Training*, 25(2-4), 168-191.

MacIntosh-Murray, A., & Choo, C. W. (2005). Informational behavior in the context of improving patient safety. *Journal of the American Society for Information Science and Technology, 56*(12), 1332-1345.

MacKenzie, I. S. (1992). Fitts' law as a research and design tool in human-computer interaction. *Human-Computer Interaction, 7*(1), 91-139.

MacKenzie, I. S. (2002). Introduction to this special issue on text entry for mobile computing. *Human-Computer Interaction, 17*(2), 141-145.

Macura, R. T., & Macura, K. (1997). Case-based reasoning: Opportunities and applications in healthcare. *Artificial Intelligence in Medicine, 9*, 1-4.

Manly, J. J., Jacobs, D. M., Sano, M., Bell, K., Merchant, C. A., Small, S. A., et al. (1999). Effect of literacy on neuropsychological test performance in nondemented, education-matched elders. *Journal of the International Neuropsychological Society, 5*(3), 191-202.

Marchibroda, J. M., & Gerber, T. (2003). Information infrastructure promises. Better healthcare, lower costs. *J Ahima, 74*(1), 28-32; quiz 33-24.

Marshall, A. H., Rachlis, A., & Chen, J. (2005). Severe acute respiratory syndrome: responses of the healthcare system to a global epidemic. *Current Opinions in Otolaryngology, Head and Neck Surgery, 13*(3), 161-164.

Marshall, M., & von Tigerstrom, B. (2002). Health information. In J. Downie, T. Caulfield & C. Flood (Eds.), *Canadian health law and policy* (2nd ed.). Markham, Ont: Butterworths.

Marsiglia, W. (1966). *Sumerian records from Drehem.* New York: AMS Press.

Massaro, T. (1993). Introducing physician order entry at a major academic medical center: Impact on organizational culture and behavior. *Academic Medicine, 68*(1), 20-25.

Massaro, T.A. (1993). Introducing physician order entry at a major academic medical center: 1. Impact on organizational culture and behavior. *Academic Medicine, 68*(1), 20-25.

McCray, A. T. (2005). Promoting health literacy. *Journal of the American Medical Informatics Association, 12*(2), 152-163.

McDonald, C. J., Overhage, J. M., Tierney, W. M., Dexter, P. R., Martin, D. K., Suico, J. G. et al. (1999). The Regenstrief Medical Record System: A quarter century experience. *International Journal of Medicine Information, 54*(3), 225-253.

McDonald, C.J., Hui, S.L., Smith, D.M., Tierney, W.M., Cohen, S.J., Weinberger, M. et al. (1984). Reminders to physicians from an introspective computer medical record: a two year randomized trial. *Annals of Internal Medicine, 100*, 130-138.

McDougall, B. S., & Hansson, A. (2002). *Chinese concepts of privacy.* Tokyo: Brill.

McInerney v. MacDonald 93 DLR (4th) 415.

McKeithen, K. B., Reitman, S. C., Rueter, H. H., & Reitman, S. C. (1981). Knowledge organization and skill differences in computer programmers. *Cognitive Psychology, 13*, 307-325.

McKnight, M. (2006). The information seeking of on-duty critical care nurses: evidence from participant observation and in-context interviews. *J Med Libr Assoc, 94*(2), 145-151.

McLaughlin, C. P., & Kibb, D. C. (2006). Information management and technology in CQI (pp. 243-278). In C. P. McLaughlin & A. D. Kaluzny (Eds.), *Continuous quality improvement in health care* (3rd ed.). New York: Jones & Bartlett.

McLaughlin, G. H. (1969). SMOG grading: A new readability formula. *Journal of Reading, 12*, 639-346.

McShane, K. E., Smylie, J. K., Hastings, P. D., & Martin, C.M. (2006). Guiding health promotion efforts with urban Inuit: A community-specific perspective on health information sources and dissemination strategies. *Canadian Journal of Public Health, 97*(4), 296-299

McSherry, B. (2004). Ethical issues in health*Connect*'s shared electronic record system. *Journal of Law and Medicine* 12,60.

Mead, N., & Bower, P. (2000). Patient-centredness: a conceptual framework and review of the empirical literature. *Social Science & Medicine, 51*(7), 1087-1110.

Mekhjian, H.S., Kumar, R.R., Kuehn, L., & et al. (2002). Immediate benefits realized following implementation of physician order entry at an academic medical center. *J Am Med Inform Assoc., 9*(5), 529-539.

Middleton, B., Hammond, W. E., Brennan, P. F., & Cooper, G. F. (2005). *Accelerating US EHR adoption: How to get there from here. Recommendations based on the 2004 ACMI Retreat.* Am Med Inform Assoc.

Militello, L. G. (1998). Applied cognitive task analysis (ACTA): A practitioner's toolkit for understanding cognitive task demands. *Ergonomics, 41*(11), 1618-1641.

Millenson, M. L. (1997). *Demanding medical excellence: doctors and accountability in the information age: With a new afterword* (Pbk. ed.). Chicago: University of Chicago Press.

Miller, R. A., Waitman, L. R., Chen, S., & Rosenbloom, S. T. (2005). The anatomy of decision support during inpatient care provider order entry (CPOE): Empirical observations from a decade of CPOE experience at Vanderbilt. *J Biomed Inform, 38*(6), 469-485.

Miller, R. H., & Sim, I. (2004). Physicians' use of electronic medical records: Barriers and solutions. *Health Affairs, 23*(2), 116-126.

Miller, R. H., & West, C. E. (2007). The value of electronic health records in community health centers: Policy implications. *Health Affairs, 26*(1), 206-214.

Miller, R. H., West, C., Brown, T. M., Sim, I., & Ganchoff, C. (2005). The value of electronic health records in solo or small group practices. *Health Aff (Millwood), 24*(5), 1127-1137.

Miller, R.H. & Sim, I. (2004). Physicians' use of electronic medical records: Barriers and solutions. *Health Affairs, 23*(2), 116-126.

Mohrmann, C. C., Coleman, E. A., Coon, S. K., Lord, J. E., Heard, J. K., Cantrell, M. J., et al. (2000). An analysis of printed breast cancer information for African American women. *Journal of Cancer Education, 15*(1), 23-27.

Molich, R. (2000). *Brugervenligt webdesign.* København: Teknisk Forlag.

Moore, C., & Kannry, J. (1997). *Improving continuity of care using a web based signout and discharge.* Paper presented at the 1997 Annual Fall AMIA Symposium, Nashville, TN.

Moore, D., Castillo, E., Richardson, C., & Reid, R. J. (2003). Determinants of health status and the influence of primary healthcare services in Latin America, 1990-98. *International Journal of Health Planning and Management, 18*(4), 279-292.

Moore, G. E. (1903). *Principia Ethica.* Cambridge: Oxford University Press.

Morris, A. H. (2002). Decision support and safety of clinical environments. *Quality Safety Healthcare, 11*, 69-75.

Morrow, D. G., Leirer, V. O., Andrassy, J. M., Hier, C. M., & Menard, W. E. (1998). The influence of list format and category headers on age differences in understanding medication instructions. *Experimental Aging Research, 24*, 231-256.

Morrow, D., Leirer, V., Andrassy, J., Tanke, E., & Stine-morrow, E. (1996). Medication instruction design: Younger and older adult schemas for taking medication. *Human Factors, 38*, 556-573.

Moss Kanter, R. (1985). *The change masters: corporate entrepreneurs at work.* London: Unwin Paperbacks.

Moss Kanter, R. (2000). Leaders with passion, conviction and confidence can use several techniques to take change or change rather than react to it. *Ivey Business Journal, 64*(5), 32-38.

Mugford, M. (2001). Using systematic reviews for economic evaluation. In M. Egger, G. Davey Smith, & D. G. Altman (Eds.), *Systematic reviews in health care: Meta-analysis in context.* London: BMJ Books.

Murff, H. J., & Kannry, J. (2001). Physician satisfaction with two order entry systems. *Journal of American Medical Information Association, 8*(5), 499-509.

Murray, M. D., Harris, L. E., Overhage, J. M., Zhou, X. H., Eckert, G. J., Smith, F. E. et al. (2004). Failure of computerized treatment suggestions to improve health outcomes of outpatients with uncomplicated hypertension: Results of a randomized controlled trial. *Pharmacotherapy, 24*(3), 324-337.

Murray, M. D., Smith, F. E., Fox, J., Teal, E. Y., Kesterson, J. G., Stiffler, T. A. et al. (2003). Structure, functions, and activities of a research support informatics section. *Journal of American Medical Information Association, 10*(4), 389-398.

Musen, M. A., Shahar, Y., & Shortliffe, E. H. (2006). Clinical decision-support systems (pp. 698-736). In T E.. Shorliffe & J. J. Cimino (Eds.), *Biomedical informatics: Computer applications in healthcare and biomedicine* (3rd ed.). New York: Springer.

Mysak, S. (1997). Strategies for promoting ethical decision-making. *Journal of Gerontological Nursing, 23*(1), 25-31.

Nagle, T. & Holden, R. (2002). *The strategy and tactics of pricing: A guide to profitable decision making.* Upper Saddle River, NJ: Prentice Hall.

National E-Health Transition Authority. (2006). *Privacy blueprint—Unique healthcare identifiers, Version 1.0.* Retrieved February 1, 2007, from http://www.nehta.gov.au/

National Electronic Health Records Taskforce. (2000). *Issues paper: A national approach to electronic health records for australia.* Retrieved December 1, 2006, from www.gpcg.org/publications/docs/Ehrissue.doc

National Health and Medical Research Council. (2004). *The regulation of health information privacy in Australia.* Retrieved January 15, 2007, from http://www.nhmrc.gov.au/publications/_files/nh53.pdf

National Health Privacy Working Group of the Australian Health Ministers' Advisory Council. (2003). *Proposed National Health Privacy Code.* Retrieved December 1, 2006, from www.health.gov.au/pubs/nhpcode.htm

National Health Service. (2005). *National Programme for IT in the NHS.* Retrieved December 1, 2006 from http://www.connectingforhealth.nhs.uk/

National Health Service. (2005). *The Care Record Guarantee: Our Guarantee for NHS Care Records in England.* Retrieved January 12, 2007, from http://www.connectingforhealth.nhs.uk/crdb/docs/crs_guarantee.pdf

National Health Service. *Direct business plan 2005-2006.* London: National Health Service.

National Institute for Health and Clinical Excellence (2007). Retrieved December 01, 2006, from http://www.nice.org.uk/

National Quality Forum. (2003). *Safe practices for better healthcare: A consensus report.* Washington, DC: National Quality Forum.

Nebeker, J. R., Hoffman, J. M., Weir, C. R., Bennett, C. L., & Hurdle, J. F. (2005). High rates of adverse drug events in a highly computerized hospital. *Arch Intern Med, 165*(10), 1111-1116.

Neilson, J., & Mack, R. (1994). *Usability inspection methods.* NY: John Wiley & Son. Usability Sciences Corporation (1994) Windows, 3.

Nelson, N. C., Evans, S., Samore, M. H., & Gardner, R. M. (2005). Detection and prevention of medication errors using real-time bed-side nurse charting. *Journal of the American Medical Informatics Association, 12*, 390-397.

NHS. (2006). *The NHS in England: The operating framework for 2007/08. Guidance on preparation of local IM&T plans.* Department of Health.

Nielsen, J. (1993). *Usability engineering.* New York: Academic Press.

Nielsen, J. (2000). *Designing web usability.* Indianapolis: New Riders Press.

Nielsen, J., & Mack, R.L. (1994). *Usability inspection methods.* New York: John Wiley & Sons.

Nielson, J. (1994). *Usability engineering.* Morgan Kaufmann.

Nøhr, C., & Boye, N. (2008). Towards computer supported clinical activity: A roadmap based on empirical knowledge and some theoretical reflections. In A.W. Kushniruk & E. Borycki (Eds.), *Human, social and organizational aspects of health information systems*. Hershey, PA: IGI Press.

Nøhr, C., Andersen S.K., Vingtoft S., Bruun-Rasmussen M., & Bernstein, K. (2004). *EHR-observatory annual report 2004*. Aalborg: EPJ-Observatoriet.

Nolan, J., McNair, P., & Brender, J. (1991). Factors influencing transferability of knowledge-based Systems. *International Journal of Biomedical Computing, 27*, 7-26.

Nordyke, R.A., & Kulikowski, C.A. (1998). An informatics-based chronic disease practice: Case study of a 35-year computer-based longitudinal record system. *Journal of the American Medical informatics Association*, (5), 88-103.

Norheim, O.F. (2006). Soft paternalism and the ethics of shared electronic patient records. *British Medical Journal, 333*, 2-3.

Norman, K. L., Slaughter, L., Schneidermn, B., & Harper, B. (1988). *Questionnaire for user interface satisfaction (Version 7)*. College Park, MD: Office of Technology Commercialization.

Nutbeam, D. (2000). Health literacy as a public health goal: A challenge for contemporary health education and communication strategies into the 21st century. *Health Promotion International, 15*(3), 259-267.

O'Connell, R. T., Cho, C., Shah, N., Brown, K., & Shiffman, R. N. (2004). Take note(s): Differential EHR satisfaction with two implementations under one roof. *Journal of American Medical Information Association, 11*(1), 43-49.

O'Neill, E. S., Dluhy, N. M., & Chin, E. (2005). Modeling novice clinical reasoning for a computerized decision support system. *Journal of Advanced Nursing, 49*(1), 68-77.

Oden, H., Langenwalter, G., & Lucier, R. (1993). *Handbook of material and capacity requirements planning*. New York: McGraw- Hill.

Ohsfeldt, R. L., Ward, M. M., Schneider, J. E., Jaana, M., Miller, T. R., Lei, Y., & Wakefield, D. S. (2005). Implementation of hospital computerized physician order entry systems in a rural state: feasibility and financial impact. *Journal of the American Medical Informatics Association, 12*(1), 20-27.

Olve, NG., Vimarlund, V. (2005).Locating ICT's benefits in elderly care. *Medical Informatics and the Internet in Medicine*, 30(4): 297-308.

Orlinkowski, W. J. & Gash, D. C. (1994). Technological frames: Making sense of information technology in organizations. *ACM Transactions on Information Systems, 12*(2), 174-207.

Orlinkowski, W. J. (1992). The duality of technology: Rethinking the concept of technology in organizations. *Organizational Science, 3*(3), 398-427.

Orlinkowski, W. J., & Yates, J. (1994). Genre repertoire: The structuring of communicative practices in organizations. *Administrative Science Quarterly, 39*(4), 541-574.

Orr, M. (2004). Evolution of New Zealand's health knowledge management system. *British Journal of Healthcare Computing and Information Management, 21*(10), 28-30.

Orr, M., & Day, K. (2004). Knowledge and learning in 'successful' IT projects: a case study. *Health Care and Informatics Review Online* Retrieved June 17, 2004, from http://www.enigma.co.nz/hcro/website/index. cfm?fuseaction=articledisplay&Feature

Orr, M., & Sankaran, S. (2005, 5-7 December). *Mutual emphathy, ambiguity and the implementation of electronic knowledge management within the complex health system*. Paper presented at the Systems Thinking and Complexity Science: Insights for Action. 11th Annual ANZSYS Conference: Managing the Complex, Christchurch, New Zealand.

Otero, J. (2002). Noticing and fixing difficulties while understanding science texts. In J. Otero, J. A. Leén, & A. C. Graesser (Eds.), *The psychology of science text comprehension* (pp. 281-307). Mahwah, NJ: Lawrence Erlbaum.

Owston, R., Kushniruk, A., Ho, F., Pitts, K., & Wideman, H. (2005). Improving the design of Web-based games and simulations through usability research. *Proceedings of Ed-Media 2005.*

Oz, E. (2005). Information technology productivity: in search of a definitive observation. *Information and management 42*, 789-798.

Pablos-Mendez, A., Chunharas, S., Lansang, M. A., Shademani, R., & Tugwell, P. (2005). Knowledge translation in global health. *Bulletin World Health Organ, 83*(10), 723.

Pan-Canadian Health Information Privacy and Confidentiality Framework. (2005). Retrieved January 3, 2007, from http://www.hc-sc.gc.ca/hcs-sss/pubs/ehealth-esante/2005-pancanad-priv/index_e.html

Panko, W. B. (1999). Clinical care and the factory floor. *Journal of the American Medical Informatics Association, 6*(5), 349-353.

Papagiunos, G., & Spyropoulos, B. (1999). The multifarious function of medical records: Ethical issues. *Method Inform Med, 38*, 317-320.

Parker, R. M., Baker, D. W., Williams, M. V., & Nurss, J. R. (1995). The test of functional health literacy in adults: A new instrument for measuring patients' literacy skills. *Journal of General Internal Medicine, 10*(10), 537-541.

Parker, R. M., Ratzan, S. C., & Lurie, N. (2003). Health literacy: A policy challenge for advancing high-quality healthcare. *Health Affairs (Millwood), 22*(4), 147-153.

Pascal, B. (2006). *Investment in health IT: Heading down the wrong road? HCIM&C, XV*(1), 6-7.

Patel, V. L., & Kaufman, D. R. (1998a). Medical informatics and the science of cognition. *Journal of the American Medical Informatics Association, 5*, 493-502.

Patel, V. L., & Kaufman, D. R. (1998b). Science and practice. *Journal of the American Medical Informatics Association, 5*, 489-492.

Patel, V. L., & Kushniruk, A. W. (1998). Interface design for health care environments: the role of cognitive science. *Proc AMIA Symp, 2937.*

Patel, V. L., Arocha, J. F., & Kaufman, D. R. (2001). *A primer on aspects of cognition for medical informatics.* Am Med Inform Assoc.

Patel, V. L., Arocha, J. F., & Kushniruk, A. W. (2002). Patients' and physicians' understanding of health and biomedical concepts: relationship to the design of EMR systems. *Journal of Biomedical Informatics, 35*(1), 8-16.

Patel, V. L., Branch, T., & Arocha, J. F. (2002). Errors in interpreting quantities as procedures: the case of pharmaceutical labels. *International Journal of Medical Informatics, 65*(3), 193-211.

Patel, V. L., Cytryn, K. N., Shortliffe, E. H., & Safran, C. (2000). The collaborative health care team: The role of individual and group expertise. *Teaching and Learning in Medicine, 12*(3), 117-132.

Patel, V. L., Eisemon, T. O., & Arocha, J. F. (1990). Comprehending instructions for using pharmaceutical products in rural Kenya. *Instructional Science, 19*(1), 71-84.

Patel, V. L., Kushniruk, A. W., Yang, S., & Yale, J. F. (2000). Impact of a computer-based patient record system on data collection, knowledge organization, and reasoning. *Journal of the American Medical Informatics Association, 7*, 569-585.

Patel, V.L., Allen, V.G., Arocha, J.F., & Shortliffe, E.H. (1998). Representing clinical guidelines in GLIF: individual and collaborative expertise. *Journal of the American Medical Informatics Association, 5*(5), 467-483.

Patel, V.L., Kushniruk, A.W., Yang, S., & Yale, J.F. (2000). Impact of a computer-based patient record system on data collection, knowledge organization and reasoning. *Journal of the American Medical Informatics Association, 7*(6), 569-585.

Pathak, M., Ketkar, Y. A., & Majumdar, R. D. (1981). Perceived morbidity, utilisation of health services and factors affecting it in a rural area. *Health and Population: Perspectives & Issues, 4*(1), 79-89.

Patterson, E. S., Cook, R. I., & Render, M. L. (2002). Improving patient safety by identifying side effects from introducing bar coding in medication administration. *JAMIA, 9,* 540-553.

Patton, R. (2001). *Software testing.* Indianapolis, IN: SAMS.

Perry, M. (2003). Distributed cognition. *HCI models, theories and frameworks: toward a multidisciplinary science* (pp. 193-223). San Francisco: Elsevier Science,.

Personal Health Information Act. (1997).*Continuing Consolidation of the Statutes of Manitoba*, chapter P33.5.

Personal Health Information Protection Act. (2004). *Statutes of Ontario*, chapter 3.

Personal Health Information Regulations, Manitoba Regulation 245/97, updated to Manitoba Regulation 142/2005.

Petersen, L. A., Orav, E. J., Teich, J. M., O'Neil, A. C., & Brennan, T. A. (1998). Using a computerized sign-out program to improve continuity of inpatient care and prevent adverse events. *Jt Comm J Qual Improv, 24*(2), 77-87.

Peterson, M. W. & Fretz, P. C. (2003). Patient use of the internet for information in a lung cancer clinic. *Chest, 123*(2), 452-457.

Phillips, D. P., & Bredder, C. C. (2002). Morbidity and mortality from medical errors: An increasingly serious public health problem. *Annual Review of Public Health, 23,* 135-150.

Piasecki, J. K., Calhoun, E., Engelberg, J., Rice, W., Dilts, D., Belser, D. et al. (2005). Computerized provider order entry in the emergency department: pilot evaluation of a return on investment analysis instrument. *AMIA Annu Symp Proceedings*, 1081.

Pinto, J. K. (2004). The elements of project success. In D. I. Cleland (Ed.), *Field guide to project management* (pp. 14-27). Hoboken, NJ: John Wiley & Sons.

Pizzi, R. (2007). Healthcare IT a key aspect of physicians' reform principles. Retrieved Janaury 15, 2007, from http://www.healthcareitnews.com/story.cms?id=6165

Pizziferri, L., Kittler, A.F., Volk, L.A. et al. (2005). Primary care physician time utilization before and after implementation of an electronic health record: A time-motion study. *Journal of Biomedical Informatics, 38,* 176-188.

Platt, R. (2007). Speed bumps, potholes, and tollbooths on the road to panacea: making best use of data. *Health Aff (Millwood), 26*(2), w153-155.

Plesk, P. (2001). Redesigning health care with insights from the science of complex adaptive systems. In Institute of Medicine (ed.), *Crossing the quality chasm: A new health system for the 21st century* (pp. 309-322). Washington, DC: National Academy Press.

Plesk, P. E., & Greenhalgh, T. (2001). Complexity science. The challenge of complexity in health care. *British Medical Journal, 323,* 625-628.

Polson, P. G., Lewis, C., Rieman, J., & Wharton, C. (1992). Cognitive walkthroughs: A method for theory-based evaluation of user interfaces. *International Journal of Man-Machine Studies, 36*(5), 741-773.

Poole, M. S., & DeSanctis, G. (2004). Structuration theory information systems research: Methods and controversies (pp. 206-249). In M. E. Whitman & A. B. Woszczynski (Eds.), *The handbook of information systems research.* London: Idea Group.

Poon, A. D., & Fagan, L. M. (1994). PEN-Ivory: the design and evaluation of a pen-based computer system for structured data entry. *Proc Annu Symp Comput Appl Med Care*, 447-451.

Poon, A. D., Fagan, L. M., & Shortliffe, E. H. (1996). The PEN-Ivory project: exploring user-interface design for the selection of items from large controlled vocabularies of medicine. *J Am Med Inform Assoc, 3*(2), 168-183.

Poon, E. G., Wald, J., Bates, D. W., Middleton, B., Kuperman, G. J., & Gandhi, T. K. (2003). Supporting patient care beyond the clinical encounter: Three informatics innovations from partners health care. *AMIA Annu Symp Proc*, 1072.

Poon, E. G., Wang, S. J., Gandhi, T. K., Bates, D. W., & Kuperman, G. J. (2003). Design and implementation of a comprehensive outpatient Results Manager. *Journal of Biomedical informatics, 36*(1-2), 80-91.

Poon, E.G, Blumenthal, D., Jaggi, T. et al. (2003). Overcoming the barriers to the implementing computerized physician order entry systems in U.S. hospitals: Perspectives from senior management. *AMIA Annual Symposium Proceedings*, 975.

Poskela, J., Dietrich, P., Berg, P. et al. (2005). Integration of Strategic Level and Operative Level Front-end Innovation Activities. *IEEE Conference Proceedings*, 197-211.

Potts, A. L., Barr, F. E., Gregory, D. F., Wright, L., & Patel, N. R. (2004). Computerized physician order entry and medication errors in a pediatric critical care unit. *Pediatrics, 113*(1 Pt 1), 59-63.

Powell, J. (2004). *Speech from the Chairman of the IT Committee*. British Medical Association. Retrieved December 1, 2006, from http://www.bma.org.uk/ap.nsf/Content/ARM04chIT?OpenDocument&Highlight=2, john,powell

Powell, J., & Buchan, I. (2005). Electronic health records should support clinical research. *J Med Internet Res, 7*(1), e4.

Pratt, W., Reddy, M. C., McDonald, D. W., Tarczy-Hornoch, P., & Gennari, J. H. (2004). Incorporating ideas from computer-supported cooperative work. *Journal of Biomedical Informatics, 37*(2), 128-137.

Pressman, R. (2005). *Software engineering: A practitioner's approach* (6th ed.). New York: McGraw Hill.

Price Waterhouse (1997). *Without change there is no progress—Coping with chaos, a global survey*. London: Price Waterhouse.

Pringle, D. M., & White, P. (2002). Happenings. Nursing matters: The nursing and health outcomes project of the Ontario ministry of health and long-term care. *Canadian Journal of Nursing Research, 33*, 115-121.

Pringle, D., & Doran, D. M. (2003). Patient outcomes as an accountability. In D. M. Doran (Ed.), *Nursing-sensitive outcomes: State of the science* (pp. 1-25). Sudbury, MA: Jones and Bartlett.

Privacy Commissioner of Canada. (2001). *Annual Report to Parliament, 2000-2001*. Retrieved December 15, 2006, from http://www.privcom.gc.ca/information/ar/02_04_09_e.asp

Project Management Institute. (2000). *A guide to project management body of knowledge (PMBOK Guide)* (2000 ed.). Newtown Square: Project Management Institute.

Protti, D.J., & Johansen, I. (2003). Further lessons from Denmark about computer systems in physician offices. *Electronic Healthcare*, 2(2), 36-43.

Public Health Agency of Canada. (2006). Disease surveillance on-line. Retrieved June 7, 2007, from http://www.phac-aspc.gc.ca/dsol-smed/

Quinn, J. (2004). Vendor perspectives: Critical do's and dont's. In Spring AMIA 2004 (Ed.). McClean, Va.

Qvortrup, L. (2003). *The hypercomplex society—Digital formations* (vol. 5). New York: Peter Lang Publishing.

Randolph, A. G., Haynes, R. B., Wyatt, J. C., Cook, D. J., & Guyatt, G. H. (1999). Users' guides to the medical literature: XVIII. How to use an article evaluating the clinical impact of a computer-based clinical decision support system. *Jama, 282*(1), 67-74.

Ratzan, S. C. & Parker, R. M. (2000). Introduction. *National Library of Medicine Current Bibliographies in Medicine: Health Literacy* Retrieved May 25, 2007, http://www.nlm.nih.gov/archive//20061214/pubs/cbm/hliteracy.pdf

Registered Nurses' Association of Ontario. (2005a). *Nursing care of dyspnea: The 6th vital sign in individuals with chronic obstructive lung disease (COPD)*. Toronto, Canada: Registered Nurses' Association of Ontario.

Registered Nurses' Association of Ontario. (2005b). *Prevention of falls and fall injuries in the older adult (revised)*. Toronto, Canada: Registered Nurses Association of Ontario.

Retchin, S. M., & Wenzel, R. P. (1999). Electronic medical record systems at academic health centers: advantages and implementation issues. *Acad Med, 74*(5), 493-498.

Ries, N.M. (2006) Patient privacy in a wired (and wireless) world: Approaches to consent in the context of electronic health records" *Alberta Law Review, 43*(3), 681-712.

Ries, N.M., & Moysa, G. (2005). Legal protection of electronic health records: Issues of consent and security. *Health Law Review, 14*(1), 18-25.

Rigby, M. (2001). Evaluation: 16 powerful reasons why not to do it--and 6 over-riding imperatives. Medinfo 2001 10(Pt 2), 1198-1202.

Rigby, M. (2006). Evaluation—the Cinderella science of ICT in health. *IMIA Yearbook of Medical Informatics, 2006*, 114-120.

Rind, D. M., & Safran, C. (1993). Real and imagined barriers to an electronic medical record. *Proc Annu Symp Comput Appl Med Care*, 74-78.

RNAO Registered Nurses Association of Ontario. (2002). *Nursing Best Practice Guideline Shaping the future of nursing: Risk assessment & prevention of pressure ulcers.* Toronto, On: RNAO.

RNAO Registered Nurses' Association of Ontario. (2005). *Nursing best practice guidelines shaping the future of nursing: Assessment and management of pain.* Toronto: Ontario.

Roberts, H.J., & Barrar, P.R.N (1992). MRP II implementation: Key factors for success. *Computer Integrated Manufacturing Systems, 5*(1), 31-39.

Rodden, T. (1991). A survey of CSCW systems. *Interacting with Computers, 3*(3), 319-353.

Rogers, E. M. (1995). *Diffusion of innovations* (4th ed.). New York: Free Press.

Rogers, Y., & Ellis, J. (1994). Distributed cognition: An alternative framework for analysing and explaining collaborative working. *Journal of Information Technology, 9*(2), 119-128.

Romanow, R. J. (2002). Commission on the future of health care in canada. *Building on Values: The Future of Health Care in Canada-Final Report.*

Rosario, J.G. (2000). On the leading edge: Critical success factors in implementation projects. *BusinessWorld*

Rosenthal, D.A. (2002). Managing non-technical factors in healthcare IT projects. *Journal of Healthcare Information Management, 16*(2), 56-61.

Rosenthal, J., & Booth, M. (October 2004). *State patient safety centers: A new approach to promote patient safety.* Portland, ME: National Academy for State Health Policy.

Roth, E. M., Patterson, E. S., & Mumaw, R. J. (2001). Cognitive engineering: Issues in user-centered system design. *Encyclopedia of Software Engineering* (2nd ed.) New York: Wiley-Interscience, John Wiley & Sons.

Rozovsky, L.E., & Inions, N.J. (2002). *Canadian Health Information* (3rd ed.). Markham, Ont: Butterworths Canada Ltd.

Rycroft-Malone, J., Kitson, A., Harvey, G., McCormack, B., Seers, K., Titchen, A., et al. (2002). Ingredients for change: Revisiting a conceptual framework. *Quality and Safety in Healthcare, 11*(2), 174-180.

Saba, V., McCormick, K. (2005). *Essentials of Nursing Informatics.* McGraw Hill.

Sackett, D. L., Richardson, W. S., Rosenberg, W. M., & Haynes, R. B. (1997). *Evidence-based medicine: How to practice teach EBM.* New York: Churchill Livingstone.

Safeer, R. S., & Keenan, J. (2005). Health literacy: the gap between physicians and patients. *American Family Physician, 72*(3), 463-468.

Safran, C., Jones, PC., Rind, D., et al. (1998). Electronic communication and collaboration in a health care practice. *Artificial Intelligence in Medicine, 12*(2), 137-151.

Safran, C., Sands, D. Z., & Rind, D. M. (1999). Online medical records: a decade of experience. *Methods Inf Med, 38*(4-5), 308-312.

Saini, F., & Rowling, L. (1997). It's more than literacy: The assimilation effect of the translation model. *Ethnicity and Health, 2*(4), 323-328.

Sakallaris, B. R., Jastremski, C. A., & Von Rueden, K. T. (2000). Clinical decision support systems for outcome measurement and management. *AACN Advanced Critical Care, 11*(3), 351-362.

Saleem, J.J., Patterson, E.S., Militello, L., et al. (2005). Exploring barriers and facilitators to the use of computerized clinical reminders. *J Am Med Inform Assoc., 12*(40), 438-447.

Sales, G. C. (2002). *A quick guide to e-learning.* Andover, MN: Expert Publishing.

Sandelowski, M. (2000). *Devices and desires.* Chapel Hill: The University of North Carolina.

Sands, D. Z., Libman, H., & Safran, C. (1995). Meeting information needs: analysis of clinicians' use of an HIV database through an electronic medical record. *Medinfo, 8 Pt 1,* 323-326.

Sang, B. (2004). Choice, participation, and accountability: Assessing the potential impact of legislation promoting patient and public involvement in health in the UK. *Health Expectations, 7,* 187-190.

Savitz, L. A., & Bernard, S. L. (2006). *Measuring and assessing adverse medical events to promote patient safety* (pp. 211-225). In C. P. McLaughlin & A. D. Kaluzny (Eds.), *Continuous quality improvement in health care* (3rd ed.). New York: Jones & Bartlett.

Schillinger, D., Grumbach, K., Piette, J., Wang, F., Osmond, D., Daher, C., et al. (2002). Association of health literacy with diabetes outcomes. *Journal of the American Medical Association, 288*(4), 475-482.

Schmidt, K., & Bannon, L. (1992) Taking CSCW seriously. *Computer Supported Cooperative Work (CSCW), 1*(1), 7-40.

Schneider, D. M., & Goldwasser, C. (1998). Be a model leader of change. *Management Review, 87*(3), 41-45.

Schoen, C., Osborn R, Huynh, P. T., Doty, M., Peugh, J., & Zapert, K. (2006). On the front line of care: primary care doctors' office systems, experiences, and views in seven countries. *Health Affairs 25*(6), w555-w571. Retrieved June 9, 2007, from http://content.healthaffairs.org/cgi/content/abstract/hlthaff.25.w555?ijkey=3YyH7yDwrJSoc&keytype=ref&siteid=healthaff

Schon, D. (1983). *The reflective practioner: How professionals think in action.* New York: Basic Books.

Schraagen, J. M., Chipman, S. F., & Shalin, V. L. (2000). *Cognitive task analysis.* Lawrence Erlbaum Associates.

Schumaker, A.M. (2002). Interorganizational networks: Using a theoretical model to predict effectiveness. *Journal of Health and Human Services Administration, 25*(3/4), 371-380.

Schwartz, L. M., Woloshin, S., Black, W. C., & Welch, H. G. (1997). The role of numeracy in understanding the benefit of screening mammography. *Annals of Internal Medicine, 127*(11), 966-972.

Senge, P. M. (1994). *The fifth discipline: The art & practice of the learning organization.* New York: Doubleday.

Seufert, T. (2003). Supporting coherence formation in learning from multiple representations. *Learning and Instruction, 13,* 227-237.

Sharp, H., Rogers, Y., & Preece, J. (2007). *Interaction design: beyond human-computer interaction* (2nd ed.). New York: John Wiley & Sons.

Shendure, J., Mitra, R. D., Varma, C., & Church, G. M. (2004). Advanced sequencing technologies: Methods and goals. *Nat. Rev. Genet., 5,* 335-344.

Sherrard, R. (1998). Enterprise resource planning is not for the unprepared. *ERP World Proceedings.* Retrieved January 1, 2007, from http://www.erpworld.org/proceed98

Shin, N., & Jemella, D. F. (2002). Business process reengineering and performance improvement. *Business Process Management Journal, 8*(4), 351-363.

Shore, B. (2005). Failure rates in global IS projects and the leadership challenge. *Journal of Global Information Management, 8*(3), 1-5.

Shortliffe, E. H. (1999). The evolution of electronic medical records. *Academic Medicine, 74*(4), 441-419.

Shortliffe, E. H. (2001). *Medical informatics: Computer applications in health care and biomedicine* (2nd ed.). New York: Springer.

Shortliffe, E. H., & Cimino, J. J. (2006). *Biomedical informatics: Computer applications in healthcare and biomedicine* (3rd ed.). New York: Springer.

Shrader, G., Williams, K., Lachance-Whitcombe, J., Finn, L.-E., & Gomez, L. (2001). Participatory design of science curricula: The case for research for practice. Paper presented at the annual meeting of the American Educational Research Association, Seattle, WA.

Sicotte, C., Denis, J.L., & Lehoux, P. (1998). The computer based patient record: A strategic issue in process innovation. *Journal of Medical Systems, 22*(6), 431-443.

Sidorov, J. (2006). It ain't necessarily so: The electronic health record and the unlikely prospect of reducing healthcare costs. *Health Affairs, 25*(4), 1079-1085.

Silfverberg, M., MacKenzie, I. S., & Korhonen, P. (2000). Predicting text entry speed on mobile phones. *Proceedings of the SIGCHI conference on Human factors in computing systems* (pp. 9-16).

Sim, I., Olasov, B., & Carini, S. (2003). The trial bank system: Capturing randomized trials for evidence-based medicine. *AMIA Annu Symp Proc*, 1076.

Sim, I., Owens, D. K., Lavori, P. W., & Rennels, G. D. (2000). Electronic trial banks: A complementary method for reporting randomized trials. *Med Decis Making, 20*(4), 440-450.

Sim, I., Wyatt, J., Musen, M., & Niland, J. (1999). *Towards an open infrastructure for clinical trial development and interpretation.* Paper presented at the 1999 Fall AMIA Symposium, Washington DC.

Simon, J. C. (2001). *Introduction to information systems.* John Wiley & Sons.

Simon, S. R., Kaushal, R., Cleary, P. D., Jenter, C. A., Volk, L. A., Orav, E. J. et al. (2007). Physicians and electronic health records: A statewide survey. *Arch Intern Med, 167*(5), 507-512.

Sinatra, G. M., Southerland, S. A., McConaughy, F., & Demastes, J. W. (2003). Intentions and beliefs in students' understanding and acceptance of biological evolution. *Journal of Research in Science Teaching, 40*(5), 510-528.

Singer. P. (2000). Recent advances: Medical ethics. *British Medical Journal, 321,* 282-285.

Singh, J. (2003). Research briefs: Reading grade level and readability of printed cancer education materials. *Oncology Nursing Forum S, 30*(5), 867-870.

Siro, C. A., Segal, R. J., Muto, C. A., Webster, D. G., Pisowicz, V., & Feinstein, K.W. (2003). Pittsburgh regional healthcare initiative: A systems approach for achieving perfect patient care. *Health Affairs, 22*(5), 157-165.

Sjöberg, C., & Timpka, T. (1998). Participatory design of information systems in health care. *Journal of the American Medical Informatics Association, 5,* 177-183.

Skov, M., & Stage J. (2005). Supporting problem identification in usability evaluations. In Proceedings of the Australian Computer-Human Interaction Conference 2005 (OzCHI'05). ACM Press.

Slack, W. V., & Bleich, H. L. (1999). The CCC system in two teaching hospitals: a progress report. *International Journal Medicine Information, 54*(3), 183-196.

Smart, J. M. & Burling, D. (2001). Radiology and the Internet: A systematic review of patient information resources. *Clinical Radiology, 56*(11), 867-870.

Smith, A. C. T. (2004). Complexity theory and change management in sport organizations. *Emergence: Complexity & Organization, 6*(1-2), 70-79.

Smith, P.D. (2003). Implementing an EMR system: One clinic's experience. *Family Practice Management, 10*(5), 37-42.

Snyder-Halpern, R. (1999). Assessing healthcare setting readiness for point of care computerized clinical decision support system innovations. *Outcomes Management for Nursing Practice, 3*(3), 118-127.

Soanes, C., & Stevenson, A. (2004). *Concise Oxford English dictionary* (11ᵗʰ ed.). Oxford: Oxford University Press.

Social Sciences and Humanities Research Council of Canada (2006). *Knowledge Impact on Society: A SSHRC Transformation Program*. Retrieved June 9, 2007, from http:// http://www.sshrc.ca/Web/apply/program_descriptions/knowledge_impact_e.asp

Solow, R. M. (1987). We'd Better Watch Out. *New York Times Book Review*, July 12.

Somers, T.M., Nelson, K., & Ragowsky, A. (2000). Enterprise resource planning for the next millennium: development of an integrative framework and implications for research. *Proceedings of the American Conference on Information Systems (AMCIS)* (pp. 998-1004).

Southan, F.C.G., Sauer, C., & Dampney, C.M.G. (1997). Information technology in complex health services: Organizational impediments to successful technology transfer and diffusion. *Journal of the American Medical Informatics Associatio, 4,* 112–124.

Southton, F. C., Saur, C., & Grant, C. N. (1997). Information technology in complex health services: Organizational impediments to successful technology transfer and diffusion. *JAMIA, 4*(2), 112-124.

Spencer, D. C., Leininger, A., Daniels, R., Granko, R. P., & Coeytaux, R. R. (2005). Effect of a computerized prescriber-order-enry system on reported medication errors. *American Journal of Health System Pharmacy, 62*, 416-419.

Speros, C. (2005). Health literacy: concept analysis. *Journal of Advanced Nursing, 50*(6), 633-640.

Spyropoulos, B., & Papagiunos, G. (1995). A theoretical approach to artifical intelligence systems in medicine. *Artifical intelligence in Medicine, 7*, 455-465.

Srinivasan, A., McDonald, L. C., Jernigan, D., et al. (2004). Foundations of the severe acute respiratory syndrome preparedness and response plan for healthcare facilities. *Infection Control and Hospital Epidemiology, 25*(12), 1020-1025.

Stagger, N., Thompson, C. B., & Snyder-Halpern, R. (2001). History and trends in clinical information systems in the United States. *Image: Journal of Nursing Scholarship, 33*(1), 75-81.

Staggers, N., & Kobus, D. (2000). Comparing response time, errors, and satisfaction between text-based and graphical user interfaces during nursing order tasks. *Journal of the American Medical Informatics Association, 7*(2), 164.

Stead, W. W. (1999). The challenge to health informatics for 1999-2000: Form creative partnerships with industry and chief information officers to enable people to use information to improve health. *Journal of American Medical Information Association, 6*(1), 88-89.

Stead, W. W., & Lorenzi, N. M. (1999). Health informatics: Linking investment to value. *Journal of American Medical Information Association, 6*(5), 341-348.

Stead, W. W., Kelly, B. J., & Kolodner, R. M. (2004). Achievable steps toward building a national health information infrastructure in the United States. *Journal of American Medical Information Association.*

Stead, W. W., Miller, R. A., Musen, M. A., & Hersh, W. R. (2000). Integration and beyond: Linking information from disparate sources and into workflow. *Journal of American Medical Information Association, 7*(2), 135-145.

Stone, R., & McCloy, R. (2004). *Ergonomics in medicine and surgery*. Br Med Assoc.

Strategos Inc. Lean Manufacturing History. Retrieved June 18, 2007, from http://www.strategosinc.com/just_in_time.htm

Strauss, A., & Corbin, J. (1994). Grounded Theory Methodology: An Overview. In N.K. Denzin & Y.S. Lincoln (Eds.), *Handbook of qualitative research* (pp. 273-285). Thousand Oaks: Sage.

Stravri, P. Z., & Ash, J. (2003). Does failure breed success: narrative analysis of stories about computerized provider order entry. *International Journal of Medical Informatics, 72*, 9-15.

Streitenberger, K., Breen-Reid, K., & Harris, C. (2006). Handoffs in care—can we make them safer? *Pediatr Clin North Am, 53*(6), 1185-1195.

Studer, M. (2005). The effect of organizational factors on the effectiveness of EMR system implementation—what have we learned? *Electronic Healthcare, 4*(2), 92-98.

Sumner, M. (1999). Critical success factors in enterprise wide information management systems projects. *Proceedings of the Americas Conference on Information Systems (AMCIS)* (pp. 232-235).

Sundhedsstyrelsen. (SeSI). Beskrivelse af GEPJ - på begrebsniveau. (2005). Sundheds-styrelsen.

Sussman, S., Valente, T. W., Rohrbach, L. A., Skara, S., & Pentz, M. A. (2006). Translation in the health professions: Converting science into action. *Evaluation and the Health Professions, 29*(1), 7-32.

Swanson, T., Dostal, J., Eichhorst, B.,et al. (1997). Recent implementations of electronic medical records in four family practice residency programs. *Academic Medicine, 172*(7), 607-612.

Talmon, J. L., & Hasman, A. (2002). Medical informatics as a discipline at the beginning of the 21st century. *Methods Inf Med, 41*(1), 4-7.

Ta-Min, R., Arocha, J. F., & Hoffman-Goetz, L. (2007). *Assessing readability and comprehensibility of Web-based cancer information.* Paper presented at the ITCH: Today's Information for Tomorrow's Improvements, Victoria, BC.

Tan, J., Wen, H. J., & Awad, N. (2005). Health care and services delivery systems as complex adaptive systems. Examining chaos theory in action. *Communications of the ACM, 48*(5), 37-44.

Tape, T.G., & Campbell, J.R. (1993). Computerized medical records and preventive healthcare: success depends on many factors. *Am J Med., 94*(6), 619-625.

Teich, J. M., Glaser, J. P., Beckley, R. F., Aranow, M., Bates, D. W., Kuperman, G. J. et al. (1999). The Brigham integrated computing system (BICS): Advanced clinical systems in an academic hospital environment. *International Journal Medicine Information, 54*(3), 197-208.

Teng, J. T. C., Grover, V., & Fiedler, K. D. (1996). Developing strategic perspectives on business process reengineering: from process reconfiguration to organizational change. *International Journal of Management Science, 24*(3), 271-294.

Thiede, M. (2004). Information and access o health care: Is there a role for trust? *Social Science and Medicine, 61*(7), 1452-1461.

Thinking About...Implementing the EMR [Electronic (2006). Version]. *Digital Office, Volume 1.* Retrieved January 15, 2007 from http://www.himss.org/Content/files/digital_office_enews/digitaloffice_200606.html

Thomas, E. J., Studdert, D. M., Runchiman, W. B., et al. (2000). A comparison of iatronic injury studies in Australia and the USA I: context, method, case mix, population, patient and hospital characteristics. *International Journal of Quality in Health Care, 12*(5), 371-378.

Thornicroft, G., & Tansella, M. (1999) Translating ethical principles into outcome measures for mental health service research. *Psychological Medicine, 29*(4), 761-767.

Tierney, W. M., Overhage, J. M., & McDonald, C. J. (1994). A plea for controlled trials in medical informatics. *Journal of the American Medical Informatics Association, 1*(4), 353-355.

Tierney, W.M. (2001). Improving clinical decisions and outcomes with information: a review. *International Journal of Medical Informatics, 62*(1), 1-9.

Tierney, W.M., McDonald, C.J., Hui, S.L., & Martin, D.K. (1988). Computer predictions of abnormal test results: effects on outpatient testing. *Journal of the American Medical Association, 259*, 1194-1198.

Tierney, W.M., McDonald, C.J., Martin, D.K., Hui, S.L., & Rogers, M. P. (1987). Computerized display of past test results: effects on outpatient testing. *Annals of Internal Medicine, 107*, 569-574.

Tierney, W.M., Miller, M.E., & McDonald (1990). The effect on test ordering of informing physicians of the charges for outpatient diagnostic test. *New England Journal of Medicine, 322*, 1499-1504.

Tierney, W.M., Miller, M.E., Overhage, J.M., & McDonald, C.J. (1993). Physician inpatient order writing on microcomputer workstations: Effects on resource utilization. *Journal of the American Medical Association, 269*, 379-383.

Tilghman, C., Tilghman, J., & Johnson, R. W. (2006). Integration of technology in a clinical research setting. *Abnf J, 17*(3), 112-114.

Timpka, T. (1994). Organizational learning in the continuo development of healthcare: Making use of information technology to increase the total service quality. *Human Factors in Organizational Development and Management, IV*, 505-510.

Timpka, T., & Marmolin, H. (1995). Beyond computer-based clinical reminders: Improvement of the total service quality by small-group based organizational learning in primary care. *Medinfo, 8*(Pt 1), 559-563.

Timpka, T., Sjoberg, C., Hallberg, N., Eriksson, H., Lindblom, P., Hedblom, P., et al. (1995). Participatory design of computer-supported organizational learning in health care: Methods and experiences. *Proc Annu Symp Comput Appl Med Care, 800*, 4.

Tonnesen, A.S., LeMaistre, A., & Tucker, D. (1999). Electronic medical record implementation: Barriers encountered during implementation. *AMIA Annual Symposium Proceedings* (pp. 624-626).

Topol, E. J. (2004). Failing the public health- Rofecoxid, Merck and the FDA. *New England Journal of Medicine, 351*(17), 1707-1709.

Townes, P.G., Benson, D.S., Johnson, P. et al. (2000). Making EMRs really work: The Southeast Health Center experience. *Journal of Ambulatory Care Management, 23*(2), 43-52.

Tugwell, P., Robinson, V., Grimshaw, J., & Santesso, N. (2006). Systematic reviews and knowledge translation. *Bulletin World Health Organ, 84*(8), 643-651.

Turban, E. (1995). *Decision support and expert systems: Management support systems.* Englewood Cliffs, NJ: Prentice Hall.

Turner, J. R., & Muller, R. (2005). The project manager's leadership style as a success factor on projects: a literature review. *Project Management Journal, 36*(2), 49-61.

Tuttle, M. S. (1999). Information technology outside healthcare: What does it matter to us? *Journal of the American Medical Informatics Association, 6*(5), 354-360.

U.S. Renal Data System (2006). *U.S.RDS 2006 annual data report. Atlas of end-stage renal disease in the United States.* Bethesda, MD: National Institutes of Health, National Institute of Diabetes and Digestive and Kidney Diseases.

U.S.Department of Health and Human Services (2007). Office of the National Coordinator for Health Information Technology. Retrieved December 1, 2006, from http://www.hhs.gov/healthit/

Umble, E.J., Haft, R.R., & Umble, M.M. (2003). Enterprise resource planning: Implementation procedures and critical success factors. *European Journal of Operational Research, 146*, 241-257

United Nations Millennium Declaration. (2000). Section III. 19 of the General Assembly resolution 55/2 of 8 September 2000. Retrieved June 9, 2007, from http://www.ohchr.org/english/law/millennium.htm

United Nations. (1948). *Universal Declaration of Human Rights.* Retrieved from http://www.un.org/Overview/rights.html

University of Alberta Health Law Institute and University of Victoria School of Health Information Science. (2005). *Electronic health records and the Personal Information Protection and Electronic Documents Act.* Retrieved

December 12, 2006, from http://www.law.ualberta.ca/centres/hli/pdfs/ElectronicHealth.pdf

University of Calgary Health Telematics Unit. (2005). Glossary of telhealth related terms, acronyms and abbreviations. Retrieved June 7, 2007, from http://www.fp.ucalgary.ca/telehealth/Glossary.htm

University of Iowa Health Informatics. (2005). What is Health Informatics? Retrieved June 7, 2007 from http://www2.uiowa.edu/hinfo/academics/what_is_hi.html

US Department of Health and Human Services. (2000). *Healthy people 2010: Understanding and Improving Health*. Retrieved December 12, 2006, http://www.healthypeople.gov/

USA Patriot Act. (2001, rev. 2005). *Uniting and Strengthening America by Providing Appropriate Tools Required to Intercept and Obstruct Terrorism Act*, HR 3162 revised as *USA Patriot Improvement and Reauthorization Act*, H.R. 3199.

van Bemmel, J.H., & Musen, M.A. (1997). *Handbook of medical informatics*. Bohn: Springer.

van Ginneken, A. M. (2002). The computerized patient record: balancing effort and benefit. *International Journal of Medicine Information, 65*(2), 97-119.

Venkatraman, N. (1994). IT-enabled business transformation: From automation to business-scope redefinition. *Sloan Management Review, 35*(2), 73-87.

Venter, J. C., Adams, M. D., Myers, E. W., Li, P. W., Mural, R. J., Sutton, G. G., et al. (2001). *The sequence of the human genome.*

Vicente, K. (2003). *The human factor.* Toronto: Vintage Canada.

Vijaya, K. (2004). Teleradiology Solutions: Taking expertise to hospitals in US. *Express Healthcare Management*, Issue dtd. 16th to 29th February 2004, from http://www.expresshealthcaremgmt.com/20040229/innews07.shtml

Vimarlund, V., Olve, N.G. (2005). Economic analyses for ICT in elderly healthcare: Questions and challenges. *Health Informatics Journal, 4*(11), 293-305.

Vimarlund, V., Sjöberg, C., Timpka, T. (2003). A theory for classification of healthcare organisations in the New Economy. *Journal of Medical Systems, 27*(5), 467-475.

Vimarlund, V., Timpka, T., Patel, V. (1999).Information technology and knowledge exchange in health-care organisations. *Proceedings of AMIA'99, American Medical Informatics Association* (pp. 632-636). Philadelphia: Hanley & Belfus Inc.

Vincent, C., Neale, G., & Woloshynowych, M. (2001). Adverse events in British hospitals: preliminary retrospective record review. *British Medical Journal, 322*, 517-519.

Vingtoft, S., Bernstein, K., Bruun-Rasmussen, M., From, G., Nøhr, C., Høstgaard, A.M., et al. (2004). *GEPKA-projektet. Klinisk afprøvning.* Aalborg: EPJ-Obseervatoriet.

Vingtoft, S., Bruun-Rasmussen, M., Bernstein, K., Andersen, S.K., & Nøhr, C. (2005). *EHR-observatory annual report 2005.* Aalborg: EPJ-Observatoriet.

Von Wright, G. H. (1983). The foundation of norms and normative statement. In G.H. Von Wright, (Ed.), *Practical reason* (pp. 67-82). Basil Blackwell: Oxford.

Wager, K.A., Lee, F.W., & White, A.W. (2001). *Life after a disastrous electronic medical record implementation: One clinic's experience.* Hershey, PA: Idea Group Publishing.

Waitman, L.R., & Miller, R.A. (2004). Pragmatics of implementing guidelines on the front lines. *Journal of the American Medical Informatics Association, 11*(5), 436-438.

Walker, J. (2003). Clinical-information connectivity nationwide. Healthcare can use the model of success frontiered by banks. *Healthc Inform, 20*(10), 62-64.

Walker, J., Pan, E., Johnston, D., Adler-Milstein, J., Bates, D. W., & Middleton, B. (2005). The value of healthcare information exchange and interoperability. *Health Affairs, Supplemental Web Exclusives).* Retrieved December 01, 2006 from http://content.healthaffairs.org/cgi/content/abstract/hlthaff.w5.10v1 percent20

Walker, L. O. & Avant, K. C. (2005). *Strategies for theory construction in nursing* (4th ed.). Upper Saddle River, N.J: Pearson/Prentice Hall.

Walsh, S. H. (2004). The clinician's perspective on electronic health records and how they can affect patient care: Br Med Assoc.

Walsham, G. (1993). *Interpreting information systems in organizations*. Chichester: Wiley.

Wang, S. J., Middleton, B., Prosser, L. A., Bardon, C. G., Spurr, C. D., Carchidi, P. J. et al. (2003). A cost-benefit analysis of electronic medical records in primary care. *Am J Med, 114*(5), 397-403.

Ware, C. (2003). Design as applied perception. In J.M. Carroll (Ed.), *HCI models, theories, and frameworks: Towards a multidisciplinary science.* San Franscisco: Morgan-Kaufmann.

Wateridge, J. (1998). How can IS/IT projects be measured for success? *International Journal of Project Management, 16*(1), 59-63.

Watson, N., & Halamka J. (2006). Patients should have to opt out of national electronic care records. *British Medical Journal, 333*, 39-42.

Wears, R.L., & Berg, M. (2005). Computer technology and clinical work: Still waiting for Godot. *JAMA, 293*(10), 1261-1263.

Weerakkody, G., & Ray, P. CSCW-based system development methodology for health-care information systems.

Weinger, M. B., & Slagle, J. (2002). Human factors research in anesthesia patient safety techniques to elucidate factors affecting clinical task performance and decision making. *Journal of the American Medical Informatics Association 2002.*

Weir, C., Lincoln, M., Roscoe, D. et al. (1995). Dimensions associated with successful implementation of a hospital based integrated order entry system. *Proceedings of AMIA Annual Fall Symposium*, 653-657.

Weiss, B. D., Mays, M. Z., Martz, W., Castro, K., Dewalt, D. A., Pignone, M. P., et al. (2005). Quick assessment of literacy in primary care: The newest vital sign. *Annals of Family Medicine, 3*(6), 514-522.

Welch, W. P., Bazarko, D., Ritten, K., Burgess, Y., Harmon, R., & Sandy, L. G. (2007). Electronic health records in four community physician practices: impact on quality and cost of care. *Journal of American Medical Information Association, 14*(3), 320-328.

Wenzel, R. P., Bearman, G., & Edmond, M. B. (2005). Lessons from severe acute respiratory syndrome (SARS): Implications for infection control. *Achieves of Medical Research 36*(6), 610-6.

Wharton, C., Bradford, J., Jeffries, R., & Franzke, M. (1992). Applying cognitive walkthroughs to more complex user interfaces: experiences, issues, and recommendations. *Proceedings of the SIGCHI conference on Human factors in computing systems* (pp. 381-388).

WHO Division of Health Promotion Education and Communications. (1998). *Health promotion glossary.* Retrieved May 31, 2007, http://www.who.int/hpr/NPH/docs/hp_glossary_en.pdf

Wideman, H.H., Owston, R., Brown, C., Kushniruk, A., Ho, F. & Pitts, K. (2007). Unpacking the potential of educational gaming: A new tool for gaming research. *Simulation & Gaming.*

Wikipedia. Just In Time. Retrieved June 18, 2007, from http://en.wikipedia.org/wiki/Just_In_Time

Wilcox, R. A., & Whitham, E. M. (2003). Personal Viewpoint Reduction of medical error at the point-of-care using electronic clinical information delivery. *Internal Medicine Journal, 33*(11), 537-540.

Wilkinson, J. (2006). Commentary: What's all the fuss about? *British Medical Journal, 333*, 42-43.

Williams, B. (2005). Models of organizational change and development. *Futurics, 29*(3 & 4), 1-22.

Williams, M. V., Baker, D. W., Parker, R. M., & Nurss, J. R. (1998). Relationship of functional health literacy to patients' knowledge of their chronic disease. A study of patients with hypertension and diabetes. *Archives of Internal Medicine, 158*(2), 166-172.

Williams, R.B. (2002). Successful computerized physician order entry system implementation. Tools to support physician-driven design and adoption. *Healthc Leadersh Manag Rep., 10*(10), 1-13.

Wilson , R.M., Runciman, W.B., Gibberd, R.W. et al. (1995). The Quality of Australian Health Care Study. *Medical Journal of Australia, 163*, 458-471.

Wilson, F. L., & Williams, B. N. (2003). Assessing the readability of skin care and pressure ulcer patient education materials. *Journal of Wound, Ostomy & Continence Nursing, 30*(4), 224-230.

Wilson, R.M., Runciman, W.B., Gibberd, R.W., Harrison, B.T., Newby, L., & Hamilton, J.D. (1995). The quality of the Australian healthcare study. *Medical Journal of Australia, 163*(9), 458-476.

Woolf, S.H., Chan, E., Harris, R. Sheridan, B.C, Kaplan, R., Krist, A., et al. (2005). Promoting informed choice: Transforming health care to dispense knowledge for decision making. *Annals of Internal Medicine, 143*(4), 293-300.

Working Group for Assessment of Health Information Systems of the European Federation for Medical Informatics (EFMI) (2007b). Retrieved June 01, 2007, from http://iig.umit.at/efmi/

World Health Organization (2006). WHO Partnership—The Africa Health Infoway (AHI). Retrieved June 7, 2007 from http://www.research4development.info/projectsAndProgrammes.asp?ProjectID=60416

World Health Organization. (2004). World Alliance for Patient Safety: Forward Programme 2005, Switzerland: WHO.

World Health Organization. (2007). Epidemic and pandemic alert and response (EPR). Retrieved June 7, 2007 from http://www.who.int/csr/en/

Wright, P. (1999). Designing healthcare advice forward reasoning the public. In T. Durso (pp. 695-723). Chichester, UK: Wiley.

Xiao, Y. (2005). Artifacts and collaborative work in healthcare: methodological, theoretical, and technological implications of the tangible. *J Biomed Inform, 38*(1), 26-33.

Yasnoff, W. A., Humphreys, B. L., Overhage, J. M., Detmer, D. E., Brennan, P. F., Morris, R. W. et al. (2004). A consensus action agenda for achieving the national health information infrastructure. *Journal of American Medicine Information Association, 11*(4), 332-338.

Zachary, W., Ryder, J. M., & Hicinbothom, J. H. (1998). Cognitive task analysis and modeling of decision making in complex environments. *Making decisions under stress* (pp. 315-344) Washington, DC: APA.

Zaroukian, M. H., & Sierra, A. (2006). Benefiting from ambulatory EHR implementation: Solidarity, six sigma, and willingness to strive. *Journal of Healthcare Information Management, 20*(1), 53-60.

Zhang, J., Johnson, T. R., Patel, V. L., Paige, D. L., & Kubose, T. (2003). Using usability heuristics to evaluate patient safety of medical devices. *Journal of Biomedical Informatics, 36*(1/2), 23-30.

Zhang, J., Patel, V. L., & Johnson, T. R. (2002). Medical error: Is the solution medical or cognitive? *Journal of the American Medical Informatics Association, 9*(90061), 75.

Zhang, T., Aranzamendez, G., Rinkus, S., Gong, Y., Rukab, J., Johnson-Throop, K. A., et al. (2004). An information flow analysis of a distributed information system for space medical support. *Medinfo, 2004*, 992-998.

Zion, A. B., & Aiman, J. (1989). Level of reading difficulty in the American College of Obstetricians and Gynecologists patient education pamphlets. *Obstetrics and Gynecology, 74*(6), 955-960.

About the Contributors

Andre W. Kushniruk is an associate professor and director of the School of Health Information Science at the University of Victoria. Kushniruk conducts research in a number of areas including: evaluation of the effects of technology, human-computer interaction in health care, and other domains as well as cognitive science. His work is known internationally and he has published widely in the area of health informatics. He holds undergraduate degrees in psychology and biology, as well as an MSc in computer science and a PhD in cognitive psychology. He focuses on developing new methods for the evaluation of information technology and studying human-computer interaction in health care and he has been a key researcher on a number of national and international collaborative projects.

Elizabeth M. Borycki teaches health information science at the School of Health Information Science at the University of Victoria. She has a unique blend of industry, consulting, and academic experience. She has worked on the implementation of electronic health record systems in major hospital settings. She has an MS in nursing and has worked in healthcare and health informatics positions related to improving use of information in healthcare for more than 10 years. She completed her doctorate degree in management and organization in healthcare at the University of Toronto and is involved in numerous national and international projects in health informatics, with a focus on understanding the impact of information technology on healthcare work and information processing.

* * *

James Anderson, PhD, earned a BES in chemical engineering, an MSE in operations research and industrial engineering, an MAT in chemistry and mathematics, and a PhD in education and sociology from the Johns Hopkins University. He is the former director of the Division of Engineering of the Evening College at Johns Hopkins University. At Purdue, he has served as assistant dean for analytical studies of the School of Humanities, Social Sciences and Education (1975-1978, director of the Social Research Institute (1995-1998), and co-director of the Rural Center for AIDS/STD prevention (1994-2006). He is the author/co-author of five books including: *Evaluating the Organizational Impact of Health Care Information Systems*; *Ethics and Information Technology: A Case-Based Approach to a Health Care System in Transition*; and *Evaluating Health Care Information Systems: Methods and Applications*.

Kevin Anstrom's research interests include: clinical trial design, cost-benefit analysis, health economics, semiparametric estimation, inverse probability weighted estimation, and propensity score techniques. Anstrom holds a PhD in statistics from North Carolina State University. He also has an

Copyright © 2008, IGI Global, distributing in print or electronic forms without written permission of IGI Global is prohibited.

MS in biostatistics from the University of North Carolina at Chapel Hill. He has worked at the Duke Clinical Research Institute for more than 10 years and studied a variety of techniques used to reduce the bias caused by non-random treatment selection and missing data.

Jose F. Arocha is an associate professor in the Department of Health Studies and Gerontology. He has extensive experience in the human aspects of health informatics, including the study of how health professionals and users of health services understand and use health information to make decisions. His current interests include the study of the application of cognitive theories to the evaluation and development of information systems, including the investigation of cognitive aspects of design and utilization of health information by lay people. Other interests include the development of methods for the in-depth investigation of health comprehension and decision making.

John Bosomworth graduated from the University of British Colombia, Faculty of Medicine in 1968. He served as a family practitioner in Princeton, B.C., Canada. Currently, he is a locum and emergency physician in Princeton. He is also the clinical instructor in the Faculty of Medicine in the Department of Family Practice at the University of British Columbia, Vancouver, B.C. He recently participated as a practitioner trainee in the CIHR health informatics PhD/postdoc strategic training program.

Niels Boye, MD, is a specialist in internal medicine and endocrinology by education. He started out as a scientist in molecular medicine more than 30 years ago, but from the introduction on the market of the IBM personal computer around 1982 his focus gradually shifted from laboratory methods to computer methods for science and in the last 10 years for support of clinical activity and the delivery of health care. He is working as a clinician and in the field of ICT as teacher, scientist, developer and evaluator in international and national relationships.

Jytte Brender's scientific focus is on the theoretical and practical aspects of quality management and technology assessment, the topic of her European Doctorate and PhD in medical informatics (1997). Presently, she is an associate research professor. Her research and interest range from constructive assessment (dynamic, self-reflective, purpose-driven and corrective evaluation), to holistic analysis of information flow, covering the breadth of organizational change and including the theoretical aspects of the quality of semantic aspects of medical knowledge. While she is a computer scientist, all things human-centered interest her, as does the multifaceted realm of asymmetric abstraction. Her latest work is a 360-page handbook of evaluation methods for IT-based solutions. She is author/co-author of five books, has an extensive list of peer-reviewed publications in scientific journals, books, and technical reports, numerous invited presentations and two keynotes. Furthermore, she is (co-)editor of proceedings of international congresses, workshops, and one special issue of a scientific journal. She is editorial board member of *IJMI*.

John Copen is an assistant professor of psychiatry at the Northern Ontario School of Medicine. He is a Royal College certified psychiatrist, practicing privately and for multiple agencies and hospitals. He completed his psychiatric residency at the University of Ottawa, followed by a clinical-research fellowship in telemedicine and addictions at the University of Western Ontario, post-doctoral training and research via the CIHR health informatics PhD/postdoc strategic training program, and is busy completing his MS degree in health information science via the University of Victoria distributed graduate program. He is president and CEO of Med-Nexus Inc., a private Canadian corporation that is developing advanced adaptive health knowledge translation and management software for the semantic Web and other applications.

Karen Day, PhD, has a special interest in health informatics, change in health organizations and how we adapt to change when it is linked to health IT projects. Her concern about the application of theory in the workplace, as well as our capacity to learn and adapt as we develop professionally, resulted in her discovery of action research. Her experience in nursing, health service management, health insurance, managed care, and health IT project management is now being used in her role as health informatics co-ordinator at the University of Auckland. Day teaches health informatics principles, knowledge management, and qualitative research. She is also involved in the establishment of a National Institute for Health Innovation. Day is completing her PhD on change management linked to health IT projects using action research.

Tammie Di Pietro, RN, MN, is a doctoral student at the Lawrence S. Bloomberg Faculty of Nursing at the University of Toronto. Prior to entering the doctoral program, she worked as a staff nurse in the emergency department. Her research interests focus on health informatics, knowledge translation, evidence-based guidelines, geriatrics, emergency medicine, nursing-sensitive patient outcomes and patient safety. Her PhD thesis will explore the impact of a knowledge translation intervention with emergency nurses on the adaptation and implementation of a falls prevention/screening program in the elderly, aged 65 and older.

Diane Doran, RN, PhD, FCAHS, joined the Lawrence S. Bloomberg Faculty of Nursing at the University of Toronto in 1995, where she served as associate dean of research and international relations (2000-2006), interim dean (2005), and is currently a full professor. Dr. Doran is a recipient of the Ontario Premier's Research Excellence Award and is a fellow of the Canadian Academy of Health Sciences. Her research has been recognized by the Canadian Association of University Schools of Nursing Award of Excellence, and the Dorothy Pringle Research Excellence Award, Sigma Theta Tau International, Lambda Pi Chapter. Her recent research focuses on health informatics, the design and measurement of nursing sensitive patient outcomes, knowledge translation, and patient safety. She is currently engaged in an innovative investigation into the use of handheld devices to improve nurses' collection, utilization, and communication of health information at the point-of-care. Dr. Doran is a co-investigator with the Nursing Health Services Research Unit in the Lawrence Bloomberg Faculty of Nursing at the University of Toronto. She is a member of the Research and Evaluation Committee of the Canadian Patient Safety Research Institute.

Eric Eisenstein is the 1993 recipient of the American Medical Informatics Association's Martin Epstein award. After completing a post-doctoral fellowship in clinical economics, he joined the faculty of the Duke Clinical Research Institute where his research has explored relationships between health-care management practices and the clinical and economic outcomes of patients. Eisenstein has served as principal investigator for phase II, III, and IV economic studies conducted alongside randomized clinical trials in cardiovascular, emergency, public health, and pulmonary medicine. He also serves as co-convenor for the Campbell and Cochrane Economic Methods Group, which seeks to incorporate economic evaluations into systematic reviews of criminal justice, education, healthcare, and social welfare interventions.

Francis Ho is a research fellow in the University of Victoria. He practiced family medicine in Ontario for 26 years before devoting his time to medical informatics research. He is an experienced Webmaster and programmer, with a diploma in education program for software professionals from the University of Waterloo. He is studying for an MSc in healthcare informatics from the University of Bath, UK, and participating in the CIHR HI PhD/postdoc strategic training program in Canada. His research interests include Internet usability studies, consumer health informatics, palliative care informatics and medical data translation.

Laurie Hoffman-Goetz is a professor in the Department of Health Studies and Gerontology. She received her PhD from the University of Michigan (1979) and an MPH from The George Washington University School of Public Health (1997). From 1995-1997, she was a Cancer Prevention Fellow at the National Institutes of Health/National Cancer Institute focusing on dissemination of cancer information for underserved and minority populations. She teaches health and risk communication and conducts research on the impact of health literacy on understanding cancer risk information, identification of best practices for dissemination of cancer information to diverse populations, media framing of health risks, and consumer health informatics.

Joseph Kannry, MD, has dual appointments in IT and medicine at Mount Sinai Medical Center in New York. He is chief for the division of clinical informatics at Mount Sinai Center and director of the Center for Medical informatics and Director of IT for the Department of Medicine. Dr. Kannry is an assistant professor in medicine and a practicing board certified Internist. In 2004, Dr. Kannry successfully led the Ambulatory EMR Selection process for Mount Sinai Medical Center and in 2005 was the informaticist in charge of EMR implementation.

Karim Keshavjee is a family physician with a part-time practice in Mississauga. He spent five years in the pharmaceutical industry managing clinical trials and an electronic drug utilization project. He is currently an associate member of the Centre for Evaluation of Medicines, an independent academic research institute affiliated with McMaster University in Hamilton, Ontario. Keshavjee is also a physician consultant to Canada Health Infoway for the pan-Canadian electronic prescribing project and the inter-operable electronic health record project. He is also a mentor on a pan-Canadian health informatics research training program for post-graduate students. He has recently licensed EMR implementation methodology from McMaster to assist primary care physicians be more successful with EMR implementations and he has also licensed the P-PROMPT™ service to help primary care physicians be more successful with managing preventive services and chronic disease management.

Kendall Ho is the associate dean in the Division of Continuing Professional Development and Knowledge Translation and executive director of Technology Enabled Knowledge Translation Investigative Centre of the Faculty of Medicine at the University of British Columbia. He is a medical consultant to the Division of Knowledge Management and Technologies, Ministry of Health, Province of British Columbia, and assists the Ministry in the provincial engagement of health professionals in e-health adoption. His research focuses on the innovative adoption of information technologies in health services and policy translation. He helps develop medical training in electronic health record uptake, and introduction of health informatics to life sciences students at UBC. He is a member of the Canada Health Infoway Academic advisory committee and co-chair of the change management evaluation committee. He is a member of the Universitas 21 e-health steering committee, and chairs the interprofessional eHealth committee. He is a practicing emergency physician in Vancouver, B.C., Canada.

Beste Kucukyazici is a PhD candidate in management science at McGill University. She received her BSc in industrial engineering, an MSc in system engineering, and is currently studying her PhD with the research interests of stochastic modeling of health care systems, decision analytical modeling and process improvement in health care via technology integration. She is also a research and teaching assistant in management science in the Department of Management at McGill University. She recently participated as a practitioner trainee in the CIHR Health Informatics PhD/postdoc strategic training program.

Shigeki Kuwata has a PhD from Osaka University in Japan, where he had conducted research on healthcare databases, inter-hospital networking and their related security issues as staff of Department of Medical Information Science at Osaka University Hospital. Since 2003, he has been an assistant professor in Tottori University as well as a deputy director of Division of Medical Informatics at Tottori University Hospital. His major research interests include development of hospital information systems, implementation of electronic patient records and risk/quality management in hospital.

Craig E. Kuziemsky is an assistant professor in the Telfer School of Management at the University of Ottawa. Craig completed his PhD in health information science at the University of Victoria in 2006. His research interests include applying methodological approaches to understanding how health information systems (HIS) impact clinical practice in day-to-day settings. Craig's research has focused on the development and use of ontologies and problem solving methods as a means of understanding and contextualizing end user needs for HIS design, implementation and evaluation.

James Lai has been a full service family physician in Vancouver since 1986 and practices in a fully implemented EMR primary care office. He recently participated as a practitioner trainee in the CIHR health informatics PhD/postdoc strategic training program. He is a representative on a number of provincial and local health authority e-health strategic planning committees, working group member on IT projects in areas of privacy, end-user networking, and physician information Web portal design, and currently also serves as an IT advisor to the B.C. Practice Support Program for primary health care reform. He is affiliated with the Faculty of Medicine at the University of British Columbia as clinical associate professor in the Department of Family Practice.

In addition to his research, **David Lobach** is a practicing endocrinologist and internist, a fellow of the American College of Medical Informatics and in the American College of Physicians. Dr. Lobach has served on several national advisory committees related to informatics including the committee of the Office of the National Coordinator for Health Information Technology for the development of *A National Roadmap for National Action on Clinical Decision Support*. His research interests in medical informatics include: development and evaluation of clinical decision support systems, human-computer interface design, and electronic health record systems.

Christian Nøhr, MSc, PhD, is an associate professor of technology analysis and health care planning at Department of Development and Planning, Aalborg University, Denmark. Christian Nøhr has been working with health care informatics for more than 20 years. His main research field is organizational change and implementation of information systems in health care. He has been project manager of several national research projects, and participated in a number of European projects. He is currently a member of the EHR Observatory—an ongoing project, which monitors the development and implementation process of electronic health record systems in Denmark.

Tony Norris is a professor of information systems at Massey University in Auckland, New Zealand. His research interests are in the strategic role of information technology and information management in the health sector and include the cultural and business issues associated with the application of IT, data quality, privacy, and telehealth. Professor Norris is the author of the book, *Essentials of Telemedicine and Telecare*, published by Wiley in 2002. He is also the author of more than 35 research papers in the field of health informatics as well as numerous papers in his first research areas of chemistry and mathematics.

Maqui Ortiz is a graduate of the North Carolina School of Science and Mathematics and is currently enrolled in the college transfer program at Alamance Community College. Her research at Duke University has focused on complex interventions in health care and education and has highlighted their economic implications. She has been a member of a wide spectrum of projects including economic analysis of health interventions, analysis of systematic review structure, and the integration of health-related economic analysis methodology into non-health fields. With Dr. Eisenstein, she recently completed a systematic review of economic analyses and health information technology evaluation studies and is currently working on a Campbell Collaboration review of a novel intervention for children with early language learning problems.

Morgan Price is a family physician practicing in British Columbia. He is a clinical assistant professor at the University of British Columbia in the Department of Family Practice, where he is also lead faculty for informatics. Price is an adjunct professor in computer sciences at the University of Victoria. He is currently completing a PhD in health information science exploring the application of cognitive usability models and methods in the design and evaluation of health information systems.

Denis Protti was the founding director of the University of Victoria's School of Health Information Science in 1981, a position he relinquished in 1994. His research and areas of expertise include: national health information management and technology strategies, electronic health records, primary care computing, and evaluating clinical information systems. He has hundreds of publications in books and journals and has given even more presentations to a wide range of audiences around the world. He is on the advisory board of a number of overseas academic programs in Health Informatics. He regularly advises and sits on expert panels for health care organizations and government agencies in both Canada and abroad.

Nola M. Ries, BA (Hons.), LLB, MPA, LLM, teaches in the areas of health law and privacy law at the University of Victoria School of Health Information Science and Faculty of Law. She is also affiliated as a research associate with the Health Law Institute, University of Alberta. Her work addresses legal issues in health information and privacy, with particular focus on electronic health records and use of personal information for health research. Other areas of research include public health law, legal issues in health system reform and regulation of genetics and biotechnology. Professor Ries is a member of the Bar of British Columbia and has practiced constitutional and human rights law.

Tina Saryeddine is a doctoral student in the Department of Health, Policy, Management and Evaluation in the Faculty of Medicine at the University of Toronto and a project manager/senior planner at the GTA Rehab Network. As project manager/senior planner at the GTA Rehab Network, she works with multi-stakeholder groups in the areas of knowledge transfer, system integration and musculoskeletal rehabilitation. Her projects have received several grants and awards such as the Ted Freedman Award for Innovation in Education, the Hygeia Award, and a grant from the Canadian Nurses Foundation and the Change Foundation. She holds an MS in health administration from the University of Ottawa and undergraduate degrees in sociology and biology. Saryeddine is a member of the Canadian College of Health Service Executives from which she holds the Certified Health Executive designation. Prior to joining the GTA Rehab Network, Saryeddine was awarded a one year Administrative Fellowship, which she completed at the Rouge Valley Health System.

Vivian Vimarlund is an associate professor (faculty lecturer and docent) in the Department of Computer and Information Science at Linköping University, Sweden. She was awarded a PhD in informatics at the Institute of Technology in October 1999. Vimarlund was a postdoctoral fellow and research scientist at UCD, Davis. She also worked as consult and scientist at the Systems Research and Applications Corporation, SRA International, Inc., in Washington, D.C. Vimarlund is currently member of the national reference group of experts for the EU-PUBLIN consortium, reviewer for international journals and member of the OECD expert group: models to evaluate, and incentives for the implementation of information, communication technologies in the health sector.

Index

Copyright © 2008, IGI Global, distributing in print or electronic forms without written permission of IGI Global is prohibited.